Honeymoon Vacations For Dummies, 1st Edition

O9-AIG-875

Cheat Sheet

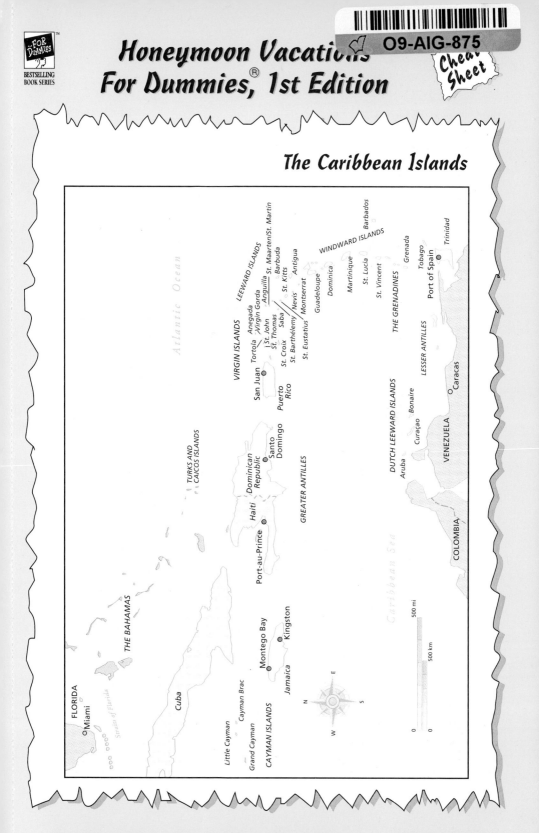

The Caribbean Islands

Atlantic Ocean

LEEWARD ISLANDS

St. Martin/St. Maarten
Anguilla
Barbuda
Barbados
St. Kitts
Antigua
Nevis
Montserrat
St. Barthélemy
St. Eustatius
Guadeloupe
Dominica
Martinique
St. Lucia
St. Vincent

WINDWARD ISLANDS

Grenada
Tobago
Trinidad
Port of Spain

VIRGIN ISLANDS

Anegada
Virgin Gorda
Tortola
St. John
St. Thomas
Saba
St. Croix

THE GRENADINES

LESSER ANTILLES

San Juan
Puerto Rico

Caracas

TURKS AND CAICOS ISLANDS

DUTCH LEEWARD ISLANDS

Bonaire
Curaçao
Aruba

VENEZUELA

Dominican Republic
Santo Domingo
Haiti

GREATER ANTILLES

COLOMBIA

Port-au-Prince

Caribbean Sea

500 mi
500 km

THE BAHAMAS

Montego Bay
Kingston
Jamaica

Cuba

N
E
S
W

FLORIDA
Miami

Straits of Florida

Little Cayman
Cayman Brac
Grand Cayman
CAYMAN ISLANDS

0
0

For Dummies: Bestselling Book Series for Beginners

For Dummies
BESTSELLING
BOOK SERIES

Hawaii

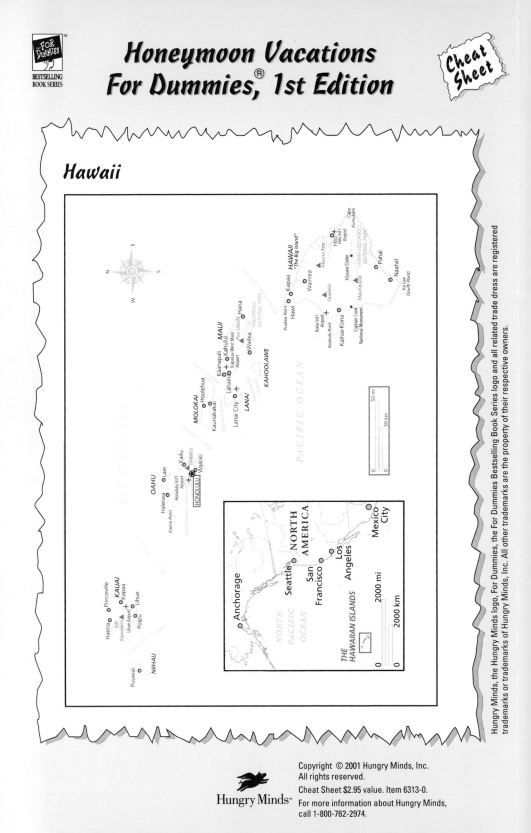

Hungry Minds™

For Dummies: Bestselling Book Series for Beginners

Honeymoon Vacations FOR DUMMIES®

1ST EDITION

Reid Bramblett, Rachel Christmas Derrick,
Echo & Kevin Garrett,
Fran Wenograd Golden, Cheryl Farr Leas,
David Swanson, and Risa R. Weinreb

Hungry Minds™

Best-Selling Books • Digital Downloads • e-Books • Answer Networks
e-Newsletters • Branded Web Sites • e-Learning

New York, NY ◆ Cleveland, OH ◆ Indianapolis, IN

Honeymoon Vacations For Dummies®, 1st Edition

Published by:
Hungry Minds, Inc.
909 Third Avenue
New York, NY 10022
www.hungryminds.com
www.dummies.com

Library of Congress Control Number: 2001092744

ISBN: 0-7645-6313-0

ISSN: 1534-9136

Printed in the United States of America

10 9 8 7 6 5 4 3 2 1

1B/QX/QZ/QR/IN

Distributed in the United States by Hungry Minds, Inc.

Distributed by CDG Books Canada Inc. for Canada; by Transworld Publishers Limited in the United Kingdom; by IDG Norge Books for Norway; by IDG Sweden Books for Sweden; by IDG Books Australia Publishing Corporation Pty. Ltd. for Australia and New Zealand; by TransQuest Publishers Pte Ltd. for Singapore, Malaysia, Thailand, Indonesia, and Hong Kong; by Gotop Information Inc. for Taiwan; by ICG Muse, Inc. for Japan; by Intersoft for South Africa; by Eyrolles for France; by International Thomson Publishing for Germany, Austria and Switzerland; by Distribuidora Cuspide for Argentina; by LR International for Brazil; by Galileo Libros for Chile; by Ediciones ZETA S.C.R. Ltda. for Peru; by WS Computer Publishing Corporation, Inc., for the Philippines; by Contemporanea de Ediciones for Venezuela; by Express Computer Distributors for the Caribbean and West Indies; by Micronesia Media Distributor, Inc. for Micronesia; by Chips Computadoras S.A. de C.V. for Mexico; by Editorial Norma de Panama S.A. for Panama; by American Bookshops for Finland.

For general information on Hungry Minds' products and services please contact our Customer Care department; within the U.S. at 800-762-2974, outside the U.S. at 317-572-3993 or fax 317-572-4002.

For sales inquiries and resellers information, including discounts, premium and bulk quantity sales and foreign language translations please contact our Customer Care department at 800-434-3422, fax 317-572-4002 or write to Hungry Minds, Inc., Attn: Customer Care department, 10475 Crosspoint Boulevard, Indianapolis, IN 46256.

For information on licensing foreign or domestic rights, please contact our Sub-Rights Customer Care department at 212-884-5000.

For information on using Hungry Minds' products and services in the classroom or for ordering examination copies, please contact our Educational Sales department at 800-434-2086 or fax 317-572-4005.

Please contact our Public Relations department at 317-572-3168 for press review copies or 317-572-3168 for author interviews and other publicity information or fax 317-572-4168.

For authorization to photocopy items for corporate, personal, or educational use, please contact Copyright Clearance Center, 222 Rosewood Drive, Danvers, MA 01923, or fax 978-750-4470.

Hungry Minds™ is a trademark of Hungry Minds, Inc.

About the Authors

Reid Bramblett (Paris)

Reid Bramblett has lived in Europe on and off since he was 11. Reid splits his time between his native Philadelphia and Rome, Italy while researching and writing such guides as *Frommer's Italy from $70 A Day, Europe For Dummies,* and *Frommer's Tuscany & Umbria.*

Rachel Christmas Derrick (Bahamas)

When it comes to islands in the Bahamas — from the best known to the barely known — Rachel Christmas Derrick has spent years poking around virtually all of them. She is the author of *Bahamas For Dummies.* Her travel articles have been published in *The New York Times, The Washington Post, The Boston Globe, The Miami Herald, Los Angeles Times, Islands, Travel & Leisure, Essence, Caribbean Travel & Life, Modern Bride,* and *Newsweek,* among many others. In addition to the Bahamas, assignments have sent her off to Bora Bora, Moorea, Australia, Hawaii, England, Wales, Brazil, Costa Rica, Mexico, Bermuda, the Turks and Caicos, and throughout the Caribbean.

Echo & Kevin Garrett (Bermuda, Caribbean, Mexico, Part of Tens)

Since Echo and Kevin Garrett, authors of *Caribbean For Dummies,* are frequently in the tropics as part of their jobs, all their friends ask their advice on where to go for their honeymoons and anniversaries. The Garretts also cover the Caribbean for Expedia.com. The Garretts, who kicked off their wedded bliss honeymooning in the Bahamas and who reside in Marietta, Georgia, still haven't decided where to celebrate their upcoming twentieth anniversary. But they agree it will be some place warm.

Kevin is author of *Fielding's Caribbean.* His articles have appeared in *Affordable Caribbean, Atlanta Homes and Lifestyles, The Atlanta Journal-Constitution, Biztravel.com, Bridal Guide, Chicago Magazine, Coastal Living, Elegant Bride, Executive Getaways, Fantastic Flyer, Great Outdoor Recreational Pages, Investor's Business Daily, Islands, Modern Bride, Second Home,* and *The Self-Employed Professional.* He and Echo updated/wrote chapters on Aruba, Bonaire, and Curaçao for *Rum & Reggae's Caribbean 2000.* An international award-winning photographer and member of the American Society of Media Photographers, Kevin's images (www.kevingarrett.com) have run in several of the above publications as well as *Voyages: The Romance of Cruising* (Tehabi Books), *Hemispheres, Los Angeles, Management Review, Sky, Smart Money, Southern Accents, Travel Holiday, Travel & Leisure, Weight Watchers,* and *World Trade.*

Echo worked as an editor at *McCall's,* then *Venture,* before going free-lance in 1988, racking up credits in more than 50 national publications from *The New York Times* to *Money,* where she became a contributing writer covering travel. She was a founding editor for an award-winning Web site, *BizTravel.com,* responsible for *Executive Getaways;* a contributing writer for "News For You," the best-read, front-page column in *Investor's Business Daily*; and a contributing writer covering hospitality and restaurants for *The Atlanta Business Chronicle.*

Fran Wenograd Golden (Cruises)

Fran Wenograd Golden writes about cruises and travel for the *Boston Herald,* Conceirge.com, cruiesmates.com, and Consumer Reports Travel Letter. She is also the author of *Cruise Vacations For Dummies, Frommer's European Cruises and Ports of Call,* and *Tvacations: A Fun Guide to Sites, the Stars and the Inside Stories Behind Your Favorite TV Shows* (Pocket Books, 1996) and coauthor of *Frommer's Alaska Cruises & Ports of Call* and *Frommer's Greece.* She lives north of Boston with her husband Ed, and two kids, Erin and Eli.

Cheryl Farr Leas (Hawaii)

Cheryl Farr Leas may live on the mainland, but she's a Hawaii girl at heart. She fell in love with Diamond Head, aloha wear, and mai tais in 1994, and has had trouble staying away ever since. Whenever she's not in the islands — and until she can figure a way to trade in her Brooklyn co-op for a Lanikai beach house — she and her husband Rob call New York City home.

Before embarking on a writing career, Cheryl served as a senior editor at Macmillan Travel (now Hungry Minds, Inc.), where she edited the *Frommer's Hawaii* travel guides for the better part of the '90's. Now happy to be a globetrotting freelancer, Cheryl also authors *Hawaii For Dummies, California For Dummies,* and *Frommer's New York City* travel guides.

David Swanson (Walt Disney World & Orlando)

Although David Swanson's first travels were in the back of a Volkswagen bus as part of annual cross-country treks with his parents, he has been hoofing the globe enthusiastically since a trip to Europe in 1982. Born and raised in San Diego (where he resides today), Swanson spends his down time bicycling, hiking, or enjoying obscure movies, and occasionally he ponders his former career in film marketing and publicity. Swanson's writing and photography has appeared in more than 50 North American newspapers, including the *Los Angeles Times, Boston Globe, San Francisco Chronicle, Chicago Sun-Times, Dallas Morning News,* and *Toronto's Globe and Mail.* Among magazines, his stories and photos appear in *National Geographic*

Traveler, American Way, Bride's, and *Travelocity,* and he is a monthly columnist for *Caribbean Travel & Life.* Swanson is also the author of *Fielding's Caribbean* (1996, 1997, and 1998 editions) and *Fielding's Walt Disney World and Orlando* (1996 and 1998) guidebooks, and a contributing editor to the *Rum & Reggae Caribbean* (2000, 2002).

Risa R. Weinreb (Introduction, Part I, Part II, Part of Tens)

A romantic at heart, Risa R. Weinreb is the former travel editor of *Modern Bride* magazine. She still writes for that publication, as well as for several other leading national magazines. Nicknamed "The Honeymoon Queen," she has been interviewed by *The New York Times* and *Travel Weekly,* and has appeared on CNN and Live With Regis Philbin. The editor of *Specialty Travel Index* magazine and its Web site (www.specialtytravel.com), she also frequently covers adventure travel, with exploits ranging from tracking rhinos in the African moonlight to sharing cough drops with former (hopefully) headhunters in Irian Jaya.

Publisher's Acknowledgments

We're proud of this book; please send us your comments through our Online Registration Form located at www.dummies.com.

Some of the people who helped bring this book to market include the following:

Editorial

Editors: Amy Lyons, Development Editor; Mary Goodwin, Project Editor

Copy Editor: Mary Goodwin

Cartographer: John Decamillis

Editorial Manager: Jennifer Ehrlich

Editorial Administrator: Michelle Hacker

Editorial Assistant: Jennifer Young

Senior Photo Editor: Richard Fox

Assistant Photo Editor: Michael Ross

Cover Photos: Front cover: Cabo San Lucas, Mexico. © Hollenbeck Photography

Project Coordinator: Dale White

Layout and Graphics: LeAndra Johnson, Barry Offringa, Jill Piscitelli, Jacque Schneider, Julie Trippetti

Proofreaders: TECHBOOKS Production Services

Indexer: TECHBOOKS Production Services

General and Administrative

Hungry Minds, Inc.: John Kilcullen, CEO; Bill Barry, President and COO; John Ball, Executive VP, Operations & Administration; John Harris, CFO

Hungry Minds Consumer Reference Group

Business: Kathleen Nebenhaus, Vice President and Publisher; Kevin Thornton, Acquisitions Manager

Cooking/Gardening: Jennifer Feldman, Associate Vice President and Publisher; Anne Ficklen, Executive Editor; Kristi Hart, Managing Editor

Education/Reference: Diane Graves Steele, Vice President and Publisher

Lifestyles: Kathleen Nebenhaus, Vice President and Publisher; Tracy Boggier, Managing Editor

Pets: Dominique De Vito, Associate Vice President and Publisher; Tracy Boggier, Managing Editor

Travel: Michael Spring, Vice President and Publisher; Brice Gosnell, Publishing Director; Suzanne Jannetta, Editorial Director

Hungry Minds Consumer Editorial Services: Kathleen Nebenhaus, Vice President and Publisher; Kristin A. Cocks, Editorial Director; Cindy Kitchel, Editorial Director

Hungry Minds Consumer Production: Debbie Stailey, Production Director

◆

The publisher would like to give special thanks to Patrick J. McGovern, without whom this book would not have been possible.

◆

Contents at a Glance

Cartoons at a Glance

By Rich Tennant

"So far this has been a perfect honeymoon. I haven't had to use a dictionary once."

page 7

"The hotel said they were giving us the 'Indiana Jones' suite."

page 413

"Oooo! Back up Robert. There must be a half dozen Lightening Whelks here."

page 349

"I know it's a wedding present from your niece, I just don't know why you had to wear it to the Louvre."

page 503

"Oh look! Isn't that Raoul, the ship steward you refused to tip after he fished your watch out of the pool?"

page 461

"Psst—Philip! It's not too late to fly back to a more civilized island."

page 77

"I appreciate that our room looks out onto several baroque fountains, but I had to get up 6 times last night to go to the bathroom."

page 41

WHILE TRYING TO FIND THE RENTAL RETURN AREA AT MIAMI INTERNATIONAL AIRPORT, FRANK AND MONA DISCOVER BERMUDA.

page 535

"Don't worry, they may be called St. Martin, St. John, and St. Lucia, but you're not required to act like one while you're there."

page 141

Cartoon Information:
Fax: 978-546-7747
E-Mail: richtennant@the5thwave.com
World Wide Web: www.the5thwave.com

Maps at a Glance

Table of Contents

· ·

Introduction

By Risa R. Weinreb

● ●

"*W*here should we go on our honeymoon?"

That is the first question engaged couples ask any travel writer. *Honeymoon Vacations For Dummies,* 1st Edition, can help you plan your perfect honeymoon — from deciding where to go, to booking the best table for two at an oceanfront restaurant.

Honeymoon Vacations For Dummies, makes planning your trip easy, fast — and fun. Focusing on the most popular honeymoon destinations in the world, we help you decide which is ideal for the both of you. We discuss the advantages (and disadvantages) of different locales, the best (and worst) seasons to travel, and the most romantic accommodations (in all price brackets).

This book is not an exhaustive tome detailing every musty old fort or luau. Instead, we focus on our romantic favorites — not just hotels and restaurants, but also beaches, snorkel spots, and adventures. We get to the point, give the information you need, and outline the choices you need to make. *Honeymoon Vacations For Dummies* provides you with all the practical, nuts-and-bolts information to make your "trip of a lifetime" come true.

About This Book

We try to anticipate every question about planning a honeymoon and to provide the answers. Since organizing your wedding may take up most of your time, we give you quick and easy, yet comprehensive information.

You can use *Honeymoon Vacations For Dummies,* in three ways:

✔ **As a trip planner:** If you are trying to decide between two or more different destinations, we steer you in the right direction. Then you can skip straight to the chapters on your favorite places to plan every aspect of your trip, from packing the right stuff to getting the best deal on your honeymoon suite.

✔ **As a destination guide:** Bring this book with you to your honeymoon destination because we let you know what to expect and tell you our favorite places to go — from the best beaches to the coolest bars to the most romantic restaurants.

✔ **As a fun overview:** If you want to get a good feel for the top honeymoon destinations, read this book straight through because we hit all the high points.

Please be advised that travel information is subject to change at any time — and this is especially true of prices. Therefore, we suggest that you phone or e-mail ahead for confirmation when making your travel plans. The authors, editors, and publisher can't be held responsible for the experiences of readers while traveling. Your safety is important to us, however, so we encourage you to stay alert and be aware of your surroundings. Keep a close eye on cameras, purses, and wallets, all favorite targets of thieves and pickpockets.

Conventions Used in This Book

We list our favorite — and most romantic — hotels and restaurants, as well as information about special attractions in each honeymoon locale. In our descriptions, we often include abbreviations for commonly accepted credit cards. The following lists explains each abbreviation:

AE	American Express
DC	Diners Club
DISC	Discover
JCB	Japan Credit Card
MC	MasterCard
V	Visa

We also include some general pricing information to help you decide where to unpack your bags or dine. We use a system of dollar signs to show a range of costs for one night in a hotel or a meal at a restaurant. Unless otherwise noted, the lodging rates reflect the high season rack rates. For restaurants, we give the price range for main courses. Check out the following table to decipher the dollar signs.

Cost	Hotel	Restaurant
$	$100 or less per night	Less than $15
$$	$100-$150	$15-$20
$$$	$150-$225	$20-$25
$$$$	$225-$300	$25-$30
$$$$$	More than $300 per night	$30 and up

Foolish Assumptions

As we wrote this book, we made some assumptions about you and what your needs may be for your honeymoon. Here's what we believed:

- You're madly in love and want to spend every minute in the most romantic surroundings possible.

- You may be inexperienced travelers looking for guidance about where to go on your honeymoon, and how to plan your trip.

- You may be experienced travelers, but you don't have a lot of time to devote to honeymoon planning. You want expert advice on how to maximize your time and enjoy a hassle-free trip.

- You're not looking for a book that provides every bit of information available about these different destinations or that lists every hotel, restaurant, or attraction. Instead, you're looking for a book that focuses on the places that give you the most romantic or unique experience on your honeymoon.

If you fit any of these criteria, then this book gives you the information that you need.

How This Book Is Organized

Honeymoon Vacations For Dummies, 1st Edition, is divided into nine parts. The chapters in each part cover specific topics or destinations in detail. Feel free to skip around; you don't have to read this book in order. Just like a buffet dinner: You can pick and choose what you like.

Part I: Starting Your Honeymoon Planning

Part I provides an easy-to-use introduction to honeymoon planning and choosing the best destination *for you both*. Note that emphasis — no matter what your friends or relatives say, there is no #1, one-size-fits-all hideaway that's right for every couple. To help you decide where *you* should go, we describe the most popular honeymoon destinations and compare and contrast what they offer. Each destination is unique, so you need to consider carefully which one sounds like the best fit. We also explain in detail the various "seasons" that are used to describe more- and less-popular times of year for people to visit each place. We discuss what kind of prices and weather you can expect throughout the year. In addition, we offer tips for couples planning a destination wedding and provide advice for people who are marrying for a second time.

Part II: Ironing Out the Details

Here we help you decide whether to use a travel agent, a packager, or the Internet when planning your trip. We provide pointers about how to choose your honeymoon accommodations and explain the advantages — and disadvantages — of all-inclusive resorts. Part II also provides information about everything from establishing a honeymoon budget to finding bargain airfares on the Internet. Finally, we explain how to cope with honeymoon stress.

Parts III through VIII: The Destinations

Now we get to the fun stuff. For each destination — from Hawaii to Paris to the U.S. Virgin Islands — we give you the scoop on the hotel scene; what you can expect when you actually arrive (from the airport to taxi drivers or car rentals); what restaurants you should consider; and finally, where to go and what to do to oomph the most fun into your honeymoon.

Part IX: The Part of Tens

Every *For Dummies* book has a Part of Tens. Here we give you helpful hints so you'll travel like an ace, not like an amateur.

At the back of the book, we also include a bunch of worksheets to make your travel planning easier. Among other things, you can determine your vacation budget, create specific itineraries, and keep a log of your favorite restaurants so that you can hit them again when you return for your second honeymoon. You can find these worksheets easily because they're printed on yellow paper.

Icons Used in This Book

 The Romance icon signals the most romantic restaurants, hotels, and attractions. Selecting these very special places is one of the favorite parts of our job, and we try to test out the romance factor personally.

 Ring in the bridesmaids and flowers — the Wedding Bells herald accommodations that offer superb destination weddings.

 Hey — we want to tell you what to avoid, too. The Heads Up icon identifies annoying or potentially dangerous situations, such as tourist traps, unsafe neighborhoods, rip-offs, and other things to beware.

 Travel like a pro. The Tip icon provides useful advice on how to make the best use of your time and money.

 Just like everyone loves a lover, lovers adore saving money. The Bargain Alert icon flags money-saving tips or great deals.

Where to Go from Here

Start planning what clothes to pack and maybe buy that new digital camera. The trip you've always longed for is here — and *Honeymoon Vacations For Dummies,* 1st Edition, travels with you each step of the way to make sure that everything turns out the way you imagined. Here's to the start of a perfect honeymoon!

Part I

Starting Your Honeymoon Planning

The 5th Wave   By Rich Tennant

"So far this has been a perfect honeymoon. I haven't had to use a dictionary once."

In this part . . .

We start off with some facts of life — Bali Hai and Shangri-La do not exist. But the perfect honeymoon destination for you does, and we help you find where in this section.

First we cover the basics: What is each destination like and which one best matches your fantasy island (or cosmopolis)? Next comes the details — choosing the best places to go during the time of year you'll be honeymooning. Finally, we provide pointers for couples planning a destination wedding and offer special advice to brides or grooms who are marrying for a second time. The trip of a lifetime begins here and now.

Chapter 1

Choosing Your Honeymoon Destination

By Risa R. Weinreb

. . . .

In This Chapter

▶ Uncovering your honeymoon desires

▶ Reviewing the top honeymoon destinations

▶ Weighing the pros and cons of different locales

. . . .

Choosing the best honeymoon locale is a lot like picking a mate. You're looking for compatibility and shared interests — physical attractiveness is a bonus, as is a sunny disposition.

In short, where you should go depends on what you both like to do. Hiking in the rainforest or hitting some tennis balls? Snorkeling or shopping? Sinking a putt or getting a massage?

Did you say "yes" to all of the above? No problem! *Honeymoon Vacations For Dummies,* 1st Edition, can help you find the perfect destination.

Choose your honeymoon destination based on your interests. Not on where your best friend went. Not on the recommendation of your Dad's doubles partner. Not on the ad for some tropical paradise posed in the pages of a bridal magazine.

Start by talking with each other about what you want from your honeymoon. Relaxation? Adventure? New scenery? Ask each other the following questions:

✔ What have you enjoyed doing most on past vacations?

✔ What do you most want to do on your honeymoon?

✔ What are your main interests? Sports? Nightlife? Casinos?

✔ What would be a perfect honeymoon day — from the moment you wake until you go to sleep?

   ✔ What's the view you would like to have from your room?

   ✔ What are one or two things you'd like to do during the day?

Often, couples have a fantasy of what the *perfect* honeymoon should be. One of the biggest misconceptions, travel agents report, is that couples think they should hide away for the week, lolling on a deserted beach, then retreating to a secluded cottage with chirping crickets providing the only evening entertainment. But if you've never spent a considerable amount of time deprived of television and direct-dial phones, you may find yourselves bored silly.

Testing Your H.Q. (Honeymoon Quotient)

The following his 'n' hers quiz is designed to help you realize what activities and lifestyles you desire for your honeymoon. Recognizing what you want to do on your trip can narrow down which destinations best suit your interests. Have fun!

Step #1: Comparing Your Interests

Individually, you and your betrothed indicate whether you think a characteristic or quality is for your trip is . . .

   A. very important

   B. moderately important

   C. not at all important

	He says	She says
A. Romance	A B C	A B C
B. Warm, sunny weather	A B C	A B C
C. Beautiful natural scenery	A B C	A B C
D. Gorgeous beaches	A B C	A B C
E. Lots of sports activities	A B C	A B C
F. Exploring a foreign country	A B C	A B C
G. Outdoor adventures	A B C	A B C
H. Casinos and gaming	A B C	A B C
I. Culture and history	A B C	A B C

J. Fine restaurants	A B C	A B C
K. Lots of nightlife	A B C	A B C
L. Being on the open seas	A B C	A B C
M. Staying in luxury accommodations	A B C	A B C
N. Great diving and snorkeling	A B C	A B C
O. Playing tennis	A B C	A B C
P. Playing golf	A B C	A B C
Q. Learning something	A B C	A B C
R. Lots of seclusion	A B C	A B C
S. Making everything as easy as possible	A B C	A B C
T. Saving money	A B C	A B C
U. Easy to reach from the U.S. east coast	A B C	A B C
V. Easy to reach from the U.S. west coast	A B C	A B C

Step #2: Analyzing the Results

Now, see how the different honeymoon destinations stack up with your preferences.

The following chart indicates a destination or honeymoon type (such as a cruise) with from 1 to 5 points, based on how well each matches an interest or activity. Five points is the highest rating, one the lowest. (But if a category does not apply to a destination — for example, gambling is illegal in Hawaii — the choice is blank.)

To keep things simple, we've generalized about each region or category. For example, the Caribbean encompasses about 30 different countries. Some have terrific golf courses; others offer happening dance clubs or amazing scuba diving. Ditto for Hawaii, which has six main islands for tourism. And although Mexico is one country, each beach resort is as different from its siblings as flan is from guacamole. Cruise lines and their ships are equally varied, offering different levels of accommodations and service — all at a wide range of prices. Nonetheless, overall patterns prevail: Getting a suntan is unlikely in Paris, and the flight from Boston to Hawaii is at least 10 hours.

Finally, tally the score for each locale. The winner — the destination with the highest total score — is the top choice for you to consider.

The Final Score Card

Points For	Disney World/ Orlando	Hawaii	Mexico	Caribbean	Paris	Cruises
A. Romance	4	5	5	5	5	5
B. Warm, sunny weather	4	5	5	5	2	5
C. Beautiful natural scenery	1	5	5	5	2	4
D. Gorgeous beaches	0	5	4	5	0	3
E. Lots of sports activities	3	5	5	5	1	3
F. Exploring a foreign country	0	0	4	4	5	3
G. Outdoor adventures	2	5	5	5	1	2
H. Casinos and gaming	0	0	0	4	1	4
I. Culture and history	1	4	4	3	5	3
J. Fine restaurants	3	4	4	4	5	4
K. Lots of nightlife	4	3	3	3	5	4

Points For	Disney World/Orlando	Hawaii	Mexico	Caribbean	Paris	Cruises
L. Being on the open seas	0	0	0	0	0	5
M. Staying in luxury accommodations	3	4	4	4	5	3
N. Great diving and snorkeling	0	3	4	4	0	3
O. Playing tennis	3	4	4	4	1	1
P. Playing golf	3	5	4	4	1	1
Q. Learning something	2	4	4	4	5	3
R. Lots of seclusion	2	4	4	4	2	4
S. Making everything as easy as possible	4	3	3	3	2	5
T. Saving money	5	3	4	3	1	4
U. Easy to reach from the U.S. east coast	5	1	4	4	3	4
V. Easy to reach from the U.S. west coast	3	4	5	1	1	5
TOTAL SCORE:						

Taking a Look at Our Suggestions

So . . . what destination scored best — and what do the results mean for your honeymoon destiny?

Although practically all the places in *Honeymoon Vacations For Dummies* offer sun, fun, and tons of romance, they contrast as much as diamonds and emeralds. We give complete details in the chapters devoted to each destination, but meanwhile, here's an introduction to the top locales.

Honeymooning in Hawaii

Waterfalls. Black-sand beaches. Red-hot volcanoes that sizzle into the sea. No wonder Hawaii is the most popular honeymoon destination outside the continental United States.

Hawaii comprises six main islands: Oahu (the setting for Waikiki Beach and Honolulu), plus the Neighbor Islands: Maui, Molokai, Lanai, Kauai, and Hawaii (known as the Big Island to distinguish it from the state). Each island has a unique personality, set of attractions, and appeal.

Oahu

Home to the world-famous Waikiki Beach, with white sands, shocking-blue water, and those killer views of Diamond Head. Oahu also offers some of Hawaii's most interesting cultural experiences (including Iolani Palace and the Bishop Museum), as well as the best restaurants, shopping, and nightlife. When you get beyond the Honolulu-Waikiki metropolis, the natural beauty and genuine Hawaiian spirit rivals any on the Neighbor Islands, especially along the north shore and in Windward Oahu.

Maui

Want gourmet restaurants, flashy clubs, world-class golf courses, and opulent hotels where peacocks preen and golden Buddhas glitter? Maui's got them, not to mention 42 miles of beaches, emerald-green rainforests, and Haleakala, a dormant volcano with a crater big enough to swallow the island of Manhattan whole. Lahaina, a former whaling town, now burgeons with boutiques, restaurants, and art galleries. *Maui no ka oi*, Hawaiians like to say. "Maui is best."

The Big Island

By far the largest of the Hawaiian islands — twice the size of all the others combined (and still growing!), the Big Island also packs in an amazing variety of experiences including fire-breathing volcanoes and snow-capped summits. In addition to exploring ancient *heiaus* (shrines), you can loll on beaches colored white or gold, black or green. The west side of the island is hot, arid, and studded with expansive, ultra-deluxe beach resorts. To the east, the topography is lush, wet, and fragrant with tropical flowers — almost primeval.

Kauai

With its razor-sharp peaks, lush vales, and long, golden strands where coconut palms sway like a line of hula dancers, Kauai is imbued with sublime tropical beauty. Beaches along the north shore are favorites of Hollywood filmmakers (scenes from *South Pacific* and *Jurassic Park* were shot here). Only 20 percent of the island is accessible by car, which makes for terrific adventure opportunities: hikes along the Na Pali coast, bike rides down from Waimea Canyon, plus snorkel trips and whale-watching voyages.

Top aspects of a Hawaiian honeymoon include the following:

- **Warm, sunny weather:** The climate is consistently good all year. Daytime temperatures average 78 degrees during the winter, 85 degrees in the summer.

- **Easy to reach from the U.S. west coast:** Less than a five-hour flight from Los Angeles or San Francisco.

- **Still in the U.S.A.:** Since Hawaii is the 50th U.S. state, you don't need a passport and the currency is the U.S. dollar.

But also consider the following:

- **Prices can be high.** Not only are hotels expensive, so are rates for most sightseeing activities.

- **Main resort areas can get crowded.** Especially during winter high season and school breaks, traffic jams at the malls and the difficulty getting restaurant reservations can be frustrating.

- **You face a long flight from the U.S. east coast.** Count on ten hours of flight time and five hours of time difference — not practical if you only have a week for your honeymoon.

Honeymooning in the Caribbean, Bahamas, and Bermuda

That sweep of blue-on-blue sea called the Caribbean stretches nearly 2,000 miles from Miami to the coast of South America. The region encompasses about 30 different nations — an estimated 7,000 islands — all as varied as the colors in a tropical sunset.

Nonetheless, the islands in the Caribbean region share certain characteristics. Balmy weather, for one — temperatures average about 80 degrees year round. The beaches are spectacular; from long arcs of pearl-white sands to tiny coves where — it may be rumored — pirates stashed their treasure three centuries ago. Here's a preview of the most popular Caribbean destinations.

Aruba

Sugar-white beaches. Splashy casinos. A stark, cactus-strewn interior known as the *cunucu*, where *divi-divi* (watapana) trees have been folded at 45-degree angles by the constant trade winds. These are the contrasts of Aruba, an independent country within the Kingdom of the Netherlands. The island is justly famous for its seven-mile stretch of white-sand beach, where most major hotels are located. Aruba lies outside the usual hurricane belt, and it gets only 17 inches of rainfall annually.

The Bahamas

Strictly speaking, the 700 Bahamian Islands (part of the British Commonwealth) are not located in the Caribbean Sea at all, but instead are completely surrounded by the Atlantic Ocean. And what a body of water — so clear that underwater scenes for many films have been shot here, including several James Bond flicks. Top honeymoon destinations include Nassau, Paradise Island, and Freeport, where you can lounge on exquisite beaches by day, and woo Lady Luck in the casinos at night.

Bermuda

Yes, the sands are pink, tinged by flecks of coral. Both prim cottages and sprawling mansions are painted gumdrop shades of peach, lemon, and mint. Horse-drawn carriages clip-clop down Front Street, and British traditions prevail, such as serving a proper afternoon tea. Like the Bahamas, Bermuda lies in the Atlantic Ocean (about 600 miles east of North Carolina) and has a subtropical climate. Expect top-notch sports facilities: the island has eight challenging golf courses and over 100 tennis courts.

Cayman Islands

Legendary among scuba divers, the trio of islands know as the Caymans is known for its awesome walls (coral-inlaid cliffs that hurtle into deep blue). Grand Cayman, with its Seven Mile Beach, forms the main tourist center, complete with snazzy hotels, duty-free shopping, plus sporting diversions like tennis and golf. For underwater pursuits, one of the best-loved sites is Sting Ray City, where the friendly fish hover like aquatic Frisbees. Meanwhile, the low-key sister islands of Cayman Brac and Little Cayman offer world-class dives such as Bloody Bay Wall.

Jamaica

Here, tropical fun sways to a reggae beat, whether you're rafting down a diamond-clear river or racing each other to the top of a bridal-veil-like waterfall. Landscapes start with 200 miles of beaches, then soar to the 7,400-foot summits of the Blue Mountains. The island owes part of its romantic success to the prevalence of all-inclusive resorts, which were first popularized here. The four main honeymoon destinations are Montego Bay, Negril, Ocho Rios, and Port Antonio.

Puerto Rico

La vida loca rules in Puerto Rico, with its high-rise luxury hotels and high-action casinos (not to mention favorite son Ricky Martin). But the island also lures couples to hidden beaches, romantic *paradores* (country inns), El Yunque rainforest, and the Old City of San Juan, where the hulking El Morro Castle has guarded the waterfront for 400 years. Since Puerto Rico is a commonwealth of the United States, Americans don't need a passport or to clear Customs after a visit.

St. Lucia

St. Lucia has some of the most heart-stopping vistas this side of the South Pacific. Jagged mountains claw the sky, while palm trees ripple along 100 beaches, including some with dusky black sands. The scenery crescendos at the Pitons (double summits that rise from the sea and are actually the tops of a collapsed volcano). Recently, the island has enhanced its honeymoon appeal with the introduction of several all-inclusive resorts.

U.S. Virgin Islands

Blessed with transparent waters like molten gemstones, the U.S.V.I. encompasses three main islands. St. Thomas is the most cosmopolitan of the trio, as celebrated for its duty-free shopping and gourmet restaurants as for its lovely beaches. Nature reigns supreme on St. John, where two-thirds of the land is a National Park. St. Croix embodies contrasts, with white-sand beaches, cactus-thorned plains, and the old Danish capital of Christiansted. Since the islands are an American territory, English is spoken, the currency is the dollar, and U.S. citizens don't need a passport.

Top aspects of a Caribbean honeymoon include the following:

- **The variety.** The activities to choose from are seemingly endless. Many of the beaches earn best-in-the-world status, with soft coral sands and turquoise water.

- **Easy to get to from the U.S. east coast.** Most of the islands are served by nonstop air service. The Bahamas lie just 50 miles off the coast of Florida, and even Aruba (the most distant island) is just a four-and-a-half-hour flight from New York.

- **Warm weather.** Temperature fluctuations in the Caribbean are surprisingly slight, averaging between 75 degrees and 85 degrees in both winter and summer. But beware of hurricane season (read on).

But also consider the following:

- ✔ **It's expensive.** Especially during the winter season, hotel rates can be stratospheric. Ditto for prices in restaurants, since most food is imported from the U.S., South America, or Europe.

- ✔ **The crowds.** Unless you're heading off the beaten path, the beaches and bar stools are packed.

- ✔ **Beware hurricane season.** June 1 to November 30 is officially classified as hurricane season. During those months, even if you don't get walloped by a category-five storm, you can encounter days of rain at a time (although you can luck into beautiful weather, too).

Honeymooning in Mexico

Imagine a vast and varied country that stretches 1,200 miles from north to south, bordering on four different seas and three nations. Add in landscapes that range from sun-parched desert to sultry jungle plus wave-sculpted promontories and limpid blue bays where 40-ton whales are so friendly, they may even swim right up to be stroked by your hand. All these juxtapositions come together in Mexico, where the old world of Mayan pyramids and Spanish conquistadors rubs up against the tomorrowland of laser-zapped dance clubs and swank hotels.

Over 6,000 miles of sun-kissed beaches frame Mexico's coastlines. Each resort destination is unique. Here are some of the best for honeymooners.

Cancun

A gilt-edged sandbox, Cancun is actually a Caribbean island, located just off Mexico's Yucatan peninsula. Known for its electric-blue water, the region offers 12 miles of soft, white beaches, perfect for pastimes from windsurfing to kayaking. Sophisticated hotels, air-conditioned malls, and pulsating dance clubs contrast with the impressive monuments of the Mayan civilization: Tulum, Chichén Itzá, and Uxmal are just a short drive away. In addition, the region offers practically goof-proof weather, with temperatures averaging in the 80s and about 240 sunny days a year.

Cozumel

If Cancun is high heels, late-night clubs, and piña coladas by the pool, Cozumel means flip-flops, hammocks at sunset, and Jacques Cousteau-like underwater adventures. Although increased cruise ship calls (Cozumel is Mexico's largest passenger port) have brought more glittery trinkets to the duty-free shops in San Miguel, Cozumel is still largely unspoiled. Most of all, the island is known for its superb scuba diving on Palancar Reef, part of the second-longest coral reef system in the world. Hotel prices tend to be reasonable.

Acapulco

The setting is awesome: 20 miles of golden sands surround a broad, blue bay, all cupped by the jungle-clad Sierra Madre Mountains. A 24-7 vacation paradise, Acapulco is as famed for its nonstop dance clubs as its beachside fun. Action centers on the Costera Miguel Alemán (also called the Costera or "Strip") where the high-rise hotels, boutiques, and restaurants are located. The city basks in an average of 360 days of sunshine a year.

Ixtapa/Zihuatanejo

Enjoy two unique resort towns for the price of one. A luxury resort developed by the Mexican government, Ixtapa (eeks-*tah*-pah) lolls beside the two-mile-long Palmar Beach. The sports facilities are first rate, with choices such as horseback riding, tennis, deep-sea fishing, as well as golf on a championship 18-hole Robert Trent Jones course. Just four miles away, Zihuatanejo (see-*whah*-tah-neh-hoe or see-*wah* for short), is a former fishing village, which now offers sophisticated restaurants, boutiques, and small hotels.

Puerto Vallarta

Located on the Pacific coast, Puerto Vallarta is tucked along Banderas Bay, Mexico's largest natural harbor. Over 100 miles of coastline surrounds the vast inlet, all surrounded by the Sierra Madre mountains. Despite the arrival of big-name hotels and hard-rocking discos, Puerto Vallarta remains largely unsullied by all the touristy hullabaloo. Cobblestone streets zigzag around whitewashed houses with red-tile roofs, and burros jostle past taxicabs on the Malecón (seaside promenade). The art galleries and restaurants are among the best in Mexico.

Los Cabos

Here, where desert meets the deep-blue sea at the tip of Baja California, the twinned towns of Cabo San Lucas and San Jose del Cabo — collectively known as Los Cabos (The Capes) — have become Mexico's boom resort destination for the 21st century. Long celebrated for número uno sport fishing (especially for blue and striped marlin) the region has recently added golf to its repertoire, with the debut of several sensational courses. The region averages 360 sunny days every year, with temperatures hovering around 75 degrees.

Top aspects of a Mexican honeymoon include the following:

- ✔ **Foreign — yet close.** Two-thousand-year-old pyramids, gilt-trimmed cathedrals built by the conquistadors — Mexico's got them. At the same time, its modern airports are easy to reach from cities throughout the United States. You don't need a passport to enter Mexico, and most people speak English in the tourist areas.

✔ **The price is right.** A strong U.S. dollar means affordable luxury. Rates tend to be lower than in other honeymoon destinations.

✔ **Easy to reach.** Cancun and Cozumel are short flights from the U.S. east coast, while Puerto Vallarta, Ixtapa/Zihuatanejo, Acapulco, and Los Cabos are convenient to west coast cities.

But consider the following:

✔ **Mexico is a foreign country.** A different language, shops that close from 2 p.m. to 5 p.m. in the afternoon, tortillas served at breakfast . . . you encounter novel customs and unfamiliar foods.

✔ **Hard-sell time-share pitches.** In some resort areas (especially Cancun and Puerto Vallarta), persistent sales people may pester you on the streets or even the beach to get you to attend time-share spiels.

✔ **The "slower" pace.** Service can be leisurely; sightseeing tours or dive trips may not leave on time.

Honeymooning in Walt Disney World and Orlando

Sure, you may be adults heading off on life's biggest adventure — but why shouldn't marriage start with nonstop fun? Walt Disney World and the other top attractions of Central Florida pack in enough different experiences to give you memories for a lifetime.

Heading the wish list for most couples is the chance to meet "The Big Cheese" himself — Mickey Mouse, along with Minnie, Goofy, Donald, and other friends at Walt Disney World. The Disney entertainment extravaganza enfolds four different theme parks: The Magic Kingdom (everything from the excruciatingly cute — It's a Small World — to exceedingly scary — ExtraTERRORestrial Alien Encounter); Epcot (cutting-edge technology and the World Showcase); Disney-MGM Studios (don't miss the Backlot Tour and Indiana Jones Stunt Spectacular); and Disney's Animal Kingdom (home to both rhinos and dinos — the latter are computerized but toothsome, nonetheless).

Increasingly, Walt Disney World is gearing activities to honeymooners. For example, Pleasure Island features some of the area's best nightlife, with Mannequins Dance Palace, a high-energy club. Disney even offers Fairy Tale Wedding packages, complete with Cinderella's glass coach and personal appearances by Disney characters.

Dynamic as Disney is, the parks are just part of the Orlando playground. Couples can also take in Universal Studios — both a working film studio and a theme park with adrenaline-surging rides like

Earthquake and Twister. Other area attractions range from killer whale acrobatics at SeaWorld to space shuttle launches at Kennedy Space Center, or even one of the world's most comprehensive collections of Tiffany glass at the Charles Hosmer Morse Museum.

Top aspects of a Disney honeymoon include the following:

- ✔ **The price is relatively inexpensive.** With over 100,000 hotel rooms, finding something in your price range shouldn't be difficult. Convenient flights link Orlando with practically everywhere on the planet Earth.

- ✔ **Fun is all around.** Cavorting with Disney characters, scaring yourselves silly on gravity-defying rides, watching parades — it all adds up to a good time.

- ✔ **Fantasy weddings.** No need to wish on a star — the Disney folks can arrange your dream wedding, complete with enchanted castles (and fireworks if you'd like)!

But also consider the following:

- ✔ **Krowds of kids.** Constantly being surrounded by whiney small fry — "Mommy, buy me a Little Mermaid doll" — sorta squelches the passion of the moment. During school vacations (summer, Christmas vacation, and spring break), hotel prices rise and lines at the parks seem to stretch halfway to Miami.

- ✔ **Summer is hot.** Not only do July and August bring endless lines: temperatures soar into the 90s, with sweltering humidity.

Honeymooning on the High Seas

So much romance sets sail on the open seas — think of *The Love Boat* or *Titanic* (wait — hold the iceberg!). There's something eternal about watching blue waves ripple to a limitless horizon, and seeing the sun rise unbounded by land or earthly desires.

In addition, there's a seductively practical reason to choose a honeymoon at sea: good value. Your cabin, food, plus on-board activities and entertainment are all included in the price.

When you're aboard, life is hassle-free — you just have to choose how you want to enjoy yourselves. Instead of having to pack and unpack at different hotels, your ship becomes your floating palace, bringing you to different islands, beaches, and cities. A medley of restaurants serves up fine food — and lots of it, from early-riser buffets to midnight snacks.

Top aspects of a honeymoon cruise include the following:

- ✔ **Good value.** The price of your cruise generally covers not just your cabin, but also food, on-board activities and entertainment, making budget-planning easy. In addition, good deals (for example, two-for-one offers, early-bird discounts, and add-on airfares) make cruising an affordable dream — see later chapters for complete details about how to get the most for your money.

- ✔ **The variety.** With so many different ships afloat, you're sure to find one that suits your lifestyle and budget. Itineraries span the world, with the Caribbean, Bahamas, and Mexico ruling the waves as honeymoon hot spots.

But also consider the following:

- ✔ **You give up individual freedom.** Your itinerary is tightly scheduled, so there's no chance to linger in a destination that appeals to you.

- ✔ **There are too many people.** Some mega-ships carry over 3,000 passengers, making it difficult for you to feel like you're escaping the world. Not all cruise ships offer tables for two in the restaurant, so a quiet dinner together can be difficult to arrange.

- ✔ **Limited departure dates.** Although Sunday departures are becoming more popular, some cruise ships sail on Saturday — not practical if your wedding is on Saturday.

Honeymooning in Paris

Think April in Paris . . . Bogie and Bergman . . . L'amour.

Okay, put a gun to our heads and make us 'fess up — of all the honeymoon destinations in the world, Paris radiates the most romantic sophistication. Steeped in over 2,000 years of history, it presents a past-meets-present synthesis of cathedrals and dance clubs, monuments and multiplexes.

Nicknamed "The City of Light," Paris can just as easily be called "the city of love." Romance seems to be everywhere — echoed in cobblestone alleys on the Ile de Saint-Louis, reflected in the passionate embraces of statues at the Rodin Museum, conjured in the rhapsodic heights of the Eiffel Tower and Notre Dame Cathedral. Above all, Paris is a city for people who want *haute* (highest quality) in their lives, from cuisine to couture. To find the essence of Paris, lose yourself in the city's rhythms, browsing at a quay-side bookseller's stall, strolling the gravel paths of the Tuileries gardens, or sitting for hours in a cafe.

Top aspects of a Parisian honeymoon include the following:

- ✔ **The sheer romance.** In a world beset by cell phones and pagers, a magical feeling comes over you as you marvel the medieval abbeys and royal palaces.

- ✔ **Luxurious accommodations.** The hotels rank among the best in the world for furnishings and service.

- ✔ **Top restaurants.** Paris is synonymous with great food, served up in cozy neighborhood bistros as well as Michelin-starred showplaces.

But also consider the following:

- ✔ **The cost is expensive.** Paris ranks as one of the priciest travel destinations in the world.

- ✔ **Long travel time and jet lag.** The transatlantic flight takes about six hours from the U.S. east coast, ten hours from the west coast. When you also consider the time difference (six hours between New York and Paris, nine hours between Los Angeles and Paris), a honeymoon in France is not realistic unless you can spend at least ten days abroad.

- ✔ **Winter weather.** Unless you're a fan of slush and grey drizzle, forget about a Parisian honeymoon if your trip is any time December through March. Temperatures in January, for example, average about 40 degrees.

Chapter 2

Focusing on the Practicalities

By Risa R. Weinreb

. . . .

In This Chapter

▶ Allowing realistic travel time

▶ Determining the best location for the time of year you're traveling

▶ Allocating your honeymoon funds

. . . .

Many factors influence your choice of honeymoon destination — namely, time (and time of year), money, and your honeymoon budget. In this chapter, we talk about all of these planning basics.

Scheduling Your Time

How many days can you devote to your honeymoon? Your timetable strongly influences your choice of destination. If you only have a week, you should not spend a full day traveling each way or head to a far-away place where you have to contend with excessive jet lag. For shorter honeymoons like this, consider flying five hours or less to your destination.

Deciding When to Go

Analyze what destinations offer the best weather and most interesting activities during the time of your honeymoon (which, for most couples, means right after their wedding). Sometimes, the seasonality is obvious: July in Paris is a lot different from January. Other times, variations are subtle: For example, diving visibility in the Caribbean is usually clearest from April to June. Seasonality may have nothing to do with the weather, but rather with special events and cultural activities, such as Aloha Week festivals (September) in Hawaii or Pirates Week (October) in the Cayman Islands.

Table 2-1	Pluses and Minuses for Destinations by Month	
Month	**For Better**	**For Worse**
January	**General:** January 2 through 15 — the slump after the holidays — is usually good for travel.	
	Hawaii: Prime whale-watching season, especially in Maui.	**Hawaii:** Chance of high surf and rain on the north coast of all islands, especially Kauai.
		Mexico: Temperatures can go down into the 50s in Los Cabos.
	Bermuda: Low-season rates, with discounts of 20 to 60 percent.	**Bermuda:** Generally too cool for swimming, with temperatures in the mid 60s.
		Caribbean: High season (and highest rates) throughout the region.
	Paris: Low-season rates.	**Paris:** Can be gray, wet, and cold (30s and 40s) for weeks at a time.
February		**General:** Beware Presidents Birthday dates.
	Hawaii: Prime whale watching season, especially in Maui.	**Hawaii:** Chance of high surf and rain on the north coast of all islands, especially Kauai.
	Mexico: Lots of sunshine and little rainfall throughout the country.	**Mexico:** Temperatures can go down into the 50s in Los Cabos.
	Bermuda: Low-season rates, with discounts of 20 to 60 percent.	**Bermuda:** Generally too cool for swimming, with temperatures in the mid 60s.
		Caribbean: High season (and highest rates) throughout the region.
	Paris: Low-season rates.	**Paris:** Can be gray, wet, and cold (30s and 40s) for weeks at a time.

March		
General: Avoid Spring Break/Easter dates.		
Hawaii: Prime whale watching season, especially in Maui.	**Hawaii:** Chance of high surf and rain on the north coast of all islands, especially Kauai.	
Mexico: Lots of sunshine and little rainfall throughout the country.		
	Bermuda: Generally too cool for swimming, with temperatures in the mid 60s.	
	Caribbean: High season (and highest rates) throughout the region.	
Paris: Low-season rates and (hopefully) spring-like weather.		

April		
Hawaii: Excellent for travel, with reliably great weather and off-season rates (starting mid-April).	**Hawaii:** "Golden Week" (late April/early May) is the Japanese equivalent of Easter break, and brings many tourists to the islands, especially Oahu.	
Mexico: Lots of sunshine and little rainfall throughout the country.		
Paris: Low-season rates and (hopefully) spring-like weather.	**Caribbean:** High season (and highest rates) ends approximately April 15.	

May		
Hawaii: Excellent for travel, with reliably great weather and off-season rates.		
Caribbean: Low season (and lower rates) throughout the region.		
Paris: Shoulder-season rates and generally good weather.		

Table 2-1	Pluses and Minuses for Destinations by Month	
Month	*For Better*	*For Worse*
June	**Hawaii:** Excellent for travel, with reliably great weather and off-season rates (ending mid-June).	
		Disney World/Orlando: Expect summer vacation crowds, highs in the 90s, and high humidity.
	Caribbean: Low season (and lower rates) throughout the region.	**Caribbean:** Hurricane season officially begins June 1.
		Paris: High season — and highest prices for travel.
July		**Disney World/Orlando:** Expect summer vacation crowds, highs in the 90s, and high humidity.
		Mexico: In Los Cabos, temperatures can reach 100-degrees-plus.
	Caribbean: Low season (and lower rates) throughout the region.	**Caribbean:** Hurricane season.
		Paris: High season — and highest prices for travel.
August		**Disney World/Orlando:** Expect summer vacation crowds, highs in the 90s, and high humidity.
		Mexico: In Los Cabos, temperatures can reach 100-degrees-plus.
	Caribbean: Low season (and lower rates) throughout the region.	**Caribbean:** Hurricane season.
		Paris: High season — and highest prices for travel.
September	**Hawaii:** Excellent for travel, with reliably great weather and off-season rates.	

	Mexico: Hurricanes are rare in Cancun and Cozumel, if but they hit, they tend to arrive in September and October.
	Caribbean: Hurricane season.
	Caribbean: Low season (and lower rates) throughout the region.
	Paris: Shoulder-season rates and generally good weather.
October	**Hawaii:** Excellent for travel, with reliable weather and off-season rates.
	Mexico: Hurricanes are rare in Cancun and Cozumel, but if they hit, they tend to arrive in September and October.
	Caribbean: Hurricane season.
	Caribbean: Low season (and lower rates) throughout the region.
	Paris: Shoulder-season rates and generally good weather.
November	**General:** Avoid Thanksgiving high season.
	Hawaii: Excellent for travel, with reliable weather and off-season rates.
	Mexico: In Cozumel, strong winds sometimes make conditions less than optimal for scuba diving.
	Caribbean: Hurricane season ends November 30.
	Caribbean: Low season (and lower rates) throughout the region.
December	**General:** Avoid Christmas high season.
	General: December 1 through 15, the slump before the holidays, is usually good for travel.
	Mexico: In Cozumel, strong winds sometimes make conditions less than optimal for scuba diving.
	Bermuda: Generally too cool for swimming, with temperatures in the mid 60s.

Don't write off a place just because your honeymoon is in the so-called "off" season. Some destinations — particularly Florida, Hawaii, Mexico, and the Caribbean — have virtually the same weather all year. In the Caribbean, for example, many islands only have a five-degree temperature difference between the winter and the summer. By going during the low season, you can save up to 50 percent on airline and hotel prices over the high season prices. Also, in the low season, fewer crowds on beaches, in stores, and in restaurants can be an advantage.

Table 2-1 summarizes the best — and worst — times to honeymoon in different locales. You may be surprised to see that in some cases, a destination is listed as both a "best" and a "worst" in the same months. That's because in travel (as in life and love), you deal with trade-offs. For example, lower rates on a hotel room in the Caribbean versus the remote chance of a hurricane. For complete information about weather, rainfall, festivals, and other factors influencing travel, see the individual destination chapters.

Allocating Your Budget

Exactly how much money do you want to spend on your honeymoon? No two couples earning, say, $60,000 a year want to spend their money the same way. Some may want to splurge on their trip, while others may opt for a more modest expenditure and prefer to save the money to buy a house, a car, or furniture. As a couple, you should set priorities.

Obviously, how much you're willing to allocate determines which honeymoon destinations you can realistically consider. What is not so apparent are the different ways to spend money on a vacation. Some couples devote a large chunk of their budget to flying to an exotic location, then sleep cheap when they get there. Others keep transportation costs down, but then stay in the best hotel in town. What do you two want to do? We explain all the ins and outs of budgeting — and give you some useful tips about ways you can cut expenses — in Chapter 6.

Using a honeymoon registry

You don't fancy fancy-cut crystal that doesn't fit in the dishwasher. Between your two bachelor apartments, you own enough Teflon frying pans and coffee mugs to entertain a busload of guests. And you don't really trust Aunt Alice's taste to pick out a tablecloth.

But boy, do you like to travel.

If that's the case, you may be prime candidates for a honeymoon registry. The registry operates just like registering your china, crystal, and other gifts with a store — except you're listing your honeymoon with a travel agent. The money that friends and relatives give you as a wedding gift automatically goes towards your honeymoon trip. Many travel agencies offer this service for couples.

Taking advantage of being newlyweds

When making reservations at a hotel, restaurant, or for an activity, be sure to say — "We're on our honeymoon." Just like babies and puppies always draw swarms of people, newlyweds inspire feelings of gaga enthusiasm in complete strangers — importantly, the same complete strangers that can help you snare an oceanfront room or seaside table at dinner. Often, hotels provide newlyweds with upgraded accommodations or special amenities at no extra charge.

As a correspondent recently reported in *Arthur Frommer's Budget Travel Newsletter*, he and his bride were treated to a bottle of champagne on their flight, a special, just-for-two horseback ride — even an emergency evening visit from a locksmith after their condo key broke in the lock — just from mentioning that they were on their honeymoon.

Chapter 3

Arranging a Destination Wedding

By Risa R. Weinreb

● ●

In This Chapter

▶ Weighing the option of a wedding away from home

▶ Comparing the costs

▶ Planning a destination wedding

● ●

*M*ore and more couples are saying "I do" to a wedding at their honeymoon locale; in fact, destination weddings are one of today's hottest trends in getting married. In this chapter, we guide you through all the steps of tying the knot away from home.

Taking the Plunge

Weddings away are a popular option for couples whose friends and family are geographically dispersed: The bride is from Connecticut, the groom is from Michigan, and they both live and work in San Francisco. Many people must travel some distance to the wedding anyway, and as an added bonus, everybody gets to vacation together.

Destination weddings may also reduce stress for couples who have to deal with complicated family situations (parental divorce, children, tensions surrounding different religions or backgrounds, and so on).

We're not talking elopements here, but real, planned weddings. In the past, most couples opting for away-from-home ceremonies came by themselves — just the two of them tying the knot on a beach at sunset. But increasingly, couples are flying in close friends and family members to celebrate with them, and having formal ceremonies — the works: tuxedos, long veils, and maids of honor. With the soaring price of a traditional wedding (averaging nearly $20,000 in the U.S.), perhaps flying 20 of your nearest and dearest to the Caribbean for a blow-out long weekend may be cheaper than hosting 200 people (including eccentric second-cousins and mom's ex-sorority sisters who you met all of once) back home.

How cheap is cheap for a wedding, away? Would you believe free? As *Honeymoon Vacations For Dummies* went to press, Sandals and Beaches Resorts (the all-inclusive properties) were offering a free wedding for couples booking a five-night "WeddingMoon" stay at any of their hotels. The plan included a champagne and hors d'oeuvre wedding reception, bouquet and boutonniere, Caribbean wedding cake, legal fees, a certified marriage license, and oodles more. For details, check their Web site at www.sandals.com or call ☎ 888-SANDALS.

At SuperClubs, another popular all-inclusive resort group, free weddings are included in several different vacation packages. Ceremonies have taken place everywhere from a swinging trapeze to aboard a luxury yacht. Contact www.superclubs.com or ☎ 877-GO SUPER for more information.

Even when you pay, a destination wedding saves money and hassle compared with marrying back home. Many hotels and attractions offer wedding packages, which can include everything from booking the officiant to hiring the videographer. Pick the plan you want and presto! Your wedding decisions are done. Several properties also provide the services of a wedding coordinator (either free or at a reasonable cost), who not only scouts out sweetheart pink roses, but can also handle marriage licenses and other formalities.

A wedding away can be as informal or as traditional as you like. Many wedding dresses and tuxedoes travel round-trip to Hawaii, Mexico, and the Caribbean. (Also, even some beachy destinations offer tux rentals). After they return from their honeymoon, couples often hold a reception for people who could not join them. At these parties, couples sometimes continue the theme of their wedding locale (decorate with piñatas, hire a reggae band), and show a video of their ceremony so that everyone can share in their happiness.

If you invite guests to your destination wedding, find out about group rates for hotels and airfare, which can save 20 percent or more off regular prices. Plan as far ahead as possible so that people can arrange their schedules and join you.

Organizing the Details

Even though destination weddings are exotic, they can be remarkably easy to plan. Meanwhile, here are some pointers for organizing a wedding away from home:

✔ **Requirements:** Regulations for getting married vary in different U.S. states. Some foreign countries make marrying easier for couples, while in others, getting married is practically impossible for non-citizens because of long residency requirements. Foreign marriages are recognized as legal in the U.S. as long as you comply with the laws of the country where the ceremony is performed. Equally important — make sure that you meet regulations in your home state. For example, some locales mandate a waiting period after a divorce decree before the person can remarry. (Check with the office of your state Attorney General.)

✔ **Waiting periods:** Some places require that you be in the area for a certain number of days before a license can be issued or a wedding performed. Check whether these requirements can be waived, and if you can get the marriage license in advance by mail.

✔ **Medical tests:** Find out if any blood tests or other screenings are required. Can these be done at home, or only at your destination?

✔ **Fees:** These can range from about $20 to several hundred for licenses, stamps, and so on.

✔ **Documentation:** You may have to produce either proof of identity or proof of age. Find out in advance what documents are acceptable, such as driver's license, certified birth certificate, or passport. Do they need to be translated or notarized? Also, do you need to send any papers to the country in advance? If so, do these need to be originals?

✔ **Religious ceremonies:** Some countries require a civil ceremony as well as a religious one. If you want a religious ceremony, check what papers are necessary.

✔ **Second marriages:** If either one of you is divorced or widowed, you usually have to furnish the official certificate. If you are marrying in a non-English-speaking country, you may need a translated, notarized copy of the papers.

✔ **Local rules:** These can be quite different from what you're accustomed to back home. For example, many countries require a certified document stating that there is no impediment to the marriage. Since no such record exists in the U.S., you need to execute an affidavit to that effect at the U.S. embassy or consulate in the country where you plan to wed.

✔ **Packing savvy:** If they plan to wear tuxedoes, guys should also remember to pack the accoutrements such as studs, bow ties, cummerbunds, and dress shoes. If they plan to wear pantyhose, brides should bring along extra pairs (probably the worse single item to go shopping for on a tropical isle). By all means, pack your wedding duds as carry-on baggage!

✔ **Early does it:** Plan to arrive at your wedding locale a few days early. If flights are late, you won't panic. You also have time to handle last-minute details and rest up.

Going over the Requirements

Most hotels offer onsite wedding planner assistance and should be contacted directly. They help you secure all of your paperwork, find an official to perform the ceremony, as well as the photographers (both still and video) and the florist, plus they organize the reception and make any other arrangements you may need. (Throughout the book, we highlight what we consider to be superb wedding establishments with a Wedding Bells icon.) Contact the tourism board of your preferred destination for a reputable company.

You can add special meaning to your big event by weaving local traditions into your ceremony. For example, in the U.S. Virgin Islands, you may want to hire a steel band for the music. In Hawaii, you can wear *maile leis,* which symbolize long life, health, and prosperity. Ask the tourist office, your wedding planner, or officiant about customs you may want to include.

For information on getting married on a cruise ship see Chapter 31.

Here's a quick overview of what to expect:

- ✔ **Aruba:** A destination wedding is out on Aruba — the one island where you can't officially tie the knot unless one of you is Aruban.

- ✔ **Bahamas:** You and your intended must both be in the Bahamas for at least 24 hours before you can apply for a marriage license. (You can fill out applications Monday through Friday.) For details, contact the office of the **Registrar General** (☎ **242-322-3316** in Nassau, or ☎ **242-352-4934** on Grand Bahama). If you and your partner are U.S. citizens, you need to get an affidavit to confirm this — and the fact that you're both single — from the American Embassy in Nassau. Note: The U.S. Embassy is closed on both American and Bahamian holidays. You must present proof of identity, such as a passport, and, if necessary, proof of divorce. You won't need any blood tests, however. The **Weddings and Honeymoon Unit of the Bahamas Ministry of Tourism** (☎ **888-687-8425** or 242-302-2034 for a brochure) can also provide information. For assistance with planning your nuptials in the Bahamas, you can also call your hotel or the Ministry of Tourism's People-to-People Program: Nassau, New Providence (☎ **242-328-7810**); Freeport/Lucaya, Grand Bahama (☎ **242-352-8044**). The marriage license fee in the Bahamas is $40 and an affidavit is $55 and up (U.S. Embassy or Notary Public).

- ✔ **Barbados:** Tying the knot here is easier than ever, because Barbados recently eliminated advance notice requirements to marry on the island. An official marriage ceremony can take place as soon as a license is obtained. To obtain a marriage license, apply in person at the **Ministry of Home Affairs,** General Post

Office Building in Bridgetown (☎ **246-228-8950** or fax 246-437-3794, open Mon–Fri. 8:15 a.m.–4:30 p.m.). Each partner must have a valid passport or the original or a certified copy of the applicant's birth certificate, and return airline tickets. You must also present a letter from the minister or magistrate who has agreed to perform the wedding ceremony. If either party is widowed, you must provide a copy of the previous marriage certificate and the deceased spouse's death certificate. If either party is divorced, you must provide an original decree or a certified copy of the final judgement. If neither party is a citizen or resident of Barbados, the wedding license costs $75, plus $12.50 for a stamp.

✔ **Disney World/Orlando:** Weddings are not a new niche for Mickey. WDW performs about 2,300 weddings annually — over 12,000 since the company got involved in nuptials in 1991. For more info, contact Disney's **Fairy Tale Weddings** at ☎ **407-828-3400.** Disney is the land of magic, so almost any ceremony you can dream up is possible. Sample budgets are available on the Internet at www.disneyweddings.com.

If you'd like to get married off Disney property, several wedding planners have businesses in the area. **Just Marry!** (☎ **800-986-2779** or 407-629-2747) is the best for diversity and enthusiasm. If you are doing your own planning, the clerk of courts offices at both the Orange County and Osceola County courthouses perform marriages from 8 a.m. to 4:30 p.m. Monday through Friday, excluding holidays. Bring your driver's licenses or birth certificates and Social Security numbers. If you're not American citizens, bring your passports, too. If you were previously married, you must provide the date the marriage ended. Florida residents have to wait three days before getting married. There isn't a cooling-off period for non-residents; they can marry the day they get their license. Marriage-license fees are $88.50; for another $20, clerks can perform the ceremony. Call in advance to see what times of day the marriages are performed; they're done on a first-come, first-serve basis. After your marriage license is issued, you have 60 days to use it for a ceremony. The **Orange County clerk's office** is at 425 N. Orange Ave., Orlando; ☎ **407-836-2067.** The **Osceola County courthouse** — the closest to WDW — is at 2 Courthouse Sq., Kissimmee; ☎ **407-343-3500.** Both offices take payments by cash, money order, traveler's check, MasterCard, or Visa.

✔ **Cayman Islands:** This is one of the few Caribbean destinations that allows U.S. citizens to marry the same day they arrive, instead of requiring a minimum on-island stay before the wedding. Detailed information regarding documentation can be found in "Getting Married in The Cayman Islands," a brochure available from **Cayman Islands Government Information Services,** Phase II, Cricket Square (☎ **345 949-8092;** fax 345-949-5936).

✔ **Hawaii:** For a reputable wedding planner, choose one endorsed by the **Hawaii Visitors and Convention Bureau** (☎ **800-GO-HAWAII**). See their Web site (www.gohawaii.com; click on WEDDINGS AND HONEYMOONS) for a complete list of wedding planners to suit any budget. For a rundown of the legalities, contact the **Honolulu Marriage License Office,** State Department of Health Building, 1250 Punchbowl St., Honolulu, HI 96813 (☎ **808-586-4545** or 808-586-4544). Or visit the government Web site at www.hawaii.gov/doh and click on VITAL RECORDS, where you'll find all the details, including a downloadable license form. A marriage license costs $50 and is good for 30 days from the date of issue. Both parties must be at least 18 years of age (minors must have written consent) and cannot be more closely related than first cousins (!). You'll need a photo ID, such as a driver's license; a birth certificate is necessary if you're 18 or under. No blood tests, citizenship, or residency minimum is required.

✔ **Jamaica:** Couples need certified copies of birth certificates that include the fathers' name; plus proof of divorce or the death certificate of any former spouse/s (if applicable). The is fee is Jamaican $200 (approximately US$5–$6) You must be in Jamaica for 24 hours before the ceremony, and the application must be made in advance of your trip. Call the **Ministry of National Security** at ☎ **876-922-0080.** For more information and for a list of wedding planners call the **Jamaica Tourist Board** ☎ **800-233-4582** or visit www.jamaicatravel.com.

✔ **Mexico:** Under a treaty between the U.S. and Mexico, Mexican civil marriages are automatically valid in the States. You need certified copies of birth certificates, driver's licenses, or passports; certified proof of divorce or the death certificate of any former spouse/s (if applicable); tourist cards; and results of blood tests performed in Mexico 15 days before the ceremony. Check with a local, onsite wedding planner through your hotel to verify all the necessary requirements, and obtain an application well in advance of your desired date. Contact the **Mexican Tourism Board** (☎ **800-446-3942;** Internet: www.visitmexico.com) for more information.

✔ **Paris:** It's very difficult for non-citizens to exchange "I do's" in Paris, because at least one of the partners must reside for at least 40 days in the town or city district in which the ceremony will be performed. There are two ways to get around the residency requirement. The easiest is to have your civil wedding in the U.S. and then arrange for a church ceremony in Paris (which a good wedding planner can put together for you). One of the best wedding specialists there is Patti Metzger, founder of **Weddings on The Move, Inc.** (☎ **800-444-6967;** Internet: www.idoweddings.com). Contact the **French Government Tourist Office** at www.francetourism.com for more information.

✔ **Puerto Rico:** The legal age to get married in Puerto Rico is 21. A blood test is required within 10 days of the wedding. Marriage license papers must be obtained, in person, at the **Department of Health, Demographic Registry Office** (171 Quisquella St., Hato Rey, ☎ **787-767-9120**). U.S. Citizens need an identification with photograph, and those who are divorced or widowed must bring along the certified proof of divorce or the death certificate of any former spouse/s. The marriage license and blood test results must be taken to a physician in Puerto Rico for certification. A judge or minister authorized by the government of Puerto Rico must offici-ate at the wedding ceremony.

✔ **St. Lucia:** You must be on the island for two days before you can get a marriage license. The required documentation is the following: a valid passport, birth certificate, a Decree Absolute if one of the parties is divorced, and a death certificate if a widow or widower is remarrying; you also need to allow four working days for pro-cessing documentation. For more information contact the **St. Lucia Tourist Board** (P.O. Box 221, Top floor, Sure Line Building Vide Bouteille, Castries; ☎ **758-452-4094**; in the U.S. 800-456-3984; fax 758-453-1121).

✔ **USVIs:** There is no waiting period, blood test, or residency require-ment in the U.S. Virgin Islands. A passport is not necessary to get married, but a photo identification is needed. An application must be received at least eight days prior to the planned wedding. You can obtain one from the Territorial Court of the U.S. Virgin Islands. If you are planning to get married on St. Thomas or St. John, mail your request to the **Administrator/Clerk of the Territorial Court of the Virgin Islands,** P.O. Box 70, St. Thomas, USVI, 00804 or call ☎ **809-744-6680.** To get married on St. Croix, write to the **Terri-orial Court of the Virgin Islands, Family Division,** P.O. Box 929, Christiansted, St. Croix, USVI, 00821 or call ☎ **809-778-9750** and request a marriage license application. If you are divorced, you also need to send your most recent certified divorce decree in English (with a raised seal or stamped certified copy) signed by the judge from the court in which you were divorced (not just a notarized copy). Your divorce must be final and dated 30 days prior to your wedding date. If either partner is widowed, she or he needs a certified, stamped copy of the previous spouse's death certificate. For information and to find a reputable wedding planner, contact the **USVI Division of Tourism** (☎ **800-372-8784;** Territorial Court, St. Thomas and St. John, 340-774-6680; Territorial Court, St. Croix, 340-778-9750; or visit www.virginisles.com).

✔ **Bermuda:** Just 90 minutes from the East Coast by air, Bermuda is easily accessible for the wedding party and guests. Couples need to file a Notice of Intended Marriage with the **Registrar General** (30 Parliament St., Hamilton HM 12, Bermuda; ☎ **441-297-7709;** Fax: 441-292-4568) at least two weeks prior to the wedding. The form must be accompanied by a $186 fee in money order, cashier's check, or bank draft made payable to the Accountant General, Hamilton, Bermuda. Two weeks after receiving the notice, the

Registrar General issues the marriage license, which is valid for three months. Copies of final divorce decrees must accompany the Notice of Intended Marriage if either the bride or groom has been divorced; no blood tests or health certificates are required. Contact the **Bermuda Department of Tourism** at www.bermudatourism.com for information about reputable wedding planners.

Part II
Ironing Out the Details

The 5th Wave   By Rich Tennant

"I appreciate that our room looks out onto several baroque fountains, but I had to get up 6 times last night to go to the bathroom."

In this part . . .

Setting the date. Choosing the wedding dress. Deciding where to have the reception. These count among your most important wedding arrangements. But just as you have to plan your ceremony, you need to organize your honeymoon.

In the following chapters, we demystify the world of glossy brochures and winking Web pages to help you find a travel agent, choose the right accommodations, locate a good deal on airfares, and other considerations. We want you to have the know-how to get the most for your money.

Chapter 4

Making Your Travel Arrangements

By Risa R. Weinreb

● ●

In This Chapter

▶ Planning a schedule

▶ Knowing what a travel agent offers

▶ Discovering the truth about honeymoon packages

▶ Finding a great deal on a flight

▶ Booking a car rental

● ●

*D*reaming is fun. But the real honeymoon is even better. In this chapter we calm your trip-planning jitters by showing you how to travel to your destination in the cheapest, most comfortable, and fastest way possible. By giving you up-to-date, practical information, we take the mystery out of trip planning and help you get the most for your money.

Making a Schedule

Planning your trip well in advance helps to ensure that you choose the right honeymoon destination, get the most convenient airline reservations (at the cheapest price), and reserve the most romantic room at your favorite resort. Here's a checklist for your schedule.

6 to 12 months before the wedding, do the following:

✔ Start discussing what sort of honeymoon destination you want — a beach, the country, a historic city? What kind of ambience — elegant or casual?

✔ Ask family and friends for recommendations, not only for destinations, but also for travel agents.

✔ Get travel brochures from tourist boards, hotels, and your travel agent. Research different destinations on the Internet.

4 to 6 months before the wedding, do the following:

✔ Make your airline, hotel, and car rental reservations. (Note: Do this even further in advance if you plan to head to a popular destination during its peak season, such as the Caribbean during the Christmas holidays.) Send all deposits necessary.

✔ Get passports (if needed).

2 to 4 months before the wedding, do the following:

✔ Check that you've received all your confirmations.

✔ Consider your luggage requirements and purchase any new pieces needed.

✔ Analyze your wardrobe. Shop for clothes to wear on your honeymoon.

1 month before the wedding, do the following:

✔ Reconfirm all your arrangements, either directly or through your travel agent.

✔ Check that the camera you intend to take is in good working order — shoot a roll of film just to be sure.

1 to 2 weeks months before the wedding, do the following:

✔ Reconfirm all your arrangements, either directly or through your travel agent.

✔ Pack everything except the clothes and toiletries you need for the coming week. Is everything cleaned, ironed, and repaired?

✔ Verify your PIN codes on credit cards you intend to use for cash in ATM machines. Purchase traveler's checks if desired.

✔ Arrange to stop the mail delivery, newspaper, and so on while you are away.

1 to 2 days before the wedding, do the following:

✔ Reconfirm all your arrangements, either directly or through your travel agent.

✔ Pack your remaining items.

✔ Be sure you pack your passports, airline tickets, traveler's checks, hotel confirmation, rental car confirmation, and credit cards.

Using a Travel Agent

In recent years, the Internet has made booking trips incredibly easy, so much so that you may start to wonder if you need a travel agent at all. The answer depends on you. During our travels, we've met many people who have booked their honeymoons online. Armed with this book and a do-it-yourself attitude, you should have no problem planning the trip on your own. However, if you aren't Internet savvy, if you like to talk over your choices with an expert, if you're short of time to plan your trip, or if your honeymoon is complicated (for example, if you're island-hopping or making several airline connections), the safest bet is to go through a travel agent.

Choosing the right travel agent

Any travel agent can help you find a bargain airfare, hotel, or rental car. A *good* travel agent — note the accent on "good" — can help stop you from ruining your vacation because you were trying to save a few dollars. The best travel agents can find a cheap flight that doesn't require you to change planes three times on your way to your destination, get you an oceanfront hotel room for the same price as a mountain-view one, arrange for a competitively priced rental car, and even give recommendations on restaurants.

A few years ago, airlines and resorts slashed travel agent commissions or eliminated them altogether, throwing travel agencies into turmoil. As a result, some travel agents have begun charging customers fees, such as $10 for an airline booking or up to $100 for planning a trip. More complex trip planning may be based on an hourly fee — or you may not have to pay a penny, depending on the agency's business policy.

The agent's fee may be a small price to pay, because a savvy travel agent can save you hundreds — even thousands — of dollars.

Here's how to find the right travel agent:

- ✔ Look for an agent who specializes in planning trips to the destinations that interest you. Several agencies also have honeymoon-planning experts.
- ✔ Choose an agent who has been in business for a while and has an established client base. Ask friends and family for recommendations.
- ✔ If you're pleased with the agency that books business travel at your workplace, ask them if they book personal travel, too.
- ✔ When meeting with an agent, evaluate everything from the appearance of the office to the agent's willingness to listen and answer questions.

> ✔ If you don't feel you're getting what you need from a particular travel agent — or you don't think he or she knows enough about your prospective destination to plan your trip appropriately — move on to someone who makes you feel more comfortable.

Considering a package tour

Package tours are not the same thing as escorted tours, so if you're picturing something like "five islands in six days" and being herded around in a group on a bus, don't worry.

Instead, the packages we're talking about are simply a way of buying your airfare, accommodations, and other pieces of your trip (usually airport transfers, and sometimes meals and activities) all at the same time — in one neat "package," so to speak.

For popular destinations from Paris to Puerto Rico, packages can save you a ton of money. In many cases, a package that includes airfare, hotel, and transportation to and from the airport costs less than just the hotel alone if you booked the room yourself — the reason being that packages are sold in bulk to tour operators, who resell them to the public.

In the individual destination chapters, we dish the skinny about the best packagers to each part of the world. An experienced travel agent should also be knowledgeable about different packagers, the deals they offer, and the general rate of customer satisfaction. Another good source of information is the travel section of your local Sunday newspaper, or the ads in the back of magazines like *Travel & Leisure, National Geographic Traveler,* and *Condé Nast Traveler.*

Here some "do's" and "don'ts" to help you distinguish packager winners from losers:

> ✔ **Do a little homework.** Read through this guide, decide which destination you prefer, and choose some accommodations that you find intriguing. Compare the rack rates that we give you in this book to the discounted rates offered by the packagers to see if you're actually being offered substantial savings.

> ✔ **Don't compare apples and oranges.** When you look over different packagers, compare the deals that they offer on similar properties. With most packagers, savings are greater on some hotels than others.

> ✔ **Do protect your money.** Find out if the tour operator puts your deposit and other payments into an escrow account until after the tour is completed. Often you can pay directly into the escrow account rather than to the tour operator. Also ask if the tour operator participates in a consumer protection program such as the United States Tour Operators Association (USTOA) consumer protection plan.

✔ **Do read the fine print.** Make sure you know *exactly* what's included in the price you're quoted. Is airfare covered? How many nights at the hotel? How about room taxes, which can top 17 percent in some locales? Before you sign or hand over your credit card, ask to see a copy of the contract with the tour operator, which should cover items like cancellation policy, changes in price, and items excluded.

If you decide that the available package vacations just don't meet your needs — say your heart is set on staying at a hotel that isn't offered as part of a package, or you want to use frequent-flier miles for your airline tickets, or you're a control freak who'd just rather handle everything yourself — doing so doesn't mean that you are going to get stuck paying top dollar (or peso or franc) for everything. See the rest of this chapter for tips on do-it-yourself savings.

The best deals usually coincide with low season for each destination, when room rates and airfares plunge. You may be a bit more limited in your flight dates, because airlines cut back on their schedules during the slow season, but if you're flexible, you can get some great bargains. Another tip — book your trip early. With many packagers, that can save up to $50 per person on airfare.

Consider buying trip cancellation insurance, offered by most tour operators for anywhere from $30 to $60. That way, if you need to axe your trip, you won't have to pay. For more information on insurance, see Chapter 7.

Travel agents may get better commissions from some packagers than others, which is why you need to do some studying — if you have a good idea of what's out there *before* you visit your local travel rep, you won't put yourself at risk for getting a less than ideal deal.

Evaluating Honeymoon Packages

There's another type of package you should know about — honeymoon packages (also known as "romance packages"). Unlike the fly'n'stay deals we discuss in the previous section, which are offered by tour operators, a honeymoon package is put together by a hotel or cruise line.

Honeymoon packages vary widely. In general, you get one of the best rooms in the house (with king-size bed and a great view) and a welcoming gift (such as a fruit basket or bottle of champagne). Other features run the full gamut: from sunset cocktail cruises to scuba-diving lessons. Usually, the room rate offers you significant savings over the "rack" rate (the standard price for the accommodations).

When evaluating different honeymoon packages, try to put a dollar value on all those bonus items you get (for example, how much do those flowers cost?). Even more important, ask yourselves if you are really going to take advantage of all the benefits. In order for you to compare values, we list both the rack rate for a double room and the honeymoon package rate (if available) in the destination chapters that follow.

If you or your future spouse has a special interest — tennis, golf, or scuba diving, for example — your money might be better spent on a special program incorporating the activity, rather than on a honeymoon package.

Getting the Best Airfares

Even if you decide to use a travel agent or a packager, it's a good idea to "do it yourself" a bit and research airfares to your honeymoon destinations. Doing so can help you tell whether or not you're getting a low price — important, because airfares typically account for 25 percent of the total honeymoon cost. See the individual destination chapters for information about which airlines fly to different destinations, and the best packagers for each area.

Booking your flight

Airfares are capitalism at its purest. Passengers within the same cabin on an airplane rarely have paid the same fare. Rather, they spent the market rate at the time they bought their ticket.

Business travelers usually get stuck paying the premium rate or "full fare," because they need the flexibility to purchase their tickets at the last minute, change their itinerary at a moment's notice, or want to get home before the weekend. Passengers — like honeymooners — who can book their ticket long in advance, who don't mind staying over Saturday night, or who are willing to travel on a Tuesday, Wednesday, or Thursday pay the least, usually a fraction of the full fare.

The airlines also periodically hold sales, lowering prices on their most popular routes. Although these fares usually have advance purchase requirements and date-of-travel restrictions, you can't beat the price. Check newspaper ads and the airline Web sites, and then pounce as soon as you see discounted fares. The sales and bargains tend to take place during low season, and almost never around the Christmas holidays, to warm weather destinations — like Hawaii, Mexico, and the Caribbean — from December through March, or to Europe in July or August.

Cutting costs by using a consolidator

Airfare consolidators — also known as bucket shops — are large companies that get discounts for buying airline tickets in bulk, and then pass some of the savings (sometimes 20 to 50 percent off the airlines' lowest published fare) on to you. You can find their ads in the small boxes at the bottom of the page in your Sunday newspaper travel section. Some of the most reliable ones (we've booked tickets through them all) are **Cheap Tickets, Inc.** (☎ **800-377-1000;** Internet: www.cheaptickets.com); **Economytravel** (☎ **888-222-2110;** Internet: www.economytravel.com); and **Lowestfare** (☎ **888-777-2222;** Internet: www.lowestfare.com).

All these major airline consolidators have Web sites. The next section walks you through the steps for making travel arrangements online.

Deals offered by consolidators ain't as great as they used to be. Sometimes, the rates are even higher than what you can find with the online travel agencies such as Expedia or Travelocity, or on the airlines' own sites — all with a lot fewer ticket restrictions. With the whole online travel industry in such flux (actually, turmoil is more like it), you just have to shop around.

Booking your trip online

Another way to find the cheapest fare is on the Internet. Even if you don't actually book online, top sites offer an array of research tools that can help you check airfares, hotel availability, and car rental prices.

Click Trips at www.clicktrips.com is a travel Web site specializing in romantic vacations. Click Trips features travel specials and offers advice from the experts. Best of all, you can book your honeymoon right on online.

Here's a rundown of our other favorite online travel booking sites:

- ✔ **Travelocity** (www.travelocity.com): Travelocity uses the SABRE system — the same computer reservations system (CRS) used by many travel agents — to offer reservations and tickets on 95 percent of all airline seats sold, plus more than 48,000 hotels, more than 50 car rental companies, and more than 5,000 vacation and cruise packages. Travelocity's Destination Guides include updated information on some 260 destinations worldwide, supplied by Frommer's.

- ✔ **Expedia** (www.expedia.com): Another fast, efficient online travel agency, Expedia covers more than 450 airlines, 40,000 hotels, all major car rental agencies, and more than 400 destination guides. Its airline reservations system is based on Worldspan, another computer reservations system widely used by travel agents.

✔ **Orbitz** (www.orbitz.com): Launched in June 2001, Orbitz is poised to reshape online travel booking. Featuring airfares from over 450 carriers worldwide, the site is owned by the five largest U.S. airlines (United, Delta, Continental, Northwest, and American). The site pledges to deliver a comprehensive, unbiased view of fares, schedules, and rates for destinations around the world. Customer service is state-of-the-art: the company sends updates about flight delays or cancellations to passengers beginning three hours before departure via the phone, cell phone, wireless handheld computer or e-mail.

Because each Web site changes its benefits and requirements so frequently, log on to each online travel agency for more specific information when you're ready to travel.

Using E-tickets

At some domestic airlines, over half of all passengers now use E-tickets (electronic tickets) — a voucher with a confirmation code, instead of a standard ticket. Usually, E-tickets work just fine — unless a flight gets cancelled and you need to change airlines. (Having a real-life ticket in hand can become critical if you encounter cancellations or delays; you may need to have a gate agent endorse your ticket or receipt fast so you can sprint to the next flight on another airline.)

If decide to buy E-tickets, remember to bring the credit card to which the E-ticket was charged with you when you go to the airport for your flight. Otherwise, the airline can and will refuse to give you the ticket. (This is to prevent someone from unscrupulously charging tickets to your credit card.)

Finding the fairest of the fares

Whether you find the fare yourself on the Internet, or use a travel agent or a packager, here are some tips to help you find the best deals aloft:

✔ **Book early.** Airlines offer only a small percentage of their seats at the absolutely lowest rate — and these cheapies book up fast.

✔ **Act fast.** When you find a super-low airfare, be prepared to book the flight immediately — five minutes later, that cheap fare can be gone.

✔ **Try again after midnight.** Airlines generally revise their inventory at 12 a.m., making additional low-cost seats available.

✔ **Fly weekdays.** Fares are generally lowest on Tuesday, Wednesday, and Thursday, and somewhat higher on Monday and Friday. Week-end departures tend to be the most expensive, especially to vacation destinations like Hawaii or the Caribbean.

- ✔ **Stay over on a Saturday night.** Many low fares require travelers to spend at least one Saturday night at their destination before their return flight.

- ✔ **Wiggle and jiggle.** Price out fares using various departure dates and times, as well as airports. (Most knowledgeable travel agents do this, or experiment yourself on the Internet.) If you're flying from New York, for example, check fares from JFK, LaGuardia, and Newark airports (as well as Islip, if that's convenient for you). To destinations such as Paris, price out airfares connecting through different cities.

- ✔ **Look before you book.** Most low airfares come with enough restrictions to ground a 747. Nearly all super-cheap fares are nonrefundable. Some charge a substantial fee for changes, while other itineraries can't be modified at all. Also find out if your ticket is endorsable — meaning it can be honored by other airlines if your scheduled flight is delayed or cancelled.

Reserving a Rental Car

Depending on where in the world you are going, you may or may not need to read this section. Car rentals are pretty much necessities on Hawaiian islands such as Maui or the Big Island; a definite extravagance (and maybe even a foolish hassle) in Paris. See the individual destination chapters for guidance about whether you need to make a deal on wheels.

For car rentals, the cost depends on the size of the car, the length of time you keep it, where and when you pick it up and drop it off, where you drive it, and other factors.

Asking a few key questions can save hundreds of dollars. For example, weekend rates may be lower than weekday rates. If you keep the car five or more days, a weekly rate may be cheaper than the daily rate. Some companies assess a drop-off charge if you do not return the car to the same rental location; others do not. Ask if the rate is cheaper if you pick up the car at the airport or an office in town. Don't forget to mention membership in AAA or frequent-flyer programs. These usually entitle you to discounts ranging from 5 to 30 percent. (Most car rentals are worth at least 500 miles on your frequent-flyer account!)

As with airline seats, booking your car rental on the Internet can sometimes (but not always) result in savings. All the major booking sites — **Travelocity** (www.travelocity.com), **Expedia** (www.expedia.com), and **Yahoo Travel** (http://travel.yahoo.com), for example — can search for discounted car-rental rates as well.

On top of the standard rental prices, other optional charges apply to most car rentals. The **Collision Damage Waiver** (CDW), which requires you to pay for damage to the car in a collision, is illegal in some states, but is covered by many credit card companies. Check with your credit card company before you go so you can avoid paying this hefty fee (as much as $15 per day), if possible.

The car rental companies also offer additional liability insurance (if you harm others in an accident), personal accident insurance (if you harm yourself or your passengers), and personal effects insurance (if your luggage is stolen from your car). The insurance on your car at home probably covers most of these unlikelihoods. If your own insurance doesn't cover rentals, or if you don't have auto insurance, you should consider the additional coverage (the car rental companies are liable for certain base amounts, depending on the state). But weigh the chance of getting into an accident or losing your luggage against the cost of the coverage (as much as $20 per day combined), which can significantly add to the price of your rental.

Chapter 5

Choosing Your Honeymoon Accommodations

By Risa R. Weinreb

* *

In This Chapter

▶ Looking at different types of accommodations

▶ Deciding if an all-inclusive resort is right for you

▶ Getting the best room in the house

* *

*W*here you stay is more important on your honeymoon than on any other trip. You want to share each moment together in the most romantic surroundings possible. For pragmatic reasons, choosing your lodgings carefully is also crucial because accommodations are usually one of your biggest honeymoon expenses, right up there with airfare.

This chapter covers the most popular accommodations for couples, with honest descriptions so that your honeymoon fantasy matches the reality on the other side of your hotel door. Later in the book, each destination chapter points you to the most romantic resorts and hotels for your lifestyle, love style, and budget.

Determining Your Kind of Place

Where can you find the perfect honeymoon hideaway? Here again we get into personal preferences: the "right" hotel is one that suits both of you. Before making your room reservations, you should consider what kind of accommodations you would prefer. Sky-tower hotel? A cozy little cottage?

What's the single biggest mistake couples make when choosing accommodations? Not paying those extra few dollars to book an oceanfront — or at least an ocean-view — room at a beach destination. At a tropical resort, the sunsets, the water, and the view from your room and balcony all contribute to the memories you take home. If you go *too* budget, you may not feel like you're in paradise.

Sometimes, a hotel is included as part of a package. But even if the price is right, it's *never* a good deal if you dislike the room.

Here are the major lodging categories:

- ✔ **Hotels:** Hotels usually offer a deluxe atmosphere emphasizing personal service in all its manifestations: porters, a concierge, bellhops, room service, and many amenities.

- ✔ **Motels:** Convenience and economy are the usual bywords here. At motels or motor lodges, you can drive up and park your car right outside your door, and the price is generally low.

- ✔ **Condominiums and villas:** Enjoy all the comforts of home while away on your honeymoon.

- ✔ **Self-contained resorts:** Often, these are hotels as well, but they can also be low-rise villas, condos, or cottages. What differentiates them from just plain hotels is the fact that everything necessary for human survival — even a honeymoon's survival — is located right on the property.

- ✔ **Bed-and-breakfasts:** Usually, B&Bs are private residences that take in paying guests, offering both a bedroom and breakfast (either full or continental). Be aware that not all B&B accommodations offer a private bath, but rather a shared bath down the hall.

- ✔ **All-inclusive resorts:** Absolutely, positively, these are the biggest trend in honeymoon accommodations (see the following section). As the name implies, all-inclusive resorts are properties where everything from accommodations to margaritas is covered by one set price.

Having It All at an All-Inclusive

Waking up in a tropical paradise is wonderful enough. But imagine greeting each honeymoon day knowing that you can go snorkeling or for a tennis lesson, quaff a piña colada or tour a plantation great house, all without opening your wallet. You can — if you honeymoon at an all-inclusive resort.

As the name indicates, an all-inclusive resort is a place where every-thing (okay, *practically* everything) is covered by one set price. Plans encompass not just "basics" like hotel accommodations, meals, sports, and sightseeing excursions — they also often cover afternoon cock-tails, tips to the staff, maybe even free laundry service. All-inclusive resorts are located all over the world, from Mexico to Malaysia.

Honeymooners and all-inclusive resorts are like a match made in heaven. Once you choose a hotel, you don't need to make any more decisions. All the restaurants and sports are right on the property. Because planning the wedding itself is so complicated, many couples are delighted just to relax and go on their honeymoon. As one bride confided, "I had enough stress planning my wedding. I certainly didn't need any on my honeymoon."

Because everything is paid for in advance, you know exactly how much your honeymoon costs before you even leave home. You can make a budget — and stick to it. Also, if your trip is a wedding present from your families, they can arrange to cover all your expenses, right down to the trapeze lessons.

Before you choose on an all-inclusive accommodation, consider the following:

- ✔ **You surrender freedom.** All your meals and most of your activities are at the resort.

- ✔ **Couples-only resorts can be cloying.** Being surrounded by all that connubial Noah's Ark-dom can feel oppressive for some couples.

- ✔ **The activities should appeal to you.** Because all-inclusive resorts are more expensive than regular properties, be certain that the pastimes offered are what you are looking for.

Understanding the all-inclusive

The price of the room you choose determines the price of the entire package. After that, zip up your credit cards. Most resorts offer a jam-packed schedule of activities each day — depending on the locale, options may include snorkel day-sails, aquacize workouts, sightseeing jaunts, comedy revues, or piano bars. There's no need to plan what to do each day — couples can participate in as many or few events as they like.

A property that looks "cheaper" for an eight-day/seven-night holiday may also offer you a lot less. In short — you get what you pay for. Here are some points to scrutinize when evaluating different all-inclusives:

- ✔ **Meals plans:** At least three meals a day should be included. Top properties also keep the snack bar open all day and also serve up treats like "elevenses" (mid-morning munchies often served in formerly British islands in the Caribbean), afternoon hors d'oeuvres, and midnight buffets.

- ✔ **Restaurants:** Does the resort have more than one restaurant? Because every meal you have is served at the hotel, choose an all-inclusive with a variety of dining rooms and cuisines. Also, are meals served by waiters or buffet style? Personal service is more gracious, but usually adds to the price. Are you fantasizing about having breakfast in bed on your own private verandah facing the sea? Find out if room service is an option (usually available 24 hours a day at the very best hotels).

✔ **Drinks policy:** Are alcoholic beverages included throughout the day, or only drinks with meals? What kinds of drinks — hard liquor, or just wine and beer? Also check whether the resort serves premium brands or some no-name stuff slogged from a large jug.

✔ **Rooms:** How plush are the accommodations? Are they located right on the beach? Do they offer amenities like TVs (with cable or satellite), direct-dial phones, air conditioning, and in-room hair dryers?

✔ **Sports:** What activities are offered — and are they sports that you want to do? Is there an extra charge for pastimes like water skiing, golf, or horseback riding? What kind of equipment do they have in the fitness room — the "good stuff" like Nautilus and Stairmasters, or some rusty all-in-one contraptions shoved in the corner of a utility shed? Also important — is instruction offered? If a resort offers sailing — great! However, if you don't know a main sheet from the boom tent, you won't be able to take advantage of the boats. How good are the instructors — a saxophone player from the hotel's band who also moonlights as a water-sports instructor may not be the best person to teach you windsurfing (believe me)!

✔ **Sightseeing:** Sure, playing at your resort is great — but why travel all those thousands of miles to park yourselves on just 30 acres for the week? Increasingly, resorts offer touring, or at least a shopping foray to town, among their options. Check if sightseeing excursions are offered and whether they include transportation, admission fees, guides, tips, and so on.

✔ **Airport transfers:** Look sharp — some not-so-all-inclusive properties often skimp on transfers. Getting from the airport to the hotel can tack on $50 to $100 per couple in some locales. Try to make sure that transportation is part of your plan.

✔ **Tipping policy:** Many all-inclusives cover tipping in the rates, and do not permit additional gratuities — a policy that has several advantages. First, tips can add $10 to $20 per day in expenses. Also, figuring out who to tip and how much to tip (especially in foreign currencies) demands the social savvy of Martha Stewart crossed with the accounting prowess of a CPA. Much, much better to know tipping has been taken care of beforehand.

✔ **Entertainment:** Can you enjoy different acts nightly — stand-up comedians, singers, or steel bands for dancing — or is the same combo performing throughout the week?

✔ **Ultra extras:** At the best of the all-inclusives, features can rival those found at the best hotels in the world. A concierge may be available to help handle details. Laundry service, dry cleaning, and ironing may be included. Ditto services like massages, manicures, and so on.

Finding the right resort

Just like some radio stations play Top 40 while others specialize in jazz, all-inclusive resorts tend to cater to different clienteles — couples-only, singles, or families, for example — and each set-up creates a different ambiance.

Couples-only resorts usually are the best choice for honeymooners. The mood is romantic, not frenetic — a perfect milieu for learning more about each other and celebrating the official start of your lives together. Many of the other guests are honeymooners as well — during June at some resorts, newlyweds may account for over 90 percent of the guests. Although as you are reading *Honeymoon Vacations For Dummies* now, presumably months before your wedding, the thought of spending your honeymoon surrounded by other "just-marrieds" may seem a bit odd, but doing so may make your honeymoon even more enjoyable.

Family-oriented resorts won't offer blissful serenity. Instead, the scene is filled with youngsters staging foot races in the corridors and raucous games of Marco-Polo in the swimming pool. Even the food is different, with an emphasis on kid-grub like hamburgers and pizzas on the buffet line. But family all-inclusives are perfect for couples taking along their children from a previous marriage. The kids feel included, and the range of activities and child-care options means that the newlyweds also have time for themselves.

Singles-oriented resorts usually make an unsuitable match for honeymooners — sort of like a bad blind date. First, the accommodations tend to be more basic and less luxurious. Activities are geared to getting guests to meet and mingle — the "everyone out to the beach for volleyball" approach. Finally, aren't you glad to have said good-bye to toga parties and wet T-shirt contests forever?

How can you judge the orientation of a singles resort? A good travel agent knows what kind of crowd a hotel generally draws. Most places tell you right up front in their brochures, or are happy to explain their guest policy if you call their toll-free reservations number.

Getting the Best Deal

The rate different hotel guests pay for a room varies almost as wildly as how much airline passengers pay for their seats.

The *rack rate* is the maximum price a hotel charges for a room — the tariff you have to pay if you walk in off the street and ask for a room for the night. You sometimes see the rate printed on the fire/emergency exit diagrams posted on the back of your room door.

You rarely get stuck having to pay top dollar (except, of course, during the zenith of the high season). Perhaps the best way to avoid paying the rack rate is surprisingly simple: Just ask for a cheaper or discounted rate. You may be pleasantly surprised.

Booking a Great Room

Somebody has to get the best room in the house, so why shouldn't that be you? Before you book, find out the nitty-gritty details about the following:

- ✔ **Views:** Does the room face the ocean or the parking garage?

- ✔ **Location:** Inquire, too, about the location of the restaurants, bars, and discos in the hotel; these can all be a source of irritating noise.

- ✔ **Beds:** You *are* on a honeymoon. Make sure that you reserve a room with a double, queen-, or king-size bed.

- ✔ **Corner rooms:** They often have more windows and light than standard rooms, and can be larger and quieter to boot. The big secret — they don't always cost more.

- ✔ **Non-smoking rooms:** Many hotels now offer them. If smoke bothers you, by all means ask for one.

To find out which rooms at a hotel are considered the best, call or e-mail the property directly. The reservations agents on site know which accommodations are the real staying powers. Be sure to mention the trip is your honeymoon, and that you want memorable accommodations.

White sands and blue waters are usually the number-one attribute couples require of their honeymoon locale. Many people assume that in the tropics, hotels automatically have postcard-perfect strands. Not necessarily — shores can also be rocky, shelly, seaweedy, buggy, swamped at high tide, or swept by strong currents or huge breakers that make swimming unpleasant to impossible. If a hotel has an adequate-not-awesome strand, there should be something else terrific to compensate — a drop-dead gorgeous pool or superb spa, for example.

If you aren't happy with your room after you arrive, talk to the front desk. If they have another room, they should be happy to accommodate you, within reason.

Chapter 6

Money Matters

By Risa R. Weinreb

- -

In This Chapter

▶ Making a realistic budget

▶ Using credit cards, traveler's checks, and ATMs

▶ Cutting costs

- -

*W*e know. These are the scary pages, the ones where you have to pony up cash for your fantasies. Take a deep breath and get out your pocket calculator or click open your spreadsheet program: We walk you through the reality checks, and show you that the honeymoon of your dreams *can* come true — if you plan carefully.

Your choice of destination greatly influences how much money you have to spend. A room in Paris, for instance, costs a lot more than a room in Puerto Vallarta, Mexico — and ditto for all the other expenses down the line. For that reason, in order to come up with a final figure for your trip's cost, you have to consult the individual destination chapters.

Calculating the Cost of Your Trip

Budgeting for your honeymoon isn't difficult, but keeping a close eye on costs is another matter. A good way to get a handle on expenses is to start the tally from the moment you leave home. Walk yourself mentally through the trip. Begin with transportation to your nearest airport and then add the flight cost, the price of getting from the airport to your hotel, the hotel rate per day (or hotel package cost), meals (exclude these if they're already covered in the hotel rate), activities, shopping, and nightlife. After you do all that, add on another 15 to 20 percent for good measure.

The following are the most common honeymoon expenses:

✓ **Air transportation:** Airfare is one of your greatest expenses. (Of course, if you plan to travel on frequent-flier miles, you can save some major bucks here.) Airfares fluctuate year round, what with cut-rate specials or prices hiked up for spring break. In addition, they vary widely depending on your point of origin and your destination. For example, published fares run about $400 to $600 round-trip from Los Angeles to Maui; about $800 to $1,100 round-trip from New York to Maui.

✔ **Accommodations:** If you haven't booked a package that combines the costs of airfare and a room, lodging can vie with flying as the priciest part of your trip. You can expect to shell out a lot more for a room in some destinations than in others.

✔ **Meals:** Eating out is a big potential budget buster, although still a distant third to airfare and lodging. You can dine inexpensively practically anywhere in the world (again, it's easier to find cheap eats in some places than in others).

✔ **Getting around:** Do you need a rental car? See the destination chapters for recommendations about the most reliable and cheapest ways to get around.

✔ **Sightseeing, activities, and entertainment:** If you just want to bake in the sun during the day and gaze at the stars after dinner, you don't have to budget much for activities. If, on the other hand, you're more active — planning to indulge in sightseeing tours, a snorkeling cruise, or a round of golf — you have to factor in some additional costs.

✔ **Shopping:** As always, shopping is the wild card. You can easily get away with buying a few inexpensive souvenirs at the airport, or decide to furnish your new home with hand-made heirlooms. Only you know how much you can afford. We suggest that you both agree to a firm figure and stick with it.

Interestingly enough (and not to sound like a shill for the local chamber of commerce), honeymoon couples often regret what they *didn't* buy — a beautiful wood carving, or an original watercolor of their favorite beach, for example. A meaningful purchase can bring back warm memories of your trip every time you look at it.

S-t-r-e-t-c-h-i-n-g Your Budget

We all know how quickly and easily money can be spent, but taking certain precautions can help alleviate financial stress. In each destination chapter, we include affordable options so that you can plan a trip to fit your budget. For top money-savers, scan the "Bargain Alert" selections.

Here's a quick list of some easy ways to save hard cash:

✔ **Plan ahead.** By booking far in advance, you have the best chance of getting a booking at that budget-but-adorable hotel right on the beach, as well as nabbing discount airline seats.

✔ **Go off-season.** If you can travel at non-peak times, you can find hotel prices and airfares discounted by 50 percent or more from high season. In addition, you jostle with fewer crowds and enjoy better service. See the individual destination chapters for explanations about when each area offers its lowest rates.

✔ **Don't fly on weekends.** If you can travel on a Tuesday, Wednesday, or Thursday, you may find cheaper flights to your destination. When you inquire about airfares, ask if you can get a lower fare if you fly on a different day.

✔ **Try a package tour.** Often, you can book airfare, hotel, ground transportation, and even some sightseeing just by making one call to a travel agent or packager, for a lot less than if you tried to put the trip together yourself. See Chapter 4 for specifics.

✔ **Reserve a room or condo with a kitchen.** Yes, you're on a honeymoon; no, you don't have to cook three meals a day. Even if you just pop open some yogurt, granola, and orange juice for breakfast, you can save about $20 to $30 a day.

✔ **Always ask for discount rates.** Membership in AAA, frequent-flyer plans, trade unions, or other groups may qualify you for discounted rates on plane tickets and hotel rooms. Just ask; you may be pleasantly surprised.

✔ **Try expensive restaurants at lunch instead of dinner.** Lunch tabs are usually much less than what dinner costs at most top restaurants, and the menu often includes many of the same specialties.

✔ **Avoid your minibar.** Can't you think of better ways to spend $5 than on a can of reconstituted orange juice? If your room has a minifridge, you can store drinks and snacks that you buy outside of your hotel.

✔ **Substitute less expensive activities for pricey ones.** Jet skiing can be fun, but may cost a lot, and the ride doesn't last that long. You may be better off spending a few hours snorkeling instead.

Tipping tips

Although precise etiquette varies around the world (in France, for example, restaurant bills practically always include a 15 percent service charge), tipping pretty much boils down the same globally. Figure 15 percent of the bill in a restaurant, $1 to $2 per bag to a bellhop, and $2 to $5 per night for a maid in a hotel (depending on the room price). See the destination chapters for details about local tipping customs.

Phoning home

Making long-distance calls from any foreign country can be extremely expensive. Don't ever dial direct from your hotel room, unless forking over $50 or so for a five-minute call is no big whoop to you. Some hotels charge even for attempted calls, and toll-free numbers in the U.S. are not necessarily free when you call from a foreign country.

In your room, you usually find long-distance instructions that give you some options, but you're usually best off using your calling card. Leading long-distance companies, such as AT&T (with AT&T Direct), MCI (with WorldPhone), and Sprint (with YOU), enable you to dial direct to the United States using your calling card. Placing calls is quick, easy, and comparatively inexpensive. Just dial an access code from a pay telephone or your hotel room. For the current access codes in the foreign destination(s) you plan to visit, and the rate per minute for your phone call, contact your long-distance carrier.

Another good option is to buy a telephone calling card at your destination. That way, you at least know when you've racked up that $10 talking to your brother about the football playoffs back home.

Choosing Credit Cards, ATMs, or Traveler's Checks

After you get a handle on how much you're going to spend, you need to think about *what kind* of money you're going to spend at your honeymoon destination.

Using credit cards

Credit cards are invaluable when traveling. They are a safe way to carry "money" and provide a convenient record of all your travel expenses when you return home. American Express, MasterCard, and Visa are widely accepted in the destinations covered in *Honeymoon Vacations For Dummies,* 1st Edition.

Travel with at least two different credit cards if you can. Depending on where you go, you may find MasterCard accepted more frequently than Visa (or visa versa), American Express honored or refused, and so on.

You can also use a credit card to get local currency from an ATM machine. The exchange rate for a cash advance on a credit card is better than you receive when exchanging currency in the banks. On the downside, interest rates for cash advances are often significantly higher than rates for credit card purchases. Also, you start paying interest on the advance the moment you receive the cash. On an airline-affiliated credit card, a cash advance does not earn frequent-flyer miles. To get a cash advance off your credit card, you need a PIN number. If you've forgotten your PIN — or didn't even know you had one — call the phone number on the back of your credit card and ask the bank to issue one through the mail. You should receive a letter in about 5 to 7 business days.

If your credit card is stolen, major credit card companies have emergency 800-numbers. Here's a list of numbers to call in the U.S. as well as internationally:

- ✔ **American Express** cardholders and traveler's check holders should call ☎ **800-327-2177** (U.S. toll free); ☎ **336-393-1111** (international direct-dial) for gold and green cards.

- ✔ **Visa's** toll-free U.S. emergency number is ☎ **800-336-8472**; from foreign countries, call ☎ **410-902-8012.** Your card issuer can also provide you with the toll-free lost/stolen card number for the country/countries you plan to visit.

- ✔ **MasterCard** holders need to dial ☎ **800-826-2181** in the U.S.; or 800-307-7309 from anywhere in the world; or ☎ **314-542-7111.** Also check with your card issuer for the toll-free lost/stolen card number for the country/countries you wan to visit.

Relying on ATMs

Cash-dispensing machines have gone global. Most cities all over the world have 24-hour ATMs linked to an international network that most likely includes your bank at home. Cirrus (☎ **800-424-7787**; Internet: www.mastercard.com/atm/) and Plus (☎ **800-843-7587**; Internet: www.visa.com) are some of the most popular ones; check the back of your ATM card to see which network your bank belongs to. Not only are the ATMs fast and convenient — they also give the best exchange rate if you need to convert your money into a foreign currency.

To make sure you can get cash from an ATM when you need it, before you leave be sure to verify your PIN, check withdrawal limits, and double-check your identifying code with the card issuer — and make sure that the code also works in the cities and countries where you travel. (In some foreign countries, the ATMs only work with a four-digit PIN.)

Many banks throughout the world impose usage fees ranging from 50 cents to $4 every time you use an ATM. Your own bank may also charge you a fee for using ATMs from other banks. Keep bank fees low by withdrawing larger amounts at a time; you pay the same fee whether you withdraw $20 or $100.

At home or abroad, always use ATMs during business hours, during daylight, and when there are lots of people around — and when you have access to a real live bank clerk in case the machine decides to eat your card.

Traveling with traveler's checks

Traveler's checks are something of an anachronism from the days before ATMs were invented. Still, if you want the security of traveler's checks and don't mind showing identification every time you want to cash one, you can buy them at almost any bank before you leave home. You usually have to pay a service charge ranging from 1 to 4 percent, and you may pay another service charge when you exchange them at your destination. Keep a record of the checks' serial numbers so that you can ensure a refund if they're lost or stolen.

American Express offers traveler's checks in denominations of $10, $20, $50, $100, $500, and $1,000. You pay a service charge for the checks ranging from 1 to 4 percent (though AAA members can get them without a fee at most AAA offices). You can order American Express Traveler's checks over the phone by calling ☎ **800-221-7282,** or visit their Web site at www.americanexpress.com; Amex gold and platinum cardholders who call the toll-free number are exempt from the 1-percent fee.

Visa (☎ **800-227-6811;** Internet: www.visa.com) and **MasterCard** (☎ **800-223-9920;** Internet: www.mastercard.com) also issue traveler's checks, which are available at thousands of banks and other locations across the country. Call the toll-free numbers or visit the Web sites to find a location near you. The service charge ranges between 1.5 and 2 percent; checks come in denominations of $20, $50, $100, $500, and $1,000.

Exchanging Currency

If you honeymoon somewhere that uses a different currency (such as the French franc), you have to convert U.S. dollars or dollar-denominated traveler's checks into the local money — a process known as *currency exchange.* But even in some countries with different money, such as Mexico, U.S. dollars are widely accepted. See the individual destination chapters for information about how best to handle your money, and the best places to exchange dollars if necessary.

Chapter 7

Taking Care of Details

By Risa R. Weinreb

. . . .

In This Chapter

▶ Getting a passport

▶ Going through customs

▶ Buying travel and medical insurance

▶ Dealing with honeymoon stress

. . . .

*T*he trip is planned. Now, what about all the details — passports, visas, customs regulations, and health and trip insurance, for example? This chapter answers all your questions and helps you take care of the last-minute details.

Opening Doors: The Importance of Passports

The only form of legal identification recognized around the world is a valid passport. You cannot cross most international borders without it. Several of the destinations covered in this book, including France, require a passport for entry. Getting a passport is easy, but the process takes some time.

The U.S. State Department's Bureau of Consular Affairs maintains an excellent Web site (www.travel.state.gov) that provides everything you need to know about passports, (including downloadable applications and locations of passport offices). In addition, the Web site provides extensive information about foreign countries, including travel warnings about health and terrorism. You can also call the National Passport Information Center at ☎ 900-225-5674 (35 cents per minute) or ☎ 888-362-8668 ($4.95 per call).

Applying for a U.S. passport

Apply for a passport at least a month, preferably two, before you leave. Although processing generally takes three weeks, during busy periods it can run longer (especially in spring). For people over age 15, a passport is valid for 10 years.

If you're a U.S. citizen applying for a first-time passport and are 13 years of age or older, you need to apply in person at one of the following locations:

- ✔ **A passport office:** An appointment is required for visits to the following facilities, and your departure date must be within two weeks: Boston, Chicago, Houston, Los Angeles, Miami, New York City, Philadelphia, San Francisco, Seattle, Stamford (Connecticut), and Washington, D.C. No appointments are required at the offices in Honolulu and New Orleans.

- ✔ **A federal, state, or probate court**

- ✔ **A major post office, some libraries, and a number of county and municipal offices:** Not all accept applications; call your local post office or log on to the Web site at www.usps.com for more information.

When you go to apply, bring the following items with you:

- ✔ **Completed passport application:** To apply for your first passport, fill out form DSP-11 (available online at www.travel.state.gov and www.usps.com). You can complete this form in advance to save time. However, *do not sign* the application until you present it to the person at the passport agency, court, or post office.

- ✔ **Application fee:** For people age 16 or older, a passport costs $60 ($45 plus a $15 handling fee).

- ✔ **Proof of U.S. citizenship:** Bring your old passport if you're renewing (see the following section); otherwise, bring a certified copy of your birth certificate with registrar's seal, a report of your birth abroad, or your naturalized citizenship documents.

- ✔ **Proof of identity:** Among the accepted documents are a valid driver's license, a state or military ID, an old passport, or a naturalization certificate.

- ✔ **Two identical 2-inch-by-2-inch photographs with a white or off-white background:** You can get these taken in just about any corner photo shop; these places have a special camera to make the photos identical. Expect to pay up to $15 for them. You *cannot* use the strip photos from one of those photo vending machines.

Renewing a U.S. passport by mail

You can renew an existing, non-damaged passport by mail if it was issued within the past 15 years, *and* if you were over age 16 when it was issued, *and* you still have the same name as the passport (or you can legally document your name change).

Include your expired passport, renewal form DSP-82, two identical photos (see the preceding section), and a check or money order for $40 (no extra handling fee). Mail everything (certified, return receipt requested, just to be safe) in a padded envelope to National Passport Center, P.O. Box 371971, Pittsburgh, PA 15250-7971.

Allow at least 1 month to 6 weeks for your application to be processed and your new passport to be sent.

Getting your passport in a hurry

Although processing usually takes about three weeks, it can actually take far longer, especially during busy times of year, such as the spring. If you're crunched for time, consider paying an extra $35 (plus the express mail service fee) to have your passport sent to you within seven to ten working days. In even more of a hurry? Try **Passport Express** (☎ **800-362-8196** or 401-272-4612; Internet: www.passportexpress. com), a nationwide service that can get you a new or renewed passport within 24 hours. Getting a new passport with this service costs $150 plus the $95 government fees if you need it in one to six days, or $100 plus the $95 government fees if you need it in seven to ten days. If you're renewing your passport, the government fees drop to $75. For a rushed passport, you must have proof of travel (your tickets).

For more details about getting a passport, call the **National Passport Agency** (☎ **202-647-0518**). To locate a passport office in your area, call the **National Passport Information Center** (☎ **900-225-5674**). The Web page of the **U.S. State Department** (www.travel.state.gov) also offers information on passport services, and you can download an application. In addition, many post offices and travel agencies keep passport applications on hand.

Applying for passports from other countries

The following list offers more information for citizens of Canada, the United Kingdom, Ireland, Australia, and New Zealand.

Canadian citizens

Passport information and applications are available from the central **Passport Office** in Ottawa (☎ **800-567-6868;** Internet: www. dfait-maeci.gc.ca/passport/). Regional passport offices and travel agencies also offer applications. Valid for five years, a passport costs Canadian $60. Applications must include two identical passport-sized photographs and proof of Canadian citizenship. Allow five to ten days for processing if you apply in person, or about three weeks if you submit your application by mail.

Residents of the United Kingdom

To pick up an application for a ten-year passport, visit your nearest passport office, major post office, or travel agency. You can also contact the **London Passport Office** at ☎ **0171-271-3000** or search its Web site at www.ukpa.gov.uk/ukpass/.htm. Passports are £28 for adults.

Residents of Ireland

You can apply for a ten-year passport, costing IR£45, at the **Passport Office,** Setanta Centre, Molesworth St., Dublin 2 (☎ **01-671-1633;** Internet: www.irlgov.ie/iveagh). You can also apply at 1A South Mall, Cork (☎ **021-272-525**) or over the counter at most main post offices. Those under age 18 and over age 65 must apply for a IR£10 three-year passport.

Residents of Australia

Apply at your local post office, search the government Web site at www. dfat.gov.au/passports/, or call toll-free ☎ **131-232.** Passports for adults are A$128 and for those under age 18 A$64.

Residents of New Zealand

You can pick up a passport application at any travel agency or Link Centre. For more info, contact the **Passport Office,** P.O. Box 805, Wellington (☎ **0800-225-050;** Internet: www.passports.govt.nz). Passports for adults are NZ$80, and for those under age 16 NZ$40.

Saying "I do" — passports and the bride

You just got married. What could be more romantic than putting your married name on your passport?

Wrong — it ain't gonna happen (unless you won't be honeymooning until several weeks after your wedding). You won't have proof of your new identity (your marriage certificate) until after the ceremony. If you already have a passport under your maiden name, it will remain valid. If you plan to use your husband's last name after marriage, you can have your passport amended by mail *after* you return from your honeymoon. The service is free.

Your name must appear exactly the same on your passport and your airline tickets, otherwise you'll have problems with airline check-in agents and immigrations officials. For more details, see Chapter 35.

Dealing with lost passports

Keep your passport with you at all times, preferably secured in a money belt. The only times to give it up are at the bank or money exchange, for tellers to verify information when you change traveler's checks or foreign currency; or to airline reservations agents and immigration officials when entering or leaving a country. In Europe, you may also be asked to show it briefly to the clerk at the hotel when you check in; or give it to the conductor on overnight train rides when you are crossing borders.

If you lose your passport in a foreign country, go directly to the nearest U.S. consulate. Bring all forms of identification you have, and they can start arranging a new passport.

Always carry a photocopy of the first page of your passport with you when you travel. Doing so greatly speeds up the paperwork in case your passport goes missing.

Getting through U.S. Customs

You *can* take it with you — up to a point. Technically, there are no restrictions on how many shopping goodies you can bring back into the United States from a trip abroad, but the customs authority *does* put limits on how much you can take home for free (this is mainly for taxation purposes, to separate tourists from souvenir importers).

When clearing Customs, be sure to have your receipts with you.

From most countries, you can bring home $400 worth of goods duty-free, providing you've been out of the country at least 48 hours and haven't used the exemption in the past 30 days. This includes one liter of an alcoholic beverage (you must, of course, be over 21), 200 cigarettes, and 100 cigars.

If you are returning from most Caribbean countries, the limits are $600 in goods and two liters of alcohol (one liter of which must be locally produced). From the U.S. Virgin Islands (a U.S. territory), the quota includes $1,200 in goods and five liters of alcohol (one liter of which must be locally produced). You have to pay an import duty on anything over these limits. Although the levy varies depending on what country/countries you've visited, it's generally a flat rate of 10 percent on the next $1,000 worth of purchases.

Anything you mail home from abroad is exempt from these limits. You may mail up to $200 worth of goods to yourself (marked "for personal use") and up to $100 to others (marked "unsolicited gift") once each day, so long as the package does not include alcohol or tobacco products.

Note that buying items at a duty-free shop before flying home does *not* exempt them from counting toward your U.S. customs limits (monetary or otherwise). The "duty" that you're avoiding in those shops is the local tax on the item (similar to state sales tax in the U.S.), not any import duty that may be assessed by the U.S. customs office.

For complete details, get the free, informative brochure, *Know Before You Go*. Write to the U.S. Customs Service, Office of Public Information, Room 6.3D, 1300 Pennsylvania Avenue NW, Washington, D.C. 20229 (☎ 202-354-1000; Internet: www.customs.gov).

Deciding Your Insurance Needs

Three kinds of travel insurance are available: trip-cancellation/ interruption insurance, medical insurance, and lost luggage insurance. Here are our recommendations on all three:

- ✔ **Trip-cancellation/interruption insurance protects you under a variety of scenarios.** Policies typically reimburse you for the nonrefundable components of your trip if you have to cancel — for example, if a family member gets seriously ill or your hotel is damaged by a hurricane. Refunds can also be made on the unused portion of your trip and reimbursements made on your airfare home if your trip is cut short for covered reasons. Optional add-ons for these types of policies include medical and dental expenses, tour-operator bankruptcy, and bad weather. (In addition to hurricanes, the weather coverage may include missed connections due to winter snowstorms in the U.S.)

- ✔ **Medical insurance purchased just for your trip doesn't make sense for most travelers.** Your existing health insurance should cover you if you get sick while on vacation (though if you belong to an HMO, verify whether you're fully covered in foreign countries).

- ✔ **Lost luggage insurance isn't necessary for most travelers.** Your homeowner's or renter's insurance should cover stolen luggage if you have off-premises theft coverage. Check your existing policies before you buy any additional protection. Important — if you are moving into a new house or apartment immediately after your marriage, verify when your new insurance coverage takes effect. The airlines are responsible for $2,500 on domestic flights (and up to $640 on international flights) if they lose your luggage; if you plan to carry anything more valuable than that, keep it in your carry-on bag.

Some credit cards (American Express and some gold and platinum Visa and MasterCards, for example) offer automatic flight insurance against death or dismemberment in case of an airplane crash. If you still feel you need more insurance, here some companies to contact:

✔ **Access America**, P.O. Box 90315, Richmond, VA 23286 (☎ **800-284-8300**; Internet: www.accessamerica.com).

✔ **Travelex Insurance Services,** 11717 Burt St., Ste. 202, Omaha, NE 68154 (☎ **800-228-9792**; Internet: www.travelex-insurance.com).

✔ **Travel Guard International,** 1145 Clark St., Stevens Point, WI 54481 (☎ **888-457-4602**; Internet: www.travel-guard.com).

✔ **Travel Insured International, Inc.,** 52-S Oakland Ave., P.O. Box 280568, East Hartford, CT 06128 (☎ **800-243-3174**; Internet: www.travelinsured.com).

Don't pay for more insurance than you need. For example, if you need only trip-cancellation insurance, don't buy coverage for lost or stolen property. Trip-cancellation insurance costs about 6 to 8 percent of the total value of your vacation.

Packing Like a Pro

Start your packing by taking everything you think you need and laying it out on the bed. Then get rid of half of it. You don't want to exhaust yourselves from lugging the contents of an entire walk-in closet with you. Suitcase straps can be particularly painful to sunburned shoulders.

Some necessities, no matter where you go in the world: comfortable walking shoes, a versatile sweater and/or jacket, a belt, toiletries and medications (pack these in your carry-on bag so that you have them if the airline loses your luggage), and — of course — bathing suits if you're heading for a tropical honeymoon. At most beach resorts, you probably won't need a suit or super-fancy dress, although men may want to bring a jacket (and a tie for more formal destinations) for dinner at a fine restaurant.

Don't forget your camera and film. The latter often costs w-a-y more in foreign countries.

Playing It Safe and Staying Healthy

Sure, the line about "In sickness and in health" is usually part of the marriage vows — but there's no need to test your mutual devotion on your honeymoon.

Chances are good that you won't get ill on your trip. But if you do catch a bug or sprain an ankle running for that net shot, you'll be in better shape if you're prepared.

The U.S., Caribbean, Mexico, and Europe are all considered generally safe places to travel. But if you suffer from a chronic illness, talk to your doctor before taking the trip. For such conditions as epilepsy, diabetes, or a heart condition, wear a Medic Alert Identification Tag, which immediately informs doctors anywhere in the world to your condition and gives them access to your medical records through a 24-hour hotline. The Medic Alert ID tag costs $35 plus a $20 annual fee. Contact the Medic Alert Foundation, 2323 Colorado Avenue, Turlock, CA 95382; ☎ **888-633-4298** or 209-668-3333; Internet: www. medicalert.org).

If you worry about getting sick away from home — or if you plan to pursue on-the-edge adventures in remote locales — buy medical insurance (see the preceding section on travel insurance).

Pack all the medications you need, plus a copy of your prescriptions, in case you lose them or run out. Also carry an extra pair of glasses and contacts with you. If you wear contact lenses, make sure that you bring your solutions; they can be hard to get in foreign countries or even beach destinations like Hawaii.

If you plan to bushwhack far from civilization, by all means bring a good first aid kit that includes antiseptics, bandages, and so on. However, if your trekking will be limited to the local boutiques, don't bother with anything but a little pocket or purse version containing chewable Pepto-Bismol tablets, Band-aids, aspirin, and possibly a wide-spectrum antibiotic cream to treat the odd scrape or blister.

Above all, don't forget your sunscreen, minimum SPF 15 strength and preferably water-repellent, though you want to slather on more every time you step out of the ocean or pool. Sunburn is not only unattractive; it can be uncomfortable and even dangerous to your health.

If you fall ill while traveling, ask the concierge at your hotel to recommend a local doctor. Should that not work, contact your country's embassy or consulate.

Most honeymoon maladies are self-induced — namely, too much sun and too much alcohol — a dicey combination. Don't try to pack a week of honeymoon fun into the first day of your trip.

If you have any concerns about health or personal security, check with the **U.S. State Department** (☎ **202-647-5225;** Internet: travel.state. gov) for updated information about travel to different countries.

For health information, including immunization recommendations, check with the **Centers for Disease Control** (☎ 877-FYI-TRIP; Fax: 888-232-3299; Internet: www.cdc.gov/travel).

Also see the individual chapters throughout this book for specific information regarding each destination.

Coping with Honeymoon Stress

You're madly in love. The airfare you have just paid to reach your honeymoon destination outstrips the annual budget of several small nations, and your suite out-glitters anything you've ever seen. Yet you have just burst into tears because your partner announces that s/he is heading to the beach to play volleyball with the gang instead of going antiques shopping with you. Is it all over?

Relax — you're dealing with honeymoon stress.

Honeymoon stress is just the flip side of taking *The Trip of a Lifetime.* As with anything that is important — and also costs a lot of money — you want it to be perfect. Worse, you're constantly worrying whether everything measures up. (Please note that "everything" also often includes your new mate.)

The factors contributing to honeymoon stress are varied and may include the following:

- **The wedding:** When most couples start planning their honeymoon, they don't anticipate how exhausted they'll be by the time the wedding night rolls around. Between nervousness about details that may go awry — plus the exhilaration when the ceremony and reception turn out splendidly — you'll be emotionally frazzled by the day after the wedding.

- **The commitment of marriage:** Even for couples who have been living together before marriage, a reality check sets in after the ceremony. Suddenly, there's permanence, a level of intimacy that doesn't necessarily happen when you are just living together — a real commitment.

- **Getting to know each other:** During courtship, most men and women stay on their best behavior and try to please each other. They worry that if certain of their quirks are uncovered — an inability to calculate a waiter's tip or crankiness in the morning — their mate won't love them anymore. Likewise, each partner will learn new things about the person he or she married.

- **Defining new roles:** When traveling together, each partner starts taking on new responsibilities. One person may be the car driver, the other the map reader and navigator. Until these roles are clearly defined, couples may encounter some rough spots.

✔ **Exaggerated expectations:** Duos anticipate so much from their honeymoon: perfect weather, rhapsodic compatibility, a string of magic moments. However, real life doesn't always play out like that.

✔ **Great "sexpectations:"** On their honeymoon, couples anticipate not only the hearts and flowers of intimacy, but also the rockets and fireworks of passion. Although people pressure themselves for peak sexual performance, conditions for a loving relationship are far from optimal. The wedding planning, ceremony, and reception leave most people absolutely zonked by their wedding night.

Also, travel itself is stressful, as frequent travelers will tell you — trips are always demanding. Wayfarers constantly worry about catching that flight, paying with foreign currencies, finding that left-hand turn to the hotel. Even globetrotters occasionally pull bloopers and forget to take their wallets, hotel confirmations, or passports.

The important thing to remember is that honeymoon stress is positive. With a honeymoon, you're talking about a huge rite of passage. Stress just comes with the territory.

Although some anxiety is natural, here are some ways to assure a happier honeymoon:

✔ **Consider delaying your honeymoon departure.** This is a smart move, since you may be pooped by the day after the wedding. By postponing your journey by at least a day, you can catch up with your sleep and also spend time with wedding guests visiting from out of town.

✔ **Eliminate sexual pressure.** Don't put performance burden on yourselves. Talk things over with your spouse and agree that you're tired, and just need to hang out for a day or two.

✔ **Do your honeymoon your way.** Plan your trip around what you like to do, instead of what you think you ought to do or what is romantic to do. If you want to cross-country ski with friends on your honeymoon, then by all means do just that.

✔ **Consider choosing a popular honeymoon resort.** Most newlyweds discover that they enjoy being with other just-marrieds since they have so much in common. Many favorite honeymoon resorts — especially the all-inclusive, couples-only properties — offer a wide range of activities, from party boats to volleyball games. With so much to do, you'll have plenty of new events to talk about.

✔ **Plan a realistic budget.** Be practical about what you can afford, but also allow some money for splurges. When asked about what they would have done differently on their honeymoon, most couples reply something like, "Gee, I wish we'd paid extra to get an ocean-front room" or "We should have taken the helicopter tour."

✔ **Communicate.** Part of intimacy is talking about things. Feel comfortable about saying to your partner, "You know, I'm overwhelmed. We've just gone through six months of wedding planning, and I'm exhausted." On the other hand, if your spouse tends to be supersensitive and takes things personally, you're often better off getting on the telephone with your best friend and voicing your weariness, concerns about commitment, and so on, with him or her.

✔ **Relax.** Enjoy every moment of the honeymoon, but you don't have to schedule activities for every minute. Also, you don't have to spend every moment together. Each of you needs some private time: You can even get that feeling of space while sitting on the beach side by side, each reading a book.

✔ **Keep your sense of humor.** If things go wrong on your adventures, remember that the mishaps can turn into the funniest stories that you can tell for years to come. And that's good advice for both traveling and marriage.

Embarking on a Second Honeymoon

Couples who are remarrying have some special needs. One factor to consider is the wedding itself. Whatever their previous marital history, couples today can plan a wedding that suits their lifestyle and social circle. Often, people who eloped the first time or had a very simple ceremony choose an all-out party to celebrate their new happiness. Someone who has already been through a splashy reception may prefer a quieter, intimate event.

For previously married individuals, one idea to consider is getting married at the honeymoon locale. The idyllic setting — a tropical beach, hidden waterfall, or bounteous garden — seems fitting for the new life that's beginning. Psychologically, it also frees couples from any family pressures or unstated objections regarding the marriage. For more information about combining your wedding with your honeymoon, see Chapter 3.

It should go without saying, but do not honeymoon where either of you has been with an ex-spouse. As one psychologist who specializes in family and marital practice emphasizes, "Don't do it the way you did it the first time. Try to do something different and something that speaks to the uniqueness of your own relationship, and get away as much as you can from the memories of `what was.'"

People who have been married before may feel a twinge of sadness even as they plan for their new happiness. Though a natural emotion, it's a complicated one, and you may cause some insecurities if you share it with your new spouse. Instead, therapists recommend talking it out with a close friend, your parents, or a professional.

Someone marrying for the first time who is tying the knot with a divorced person may experience some different anxieties. It's only natural that the person who has not been married before may be concerned about living up to previous experiences. If this is your situation, don't brood. Remember that this is a new life, this is a different relationship, and there is no basis for comparison. Just concentrate on being yourself.

If either of you has children by a previous marriage, the question of taking them along on your trip may already have come up. The response of the experts varies from "no — never" to a qualified "perhaps." In general, the feeling is that the partners need some time to be together as a couple. But each situation is different, and each couple should decide what works best for their family.

For most couples, taking a break from dealing with the responsibilities that are going to be such a demanding part of your everyday lives offers much needed distance and objectivity — and relaxation. There is plenty of time in the future for family vacations.

Part III
Hawaii

The 5th Wave   By Rich Tennant

"Pssst—Philip! It's not too late to fly back to a more civilized island."

In this part . . .

A loha! If you're thinking of honeymooning Hawaii, you must be told: Hawaii is paradise on earth. Each island may sound better than the next, and thus making a decision about where to go can be difficult.

Each of the islands offers something for everyone, so not to worry. They are all magical. We give you the low-down on what each island offers, where to go when you get there, what to do, and where to stay.   Planning your tropical honeymoon is easier than you think.

Chapter 8

Honeymooning in Hawaii

By Cheryl Farr Leas

· ·

In This Chapter

▶ Introducing the Islands of Aloha

▶ Getting to know Hawaii

· ·

*W*hite-sand beaches fringed with swaying palms. The scent of fragrant orchids in the breeze. Day after day of warm sun, sweet blue sky, and friendly aloha . . . No wonder so many honeymooners wing their way across the vast Pacific year after year in celebration of their brand-new union. You couldn't dream up a better place to kick back, relax, and celebrate under the tropical sun — which is why so many people call these exquisite islands Paradise.

The Gathering Place: Oahu

Home to about 80 percent of all Hawaii residents, Oahu is where you find **Honolulu,** the 11th-largest city in the U.S. — and Hawaii's biggest by far, with more about 870,000 inhabitants — world-famous **Waikiki Beach,** a densely built urban resort that stretches along the south coast of the island, and such major sightseeing attractions as Pearl Harbor.

Although you find the biggest crowds on Oahu, the island is a great destination — yes, even for honeymooners — since it's home to Hawaii's finest restaurants, sightseeing, and nightlife. It the last few years, formerly kitschy Waikiki has been reinvented along more sophisticated lines, mainly as a result of its popularity with Japanese honeymooners. And, frankly, there's no Hawaii experience more iconic than strolling hand-in-hand along torch-lit Waikiki Beach at sunset, with shapely landmark Diamond Head looming in the background, as ukulele players strum and hula dancers entertain at the beachfront lounges.

If you're up for endless diversion and don't mind a few crowds or a little kitsch with your aloha — if you're the types who revel in the glitz and energy — Waikiki is the place for you. Still, many newlyweds who visit only Waikiki leave with the wrong idea about Hawaii — that it's more crowded, overbuilt, and urbanized than it should be. So if you want to go home without feeling like you missed out on the magic, pair a stay here with a visit to at least one neighbor island. Leave Oahu off your itinerary entirely if your singular goal is to get away from it all.

The Valley Isle: Maui

Maui has become the hot destination in Hawaii. When people think Hawaiian paradise these days, they usually think Maui. Almost everybody who comes here just loves this island, and for good reason: It offers the ideal mix of unspoiled natural beauty and tropical sophistication, action-packed fun and laid-back island style. People love Maui because it's exotic, but not too foreign; ideally Hawaiian, but not too different from the mainland. Indeed, the Valley Isle is more like the mainland than any other place in Hawaii (yes, even Honolulu). The highways and L.A.-style traffic jams and mini-malls should look comfortingly familiar. Despite the mainland-style development, Maui really is a tropical paradise, with golden beach after golden beach, misty tropical cliffs, and more water-falls than anyone could count in a day. Maui also happens to be the most activity-oriented of Hawaii's islands, especially for those who like natural wonders and ocean fun.

Everybody loves Maui — so expect to battle a few crowds. Still, nothing can dull the sheen on this always romantic, ultra-gorgeous island, Maui has a wonderful small-town, easygoing vibe once you move away from the resort coasts.

The Big Island: Hawaii

If you're looking for drama in your honeymoon, this is where you can find it.

The island that gave the entire chain its name is the largest of the Hawaiian islands — twice the size of all the others combined — and a real study in contradictions: The left (Kona-Kohala) side is hot, dry, and studded with expansive, ultra-deluxe beach resorts and world-class golf courses carved out of the lava, while the right (Hilo-Volcano) side is lush, almost primal rainforest dotted with waterfalls and fragrant with orchids. In between are two of the tallest mountains in the Pacific, Mauna Kea and Mauna Loa; it's not uncommon to spot snow atop their 14,000-foot peaks while you're deep-sea fishing off the legendary Kona Coast, the Sportfishing Capital of the World, or snorkeling in the some of the Pacific's warmest waters. At the island's heart is Hawaii Volcanoes National Park, one of the coolest — sorry, hottest — places you may ever have a chance to visit in your lifetime. If you like weird places, don't miss it.

The Big Island is jaw-droppingly spectacular but beware: It doesn't exactly fulfill the average tropical dream. Flying into Kona Airport elicits downright shock from some visitors, who take exception to the chocolate brown lava fields that greet them in every direction. But the traditional tropical ideal — from picture-perfect white-sand beaches to flowering rain forests — are all here, just for the asking.

The Big Island is so big that you need time — a good, solid week — to see everything. While you may spend more time in the car here than on any other island, you may have every place pretty much to yourself once you arrive.

The Garden Isle: Kauai

Of all the Hawaiian islands, Kauai is the one that comes closest to embodying the honeymoon ideal. Tropical landscapes simply don't get any finer. Kauai boasts the kind of natural beauty that cameras can't really capture, that surpasses the memories you can keep in your mind's eye.

Kauai is the ideal place for couples to get away from it all. Come to this gorgeous, uncomplicated isle to escape the modern world, not to embrace it. Garden-like Kauai is quieter and less developed than its sister islands; rather than Cancun-style nightlife or St. Thomas-worthy shopping, you find a verdant, unspoiled island boasting wind-carved emerald cliffs, fertile valleys rich with taro, powder-fine white-sand beaches devoid of crowds, and gorgeous vistas in every direction. This is postcard-perfect Hawaii — really.

Of course, it takes a lot of rain to keep Kauai so lush, fertile, and flower-fragrant; consequently, the weather is a little less reliable than on the other islands. This is the one island where a week of rain can quash your fun-in-the-sun plans; they're at greatest risk from mid-December through March, but it's been known to happen even in May. Stick to the south shore if you want the best chance at a string of sunny days. The super-lush north shore — the most breathtakingly beautiful coastline in all of Hawaii — is best for summer vacations, when the wild winter surf transforms into a glassy, swimmable pond, and the days tend toward dry and sunny.

Chapter 9

Hawaii's Top Accommodations for Honeymooners

By Cheryl Farr Leas

- -

In This Chapter

▶ Figuring out where to stay

▶ Finding the best rates

- -

*H*awaii boasts an unparalleled collection of world-class resorts that have all the advantages for honeymooners: style, fame, elegance, an idyllic on-the-beach location, and a reputation for impeccable service. Everything you need is here — and access to lots more you don't, like twice-daily maid service, enough out-of-this-world facilities to keep you busy for a month of Sundays, and even your own personal beach boy to spritz you with bottled mineral water lest you generate a drop of sweat.

Keeping Costs in Mind

Accommodations in Hawaii can be ridiculously expensive. Resorts won't blink at charging 300 bucks — or more — a night for a partial oceanview room with not much more than a queen-size bed in it.

Don't be scared off, though, if your honeymoon budget is limited. The islands also have plenty of super-romantic places to stay that don't cost a fortune — and the reality is that it just doesn't take much luxury to make Hawaii feel like paradise, anyway.

No matter how much you have to spend, it's always a good idea to investigate all-inclusive packages, which allow you to pay one price for airfare and accommodations, often saving you big bucks in the process.

Choosing Among Hawaii's Best Accommodations for Honeymooners

If you want the best that Hawaii has to offer (this is your honeymoon, after all — you deserve it!), you've come to the right place. The listings that follow are a mix of accommodations on each of Hawaii's four main islands to suit every taste and budget: world-class resorts, moderately priced hotels and condos with a romantic bent, and one-of-a-kind honeymoon hideaways.

Please refer to the Introduction of *Honeymoon Vacations For Dummies* for an explanation of our price categories.

Oahu

Halekulani

$$$$$ **Waikiki**

For honeymooners who only want the best, Halekulani is as good as it gets. The Halekulani is the epitome of gracious and elegant aloha. Spread tropical style over five acres of Waikiki beachfront, this open, low-rise beachfront hotel is supremely luxurious, but in an understated style that keeps it from feeling too formal. About 90 percent of the rooms face the ocean, and they're all huge (around 620 feet) and done in a classy but comfortable natural-on-white style with a sitting area, a sumptuous marble bath, and a large furnished lanai. The quietly efficient service is among the best, the restaurants are first rate, the alfresco lounge, House Without a Key, is Oahu's most romantic spot for sunset cocktails accompanied by live Hawaiian music and hula, and the pool is magnificent. One niggling complaint: The stretch of beach out front is small, and the hotel offers only pool service; if you want to sit in a chair rather than on a towel, you're stuck behind a hedge — and if you recline you lose the oceanview.

2199 Kalia Rd., Waikiki. ☎ *800-367-2343, 800-323-7500, or 808-923-2311. Fax: 808-926-8004. Internet:* www.halekulani.com. *Valet parking: $10. Rack rates: $325-$520 double, from $720 suite. Deals: Good-value multi-night romance packages usually on offer, often including breakfast, limo transfers, spa services, dinner and champagne, or other extras. AE, DC, MC, V.*

Hawaiiana Hotel

$-$$ **Waikiki**

This low-rise garden motel has been pleasing budget-minded honeymooners for decades now. It's affordable, comfortable, well-located — less than a block from the prime sunning-and-swimming section of Waikiki Beach — and full of old-time aloha spirit. Every spacious studio-style

Oahu

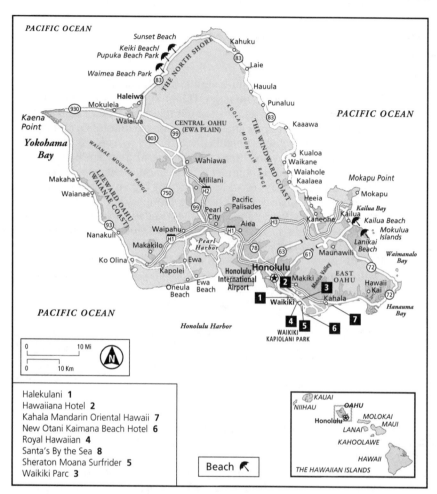

PACIFIC OCEAN

Sunset Beach
Keiki Beach/
Pupuka Beach Park
Waimea Beach Park
Kahuku
Laie
THE NORTH SHORE
Hauula
Haleiwa
Mokuleia
Punaluu
PACIFIC OCEAN
Kaena Point
Waialua
CENTRAL OAHU (EWA PLAIN)
Kaaawa
Yokohama Bay
Wahiawa
Kualoa
Waikane
Waiahole
Kaalaea
Mokapu Point
Makaha
Mililani
Heeia
Mokapu
Waianae
Pacific Palisades
Kailua Bay
Kailua
Kailua Beach
Waipahu
Pearl City
Aiea
Kaneohe
Mokulua Islands
Nanakuli
Makakilo
Pearl Harbor
Lanikai Beach
Maunawili
Waimanalo Bay
Ko Olina
Ewa
Kapolei
Honolulu International Airport
Honolulu
Makiki
EAST OAHU
Hawaii Kai
Oneula Beach
Ewa Beach
Waikiki
Kahala
Hanauma Bay
PACIFIC OCEAN
Honolulu Harbor
WAIKIKI KAPIOLANI PARK

0   10 Mi
0   10 Km

Halekulani **1**
Hawaiiana Hotel **2**
Kahala Mandarin Oriental Hawaii **7**
New Otani Kaimana Beach Hotel **6**
Royal Hawaiian **4**
Santa's By the Sea **8**
Sheraton Moana Surfrider **5**
Waikiki Parc **3**

Beach

KAUAI
NIIHAU   OAHU
Honolulu
MOLOKAI
MAUI
LANAI
KAHOOLAWE
HAWAII
THE HAWAIIAN ISLANDS

features a full kitchenette with microwave; the concrete-block walls aren't the sexiest in town, but the rooms are light and bright, most appliances are on the newer side, and maintenance is very impressive. If your wallet can handle it, splurge on one of the pricier, superior Alii studios, which boast better-quality furnishings, prime positions in the complex, bathtub-shower combos (instead of showers only), and such extras as hair dryers and bathrobes; for the ultimate in romance, book the Kamehameha studio, which has its own hot tub. Still, the standard rooms are just fine for couples on tight post-wedding budgets. Free coffee and juice are served mornings in the courtyard, and the nicely manicured grounds feature two nice pools, barbecues, and coin-op laundry.

260 Beach Walk, Waikiki. ☎ *800-367-5122, 800-628-3098, or 808-923-3811. Fax: 808-926-5728. Internet:* www.hawaiianahotelatwaikiki.com. *Parking: $8. Rack* *rates: $85-$105 studio, $135-$145 1-bedroom, $165-$190 Alii (deluxe) studio. Deals: Ask about special discounts and lower weekly rates. AE, DC, DISC, MC, V.*

Kahala Mandarin Oriental Hawaii

$$$$$ **Kahala**

If you want to see Honolulu's sights, but the bustle and crowds of Waikiki sound like a romance quasher, this magical resort lets you have your cake and eat it, too: It's just a ten-minute drive east of Waikiki, staked out on its own perfect crescent beach in one of Honolulu's most prestigious, tranquil, and gorgeous neighborhoods. The marvelous Mandarin is ideal for couples who want first-rate service and an ambiance that blends T-shirts-and-flip-flops comfort with gracious elegance. The big, beautiful rooms boast CD players and consistently high-quality everything, including super-romantic beds with gauzy canopies and the best bathrooms in the business, with vintage fixtures, extra-deep soaking tubs, plush robes, and his-and-hers sinks and dressing areas. Hoku's, one of Honolulu's most celebrated and view-endowed restaurants, is named for the most charming of the three bottlenose dolphins that live on premises; book a room with a lanai that overlooks the dolphin lagoon and sea, and the world is yours. (*Tip:* A trainer-led swim-with-Hoku session makes a wonderful one-of-a-kind wedding gift for your new spouse.)

5000 Kahala Ave., Kahala. ☎ *800-367-2525 or 808-739-8888. Fax: 808-739-8800. Internet:* www.mandarin-oriental.com/kahala. *Valet parking: $12. Rack rates: $310-$690 double, from $590 suite. Deals: Numerous package deals are always on offer, including full-service wedding packages; also inquire about AAA discounts. AE, DC, DISC, MC, V.*

New Otani Kaimana Beach Hotel

$$-$$$ **Waikiki**

Located at the quiet, pretty foot of Diamond Head, this boutique hotel is Waikiki's best beachfront bargain. It sits right on a relatively quiet, romantic stretch of Waikiki Beach, with leafy Kapiolani Park at its back door, which makes the views pleasing in almost any direction. An inviting open-air lobby leads to contemporary rooms that are more Holiday Inn than stylish, but perfectly comfortable. The most basic rooms are tiny, so spring for a superior one if you can; corner rooms boast Waikiki's finest views. With lovely living rooms and ocean views from all corners, the Waikiki and Pacific suites make a worthy splurge for honeymooners; ditto for the Robert Louis Stevenson Suite, which makes up for the lack of corner panoramas with a hot tub with a view. The airy lobby opens onto the Hau Tree Lanai, a wonderfully romantic restaurant right on the sand. Amenities include VCRs, minifridges, and coin-op laundry. An excellent value for honeymooners with mid-range budgets.

2863 Kalakaua Ave., Waikiki. ☎ *800-35-OTANI, 800-421-8795, or 808-923-1555. Fax: 808-922-9404. Internet:* www.kaimana.com. *Valet parking: $11. Rack rates: $135-$320* *double, $200-$865 junior suite or suite. Deals: Ask about room-and-car packages. AE, DC, DISC, MC, V.*

Royal Hawaiian

$$$$$ Waikiki

Tucked away from busy Kalakaua Avenue amongst blooming gardens in the heart of Waikiki, this shocking-pink oasis has been the symbol of Hawaiian luxury since 1927. Beautifully restored and now a member of Starwood's Luxury Collection, it still exudes elegance from a time when travelers arrived by Matson Line rather than jumbo jet, with steamer trunks instead of nylon totes in tow. Since the Royal was an early comer to Waikiki, it's on Waikiki's most fabulous and exciting stretch of beach; you can't dream up a better location. It's a bit more formal than you may expect in laid-back Hawaii, but no more so than the Halekulani. The crowd is a diverse one, ranging from heads of state to middle-income couples who scored a killer package deal. Every guestroom is lovely. You may end up in a modern room if you want an ocean view, but the period feeling persists. The Royal has nostalgic appeal, and the perks are very good: lei greetings, attentive concierge service, a freshwater pool, a guests-only beach area with full cocktail service, and a grand Monday-night luau (Waikiki's best).

2259 Kalakaua Ave., Waikiki. ☎ 800-325-3589 or 808-923-7311. Fax: 808-924-7098. Internet: www.royal-hawaiian.com *or* www.luxurycollection.com. *Valet parking: $13; self-parking $9. Rack rates: $335-$625 double, suites from $800. Deals: SureSaver rates from $310. Numerous package deals are also available; the romance, wedding, and honeymoon packages are legendary — and, if you're lucky, may include airport transfers in the Royal's signature pink limousine. Also ask for AAA-member and senior discounts. AE, DC, DISC, MC, V.*

Santa's By the Sea

$$ North Shore

Okay, the name sounds kitschy — but this hotel is actually ultra romantic. The fabulous beachfront location, low, low price, and cute country charm make Santa's place a wonderful choice if you want to stay on Oahu's North Shore. It's one of the very few North Shore B&Bs right on the beach — and not just any beach, but the world-famous Banzai Pipeline. Because you're the only guests, you have all the privacy you want here. The sole one-bedroom unit in the cedar home is impeccable, and boasts its own private entrance, finely crafted woodwork, bay windows, a living room with VCR and stereo, a full cook's kitchen and dining area, a full bath (shower only), and a collection of unique Santa figurines and one-of-a-kind Christmas items that appeal to the kid in all of us. On the grounds is a covered gazebo, an outside shower with hot water for after the beach, a barbecue, and a magical on-the-sand setting that would cost a fortune if you were staying at a full-fledged hotel.

Keep in mind that the north shore ocean is gentle as a lamb, perfect for swimming, in summer. But stay out of the water in winter, when only death-defying surfers take their chances with the waves. But is it fun to watch them ride the curls!

Ke Waena Rd., Haleiwa. Reservations c/o Hawaii's Best Bed & Breakfasts. ☎ 800-262-9912 or 808-885-4550. Fax: 808-885-0559. Internet:: www.bestbnb.com. Parking: Free! Rack rates: $120-$140 double. Rate includes first day's breakfast items in refrigerator. Two-night minimum. No credit cards.

Sheraton Moana Surfrider

$$$$ **Waikiki**

The Moana isn't quite as luxurious as the neighboring Royal Hawaiian, but it's more understated and intimate, and less expensive, than the Royal, and the location is equally ideal. Even with a '60s extension and a modern tower, this elegant white-clapboard Victorian — Waikiki's first hotel, built in 1901 — overflows with beachy nostalgia and old Hawaii romance. The original U-shaped building embraces a hundred-year-old banyan tree and the ocean beyond; it exudes a magical back-in-time ambiance. The Banyan rooms (in the original building) are small but over-flow with historic detail and charm. If you prefer space over ambiance, book into one of the newer wings, where you also get a lanai.

2365 Kalakaua Ave., Waikiki. ☎ 800-782-9488 or 808-922-3111. Fax: 808-923-0308. Internet: www.moana-surfrider.com or www.sheraton.com. Valet parking: $15; $9 self-parking (across the street). Rack rates: $265-$530 double, suites from $560. Deals: SureSaver rates as low as $195. Promotional rates and/or package deals are almost always available, so ask for these as well as AAA-member and senior discounts. Not-yet-marrieds should inquire about the Moana's attractive wedding packages, too. AE, DC, DISC, MC, V.

Waikiki Parc

$$$ **Waikiki**

This sister hotel to the ultra-deluxe Halekulani is a wonderful choice for honeymooners looking for impeccable service, little luxuries, and a terrific at-the-beach location at an affordable price. Boasting a cool cream-and-blue palette and an Asian-tinged island flair, the stylish designer-done rooms are even better than the price may suggest: Each one features chic rattan, tile floors with plush inlaid carpeting, a cozy sitting area, a furnished lanai with white louvered shutters, minifridges, and generous, pretty bathrooms. These are some of the best-value rooms overlooking Waikiki Beach, and phenomenal money-saving packages make this good value an even better bargain, so splurge on an oceanview room for real romance (the city views are less than inspiring). Facilities include a first-rate Japanese restaurant; the lovely Parc Cafe, which may even win over avowed buffetphobes with its high-quality, bounteous spreads; concierge and room service; coin-op laundry as well as valet service; and a gracious staff that doesn't skimp on signature Halekulani service. There's an eighth-floor pool, but why bother? The sand is 100 yards away, via a beach-access walkway.

2233 Helumoa Rd., Waikiki. ☎ 800-422-0450 or 808-921-7272. Fax: 808-931-6638. Internet: www.waikikiparc.com. *Parking: $10. Rack rates: $190-$270 double. Deals: A bevy of excellent money-saving packages are always on offer, including the Parc Sunrise (three-night stay, plus parking and breakfast, from $417) and the Parc Room & Car (three-night stay, compact car, breakfast, and parking, from $516). AE, CB, DC, JCB, MC, V.*

Maui

Grand Wailea Resort & Spa

$$$$$ Wailea

Here's the place to stay if you and your legally anointed other can afford to live large. With its lush, art-filled grounds and exclusive tropical-theme-park vibe, this wonderfully over-the-top spread is ideal for a *Lifestyles of the Rich and Famous*-meets-Disneyland escape. The 50,000-foot Spa Grande is the ultimate temple to the pampered life, while the cream-of-the-crop pool complex is a fantasy of waterfalls, rapids, slides, grottos, hidden hot tubs, and swim-up bars — ideal for honeymooners who are kids at heart. The beach is one of Maui's finest; restaurants, lounges, and shops abound; and the service is first rate. For a no-expense-spared honeymoon, opt for one of the signature named suites in the exclusive Napua Tower, which offer spectacular panoramic views over the vast property as well as individual luxuries ranging from wrap-around balconies to grand pianos. But even the least expensive room is a huge and elegantly appointed love nest with a luxurious marble bath; vault over the Terrace category to the Garden level, which gives you a wonderful view of the fantasyland grounds and easy access to the beach, pools, and spa. If you haven't already tied the knot, the seaside wedding chapel — with stained-glass windows and handmade Venetian chandeliers — makes a dramatic setting, and a wedding staff is on hand to help arrange the big day.

3850 Wailea Alanui Dr., Wailea. ☎ 800-888-6100 or 808-875-1234. Fax: 808-879-2442. Internet: www.grandwailea.com. *Valet parking: $8. Self-parking: Included in $10-per-night resort services fee, which also includes free local and 800 calls, in-room coffee, and other extras. Rack rates: $410-$760 double, from $750 suite. Deals: Wedding and honeymoon packages galore, plus an a la carte menu for indi-vidualized event planning. Also check for discounted rates (from $310 at press time) and fifth-night-free specials, plus bed-and-breakfast, room-and-car, golf, spa, and other inclusive deals. Excellent air-inclusive prices are often available through Pleasant Hawaiian Holidays and other packagers. AE, DC, DISC, MC, V.*

Maui

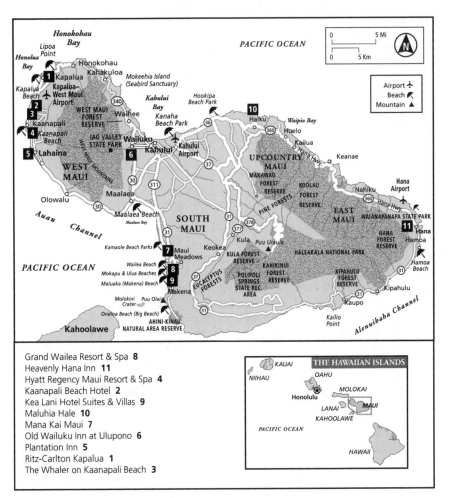

Grand Wailea Resort & Spa **8**
Heavenly Hana Inn **11**
Hyatt Regency Maui Resort & Spa **4**
Kaanapali Beach Hotel **2**
Kea Lani Hotel Suites & Villas **9**
Maluhia Hale **10**
Mana Kai Maui **7**
Old Wailuku Inn at Ulupono **6**
Plantation Inn **5**
Ritz-Carlton Kapalua **1**
The Whaler on Kaanapali Beach **3**

Heavenly Hana Inn

$$$ **Hana**

This gorgeous Japanese-style inn is a slice of heaven in Hana, an angelic spot way out at the east end of a three-hour Dramamine-inspiring drive through some of Hawaii's most breathtaking — and pristine — country. Each of the three suites is private and ultra-romantic, with its own entrance, a sitting room with a futon couch, polished hardwood floors, shoji screens, and a bedroom with a raised, luxuriantly outfitted platform bed. The private black-tiled baths boast a soaking tub (with all the Japanese implements for a good scrub, of course) and a separate shower. Fragrant flowers are everywhere, ceiling fans keep rooms cool, and host

Sheryl Filippi's two-course gourmet breakfast is both delicious and beautifully presented, on elegant Japanese dishware at a stunning hand-crafted table in an artwork-filled dining room. (Sheryl can also prepare picnic baskets and serve formal Japanese tea with notice.) A bamboo fence shuts out the world and transforms the impeccably manicured two acres into an Zen oasis, with tiny bridges crossing a meandering stream and heavy fruit trees. The closest swimming beach is Hana Bay, a 1½-mile drive away.

Hana Hwy., Hana. ☎ *and fax: **808-248-8442**. Internet:* www.heavenlyhanainn. com. *(Booking can also be made c/o Hawaii's Best Bed & Breakfasts,* ☎ ***800-262-9912** or 808-885-4550; Internet:* www.bestbnb.com.*) Parking: Free! Rack rates: $185-$250 double. Rate includes gourmet breakfast. Two-night minimum. AE, MC, V.*

Hyatt Regency Maui Resort & Spa

$$$$-$$$$$ Kaanapali

If you like the idea of a fantasy mega-resort but can't swing the price tag at the Grand Wailea, also consider this often-less-expensive alternative. While not quite as fab as the Grand Wailea's, the half-acre pool complex is no slouch here, either; there's even a manmade beach in case the spectacular Kaanapali sands out front are too crowded. The spacious guestrooms are warmly decorated in rich colors, floral prints, and Asian accents (a welcome change from the chain-standard beiges that often plague Hawaii resorts) and feature separate sitting areas and furnished lanais. The Hyatt is an excellent choice for restless honeymooners, since activities include a rooftop astronomy program (the Friday and Saturday 11p.m. show is accompanied by champagne and chocolate-covered strawberries); tennis; world-class golf within walking distance; beach gear and activities galore; a nightly luau complete with fire dancers; and snorkel sails, whale watches, and sunset cocktail cruises aboard the *Kiele V,* the resort's own 55-foot catamaran. When it's time to relax, give yourself over to the brand-new oceanview Spa Moana, whose dual treatment room is ideal for joint pampering.

200 Nohea Kai Dr., Kaanapali. ☎ ***800-233-1234** or 808-667-4440. Fax: 808-667-4498. Internet:* www.maui.hyatt.com. *Valet parking: $10. Self-parking: Included in $12-per-night resort fee, which also includes free local and 800 calls, in-room coffee, and other extras. Rack rates: $270-$575 double, from $650 suite. Deals: Special deals (including fifth night free) and packages galore. AE, DC, DISC, MC, V.*

Kaanapali Beach Hotel

$$$ Kaanapali

The Kaanapali Beach is the last hotel left in Hawaii that gives honeymooners a real resort experience in this price range. It's older and not luxurious, but it boasts a genuine spirit of aloha that's absent in so many other hotels. Set beachfront around a wide, grassy lawn with a whale-shaped pool, three low-rise wings house spacious, just-upgraded rooms;

still rather motel-like, they're nevertheless perfectly comfortable and feature Hawaiian-style decor and all the conveniences, plus lanais overlooking the pretty yard or beach. Go with an oceanfront room in the Molokai or Kauai wings — whose lanais extend practically over the waves — for spectacular views, easy beach access, and bliss-inducing ocean breezes. The folks here can even recommend a reliable wedding planner and plan a wallet-friendly reception for you. Three restaurants featuring affordable Hawaiian cuisine and a coin-op laundry are also onsite. One of Maui's most romantic oceanfront restaurants, the moderately priced Hula Grill, is just a short walk away along the beach. Pure magic for budget-watching honeymooners. Kaanapali Beach is an all-time favorite in any price range.

2525 Kaanapali Pkwy., Kaanapali. ☎ *800-262-8450 or 808-661-0011. Fax: 808-667-5978. Internet:* www.kaanapalibeachhotel.com. *Valet parking: $7. Self-parking: $5. Rack rates: $155-$275 double, $235-$585 suite. Deals: Free breakfast, free car, free night, golf, and romance packages are almost always available, as well as military and corporate discounts. AE, DC, DISC, MC, V.*

Kea Lani Hotel Suites & Villas

$$$$$ **Wailea**

This fanciful Moorish palace is one of Maui's best bargains in the luxury category. It's not quite as pricey as Maui's other top-level resorts, but it's just as fabulous and gives you so much more for your money. You get a giant one-bedroom suite, complete with a gorgeous living room and full entertainment center with VCR, CD, and DVD; a second TV in the bedroom; a wet bar with coffee maker and microwave; a mammoth marble bath with a soaking tub big enough for two, double sinks, and a separate shower; and a furnished double-size lanai (with chaises *and* a dining table) that's ideal for alfresco breakfast *à deux*. What's more, it's a bit more intimate, tranquil, and grown-up in its attitude than the neighboring Grand Wailea (see the listing earlier in this section), which makes it perfect for couples looking for a quieter, more easygoing scene. Skip the cheapest mountain-view rooms, but any other category is divine. Amenities include three swimming pools (including an adults-only pool) and two hot tubs; a spa that's second to the neighboring Grand Wailea's, but excellent nonetheless; a fitness center; a beach activities center; and excellent dining. A first-rate choice on every level.

4100 Wailea Alanui Dr., Wailea. ☎ *800-441-1414, 800-659-4100, or 808-875-4100. Fax: 808-875-2250. Internet:* www.kealani.com. *Valet parking: Free! Rack rates: $305-$625 suite; from $1,450 two- or three-bedroom villa with car. Deals: Ask about Kea Lani's terrific fifth-night-free, bed-and-breakfast, and car-included deals, which are regularly on offer. AE, CB, DC, DISC, JCB, MC, V.*

Maluhia Hale

$$ **Haiku**

Maluhia Hale *(ma-loo-HE-ah HA-lay)* is absolutely magical. The sole guest accommodation is an open-plan cottage with a wall of windows and a simple but gracious old Hawaiian vibe. A sense of peace and orderliness reigns here: You enter through an open and airy screened veranda, which leads to a glassed-in sitting room with a TV, a king-size bed impeccably made up in lacy white linen, a stocked kitchenette with nostalgic charm, and a traditional Hawaiian bathhouse with an old clawfoot tub and a wonderfully romantic indoor/outdoor shower. Innkeeper Diane Garrett has filled the cottage with a beautiful selection of antiques that make it feel cozy rather than formal. She also leaves charming notes throughout (like "Bang the top of the TV twice if the reception is bad"), which make the cottage just that much more darling. Diane does light housekeeping daily; you return at the end of the day to a softly lit place filled with sweet-smelling flowers. Not fancy, but idyllic through and through. Situated up a dirt-road turn-off part way down the Hana Highway, Maluhia Hale is not the most convenient place to stay on Maui, but its remoteness just adds to its romance. Pristine waterfall pools are just a walk away.

Off Hana Hwy., Haiku. ☎ *and fax:* ***808-572-2959.*** *Internet:* www.maui.net/~djg. *(Booking can also be made c/o Hawaii's Best Bed & Breakfasts,* ☎ ***800-262-9912*** *or 808-885-4550; Internet:* www.bestbnb.com.*) Parking: free! Rack rates: $110-$120 cottage (holiday rates slightly higher). Rates include continental breakfast. Three-night minimum. No credit cards.*

Mana Kai Maui

$$-$$$ Kihei/Wailea

Situated on a stunning white-sand beach that's one of Maui's best-kept-secret snorkel spots, Mana Kai is an eight-story hotel-condo hybrid. Almost all of the units have marvelous ocean views; about half are hotel rooms, which are smallish but offer great value. The larger apartments all have ocean views and feature full kitchens, cheery island-style furnishings, like-new kitchens and baths, and open living rooms that lead to small but view-endowed lanais — ideal for honeymooners who really want to make themselves at home. All the units are older but are kept clean and comfortable with daily maid service. The management is friendly and conscientious, a coin-op laundry is located on each floor, a restaurant and lounge is downstairs, and there's a nice pool and a grassy lawn with beach chairs in addition to that fabulous beach. But the Mana Kai's real value is in its location: on upscale Wailea's doorstep, at the quiet, prettiest end of wallet-friendly Kihei, away from the strip-mall fray. Ideal for wallet-watching couples who want a big, oceanfront bang for their mid-priced buck.

2960 S. Kihei Rd., Kihei. ☎ ***800-367-5242*** *(800-663-2101 from Canada) or 808-879-2778. Fax: 808-879-7825. Internet:* www.crhmaui.com. *Parking: Free! Rack rates: $93-$137 double, $172-$242 one-bedroom, $229-$297 two-bedroom. Deals: Excellent car-and-condo packages are usually on offer; also ask about other available specials. Ten percent discounts available on monthly stays. AE, MC, V.*

Old Wailuku Inn at Ulupono

$$ Wailuku

If you're charmed by the notion old-time Hawaii, book into this exquisite 1920s home, located in the historic and funkily charming antique shop-lined haven of Wailuku. Lovely innkeepers Tom and Janice Fairbanks have painstakingly restored the home. Each of the seven guestrooms is impeccably decorated with a Hawaiian heirloom quilt on the bed, soft woven lauhala mats underfoot, and top-quality everything, included an oversized luxury bathroom, plus modern comforts like TV and telephone. Janice has used her impeccable eye to fill the home with sumptuous fabrics and a jaw-dropping collection of bamboo and Asian antiques. Don't fear formality, however; the furnishings are oversized, cushy, and invite you to kick back and make yourself at home. There's a wonderful sitting room for curling up with a good book, and a wide lanai invites alfresco lounging. Tom and Janice are very happy to recommend activities and help you plan your days, but these gentle folks also respect your privacy if you prefer to operate on your own. The beach is a drive away, but the central location puts all of Maui within easy reach.

2199 Kahookele St., Wailuku. ☎ *800-305-4899 or 808-244-5897. Fax: 808-242-9600. Internet:* www.mauiinn.com. *Parking: Free! Rack rates: $120-$180 double. Rates include full gourmet breakfast. Two-night minimum. AE, DC, DISC, MC, V.*

Plantation Inn

$$-$$$ Lahaina

This charming Victorian-style hotel in the heart of Lahaina, West Maui's groovy old whaling/party town, offers both in-town convenience and romantic period appeal. It's actually of 1990s vintage, but the vibe is authentic. Vintage touches in the rooms — four-poster canopy beds and armoires in some, brass and wicker in others — set the tone, while modern extras like ceiling fans and A/C, soundproofing (a plus in down-town Lahaina), VCR, fridge, and private bath (some with shower only) mean you have all the comforts, too. The inn wraps around a nice large tiled pool and deck with a hot tub; deluxe rooms have lanais overlooking the gardens and pool, and a few have kitchenettes. Onsite are coin-op laundry facilities and Gerard's, an excellent indoor/outdoor garden restaurant that's one of the island's most romantic (*Bon Appetit* has called it "Maui's little French jewel"). The staff is excellent. You have to drive to a good beach, but Lahaina Harbor is a walk away (great for early-morning snorkel cruises).

174 Lahainaluna Rd., Lahaina. ☎ *800-433-6815 or 808-667-9225. Fax: 808-667-9293. Internet:* www.theplantationinn.com. *Parking: Free — and a rarity in Lahaina. Rack rates: $145-$195 double, $225-$245 suite. Rates include continental breakfast. Deals: Excellent-value three- and seven-night honeymoon packages from $669 (at press time), including deluxe room, champagne, and dinner at Gerard's. AE, DC, DISC, MC, V.*

Ritz-Carlton Kapalua

$$$$$ Kapalua

Situated at the very north tip of Maui's west coast, the Ritz is a destination resort by default alone — but it's precisely this isolation that makes this massive place hugely popular with big-budget honeymooners. Designed along the lines of a grand plantation house, the hotel is airy and graceful. The two-bedroom Ritz-Carlton Suite (room numbers 1638-40) is the most romantic room in the house, with sweeping ocean views and your very own grand piano — but even the cheapest mountain-view room wows with spectacular panoramas, soundproofing for extra privacy, and deluxe appointments. Additional across-the-board attractions include first-rate dining (including a superb sushi bar), three pools, Hawaii's largest resort tennis complex with resident pros, spa services, and a fitness center, plus unsurpassed service.

Everything you need is right at hand: The setting is breathtaking, the beach is small but fabulous, and there's a wealth of good stuff to see and do, from world-class golf on three of the nation's finest championship courses to horseback riding and guided eco-hikes. The resort feels a bit too formal for Hawaii (not the place to parade through the lobby in your cut-offs); but you get what you pay for here, and the overall grace and tranquility makes this is a great place to recover from the nuptial madness. It's also hugely popular for the main event, as the historic wedding chapel is a super-romantic place to say your I do's.

*1 Ritz-Carlton Dr., Kapalua. ☎ **800-241-3333** or 808-669-6200. Fax: 808-665-0026. Internet:* www.ritzcarlton.com. *Valet parking: $10. Self-parking: Free! Rack rates: $325-$595 double, from $550 suite. Additional $12-per-night resort fee covers area shuttle service and discounts on golf. Deals: A complete range of golf, romance, honeymoon, and other packages are available, as well as complete wedding-planning services. AE, DC, DISC, MC, V.*

The Whaler on Kaanapali Beach

$$$ Kaanapali

You may want to move in after a stay at this snazzy beachfront midrise condo complex on terrific Kaanapali Beach. It was built in the '70s and still sports a few Me Decade hallmarks, but in a good way. The relaxing ambiance starts in the clean-lined, open-air lobby and continues in the impeccably kept apartments, which make an ideal base for honeymooners just launching their nesting life. Each generous unit is privately owned and individually decorated, but all have amenity-laden kitchens, VCRs, marble baths, and big, furnished, blue-tiled lanais that overlook the lush gardens and/or sparkling sea. Opt for a mid-range — oceanview — room for the best of both worlds. Many one-bedrooms have two full, his-and-hers bathrooms. Luxuries include daily maid service, plus bell and concierge services, making this a great way to feel both independent and well cared for at the same time. The grounds are private and well-manicured, and onsite extras include an oceanfront pool and spa, an exercise room, and romantic oceanfront, tiki torch-lit dining and shopping at neighboring Whalers Village.

2481 Kaanapali Pkwy., Kaanapali. ☎ *800-367-7052 or 808-661-4861. Fax: 435-655-4844 or 808-661-8315. Internet:* www.the-whaler.com. *Parking: Free! Rack rates: $195-$240 studio, $255-$450 one-bedroom, $430-$645 two-bedroom. Deals: Car-and-condo packages, special rates, and Internet offers are often available, so always mine for specials and off-season discounts. AE, MC, V.*

The Big Island

Aston Keauhou Beach Resort

$$$ South Kona

Unveiled in 2000 after a $15-million-plus overhaul, this like-new hotel is a great choice for culture buffs, active honeymooners, or any couple in search of affordable oceanfront accommodations. Situated on a tranquil and lovely stretch of coast, the mid-rise structure boasts a central location, a genuinely romantic Hawaiian ambiance, and an award-winning Hawaiiana program with a full slate of cultural activities. The island's best snorkeling is right next door at Kahaluu Beach Park, while the hotel's own grounds feature an oceanside pool, a fitness center, tennis courts lit for night play, and one of the most authentic luaus in the islands. A grassy oceanfront area is dedicated to the easy life, with hammocks strung between coconut palms. The rooms themselves are less distinctive but perfectly comfortable. They're fresh, pleasant, and pretty, with good bedside reading lights, generous counter space and cushy towels in the bathrooms (some of which have showers only), coffee makers, and lanais, most with some kind of ocean view. Book a high-floor room oceanview or oceanfront room for prime ambiance.

78-6740 Alii Dr., Keauhou. ☎ *800-922-7866 or 808-322-3441. Fax: 808-322-3117. Internet:* www.aston-hotels.com. *Parking: $5. Rack rates: $156-$280 double, $525-$550 suite. Deals: Internet-only ePriceBreaker rates can result in substantial savings (doubles as low as $134 at press time). Ask for AAA and corporate discounts and "Island Hopper" rates (which may qualify you for 25 percent discount on weeklong stays at Aston properties). AE, DC, DISC, MC, V.*

Carson's Volcano Cottages

$$ Volcano

Warm and wonderful innkeepers Tom and Brenda Carson offer a collection of accommodations just outside the gateway to Hawaii Volcanoes National Park, including three romantic tin-roofed cottages for two nestled in the rainforest that are perfect for honeymooning couples. All three brim with island-style charm and feature full kitchens, cozy beds with goosedown comforters, plush terry robes, a wood-burning stove (a wonderful extra on cold nights), private hot tubs tucked among the ferns, and daily maid service. The magical Koa Cabin's wonderful collection of

Big Island

Airport ✈
Beach 🏖
Mountain ▲

THE HAWAIIAN ISLANDS
KAUAI
NIIHAU
OAHU
MOLOKAI
Honolulu
LANAI   MAUI
KAHOOLAWE
PACIFIC OCEAN
HAWAII
"The Big Island"

Hawi   Kapaau
270
NORTH
250   KOHALA   Waipio Bay
270   Waipio
Kawaihae   Valley   Honokaa
Harbor   Kawaihae   19
Kaunaoa (Mauna   19   Laupahoehoe
Kea) Beach   Waimea   HAMAKUA
Hapuna Beach   (Kamuela)   COAST
Waikoloa
Anaehoomalu   Village   1   19
Bay   Waikoloa Rd.   190
2   KOHALA   200   Honomu
3   COAST   ▲ Mauna Kea   220
KONA COAST   Hualalai   Hilo Bay
STATE PARK   (Kaupulehu)   19
Kona   ▲ Hualalai   Hilo   Leleiwi Beach Park
Int'l.   Saddle Rd.   10   Hilo
Airport   200   International
Honokohau   Airport
Harbor   Kailua-Kona   4   Keaau
5   Holualoa   Stainback Hwy.
Keauhou   Keauhou   KONA   Mountain View
Bay   Kahaluu Beach   COAST   11   Pahoa
6   Kealakekua   130
Kealakekua   Captain Cook   Mauna Loa ▲   HAWAII VOLCANOES   8   9   THE PUNA   132
Bay   Napoopoo   NATIONAL PARK   Volcano   REGION
Honaunau   Kilauea Caldera ■   Village   130   137
Honaunau   Keokea
Bay   Kealia
7   SOUTH
KONA
THE
KAU DESERT   HAWAII VOLCANOES
NATIONAL PARK
Miloli   Pahala   11
Punaluu   Aston Keauhou Beach Resort **5**
Punaluu (Black Sand)   Carson's Volcano Cottages **9**
Beach   Four Seasons Resort Hualalai **3**
Hale Ohia Cottages **8**
11   Naahelu   Holualoa Inn **4**
SOUTH POINT   Horizon Guest House **7**
Kanaloa at Kona **6**
0   10 Mi   Kona Village Resort **2**
N   Papakolea (Green Sand) Beach   Outrigger Waikoloa Beach **1**
0   10 Km   Shipman House
Ka Lae (Land's End)   Bed & Breakfast Inn **10**

Jadite dinnerware (Martha Stewart's favorite) and other mid-century collectibles set an ultra-charming honeymooner's scene. If you want to spend less, opt for the charming and tranquil Japanese-style Kobayashi room, which offers easy access to the resort's common outdoor hot tub. The bountiful breakfast buffet is a hearty, yummy feast — good carbo pumping for your day at the park.

501 Sixth St., Volcano. ☎ *800-845-5282 or 808-967-7683. Fax: 808-967-8094. Internet:* www.carsonscottage.com. *Parking: Free! Rack rates: $105–$115 double, $125–$155 suite, $125–$165 cottage. Full breakfast buffet included. Deals: Ask about weekly, monthly, and off-season rates. AE, DISC, MC, V.*

Four Seasons Resort Hualalai

$$$$$ **Kona Coast**

The finest resort hotel in the islands — and the Hope Diamond of the glittering Four Seasons chain, island-style luxury simply doesn't get better. Low-rise clusters of clean-lined oceanfront villas are nestled between a lovely sandy beach and a fabulous Jack Nicklaus-designed golf course (for guests only — so start dialing, club-toting couples!). You want for nothing in the huge, casually elegant, supremely comfortable rooms, done in soothing natural tones with fully furnished lanai and top-quality everything. Honeymooners should opt for one of the ground-level rooms, which boast Hawaii's most romantic bathrooms, with a private outdoor garden-and-lava rock shower that lets you rinse *au naturel* under the sun or stars. For the most romantic room in the house, ask for number 1803, a one-bedroom suite located right on the beach. Among its deluxe amenities are a private lanai with hot tub (perfect for secluded sunbathing or an intimate alfresco dinner) and a huge living room with unobstructed ocean views. The beautiful beach can be too rough for swimming, but no matter — three oceanfront pools more than compensate, including a stocked snorkel pond (with friendly stingrays!) that's ideal for beginning snorkelers. An exclusive spa, a state-of-the-art fitness center, and sublime beachfront dining round out the divine experience (book a table for two at Pahu i'a *now* so you don't miss out). Service is impeccable, of course. A wedding coordinator is onsite, as well as a range of scenic spots for the big event.

100 Kaupulehu Dr., Kaupulehu-Kona. ☎ *800-332-3442, 888-340-5662, or 808-325-8000. Fax: 808-325-8200. Internet:* www.fshr.com. *Valet parking: Free! Rack rates: $475–$675 double, from $900 suite. Deals: Ask about romance, golf, fifth-night-free, room-and-car, bed-and-breakfast, and other packages. AE, DC, DISC, MC, V.*

Hale Ohia Cottages

$$ **Volcano**

Set in the rainforest just outside the gate to Hawaii Volcanoes National Park, this charming and tranquil collection of suites and cottages for two offers an ideal opportunity to step into the past and get back to nature. The gorgeous red-shingled 1931 estate is impeccably done in a style that blends 1930s Hawaii plantation style with modern-day sophistication. The gorgeous botanical grounds are the result of 30 years' work by a master Japanese gardener. All of the accommodations are lovely and comfortable; tucked away by itself under the sugi trees, the Ihilani Cottage is a honeymooner's delight, with its own enclosed lanai with bubbling fountain. Funkier but no less romantic is the newest addition, Cottage 44, an original redwood water tank transformed into an impeccable, one-of-a-kind hideaway with vintage detailing, a small kitchenette, and a hot tub. For couples who need their space, the massive and antique-filled Master Suite (where the owner stays when he's on the island) is a steal if you can snare it. The in-room continental breakfast makes Hale Ohia an excellent choice for those who want their privacy.

On Hale Ohia Rd., Volcano. ☎ *800-455-3803 or 808-967-7986. Fax: 808-967-8610. Internet:* www.haleohia.com. *Parking: Free! Rack rates: $95-$150 double. Rates include continental breakfast. DC, DISC, MC, V.*

Holualoa Inn

$$-$$$ Upcountry Kona

Set on 40 pastoral acres in a cute-as-a-button plantation town-turned-artists' enclave high above Kailua-Kona, the Holualoa Inn is a marvelous place to have your cake and eat it, too. You get all the peace and quiet the two of you could want, with great beaches and all the conveniences just a 15-minute drive away. This gorgeous, contemporary Hawaiian home built entirely of golden woods has six spacious, South Pacific-accented guestrooms. Window-walls throughout slide away, Japanese shoji style, to let in the fragrance of tropical flowers and stunning panoramic ocean views. A favorite is the top-floor Balinese Suite, a big, airy room with a king-size bed, a separate sitting room, and its own small balcony. The garden hot tub and pool overlook the backyard coffee farm and fruit trees (which supply the morning brew and breakfast papayas) and the coastline below. Other nice extras include a romantic gazebo, a gas grill with all the supplies you need to prepare an intimate dinner for two, and a pool table to entertain yourself on quiet evenings. You feel right at home here, even in the common spaces. Service is attentive but completely non-intrusive. Holualoa Inn is perfect for solitude-seeking honeymooners.

76-5932 Mamalahoa Hwy., Holualoa. ☎ *800-392-1812 or 808-324-1121. Fax: 808-322-2472. Internet:* www.konaweb.com/HINN. *Parking: Free! Rack rates: $150-$200 double. Rates include substantial continental breakfast and sunset pupus. AE, MC, V.*

Horizon Guest House

$$$$ South Kona

This spanking-new bed-and-breakfast offers the ultimate in luxurious relaxation. Located 1,100 feet above famous Kealakekua *(kay-ah-la-ka-KOO-ah)* Bay, where Cap'n Cook met his end more than 200 years ago (and where snorkelers love to gather now for the best fish sightings in the islands), Horizon is situated on 40 acres of lush pastureland. You can see 25 spectacular miles of coastline, but not another structure. Four carefully designed one-room suites are cantilevered off the end of the house for maximum privacy. Each has its own private entry and is filled with gorgeous island antiques, hand-quilted Hawaiian bedspreads, a minifridge, coffeemaker, cushy robes, and a furnished lanai with breathtaking coastal views. A dramatic 20-by-40-foot infinity pool and a romantic hot tub are also situated to take full advantage of the view. Guests have free use of laundry facilities and beach toys galore. Gracious innkeeper Clem Classen (a refugee from the Silicon Valley) serves a gourmet buffet breakfast in the stunning artifact-filled main house, which also features a multimedia room with an extensive book and video library and a TV with VCR and DVD. Impeccable, personalized service is the elegant finishing touch that makes the high price tag well worth the splurge. Expect your fellow guests to be romantic couples looking for special moments just like you are.

Hwy. 11, Honaunau. ☎ *888-328-8301 or 808-328-2540. Fax: 808-328-8707. Internet:* www.horizonguesthouse.com. *Parking: Free! Rack Rates: $250 double. Rate includes full gourmet breakfast. Deals: 15 percent off bookings of seven nights or more. Inquire about other discounts; rates can fall as low as $175. MC, V.*

Kanaloa at Kona

$$$-$$$$ South Kona

Tucked away in a quiet and attractive neighborhood, these big, well-managed oceanfront condos are a cut above the average, and ideal for honeymooners. Comfortably furnished in quality island style with Hawaiian wood accents, the apartments have all the comforts of home and then some, including dressing rooms, cook's kitchens, huge bathrooms (plus whirlpools in oceanview suites!), and washer/dryers. Room number 3101 is a dreamy two-bedroom secluded at the end of a lava point overlooking the ocean. Tennis courts, three pools, a hot tub, and playgrounds dot the pleasant, attractively manicured grounds; the coast is lava-rock here, however, so you have to drive a half-mile to Kahaluu Beach (one of Hawaii's best for snorkeling). An excellent, super-romantic restaurant, Edward's at Kanaloa, is onsite; a big, modern, well-stocked supermarket is just up the hill, and Kailua-Kona's restaurants and shops are a ten-minute drive away. A terrific place to snuggle up for some quality time together. Expect a smart mix of families, seniors, and young couples who really know good value when they see it.

78-261 Manukai St., Keauhou. ☎ *800-688-7444 or 808-322-9625. Fax: 808-322-3618. Internet:* www.outrigger.com. *Parking: Free! Rack rates: $235-$265 one-bedroom, $270-$310 two-bedroom. Deals: Almost nobody pays rack with Outrigger, the king of package deals. Better-than-average discounts for AAA- members, corporate, government, and military, plus first-night-free, bed-and-breakfast, room-and-car, and other packages. AE, DC, DISC, MC, V.*

Kona Village Resort

$$$$$ Kona Coast

This resort is really something special: a super-deluxe version of *Gilligan's Island*, where every building is a thatched hut and it seems perfectly natural to run around barefoot and sip cocktails out of coconuts. There may be fancier and more amenity-laden resorts, but no other place is as decadent. Why? Because there's nothing to do here but *relax* — no TVs, no incoming faxes, no phone calls to distract you from the business at hand: each other.

The rates are all-inclusive (after all, going out to restaurants is so much *work*), and the food is terrific at every meal. Everybody stays in free-standing island-style bungalows called *hales (ha-LAYS)*, which are nestled in a tropical paradise of swaying palms and lagoons. All have a bedroom, a bathroom, and a lanai, ceiling fans, a grind-and-perk coffeemaker, and a fridge that's replenished daily with free sodas and bottled water; some units also have living rooms and/or hot tubs. Every hale is romantic, but consider New Hebrides Hale number 6 or Lava Tahitian number 10 if you'd like to relax in your own private oceanfront hot tub under the stars after a hard day of nothing. For those who desire utter seclusion, request Sand Marquesan number 9, the last hale on the beach; it doesn't have an oceanfront hot tub, but a jet-tub for two is in the bathroom. The dark-sand beach is small but offers first-rate snorkeling, often with green sea turtles. The grounds also feature two pools, hot tubs, and access to all kinds of water sports. There's something going on most nights, whether it's dancing to a Hawaiian trio, a cowboy cookout, or the terrific Friday-night luau. May and September are great months for honeymooners, since the resort is reserved for couples only.

Kaupulehu-Kona. ☎ *800-367-5290 or 808-325-5555. Fax: 808-325-5124. Internet:* www. konavillagehoneymoon.com *or* www.konavillage.com. *Parking: Free! Rack rates: $480-$825 studio, $785-$1,015 suite. Rates include all meals, in-room refreshments, most activities, airport transfers, and more. Deals: Three- to seven-night honeymoon packages from $1,375; complete weddings from $850; car-inclusive packages from $500. AE, DC, MC, V.*

Outrigger Waikoloa Beach

$$$$ Kohala Coast

This used to be the Kohala Coast's best value back when it was the Royal Waikoloan. The Hawaii-based Outrigger chain spent $23 million and five months reimagining it as a full-service resort; the new renovation has really lightened and upscaled the place and removed much of the budget vibe from the smallish rooms, giving them an island-fresh feeling and all-new everything, including coffee makers and minifridges. Still, the biggest plus remains the location: The resort is situated on palm-lined A-Bay, one of the island's most picturesque beaches and one of its best bays for swimming and water sports (guests from the ritzier places down the coast often come to spend the day here). An excellent beach-activities desk provides easy access to snorkeling, diving, kayaking, and windsurfing; Robert Trent Jones Jr.-designed championship golf is also on hand. All in all, the resort looks great. But the food service is less than impressive, and the service and trappings are not on par with its more luxury-minded neighbors. Still, Outrigger excels at handing out packages and discounts, so if you snare a good rate, you can have the bargain of the Kohala Coast.

69-275 Waikoloa Beach Rd., Waikoloa. ☎ *800-688-7444 or 808-886-6789. Fax: 808-886-6789. Internet:* www.outrigger.com. *Valet parking: $5. Rack rates: $265-$395 double, from $450 suite. Deals: Almost nobody pays rack with Outrigger, the king of package deals. Better-than-average discounts for AAA-members, Websurfers, corporate, government, and military, plus first-night-free, bed-and-breakfast, room-and-car, and other packages. AE, DC, DISC, MC, V.*

Shipman House Bed & Breakfast Inn

$$ Hilo

Misty, flower-filled Hilo wows nostalgics with its Victorian homes and charming downtown overlooking a romantic half-moon bay. This dreamy B&B is one of those century-old Victorians. Impeccably restored and on the National Register of Historic Places, it's right in step with Hilo's old Hawaii ambiance. Barbara Ann and Gary Andersen have kept the inn true to its original form, but they haven't lost sight of its present-day purpose. It's full of modern conveniences, including full baths with all of the amenities, ceiling fans, minifridges, and cotton kimono robes in each of the five spacious, charmingly done rooms. Most romantic is Auntie Clara's Shell Room, a corner room overlooking the lush rainforest and bay, with a claw-foot tub in the bath; Waikapu Stream, just outside, gently gurgles outside. Breakfast is a generous, island-style continental spread served on the wide veranda. Perfect for romance-seeking couples, history buffs, and national parkgoers alike, as Hawaii Volcanoes is a half-hour's drive south.

131 Kaiulani St., Hilo. ☎ *800-627-8447 or 808-934-8002. Fax: 808-934-8002. Internet:* www.hilo-hawaii.com. *Parking: Free! Rack rates: $140-$175 double. Rates include generous continental buffet breakfast. Rates $25 higher for single-night stays. AE, MC, V.*

Kauai

Gloria's Spouting Horn Bed & Breakfast

$$$$ Poipu Beach

Staying here may well be the romantic highlight of your honeymoon. One of Hawaii's very few oceanfront B&Bs — and one of its best — Gloria's is located right at the water's edge, on a simply stunning stretch of Kauai's sunny south shore. The red earth, the lush greenery, the golden sand, the white-capped waves, and the brilliant blue sky all come together in a perfect marriage of nature's most vivid hues. Gloria and Bob Merkle welcome guests (mostly youngish, active couples) into their very attractive and comfortable home, which offers three very well-stocked, well-furnished guestrooms, each with a wet bar with fridge, microwave, and coffee maker; a VCR; a huge lanai overlooking the surf and the solar-heated pool at ocean's edge; and a private bath with a Japanese-style soaking tub. Every room is ultra-romantic, but our favorite is Punana Aloha, a love nest furnished in willow. Breakfasts are elaborate buffet affairs served on linen, crystal, and china in the dining room or, for lovers who'd rather stay in bed, on a tray with flowers. Sunset is celebrated nightly with an open bar and pupus, and snacks are out all day — you won't go hungry here. The food is excellent, and the ambience is idyllic.

4464 Lawai Beach Rd., Koloa. ☎ *and fax: 808-742-6995. Internet:* www.gloriasbedandbreakfast.com. *Parking: Free! Rack rates: $250 double. Rates include full breakfast and afternoon drinks and hors d'oeuvres. Three-night* *minimum. Deals: $25 per-night discount for weekly stays. Ask Gloria about discounted car-rental rates and interisland airfares. No credit cards.*

Hanalei Colony Resort

$$$ North Shore

This small, lovely lowrise resort is the place to stay if you want to experience Kauai's breathtakingly spectacular north shore in all its remote, romantic glory. It's well past Hanalei, near the end of the road — perfect for honeymooners looking to stay off the beaten path, away from the crowds. The setting is idyllic, with lush gardens and a perfect golden beach. Each of the roomy two-bedroom, one-bath apartments is done in appealing creamy tones. Each has a lanai, a complete kitchen, ceiling fans (A/C isn't necessary here), and great views (the mountain views are just as fab as the ocean views). The atmosphere is quiet and relaxing — no TVs, stereos, or phones to interfere with the seductive sound of the shorebreak and the tropical birdsong. Any of the premium oceanfront condos (our favorite is number G-2) are tops for romance. Don't worry about being bored here. There's plenty of beach gear at hand, plus a large pool and hot tub, barbecues, Hawaiiana classes, lawn and board games, and more to keep you happy and relaxed. The spectacular Na Pali Coast offers a marvelous day hike, and more of Hawaii's most gorgeous beaches are at hand for snorkeling and ultra-romantic sunset walks. The staff loves to welcome honeymooners, so you can expect to be doted upon; a wedding coordinator can even help you plan your tropical nuptials.

5-7130 Kuhio Hwy., Haena. ☎ *800-628-3004 or 808-826-6235. Fax: 808-826-9893. Internet:* www.hcr.com. *Parking: Free! Rack rates: $155-$290 two-bedroom (to $348 during the winter holidays). Deals: Every seventh night is free. Car-and-condo packages from $185; five- to seven-night honeymoon packages from $1,415. Complete weddings from $375. AE, MC, V.*

Hyatt Regency Kauai Resort & Spa

$$$$$ Poipu Beach

The Hyatt Regency Kauai is one of Hawaii's best luxury hotels. This gorgeous, open-air, genuinely Hawaiian-style place has a wonderful retro-1930s feel, but with all of the modern amenities you could want (and then some). It's just fabulous, in an understated rather than too-grand way; everyone feels comfortable here. The location is marvelous, too, on Kauai's sunny southern Poipu coast. The most distant accommodations are a good five-minute hike from the lobby — but once you get there, you find a room that's oversized (600 square feet) and elegant, with tropical accents, luxurious marble baths, and spacious lanais (most with ocean views). Since the ocean is rough here, there's a fantasy mega-pool complex, plus a whopping five acres of swimming lagoons with islands and a manmade beach. The restaurants are elegant and satisfying (particularly award-winning Dondero's for Italian), the activity programs are terrific, and the 25,000-square-foot Anara Spa is one of the finest in the Pacific. You and your honey simply can't go wrong here. Book *well* ahead.

Kauai

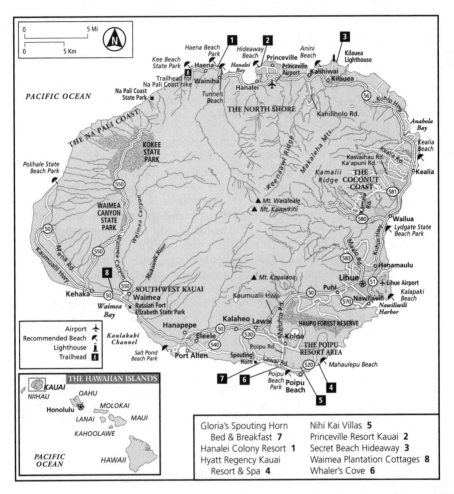

Gloria's Spouting Horn Bed & Breakfast **7**	Nihi Kai Villas **5**
	Princeville Resort Kauai **2**
Hanalei Colony Resort **1**	Secret Beach Hideaway **3**
Hyatt Regency Kauai Resort & Spa **4**	Waimea Plantation Cottages **8**
	Whaler's Cove **6**

1571 Poipu Rd., Koloa. ☎ **800-55-HYATT** or 808-742-1234. Fax: 808-742-1557. Internet: www.kauai.hyatt.com. *Valet parking: $5 (free self-parking). Rack rates: $355-$630 double, from $825 suite. Deals: Multiple packages are almost always on offer; ask about the Aloha rates (from $275 at press time), AAA discounts, romance packages, Sunshine on Sale, and other special deals. AE, DC, DISC, MC, V.*

Nihi Kai Villas

$$ Poipu Beach

This beautifully maintained Mediterranean-style condo complex is just a block from the finest stretch of Poipu Beach, and an excellent choice on all fronts. It's lovingly and meticulously run, and the tropical-style apartments are gorgeous. Each boasts a full kitchen (with microwave), ceiling fans, washer/dryer, full cable (most have VCRs), lots of windows, and at least one lanai (usually two). Everything is top-notch, from the big, comfy furniture to the well-cushioned wool carpet underfoot. The grounds are well landscaped and quiet, boasting two tennis courts, paddleball, barbecues, and two nice pools. A favorable unit for honeymooning couples is number 200, a giant (1,858 square feet) two-bedroom with a great location near the pool and fabulous ocean views.

1870 Hoone Rd., Poipu Beach. ☎ *800-325-5701, 800-742-1412, or 808-742-2000. Fax: 808-742-9093. Internet:* www.grantham-resorts.com. *Parking: Free! Rack rates: $149–$169 one-bedroom, $139–$225 two-bedroom, $275–$300 three-bedroom. Ask about minimum-stay requirements (usually five nights). Deals: Discounts on car rentals are available. DC, DISC, MC, V.*

Princeville Resort Kauai

$$$$$ North Shore

Princeville is fabulous, and the location is Hawaii's most breathtaking. Majestically set on a clifftop overlooking Hanalei Bay and Kauai's emerald, steepled mountains, the tiered resort steps down the cliff to maximize views, which are spectacular in every direction. Cupid himself couldn't create a more romance-inducing setting. Each sizeable room is done in a subdued natural-colors-and-fibers palette and outfitted with original art, oversized windows (no lanais, though), bedside controls for everything, and a "magic" shower window that you can switch in an instant from opaque to clear, allowing you to take in those awesome views as you shampoo. World-class Robert Trent Jones, Jr., golf, a first-rate spa and fitness center, a resort shuttle, first-rate dining, and a wonderful reef for snorkeling are all at hand. Needless to say, you and your sweetie won't want for anything here. Keep in mind, though, that the lush north shore can be quite rainy in winter, when the waters are too rough for swimming; in the cooler months, you're safer booking into the Hyatt on the sunny south shore.

5520 Ka Haku Rd., Princeville. ☎ *800-325-3589 or 808-826-9644. Fax: 808-826-1166. Internet:* www.princeville.com *or* www.luxurycollection.com. *Valet parking: $12. Rack rates: $395–$595 double, from $685 suite. Deals: Package deals are usually available, including two-night oceanview honeymoon packages from $890. Also ask for AAA discounts. Complete weddings from $1,600; call the resort's wedding specialist at 800-826-4400. AE, DC, DISC, MC, V.*

Secret Beach Hideaway

$$$$$ North Shore

If you want Kauai's most romantic lodgings, and money is no object, look no further: Pick up the phone now and book one of these exquisite cottages overlooking magical Sunset Beach on Kauai's fabled north shore. Featuring just three intimate cottages spread over 11 lush tropical acres and overflowing with privacy, gorgeous views, and faultless appointments, these intimate hideaways were built with honeymooners in mind. Each is tiny — about 500 square feet — but boasts the finest of everything: polished maple furnishings, granite counterops, 450-count

Italian linens, Celadon china from Chiang Mai, mini SubZero fridge in the gourmet kitchenette, TV with VCR, CD stereo, barbecue grill, washer/dryer, deck furniture, and outdoor private hot tub for soaking in the spectacular views. Each is perfect, but the jewel of the property is the Japanese-style Hale Lani. A path leads from each cottage to Secret Beach, which is only swimmable from May to October.

Next to Kilauea Lighthouse, Kilauea. Reservations c/o Hawaii's Best Bed & Breakfasts. ☎ *800-262-9912 or 808-885-4550. Fax: 808-885-0559. Internet:* www.bestbnb.com. *Parking: Free! Rack rates: $395 double, plus one-time $125 cleaning fee. Two-night minimum. No credit cards.*

Waimea Plantation Cottages

$$-$$$ Waimea

Here's Kauai's most charming place to stay. This collection of beautifully restored historic plantation workers' cottages is set among a beachfront grove of coconut palms on the sunniest section of Kauai's south shore. These comfortable tin-roofed cottages are authentically outfitted with tropical-style furniture and bark-cloth fabrics from the 1930s; stay here and you feel like you've stepped back to a time when living was simple and easy. Each has a furnished porch, ceiling fans, cable TV, a full modern kitchen, and oodles of period charm. The rooms range from cute little studios to a multibedroom estate that's perfect for an entire wedding party (and the palm-dotted grounds make a great setting for the ceremony).

The only downsides are the black-sand beach, which is lovely but not swimmable, and the location: Way out in west Kauai, 20 minutes past Poipu and a full two hours from the north shore. Still, this place is a real retro delight — and a perfect place to revel in your marital bliss. Hikers take note: Technicolor Waimea Canyon, known as "The Grand Canyon of the Pacific," is nearby.

9400 Kaumualii Hwy., Waimea. ☎ *800-992-7866 or 808-338-1625. Fax: 808-338-2338. Internet:* www.aston-hotels.com. *Parking: Free! Rack rates: $130-$140 studio, $170-$240 one-bedroom, $220-$375 two- to four-bedrooms. Deals: Internet-only ePriceBreaker rates can result in substantial savings (one-bedrooms as low as $137 at press time). Ask for AAA and corporate discounts and "Island Hopper" rate programs (which may qualify you for a 25 percent discount on stays at Aston properties of seven nights or more). AE, DC, DISC, MC, V.*

Whaler's Cove

$$$$ Poipu Beach

Condo living hardly gets better than this. The individually decorated apartments are pricey but well worth the dough. They're elegant, oversized, and held to a very high standard: Each has a full modern kitchen, a large lanai, a washer/dryer, and ceiling fans throughout; most have hot tubs in the master bath. The contemporary and stylish complex was smartly designed to give each and every unit an ocean view. Hotel-like amenities include bell service, concierge, and daily housekeeping. A very nice oceanside pool is onsite, plus hot tub and sauna. You have to drive to the beach, but there's good swimming (often with sea turtles) from a rocky cove out front.

2640 Puuholo Rd., Poipu Beach. ☎ *800-225-2683 or 808-742-7571. Fax: 808-742-1185. Internet:* www.whalers-cove.com. *Parking: Free! Rack rates: $319-$464 one-bedroom, $391-$567 two-bedroom. Two-night minimum stay. Deals: Ask about seventh-night-free, honeymoon, car-and-condo, and other package deals. AE, MC, V.*

Chapter 10

Enjoying Your Hawaiian Honeymoon

By Cheryl Farr Leas

● ●

In This Chapter

▶ Finding fun in Hawaii

▶ Discovering the best places to dine

▶ Planning romantic adventures

● ●

*N*ow it's time to kick back and enjoy the fruits of all that honeymoon planning. Here's where you plan your fun on each of the major islands — Oahu, Maui, the Big Island, and Kauai — outside of your hotel room, of course.

The state adds about 4 percent in sales tax to every restaurant bill. A 15 to 20 percent tip is standard in Hawaii, just like back home.

Going Wild On Oahu

Oahu is the place to rev up and have some fun. The island boasts more than you can see or do in the span of five vacations — much less one honeymoon!

Having fun on land and at sea

Probably the most famous beach on the planet, **Waikiki** is ground zero for Hawaii's biggest and best beach party. Sure, it gets crowded — but that's part of what makes Waikiki such a blast. **Hanauma Bay** beach may be crowded, and sometimes it seems there are more people than fish in the water — not exactly the place to tuck away for a romantic interlude. But world-famous Hanauma Bay offers some of the best snorkeling in all of Hawaii. The Windward Coast's premier beach park, **Kailua Beach,** is a two-mile-long gently sloping golden strand with dunes, palm trees, gentle waves, and gorgeous green mountains as a backdrop. With water that's about 78°F year-round, it boasts excellent swimming. **Lanikai Beach,** a Windward Coast gem, is one of the state's most tranquil and most beautiful beaches. Finally, the world-famous Mecca for surfers in winter, legendary **Waimea Beach** is a gorgeous one-of-a-kind sandy bowl whose placid summer waves are excellent for swimming, snorkeling, and bodysurfing.

Watching for sea life

Dolphin Excursions (☎ 808-239-5579; Internet: www. dolphinexcursions.com) takes you cruising Oahu's west shore in a Zodiac, a 23-foot motorized rubber raft, with a maximum of 13 others in search of friendly pods of spinner dolphins, the cutest creature in the Pacific. Zodiacs are great for getting close to the water and the dolphins — and there's nothing like seeing humpback whales breach and spyhop from such a low-slung, intimate boat in season (late December to early April). The bravest among you can pay for a "tow," in which you don a mask and snorkel and get towed behind the boat so that you can watch the dolphins in their underwater habitat.

Catching a wave

If you've always dreamed of learning to surf, Waikiki is the perfect place to do it. The beach boys who line up along the Kuhio Beach section of the beach (next to the Sheraton Moana), swear that they can teach anybody to stand up on a board and catch a wave, as long as they have basic swimming skills (and about $35 an hour). But if you're more serious-minded about learning to surf, book a lesson in advance with the **Hans Hedemann Surf School** (☎ 808-924-7778; Internet: www. hhsurf.com), whose pro instructors teach surfing and bodyboarding off the Diamond Head end of Waikiki.

Kailua Beach is the best place to learn to windsurf — and the folks to learn from are **Naish Hawaii** (☎ 800-767-6068 or 808-262-6068; Internet: www.naish.com), the domain of champion windsurfer Robbie Naish. Beginning, intermediate, and advanced lessons are available, plus equipment rentals for experienced windsurfers.

Exploring the deep

Whether you're a first-timer in search of a resort course or a veteran diver just looking for a ride, the outfitter to contact is **Aaron's Dive Shop** (☎ 888-84-SCUBA or 808-262-2333; Internet: www.hawaii-scuba.com), Hawaii's oldest and largest dive shop. Aaron's offers boat and beach dive excursions at all of Oahu's top dive spots, plus uncertified dives for beginners.

Climbing Diamond Head Crater

The 1.4-mile, 1½-hour round trip climb to the top of Hawaii's most famous landmark is easy and a lot of fun — and the 360° panoramic views from the top are spectacular. To prepare, don a reasonable pair of walking shoes (sneakers or Tevas are fine) and bring a flashlight (your hotel can usually lend you one), water, and your camera (this will be the candid honeymoon photo you send your friends and family).

Go early, before the heat of midday. Skip the stairmaster the morning you go because you climb lots of steps during the hike — but after you reach the observation post up top, the views are indescribable.

Visiting the sites

The royal **Iolani Palace** was the official residence of the last monarchs of Hawaii: King David Kalakaua and his sister, Queen Liliuokalani. The ultra-romantic Italian Renaissance palace can only be seen on a 45-minute guided tour, which tells the fascinating story of the coming of Western ways to the islands, the rebirth of Hawaiian culture in the last years of royal rule, and the sad story of the monarchy's overthrow. You must call ahead and reserve your tour spots, as tours sell out regularly. Call a few days in advance if you don't want to be disappointed (S. King and Richards sts., downtown; ☎ **808-538-1471** or 808-522-0832; Internet: alaike.lcc.hawaii.edu/openstudio/iolani).

The **USS Arizona Memorial & Museum** is quietly devastating, but well worth a few hours out of your otherwise-celebratory honeymoon. It's the nation's most enduring reminder of the Japanese attack on Pearl Harbor on December 7, 1941. Launches take you out to the stark, white memorial that spans the hull of the sunken battleship. Try to arrive early at the visitor's center to avoid the huge crowds, as advance reservations are not taken and waits of an hour or two are common. While you're waiting for the shuttle to take you out to the ship — you are issued a number and time of departure, which you must pick up yourself — you can explore the small but arresting museum, which features personal mementoes, photos, and historic documents. A 20-minute film precedes your trip to the ship. Allow about three hours for your visit. (On Battle-ship Row, Pearl Harbor; ☎ **808-422-0561**; Internet: www.nps.gov/usar; Admission: Free!)

While you're at Pearl Harbor, you can also tour the **Battleship Missouri Memorial** (☎ **877-MIGHTY-MO** or 808-423-2263; Internet: www.ussmissouri.com), the site of Japanese surrender to Douglas MacArthur and the Allied forces in 1945; and the **USS Bowfin Submarine** (☎ **808-423-1341**; Internet: www.aloha.net/~bowfin), one of only 15 World War II submarines still in existence.

Hanging around Waimea Valley

Waimea Valley, a scenic 1,800-acre river valley, is two parks in one: **Waimea Falls Park,** a botanical extravaganza with gorgeous gardens and groves blooming with flora from all over the world; a small collection of native birds and animals; remnants of old Hawaiian settlements and authentic demonstrations of ancient hula, games, and crafts; and the highlight, cliff-diving shows in which expert divers take death-defying leaps into a pool fed by a 45-foot waterfall — very cool. The other half is **Waimea Valley Adventure Park,** where adventure-seeking couples can skip the more prosaic attractions and head right for the thrills. You can go river and ocean kayaking (guided or unguided); ride rough-shod through the lush backcountry along mountain-biking trails; or tour the stunning north shore foothills on horseback. You can choose to enjoy one or both a la carte or in packages — it's up to you. (59-864 Kamehameha Hwy., Haleiwa. ☎ **808-638-8511;** Internet: www. atlantisadventures.com/hawaii/waikiki; Admission: $24 includes the falls only or $59 includes the falls, lunch, and two 20-minute activities.)

Visiting the north shore

Little more than a collection of faded clapboard storefronts with a picturesque harbor, the north shore town of **Haleiwa** has evolved into ground zero for Hawaii's surf culture, and a major roadside attraction unto itself. Exuding a sleepy tropical charm in summer, this beach town comes alive in winter, when the north shore waves swell and draw big-wave surfers from the world over. It's worth visiting whenever you're on the island.

Haleiwa sits about an hour's drive north of Waikiki, at the junction of highways 99 and 83, both called Kamehameha Highway. To get there, cruise north through Oahu's broad and fertile central valley, past Pearl Harbor, and pineapple and sugarcane fields until the sea reappears.

Haleiwa is definitely worth a stop to soak in some atmosphere, and shoppers looking for honeymoon souvenirs find an hour or two worth of good boutiquing to be had, and the surf shops are legendary. If you're captivated by surf lore (or just want to see what all the fuss is about), stop into the **North Shore Surf and Cultural Museum,** in the North Shore Marketplace at 66-250 Kamehameha Highway (☎ **808-637-8888**).

To really get into Haleiwa's surf city groove, stop into **Matsumoto's,** (66-087 Kamehameha Hwy.), for a taste of Hawaii's favorite sweet treat, shave ice — never "shaved ice" — the island version of a snow cone. Do as the locals do and order yours with a scoop of ice cream and sweet red azuki beans nestled in the middle — yum! One is more than enough for two to share. For some real food, north shore legend **Kua Aina Sandwich** (66-214 Kamehameha Hwy.; ☎ **808-637-6067**) grills up Hawaii's ultimate burger; take yours to the beach for the quintessential north shore picnic.

Enjoying sunsets and Mai Tais

Hands down, the best spot for sunset cocktails in all of Hawaii is the **House Without a Key** at the Halekulani, 2199 Kalia Rd., Waikiki (☎ **808-923-2311**). On an oceanfront patio shaded by a big kiawe tree, you can sip the best Mai Tais on the island, listen to masterful steel guitar music, and watch a traditional hula dancer (often former Miss Hawaii Kanoe

Miller) sway with the palms. Romantic, nostalgic, and simply breath-taking. Another top spot for live music (Hawaiian sounds and hula at sunset, a pianist tickling the ivories after dark), ocean views, and orchid-adorned cocktails is the oh-so-romantic **Banyan Veranda** at the Sheraton Moana Surfrider, 2365 Kalakaua Ave. (☎ 808-922-3111). Nothing sepa-rates you from the sand at the **Royal Hawaiian's Mai Tai Bar,** 2259 Kalakaua Ave. (☎ 808-923-7311), giving this place one of the most lovely views of Waikiki Beach. The Mai Tai Bar maintains an all-Hawaiian music program, which adds to the magical mood. If you're at the Diamond Head end of Waikiki, visit the **Sunset Lanai** at the New Otani Kaimana Beach Hotel, 2863 Kalakaua Ave. (☎ 808-923-1555). Shaded by a giant light-festooned hau tree and practically on the sand, it's no wonder that this magical spot is a favorite watering hole.

Dining on Oahu

If you want to splurge on one *really* fabulous meal while you're in Hawaii, you need to know only two names: **Chef Mavro** (1969 S. King St., Honolulu; ☎ 808-944-4714; Internet: www.chefmavro.com; $$$$$) and **Alan Wong's** (1857 S. King St., 5th Floor, Honolulu; ☎ 808-949-2526; Internet: www.alanwongs.com; $$$$-$$$$$). These are the two finest restaurants in the entire Pacific — and the unassuming masters behind them deserve megastar status on the world culinary map. Alan Wong's cooking brings all the goals of Hawaii Regional cuisine to their ultimate realization, while George Mavrothalassitis adds an inspired Provençal touch to gourmet Hawaii cooking that's pure genius. You're in for a transcendent dining experience at either restaurant — try squeezing both in, if you can manage it.

If you must choose between the two, Chef Mavro's is the more romantic.

Creating special memories

Duke's Canoe Club at the Outrigger Waikiki (2335 Kalakaua Ave.; ☎ 808-922-2268; $$$) is everything that Waikiki dining should be, complete with sarong-wearing cocktail waitresses, an open-air beachfront dining room, and tiki torches in the sand. Oceanfront dining hardly gets more romantic than **Orchids,** at the Halekulani hotel, 2199 Kalia Rd. (☎ 808-923-2311; $$$$), serving an impressive surf-and-turf menu that offers something for everyone. Live music adds to the romantic vibe nightly and at the legendary Sunday brunch. A casual terrace right on the sand, shaded by an ancient hau tree that twinkles with tiny lights at dinnertime, **Hau Tree Lanai,** at the New Otani Kaimana Beach Hotel, 2863 Kalakaua Ave. (☎ 808-921-7066; $$$), is one of Hawaii's most romantic beachfront restaurants. Few restaurants can make dining on Chinese feel like a special event, but the **Golden Dragon,** in the Hilton Hawaiian Village, 2005 Kalia Rd. (☎ 808-946-5336; $$$), does. Exotically elegant decor sets the stage for a class-act dining experience. Fixed-price meals give couples the best opportunity to sample the wide-ranging menu.

Finding romance for less

At **Indigo,** 1121 Nuuanu Ave., downtown Honolulu (☎ **808-521-2900;** Internet: www.indigo-hawaii.com; $$-$$$), excellent hybrid cuisine unites East and West in surprising harmony. For the ultimate in romantic dining, call ahead for a table on the magical lanai, which overlooks a charming pocket park. Intimate and affordable **Arancino,** 255 Beach Walk, Waikiki (☎ **808-923-5557;** $$), is hugely popular with visitors and locals alike thanks to its first-rate northern Italian cuisine — creative pizzas and pastas, housemade risottos, and fresh island seafood — and super-charming trattoria-style decor. **Singha Thai Cuisine,** 1910 Ala Moana Blvd., Waikiki (☎ **808-941-2898;** Internet: www.singhathai.com; $$-$$$), serves imaginative — and splendid — Thai-Hawaiian cuisine in a lovely setting. Graceful Thai dancers entertain nightly from 7 to 9 p.m.

Wowing It Up On Maui

Maui is much like a smorgasbord: Even if you have no intention of sampling everything it has to offer, you are wowed by the bounty of choices — and you plate is bound to be full well before you satisfy all of your cravings.

Having fun on land and at sea

Kaanapali Beach's four miles of grainy gold sand are lined with hotels in near-Waikiki density, but the beach tends to be populated only in pockets; you can almost always find a not-so-crowded section. **Kapalua Beach,** a gorgeous golden crescent bordered by two palm-studded points, is justifiably popular, but never too crowded. **Maluaka (Makena) Beach,** a wonderful South Maui beach park, offers a romantic off-the-beaten-path experience for couples in search of a first-rate snorkel experience or a break from Maui's ever-present crowds. If you're heading out to Hana, **Hamoa Beach,** a remote, half-moon-shaped beach at Maui's easternmost point, is breathtakingly lovely, with surf the perfect color of turquoise, gorgeous golden-gray sand, and luxuriant green hills providing a postcard-perfect backdrop.

Exploring the deep and skimming the surface

Maui boasts two prime offshore snorkel spots: the sunken crater called **Molokini,** and the waters around the island of **Lanai.** Both are great snorkel destinations, and you can visit each on day cruises. Snorkel-sails add whale watching to the agenda when the Pacific humpback whales make their annual visit to Hawaii from Alaska (generally December through March); much like many honeymooners, they seem to prefer Maui.

Some outfitters offer online booking discounts, so check.

Ecologically minded honeymooners can't do better than to give their snorkel-cruise dollars to the non-profit **Pacific Whale Foundation**

(☎ 800-942-5311 or 808-879-8811; Internet: www.pacificwhale.org), which is at the fore of Maui-based whale research, education, and conservation. Their first-rate modern catamaran fleet offers some of the best tours of Molokini and offshore Lanai — and the winter whale-watching cruises are unparalleled, of course.

Blue Water Rafting (☎ 808-879-7238; Internet: www.bluewaterrafting.com) takes small groups out on fast-flying, rigid-hulled inflatable boats for an exciting ride. Their Molokini cruises arrive in between the big boats' trips, so you have the overpopular crater largely to yourselves. They can also take you to the untouristed Kanaio Coast to visit turtles and spinner dolphins.

Trilogy Excursions (☎ 888-225-MAUI or 808-661-4743; Internet: www.sailtrilogy.com) is the Mercedes of Maui snorkel-sail operators. They feature first-rate catamarans, top-quality equipment, great food, and an A-1 crew. They have exclusive rights to land on Hulopoe Beach, one of Hawaii's best snorkel and dolphin-watching spots, and to offer ground tours; if you really want a genuine Lanai experience, don't book with anyone else. Half-day snorkel/sails to Molokini and late-morning snorkel-sails off Kaanapali Beach are also offered. Scuba upgrades are available on most Trilogy excursions for beginning and certified divers alike.

Scuba-diving honeymooners love Molokini. This crescent-shaped crater has three tiers of diving: a 35-foot plateau inside the crater basin (great for beginning divers), a wall sloping to 70 feet just beyond, and a sheer wall on the backside that plunges 350 feet below the surface. Whether you're first-timers or experienced divers, contact **Lahaina Divers** (☎ 800-998-3483 or 808-667-7496; Internet: www.lahainadivers.com), regularly lauded as a top dive operator by publications like *Scuba Diving* magazine. Another excellent option is **Ed Robinson's Diving Adventures** (☎ 800-635-1273 or 808-879-3584; Internet: www.mauiscuba.com/erd1.htm), which caters exclusively to certified divers.

Catching a wave

If you've always wanted to learn to surf, Maui is a great place to fulfill the dream, as it's known for having the easiest learning surf in Hawaii — and your best teacher is the **Nancy C. Emerson School of Surfing** (☎ 808-873-0264; Internet: www.maui.net/~ncesurf).

Hiking Haleakala

If you want to hike **Haleakala National Park,** you should go with a guide. A huge, barren, otherworldly place, the park is best seen with someone who can help you understand what you're seeing. Park rangers offer guided hikes into the park's cloud forest on weekdays; call ☎ 808-572-4400 at least a day ahead to check the current schedule, and to find out what to wear and bring (sturdy shoes and water are musts). **Hike Maui** (☎ 808-879-5270; Internet: www.hikemaui.com) has been universally lauded for the quality of their guided crater hikes. Hike

Maui also offers a number of other guided trips to various spots on the Valley Isle for all levels of hikers.

You may want to do what a lot of young, active-minded honeymooners do: Coast down the switchbacked, view-endowed road to the base of the mountain on a bike. Contact **Maui Downhill** (☎ **800-535-BIKE** or 808-871-2155; Internet: www.mauidownhill.com), Maui's oldest downhill company, to arrange a guided Haleakala bike "safari".

If you prefer a more independent — and more affordable – downhill ride, **Haleakala Bike Company** (☎ **888-922-2453** or 808-575-9575; Internet: www.bikemaui.com) can outfit you with all the gear, take you up to the top, and let you proceed down the mountain at your own pace.

Flightseeing over Maui

Flightseeing is an excellent way to see pristine parts of Maui that are unviewable by any other means. Maui-based helicopter tours also offer you the opportunity to see neighbor islands — Molokai, Lanai, even the Big Island — from the air. Helicopter tours are pricey — expect to pay anywhere from $200 to $800 for two, depending on the tour you choose — but breathtaking views make flightseeing a worthy honeymoon splurge. Excellent outfitters include **Blue Hawaiian Helicopters** (☎ **800-745-BLUE;** Internet: www.bluehawaiian.com) and **Hawaii Helicopters** (☎ **800-994-9099;** Internet: www.hawaii-helicopters.com).

Both companies offer significant price breaks if you book online in advance.

Hitting the links

Always book your tee times well in advance on popular Maui. Weekdays are best for avoiding the crowds and securing the tee times you want. Many clubs now accept online bookings. Budget-minded golfers should inquire about matinee discounts.

The views from the **Kapalua Golf Club** (☎ **877-527-2582** or 808-669-8044; Internet: www.kapaluamaui.com) are worth the pricey greens fees alone. **Kaanapali** (☎ **808-661-3691;** Internet: www.kaanapali-golf.com) poses a challenge to all golfers, from high handicappers to near-pros. The Tournament North Course is a true Robert Trent Jones design, with wide bunkers, the most contoured greens on Maui, and one of Hawaii's toughest finishing holes. Robert Trent Jones, Jr., was in top form when he designed the 36 holes at **South Maui's Makena Golf Club** (☎ **808-879-3344;** Internet: www.makenagolf.com) — and the views are spectacular. The par-72, 6,914-yard North Course is the more difficult, and more view-endowed, of the two courses. Most challenging at **Wailea Golf Club** (☎ **800-322-1614;** Internet: www.waileagolf.com) is the championship Gold Course, a classic Robert Trent Jones, Jr., design. The least difficult — and most scenic — is the Emerald Course.

Hotels around the island can often garner special rates at Wailea, so ask your concierge.

Watching the sunrise at Haleakala National Park

Home to the world's largest dormant volcano, Haleakala (ha-LEE-ah-KA-la) National Park is Maui's main natural attraction. It's a stark, barren place that's nevertheless quite beautiful in an otherworldly way. Just driving up the mountain is an experience in itself: You climb from sea level to 10,000 feet in just 37 miles. The views are magnificent and Haleakala is never more stunning than at sunrise, which becomes a truly awesome, you've-never-really-seen-a-sunrise-until-now, Technicolor sight from this lofty perch. A few folks may tell you that sunset is just as spectacular, but it's not.

To get to Haleakala Summit, take the Haleakala Highway (Hwy. 37 to Hwy. 377) to Haleakala Crater Road (Hwy. 378), where you'll start your ascent to the summit. Allow 2 hours if you're coming from Lahaina or Kihei, a little more if you're farther away. At the park entrance, you'll pay a fee of $10 per car; expect a slow, switchbacked drive the rest of the way up the hill. At Puu Ulaula Overlook, the volcano's highest point, a triangular glass building serves as a wind break and the best sunrise-viewing spot.

Taking a heavenly honeymoon drive

No Hawaii road is more celebrated than the "heavenly" **Hana Highway** (Hwy. 36), the super-curvaceous two-lane road that winds along Maui's northeastern shore, offering some of the most stunning natural sightseeing in the entire gorgeous state. The Hana Highway winds for some 52 miles east from Kahului east, crossing more than 50 one-lane bridges, passing greener-than-green taro patches, magnificent seascapes, gorgeous waterfalls, botanical gardens, and lush rainforests before passing through the little town of Hana and ultimately ending up in one of Hawaii's most beautiful tropical places: the Kipahulu section of Haleakala National Park. Kipahulu is home to Oheo *(oh-HAY-oh)* Gulch, a stunning series of waterfall pools that tumble down to sea.

Despite the draws at the end of the road, remember that this drive is about the *journey,* not the destination. It takes at least three hours — but you should allow all day for it. If you race along to arrive in Hana as quickly as you can, you end up as perplexed as so many others who just don't get it. Start out early, take it slow and easy, stop at scenic points along the way, and let the Hana Road work its magic on you.

Take these points into consideration as you plan your Hana trip:

- ✔ **Leave early to avoid the crowds.** Have breakfast (try **Charley's,** 142 Hana Hwy., in Paia — ☎ **808-579-9453** — which opens at 7 a.m.) and hit the road by 8 a.m.

- ✔ **Consider booking a place to stay in Hana.** That way, you can head out against the traffic in the afternoon, stay for a couple of nights so that you have a full day to enjoy East Maui's attractions (including its abundance of peace and quiet), and meander back at your own pace (once again avoiding the traffic) on the morning of the third day. See Chapter 9 for recommendations.

✔ **Fill up on gas before you set out.** If all else fails, make sure you stop in Paia, just east of Kahului, as the next gas is in Hana — 44 miles, 50-some bridges, and 200-plus hairpin turns down the road.

✔ **Don't bother if it's been raining heavily.** The Hana Highway is well paved and well maintained but can be extremely dangerous when wet — and it's easy to get stuck in muddy shoulders and pull-offs.

✔ **Bring your bathing suit in warm weather.** You find a number of waterfall pools along the way that are ideal for a refreshing dip, and folks love to swim in Oheo Gulch's placid summer pools.

✔ **Honk your horn.** On blind curves remember to honk to indicate that you're coming around the bend — and proceed slowly.

Ten luxuriant miles past Hana is **Oheo Gulch,** a dazzling series of water-fall pools cascading into the sea. Oheo Gulch is in the Kipahulu district of Haleakala National Park, and a ranger station sits at the back of the parking lot (☎ **808-248-7375**). Rest rooms are available but no drinking water, so be sure to pick some up in Hana if you're out. There is no fee for visiting this area of the park. The easy, half-mile Kuloa Point Loop Trail leads to the lower pools, where you can take a dip when the weather is warm and the water is placid. This well-marked 20-minute walk is a must for everyone.

Stay out of the Oheo Gulch pools in winter or after a heavy rain, when the otherwise placid falls can wash you out to sea in an instant, to the waiting sharks below. (No kidding.) If you do get to take a dip, always keep an eye on the water in the streams in any season, as upland rain can cause flood waters to rise quickly.

Just west of historic Wailuku in Central Maui, the transition between town and wild is so abrupt that most folks who drive up into Iao Valley are stunned by the rain forest that greets them. A gorgeous canyon, Iao Valley is great for a little quiet together time. Two paved walkways loop the 6.2-acre park; a leisurely ⅓-mile loop walk takes you past lush vege-tation and lovely views of the Iao Needle, an impressive spire jutting 2,250 feet above sea level. An architectural heritage park of Hawaiian, Japanese, Chinese, Filipino, and New England-style houses stands in harmony by Iao Stream at Kepaniwai Heritage Garden, which makes a good picnic spot. You can see ferns, banana trees, and other exotic plants in the streamside botanic garden. (On Iao Valley Rd., at the end of Main St., Wailuku. To get there: From Kahului, follow Kaahumanu Ave. east directly to Main St. and the park entrance. Admission: Free! Open: Daily 7 a.m.-7 p.m.)

Antiquing in Old Wailuku

For antiques-loving couples, there's nothing more romantic than the hunt. Historic Wailuku is the epicenter of antiquing in Hawaii. It's a mixed bag, but treasure hounds are sure to come away with a find or two. Market Street north of Main is the main shopping drag. Highlights include **Memory Lane,** 130 N. Market St. (☎ 808-244-4196) for 20th-century collectibles; **Brown-Kobayashi,** 160 N. Market St. (☎ 808-242-0804), for graceful and stylish Asian-accented finds; and **Bird of Paradise Unique Antiques,** 56 N. Market St. (☎ 808-242-7699), for glassware, pottery, and Hawaiiana.

Indulging at the spa

There's no better way to unwind than with a few pampering spa treatments. The best spa in Hawaii is the luxurious **Spa Grande at the Grand Wailea Resort** (☎ 800-888-6100 or 808-875-1234; Internet: www.grandwailea.com), a 50,000-square-foot temple to the good life with a massive East-meets-West spa menu, a first-rate army of therapists, and a full hydrotherapy circuit that's worth the treatment price alone. For a more intimate, personalized experience in South Maui, book treatments *à deux* at **Spa Kea Lani at the Kea Lani** (☎ 800-441-1414 or 808-875-4100; Internet: www.kealani.com). In West Maui, your top choice is **Spa Moana at the Hyatt Regency Maui** (☎ 800-233-1234 or 808-667-4440; Internet: www.maui.hyatt.com), a brand-new oceanview spa with an extensive menu that includes couples' treatments.

Living it up in Lahaina

A charming harbor town, **Lahaina** takes on a real party atmosphere as sunset nears. All of the restaurants along oceanfront Front Street boast stellar views and bars that are party scenes unto themselves, with lively bar scenes and live music. Your best bet is to just start at one end of Front Street and stroll along, dropping into whichever spots catch your fancy.

'Ulalena, at the Maui Myth & Magic Theatre (878 Front St.; ☎ 877-688-4800 or 808-661-9913; Internet: www.ulalena.com), is an incredible, Broadway-quality 75-minute live performance that interweaves the natural, historical, and mythological tales of the birth of Hawaii using a near-perfect mix of original music and dance, ancient chant and hula, creative lighting, gorgeous costumes, visual artistry (including some mindblowing puppets), and live musicianship. This hugely popular show is performed nightly. Don't miss it!

For something completely different, spend an evening at **Warren & Annabelle's** (900 Front St.; (☎ 808-667-6244; Internet: www.hawaiimagic.com). This genuinely fun and surprisingly uncheesy mystery-and-magic cocktail show stars illusionist Warren Gibson and "Annabelle", a ghost who plays a grand piano — yep, even your requests. Expect the requisite audience participation. Very popular, so book at least a few days in advance.

The Old Lahaina Luau (1251 Front St.; ☎ **800-248-5828** or 808-667-1998; Internet: www.oldlahainaluau.com) is Hawaii's most authentic and accolade-endowed luau. The oceanfront luau grounds provide a stunning setting, both the luau buffet feast and riveting hula show serve as a wonderful introduction to island culture, and the staff practices warm aloha. When you book, choose between Hawaiian-style seating, on mats and cushions set at low tables at the foot of the stage (most romantic), or traditional seating at generously portioned common tables; all tables have great views, but earlier bookings garner the best seats. Tickets are $70 per person, including food and cocktails.

The luau is offered nightly, but often sells out a week or more in advance, so book before you leave home to avoid disappointment.

Honeymooners looking for a more refined, grown-up experience prefer the **Feast at Lele,** 505 Front St. (☎ **808-667-5353;** Internet: www.feastatlele.com). This winning new concept in luaus (from the folks behind the Old Lahaina Luau) is ideal for romance-seeking couples who don't mind paying more for an intimate setting, a private table, and an excellently prepared five-course meal. Each course is dedicated to a Pacific island culture — Hawaii, Tonga, Tahiti, and Samoa — and comprised of gourmet versions of dishes from the native cuisine, followed by a dazzling native song and dance performance on a water's-edge stage. Offered Tuesday through Sunday; tickets are $89.

Dining on Maui

The Valley Isle has attracted so many top chefs from around the globe that choosing among their restaurants can be trying business. (Life should always be this rough, shouldn't it?)

Creating special memories

Pegged "Maui's little French jewel" by *Bon Appétit,* **Gerard's,** in the Plantation Inn, 174 Lahainaluna Rd., Lahaina (☎ **877-661-8939** or 808-661-8939; Internet: www.gerardsmaui.com; $$$$), is an excellent choice for couples in love. **David Paul's Lahaina Grill,** 127 Lahainaluna Rd., Lahaina (☎ **808-667-5117;** Internet: www.lahainagrill.com; $$$$), is consistently voted "Best of Maui". Overlooking luxuriant golf greens and the stunning Kapalua coastline, the **Plantation House,** 2000 Plantation Club Dr., Kapalua (☎ **808-669-6299;** Internet: www.theplantationhouse.com; $$$$), boasts an utterly glorious setting — and Chef Alex Stanislaw's one-of-a-kind Asian-Mediterranean fusion menu. **Nick's Fishmarket,** in the Kea Lani Hotel (4100 Wailea Alanui Dr., Wailea, ☎ **808-879-7224;** Internet: www.tri-star-restaurants.com; $$$$-$$$$$), is the top choice for romance in South Maui. A top-quality Mediterranean-accented seafooder, Nick's gets everything right: food, wine list, setting, and service. **Joe's Bar & Grill,** at the Wailea Tennis Center (131 Wailea Ike Dr., Wailea ☎ **808-875-7767;** $$$$), is another wonderful South Maui choice. Joe's serves a pleasing menu of upscale

American home cooking with island twists, and dim lighting and well-spaced tables make for a surprisingly romantic ambience after dark.

Searching for the sea

You can't get closer to the ocean than the alfresco tables at **I'o** (505 Front St., Lahaina ☎ **808-661-8422;** $$$$). I'o is a multifaceted joy, with a winningly innovative, mostly seafood menu, first-rate service, and a top-notch wine list. **Hula Grill** (Whaler's Village, 2435 Kaanapali Pkwy.; ☎ **808-667-6636;** $$$) serves an excellent steak-and-seafood menu and overflows with quintessential Hawaii charm. At **Mama's Fish House** (just off the Hana Hwy., 799 Poho Place, Paia; ☎ **808-579-8488;** Internet: www.mamasfishhouse.com; $$$$$) the fresh fish is as fabulous as it can be, and the beachfront tiki-room setting is quintessential romantic Hawaii. The service is sincere if dated ("And what will the lady have?"), but it suits the mood, as does the lengthy list of tropical drinks — with umbrellas!

Finding romance for less

Aloha Mixed Plate (1285 Front St., Lahaina; ☎ **808-661-3322;** $) serves casual island cuisine all day long at low, low prices — and with an ocean view, no less. At **Cheeseburger in Paradise** (811 Front St., Lahaina; ☎ **808-661-4855;** $), there's an idyllic harbor view from every seat, and it comes with a first-class burger: Big, juicy, gooey, and served on fresh-baked buns, they're guaranteed to satisfy even the most committed connoisseur. Chef Roy Yamaguchi has parlayed Hawaii Regional Cuisine into an international reputation. Of his two side-by-side Maui restaurants, **Roy's Kahana Bar & Grill,** in the Kahana Gateway Shopping Center (4405 Honoapiilani Hwy., Kahana; ☎ **808-669-6999;** $$$), has a lively atmosphere that's well suited to ordering a wallet-watching but wholly satisfying spread of Asian-accented appetizers and creative wood-oven pizzas.

Living Large on the Big Island

Beautiful beaches, lava fields, snorkeling, fishing, golf, and more — the Big Island has it all!

Having fun on land and at sea

The popular **Anaehoomalu Bay (A-Bay)** at Waikoloa is the most beautiful of the island's salt-and-peppery beaches. Boasting pretty fine-grained sand and a lovely grove of coconut palms, the beach fronts the Outrigger Waikoloa, but it's easily accessible, and it's so nice that even locals come. **Hapuna Beach State Park** has all the assets: glorious turquoise surf, a half-mile of the finest white sand, green lawns that allow you to picnic without getting sand in your lunch, and grade-A facilities. Hapuna is magical, especially in the gentle seasons, when the beach is widest, the ocean is calmest, and locals and visitors alike come out to swim, play, and ride the easy waves. If you've never snorkeled before, **Kahaluu Beach Park** is the place to start. The most popular beach on the Kona Coast, the water's so clear that you don't even need a mask — you can just wade in and look down; you may even spot a sea turtle or two. Separated from civilization by nearly two miles of vast lava fields, **Kona Coast (Kekaha Kai) State Park** is a great place to escape the crowds and get away from it all. The road to the beach is a bit rough going, but what awaits at the end is worth the drive for solitude-seeking honeymooners: a half-dozen unspoiled gold-sand beaches, with well-protected coves that are great for swimming in the gentle seasons. **Punaluu (Black Sand) Beach Park** is on the southeast coast enroute from Volcano to Kona (or vice versa). Stop here if you want to see a genuine black-sand beach. Stay out of the water year-round, as the offshore currents are strong.

Snorkeling Kealakekua Bay

One of Hawaii's absolute best snorkel spots is **Kealakekua Bay,** a stunning underwater marine preserve whose calm, clear waters teem with a kaliedoscope of colorful reef fish, plus playful spinner dolphins who often come by to say hi. The bay can only be reached by boat, however. The best snorkel cruises are offered by **Fair Wind** (☎ **800-677-9461** or 808-322-2788; Internet: www.fair-wind.com). The *Fair Wind II* is a state-of-the-art 60-foot catamaran complete with easy-access stairs (so you can literally walk into the water) and a water slide. Another option is to kayak. If you're new at this, take a guided tour with **Aloha Kayak Co.,** 79-7428 Mamalahoa Hwy., at the 114 mile marker (☎ **877-322-1444** or 808-322-2868; Internet: www.alohakayak.com). Experienced kayaking couples can rent singles or doubles and snorkel gear from the friendly shop, which can direct you to the best launch spots.

Watching for whales

Have your hearts set on whale watching, even though it's summer? Maybe you're visiting in winter, but you want to spot humpbacks with the most qualified expert around? Then call **Captain Dan McSweeney's Year-Round Whale-Watch Learning Adventures** (☎ **888-942-5376** or 808-322-0028; Internet: www.ilovewhales.com). The search is for visiting humpback whales in season, of course (roughly December to April); the rest of the year (except for May and June), Dan takes visitors looking for pilot, sperm, false killer, melon headed, pygmy killer, and beaked whales. Because Dan has been a whale researcher for 25 years and works daily with the whales, he has no problem finding them; he guarantees a sighting, or he takes you out again for free.

Diving into the deep

With calm, warm waters, 100-plus-feet visibility, and an open drop-off that supports a wealth of colorful marine life, the Kona-Kohala Coast offers some of the best scuba diving in the world (including excellent opportunities to swim with manta rays). Highly regarded outfitters for both beginners and seasoned pros alike are **Eco Adventures** (☎ 800-949-3483 or 808-329-7116; Internet: www.eco-adventure.com) and **Jack's Diving Locker** (☎ 800-345-4807 or 808-329-7585; Internet: www.jacksdivinglocker.com), both located in Kailua-Kona town. If you want a dive operator on the Kohala Coast, contact **Red Sail Sports** (☎ 877-RED-SAIL or 808-886-2876; Internet: www.redsail.com/hawaii-d.html).

Hooking the big one

Gigantic marlin, spearfish, ahi, mahi, ono (wahoo), and other good-eating big-game fish roam the warm Kona waters — the sportfishing capital of the world. Arrange a charter through **The Charter Desk at Honokohau Marina** (☎ 888-KONA-4-US or 808-329-5735; Internet: www.charterdesk.com), 2½ miles south of Kona Airport. The booking agents are real pros; they sort through the more than 50 available boats, fishing specialties, and personalities to match you up with the boat and crew that's right for you. When you book with the Charter Desk, you can be sure that your boat captain is USCG-licensed and that the boat is fully insured.

Most big-game charter boats carry six passengers max. Half-day and full-day charters are available, and the boats supply all equipment; no license is required. Prices start around $70 per person for a half-day share (where you share the boat with strangers), and $250 for a private charter. If you go for a share, you have to rotate rods (you won't get a full four hours of fishing in), so on a time-for-dollar basis, it's probably better to book your own boat if you're both interested and the two of you can afford it.

Craving adventure

An expert guide can really help you appreciate the majesty and power of this fantastic, multifaceted island in a way that you just can't on your own. Top is **Hawaii Forest & Trail** (☎ 800-464-1993 or 808-331-8505; Internet: www.hawaii-forest.com). Naturalist and educator Rob Pacheco or one of his well-trained guides takes small groups (usually no more than ten) out in plush four-wheel drive vehicles to explore some of the Big Island's most remote and pristine natural areas. All of the guides are well-schooled in natural history, ecology (both native and introduced flora and fauna), vulcanology, and island culture and history. A full slate of half- and full-day trips are available, all personalized to the groups' interest and ability levels, and they usually feature easy or moderate walking. A favorite adventure is the **Kohala Mule Trail Adventure.** An island-born guide takes you down a steep 500-foot trail on sure-footed mules to explore the stunningly pristine, history-rich, and otherwise inaccessible Pololu Valley. Full-day adventures include the **Volcanoes Adventure,** a 12-hour trip from the Kona-Kohala Coast to Hawaii Volcanoes National Park. Volcano Adventure is the best introduction to the active volcano and vulcanology that there is — and the absolute best way to see the volcano if you only have one day to do it.

Prices for half-day trips usually cost about $95 per person, while full-day trips are around $145 per person; rates include food and all the gear you need. Reservations should be made at least a week in advance.

Flightseeing over the Big Island

Taking a helicopter ride is a marvelous way to explore this large, dynamic isle — and there's no better way to see the bubbling volcano, especially if the current flow is too far from civilization to see from accessible points in the national park. Tours are pricey — expect to pay anywhere from $300 to $600 for two, depending on the tour you choose — but breathtaking views make flightseeing a worthy honeymoon splurge. The island's best is **Blue Hawaiian Helicopters** (☎ **800-745-BLUE;** Internet: www.bluehawaiian.com).

Blue Hawaiian offers a 15 percent price break if you book online in advance.

Hitting the links

The Kohala Coast is home to some of the finest golf challenges in the world.

Always book your tee times well in advance. Budget-minded golfers should inquire about matinee discounts.

The championship **Hapuna Golf Course** (☎ **808-880-3000** or 808-880-1111; Internet: www.hapunabeachprincehotel.com) is one of Arnold Palmer and Ed Seay finest designs. The 6,027-yard links-style course is gorgeous, with pastoral mountain views on one side and sweeping ocean views on the other. Around since 1964, the Robert Trent Jones, Sr.-designed **Mauna Kea Golf Course** (☎ **808-882-5400** or 808-882-7552) is the grande dame of Big Island courses. The legendary architect called the 3rd one of his favorite holes of all time; don't miss it if you can manage. Carved out of an ancient lava flow, the championship **Mauna Lani Frances H. I'i Brown** courses (☎ **808-885-6655;** Internet: www.maunalani.com/golf) are both winners. The North Course may not have the same drama as the oceanfront South Course, but old-growth greenery gives the course a Scottish feel.

The island's newest course, at the **Big Island Country Club** (☎ **808-325-5044**), is a 6,114-yard Pete and Perry Dye design situated at 2,500 feet elevation above the Kohala Coast, offering welcome relief from the perennially hot coastal weather — and the perennially high greens fees at most island courses. Expect to pay a third or quarter of what you'd pay elsewhere. What's more, the mountain and ocean views are incredible.

Braving a volcano

The top natural attraction in the islands, **Hawaii Volcanoes National Park** is the only rainforest in the U.S. National Park system — and the only national park that's home to a live, lava-pumping volcano. You can explore the park in one day if you don't mind the whirlwind tour, but you need at least two if you want to do some hiking. No matter how long your visit is, plan to stay until after dark at least one evening. That's when — if you're lucky — you can witness the miracle of creation as erupting Kilauea volcano spews glowing, red-hot lava.

At press time, the lava was flowing strong and shows no signs of stopping anytime soon, vulcanologists say — but Madame Pele, Hawaii's volcano goddess, doesn't run on a fixed schedule. The volcano could be shooting fountains of lava, or it could be shut down on the day you arrive in the park — and even if it is flowing, there's no guarantee that you'll get to see it. On many days, you can get as close to the lava flow as the heat allows; at other times it flows miles away, and is visible only in the distance (or via helicopter) or not at all (when it stays underground).

If you happen to visit during a period when the lava isn't visible, don't be too disappointed. You can still have a terrific day in the park even without seeing a speck of red — visiting the park is a once-in-a-lifetime experience even without the lava show.

The park is about 30 southwest of Hilo on the Hawaii Belt Road (Hwy. 11). From Kailua-Kona it's about 100 miles, or a three-hour drive. If you stay in Volcano village, the entrance is within a mile. At the entrance, you pay $10 (per car) admission, which lets you come and go for seven days.

Keep these tips in mind as you plan your park visit:

- ✔ You need two or three days to explore the park thoroughly, so book yourself a stay in Volcano village, at the park's gateway, or Hilo, about a 45-minute drive away. But don't stay away if you can't dedicate so much time; you can see a lot of the park if one full day is all you have.

- ✔ If you stay exclusively on the west (Kona-Kohala) coast and you can only see the park on a day trip, consider booking a guide-led nature tour of the park with Hawaii Forest & Trail (see the information earlier in this chapter).

- ✔ It's always colder here, so dress accordingly. Expect it to be at least 10 to 20°F cooler than it is on the Kona side; bring a light jacket and long pants. In winter, be prepared for temperatures in the 40s or 50s. Always have rain gear, especially in winter, and sturdy close-toed shoes.

- ✔ *Always* bring a hat, sunglasses, and sunscreen. Take it from us, who came away with quite a sunburn on a day that started with a downpour. Bring water, too, as it isn't readily available in most areas of the park.

- ✔ Pregnant visitors may want to skip the national park altogether, as it's not a good idea to expose yourself or your baby to the ever-present sulfuric fumes. Those with heart or breathing problems may also want to stay away. Otherwise, the park is perfectly safe for visitors.

For more information, contact park headquarters at ☎ **808-985-6000** (which also serves as a 24-hour eruption update and weather hotline) or visit www.nps.gov/havo. Visit the U.S. Geological Survey at www.usgs.gov and click on "Volcanoes" for more information on Kilauea's recent eruption activity. Another excellent site is www.hawaii.volcanoes.national-park.com.

Just inside the park is Kilauea Visitor Center. Here you can get up-to-the-minute reports on eruption viewing and good access points, pick up trail maps, check out exhibits that show you how volcanoes work, watch a 20-minute film on eruptions (shown hourly), and review the day's schedule of activities. An easy, 45-minute guided summit walk leaves daily at 9:45 p.m.; it offers an excellent introduction to the park and its flora, fauna, and volcanic geology, so begin your visit to the park with it. The guide is happy to make instructive recommendations on planning your time.

Use the rest room if you're heading into the depths of the park, because they're not readily available in the wilds.

Venturing to Puuhonua o Honaunan

If you only visit one historic site on your honeymoon, make it **Puuhonua o Honaunau National Historical Park.** No other place illustrates better what ancient island life was like — and, boy, is this place cool. With its fierce, haunting totem-like idols, this sacred site on the ocean looks mighty intimidating. To the ancients, though, it was a welcome sight — especially for defeated warriors and taboo breakers, because it was a designated sanctuary; as long as the troubled Hawaiians made it inside the massive rock wall, they were absolved. Wear shoes or sandals with good traction that are attached to your feet, and you can crawl around on the oceanfacing lava flats — fun! Launch your visit with a half-hour ranger-led orientation talk; all in all, allow two to three hours.

The park is located at the end of Hwy. 160, Honaunau (about 22 miles south of Kailua-Kona). To get there: Turn off Mamalahoa Hwy. (Hwy. 11) at Hwy. 160, between mile markers 103 and 104, and proceed the 3½ miles to the park entrance. ☎ **808-328-2326** or 808-328-2288. Internet: www.nps.gov/puho. Admission: $2 adults. Open: Visitor center, daily 8 a.m.-5:30 p.m.

Exploring North Kohala

North Kohala is the see a mountainous peninsula protruding from the top of the Big Island. If you want to experience old-style, plantation-minded Hawaii, North Kohala is the place to do it.

The hour-long drive along the Akoni Pule Highway (Hwy. 270) from Kawaihae (at the north end of the Kohala Coast) to the north tip is one of our favorite drives in all of Hawaii. It takes you past gorgeous rolling ranchlands with remarkable ocean vistas and through two charming old plantation towns, Hawi and Kapaau, both of which have been transformed into havens for shoppers in search of quality island crafts and unique gifts. After you finish browsing Hawi and Kapaau, continue a few miles to the end of Hwy. 270 and the Pololu Valley Lookout, a gorgeous scenic overlook that takes in a panoramic view of foaming waves and sheer seacliffs.

After all this sightseeing, you're bound to be hungry; retro-charming **Bamboo** (Akoni Pule Hwy., Hwy. 270, Hawi; ☎ **808-889-5555**), in Hawi, is an ideal stop for lunch (see the section "Dining on the Big Island" later in this chapter for more information).

Visiting Akaka Falls

One of Hawaii's most scenic waterfalls is **Akaka Falls,** a dramatic 420-footer tucked away in the misty rainforest eight miles north of Hilo. To reach it, turn off Hwy. 19 in Honomu left onto Akaka Falls Road (Hwy. 220) and follow it for 3.6 miles to the trailhead. It's an easy one-mile paved loop along a fragrant path that takes you past bamboo and ginger and down to an observation point, where you have a perfect view. You can also see nearby Kahuna Falls, which is a mere 100-footer. Keep your eyes peeled for rainbows.

Seeing Waipio Valley

The gorgeous **Waipio Valley** at the end of the road on the northeast (Hamakua) coast is one of the Big Island's most spectacular views. From the black-sand bay at its mouth, Waipio sweeps back six breathtaking miles, boasting green-as-can-be taro patches rustling in the wind between sheer cliffs almost a mile high. Take Hwy. 19 to Honokaa, then turn onto Kukuihaele Highway (Hwy. 240), which leads to Waipio Valley Lookout. This grassy park has splendid views of the Eden-like valley below, and makes an ideal spot to unpack a picnic.

Hanging around Hilo

Although **Hilo** is Hawaii's second-largest city, this pretty bayfront city really feels like a funky old plantation town. Some people just don't understand Hilo's appeal; you really have to be vintage-minded romantics to appreciate it. If you are, it's worth checking out, especially for the charming mix of fine and funky shopping centered in the wooden Wild West storefronts along oceanfront Kamehameha Avenue and the adjacent side streets.

But even if you just drive through on your way to Hawaii Volcanoes National Park, take a few minutes to cruise down Banyan Drive, the shady lane that curves along the waterfront, offering fabulous Hilo Bay views. Along Banyan Drive is postcard-pretty Liliuokalani Gardens, the largest formal Japanese garden this side of Tokyo.

Dancing the Hula at a luau

You'd be hard-pressed to find a better luau than the Friday-only **Kona Village Luau,** at Kona Village Resort (☎ **800-367-5290** or 808-325-5555). The setting is lovely (if not oceanfront), the food is excellently prepared, the traditional imu (underground pig roasting) ceremony is fascinating, and the South Pacific revue is top-quality, fast-moving, and lots of fun, if not 100 percent authentic — but the fire dancer is a show-stopper. The luau is large-scale, but manages to feel intimate, and the spirit of aloha shines from start to finish. It's $74 per person, beer and wine included. Reserve well ahead.

The **Traditions at Kahaluu** luau, at South Kona's Aston Keauhou Beach Resort (☎ **877-532-8468** or 808-322-3441), takes its job as cultural ambassador seriously, so expect an authentic Hawaiian experience. You won't be disappointed by the live entertainment — the hula troupe has won multiple world championships. Offered Sunday and Thursday; $67.50 per person, one mai tai included (full cash bar available).

Dining on the Big Island

The Big Island is home to some wonderful restaurants, including a handful of special-occasion oceanfront spots that are just right for some grand island-style wooing. But you don't have to spend a fortune to eat well; in fact, the Big Island is home to some of our favorite affordable and ethnic restaurants in the state.

Creating special memories

On-the-beach dining experiences don't come finer than **Brown's Beach House,** at the Orchid at Mauna Lani (1 North Kaniku Dr., Kohala Coast; ☎ **808-885-2000**; $$$$). An excellent alfresco restaurant, Brown's consistently shines in all categories: food, service, and setting. It's not on the sand like Brown's, but **Pahu i'a,** at the Four Seasons Resort Hualalai (seven miles north of Kona Airport; ☎ **808-325-8000**; $$$$), is intimate, candlelit, and one of the most beautiful restaurants in Hawaii — and the sublime food and faultless service live up to the setting in every respect. Neither residents nor visitors mind the long drive upcountry (20 minutes from the Kohala Coast, an hour from Kona or Hilo) when the reward is **Merriman's** (Opelo Plaza, Hwy. 19, Waimea (☎ **808-885-6822**; $$$$), one of the best Hawaii Regional restaurants in the state. **Roy's Waikoloa Bar & Grill** (Waikoloa Resort on the Kohala Coast; ☎ **808-886-4321**; Internet: www.roysrestaurant.com; $$$-$$$$) delivers excellent Asian-accented Hawaii Regional cuisine, excellent top-notch surf-and-turf, and a spectacular over-the-ocean setting — it's a proven **Chart House** recipe, and the Kailua-Kona version (75-5770 Alii Dr.; ☎ **808-329-2451**; $$$$), succeeds in spades. Koa-wood touches, an aloha-friendly staff, and that fabulous view personalize the chain's formula.

Finding affordable oceanfront allure

It's amazing that the über-expensive Four Seasons resort offers such an unpretentious place as the **Beach Tree Bar & Grill** (☎ 808-325-8000; $$$-$$$$). At this lovely outdoor patio on the sand, every table is angled to make the most of surf and sunset views. At sunset, music and hula make an already enchanting setting simply exquisite. Little more than a covered pier jutting over the water, **Edward's at Kanaloa,** 78-261 Manukai St., Keauhou (☎ 808-322-1003; $$$-$$$$), is one of Hawaii's most romantic restaurants. The **Coffee Shack,** on Hwy. 11 between mile markers 108 and 109 (☎ 808-328-9555; $), is a bare-bones South Kona charmer serving up first-class breakfasts, terrific home-baked pizzas, and the best sandwiches on the coast on an open-air patio with fantastic coastal views. Breakfast and lunch only.

Discovering out-of-the-way gems

The generous island-style sandwiches and home-baked goodies at **Maha's Café** (Waimea Center, 65-1148 Mamalahoa Hwy. (Hwy. 19), Waimea; ☎ 808-885-0693; $) are really something special. Hers is simple homestyle cooking, but Maha has the magic touch. Cute as a button, too. Well worth a visit for a memorable breakfast or lunch.

For the perfect excuse to venture up to pastoral North Kohala, reserve a table at **Bamboo Restaurant & Gallery** (Akoni Pule Hwy., Hwy. 270; ☎ 808-889-5555; $$-$$$). Bamboo bubbles over with nostalgic charm — like Trader Vic's without the kitsch. It's a perfect setting for pleasing island-style food that's absolutely wonderful but devoid of any "gourmet" pretentions. Fab passion-fruit margaritas, too.

Romancing on the right coast

A Volcano favorite is the rustic-romantic dining room at **Kilauea Lodge** (19-4055 Volcano Rd.; ☎ 808-967-7366; $$$-$$$$), tucked away in the rainforest just outside Hawaii Volcanoes National Park. Chef/owner Albert Jeyte prepares an Old World European menu that never disappoints, and the bartender shakes Manhattan-worthy cocktails. A lovely setting and top-flight Thai cuisine make **Thai Thai Restaurant** (19-4084 Old Volcano Rd.; ☎ 808-967-7969; $$) a real find in restaurant-poor Volcano village. Hilo's top special-occasion restaurant, **Pescatore** (235 Keawe St.; ☎ 808-969-9090; $$$). is an Old World affair, complete with wood-paneling, lace curtains, and traditional Italian fare that's well-prepared and pleasing.

Kicking Back on Kauai

Kauai's stunning north shore beaches are excellent for swimming and snorkeling in the warmer months, but they are not safe for swimming in the winter months, when the swells come and a powerful undertow takes over. Head to the south shore if you want to take a winter dip.

Having fun on land and at sea

Anini Beach is tucked away in a million-dollar residential neighborhood. This secret beach is one of the most gorgeous — and safest — swimming beaches on Kauai. The three-mile-long gold-sand beach is shielded from the open ocean by the longest, widest fringing reef in the islands. The north shore's half-moon **Hanalei Bay** has one of the most beautiful beaches anywhere: Gentle waves roll up the wide, golden sand; towering palms sway in the tradewinds; waterfalls vein an emerald accordion rising sharply in the distance. The whole bay is excellent for swimming and kayaking in summer; in winter, stick to the westernmost curve. Little-known and super-secret **Hideaway Beach** is a perfectly monikered beach, a gorgeous pocket of sand in the Princeville Resort that takes some work to reach — but it's worth the effort for seclusion-seeking couples. Swaying palms, a shelter of ironwoods, and gorgeous gold sand along a curvaceous shore make **Tunnels Beach** one of Hawaii's most beautiful beaches. The sand here is rougher, more pumice-textured than elsewhere, but somehow it's all the more luxurious for it. Go for perfect sunsets.

For amour amongst the south shore's unspoiled beauty, head to one of the finest stretches of untouched sands in Hawaii: **Mahaulepu Beach.** Two miles of grainy, reddish-gold sand tucked away among rocky cliffs, sand dunes, and a forest of casaurina trees, this idyllic stretch is perfect for beachcombing, sunbathing, or just cuddling up with your cutie and watching the endless waves roll in. Nobody should miss the big, wide **Poipu Beach Park,** the perfect beach playground, where grassy lawns with big, leafy shade trees skirt abundant white sand at the water's edge. **Lawai Beach** (Beach House Beach), a little, rocky white-sand beach just west of the Beach House Restaurant isn't the south shore's most beautiful, but snorkelers love it. The water is warm, shallow, clear, and silly with clouds of tropical fish.

Kayaking on the ocean and river

Kauai is made for kayaking. Even beginners can paddle down the Huleia River into **Huleia National Wildlife Refuge,** the last stand of Kauai's endangered birds, or follow the curving **Hanalei River** out to beautiful Hanalei Bay. Skilled kayakers can set out for the majestic **Na Pali Coast** for some real excitement. Our favorite island outfitter is **Kayak Kauai Outbound,** a mile past the Hanalei Bridge on Highway 56 (look for them on the ocean side of the road, across from Postcards Cafe) in Hanalei (☎ **800-437-3507** or 808-826-9844; Internet: www.kayakkauai.com), which offers a range of guided trips for all levels, as well as rentals. A second shop is on the Coconut Coast at the Coconut Marketplace, on Kuhio Highway (Hwy. 56), Wailua (☎ **808-822-9179**).

Diving into the deep

In winter, when heavy swells and high winds hit Kauai, diving is generally limited to the south shore. After the winter swells disappear and the easygoing summer conditions move in, the magnificent north shore opens up. Among the top outfitters are **Fathom Five Divers** (☎ **808-742-6991;** Internet: www.fathomfive.com) and **Dive Kauai** (☎ **800-828-3483** or 808-822-0452; Internet: www.divekauai.com).

Cruising Na Pali Coast

The most spectacular coastline in all of Hawaii is Kauai's remote **Na Pali Coast,** on the island's northwestern edge, which is best seen from a boat. Most cruises combine snorkeling with sightseeing, plus humpback whale watching in winter.

Mornings are usually calm, but the surf tends to seriously kick up later in the day — especially in winter, but not exclusively so. Those of you with sensitive tummies should take Dramamine or other motion-sickness meds well before you set out; after you're already on the high seas, it's too late.

Hawaiian-owned and -operated **Liko Kauai Cruises** (☎ **888-SEA-LIKO** or 808-338-0333; Internet: www.liko-kauai.com) offers 4½-hour Na Pali Coast cruises aboard a sleek, fast 49-foot power catamaran. You peek into sea caves and lush valleys, and glimpse waterfalls and miles of white-sand beaches. The narration is in-depth, culturally as well as naturally oriented, and very good. Tours leave from Waimea on the island's southwest shore.

Captain Sundown (☎ **808-826-5585;** Internet: www.captainsundown.com) is the only operator to offer cruises year-round from the north shore. Their 40-foot sailing catamaran carries only 15 passengers, so Captain Sundown is an excellent choice for couples looking for an intimate trip. Options include Na Pali sails, with an emphasis on snorkeling in summer, whale-watching in winter; plus a sunset sail option that offers a stunning view of the Bali Hai cliffs. All trips include an exciting short paddle out to the boat in a Hawaiian Outrigger canoe. Reserve well in advance.

Hiking Na Pali Coast State Park

Na Pali Coast State Park is the most spectacular place in the Hawaiian Islands. This 22-mile stretch of green-velvet fluted cliffs wrap around the island's northwest shore. Seven valleys crease the soaring cliffs; hidden within are spectacular waterfalls, remote beaches, and other wonders of nature that are too beautiful to be real.

Na Pali takes effort to explore. You can sail by on a boat (see the preceding section), fly over it in a helicopter (see the following section), or hike in. The north shore trailhead is at the end of Kuhio Highway (Hwy. 560), at Kee Beach, about 7½ miles past Hanalei. The hike along the Kalalau Trail is too much for most (including us); it winds for 11 grueling miles through the remote park, requires a permit, and takes about eight hours each way. Try hiking just the first two miles, to Hanakapiai Beach. Even this first stretch is tough — it's never level, it's rocky the entire way, and the first mile's all uphill. The beach at the end is breathtaking, but you have to climb over big boulders at the end of the trailhead to do it (eminently doable, but be forewarned), and the water's *way* too rough for swimming even in summer. However, the payoff is more than worth the trouble. Expect it to take 1½ to 2 hours to reach the beach. Wear good hiking shoes with ankle support if you have them, tennis shoes with good traction if you don't. Wear a hat and bring lots of water, as there's little cover along the trail.

If it sounds like too much for you, in terms of effort or time, you can get a big reward by just hiking in the first half-mile, which gives a good hint at the breathtaking natural beauty that lies ahead.

Flightseeing over Kauai

Kauai is the helicopter capital of Hawaii; if you want to splurge on a flightseeing tour just once, do it here. No other island has so much startling, but otherwise unreachable, natural beauty. **Island Helicopters** (☎ **800-829-5999** or 808-245-8588; Internet: www.islandhelicopters.com) is one of the most well-established and safest air-tour operators in the business. Other excellent options are **Jack Harter (☎ 888-245-2001** or 808-245-3774; Internet: www.helicopters-kauai.com), and **Will Squyres Helicopter Tours (☎ 888-245-4354** or 808-245-8881; Internet: www.helicopters-hawaii.com).

Book your flight in advance, at least a week in high season. If weather conditions look iffy on the day of your flight, reschedule.

Most operators offer discounts to those who book in advance via their Websites.

Hitting the links

Stars of the show are the **Princeville Resort Courses (☎ 800-826-1105** or 808-826-5070; Internet: www.princeville.com/play), two accolade-laden Robert Trent Jones, Jr., designs. This devil of a course is sculpted to offer ocean views from every hole; golfers in the know often name it the best-designed course in the state. Accuracy is key here — if you miss the fairway, your ball's in the drink. The Makai Course is more forgiving, but not by much.

In Lihue are the **Kauai Lagoons Courses (☎ 800-634-6400** or 808-241-6000). Both of the Jack Nicklaus-designed courses are excellent: *Golf Digest* awarded Kauai Lagoons its gold medal in 2000, calling the Kiele Course "one of the four finest courses in the country", while the Mokihana is a Scottish-style layout that's ideal for recreational golfers.

Here's a sunny south shore challenge for low-handicap honeymooners: The 6,959-yard, par-72 **Poipu Bay Resort Golf Course (☎ 800-858-6300** or 808-742-8711; Internet: www.kauai-hyatt.com/golf) has a links-style layout by Robert Trent Jones, Jr., that's a favorite among avid golfers — including, no doubt, Tiger Woods, who has won the PGA's Grand Slam of Golf here more than once.

Tops for wallet-watching honeymooners is Poipu's exciting **Kiahuna Golf Club** (☎ 808-742-9595; Internet: www.kiahunagolf.com), whose Robert Trent Jones, Jr., links design plays around four archaeological sites. Greens fees are a half or third of what most resort courses charge.

It's usually not too tough getting tee times on Kauai, but honeymooners with golf on their minds should book in advance.

Gracing Allerton Garden

Allerton Garden is a former turn-of-the-century private estate that has been transformed into a nationally chartered research facility for the study and conservation of tropical botanics. It's home to an extraordinary collection of tropical fruit and spice trees, rare introduced and native Hawaiian plants, hundreds of varieties of flowers, a marvelous palm collection, a series of Green Giant-sized Moreton Bay fig trees that were featured in *Jurassic Park,* and some spectacular examples of landscape gardening featuring outdoor "rooms" and gravity-fed fountains. You can only visit the garden on a docent-led guided tour; it's a well-spent 2½ hours for serious green thumbs and novices alike that's well worth the high price tag. Be sure to look for the secret beach that you pass at the start of the tour — the views are awe-inspiring.

Reservations are required. Reserve at least a week in advance in summer. Wear walking shoes and long pants, and bring insect repellent. On Lawai Rd. (across from Spouting Horn), Poipu Beach. ☎ 808-742-2623. Internet: www.ntbg.org/allerton.html. 2½-hour tours: $30. Times: Tues-Sat at 9 a.m., 10 a.m., 1 p.m., and 2 p.m.

Going to Waimea Canyon and Kokee State Park

Waimea Canyon and Kokee State Park is a great gaping gulch that is fondly called the "Grand Canyon of the Pacific" — and the nickname is apt, for the valley's reddish lava beds remind everyone who sees it of Arizona's Grand Canyon. Kauai's version is much smaller: only a mile wide, 3,567 feet deep, and 12 miles long. As you drive north — and up in elevation — the first good vantage point you reach is Waimea Canyon Lookout, between the 10- and 11-mile markers on Waimea Canyon Road. A few more lookout points dot the route, each offering spectacular views; Puu Hina Hina Lookout, between the 13 and 14 mile markers, is a particular gem.

Keep going upland and inland through Waimea Canyon, all the way to the top, and you find a high-altitude treat: **Kokee State Park,** a cloud forest at 4,000 feet. This cool, wet forest is full of beautiful native plants and imports, plus pigs, goats, black-tailed deer, and a wealth of native birds. The trails up here are a must for serious hikers.

Getting there: from Kaumualii Hwy. (Hwy. 56), turn north onto Hwy. 550, Waimea Canyon Dr., which eventually becomes Kokee Rd. Park:

☎ 808-335-9975. Internet: www.aloha.net/~kokee. Admission: Free! Open: Museum, daily 10 a.m.-4 p.m.

Touring the north shore

The most enticing thing about Kauai is its natural beauty — and it's just outside your car window. Even if you don't stay on the north shore, take Kuhio Highway up for the day, surveying the beauty as you go. Stop to take in the beautiful vistas along the way, have lunch and explore laid-back Hanalei, and kick back at one of the fabulous beaches along this shore. Finish the day at our favorite sunset-watching perch, on the north shore in the cute little town of **Kilauea,** at the end of Kilauea Lighthouse Road (seven miles before Hanalei town; turn off the Kuhio Highway at the Menehune Mart and gas station). Look west to watch the sun sink into the horizon beyond Hanalei Bay, brilliantly illuminating the luxuriant Bali Hai cliffs with its warm orange rays. It's the best, most romantic sightseeing you can do on Kauai; it lives on in your memory for a long time to come.

Indulging at the spa

There's nothing more relaxing than a spa day at the **Hyatt Regency Kauai's Anara Spa,** Poipu Beach (☎ 808-742-1234; Internet: www.kauai-hyatt.com/anara), one of Hawaii's finest spa facilities. "Anara" is an acronym for "A New Age Restorative Approach," which sets the tone for Anara's touchy-feely, homeopathic-minded mission — and God bless them for it. The phenomenal facility is the perfect place to spend the day — and the spa's masterminds know it, which is why they designed a full slate of spa packages. This place is always booked up, so reserve well ahead. Ask about massages for two, in which a therapist teaches each of you to work massage magic on each other.

On the north shore, **Princeville Health Club & Spa** (☎ 808-826-5030; Internet: www.princeville.com) isn't quite so extensive, mission-oriented, or eye-catching, but its facilities are comfortable, its spa menu appropriately lengthy, and its technicians first-rate.

Sailing into the sunset

What better way to celebrate the end of another fine day in Paradise than with a sunset cocktail cruise? **Bluewater Sailing** (☎ 808-828-1142; Internet: www.sail-kauai.com), **Captain Andy's Sailing Adventures** (☎ 808-335-6833; Internet: www.sailing-hawaii.com), and **Captain Sundown** (☎ 808-826-5585; Internet: www.captainsundown.com) offer regular sunset sails.

Dining on Kauai

Whether you're looking for a romantic candlelit dinner, quality seafood in an oceanfront setting, or simply a great island-style burger, choices abound on the Garden Isle.

Creating special memories

The oceanfront **Beach House Restaurant** (5022 Lawai Rd., Poipu Beach; ☎ 808-742-1424; $$$$) is a favorite special-occasion restaurants. The long, Japanese-reminiscent room is lined with shoji-like windows that make sunset a celebration every night, and let in a symphony of surf after dark. At super-elegant **Dondero's,** at the Hyatt Regency Kauai, Poipu Beach (☎ 808-742-6241; $$$$$), you can always count on a beautifully prepared regional Italian menu. A shining star on the Hawaii dining scene is **A Pacific Cafe,** in the Kauai Village Shopping Center (4-831 Kuhio Hwy., Kapaa; ☎ 808-822-0013; $$$$), one of the state's top showcases for gourmet Hawaii Regional cooking. A sublime — and thoroughly enjoyable — dining experience every time. Easygoing **Roy's Poipu Bar & Grill,** in the Poipu Shopping Village (2360 Kiahuna Plantation Dr., Poipu Beach ☎ 808-742-5000; $$$-$$$$), is perfect for gourmet-minded honeymooners who want to keep it casual. **Cafe Hanalei,** at the Princeville Resort (☎ 800-325-3589 or 808-826-9644; Internet: `www.princeville.com`), satisfies the perfect north shore mood. They offer a romantic indoor-outdoor setting with breathtaking views, and a marvelous menu with alternating Asian and Mediterranean accents.

Romancing for less

Keoki's Paradise, in Poipu Shopping Village (2360 Kiahuna Plantation Dr., Poipu Beach; ☎ 808-742-7534; $$), boasts alfresco allure galore, complete with tiki torches, aloha-friendly service, a lengthy menu, and live Hawaiian music that heightens the tropical ambience on weekends. The eclectic cafe-cum-art gallery called **Caffè Coco,** on the Coconut Coast (4-369 Kuhio Hwy., Wailua; ☎ 808-822-7990; $$), is tops for low-budget romance. The worldwise, everything-from-scratch food is creative and wonderful, and the flickering tiki torches set the perfect mood. Cool, dimly lit **Norberto's El Cafe,** on the Coconut Coast at 4-1373 Kuhio Hwy., Kapaa (☎ 808-822-3362; $-$$), marries fresh-grown island greens and fish with traditional south-of-the-border recipes, resulting in Mexican fare that's both top-quality and pleasingly authentic.

Finding a local favorite

Set in a historic plantation house on the edge of Hanalei, **Postcards Cafe** (5-5075A Kuhio Hwy.; ☎ 808-826-1191; $$$) boasts a creative pan-cultural menu that emphasizes fresh fish and locally grown greens. Postcards is also a great place to start your day with vegetarian breakfasts (stellar smoothies!). Fresh-off-the-boat seafood and a romantic tropical garden setting on the banks of the Hanalei River makes **Hanalei Dolphin** (5-5016 Kuhio Hwy. Hanalei; ☎ 808-826-6113; $$$) a very pleasing choice for cocktails and dinner. The name says it all: **Sushi, Blues & Grill,** in Ching Young Village, (5-8420 Kuhio Hwy., Hanalei; ☎ 808-826-9701; $$$). Neither raw fish nor live entertainment (usually live jazz, blues, or dance music) gets better on Kauai, and the terrific sake and cocktail menu means you'll be content 'til the cows come home.

Chapter 11

Making Plans and Settling In

By Cheryl Farr Leas

● ●

In This Chapter

▶ Making your way to Hawaii

▶ Getting around once you arrive

▶ Knowing all the details

● ●

*P*lanning your trip may not really be half the fun, but it's a necessary step.

Getting to Hawaii

Most trans-Pacific flights arrive on Oahu, but an increasing number land directly on Maui, the Big Island, and Kauai. Flying direct to the island of your choice is the most convenient thing to do, as it can save you a two-hour layover in Honolulu and an interisland plane ride — a process that can add another three or four hours to your total travel time. However, expect to pay for the privilege of flying direct, as mainland flights to the neighbor islands are generally more expensive than those that arrive in Honolulu.

The following major airlines fly between mainland North America and one or more of Hawaii's major airports: **Air Canada** (☎ **888-247-2262;** Internet: www.aircanada.ca); **Aloha Airlines** (☎ **877-TRY-ALOHA** or 800-367-5250; Internet: www.alohaair.com); **American Airlines** (☎ **800-433-7300;** Internet: www.americanair.com); **Continental Airlines** (☎ **800-525-0280;** Internet: www.continental.com); **Delta Airlines** (☎ **800-221-1212;** Internet: www.delta-air.com); **Hawaiian Airlines** (☎ **800-367-5320;** Internet: www.hawaiianair.com); **Northwest Airlines** (☎ **800-225-2525;** Internet: www.nwa.com); **TWA** (☎ **800-221-2000;** Internet: www.twa.com); and **United Airlines** (☎ **800-241-6522;** Internet: www.ual.com).

Flying Between the Islands

The only way to travel from island to island is by airplane. There are two major interisland carriers: **Aloha Airlines** (☎ **800-367-5250**, 877-TRY-ALOHA, or 808-484-1111; Internet: www.alohaairlines.com) and **Hawaiian Airlines** (☎ **800-367-5320**, 800-882-8811, or 808-838-5300; Internet: www.hawaiianair.com). Both offer similar interisland jet service — flights between the major islands every hour or so — and competitive pricing.

At press time, the full interisland fare was about $104 per one-way segment, with fares dropping as low as $50 on occasion, depending on the dates and routes you wish to fly.

Arranging for a Rental Car

Unless you and your new spouse want to just park yourself at a resort for your entire trip — not a great idea since Hawaii has so many fabulous things to see and do — you need a rental car on each of the islands. The only island that's navigable without a car is Oahu, but you are stuck in Waikiki if you don't have your own wheels.

The following companies rent cars on all of the major Hawaiian islands:

- **Alamo:** ☎ **800-GO-ALAMO;** Internet: www.alamo.com
- **Avis:** ☎ **800-230-4898;** Internet: www.avis.com
- **Budget:** ☎ **800-527-0700;** Internet: www.budget.com
- **Dollar:** ☎ **800-800-4000;** Internet: www.dollar.com
- **Enterprise:** ☎ **800-325-8007;** Internet: www.enterprise.com
- **Hertz:** ☎ **800-654-3131;** Internet: www.hertz.com
- **National:** ☎ **800-227-7368;** Internet: www.nationalcar.com
- **Thrifty:** ☎ **800-THRIFTY;** Internet: www.thrifty.com

Book your rental cars well ahead. Rental cars are almost always at a premium on Kauai, and may be sold out on all neighbor islands on weekends.

Fast Facts: Hawaii

American Automobile Association (AAA)

The only local AAA office is in Honolulu, on the island of Oahu, at 1270 Ala Moana Blvd., between Piikoi Street and Ward Centre (☎ 800-736-2886 or 808-593-2221; Internet: www.aaa-hawaii.com). For roadside assistance or information on becoming a member, call ☎ 800-AAA-HELP or point your Web browser to www.aaa.com.

American Express

Cardholders and traveler's check holders should call ☎ 800-221-7282 for all money emergencies. To make inquiries or to locate other branch offices, call ☎ 800-AXP-TRIP or visit www.americanexpress.com. American Express has branch offices:

On Oahu at 1440 Kapiolani Blvd., Suite 104, Honolulu (☎ 808-946-7741); in the Tapa Tower at Hilton Hawaiian Village, 2005 Kalia Rd., at Ala Moana Boulevard, Waikiki (☎ 808-951-0644); and at the Hyatt Regency Waikiki, 2424 Kalakaua Ave. (☎ 808-926-5441).

On Maui at One in Kaanapali at the Westin Maui, 2365 Kaanapali Pkwy. (☎ 808-661-7155); and in South Maui at the Grand Wailea Resort & Spa, 3850 Wailea Alanui Dr., Wailea (☎ 808-875-4526).

On the Big Island's Kohala Coast at Hilton Waikoloa Village, 425 Waikoloa Beach Dr., off Hwy. 19 in the Waikoloa Resort (☎ 808-886-7958).

On Kauai there is no AmEx office at this time.

Area Code

All of the Hawaiian Islands are in the 808 area code. When dialing, you can leave the area code off if you're calling someone on the same island that you're on. If you call someone on a different island, you must dial 1-808 before the seven-digit phone number.

If you call from one island to another, the call will be billed as long distance, which can be more expensive than calling the mainland from Hawaii. So use your long-distance calling card when calling between islands to avoid adding inflated phone charges to your hotel bill.

ATMs

ATMs are plentiful in the major resort areas, and all are connected to all the global ATM networks. Do yourself a favor, though, and don't head to a remote area — the north shore of Kauai, say, or the Big Island's North Kohala peninsula or Volcano area — without stocking up on cash first.

One of Hawaii's most popular banks, with branches throughout the state, is **Bank of Hawaii**, which is linked with all the major worldwide networks. To find the one nearest you, call them at ☎ 808-643-3888 or visit www.boh.com/locations/atmdir.asp. You can also find ATMs on the **Cirrus** network via ☎ 800-424-7787 or www.mastercard.com/atm; to find a **Plus ATM,** call ☎ 800-843-7587 or visit www.visa.com/atms.

Doctors

On Oahu, **Straub Doctors on Call** (☎ 808-971-6000; Internet: www.straubhealth.org) offers around-the-clock care at their 24-hour health clinic, on the ground floor of the Sheraton Princess Kaiulani Hotel, 120 Kaiulani Ave., just north of Kalakaua Avenue in the heart of Waikiki.

On Maui, walk-in patients are accepted at **West Maui Healthcare Center,** Whaler's Village, 2435 Kaanapali Pkwy., second floor, Kaanapali (☎ 808-667-9721); and in South Maui at **Urgent Care Maui,** 1325 S. Kihei Rd. (at Lipoa Street), Kihei (☎ 808-879-7781).

On the Big Island, **Hualalai Urgent Care** is at 75-1028 Henry St. (opposite Safeway), Kailua-Kona (☎ 808-327-4357).

On Kauai, walk-ins are accepted at the **Kauai Medical Clinic,** 3420-B Kuhio Hwy. (next to Wilcox Hospital), Lihue (☎ 808-245-1500); and at **Kilauea North Shore Clinic,** on Oka Street (turn right off Kilauea Lighthouse Road), Kilauea (☎ 808-828-1418).

Emergencies

No matter where you are in Hawaii, dial **911** from any phone.

Information

The **Hawaii Visitors and Convention Bureau** operates an office on the fourth floor of the Royal Hawaiian Shopping Center, 2233 Kalakaua Ave., in the heart of Waikiki (☎ 800-464-2924 or 808-923-1811; Internet: www.gohawaii.com). Island-specific information is available from the **Oahu Visitors Bureau** (☎ 877-525-OAHU or

808-524-0722; Internet: www.visit-oahu.com); the **Maui Visitors Bureau** (☎ 800-525-6284 or 808-244-3530; Internet: www.visitmaui.com), which can also provide information at Molokai and Lanai; the **Big Island Visitors Bureau** (☎ 808-886-1655 on the Kona-Kohala Coast, ☎ 808-961-5797 in Hilo; Internet: www.bigisland.org); and the **Kauai Visitors Bureau** (☎ 800-262-1400 or 808-245-3971; Internet: www.kauaivisitorsbureau.org).

Liquor Laws

The legal drinking age in Hawaii is 21. Bars are allowed to stay open daily until 2 a.m.; places with cabaret licenses can keep the booze flowing until 4 a.m. Grocery and convenience stores are allowed to sell beer, wine, and liquor seven days a week.

Mail

To find the U.S. Postal Service branch nearest you, call ☎ 800-275-8777 and be prepared to give the operator the local zip code.

Maps

All of the rental-car companies hand out very good free map booklets on each island, which is all you need to navigate your way around. AAA supplies excellent maps of Hawaii to members only.

If you want more complete topographic maps of each island, the best are printed by the University of Hawaii Press. They're available from just about any bookstore in the islands. If you'd like to order them before you leave home, contact **Basically Books,** 160 Kamehameha Ave., Hilo, HI 96720 (☎ 800-903-MAPS or 808-961-0144; Internet: www.basicallybooks.com).

Newspapers

The *Honolulu Advertiser* (www.honoluluadvertiser.com) is the statewide paper. The main weekly

entertainment rag is Oahu's *Honolulu Weekly* (www.honoluluweekly.com).

Smoking

It's against the law to smoke in just about all public buildings. Hotels have nonsmoking rooms available, restaurants have nonsmoking sections, and car-rental agencies have nonsmoking cars. Most bed-and-breakfasts prohibit smoking inside their buildings.

Taxes

Hawaii's sales tax is 4 percent. Expect taxes of about 11.42 percent to be added to your final hotel bills.

Time

Hawaii Standard Time is in effect year-round. Hawaii is two hours behind Pacific Standard Time and five hours behind Eastern Standard Time — so when it's noon in Hawaii, it's 2 p.m. in California and 5 p.m. in New York. Hawaii does not observe daylight savings time, however, so when daylight savings time is in effect on the mainland — summertime, from April through October — Hawaii is three hours behind the West Coast and six hours behind the East Coast (making it noon in Hawaii when it's 3 p.m. in California and 6 p.m. in New York). For the exact local time, call ☎ 808-245-0212.

Weather and Surf Reports

Call ☎ 808-935-5055 for statewide conditions; ☎ 808-973-4382 for statewide marine reports; ☎ 808-973-6114 for statewide coastal wind reports. For local conditions and forecasts, call: Oahu (☎ 808-973-4380); Maui (☎ 808-877-5111); Big Island (☎ 808-961-5582); Kauai (☎ 808-245-6001). For online forecasts, visit www.hawaiiweathertoday.com; you might also check with www.weather.com or www.cnn.com/weather.

Part IV
The Caribbean, the Bahamas, and Bermuda

The 5th Wave   By Rich Tennant

©RICHTENNANT

"Don't worry, they may be called St. Martin, St. John, and St. Lucia, but you're not required to act like one while you're there."

In this part . . .

*P*lanning a honeymoon to a place you only know as a dot on the map? Before you commit to anything, relax and let us take you on a whirlwind tour of one of the world's most beautiful regions. In this part, we help you judge the romance quotient of our favorite islands.

First, we cover the basics: What each island is like and which one can make your dreams come true. Next come the details, like where to stay, eat and play, and — most importantly — those places and experiences sure to put you in the mood for love.

Chapter 12

Getting to Know the Islands

By Echo & Kevin Garrett with Rachel Christmas Derrick

• •

In This Chapter

▶ Taking a quick look at the each island

▶ Knowing who flies where

• •

*W*hatever sets your pulse racing — and fits your budget — rest assured that you can cast the right backdrop to play out your big-screen romance in the Caribbean. After all, that sweep of aquamarine blue-on-blue sea stretches nearly 2,000 miles from Cuba to South America and encompasses more than 30 different nations and a mind-boggling 7,000 islands.

From the flat, sunny, windy, Arizona-like Aruba, to the lush, mountainous, jungle-like rain forests of Puerto Rico, Jamaica, and St. Lucia, terrain varies tremendously from island to island. The islanders themselves are also a diverse group, representing 100 different cultures, a spicy melting pot from African to East Indian to European, as evidenced by everything from eye-popping art to the pulsating music to food. So take a quick tour through this vibrant region. The Caribbean, the Bahamas and Bermuda have stolen our hearts. We bet one of these magical places captures yours, too.

In this chapter, we hit the highlights on a whirlwind tour of some of our favorite islands, leaving the wonderful history and culture of this fascinating part of the world for you to discover on your own . . . or not. Here are the Caribbean's most popular destinations.

Aruba: Guaranteed Sunshine

Sugar-white beaches. Splashy casinos. A stark, otherworldly, cactus-dotted landscape known as the *cunucu,* where divi-divi (watapana) trees have been bowed to a 45-degree angle by the constantly blowing trade winds. Think Arizona with a beach, and you've got Aruba, an independent country within the Kingdom of the Netherlands.

Located a scant 15 miles north of Venezuela, this Dutch treat has a diverse heritage and is surprisingly small. Popular with honeymooners, the package-tour crowd, cruise ship daytrippers, and families (particularly in the summer) — and is famed for its wide, seven-mile stretch of white-sand beach, where most of its 30 hotels are tightly packed. Aruba's tiny capital, Oranjestad — with its pastel, stucco walls topped by wedding-cake cupolas and terra-cotta roofs — makes for a nice afternoon stroll. In the evenings, Oranjestad's club scene — heavily influenced by neighboring Latin American countries — offers festive and fun dancing.

If you want a hassle-free, relaxing honeymoon in the Caribbean and wonderful dining, Aruba should be high on your list. The hotels offer great honeymoon packages, and several of them have added spas recently. Even though Aruba is one of the more far-flung islands, you can get a direct flight from several major cities in the U.S. and Europe. What we like most about Aruba is the fact that the island is easy to navigate, and the people are hospitable. However, sophisticated travelers find little appeal on Aruba. We were disappointed to see the bland buildup along its stunning beaches. A moratorium now restricts new construction, but to our minds, the island had long ago reached the saturation point anyway. Although we had lots of fun on this island, Aruba is far from our definition of a tropical getaway. If you're envisioning a place where you two can find lots of time alone, look elsewhere.

Bahamas: The Islands with Variety

It is the Atlantic, not the Caribbean that actually surrounds the more than 700 islands that make up the Bahamas. Without question, these islands have beautiful beaches, superb snorkeling, sensational scuba diving, big-time boating, and fantastic fishing. However, each island also boasts its own special look, character, and atmosphere. All this variety means that tailoring a trip to almost any desire or budget is easy.

The busiest, most developed, and most popular islands in the Bahamas are New Providence (home to Nassau, Cable Beach, and adjoining Paradise Island) and Grand Bahama (the home of Freeport and Lucaya). Those are the islands that we cover in this book. Here you find glittering casinos, many restaurants (both gourmet and local), plenty of nightlife, and a wide range of hotels — whether you want something small and economical or a lavish, sprawling, break-the-bank lodging. New Providence and Grand Bahama are where most of the dry-land sightseeing is concentrated, from forts, museums, and horse-drawn carriages to aquariums, gardens, and nature preserves. A couple of straw markets plus scores of stores and boutiques duke it out for your attention — well, actually, your wallet. Most visitors don't mind, though, because the duty-free shopping on these islands can save you serious cash on an array of international imports.

We don't cover them in this book, but you may consider heading to the Bahamas Out Islands for your honeymoon. These islands include all those in the Bahamas other than the big three (New Providence, Paradise Island, and Grand Bahama). Most Out Island hotels are small, low-rise accommodations where the staff quickly gets to know you by name. The islands boast miles of empty, flour-white beaches and glass-clear, turquoise water. For more information on these islands pick up a copy of *Bahamas For Dummies,* by Rachel Christmas Derrick, published by Hungry Minds, Inc.

Barbados: A Tropical English Outpost

Steeped in English tradition and more straitlaced than some of its neighbors, Barbados has been giving the wealthy and famous the royal treatment for centuries. The easternmost of the Caribbean's Lesser Antilles chain, Barbados juts out into the Atlantic Ocean and used to serve as a gateway to the West Indies for ships coming to and from Europe and South America. As a result, its islanders got first pick of the bounty flowing into the Caribbean.

Known for its posh resorts from Sandy Lane to Royal Pavilion (think *Lifestyles of the Rich and Famous* and you've got the picture), Barbados offers a range of accommodations. You can receive the royal treatment from the moment you are greeted at the airport and are whisked away to your hotel. You pay for it, too.

High tea by the pool may seem odd at first, but by the second day, guests get into the spirit and join in this tradition. Another tradition to be aware of is dressing up for dinner — a must on Barbados. We quickly learned firsthand why Barbados has garnered international acclaim for its restaurants.

The mood on Barbados is unmistakably civilized — so much so that we felt a little stifled and hamstrung by all the tradition. We were relieved to come upon surfers hanging out near Bathsheba. With their hip attitudes, they definitely clashed with the island's character, but they actually made us feel more at home. Barbados residents, called Bajans (pronounced *bay-johns*), cut loose only when it comes to rum. Bajans are extremely proud of the locally made rums, and several little dives around the island serve rum at all hours.

Bermuda: A British Gem

Located in the Atlantic Ocean, about 600 miles east of North Carolina, the island of Bermuda has long been a favorite for its picture-perfect beauty, gorgeous pink beaches, and clear blue waters. The climate is subtropical, and during the winter months the temperatures are springlike — averaging in the low 60s to 40°F. Bermuda is convenient for those living on the east coast, and has long been a favorite locale for destination weddings.

Bermuda offers many fun things to do and places to explore. There are eight golf courses, numerous tennis courts, sailing, wreck diving, and other water sports. Visitors enjoy exploring Bermuda's historic towns, strolling through a lush garden, or wandering through one of the museums.

Distinctly British, Bermuda is a reserved island. There is no sparkling nightlife, so if you are looking to party on your honeymoon, you'll be disappointed. And it can be expensive. But visitors are charmed by this little gem. It's safe, clean, and — most importantly — romantic.

Grand Cayman: For the Quiet Set

The Cayman Islands, the birthplace of the Caribbean's recreational diving, rely on a good reputation for their relatively healthy reefs and dramatic wall dives with almost 200 dive sites and visibility up to 100 feet. Of the trio that makes up the Cayman Islands — Grand Cayman, Cayman Brac, and Little Cayman, just south of Cuba — Grand Cayman is the primary draw with its famed 5½ mile-long Seven Mile Beach.

Diving aside, Grand Cayman is easy to reach and easy to navigate when you're there. The island is safe and sanitized in every way — the kind of place where you can go to sleep in your beach chair, wake up, and still have all your stuff intact. English is spoken, U.S. dollars are accepted, and, most importantly, you are made to feel welcome.

Grand Cayman's top-drawer restaurants, cool attractions, tidy beaches, and plethora of watersports make it a popular choice with families, honeymooners, and divers who are traveling with nondivers.

If you crave glittery nightlife, don't go to Grand Cayman; go to Puerto Rico or Aruba instead. Even though the banking industry has made this island wealthy, flashing affluence at trendy clubs or gambling it away at casinos isn't the thing here. Expect to be in the company of the old money crowd, whose idea of fun is watching the sun set from a lantern-festooned deck while celebrating happy hour at a British-style pub.

Jamaica: Rugged Beauty

Does your island fantasy include rafting a river and swimming in a blue lagoon? How about racing to the top of a waterfall, or sitting on a verandah sipping your morning coffee while overlooking the bushes from which the coffee beans were plucked? Choose your favorite sunny spot from Jamaica's 200 miles of beaches. Hike the 7,400-foot summits of the Blue Mountains. Cuddle under a heated duvet to ward off the cool mountain air at night.

Jamaica has four main resort areas — Montego Bay, Negril, Ocho Rios, and Port Antonio — each tempting in a different way with tennis, golf, horseback riding, and water sports. The island owes part of its success to the prevalence of all-inclusive resorts — several of them are reserved for couples only — which were first popularized here and have spread to several other Caribbean islands. However, these compounds have proven both a blessing and a curse. Many honeymooners like them because they take a lot of the guesswork out of your trip, letting you control costs up front.

We have a love/hate relationship with the island. We adore the less-touristy parts and the way people quickly warm up if you are kind to them and show interest in their country. We abhor the brazen approaches of shady characters peddling drugs and prostitutes that you're likely to encounter on the beaches and outside the resorts' gates. On the other hand, if you are looking for local color and are genuinely interested in this beautiful country, you can make friends for life here.

Puerto Rico: Pleasurable Paradise

Everything that your heart could desire in an island honeymoon, Puerto Rico is a stunner dished out with a steamy Latin beat. The colonial city of Old San Juan, with its well-preserved forts and narrow stone streets overhung with balconies brimming with flowers, has managed to avoid the T-shirt tackiness that mars so many of this hemisphere's port cities. Yet with its chic art galleries and incredible restaurant scene, Old San Juan gracefully bridges the gap between old and new.

Those who want high-rise hotels with happening beach scene, high-energy discos, and frenetic casinos can find them on Condado and Isla Verde in San Juan. Puerto Rico has enough natural wonders — dramatic caves for spelunking, extensive rainforests for hiking, phosphorescent lakes and good corals for diving, and 272 miles of Atlantic and Caribbean coastline for horseback-riding, swimming, surfing, whale watching, and walking hand-in-hand — to keep you more than occupied. The island also scores with people who love golf and deep-sea fishing.

As for accommodations, Puerto Rico arguably has the broadest range of choices in the Caribbean: from a hotel converted from a 500-year-old convent to mega-resorts with all the bells-and-whistles. It also offers gems called *paradores* — clean, comfortable, and reasonably priced bed-and-breakfasts that must pass government inspection.

Puerto Rico packs sizzle to spare with a sexy nightlife scene. This island is considered paradise for eco-hounds and sports nuts as well as those souls who are content to sit on the beach sipping margaritas.

St. Lucia: A Little Bit of Hawaii

Ahhhh, St. Lucia. An often-overlooked gem, St. Lucia yields one surprise after another: a steamy volcano, secluded waterfalls, dramatic mountain vistas, lush rain forests, even private mineral baths used by Napoleon's muse Josephine, who grew up on one of the island's plantations. The crowning glory of St. Lucia (pronounced *loo-sha*) is the Pitons, postcard-perfect twin volcanic peaks rising majestically out of the sea. To the east, the Atlantic Ocean crashes against the coast; to the west lies the serene beauty of the Caribbean.

We particularly like the low-key resorts and hotels tucked into the mountainous terrain around Soufrière, a small fishing village near the Pitons. Rustic, yet beautiful, they remind of us of what we imagine the Caribbean used to be. And the protected marine park around the Pitons and Anse Chastanet is the home of some of our favorite Caribbean snorkeling and dive sites. Many of the secluded beaches are accessible only by boat. Near Castries, the capital, are several all-inclusives and sprawling resorts that are popular with honeymooners, especially Europeans (primarily from England, Ireland, France, and Germany). For reasons that are beyond us, St. Lucia hasn't quite caught on with the U.S. market. However, a new Hyatt and an expanded Sandals should help remedy that.

The U.S. Virgin Islands: Plenty to Love

Blessed with about 300 sunny days a year, the U.S. Virgin Islands have deservedly been dubbed America's Paradise. The island group encompasses St. Thomas, St. John, and St. Croix, plus another 50 islets and cays, most of them uninhabited.

As a U.S. territory, the USVI is a breeze for U.S. citizens to visit. English is spoken everywhere, the currency is the dollar, and you don't need a passport. The other cool thing is that you can easily and conveniently visit more than one of these beautiful islands, awash in flowers ranging from brilliantly colored bougainvillea to fragrant jasmine to the cheekily named "jump-up-and-kiss-me," which has ruby-red blossoms. And you may want to visit more than one island, because they each have such distinctive personalities. In fact, we highly recommend arranging your honeymoon with more than one island on the agenda. If you only have a week, though, pick two and save the third for next time.

The most populous, **St. Thomas,** is also one of the busiest cruise ports in the Caribbean. Shoppers surge through its capital, Charlotte Amalie, scooping up jewelry, perfume, clothes, and trinkets. Eco-lovers flock to **St. John,** where two-thirds of the island is preserved as a national park and visitors who are in the know reserve tents in its popular, luxury campgrounds at least eight months in advance. The largest of the three islands, **St. Croix,** sometimes gets overlooked, but it embraces some of the best aspects of the other two. It has the beautiful architecture of Charlotte Amalie in its two small Dutch Colonial towns, with a nice selection of shops and good restaurants. You can walk the streets and get a sense of history without being distracted by commercialism. St. Croix's natural beauty hasn't been swallowed up by development, either. In fact, its agricultural roots are still much in evidence.

Flying to the Islands

Getting to the Caribbean from the U.S. is relatively easy. In fact, with improved connections from the West Coast of late, many islands are getting a increased number of West Coast honeymooners who want to experience something other than Hawaii.

Here are the airlines that currently service the Caribbean; please note that air service is always subject to change:

- ✔ **Air Canada** (☎ **800-776-3000;** Internet: www.aircanada.ca) flies direct from Toronto to Barbados; Montego Bay and Kingston in Jamaica; and St. Lucia.

- ✔ **Air Jamaica** (☎ **800-523-5585;** Internet: www.airjamaica.com) has more than 330 flights a week with direct service from Atlanta, Baltimore, Chicago, Fort Lauderdale, Houston, London, Los Angeles (daily service with 10 weekly flights), Miami, Newark, New York's JFK, Orlando, Philadelphia, Phoenix, Toronto and Washington, D.C./Dulles, to Montego Bay and Kingston, Jamaica, airports. You can make connections to Barbados, Bonaire, Grand Cayman, Grenada and St. Lucia. It flies from Jamaica to Cuba, Trinidad, and Tobago. It also flies non-stop from New York's JFK to Barbados. In addition, its codeshare agreement with Delta Air Lines, and joint fare arrangements and compatible schedules with United, help extend access to more than 150 cities in the U.S.

- ✔ **American Airlines** (☎ **800-433-7300;** Internet: www.aa.com) and American Eagle service almost every destination in the Caribbean from several U.S. cities. For non-stop flights, American Airlines often can't be beat for U.S. travelers.

- ✔ **British Airways** (☎ **800-247-9297,** in the U.K. ☎ 0845 77 333 77; Internet: www.british-airways.com) flies from London to Kingston and Montego Bay in Jamaica, Grand Cayman, and St. Lucia.

✔ **BWIA West Indies Airways** (☎ **800-538-2942** or 718-520-8100) has service from New York, NY; Miami, FL; and Toronto, Canada to Barbados and St. Lucia.

✔ **Canadian Holidays** (☎ **416-620-8050**) charters from Toronto, Canada to Barbados, Grand Cayman, San Juan and Tortola.

✔ **Cayman Airways** (☎ **800-422-9626** or 305-266-6760) has service from Atlanta, GA; Houston, TX; Miami and Tampa, FL to Grand Cayman.

✔ **Comair** (☎ **800-354-9822** or 606-767-2550) has connecting service with Delta's routes.

✔ **Continental Airlines** (☎ **800-525-0280**; Internet: www. continental.com) flies nonstop from New York, NY and Newark, NJ to St. Maarten, San Juan, and Jamaica, and from Houston to Aruba.

✔ **Delta Airlines** (☎ **800-221-1212**; Internet: www.delta-air.com) flies direct from Atlanta, GA to Aruba, San Juan, St. Croix and St. Thomas and from New York's JFK to Aruba.

✔ **Martin Air** (☎ **561-391-1313**; Internet: www.martinair.com) flies from Miami to Aruba on Tuesday and Saturday.

✔ **Northwest World Vacations** (☎ **800-727-1111** or 612-470-1111 has scheduled service from all Northwest hubs to Jamaica and Grand Cayman.

✔ **United Airlines** (☎ **800-241-6522**; Internet: www.ual.com) flies direct daily from Chicago's O'Hare to Aruba and St. Thomas and from Washington, D.C. to St. Thomas on the weekends.

✔ **US Airways** (☎ **800-428-4322**; Internet: www.usairways.com) has service between Baltimore, MD and Grand Cayman, San Juan, St. Croix, Sint. Maarten and St. Thomas; between Charlotte, N.C. and Grand Cayman, Montego Bay, San Juan and Sint Maarten; Philadelphia and Aruba, Grand Cayman, San Juan, St. Thomas and Sint Maarten.

✔ **Virgin Atlantic Airways** (☎ **800-862-8621,** from the U.K.: Flight information ☎ 01293 511 58, Reservations 01293 747 747; Internet: www.virgin.com) flies to Barbados and St. Lucia from London.

Investing in a Dining Plan

If you visit **Aruba, Puerto Rico, St. Thomas, Jamaica,** or **Barbados,** you probably want to try some of the good local restaurants that each island is known for. But you also want to keep costs in check, so ask if your hotel has offers a dine-around plan. That way you won't get stuck in a culinary rut or shell out tons of money for food. Dine-around plans are not identical, but you usually pay a flat fee for a certain number of gourmet meals (say three to five for the week). You then get to use your dine-around credits with the hotels/restaurants that are part of the program.

Most hotels offer a **European Plan (EP),** which means that no meals are included. If you see a **Continental Plan (CP)** listed, that means you get only Continental breakfast — juice, coffee, and some kind of bread. A **Breakfast Plan (BP)** signifies a full American-style breakfast. Another popular option, which leaves couples to figure out the evening meal on their own, is the **Modified American Plan (MAP),** which provides two full meals daily. Finally, **all-inclusives** means you get three all-you-can-eat meals a day and (often) all the alcohol you can guzzle — sometimes included premium liquors and great wines. We indicate in the listing info if one or more of the meal plans is available.

Chapter 13

Honeymooning in Aruba

By Echo & Kevin Garrett

• •

In This Chapter

▶ Finding the best honeymoon accommodations

▶ Discovering the fun and romance of Aruba

▶ Uncovering all the details

• •

*A*ruba's best asset is its people, who are the friendliest in the Caribbean. They not only deal with the teeming masses of tourists, but they also handle visitors with aplomb and a smile. Aruban hospitality is even more refreshing when juxtaposed against the concrete and plastic world of Aruba's hotel district, which sprouted in the 1980s along the island's best beaches.

Few lodging properties on Aruba capitalize on the island's surreal natural beauty. Familiar U.S.-based chains, condos, and timeshares and a few small, individually-owned hotels are congregated on the island's southwest edge. Most of Aruba's hotel developments look like the architects watched too many reruns of the opening minutes of the old TV show *Hawaii 5-0*.

Aruba hosts a big share of U.S. travelers looking for an easy sun-and-sand vacation package in the Caribbean. A sprinkling of European tourists come as well, but most Europeans opt for neighboring Curaçao, which has far more architectural charm and is almost unknown to most U.S. tourists. Wealthy South Americans like Aruba for its proximity — only a few miles north of Venezuela — as well as its dizzying dance club scene and casinos. Most of the large resorts have attached the words "& Casino" to their names in the past several years, and several have added

Aruba

| Aruba Marriott Resort & Stellaris Casino **1** |
| Aruba Sonesta Resorts & Casino at Seaport Village **6** |
| Bucuti Beach Resort **5** |
| Holiday Inn Aruba Beach Resort & Casino **3** |
| Hyatt Regency Aruba Resort & Casino **2** |
| Manchebo Beach Resort **6** |
| Radisson Aruba Caribbean Resort **4** |

spas, too, with a handful of full-service spas. Safe and clean, Aruba is also a consistent choice for the cruise ship lines because it lies outside of the hurricane belt. All these factors make it wildly popular with active honeymooners who aren't looking for a secluded tropical paradise — just lots of fun in the sun.

The romance market is ultra-competitive, and most Caribbean resorts throw in all kinds of extras and upgrades for honeymooners, but you must ask to receive. Book early! We recommend making your reservation with the resort directly, after you've checked it out on the Web. Let the on-site reservationist know of any special room requests. The toll-free numbers usually connect you to a U.S.-based operator, who may not have seen the resort.

A destination wedding is out on Aruba — the one island where you can't officially tie the knot (unless you fall for an Aruban).

Figuring Out Where You Want to Stay

While Aruba doesn't have the range of accommodation choices you find on islands like Puerto Rico and Jamaica — no secluded little hideaways or unique inns — it makes up for the fact with good service and guaranteed sun. Almost all of Aruba's hotels (with more than 7,000 hotel rooms) are jammed adjacent to the wide, white sand beaches on the island's calm southwest coast (see the map of Aruba in this chapter). The resort farthest from the airport is only a 20-minute ride. Bordering a string of high-rise resorts is Aruba's most famous and aptly named beach: **Palm Beach,** which is popular with North and South Americans.

Low-rise hotels (as they're called by the locals) hug **Eagle** and **Manchebo beaches,** a quieter area that appeals more to Europeans. The most tranquil and widest point of Eagle Beach is in front of one of our favorite small hotels, **Bucuti Beach Resort.** Because the hotel caters exclusively to adults and the resort is popular with Europeans, you may see a few topless sunbathers on the beach (however, the practice is officially frowned upon in conservative Aruba).

If you need to keep a close tab on expenses, many Aruba properties now offer an all-inclusive option. However, we strongly urge you to skip it and splurge on Aruba's sparkling dining scene (see "Dining in Aruba" later in this chapter).

Aruba's "One Cool Honeymoon" package is extremely generous — the best overall that we've seen an island offer as a whole — with two dozen different freebies and discounts. This package is offered year-round. Newlyweds just need to identify themselves as honeymooners when they make reservations and remind the hotel (almost all participate) upon check-in that they wish to participate in the package.

Choosing Among Aruba's Best Accommodations for Honeymooners

All of the honeymoon accommodations we chose are air-conditioned — gotta have that luxury on the Caribbean's hottest island — and all, except the Sonesta, are located on Palm, Eagle, or Manchebo beaches.

Although we haven't stayed there ourselves, we've heard many complaints of late regarding both the food and service at Aruba Allegro Resort, an all-inclusive that has undergone an ownership change.

The rack rates that appear for each accommodation are in U.S. dollars, and they represent the price range for a standard double room during high season (mid-December to mid-April), unless otherwise noted. Lower rates are often available during the off-season summer months and the shoulder seasons of late spring and fall.

Please refer to the Introduction of *Honeymoon Vacations For Dummies* for an explanation of our price categories.

Aruba Marriott Resort & Stellaris Casino
$$$$$ Palm Beach

This five-star high-rise resort with 413 guestrooms, including 20 suites, occupies a prime spot on Palm Beach. At the far end of the high-rise hotel district, it offers great views of the ocean. The biggest plusses here are the oversized, sun-drenched guestrooms, 500 square feet apiece, with roomy 100-square-feet balconies that give you unfettered sea views. Request a room on the higher floors for a more dramatic vista. The rooms also have walk-in closets. Marriott's elegant 16,500 square-foot Mandara Spa is the island's largest. The bi-level fitness center with floor-to-ceiling windows boasts the latest equipment in a sunny, air-conditioned space near the magnificent free-form pool with a popular swim-up bar looking out at the sea. An iguana habitat is adjacent to the pool. The Stellaris Casino — 10,700 square feet of gaming space — and a shopping mall are adjacent to the cavernous lobby where marble, tropical plants, and splashing fountains abound. One quibble: the cheesy, fake tropical plants in the atrium.

L.G. Smith Blvd. 101, Palm Beach. ☎ *800-223-6388 or 297-86-9000. Fax: 297-86-0649. Internet:* www.offshoreresorts.com. *Rack rates: $310-$495 double. All-inclusive and special romance packages are available. AE, MC, V. MAP.*

Aruba Sonesta Beach Resort at Seaport Village
$$$$ Oranjestad

Located in the heart of Aruba's quaint capital and convenient to its fun discos and bustling shopping areas, this luxury hotel is perfect for couples who like to be in the middle of all the action, yet want the option of privacy when they need it. This 556-room and suite resort fronts a marina rather than a beach, but Sonesta cleverly turned a negative into an asset by acquiring a 40-acre private island just five minutes away by motorboat and transforming it into a lovely alternative to Aruba's somewhat crowded beaches. You step off the elevator in the lobby to a waiting motorboat launch, which whisks you to Sonesta Island, where you get full facilities, including a tennis court, watersports fitness center, tropical bird sanctuary, outdoor restaurant, and bar. One path on the island leads to the adults-only section, where hammocks beckon and you can reserve a private mangrove cove with your own butler for the day.

Regular guestrooms are on the small side. Go for the suites if budget permits. The resort has two busy casinos (one is open 24 hours a day), 15 restaurants, six bars, and lounges. The resort also features three swimming pools, two fitness centers, and the Okeanos Spa. Guests also have access to the nearby Tierra del Sol, a championship golf course designed by Robert Trent Jones II.

Honeymooners also receive a free night at the resort on their first anniversary.

L.G. Smith Blvd. 9, Oranjestad. ☎ *800-766-3782 or 297-83-6000. Fax: 297-83-4389. E-mail:* reservations@sonesta.aw. *Internet:* www.arubasonesta.com. *Rack rates: $215 double, $335-$450 suite; Island Romance honeymoon package $310-$330 a night, includes oceanview accommodations, a rubdown for two in the resort's spa Okeanos, candlelight dinner for two, tickets to a show at the Stardust Theater, a sunset sail for two, a bottle of wine, and a gourmet island picnic for two. AE, DC, MC, V. MAP.*

Bucuti Beach Resort
$$$ Eagle Beach

If you don't feel like shelling out for one of the top-drawer hotels, this place is a great lower-priced alternative with its cheerful staff and low-key mood. Bucuti is also one of the few resorts geared exclusively to couples and adult guests — perfect for honeymooners. This small boutique resort has an ideal location on the widest section of pristine Eagle Beach, far from the madding crowds. Bucuti's 16-acre grounds are handsomely landscaped with labeled native plants. Constructed in a low-slung, hacienda style, Bucuti has big, sunny rooms, all stylishly decorated in bright Caribbean colors, with handmade furnishings custom-designed for the resort. Its guest rooms meld contemporary luxury with tropical chic and come with ceiling fans, microwave ovens, mini-bars, refrigerators, and coffeemakers. All have either queen or king-size beds. There's an on-site grocery store, free e-mail and Internet access for guests, a place to do laundry, and a well-equipped workout area shaded under a huge beach hut.

L.G. Smith Blvd. 55B (P.O. Box 1299, Eagle Beach). ☎ *800-223-1108 or 297-83-1100. Fax: 297-82-8161. E-mail:* bucuti@setarnet.aw. *Internet:* www.bucuti.com. *Rack rates: $240-$320 double, honeymoon packages available in the summer only at $1,135 for 7 nights. AE, MC, V. MAP.*

Holiday Inn SunSpree Aruba Beach Resort & Casino
$$$ Palm Beach

This sprawling resort — which had a multimillion-dollar facelift along with a redo of its Excelsior Casino in 1999 — was one of the first hotels on Aruba and boasts more than 600 guest-rooms. You need a map to figure out where everything is. This busy place, centered right on a quarter mile of the island's most popular beach, is popular with honeymooners who can't quite afford the elegant digs at the Hyatt nearby. For water lovers the Holiday Inn offers Pelican Watersports, a Gold Palm five-star PADI (Professional Association of Diving Instructors) dive operation onsite, as well as parasailing, snorkeling, windsurfing, or boating. Or you can rent one of the floating sea mats and loll in the calm Caribbean in front of the hotel.

Be forewarned that the Holiday Inn is also popular with families with young kids. But there's enough going on to keep everybody happy. The friendly staff is eager to please, and the sparsely decorated guestrooms are unusually large and come with direct-dial phone with dataport, hairdryer, coffeemaker, iron, and ironing board.

J.E. Irausquin Blvd. #230. ☎ *800-934-6750 or 297-86-3600. Fax: 297-86-5165 (reservations), 297-86-3478 (guest). E-mail:* holidayinn@setarnet.aw. *Internet:* www.holidayinn-aruba.com. *Rack rates: $219-$300. AE, DC, MC, V.*

Hyatt Regency Aruba Resort & Casino
$$$$$ Palm Beach

Set on 12 acres fronting one of the more action-packed stretches of Palm Beach, this Mediterranean-style tropical oasis easily ranks as one of the most romantic resorts on the island. It embraces a three-level landscaped waterpark with a 5,000-square-foot lagoon and a two-story waterslide.

If you are an active couple who want plenty to do but hate the frantic atmosphere that plagues some resorts, this place is sure to satisfy your restlessness without sacrificing your privacy. Although the resort has 360 rooms, you never feel overrun by other guests — important on a honeymoon. The tastefully furnished guestrooms come with an arsenal of amenities. Unfortunately, the balconies are too small to enjoy. The pool area is so incredible, however, that you won't want to hang in your room anyway. The resort has five restaurants, four bars, a lively casino, onsite shops, a health and fitness center with sauna, steam, and massage, Red Sail Sports — in case you want to scuba dive, jet ski, or windsurf — and aerobics on the sun deck. The Spa at the Hyatt Regency Aruba is a full-service spa and exercise center with a variety of massage options, including the unique "Conchi Splash" massage in a hydrotherapy tub.

Upgrades for honeymooners depend on hotel occupancy, and no honeymoon packages are available.

J.E. Irausquin Blvd. 85. ☎ *800-55-HYATT or 297-86-1234. Fax: 297-86-1682. E-mail:* res.hyattraruba@setarnet.aw. *Internet:* www.hyatt.com. *Rack rates: $365-$535 double, $650-$2,150 suite. AE, DISC, DC, MC, V.*

Radisson Aruba Resort and Casino
$$$$$ Palm Beach

Following a $55 million transformation of one of Aruba's original Palm Beach resorts, this beautiful new Radisson has raised the bar on the upscale market, bringing South Beach chic to Aruba. Its open-air lobby marries tropical cool with a grand statement, instantly relaxing arriving guests and cooling them off with Evian upon arrival. The 14-acre tropical landscaping, replete with parrots and macaws, and good use of colonial West Indian-style design and heavy mahogany furnishings make this resort a visual feast. The grounds of the 358-room resort (including 32 suites) are laced with lagoons and waterfalls. You can opt for lazing on the resort's 1,500-foot beach with 50 shade palapas, or chill out in one of the twin beachfront zero-entry free-form swimming pools. There is a casino, four restaurants, two lighted tennis courts, a fitness center and salon (a full-service spa is in the plans), and a watersports center offering scuba and PADI (Professional Association of Diving Instructors) certification.

The top two floors of the nine-story Aruba Tower are concierge floors. The stylish guestrooms have roomy marble bathrooms, plush bathrobes, and many amenities. All rooms have spacious balconies with teak patio furniture. For sea views, you need to be above the fourth floor.

4400 J.E. Irausquin Blvd. 81, Palm Beach. ☎ *800-333-3333 or 297-86-6555. Fax: 297-86-3260. Internet:* www.radisson.com. *Rack rates: $255-$550 double, $510-$1,850 suite, Ultimate Honeymoon package $1,493 for 3 nights, $3,193 for 7 nights (additional nights $425), includes champagne and chocolates upon arrival, nightly turndown service, daytime tennis, breakfast buffet daily, one-day Jeep rental, one sunset sail for two, one dinner, and souvenir keepsake bathrobes. AE, DISC, DC, MC, V.*

Enjoying Your Aruban Honeymoon

In this section, our focus is on fun! We offer plenty of suggestions for activities to help you take advantage of Aruba's chief natural assets: water, sand, and sun. The island offers watersports galore, including world-class windsurfing and wreck scuba diving. If you prefer to be on solid ground, consider driving a four-wheeler through the desert or golfing on one of the Caribbean's most unique courses. We also take a look at Aruba's vibrant nightlife and dining scene — both among the most dynamic in the Caribbean.

Before you go, order a nifty discount card ($10) that gives you whopping savings and freebies on activities and restaurants by going to www.visitaruba.com.

Exploring Aruba's beaches

Aruba's main draws are its glorious powder-white beaches (all public) and its virtually guaranteed sunshine. When people talk about the **leeward** side of Aruba, they refer to the calmer waters of the northwest and southwest coasts, from Arashi down to Baby Beach on the southern tip. The **windward** or north side of the island spans the northeast to southeast coasts. The windward side experiences much rougher waters and has surrealistic coral landscapes carved out by the pounding waves. The wild surf crashing against odd rock formations on the windward side translates into only a few beaches that are worth investigating, though they do offer a truly unique experience. (See the map of Aruba earlier in this chapter.)

Aruba's best-known beaches — **Palm, Eagle,** and **Manchebo** — are located on the leeward side, where the low-rise and high-rise hotel districts are located. Despite the constantly blowing trade winds, the Caribbean's clear, blue waters are remarkably smooth and boast visibility up to 100 feet.

Try to get out on the beach before 10 a.m. so that you can enjoy some quality time before the sun goes into high-broil mode, which lasts from noon to 3 p.m. And don't forget to slather on that sunscreen; you are, after all, just a few degrees above the equator.

Putting wind in your sails

When you tire of soaking up the rays on the beach, Aruba offers plenty of other options for having a good time — in, on, and around the beautiful, bountiful beaches

Vela Windsurf Aruba (Aruba Marriott Resort; ☎ **800-223-5443** or 297-86-9000, ext. 6430; E-mail: info@velawindsurf.com; Internet: www.velawindsurf.com) rents boards for $60 a day. Beginner lessons run $55 an hour and include a board. **Sailboard Vacations** (☎ **800-252-1070**, stateside 617-829-8915; Internet: www.sailboardvacations.com) offers windsurfing and accommodations packages on Malmok Beach, which has a little more of the surfer dude feel to it ($50 to rent a board, $55 for beginner's lesson including board).

Dining and dancing on the water

Our favorite dinner and dance cruise combo is aboard the **Sea Star** (☎ **297-86-2010**), which sails to a waterfront marina restaurant for a candlelit meal accompanied by island music. After dinner you return to the boat for merengue and salsa dance lessons. Book through **De Palm Tours** (L. G. Smith Blvd. 142; ☎ **297-82-4400**; Internet: www.depalm.com) for $59.50 a person. Or reserve an evening for dirty dancing on **Tattoo** (☎ **297-86-2010**), a party boat with a buffet dinner. The cost is $49 per person for a four-hour tour. If you're feeling frisky, wear your swimsuit under your clothes and take the plunge from the boat's rope swing.

Diving right in

Aruba ranks right behind Bermuda for wreck diving. The **Antilla,** a hulking German freighter that sunk off Malmok Beach during WWII, is one of the Caribbean's largest and most notable wrecks. The **California,** a wooden cargo ship that sank while trying to deliver general merchandise from Liverpool to South America, is also a popular wreck dive. Keep in mind that you must be a qualified diver.

For those less enamored of making like Jacques Cousteau, Aruba has many less challenging dive and snorkeling sites where you can see manta rays, lobsters, groupers, sea fans, corals, sea turtles, and octopuses. One option is **SNUBA**, which is safe and easy to learn and has recently become popular on the island. SNUBA goes beyond snorkeling; you wear a mask, but you can go to 20 feet beneath the surface and breathe without having to wear all the heavy diving tanks.

De Palm Tours (L. G. Smith Blvd. 142; ☎ **297-82-4400;** Internet: www.depalm.com) offers SNUBA, diving, and snorkeling instruction and equipment. De Palm Tours offers a terrific combo package for $77.50 per adult. The deal includes snorkeling at De Palm Island, a tour of Aruba, and sailing and snorkeling from De Palm's *Fun Factory* catamaran. De Palm's honeymoon package ($269 a couple) includes a sail and snorkel, a Jeep tour, and a fantasy dinner and dance cruise.

Another excellent operator, centrally located on Palm Beach between Holiday Inn Sunspree and Playa Linda, is **Pelican Adventures N.V. Tours & Watersports** (P.O. Box 1194, Oranjestad; ☎ 297-87-2302; Fax: 297-87-2315; E-mail: pelican-aruba@setarnet.aw; Internet: www.pelican-aruba.com). Pelican has a PADI (Professional Association of Diving Instructors) Gold Palm five-star facility with custom-built dive boats and numerous dive packages. Other good operators include **Unique Sports of Aruba,** the third largest operator on the island (L. G. Smith Blvd. 79; ☎ 297-86-0096); **Fly 'n Dive,** which has multiple dive sites on Aruba as well as on neighboring islands (Shiribana 9-A Paradera; ☎ 297-87-8759); **Native Divers**, a husband-and-wife team that takes groups of two to six experienced divers and offers far more flexibility than other operators (Koyari 1; ☎ 297-86-4763); and **Aruba Pro Dive** (Ponton 88; ☎ 297-88-5520).

If snorkeling is more your speed, you can also book a trip for $48 per person on the **Mi Dushi** (☎ 297-86-2010), a 78-foot Swedish sailing vessel built in 1925, which has a fun rope swing. It specializes in four-hour guided snorkel trips (we hit three good spots, including the famed wreck of the *Antilla*) crowned with a hot barbecue lunch.

Cruising the depths while staying dry

For $75 per person, **Atlantis Adventures** (L. G. Smith Blvd. 82; ☎ 297-83-6090) offers a two-hour submarine cruise. The sub plunges 150 feet below the surface off Sonesta Reef, allowing you close views of the wrecks of *Mi Dushi* (a 70-year-old wooden sailing yacht), *Morgenster* (a steel-hulled 110-foot-long ship), and several airplanes. Okay, so the sub is not yellow — but it's a real one and a great solution for those who don't like the idea of diving but still want to explore the ocean depths

The experience may bore divers, and if you get claustrophobic, forget it.

Swinging a round of golf

Aruba's deluxe hotels offer golf at the island's **Tierra del Sol** (Malmokweg; ☎ 297-86-0978; E-mail: tierra.rent@setarnet.aw; Internet: www.tierradelsol.com), an 18-hole championship course designed by famed golf-course designer Robert Trent Jones Jr. You can view the sea from an astounding 15 holes. Located near the California Lighthouse, this par-71, 6,811-yard course allows you to admire the rugged beauty of Aruba's northwest coast.

The trade winds add an extra challenge to your swing, but Tierra del Sol is not an overly difficult course. Even beginners enjoy trying their hand at the game here. The surroundings are beautiful, and the pros have a sense of humor. (If you don't know your eight irons from your Tiger Woods, check out the club's "No Embarrassment" golf clinics.)

The $120 greens fee includes a golf cart, and club rentals are an extra $25 to $45. The golf clinic is a real bargain: $50 for a half day, which includes an excellent lunch at Ventanas del Mar, where floor-to-ceiling windows overlook the course.

Communing with Mother Nature

Near the Wyndham and Radisson resorts is **The Butterfly Farm** (Palm Beach; ☎ 297-863656), where a $10 fee gives you an entry pass for your entire vacation to this 1,500 square-foot netted garden of butterflies and moths. We loved having our early morning coffee in this mini-piece of paradise, sitting among the tropical garden and watching the winged beautifies flit in the sunlight. Tony Cox, the gregarious owner, peppers his talks with tidbits about why certain caterpillars are colored certain ways and why moths don't have mouths. Our favorite inhabitant was the iridescent blue morpho butterfly — it was the size of a man's hand!

Having fun in the cunucu

While **De Palm** (L. G. Smith Blvd. 142; ☎ 297-82-4400; Internet: www. depalm.com) offers a variety of island tours, our favorite is an off-road excursion through the *cunucu* (or countryside). You start out at the picturesque California Lighthouse. And yes, you actually do your own driving. You follow your leader along the rugged (and dusty) north coast, so try to get as close to the front of the line as possible. The big highlight is the **Natural Bridge,** a dramatic coral structure that stretches for 100 feet and hangs 25 feet above the wild surf that created it in the first place. The bridge is the Caribbean's highest coral structure and Aruba's most photographed site.

Driving the rugged north coast can be a sunny, dusty trip. Bring some bottled water, sunglasses, extra sunscreen, and a bandana. Then get ready to eat some trail dust.

Taking in Aruban culture

The **Bon Bini Festival** is held every Tuesday starting at 6:30 p.m. at small Fort Zoutman (Zoutmanstraat Z/N, Oranjestad; ☎ 297-82-6099), which houses an even smaller historical museum in its tower. The festival is well worth an hour or so of your time and only costs $3 per person. The folkloric dancing and music give you a feel for Aruba's warm-hearted people and their culture.

The event is joyous and homespun, so expect lots of families. Skip the museum, though: The faded labeling is all in Dutch.

Living it up in Aruba's nightlife

Feeling lucky? Almost every major Aruban hotel (11 at last count) comes with a casino attached. The **Sonesta's Crystal Casino** (Sonesta Resort, Oranjestad) stays open all day and all night. We prefer the Crystal because it draws a more upscale crowd and is centrally located downtown — a plus if you tire of blackjack and decide to go to a disco.

Aruba's club scene is also worth exploring. Go late — the Latin influence means that the action doesn't even get started until around 11 p.m. — and dress in your best resort wear.

At press time, there were several hip joints to hit. But when in doubt, ask your concierge to steer you. Be sure to check and make sure that the following are still happening:

- ✔ **The Cellar** (☎ 297- 82-8567), one block behind the Sonesta and located between two Benetton shops, is a trendy downtown pub that alternates between a live band and a DJ.

- ✔ **Mambo Jambo** (☎ 297-83-3632) in the Royal Plaza Mall is a funky Caribbean hangout that attracts locals and tourists.

- ✔ **La Fiesta** (☎ 297-83-5896) in the Aventura Mall is a casually hip place to dance or just be seen.

- ✔ **Club E** (Weststraat 5; ☎ 297-93-6784) is a techno-chic inspired nightclub that has a spectacular house band playing a mix of musical styles.

- ✔ **Carlos 'N Charlie's** (Weststraat; ☎ 297-82-0355) plays a heady mix of Latin American hits and U.S. disco favorites.

Dining in Aruba

With more than 40 nationalities represented on this small island, finding a restaurant among the more than 100 choices isn't a problem. The local cuisine, a combination of Dutch and Caribbean, tends to use a lot of fine cheeses and meats with heavy sauces along with fresh seafood and curries. Try at least one local specialty while you're on the island, although sensitive stomachs may find local food too rich. The cuisine often has a strong South American influence lending additional spice, because Aruba is so close to that part of the world.

The local Dutch-meets-Caribbean cuisine tends to be lower-priced than other choices, but another way to save money is through the **Dine-Around Program.** This unique program allows you to purchase cou-pons redeemable for 3, 5, 7, or 10 meals at 20 of the island's better restaurants. The price for 3 dinners is $109; 5 for $177; 7 for $245; and 10 for $339. The meals include appetizer, main course, dessert, coffee, and service charge. Beverages are not included, and surcharges apply to some menu items. For information, call the **Aruba Gastronomic Association** (☎ 800-477-2896 or 297-86-2161; Fax: 297-86-2162; E-mail: aga@setarnet.aw; Internet: www.arubadining.com). The VIP Gourmet Selection ($60 per dinner per person with a minimum purchase of three dinners) lets you choose a multi-course gourmet dinner with a special menu, including service charge.

Stray cats often wander into even the finest restaurants. Also, you must request the check on Aruba, which is a European way of doing things. Arubans never want to rush you.

Please refer to the Introduction of *Honeymoon Vacations For Dummies* for an explanation of our price categories.

Creating special memories

If you're going to splurge, go for dinner at **Chez Mathilde** (Havenstraat 23, Oranjestad; ☎ 297-83-4968; $$$$) housed in an elegant house built in the 1800s. Ask for a private nook in the Pavilion Room, awash in tasteful beige and Italian and French antiques. Another winner is **Chalet Suisse** (J. E. Irausquin Blvd. 246; ☎ 297-87-5054; $$$$), soothed by romantic lighting and an attentive waitstaff.

Before you hit the gaming tables, we recommend dining at the elegant French/Caribbean **L'Escale** (Aruba Sonesta Resort at Seaport Village; ☎ 297-83-6000, ext. 1791; $$$$) where a strolling string trio adds to the romantic ambience. Request a table away from the casino by the windows overlooking the seaport. If you are looking for a leisurely evening on a moonlit night, dinner is served at **Papiamento** (Washington 61, Oranjestad, Noord; ☎ 297-86-4544; $$$$) poolside amidst riotous tropical gardens studded with gargantuan terra-cotta pots Chatêaubriand for two and Caribbean lobster are winners.

Ruinas del Mar (Hyatt Regency, J. E. Irausquin Blvd. #85; ☎ 297-86-1234; $$$$), built to look like the old stone gold mine ruins on the island and lit by torches and candlelight, is an absolute stunner, and the native Aruban chef is masterful with seafood and steaks.

The terrace tables next to the lagoon at Ruinas del Mar are in high demand, so put your request in early.

If sleek, open South Beach design appeals to your aesthetics, head to **Sunset Grille** (Radisson Aruba Caribbean Resort and Casino, 4400 J.E. Irausquin Blvd. 81, Palm Beach; ☎ 800-333-3333 or 297-86-6555; $$$$). Besides the excellent cuisine, diners enjoy fantastic terrace views of the gardens, cascading waterfalls, and the Caribbean beyond.

After more than a decade of living in New York, we consider ourselves somewhat snobbish when it comes to Italian food, yet **Tuscany** (Aruba Marriott, L. G. Smith Blvd. 101, Palm Beach; ☎ 297-86-9000; $$$$). managed to exceed our expectations and then some. With paintings of the Tuscany countryside, sparkling chandeliers, and the tinkling of a piano in the background, the place manages to be romantic.

Looking for fun

Boonoonoonoos — pronounced *boo-new-new-news* — (Wilmelminastraat 18A, Oranjestad; ☎ 297-83-1888; $$) is a fun surprise and fun to say. The word is Jamaican slang for "extraordinary."

The hip, carefree windsurfing crowd flocks to **Madame Janette** (Cunucu Abao 37; ☎ **297-87-0184**; $$) for the young European chef's spicy, old-style French creations with a Caribbean flair. Request one of the tables near the fans, though, because you don't have the sea breeze to cool you off.

Enjoying spectacular water views

You can lose yourself counting the many shades of blue in the Caribbean from your table at the water's edge table at **The Pirates' Nest** (Bucuti Beach Resort, L. G. Smith Blvd. 55B; ☎ **297-83-1100**; $$$), a fake Dutch galleon designed to look as if though sinking in the sands of Eagle Beach. With 24-hours notice, you can be assigned a private server.

Request the five-course chef's choice for two, which includes a bottle of wine and cappuccino, coffee, or tea for $75 per couple. In the mornings, you can get a lavish champagne buffet breakfast here, too.

Killer views await at the aptly-named **Ventanas Del Mar** (windows of the sea) (Tierra del Sol; **297-867800**; $$), where the soaring windows and the terrace allow unfettered views of the sea and this unique desert golf course. The Gold Medal-award winning chef whips up dazzling dishes to match the elegant setting. Friday nights you can get a grilled seafood dinner with all the extras for $19.95.

Finding a local favorite

On the day you head to Baby Beach or Boca Grandi, stop in at **Charlie's Bar** (Main St. 56, Zeppenfeldstraat 56, San Nicolas; ☎ **297-84-5086**; $), which has been operating since 1941 and is now run by the late Charlie's gregarious grandson Charlito. While away an hour or two with the locals, artists, sailors, musicians, and other tourists drinking Balashis (the locally made beer) and nibbling on platters of Creole calamari and jumbo shrimp, accompanied by local bread and Aruban-style french fries (fat and freshly cut). The walls are cluttered with oddities left behind — from tennis shoes to license plates.

In a traditional country house, **Gasparito** (Gasparito #3, Noord, near the high-rise hotel section; ☎ **297-86-7044**; $$) a kitschy combination restaurant/art gallery, turns out some of the best local cuisine around. A dining experience here leaves little doubt why the chef frequently wins awards in Caribbean cooking competitions.

For years, **Hadicurari Fisheries Center,** (Centro di Pesca or The Fishery Center, L. G. Smith Blvd; ☎ **297-86-0820**; $), was a gathering place for local fishermen to anchor their colorful wooden boats and swap tales. It has become an excellent casual dining spot in the heart of the action on Palm Beach — and one of our favorite spots to watch the sunset colors over the sea.

A steel-pan band plays here every Saturday and Sunday from noon to 4 p.m. Have some fun dancing on the beach with a mix of locals (including many middle-aged Arubans) and tourists from the surrounding hotels. On Sundays, the beach party goes on until 9 p.m.

Settling into Aruba

Aruba's declaration of independence from the Kingdom of the Netherlands on July 1, 1986, coincided with this small island's enthusiastic embrace of tourism as its future. Its warm, friendly people — among the Caribbean's most highly educated, because a quarter of the national budget is devoted to education — are known for their hospitality. In fact, many of the island's natives study at Europe's finest hotel schools before returning home to work in the tourism trade. In this section, we help you get settled into Aruba, and we cover all those essentials like arriving and getting around.

Arriving in Aruba

Arriving in the Caribbean doesn't get any easier than it does in Aruba. Having welcomed more than 1 million visitors in 2000, the people of tiny Aruba (population 94,000) sure knows what they're doing. After you get off the plane, you can whisk right through customs and passport control.

Thanks to a $64 million expansion that tripled its capacity, Aruba's busy, busy **Queen Beatrix International Airport** (☎ **297-82-4800;** E-mail: airportaruba@setarnet.aw; Internet www.arubaairport.com) makes a much better first impression than it used to. It handles jumbo jets and charters that arrive from all over the world, disgorging tourists from the U.S., South America, and Europe amazingly well. The airport is clean, bright, and well-staffed.

Pick up free copies of the excellent magazines **Aruba Experience** (☎ **297-83-4467;** Internet: www.aruba-experience.com) and **Aruba Nights** (Internet: www.nightspublications.com). Coupons are often inside for car rentals and restaurants. Cheerful tourist-board representatives chirping *bon bini* (the Papiamento phrase for "welcome") patrol the orderly lines looking for tourists to assist.

Traveling from the airport to your hotel

Right after you claim your bags and clear customs, find the spiffy taxis lined up at the curb. Courteous drivers quickly approach when you beckon. The capital of Aruba, Oranjestad, is a 5- to 10-minute ride from the airport, which costs between $5 and $8. The Aruba Marriott, an easy 20-minute, $20 ride, is the farthest hotel from the airport. The average tab runs $14 to $20 along the hotel strip. Though not mandatory, you can tip from 10 to 15 percent of the fare.

Your transfer from the airport may be included in your hotel package, in which case, look for a driver holding a sign with your name or the name of your hotel on it.

If you rented a car, you can pick it up across from the airport building, along with easy-to-follow directions to your hotel.

Getting around Aruba

Because most of the hotels are lined up along the island's fabulous beaches (see the map of Aruba earlier in this chapter), you may not feel the need to wander far from the hotel pool and the milky teal blue calm of the Caribbean.

You definitely don't need a car to tour downtown Oranjestad. A leisurely stroll through the picturesque town with its charming Dutch architecture is all that's required to take in the entire shebang.

Walking

The hassle-free, pristine beaches of Aruba are perfect for long walks. If you like to walk, Oranjestad is a good spot, too. Nature lovers and adventurers may want to take the easy hike around **Arikok National Park.** Ask your hotel to refer you to a guide, or contact the park at Piedra Plat 42; ☎ **297-82-8001;** Fax: 297-82-8961; E-mail: PNA@setarnet.aw; Internet www.arubanationalparks.com.

Taking a bus

Aruba has a reliable public bus system — air-conditioned blue-and-white Volvos — that runs hourly trips between the hotels fronting Palm and Eagle beaches and Oranjestad, as well as down the coast between Oranjestad and San Nicolas. Each trip costs $1 each way, and U.S. dollars are accepted. You can pick up a current schedule at your hotel's front desk. The terminal is on Oranjestad's main drag across from the waterfront, next to the Royal Plaza shopping center.

Hailing a taxi

Fixed fares are set by the government. After midnight, you pay an additional $1 surcharge for trips. Tell the driver where you want to go before you climb in and ask for the fare quote in U.S. dollars. Taxis are also available for sightseeing tours; an hour-long tour for one to four people costs $25. For the airport dispatch office, dial ☎ **297-82-2116** or

297-82-1604. Or ask your hotel to call a taxi for you. In town, you can easily flag one by raising your hand.

Renting a car

Car rental companies on Aruba are eager for your business, and a free day's rental is often rolled into package deals, especially during generous summer promotions. We think that renting a car for a day here — especially if a freebie is involved — is a fun idea, because Aruba is so safe and friendly. You probably also get extras like free pickup and delivery.

Still, during high season, call ahead and reserve. And keep in mind that gas prices are sky-high on Aruba — about $5 a gallon at press time.

Whether you reserve your car ahead of time or not, look for coupons in the handy tourist guides you grabbed when you got off the plane and present them when you start the transaction. Or simply ask about any special discounts. All rental companies offer unlimited mileage; with an island measuring 19 miles long by 6 miles wide, the proposition is no-lose. Without a coupon, expect to spend about $50 a day. Local rental car agencies are sometimes slightly less expensive. The main rental vehicles are Toyotas and Suzuki Samurais. Ask about the age of the car before agreeing to rent it.

Request a 4-wheel drive vehicle if you plan on touring the island's less-developed countryside, the *cunucu,* which is kind of like Australia's Outback. The weather's hot, so don't forget air-conditioning. A day's rental is all you need to tour the entire island. (But a cheaper way to accomplish the same thing is to book one of the 4-by-4 tours of Aruba.)

All the roads in Oranjestad and toward the hotels are well-marked and in good shape. On other parts of Aruba, though, the signage quickly dwindles down to sketchy at best, and the same goes for the roads at certain points. Think rural Arizona.

You would think it'd be tough to get lost on such a small island, but we've even been with a few local drivers who appeared confused sometimes. Locals who live near popular tourist sites in the countryside have taken to posting home-made signs, because they are asked for directions so often. Also, you may be unfamiliar with the road signs here, which use international symbols, and the European-style traffic lights. And speaking of signs, keep an eye out for one-way streets in Oranjestad.

If you do rent a car, study the local rules of the road before setting out, bring a map (but feel free to ask directions), drive defensively, and remember: *do not* turn right on red.

Parking is free and traffic isn't bad. You get a few mild jam-ups in Oranjestad when people get off work or during a celebration, which, come to think of it, happens with great frequency.

Choosing a bicycle, moped, or motorcycle

The flat terrain makes Aruba a fun place to bike or ride, but because of the ferocious intensity of the sun and wind, we recommend bicycles only for masochists or for those in good shape.

Stay off Routes 1 and 2, which have busy traffic around the hotel strip and town. And take plenty of water and sunscreen.

Bicycles are available through many hotels. **Pablito Bike Rental** (☎ 297-87-8655) in Oranjestad rents mountain bikes for a full day for $12. Olympian triathlete Gert Van Vliet rents mountain bikes through his **Tri Bike Aruba** (☎ 297-85-2734) in Papilon 65A.

Motor scooters and motorcycles, which rent for $40 to $100 a day, can be found at **George's Scooter Rentals** (☎ 297-82-5975) or **Nelson Motorcycle Rentals** (☎ 297-86-6801). Motorcycle Mamas and Papas who want to go whole hog can rent Harleys at **Big Twin Aruba,** L.G. Smith Blvd. 124-A, (☎ 297-82-8660; Fax: 297-83-9322). Or at least have your picture taken with Big Twin's 1939 Harley Davidson Liberator.

Fast Facts: Aruba

ATMs

There are two ATMs at the airport. Several machines are available in town in the shopping areas: Noord Branch Palm Beach 4B; Seaport Marketplace, L.G. Smith Blvd.; Playa Linda Beach Resort, L.G. Smith Blvd. 87; Sun Plaza Building, L.G. Smith Blvd. 160. For a complete listing, look in the back of the handy guide you get at the airport. Instructions are in English, Dutch, Spanish, and Papiamento. You can get U.S. dollars or the local currency, florins.

Banks

ABN/AMRO Bank (Caya G.F. Betico Croes 89) and Caribbean Mercantile Bank are in Oranjestad. Hours are weekdays 8 a.m. to 4 p.m. (Banks do not close for lunch in Aruba.)

Credit Cards

Major credit cards and traveler's checks (with ID) are readily accepted. Casinos cash traveler's checks for free, while banks charge a small fee for the service.

Currency Exchange

The official currency is the Aruban florin (also called the Aruban guilder), written as Af or Afl. U.S. dollars are happily accepted everywhere: U.S. $1 = Afl $1.78 at press time. You really don't need to exchange money, unless you want pocket change for soda machines or a few coins to collect, because they are cool-looking.

U.S. dollars are the only foreign currency readily accepted on Aruba; however, other monies can be easily converted at any local bank. All exchange rates are posted in the bank, or check the Internet at www.xe. net/ucc/.

Doctors

Hotels have doctors on call.

Emergencies: Call ☎ 115 (fire and ambulance).

Hospitals: Horacio Oduber Hospital, J.E. Irausquin Blvd., can be reached at ☎ 297-87-4300.

Information

You can find a tourist office in the airport. Prior to your visit, contact the Aruba Tourism Authority (1000 Harbor Blvd., Weehawkien, NJ 07087; ☎ 800-862-7822 or 800-TO-ARUBA in the U.S.; 416-975-1950 in Canada; 800-268-3042 in Quebec and Ontario; Internet: www.aruba.com).

Language

Dutch is the official language, but Arubans also speak English and Spanish. The everyday language of the people is Papiamento. Locals often mix three or four languages in the same conversation; keep your ears tuned for some interesting exchanges, even if you can't understand what's being said.

Maps

Maps are available throughout the island and in the back of free guides.

Newspapers/Magazines

Boulevard Drug & Bookstore (☎ 297-82-7385) in the Seaport Village Mall can keep you in touch with current events, and the store sells stamps and road maps as well.

Pharmacies

For prescriptions and other needs, visit Boulevard Drug & Bookstore (☎ 297-82-7385) in the Seaport Village Mall. Or look for the word "Botica."

Police

Call ☎ **100**.

Post Office

The post office is at 9 J. E. Irasquin Blvd., Oranjestad (☎ 297-82-1900), but your hotel's front desk can also mail your letters and postcards.

Safety

Crime is extremely rare on Aruba, which is a prosperous island. You can walk about freely, but common-sense rules apply. Don't leave valuables wrapped in your towel on the beach or have your camera dangling behind you while you look at the shops along the waterfront.

Taxes

The government room tax is 7.6 percent, and hotels charge an additional 10 percent service charge for room, food, and beverages. The Departure Tax is $23, plus $3.25 for those making use of the U.S. Departure terminal and, therefore, U.S. INS/Customs services in Aruba. The Departure Tax, officially referred to as the Passenger Facility Charge, is included in the airline ticket price.

Telephone

To call Aruba from the U.S., dial 011, then 297, and then the 6-digit local number.

International calls made from hotels carry heavy service charges resulting in a charge five times the normal rate (about $15 for a 3-minute call). Walking or driving to a nearby SETAR teleshop is worth the time, resulting in a comparatively low cost of one U.S. dollar per minute. In your hotel room, you can find a guide that lists the codes to reach the major carriers and also alerts you to which one the hotel deals with. Or you can call your hotel operator, who can usually quickly and efficiently connect you to the long-distance carrier you desire. You can reach **AT&T** at ☎ 800-462-4240; **Sprint** at ☎ 800-877-8000; and **MCI** at ☎ 800-888-8000.

Time Zone

Aruba is on Atlantic Standard time year-round, so most of the year Aruba is one hour ahead of Eastern Standard time (when it's 10 a.m. on Aruba, it's 9 a.m. in New York). When daylight saving time is in effect in the United States, clocks in Aruba and New York show the same time.

Tipping

The standard is 15 percent if the tip is not already included, and $1 per day for maids and $1 per bag for bellhops. Many restaurants tack on 15 percent service charges to their bills, so check before you leave a double tip.

Water

The water's fine to drink; it comes from the island's desalinization plant, the second largest in the world.

Chapter 14

Honeymooning in the Bahamas

By Rachel Christmas Derrick

In This Chapter

▶ Finding the best honeymoon accommodations

▶ Discovering the fun and romance of the Bahamas

▶ Uncovering all the details

*B*eginning just off the tip of Florida and scattered southeast across some 100,000 square miles of the Atlantic Ocean, the islands of the Bahamas couldn't be more diverse — this country is an archipelago of some 700 islands. You'll be stunned by the beaches, the translucent water that shimmers in shades from pale aquamarine to electric sapphire, and the fish-packed coral reefs below the gentle waves.

Contrary to popular belief, the Bahamas is not in the Caribbean Sea. Because they're so close geographically and culturally to the Caribbean, they're often considered part of that region, even though they are actually in the Atlantic.

 Remember, though, that the northern locale of these islands means that, during winter months, the weather is sometimes cooler than the always-warm Caribbean.

Figuring Out Where You Want to Stay

The most popular islands in the Bahamas are **New Providence** (home to Nassau, Cable Beach, and adjoining Paradise Island) and **Grand Bahama** (the home of Freeport and Lucaya). On both of these islands, you find glittering casinos, golf courses, many restaurants (both gourmet and local), plenty of nightlife, and a wide range of hotels — whether you want something small and economical or a lavish, sprawling, break-the-bank lodging.

New Providence Island

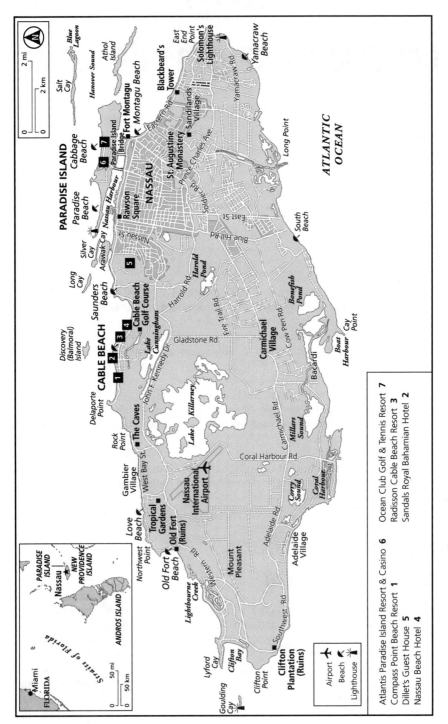

2 mi
2 km

Blue Lagoon
Salt Cay
Hanover Sound
Athol Island
East End Point
Solomon's Lighthouse
Yamacraw Beach
Blackbeard's Tower
Montagu Beach
Fort Montagu
PARADISE ISLAND
Cabbage Beach
Paradise Island Bridge
Paradise Beach
Sandilands Village
Yamacraw Rd.
Eastern Rd.
St. Augustine Monastery
Prince Charles Ave.
Soldier Rd.
NASSAU
ATLANTIC OCEAN
Long Point
Silver Cay
Arawak Cay
Nassau Harbour
Rawson Square
Nassau St.
East St.
Blue Hill Rd.
South Beach
Long Cay
Saunders Beach
Cable Beach Golf Course
Lake Cunningham
Harold Rd.
Harold Pond
Bonefish Pond
Cay Point
Discovery (Balmoral) Island
CABLE BEACH
Gladstone Rd.
Fire Trail Rd.
Cow Pen Rd.
Boat Harbour
Delaporte Point
John F. Kennedy Dr.
Carmichael Village
Bacardi
Rock Point
The Caves
Lake Killarney
Carmichael Rd.
Millars Sound
Coral Harbour Rd.
Gambier Village
West Bay St.
Nassau International Airport
Coral Harbour
Love Beach
Tropical Gardens
Old Fort (Ruins)
Old Fort Beach
Adelaide Rd.
Corry Sound
Northwest Point
Lightbourne Creek
Mount Pleasant
Adelaide Village
Western Rd.
Southwest Rd.
Lyford Cay
Clifton Bay
Clifton Plantation (Ruins)
Clifton Point
Goulding Cay

Inset map
PARADISE ISLAND
NEW PROVIDENCE ISLAND
Nassau
ANDROS ISLAND
Straits of Florida
Miami
FLORIDA
50 mi
50 km

Legend
Airport
Beach
Lighthouse

Atlantis Paradise Island Resort & Casino **6**
Compass Point Beach Resort **1**
Dillet's Guest House **5**
Nassau Beach Hotel **4**
Ocean Club Golf & Tennis Resort **7**
Radisson Cable Beach Resort **3**
Sandals Royal Bahamian Hotel **2**

All-inclusive resorts — where one price covers your room, all meals, beverages, entertainment, most activities, tips, taxes, as well as airfare, if you like — are very popular among newlyweds. To stay busy day and night, you need never leave these self-contained vacation playgrounds until it's time to go home. **Sandals Royal Bahamian**, on New Providence, is for couples only. On Grand Bahama, think about **Club Viva Fortuna**.

If you don't necessarily want an all-inclusive setting but you like a blizzard of action, you can't go wrong with **Atlantis Paradise Island Resort & Casino** off New Providence. You can also find plenty to see and do in and around **Our Lucaya** on Grand Bahama.

Some couples prefer quieter, more remote resorts, where the sun, the sand, and each other are the main draws. The elegant **Ocean Club Golf & Tennis Resort,** the funky, startlingly colorful **Compass Point Beach Resort**, and home-like **Dillet's Guest House** are excellent honeymoon haunts on New Providence.

Choosing Among the Bahamas' Best Accommodations for Honeymooners

Quite a few accommodations, particularly the larger ones, feature honeymoon packages. These packages aren't usually money-savers, but they do include special extras such as a corner room, king-size bed, champagne, maybe a gourmet meal or two, and sometimes transportation in limousines between your hotel and the airport. Each hotel boasts a somewhat different set of perks, so make sure that you ask exactly what your package includes when you make your reservation. Here's a rundown of the best places for pillow talk.

Please refer to the Introduction of *Honeymoon Vacations For Dummies* for an explanation of our price categories.

Atlantis Paradise Island Resort & Casino
$$$$$ Paradise Island, off New Providence

Some people consider this larger-than-life resort over the top, with its gold-leaf dome ceilings, Mayan temple with aqua-slides, and elaborate waterfalls, fountains, and high-rise towers, yet for others it's pure fun — albeit expensive fun. You may find the polished, ultra-professional service here refreshing. After all, your honeymoon is a once-in-a-lifetime event, right? So what's wrong with a little over-the-top? The $850-million, 2,300-room resort dominates Paradise Island and sprawls from one shore to the other. Dozens of restaurants, bars, lounges, designer boutiques, and a huge casino that's open all day and all night make it easy never to leave the premises.

According to the legend of Atlantis, whose theme plays out all over the resort, an earthquake put this flourishing, utopian civilization at the bottom of the ocean around 1500 B.C. In staying true to that theme, the centerpiece of the hotel is its thrilling waterscape of aquariums, swimming pools, snorkeling lagoons, waterslides, and — almost forgot — a wonderful beach.

The resort's comfortable, pleasantly decorated rooms vary in size, view, and location. Although all have balconies, many of those in plush Royal Towers (the newest and priciest section) are only wide enough for a couple pairs of feet. The Beach Tower is the least expensive wing, with Coral Towers in the middle. Room service is available around the clock, and you can stay busy on the tennis, volleyball, and basketball courts, the putting green, in exercise classes, or at the spa.

Adjacent to the Atlantis Casino. ☎ ***800-ATLANTIS*** *or 242-363-3000. Fax: 242-363-3524. Internet:* `atlantisresort.com`. *Rack rates: $435-$560. A romance package is available. AE, MC, V.*

Club Viva Fortuna

$$$$ Fortune Beach, Grand Bahama

Most of Club Viva Fortuna's guests are young couples, some of whom start their honeymoons with weddings on the premises. (For help with your own nuptials, contact the hotel wedding coordiantor.) This European-owned resort has a definite Italian accent. You hear more *ciaos* than hellos, see folks playing bocce ball on the beach, and dine mostly on Italian (and some Bahamian) cuisine. Not far from the Bahamas National Trust Rand Memorial Nature Centre and Lucayan National Park, this beach resort has a one-size-fits-all price tag. You don't need to dig into your pocket for food, drinks, nightly entertainment, or most activities. You may have to pay extra for scuba diving, fishing, waterskiing, and horseback riding, but tennis, windsurfing, kayaking, snorkeling, and sailing are among the diversions that come with your room. The gym and sauna are also free to guests.

Four miles from Lucaya (where the Port Lucaya Marketplace is located) and six miles from Freeport (where you can find the Casino at Bahamia and the International Bazaar shopping complex), this 26-acre resort is an attractive getaway. Marble and vaulted wooden ceilings highlight the lobby. Flowers line walkways that wind through the property, which hugs a beautiful broad beach. More than half the comfortable rooms have views of the water while the others overlook the colorful gardens. If you want an accommodation in an isolated setting, then you won't mind staying here and having to rent a car to explore the rest of the island.

Doubloon Rd. and Churchill Dr., four miles east of Lucaya. ☎ ***800-898-9968*** *or 242-373-4000. Fax: 242-373-5594 or 242-373-5555. E-mail:* `club.fortuna@viva resorts.com`. *Internet:* `www.vivaresorts.com`. *Rack rates: $300-375 double, including all meals and most activities. AE, MC, V.*

Compass Point Beach Resort
$$$-$$$$$ New Providence

This startlingly colorful beach resort is New Providence's most whimsi-cal place to stay. Octagonal cottages with louvered windows are painted the vivid hues — canary, tangerine, teal, lavender, and sky blue — of the Bahamian Christmastime Junkanoo festival. These wooden buildings, some on stilts, stud the waterfront and gently sloping hillside. The beach in front of the hotel may be small, but larger Love Beach (popular for snor-keling) is just next door. Most units aren't air-conditioned, but ceiling fans and cross ventilation keep you cool. Welcome extras include sweet-smelling toiletries, hairdryers, irons and ironing boards, coffeemakers, satellite TV/VCRs, CD players, and CDs. All units have refrigerators, and some come with open-air kitchenettes and dining patios, but don't even think about whipping up more than snacks. (The hotel's oceanfront restaurant offers some of Nassau's most imaginative cooking.)

With help from the resort's staff, you can easliy arrange watersports (including scuba diving), along with golf, tennis, and sightseeing excur-sions. Cable Beach (with its casino) is less than a ten-minute drive away, but most people who choose this hotel want peace and quiet, not tall build-ings and crowds. However, the airport is just eight convenient minutes from here, so the down side of this proximity is, of course, that the rumble of planes overhead periodically shatters Compass Point's tranquility.

Adjacent to Love Beach, about a ten-minute drive west of Cable Beach. ☎ *800-688-7678 or 242-327-4500. Fax: 242-327-3299. E-mail:* cpoint@bahamas. net.bs. *Internet:* www.islandoutpost.com. *Rack rates: begin at $200 for two people in a double room. AE, MC, V.*

Dillet's Guest House
$$ New Providence

Located in a quiet residential neighborhood, this bed-and-breakfast is within leisurely strolls of Saunders Beach, downtown Nassau, and bus stops. Iris Knowles, who runs Dillet's with her daughter, Danielle, was raised in this handsome home, built in 1928 by her father. Its arched entryway has welcomed visitors since 1990. Talk about personal atten-tion! The inn has only seven rooms, so you really feel as if you're visiting old friends. Decorated with white wicker and pastels, all the guest quar-ters offer sitting areas, cable TV, clock radios, and both air-conditioning and ceiling fans. The bathrooms are also attractive, if a bit small. You won't find a telephone in your room, but you can use the pay phone in the living room for outgoing calls, and you can receive incoming calls on the mobile phone.

Taking up an entire block, the grounds — which include a small swim-ming pool — are wonderfully lush with tropical greenery. The pictur-esque gazebo is popular for weddings. Breakfast may consist of johnnycake (a mildly sweet bread something like a flat baking powder biscuit), banana bread, potato bread (flavored with coconut), fresh fruit, and cereal, with coffee or tea. You pay extra for lunch or dinner, perhaps consisting of baked grouper with broccoli, peas and rice, and chocolate cake. You get to know other guests during afternoon tea.

Dunmore Ave. and Strachan Street. ☎ *242-325-1133. Fax: 242-325-7183. E-mail:* dillets@batelnet.bs. *Internet:* www.islandeaze.com. *Rack rates: $100-$125 double, including breakfast. AE, MC, V.*

Nassau Beach Hotel
$$-$$$ New Providence

Next door to its sister property, the flashier Nassau Marriott Resort & Crystal Palace Casino, and across the road from the Cable Beach Golf Course, the Nassau Beach Hotel has been going strong since the 1940s. Spruced up during the 1990s, it has weathered competition from the newer, glitzier resorts that reside near it. Claiming a prime slice of the beachfront, this hotel is one of the more dignified in the area. But don't let the Georgian-style architecture, gleaming marble and tile lobby, and hushed hues fool you. The Nassau Beach Hotel knows how to party hearty. Check out the nightly Bahamian revue at the popular King & Knights club, the loud Friday evening Junkanoo parade at Café Johnny Canoe out front, or one of the hotel's various bars. When hunger hits, you can choose decent restaurants, from casual to not-so-casual, inexpensive to not-so-inexpensive.

All the rooms come with a balcony or patio, but be sure to ask about your view. Although you can see the ocean from most, some rooms overlook buildings instead. The watersports are extensive, and there are also two swimming pools, six tennis courts (four are floodlit for play under the stars), and a fitness center.

Near the Crystal Palace Casino. ☎ ***888-NASSAU-B*** *or 242-327-7711. Fax: 242-327-8829. Internet:* www.nassaubeachhotel.com. *Rack rates: $150-$320 double, $255-$485 suite. AE, MC, V.*

Ocean Club Golf & Tennis Resort
$$$$$ Paradise Island, off New Providence

Tucked away on the quiet eastern side of Paradise Island, this upscale colonial-style resort is as understated as Atlantis is extravagant (see the listing for Atlantis, earlier in the chapter At Ocean Clubs's core are formal terraced gardens, inspired by Versailles, where stone steps, hand-laid rock ridges, and European bronze and marble statues set off bright bougainvillea and hibiscus flowers. Striking stone arches of a twelfth-century Augustinian cloister overlook the gardens and the harbor (where the sunsets are fabulous). Get a load of the cloister at night when it's lit — talk about eye candy!

When you arrive, the concierge escorts you to your new digs. The guest rooms are spacious, with views of the gardens or the beach and ocean. All rooms come with patios or balconies, DVD and CD players, minibars, and Internet access. Some rooms have king-size mahogany four-poster beds that seem designed for newlyweds. The unobtrusive staff is there whenever you need assistance. (Each afternoon, champagne and strawberries mysteriously appear in your room.) You can dine seaside at Dune or by the fountains in the romantic Courtyard Terrace. Tennis courts, a pool, and a spa are also on the premises. Take the shuttle bus or a short walk to the 18-hole championship golf course. Because Atlantis and Ocean Club share the same owners (Sun International), Ocean Club guests have full access to all the facilities at theme-park-like Atlantis. Therefore, Ocean Club is a good choice if you like spending most of your time in a subdued atmosphere, but want to add a little dazzle now and then.

Paradise Island Dr. ☎ ***800-321-3000*** *or 242-363-2501. Fax: 242-363-2424. Internet:* www.sunint.com. *Rack rates: $700-$775 double. A romance package is available. AE, MC, V.*

Our Lucaya

$$$-$$$$ **Lucaya, Grand Bahama**

With a wedding coordinator on staff ready to help you plan the perfect ceremony, Our Lucaya is an excellent choice if you want your honeymoon to begin the instant you say, "I do!" This expansive beachfront resort offers plenty of action — wet and dry, by day and by night. Making its debut in April 1999, Reef Village (the first of three towers) houses spacious rooms, with and without balconies and ocean views. All are brightly decorated in the startlingly bold colors of Junkanoo (the Bahamian festival featuring wild music and dance and even wilder costumes).

Head outdoors and you find a gorgeous 7½-acre beach, complete with paraphernalia for scuba diving, snorkeling, jet skiing, banana boat rides, and parasailing, among other activities. In the midst of this oceanfront action is the free-form swimming pool with its sugar mill tower waterslide. When you're ready to tee off, you can check out the 18-holer at the Lucayan Course (designed by the renowned architect Dick Wilson), a 45-minute drive from the hotel. Before booking a room at Our Lucaya, check the status of the second championship golf course, Our Lucaya Reef course (by the equally renowned Robert Trent Jones, Jr.), additional guest rooms and restaurants, the spa and fitness center, tennis courts, shopping promenade, and new casino.

Royal Palm Way, across from Port Lucaya Marketplace. ☎ ***877-687-5822*** *or 242-373-1333. Fax: 242-373-8804. Internet:* www.ourlucaya.com. *Rack rates: $200-$275 double. Honeymoon packages are available. AE, MC, V.*

Radisson Cable Beach Resort

$$$-$$$$ **New Providence**

With a far wider and longer beach than the neighboring Nassau Marriott Resort & Crystal Palace Casino, the Radisson is a great choice for newlyweds looking for action. Go snorkeling, scuba diving, sailing, or play some tennis. Featuring three swimming pools, the hotel's tropical waterscape also includes rock formations, waterfalls, and whirlpools. There's a fitness center on the premises, and a golf course is across the road. You can dine at several good restaurants and, at night, listen to live music at the hotel. If you prefer, however, head to the adjoining casino complex for other eats, shops, and entertainment.

All with balconies, the 700 guest rooms in two nine-story wings form a U to cup the pools and beautiful sandy shore. Depending on the location of your room, you can get plenty of exercise going to and from the elevator, because the corridors are super long. The views from the lower floors showcase the gardens while higher rooms overlook the ocean.

If you book the all-inclusive Wedding Package with a minimum three-night stay, you get a decorated wedding cake, flowers, a bottle of champagne, a clergyman, and the expertise of the onsite wedding consultant to help you make all other arrangements, from choosing the locale (beach or wedding gazebo, maybe?) to obtaining your marriage license.

Adjacent to the Crystal Palace Casino. ☎ *800-333-3333 or 242-327-6000. Fax: 242-327-4728. E-mail:* rcbgroups@aol.com. *Internet:* www.radisson.com. *Rack rates: $200-$350 double. AE, MC, V.*

Sandals Royal Bahamian Hotel

$$$$$ **New Providence**

With its Romanesque statues, European spa, gourmet restaurants, and pools surrounded by stately columns, Sandals Royal Bahamian is an elegant all-inclusive. A brief shuttle ride or a leisurely stroll west of the Crystal Palace Casino, the hotel is removed from the busiest section of gorgeous Cable Beach. Therefore, it's no surprise that Sandals appeals to newlyweds, and many couples start their honeymoons by having their weddings on the hotel's grounds. (A professional wedding coordinator is on staff to help with all your arrangements.) With romantic touches such as four poster beds and luxurious baths, the individual rooms, suites, and villas at Sandals are exclusively for couples.

As soon as you enter the lobby that's decked out in glistening marble with sparkling chandeliers hanging from fresco-painted ceilings, you feel regal. You can spend a week here and splash in a different pool every single day. To relax, sip a cocktail at a swim-up bar (yes, you can really order drinks without leaving the pool!) while listening to the soothing sounds of a waterfall. Or, stretch out by the misting pool and see if your revitalized skin doesn't thank you. You can even sail off to the hotel's private island, complete with its own pool and restaurant. Whether you're in the mood for snorkeling, scuba diving, or waterskiing, Sandals offers it all.

If you're a landlubber, you can hit the billiards room, play basketball, tennis, or volleyball, or work out. When it's time to dine, you certainly won't experience culinary boredom at this resort. The food at more than half a dozen restaurants ranges from homestyle Bahamian and Japanese Teppanyaki to classic French and Northern Italian. After dark, head to the theater for live performances by local bands, dancers, and other entertainers, or spend a quiet evening at the piano bar.

A short drive or comfortable walk from the Crystal Palace Casino. ☎ 800-SAN-DALS or 242-327-6400. Fax: 242-327-6961. E-mail: `srb.gm@batelnet.bs`. *Internet:* `www.sandals.com`. *Rack rates: $650 double, including all meals, beverages, and most activities. Minimum two-night stay. AE, MC, V.*

Xanadu Beach Resort and Marina

$$-$$$ Grand Bahama

Overlooking its own beach and marina, Xanadu sits apart from the main tourist areas. Elegant touches, such as gold lion heads, mosaic tiles, and large terra-cotta urns, adorn the entranceway and hark back to the hotel's grand old days as a private club and hideaway of billionaire Howard Hughes. But that was then and this is now. So be sure to ask for a renovated room in the 12-story tower or in the three-story pool wing of this high-rise resort. Although rooms and suites are airy and many have expansive views of the ocean, some are badly in need of facelifts. You can learn to scuba dive through the dive shop, or you can try windsurfing, parasailing, or jet skiing. Three tennis courts are on the premises, and golf courses aren't far away. You have a couple of choices for restaurants — casual or formal — but don't expect to be blown away by the food. Xanadu hosts live entertainment several nights a week.

The medium-sized beach across the road from the hotel is popular among cruise ship day-trippers and guests of beachless hotels. So don't be surprised if you find it packed at times.

Sunken Treasure Dr., Xanadu Marina, near the International Bazaar, casino, and the airport. ☎ 242-352-6782. Fax: 242-352-6299. E-mail: `xanadu@batelnet.bs`. *Internet:* `www.bahamasvg.com/xanaduhotel.html`. *Rack rates: $135-$225 double. AE, MC, V.*

Enjoying Your Bahamian Honeymoon

The Bahamas offer a virtually endless array of honeymoon options. Do you want to celebrate your new lives together by partying 'til dawn, making a killing at a casino, and dining in a different elegant restaurant each night? Would you like to scuba dive or snorkel through schools of cartoon-colored fish?

Is visiting crumbling old forts, botanical gardens, and pint-sized museums more your style? Or would you rather just stroke each other on a sandy beach or sip potent rum punch while watching the sun slide into the ocean? In the Bahamas you can do it all — or do nothing at all.

Having fun in New Providence

New Providence island, home of Nassau (the Bahamas' colonial capital) and luscious Cable Beach, is linked to Paradise Island by bridges. The staff at your hotel can help you make arrangements for watersports, tennis, golf, sightseeing, and dining.

Playing in the sun and surf

If the issue is popularity, then hotel-studded **Cable Beach,** on New Providence, and **Paradise Island Beach** win hands down. Jet skiing, parasailing, banana boat rides, water-skiing, and windsurfing are available on the beaches in front of the hotels along these gorgeous stretches of sand.

To get away from the crowds, head to cozy **Love Beach** (on New Providence), which is great for snorkeling, or **Cabbage Beach** (on Paradise Island).

For a change of scenery, many newlyweds board tour boats to **Blue Lagoon Island** and **Rose Island,** two popular cays just offshore. Through **Dolphin Encounters** (☎ 242-363-1003) on Blue Lagoon island, you can pet or even swim with these friendly aquatic mammals.

Take a 90-minute horseback ride along wooded and beachside trails with **Happy Trails Stables** (☎ 242-362-1820). If you'd rather move under your own steam, try **Pedal and Paddle Ecoventures** (☎ 242-362-2772) bicycle and kayak excursions along New Providence's southwestern coast.

You have lots of choices when it comes to hitting the links. The 18-hole **Cable Beach Golf Course** (☎ 242-327-6000) is the island's oldest and the redesigned 18-holer at the **Ocean Club** (☎ 800-321-3000) on Paradise Island is the newest.

Taking in the sites

Not quite ready for scuba? Then try helmet diving with **Hartley's Undersea Walk** (☎ 242-393-8234; Internet: www.underseawalk.com) at the Nassau Yacht Haven. Getting up close and personal with colorful marine life, you walk on the ocean floor while wearing a lead helmet attached to an air tube.

Head to Paradise Island for a guided tour through parts of **Atlantis Aquarium** (☎ 242-363-3000), said to be the world's largest tropical marine habitat. Wander through the entertainment complex of this extravagant mega-resort. Try your luck at the casino, stop at the shops, or wine and dine.

Save some time for a ride in a horse-drawn carriage or a leisurely hand-in-hand stroll through the charming streets of **Nassau**, the Bahamas' colonial capital. Be sure to climb the 65 steps of **Queen's Staircase,** which leads to **Fort Fincastle** and the **Water Tower**, which both offer fabulous views of Nassau and the harbor. If you're in town on a Saturday morning, you might catch the **Changing of the Guard,** the dignified ceremony that takes place, British-style, at pink and white **Government House.** Then poke around the open-air **Straw Market,** packed with vendors selling everything from straw hats to clothing made from colorful African and Indonesian fabric.

For the ultimate in romance, take a two-hour champagne sunset cruise with **Barefoot Sailing Cruises** (☎ 242-393-0820). No Bahamian honeymoon is complete without a visit to **Versailles Gardens and Cloister**, a romantic oasis on Paradise Island. Bronze statues are scattered throughout meticulously landscaped, terraced gardens. Follow the central stone path leading to the rise topped by the twelfth-century stone cloister that was brought from France and reassembled here. The nearby gazebo, overlooking Nassau's beautiful harbor, may make you want to repeat your vows. And what a perch for watching the sunset!

Living it up in New Providence's nightlife

The newer of New Providence's dynamic duo, the casino complex at **Atlantis Paradise Island Resort** is the largest in the Bahamas or Caribbean. Along with **Voyagers Disco** (☎ 242-363-3000, open 10 p.m. to 1 a.m.), all kinds of bars draw the party crowd. You can find the **Crystal Palace Casino** between the Nassau Marriott and Radisson resorts on Cable Beach. Here in this busy entertainment complex, the **Rainforest Theatre** (☎ 242-327-6200) is the setting for the twice-a-night Las Vegas-style music and dance extravaganza.

Conveniently located on West Bay Street (across from Saunders Beach) between Cable Beach and downtown Nassau, the **Zoo Nightclub** (☎ 242-322-7195) is, by many accounts, the hottest dance club in town. Often featuring live bands, **Club Waterloo** (☎ 242-393-7324), on East Bay Street, just east of the Paradise Island exit bridge, is another popular dance spot with a choice of bars.

Dining in New Providence

New Providence and Paradise Island are the culinary heart of the Bahamas. In everything from unassuming diners to elegant dining rooms, countless chefs compete to please your palate. Men are required to wear jackets at only a couple of the most expensive restaurants.

Creating special memories

Book a candlelit table at **Buena Vista** (Delancy and Augusta Streets, Nassau; ☎ 242-322-2811; $$$$$), set in a 19th-century mansion, where the creamy garlic soup and rack of lamb are unforgettable. Handsome antiques, elegant china, and old English silverware also make dining a romantic experience at **Graycliff** (West Hill Street and Blue Hill Road, Nassau; ☎ 242-322-2796; $$$$$), known for its gourmet French and Italian creations with a Bahamian twist. Candle flames flicker in the breeze as you dine by the rock pool on the patio at **Sun And . . .** (Lakeview Rd. off Shirley St., Nassau; ☎ 242-393-1205; $$$-$$$$), where the dessert souffles are a big hit.

At **Courtyard Terrace** (Ocean Club, Paradise Island; ☎ 242-363-2501; $$$$$), diners sit beside a pool with a fountain as fronds of stately palm trees rustle overhead. Try the imaginatively prepared grouper, snapper, or lobster, or the flourless chocolate rum cake. Have breakfast, lunch, cocktails, or dinner with ocean breezes at **Dune** (also at Ocean Club, Paradise Island; ☎ 242-363-2501; $$$$$), perched on a rise above the beach. Even if you don't win a bundle at the adjacent casino, you can't lose at **Five Twins** (Atlantis Resort, Paradise Island; ☎ 242-363-3000; $$$$$). Revolving around seafood, the Thai-Japanese-Indonesian cuisine here is contemporary Pacific Rim with a European flair.

Looking for a casual experience

The Poop Deck , (East Bay St. next to Nassau Yacht Haven, Nassau; ☎ 242-393-8175; $$), an open-air waterside restaurant, offers everything from grilled chicken Caesar salad and burgers to crab-stuffed mushrooms and fried lobster, along with a spectacular view of the busy marina. For more upscale indoor or outdoor beachside dining, check out the restaurant's other location five minutes west of Cable Beach (at Sandypoint, west of Nassau; ☎ 242-327-3325; $$-$$$). Sit on the oceanfront patio or in the brightly decorated dining room for some scrumptious Caribbean-Asian-American dishes at **Compass Point** (Gambier Village; ☎ 242-327-4500; $$-$$$), a small, distinctive hotel about ten minutes west of Cable Beach.

Café Skan's (Bay Street at Market Plaza, Nassau; ☎ 242-322-2486; $) makes a good breakfast stop when you're in the mood for a stack of pancakes, a fluffy omelet, or French toast. For pizza topped with grilled seafood, cannelloni with lobster sauce, or other Northern Italian-style seafood dishes, head to **Café Matisse** (Bank Lane at Bay Street, Nassau; ☎ 242-356-7012; $$$). Ask for a table in the peaceful ground floor garden. Brightly decorated with Bahamian artwork, **Anthony's Caribbean Grill** (Casino Dr., Paradise Island; ☎ 242-363-3152; $$) has an extensive menu that includes peppery jerk chicken on Rasta pasta, twin lobster tails, and a 20-ounce Junkanoo Steak, along with well-seasoned vegetarian dishes.

Grand Bahama

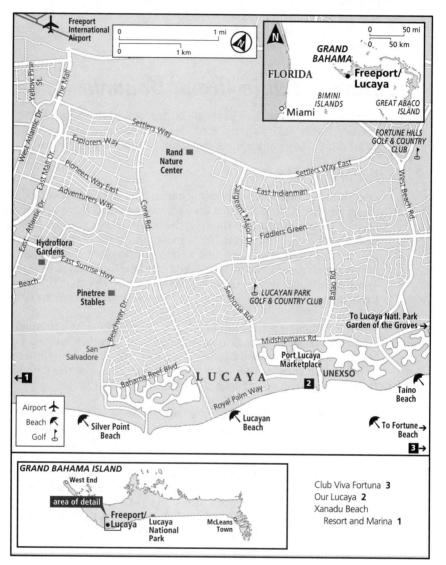

Finding a local favorite

You may think that you're visiting the home of old friends as you sample the fried grouper or steamed snapper at **Mama Lyddy's Place** (Market Street at Cockburn Street, Nassau; ☎ **242-328-6849; $**), located in a handsome house built during the 1800s. Starting around 8 p.m. on Friday nights at **Café Johnny Canoe** (Nassau Beach Hotel, West Bay St., Cable Beach; ☎ **242-327-3373; $-$$**), a Junkanoo band turns this busy restaurant into a party. As you tap your feet to the beat, munch the cracked conch with peas and rice, followed by guava duff for dessert.

At the edge of downtown Nassau, **Conch Fritters Bar & Grill** (Marlborough Street, Nassau; ☎ 242-323-8801; $-$$) is a convenient spot for sampling Bahamian specialties such as a Bahama Mama (a popular rum-based cocktail), cracked conch, and, of course, those fritters that gave the place its name.

Having fun in Grand Bahama

Compared to Nassau and Paradise Island, Grand Bahama may be low-key. But while its sights, activities, and dining spots may not be as plentiful, they pack just as much fun for active newlyweds.

Fun in the surf 'n' sun

From booze cruises and snorkeling excursions to banana boat rides and kayak paddles, Grand Bahama keeps water lovers as busy as they wanna be. The variety of beaches rimming the island allows couples to keep changing the sandy scenery. The busiest (and some of the prettiest) beaches are in **Lucaya,** the island's watersports mecca, where the resort hotels are clustered. Many newlyweds get their first glimpse of scenic **Taino Beach,** just east of Lucaya, when they stop to eat at **The Stoned Crab** restaurant (see the section "Dining in Grand Bahama" for details).

When it comes to scuba and snorkeling, Grand Bahama's premier operator is **UNEXSO** (Underwater Explorer's Society; Port Lucaya Marketplace; ☎ **888-365-3483** or 242-373-1244). Whether you want to stroke, swim with, or dive with dolphins, you can do it through **The Dolphin Experience** (☎ **888-365-3483** or 242-373-1250).

In the mood for a floating party? Climb aboard a 72-foot catamaran with a Bahama Mama Booze Cruise hosted by **Superior Watersports** (☎ **242-373-7863**).

Landlubbers enjoy excellent golf at a choice of courses, including championship **Our Lucaya Reef,** where 13 of the 18 holes bring water into play. Cascading waterfalls and a lake set off the eighteenth hole of **The Lucayan** (☎ **242-373-1066** for both courses). For horseback riding, try **Pinetree Stables** (☎ **242-373-3600**).

Sights you shouldn't miss

Spend some time at **Port Lucaya Marketplace,** a six-acre, open-air shopping and dining complex that sprawls along the waterfront. Some afternoons and most evenings, live music spills from the lacy harborside gazebo at **Count Basie Square.** If you're still in the market for some honeymoon mementos, also hit the older **International Bazaar** and the adjoining **Straw Market** in Freeport.

Rent a car for the 20-minute drive from the hotels of Lucaya to secluded **Gold Rock Beach,** at **Lucayan National Park.** This is an excellent spot for a just-you-and-me-kid picnic.

Save a day for a guided snorkeling and sightseeing excursion with **Kayak Nature Tours** (☎ 242-373-2485). You spend 90 minutes of this six-hour adventure paddling double kayaks along a tranquil tidal creek, through a mangrove forest with branches creating a shady canopy.

Finding fun after dark

Most of the action centers around Freeport's **Casino at Bahamaia,** under a dramatic Moorish-style dome. For an evening with more island appeal, try the **Yellowbird Showroom** (Castaways Resort; ☎ 242-352-6682). To be wined, dined, and entertained at sea, take a moonlit dinner cruise with **Superior Watersports** (☎ 242-373-7863).

Dining in Grand Bahama

Grand Bahama may not match New Providence and Paradise Island in numbers when it comes to places to dine. However, this quieter island has more than enough excellent restaurants to satisfy any honeymooning couple.

Creating special memories

Make a reservation at **The Arawak** (Our Lucaya Lucayan Golf Course, Bishop Lane; ☎ 242-373-1066; $$), where walls of windows look out to the expansive golf course by day and an illuminated waterfall at night. Consider the lobster tails or the chateaubriand. Seafood crepes, escargot, and scampi flambéed with cognac are among the gourmet treats at **Luciano's** (Port Lucaya Marketplace; ☎ 242-373-9100; $$$-$$$$). If you'd like to stay close to the blackjack table, you can bet on **The Crown Room** (The Casino, the Resort at Bahamia; ☎ 242-352-7811; $$$) for excellent Caesar salad, rack of lamb, and seafood.

For some romantic sunset watching, try **Pier I** (near the cruise ship dock, Freeport; ☎ 242-352-6674; $$$), where you can dine indoors or out. Europe meets the islands at **Ruby Swiss European Restaurant** (West Sunrise Highway and Atlantic Drive, next to the Resort at Bahamia; ☎ 242-352-8507; $$-$$$). The candlelit, beachside setting of **The Stoned Crab** (Taino Beach; ☎ 242-373-1442; $$$) may make you fall in love all over again.

Looking for a casual experience

Catch a glimpse of some of the colorful garb worn during the Bahamian Christmastime festival at the **Junkanoo Sports Bar & Grill** (Port Lucaya Marketplace; ☎ 242-373-6170; $-$$). Put yourself in the mood for a trip down under at **The Brass Helmet** (above the headquarters of the Underwater Explorer's Society (UNEXSO), Port Lucaya Marketplace; ☎ 242-373-2032; $-$$). Here underwater videos are always playing on the large screen TV and a vicious-looking shark has "burst" through the restaurant wall. Call ahead for complimentary transportation to **Club Caribe** (Churchill Beach, Mather Town; ☎ 242- 373-6866;

$), and don't forget your snorkel gear! Serving cracked conch and blackened mahi-mahi with peas and rice, along with ribs, sandwiches, and salads, this seaside restaurant turns a meal into a beach party.

Fish and chips, shepherd's pie, and steak-and-ale pie are among the pub fare on the menu at **The Pub at Port Lucaya** (Port Lucaya Marketplace; ☎ 242-373-8450; $-$$). In a tranquil spot away from the crush of shops and hotels, **Ferry House Restaurant** (Bell Channel, near Port Lucaya Marketplace; ☎ 242-373-1595; $-$$) offers views of pleasure boats and ferries along with creative renditions of sandwiches, salads, seafood, chicken, and beef.

Finding a local favorite

Ask for a table on the breezy balcony overlooking the water at **Fatman's Nephew** (Port Lucaya Marketplace, Lucaya; ☎ 242-373-8520; $-$$), the place to go for spicy Cajun-style fish and Bahamian peas and rice. There's nothing fancy about **Geneva's Place** (Kipling Lane, the Mall at West Sunrise Highway, Freeport; ☎ 242-352-5085; $), but the cracked conch and steamed grouper are scrumptious.

No matter what time of day you get to **Becky's** (East Sunrise Highway at East Beach Drive, Freeport; ☎ 242-352-8717; $-$$), you can feast on pancakes, eggs, or local breakfast favorites such as stewed fish with grits. For lunch or dinner, try the steamed snapper or pan-fried grouper, and wash it down with a Becky's Special, a coconut rum-vanilla ice cream-brandy concoction. Another good alternative to hotel restaurants for breakfast is **Cowboy's** (Port Lucaya Marketplace; ☎ 242-373-8631; $-$$), where the portions of steak and eggs are hefty. For lunch or dinner, order the Butch Cassidy Combo, a finger-lickin'-good pairing of barbecued chicken and ribs.

Making Plans and Settling In

When planning the perfect honeymoon (and tropical wedding), who wants hassles? Here are some tips to help you save plenty of time, confusion, and money. After all, putting the details in place now can pay off big time when you're snuggling with your honey as the warm island breeze swirls around you.

Getting to the Bahamas

The following airlines currently service the Bahamas. Please note that air service is always subject to change:

- ✓ **Air Canada** (☎ 888-247-2262) swoops down on Nassau from Toronto.

- ✓ **American Airlines/American Eagle** (☎ 800-433-7300; Internet: www.aa.com) is big man on campus when it comes to getting to the Bahamas from the U.S. Although most flights are from Miami, some are from Ft. Lauderdale, Orlando, or Tampa. About a dozen daily flights link Miami with Nassau (New Providence) and some seven flights a day connect with Freeport (Grand Bahama).

✔ **Bahamasair** (☎ **800-222-4262**; Internet: www.bahamasair.com), the Bahamas' national carrier, takes off from Miami, Ft. Lauderdale, and Orlando for Nassau. Bahamasair also flies from Nassau to Freeport (Grand Bahama).

✔ **British Airways** (☎ **0845 77 333 77** in the U.K., 800-247-9297 in the U.S.; Internet: www.britishairways.com) offers British travelers direct flights from Gatwick Airport to Nassau.

✔ **Continental Airlines** (☎ **800-525-0280**; Internet: www.continental.com) offers daily flights to Nassau (New Providence) from Newark, New Jersey, Miami, Ft. Lauderdale, or West Palm Beach. There aren't as many flights from which to choose, but Continental also serves Freeport (Grand Bahama) daily from Miami, Ft. Lauderdale, and West Palm Beach.

✔ **Delta** (☎ **800-221-1212**; Internet: www.delta.com) flies daily to Nassau (New Providence) from New York, Atlanta, Cincinnati, and Orlando.

✔ **Lynx Air International** (☎ **888-596-9247**), a small carrier, travels from Ft. Lauderdale to Freeport (Grand Bahama).

✔ **Trans World Airlines (TWA)** (☎ **800-221-2000**; Internet: www.twa.com) offers daily flights from New York and Miami to Nassau (New Providence), as well as from New York and Miami to Freeport (Grand Bahama).

✔ **US Airways** (☎ **800-428-4322**; Internet: www.usairways.com) connects Philadelphia and Charlotte to Nassau daily.

If you're a U.S., Canadian, or British citizen, you don't need a passport to enter the Bahamas, as long as you have two other acceptable forms of identification. If you don't have a passport, you must take the following papers with you:

✔ A certified or original copy of your birth certificate (it must have a raised seal)

✔ An official photo identification, such as a valid driver's license

✔ A return or ongoing airplane ticket

You may enter the Bahamas with an expired passport, as long as it has expired within the last five years.

Knowing the Bahamas

Shaped by indigenous Indian, West African, and British heritages, the Bahamas also have strong American and Canadian influences.

Newlyweds find plenty that's familiar here — and lots that's not. Sure, English is the national tongue, but in these islands the language has its own special lilt and lingo. "So you wisitin', ay?" a Bahamian might ask you. (Translation: "So you're visiting, are you?") Another thing you have to get used to is that life in these islands moves much more slowly than in many other parts of the world. Perfect, right? Because who wants to rush a honeymoon?

When you're in the Bahamas, don't be a member of the Ways and Means Committee — offending with your foreign ways when you don't mean to do so. For instance, would you show up at a movie theater wearing your bra and underpants or your boxers? We hope not, but that's what it looks like to island residents when visitors wander anywhere but the beach or pool in bathing suits, short shorts, and even beach cover-ups. Residents may feel as if you're treating them like nothing more than walking information booths when you ask for directions without saying hello first. Also, many people who were born in these islands don't like being referred to as "natives," because the term can sound condescending. "Locals" and "residents" are more acceptable terms. (But to confuse the issue, using native as an adjective, as in "native restaurant" is okay.)

For more information about the Bahamas please refer to *Bahamas For Dummies,* by Rachel Christmas Derrick.

Fast Facts: The Bahamas

American Express

In Nassau, visit the American Express office at Playtours on Shirley Street (☎ 242-322-2931). On Grand Bahama, the Scotiabank ATM accepts American Express cards for cash; call ☎ 800-221-7282 if you have a problem with traveler's checks.

ATMs and Credit Cards

Most banks on New Providence and Grand Bahama have ATMs with 24-hour access. However, some only accept cards in the Cirrus network (☎ 800-424-7787 or 800-4CIRRUS; Internet: www.mastercard.com/atm/) while others only take Plus (☎ 800-843-7587; Internet: www.visa.com/atms).

Currency

U.S. dollars are used throughout the Bahamas. The Bahamas also has its own currency, with a $1 for $1 exchange rate with U.S. green.

Driving

There's no need to rent a car in the Bahamas unless you want to, since getting around is hassle-free in public buses, taxis, ferries, and on foot.

Electricity

Go ahead — pack that blow dryer. North American appliances work fine in the Bahamas, which uses the same electrical current.

Emergencies

Dial ☎ 919.

Information and Maps

On New Providence, contact the **Ministry of Tourism** (☎ 242-322-7500). On Grand Bahama, call the **Grand Bahama Island Tourism Board** (☎ 242-352-8044).

Internet Access

If your New Providence hotel doesn't offer Internet access, contact **ASAP** (☎ 242-394-6447), a dowtown business center. On Grand Bahama, ask at your hotel or visit the **CyberCafe** (☎ 242-351-7283).

Language

English is the official language in the Bahamas.

Safety

The Bahamas are relatively safe. However, you should use the same common sense you would at home: Don't venture into desolate areas at night and don't leave valuables lying around.

Taxes

Although total charges vary from hotel to hotel, here's roughly what you can expect to pay: In the Bahamas, 12 percent resort tax plus about $8 per day, per guest, for housekeeping gratuity and energy surcharge (for use of electricity).

Don't forget to save $15 to $17 each for the departure tax that is collected before you can board the plane on your way home.

Telephone

Many hotels charge you at least 75 cents to $1 per phone call, whether or not you are calling a toll-free number, and sometimes whether or not you get through to the person you're calling. And don't even *think* about calling long distance direct, unless you have money to burn. The least expensive way to call overseas is with a phone card — either pre-paid or one that is connected to your home phone service — from a pay phone.

Drinking the water

Most folks in the Bahamas sip bottled water these days. However, the tap water is perfectly safe to drink on all the main islands and most of the smaller islands as well.

Tipping

Most restaurants make tipping easy by adding a 15 percent service charge to your bill. If you're not sure whether or not this has been done, don't be afraid to ask. Taxi drivers expect 15 percent of the fare, and baggage carriers, about $1 per bag. With tour guides, the guideline is a bit looser; many visitors give $3 or $4 per couple for a group tour.

Weather Updates

To check the forecast on New Providence or Grand Bahama, call ☎ 915.

Web Sites

Top destination Web sites for the Bahamas include The Bahamas Ministry of Tourism (www.bahamas.com); Bahamas Tourist Guide (www.interknowledge.com/bahamas); Bahamas Vacation Guide (www.bahamasvg.com); Bahamasnet: The Bahamas Vacation, Hotel, and Travel Guide (www.bahamasnet.com); and Virtual Voyages Bahamas Directory (www.virtualvoyages.com).

Chapter 15

Honeymooning in Barbados

By Echo & Kevin Garrett

. . . .

In This Chapter

▶ Finding the best honeymoon accommodations

▶ Discovering the fun and romance of Barbados

▶ Uncovering all the details

. . . .

*B*arbados's range of accommodations can't be beat. The island is home to some of the Caribbean's most over-the-top resorts, places that are luxurious to the point of absurdity. The ultra-exclusive Sandy Lane, which just reopened after being closed for three years of renovations — at a cost in excess of $200 million — leaps to mind. Barbados has villas, classy resorts, small boutique hotels, timeshares, and a handful of all-inclusive resorts. But you won't find big familiar-name chains. The biggest operator on Barbados, with a total of 572 luxury rooms at five different resorts, is the **Elegant Hotels Group** (☎ **800-326-6898**), which owns Colony Club, Crystal Cove, Coconut Creek, Tamarind Cove, and Turtle Beach Resort.

Barbados is not the place for romantic secluded retreats like you find on the British Virgin Islands or Jamaica. Nor is Barbados the place to find stunning structures; most hotels have less than 100 rooms, and, with few exceptions, the architects who designed them didn't go for the cutting-edge look. Most resorts have relied instead on Barbados's beautiful beaches and lush gardens to enchant visitors.

Barbados can claim some of the region's more sophisticated and charming hoteliers. Many properties are exquisitely managed with a careful eye toward making guests feel welcome. (One of our favorite hosts is Hamish Watson at Cobblers Cove. The affable Antigua-born Watson, who now calls Barbados home, genuinely makes you feel like you're the honored guest of an English country gentleman.)

Barbados

Bougainvillea Beach Resort **9**
Cobblers Cove **1**
Coral Reef Club **4**
Divi Southwinds Beach
    Resort and Racquet Club **8**
Glitter Bay **2**
Royal Pavilion **3**
Sandy Beach Island Resort **6**
Silver Rock Resort **10**
Tamarind Cove Hotel **5**
Turtle Beach **7**

Caribbean Islands

Barbados

North Point

Archer's Bay
Stroud Bay
Harrison Point
Maycock's Bay
Half Moon Fort
Six Men's Bay
Heywoods Beach
Mullins Beach
Gibbs Beach
Church Point
Paynes Bay
Paradise Beach
Brighton Beach
Brandon's Beach
Deep Water Harbour

River Bay
Cuckold Point
Gay's Cove
Pico Teneriffe
Fairfield
Coleton
ST. LUCY
Morgan Lewis Beach
Greeland
St. Andrew's Church
ST. PETER
Speightstown
SCOTLAND
ST. ANDREW
Weston
Chalky Mount
Turner's Hall Woods
Cattlewash
Lower Carlton
Tent Bay
ST. JAMES
Flower Forest
Bathsheba
Welchman Hall Gully
FOLKSTONE UNDERWATER PARK
Welchman Hall
ST. JOSEPH
Martin's Bay
Congor Rocks
Holetown
Blackmans
ST. JOHN
Consett Bay
Sunset Crest
Harrison's Cave
CULPEPPER ISLAND
Ragged Point Lighthouse
Lazaretto
ST. THOMAS
Groves
Francia Plantation
Three Houses
Kitridge Point
Prospect
Warrens
ST. GEORGE
Gun Hill Signal Station
Sunbury Plantation House
Bushy Park
Sandford
Bottom Bay
ST. MICHAEL
ST. PHILIP
Sam Lord's Castle
Black Rock
Long Bay
Marchfield
Beachy Head
Heritage Factory & Rum Park
Crane Beach
Queen's Park
CHRIST CHURCH
Crane Beach Hotel
Bridgetown
Tyrol Cot Heritage Village
Carlisle Bay
Hastings Worthing
St. Lawrence
Grantley Adams Int'l Airport
Needham's Point
Maxwell
Rockley Beach
Sandy Beach
Casuarina Beach
Oistins
Long Bay
South Point
Silver Sands Beach

Atlantic Ocean

Caribbean Sea

Airport ✈   Beach ↖   Church ⸸   Lighthouse ☀

0   5 Mi
0   5 Km

Figuring Out Where You Want to Stay

Barbados is developed, so don't expect to find a little gem tucked into the edge of jungle-like growth. Most of our recommendations are in fashionable St. James, St. Peter, or St. Michael parishes. (Parishes are like counties in the U.S.) All three are on Barbados's western shore where the Caribbean waters are calm — nicknamed the Platinum Coast, supposedly for the color of the sand (but we think the name is such because you need a platinum card to pay the hotel bill at many of the resorts in this region). See the map of Barbados in this chapter.

The resorts on the **Platinum Coast** tend to be self-contained. If you stay on the Platinum Coast, don't expect to be able to walk to a nearby restaurant; two-lane Highway 1 runs along the coast, and is too busy to safely stroll for any distance.

Hotels on the south coast in **Christ Church parish** (near Bridgetown) are a bit less pricey. If you like to restaurant-hop and enjoy nightlife, we recommend staying near here. A few of our picks are on the scenic Atlantic side where the waves crash against the shoreline. Villas, private homes, and condos are available south of Bridgetown, in the Hastings-Worthing area, and along the west coast in St. James and in St. Peter.

Many of the resorts are located near busy roads, and, unfortunately, some truck drivers on the island apparently find it great fun to merrily toot their horns as they roll by the hotels — especially in the wee hours of the morning. If traffic noise bothers you, ask for a room as close to the sea as possible.

Truth be told, if you're on a budget, Barbados isn't the best choice, unless you go during the summer low season. Barbados boasts exclusive properties in demand among the old-money set as well as hotels that have tapped into the European and Canadian charter market. Because of the dual demand, rates fluctuate inexplicably, which can be maddening when you're trying to plan a vacation without breaking the bank.

During the winter, many Barbados hotels insist that guests purchase the meal plans. We find doing so is limiting, however, especially because Barbados is known for having great restaurants.

You're always better off with at least a weeklong package (and you are, after all, going to be on your honeymoon). Hotel prices in Barbados are geared to the longer vacation times of Europeans, not the U.S. vacationers' habit of popping onto an island for three or four days. As a result, several per-night rates listed in this chapter may curl your hair — or even shock it into dreadlocks.

The **Barbados Super Saver Program** (☎ 246-228-4221), which runs from April 15 to December 15, offers discounts on airfare, hotels, meals, car rentals, and attractions. Guests who book the package receive a range of information helpful for busy travelers including a full color ticket-size voucher that includes a summary of the package, a list of discount specials, a 24-hour hotline number, a list of participating hotels, a full description of all the "Meet and Mingle" options, and reservation numbers to book any of the offers. The package also contains a sheet of tickets that can be redeemed for free meals and discounts when presented at participating vendors. The program includes round-trip air on American Airlines, Air Jamaica, or BWIA, transfers in Barbados, the first night free with a minimum five-night stay, full breakfast daily, and a "Bajan Meet-and-Mingle Meal Event." More than 20 hotels participate in the program.

Between Barbados's hefty room tax and the 10 percent surcharge, expect your final hotel bill to jump by about 17 to 25 percent of the subtotal.

Choosing Among Barbados's Best Accommodations for Honeymooners

The rack rates listed in this chapter are in U.S. dollars and are for a standard double room during high season (mid-December to mid-April), unless otherwise noted.

Please refer to the Introduction of *Honeymoon Vacations For Dummies* for an explanation of our price categories.

Bougainvillea Beach Resort
$$$ **Christ Church**

Bougainvillea is a lovely beachfront resort, one of the newer properties on the island — surrounded by lush gardens and towering palms on Maxwell Beach — and offers a terrific value for couples. You can rent a spacious time-share apartment in a four-story building by the week in high season or for a three-day minimum during off-season. The accommodations come with an in-room safe and daily maid service. All units have a terrace or balcony with a beautiful water view or a view of the riotous gardens; three units have plunge pools. The resort has three pools; one is especially large and has a swim-up bar. Kayaks, sunfish, boogie boards, and snorkeling gear are available for the asking. A car-rental desk and a restaurant are onsite, and several restaurants are within walking distance. A tennis court and exercise room round out the offerings.

Ask about the extensive wedding package.

Maxwell Coast Rd., Christ Church. ☎ *800-988-6904, 800-742-4276, or 246-418-0990. Fax: 246-428-2524. E-mail:* centralres@sunbeach.net. *Internet:* www.bougainvillearesort.com. *Rack rates: $218-$480 studios and two-bedroom suites. AE, DC, MC, V. EP.*

Cobblers Cove

$$$$$ St. Peter

Built on the site of a former British fort, Cobblers Cove is adjacent to a small but pleasant crescent beach situated on a placid cove on Barbados's famed Platinum Coast. A small resort, Cobblers Cove is a favorite of gourmands and older European visitors. The resort is not splashy, but ripe with a cozy elegance. The centerpiece of the three-acre grounds is the pink-washed great house, which has two sun-drenched suites upstairs, the Camelot, and the Colleton, each with plunge pools, king-size four-poster beds, fresh orchids, and island murals. Only bedrooms are air-conditioned. Suites have wide sitting areas, big bathrooms, wet bars with snacks, and kitchenettes. (Some are a bit too close to the busy highway; ask for suites 1 through 8, toward the sea.) Afternoon tea is served poolside near the clubby lounge/library. The small resort also has a generous dine-around plan that allows you to sample other top restaurants.

Guests get complimentary water-skiing, windsurfing, snorkeling, and sunfish sailing (instruction included), as well as guaranteed tee times at the Royal Westmoreland Golf Club. From January 5 to March 24, the atmosphere is adults-only.

Road View, Speightstown, St. Peter. ☎ *800-890-6060 or 246-422-2291. Fax: 246-422-1460. E-mail:* cobblers@caribsurf.com. *Internet:* www.barbados.org/hotels/cobblers.htm. *Rack rates: $740-$1,104 suite, $1,868-$2,115 Camelot/Colleton suites. MAP supplement adds $94 a person per day. AE, MC, V.*

Coral Reef Club

$$$$$ St. James

A small, family owned and managed resort, the Coral Reef Club has set the pace for Barbados's luxury resorts for four decades. But the Coral Reef Club is anything but stuffy. Public areas are strung along the sandy white beach adjacent to the calm, bathlike Caribbean, and small coral-stone cottages are scattered over 12 flower-filled acres. (Those farthest from the beach require a hike to the main house.) Fresh flowers grace the spacious accommodations. Each room has a small patio and amenities such as radios and hair dryers. Junior suites have a sitting area and large private balcony or patio; cottage-style suites have an additional single bed and dressing room. We recommend splurging on the ultra-spacious luxury plantation suite, if your budget allows. Each has a private terrace and an open sundeck with a 9-by-9-foot pool. A beauty salon, masseuse, three tennis courts, exercise room, billiards, windsurfing, boating, and waterskiing are also available. A TV is available by request only and carries an extra charge. Guests on the Modified American Plan, which includes two full meals daily, have dining and golf privileges at Royal Westmoreland Golf Club. Another convenience is the free weekday shuttle into Bridgetown. No children under age 12 allowed.

Hwy. 1, Holetown, St. James. ☎ 800-223-1108, 800-525-4800, or 246-422-2372. Fax: 246-422-1776. Rack rates: $480-$740 double, $1,805 Luxury Plantation suite. AE, MC, V. MAP.

Divi Southwinds Beach Resort and Racquet Club
$$$ St. Lawrence

An ultra-busy resort, Divi is for couples who like being in the center of the action — the resort is only steps from a sandy white beach in the heart of the restaurant district and Bajan nightlife in St. Lawrence Gap. The buildings on 20 lush acres are vanilla-plain, but Divi is the the sort of place where you don't spend much time in the room anyway. The friendly staff goes out of its way to make sure that you're having fun. We favor taking one of the larger rooms, with a kitchenette and a balcony overlooking the gardens and pool. If you're a beach bunny, the trade-off for being right by the beach is taking a smaller, older room. The hotel has two restaurants and two bars, or you can cook in your room. Onsite you also find two pools, a beauty salon, a putting green, two lighted tennis courts, basketball, volleyball, a dive shop, and other shops.

St. Lawrence Gap, Christ Church. ☎ 800-367-3484 or 246-428-7181. Fax: 246-428-4674. E-mail: reserve@diviresorts.com. *Internet:* www.diviresorts.com. *Rack rates: $197-$320 double. AE, DC, MC, V.*

Glitter Bay
$$$$$ Porters

In the case of Glitter Bay, a classy resort, all that glitters is . . . everything — from the accommodating staff to the 76 polished suites to the sparkling Caribbean. Glitter Bay is such a favorite with repeat guests that you need to book nearly a year in advance to get a room in high season. English shipping magnate Sir Edward Cunard built this Moorish-style stucco estate in the 1930s to resemble his palazzo in Venice. Now the Great House serves as the reception area for this elegant resort, which is set amid grand gardens that sweep to a half-mile-long stretch of palm-lined, golden-sand beach. Glitter Bay's beachside hotel restaurant also deserves high marks for romance.

Glitter Bay is more casual than its next-door neighbor, the Royal Pavilion. These two sister resorts share facilities, including watersports and dining privileges. Guests enjoy privileges at Royal Westmoreland Golf Club (with complimentary transportation). A beauty salon, masseuse, two lighted tennis courts, exercise room, and shops are onsite.

Porters, St. James. ☎ *800-223-1818 or 246-422-5555. Fax: 246-422-3940. E-mail:* glitterbay@fairmont.com. *Internet:* www.fairmont.com. *Rack rates: $529–$1,199 suite. AE, DISC, DC, MC, V. EP, MAP.*

Royal Pavilion

$$$$$ Porters

The Royal Pavilion, an elegant Spanish mission-style resort, located next door to its sister resort (the more casual though still pricey Glitter Bay), is one of our favorites on Barbados. Like Glitter Bay, it stays almost fully booked in the winter months. The resort attracts a sophisticated clientele who want an idyllic respite with a little water fun tossed in. Of the 75 suites here, 72 are oceanfront; the remaining three are ensconced in a two-story garden villa. Take one of the oceanfront, ground-floor suites (with cool marble floors and comfy king-size beds); you can walk ten steps to the white-sand beach.

Royal Pavilion shares amenities and management with Glitter Bay. Two lit tennis courts, nonmotorized watersports, 24-hour concierge, laundry, and limousine service are part of the eye-popping rates. Breakfast and lunch are served alfresco at the edge of the beach. Afternoon tea and dinner are in the Palm Terrace. Royal Westmoreland Golf Club is almost across the street. The welcome mat is yanked for children ages 12 and under. Housekeeping and the front desk can be snappier — especially at these prices.

Weddings are often performed onsite here. The honeymoon package includes complimentary his/hers massage, champagne, orchids and chocolate dipped strawberries on arrival; dinner for two at the Palm Terrace Restaurant; a sail on a catamaran; and accomodations with a private balcony.

Porters, St. James. ☎ *800-223-1818 or 246-422-4111. Fax: 246-422-3940. E-mail:* royalpavilion@fairmont.com. *Internet:* www.fairmont.com. *Rack rates: $679–$1,200 suite. AE, DISC, DC, MC, V. EP, MAP.*

Sandy Beach Island Resort

$$ Worthing

One of Barbados's better values, Sandy Beach Island Resort is a comfortable hotel located on an excellent wide swath of beach and boasts efficient and friendly staff members who want guests to have fun. The rooms — one- and two-bedroom suites with full kitchens and dining areas — sport tropical colors rather than the hotel-bland palette of many Barbados resorts. The hotel is a convenient walk to the good restaurants of St. Lawrence Gap, and the onsite Beachfront Restaurant serves a West Indian buffet Tuesday and Saturday nights. This 127-room hotel has a boardwalk gazebo, a roof garden, and a free-form pool with a poolside bar. The staff can help you arrange dive certification, deep sea fishing, harbor cruises, windsurfing, snorkeling, and catamaran sailing.

Worthing, Christ Church. ☎ *800-742-4276, 800-448-8355, 800-223-9815, 800-GO-BAJAN, or 246-435-8000. Fax: 246-435-8053. Internet:* www.funbarbados.com. *Rack rates: $130-$335 double. AE, DC, MC, V.*

Silver Rock Resort

$ Silver Sands

Ideal for professional windsurfers and adventure seekers, Silver Rock Resort opened in January 2000. A range of beachfront, ocean-view, and garden-view accommodations are available. The hotel's open-air restaurant, Jibboom, serves tasty local and international dishes and has occasional theme nights. Guests frequently take part in the Friday Night Street Party at nearby Time Out at the Gap. Other sports popular with the hardbodies who populate the Silver Rock Resort include scuba diving, snorkeling, boogie-boarding, surfing, hiking, beach volleyball, and sea kayaking. All guests receive reduced greens fees and preferential tee times at the newly opened Barbados Golf Club, the island's only public championship golf course.

Silver Sands, Christ Church. ☎ *246-428-2866. Fax: 246-428-3687. E-mail:* silver@gemsbarbados.com. *Internet:* www.gemsbarbados.com. *Rack rates: $115-$275 double. AE, MC, V.*

Tamarind Cove Hotel

$$$$ Paynes Bay

You think you've taken a magic carpet ride when you encounter the Spanish Moorish architecture at Tamarind Cove. Its expansive courtyard is a visual feast with brilliantly hued bougainvillea. All 164 rooms have king-size beds, a mini-refrigerator, and a private balcony or patio facing the sea. Honeymoon suites have lavish extras such as private Jacuzzis or plunge pools. You get a smorgasbord of watersports, including water skiing, sailing, and snorkeling. And the resort has — we're not kidding — eight freshwater pools. Twice a week, Tamarind Cove hosts a candlelight dinner served directly on the hotel's magnificent stretch of white-sand beach. Set against the backdrop of waves gently breaking against the shore, enveloped by a night sky blanketed with stars, the five-course gourmet dinner is served to an intimate group of no more than 20 guests, so reserve early.

The hotel offers an extensive wedding package for $645 per couple.

Paynes Bay, St. James. ☎ *800-326-6898 or 246-432-1332. Fax: 246-432-6317. E-mail:* elegantna@earthlink.com. *Internet:* www.eleganthotels.com. *Rack rates: $227-$380 double. AE, MC, V. EP.*

Turtle Beach
$$$$$ Christ Church

Set on a wide, 1,500-foot-long white strand of beach on the south coast, this three-story hotel opened in 1998 as the flagship of the Elegant Hotel Group. It gets its name from the sea turtles that occasionally nest on the beach — although based on our experience in the Caribbean, whenever a property lays claim to turtles, sightings quickly become a rarity. Nonetheless, Turtle Beach, a well-done, 166-suite all-inclusive, is a good addition to the Barbados hotel scene, and a good choice for active types who love golf and the nightlife of Bridgetown, just 15 minutes away. Included in the price, you get instruction and the equipment to participate in scuba diving, waterskiing, snorkeling, kayaking, sailing, and boogie-boarding. Set in six acres of lush gardens, the hotel promises you ocean views from every suite. Tennis equipment is provided; golfers get special rates and times at Royal Westmoreland Golf Club.

Turtle Beach offers an extensive wedding package for $645 per couple.

Dover. ☎ *800-326-6898 or 246-428-7131. Fax: 246-428-6089. Rack rates: $626-$742 suite. Rates are all-inclusive. AE, DC, MC, V.*

Enjoying Your Honeymoon in Barbados

Because both of us have recently discovered that our Irish and Scottish ancestors immigrated to Barbados before entering the U.S., we must confess that we've suddenly developed a soft spot for Barbados, where polo and cricket are considered great fun. We're a bit more inclined now to overlook the fact that the island is overdeveloped, crowded, and geared to the package-tour groups from Canada and the United Kingdom who are perfectly happy to spend their entire holidays at their respective resorts.

The mood on Barbados is unmistakably civilized. Despite more than three decades of independence from Great Britain, the island still exudes a British air of formality — so much so that we have personally felt a little stifled there at times. Still, when it comes time to play, the Bajans cut loose — and the locally-made rum can thaw the frostiest of demeanors.

What else can you do on Barbados besides play polo and drink rum? Plenty. In this section, we guide you toward Barbados's best beaches and activities.

Basking on the beaches

With more than 70 miles of coastline, Barbados has a great selection of beaches, from stretches of soft white sand lapped by calm, turquoise Caribbean water to the rough, windswept Atlantic Ocean coastline.

The wind swept **Bathsheba/Cattlewash,** where magnificent boulders frame pounding waves, is a great place to watch the sunrise. We were surprised to find a gaggle of surfers already there to catch the waves. It turns out that Bajans ride the waves here almost daily. If you decide to try surfing, be sure to get a local's advice on where to enter the water.

 Although the east coast has miles of untouched beach along the island's wildest, hilliest, and most beautiful stretch of coast, swimming at Bathsheba or along the Atlantic coast can be extremely dangerous. Save your swimsuit for the calmer waters of the south or west coast beaches.

South coast

The medium waves of the south coast beaches generally draw a young, energetic crowd. These bustling beaches are consistently broad with white powdery sand; the reef-protected waters are crystal clear and safe for swimming and snorkeling. **Accra Beach** in Rockley is popular — lots of people, activity, food, and drink are nearby. Rental equipment is available here for snorkeling and other watersports. **Casuarina Beach,** at the Casuarina Beach Hotel, (east end of St. Lawrence Gap area) is a big, wide breezy beach with a fair amount of surf. Public access is available from Maxwell Coast Road.

One of the island's best beaches, **Needham's Point** and its lighthouse are at the south end of Carlisle Bay, just outside Bridgetown. It's crowded with local people on weekends and holidays. The Carlisle Bay Centre has changing rooms and showers to accommodate cruise-ship passengers spending a day at the beach. In Worthing, **Sandy Beach** has shallow, calm waters and a picturesque lagoon. Parking is available on the main road, and there are plenty of places nearby to buy food or drink.

 To fully appreciate the rugged beauty of Barbados, we recommend the lovely cove at **Bottom Bay,** north of Sam Lord's Castle. Follow the steps down the cliff to a strip of white sand lined by coconut palms and washed by an aquamarine sea. You may even find a cave to explore, and you won't see another soul for miles around — perfect for a picnic for two. Most of the hotels can prepare a scrumptious picnic basket if you put in your request 24 hours in advance.

For a classic beach that's a favorite of many visitors, check out the cliffs, dunes, pink sands, and beautiful water of **Crane Beach,** on the southeast coast. "Lifestyles of the Rich and Famous" named it one of the best beaches in the world. **Silver Rock Beach,** close to the southernmost tip of the island, has a beautiful expanse of white-sand beach with a stiff breeze that attracts windsurfers who use Silver Rock Hotel as their base.

West coast

If you want to dip your toes in the calm, magnificently clear Caribbean, head for the west coast, nicknamed the "Platinum Coast." Here in the stunning coves and sandy beaches are excellent water sports and swimming. The water is so smooth (especially early in the morning) that you can even water-ski here.

This almost unbroken chain of beaches between Speightstown (in the north) and Bridgetown is lined with elegant private villas and luxurious boutique resorts. The beaches aren't crowded, but they aren't private either. You won't find concession stands, but hotels welcome nonguests for terrace lunches as long as they are wearing a decent cover-up. You can park on the main road and walk to **Mullins Bay** and **Gibbs Beach,** just south of Speightstown. Its glassy blue waters are ideal for swimming and snorkeling. Pretty **Paynes Bay,** south of Holetown, has a number of luxury hotels and plenty of white-sand beach to match. Parking areas and public access are available opposite the Coach House Pub. Grab a bite to eat and liquid refreshments at Bombas Beach Bar.

 Serious snorkelers should head to **Folkstone Underwater Park** at Church Point, just north of St. James church. Gear is available to rent. Because there is so much traffic in the water here, however, always take along a brightly-colored buoy when you go snorkeling.

Exploring dive sites

Barbados hasn't become known among divers, and there's a reason. Fishing is still big business here, and you rarely see any large fish on its reefs. But if you're a beginning diver who wants to get in a few dives between rounds of golf, Barbados is a good choice. Visibility is generally around 80 to 90 feet, but may be much less than that during the rainy season from June to January.

The most popular dive site is at **Dottin's Reef** off Holetown — a gorgeous reef festooned with sea fans, gorgonians, and brain coral. You can see parrotfish, snappers, barracuda, and a few turtles starting at depths of 65 feet. South of Dottin's Reef is the **Stavronikita,** a 356-foot Greek freighter that lies about 135 feet under water and is a good wreck to explore (though often crowded with tourist divers). Virtually every part of the ship is accessible, but its depth is not for less experienced divers.

A one-tank dive on Barbados runs about $55; a two-tank dive costs about $90. All gear is supplied, and you can purchase multi-dive packages. **The Dive Shop, Ltd.** (Aquatic Gap near Bay Street, St. Michael; ☎ 800-348-3756 or 246-426-9947; Internet: www.barbados.org/diving/diveshop/diveshop.html) is the oldest dive shop on Barbados and teaches all levels of certification. On the west coast, **Hightide Watersports** (Coral Reef Club, St. James; ☎ 800-513-5763 or 246-432-0931; Fax: 246-432-0931; Internet: www.divehightide.com) specializes in small groups. Hightide offers one- and two-tank dives, night reef/wreck/drift dives, the full range of PADI instruction, and free transportation.

For snorkeling, we suggest booking with **Ocean Adventures** (☎ 246-436-2099; E-mail: oceanadventure@sunbeach.net), which has an excellent 3½-hour snorkeling tour on its 30-foot custom-built snorkeling boat. The trip includes a trip to the island's best reef and snorkeling over some shallow wrecks, as well as a beach stop and a swim with greenback turtles.

Taking a ride under the sea

Atlantis Submarines (Shallow Draught, Bridgetown; ☎ 246-436-8929) offers enormously popular mini-submarine voyages for those who are curious about what's under the sea but don't want to dive or snorkel. Two trips are submarine trip are offered on Barbados:

✔ **Atlantis III**, a 48-passenger, 65-foot boat, offers a 45-minute tour (for $80 a pop) of wrecks and reefs as deep as 150 feet. Special nighttime dives, using high-power searchlights, are spectacular.

✔ **The Atlantis SEATREC** (Sea Tracking and Reef Exploration Craft) essentially lets you experience the same views you'd get snorkeling without getting wet. The 46-passenger vessel has large viewing windows six feet below the surface, where you enjoy the underwater marine life on a near-shore reef from the air-conditioned craft.

If you even think that you may be claustrophobic, don't try the submarine.

Riding the wind

Barbados is one of the top spots in the world for windsurfing and is part of the World Cup Windsurfing circuit. If you want to try your hand, here are the best operators on the island:

✔ **Mistral Windsurfing School** is at Grand Barbados Beach Resort in Carlisle Bay, south of Bridgetown (Aquatic Gap, St. Michael; ☎ 246-426-4000).

✔ **Silver Rock Windsurfing Club** is at Silver Rock Hotel (Silver Sands Beach, Christ Church; ☎ 246-428-2866).

Winds are strongest between November and April and at the island's southern tip, where the Barbados Windsurfing Championships are held in mid-January. Boards and equipment are often free of charge for guests at the larger hotels; ask whether lessons are part of your package.

Sailing away

Party boats depart from the Careenage or Bridgetown Harbour area for lunchtime snorkeling or cocktail-hour sunset cruises. Prices are around $50 to $55 per person. Catamaran cruises are available on **Limbo Lady** (☎ 246-420-5418), **Tiami** (☎ 246-430-0900), and **Tropical Dreamer** (☎ 246-427-7245). **Secret Love** (☎ 246-432-1972; E-mail: yachts@caribsurf.com), a 41-foot Morgan yacht, offers daily lunchtime or evening snorkel cruises and specializes in private charters. The red-sailed **Jolly Roger** "pirate" ship (☎ 246-436-6424) runs lunch-and-snorkeling sailing cruises (with complimentary rum punches) along the west coast.

A fun, new option is taking a coastal kayak tour through **Ocean Adventures** (☎ 246-436-2099; E-mail: oceanadventure@sunbeach.net).

Exercising on-land options

If your sea legs need a break from all that fun in and on the water, check out some of the options Barbados offers on dry land.

Teeing off

Bajans love golf, but until recently, the island didn't make itself too welcoming to outsiders looking to play a game. All that's changed. Barbados has debuted three new 18-hole championship courses of late, but play remains some what restricted, so call ahead to find out if you can get on the course. Greens fees range from $75 for 9 holes at Club Rockley to $145 for 18 holes at Royal Westmoreland Golf Club. During low season, prices fall by almost half.

In July 2000, the redesigned and reconstructed **Barbados Golf Club** (Durants, Christ Church; ☎ 246-434-2121; Fax: 256-418-3131; Internet: www.barbadosgolfclub.com) on the south coast opened as Barbados's first public championship golf course. The 6,905-yard, par-72 course, designed by architect Ron Kirby, has been approved and sanctioned to host the PGA Seniors Tournament in 2002. Greens fees for 18 holes are $99 plus $13 for a cart and $20 for Callaway club rentals. A three-day unlimited golf pass during high season is $225.

The **Royal Westmoreland Golf Club** (St. James; ☎ 246-422-4653) has a world-class Robert Trent Jones, Jr., 18-hole championship course that meanders through the 500-acre Westmoreland Sugar Estate. To play at this exclusive course, you must stay at a hotel with access privileges (such as Cobblers Cove, Coral Reef Club, Glitter Bay, Royal Pavilion, or Turtle Beach).

Club Rockley Barbados (Rockley, Christ Church; ☎ 246-435-7873), on the southeast coast near Sam Lord's Castle, has a challenging 9-hole course that can be played as 18 from varying tee positions. The course is open to the public daily, and trolleys and clubs can be rented inexpensively. Greens fees are $75 during high season.

The prestigious **Sandy Lane Golf Club** (St. James; ☎ 246-432-2829) has undergone a dramatic redesign by renowned course architect Tom Fazio. Eventually Sandy Lane plans to boast 45 holes with two 18-hole championship courses, both designed by Fazio.

Watching from the sidelines

Barbados's spectator sports include these thoroughly British options.

Cricket

Not Jiminy Cricket — just plain cricket. Barbados is mad for the game, which has a season from May to late December. International test matches are played from January to April. Newspapers give the details of the times and places. Tickets to cricket matches at Kensington Oval, Bridgetown, range from $5 to $25. For information, call the **Barbados Cricket Association** (☎ 246-436-1397).

Polo

Never experienced a polo match? Here's a great opportunity. Polo matches here are much more casual than at other places, so spectators are more than welcome. Matches are played at the **Barbados Polo Club** in Holders Hill, St. James (☎ 246- 427-0022) on Wednesdays and Saturdays from October through April.

Touring historic sites

To encourage you to tour the island's many historic sites, the Barbados National Trust has designed the Heritage Passport, a free pass to some of the island's most popular attractions and historic sites. When the holder pays full admission to visit some attractions, the passport is stamped to validate free admission to other sights. Passports are free and can be picked up at displays in supermarkets, shops, hotels, and restaurants.

Every Wednesday afternoon from mid-January through mid-April, the Trust offers a bus tour of historic great houses and private homes open for public viewing, including **Tyrol Cot Heritage Village** (St. Michael); **St. Nicholas Abbey** (St. Peter); **Francia Plantation, Drax Hall,** and **Brighton Great House** (St. George); **Villa Nova** (St. John); and **Sam Lord's Castle** and **Sunbury Plantation House** (St. Philip). The cost is $18 per person, which includes transportation to and from your hotel. (If you wish to visit the homes on your own, they're open on those Wednesday afternoons from 2:30 to 5:30 p.m.; entrance fees at each range from $1.25 to $5.)

History-rich Barbados has much to offer to those interested in the past. Thanks to the British influence, it also boasts some of the Caribbean's finest gardens. Here are our favorite picks to get a flavor for both:

- ✔ **Barbados Wildlife Reserve:** Home to herons, land turtles, a kangaroo, screeching peacocks, lots of green monkeys, geese, brilliantly colored parrots, and a friendly otter, this lovely reserve has a giant walk-in aviary and natural-history exhibits. Across from Farley Hill, St. Peter. ☎ 246-422-8826. $10. Open daily from 10 a.m. to 5 p.m.

- ✔ **Farley Hill:** At this national park in northern St. Peter, the imposing ruins of a plantation great house are surrounded by gardens, lawns, an avenue of towering royal palms, and gigantic mahogany, whitewood, and casuarina trees. St. Peter. $1.50 per car; walkers free. Open daily 8:30 a.m. to 6 p.m.

- ✔ **Folkestone Marine Park & Visitor Centre:** At this park north of Holetown, a museum explains Barbados's marine life. It also has an underwater snorkeling trail around Dottin's Reef. A glass-bottom boat ride allows youngsters and nonswimmers to get a good look, too, at a barge sunk in shallow water teeming with reef fish. Church Pt., Holetown, St. James. ☎ 246-422-2314. Admission 60 cents (the boat ride costs extra). Open weekdays from 9 a.m. to 5 p.m.

- ✔ **Andromeda Gardens:** We spent an entire afternoon here, where six acres of gardens are nestled among streams, ponds, and rocky outcroppings above the Bathsheba coastline. The orchid collection is especially beautiful. Bathsheba, St. Joseph. ☎ 246-433-9384. Adults $6; children $3. Open daily from 9 a.m. to 5 p.m.

- ✔ **Flower Forest:** Walk amid the fragrant flowering bushes, cannas, ginger lilies, puffball trees, and more than a hundred other species of tropical flora. A ½-mile (1-km) path winds through the 50 acres of grounds. Richmond Plantation, Hwy. 2, St. Joseph. ☎ 246-433-8152. Adults $7; children $3.50. Open daily from 9 a.m. to 5 p.m.

- ✔ **Gun Hill Signal Station:** The 360-degree view from windswept Gun Hill, built in 1818 at 700 feet above sea level, was what made this location of strategic importance to the 19th-century British army. Today, Gun Hill is a cool place to get the best view on the island. St. George. ☎ 246-429-1358. $5.00. Open Monday through Saturday from 9 a.m. to 5 p.m.

- ✔ **Sam Lord's Castle:** The Regency house built by the buccaneer Sam Lord is considered by many to be the finest mansion in Barbados. Built in 1820 and now part of a resort, the house is decorated with fine furninshings that Sam Lord is reputed to have pillaged from passing ships. The pirate supposedly lured ships onto Barbados's treacherous reefs by hanging lanterns in palm trees to simulate harbor lights. Long Bay, St. Philip. ☎ 246-423-7350. Admission $5; resort guests free. Open daily from 10 a.m. to 4 p.m.

Partying on Barbados

Just a quarter of a century after Barbados was settled in 1627, Bridgetown already had more than 100 bars. That tradition continues today. We've never seen a Caribbean island with so many watering holes. The nightclubs open around 9:30 p.m., but the action doesn't really heat up until at least 11 p.m. and may go on until 3 a.m. For most nightlife venues, women wear dresses or skirts, although nice pants are fine. Men can be found in khaki pants, collared shirts, and dress shoes.

Always exercise caution, especially if you're out late after the wallop of a few Planter's Punches has settled in. Take a cab back to your resort if you've had much to drink — the roads on Barbados are narrow and dark.

Baku Beach (Holetown, St. James; ☎ 246-432-BAKU) and its sister nightclub the **Casbah,** a Moroccan theme with Euro flair, are currently the hot spots on Barbados. The trendy crowd at Baku, open nightly from 6:30 p.m., consists of locals and tourists alike. Some of the hottest bands on the island perform at its cocktail bar. The Casbah, open nightly from 10 p.m. to 3 a.m., resembles a New York City lounge with a DJ spinning tunes all night. Vintage Wine Bar, also at the Baku complex, serves light tapas, and a choice of champagnes, wines, and cigars.

The Gap, or St. Lawrence Gap, situated on the south coast in the Worthing Area, has long had a reputation as the place for late-night limin'. Its "hip strip" boasts a mind-boggling 40 bars, pubs, clubs, and restaurants. **Café Sol** (St. Lawrence Gap, Christ Church; ☎ 246-435-9531) has a wraparound terrace with a great view of the St. Lawrence Gap strip. One of the best-known nightspots is the **Ship Inn** (St. Lawrence Gap, Christ Church; ☎ 246-435-6961), a friendly pub with live local bands every night for dancing.

On the south coast, the hot spot is **The Boatyard** (Bay Street on Carlisle Bay five minutes from Bridgetown; ☎ 246-436-2622). It has a pub atmosphere with both a DJ and live band music. From happy hours (twice daily: 3 to 6 p.m. and 10 to 11 p.m.) until the wee hours, The Boatyard is packed with mingling locals and visitors.

The Rusty Pelican (the Careenage, Bridgetown, St. Michael; ☎ 246-436-7778) overlooks the bustling waterfront of the Careenage and features an easy-listening guitarist. Upstairs at Olives (Holetown, St. James; ☎ 246-432-2112) is a sophisticated watering hole that's open late.

Savoring a Taste of Barbados

Interestingly enough, there's a strong culinary connection between Barbados and South Carolina; both share a spicy West Indian flair. Of course, catches from the Atlantic and Caribbean figure heavily into the menus here. Flying fish, the national bird — oops, we mean fish — leaps onto menus all over the island. Sides of rice and peas are important, as are spicy stews. Fresh fruit finds its way into many dessert concoctions.

We urge you to dine at some swank spot at least once, and dressing up is the way they do it here. Shorts generally elicit raised eyebrows in the evenings.

Following British custom, your waiter does not present your final bill until you signal that you're ready for it.

Please refer to the Introduction of *Honeymoon Vacations For Dummies* for an explanation of our price categories.

Creating special memories

Our top choice for romance is **The Cliff** (Derricks, St. James; ☎ 246-432-1922; $$$), a dramatically positioned, open-air restaurant, built atop a 10-foot coral cliff adjacent to the Coconut Creek Hotel. Imaginative art accents the tiered dining terrace, and every candlelit table has a view of the sea. The artistry extends to the innovative menu, which offers excellent cuts of prime meat and fresh fish, creatively presented with nouvelle accents.

A popular spot for weddings, **The Emerald Palm** (Porters, St. James two miles north of Holetown; ☎ 246-422-4116; $$$) occupies a coral stone-and-tile country house on Barbados's fashionable West Coast amidst a tropical garden dotted with a trio of gazebos. Chef David Jones whips out zesty dishes packed with international and island flavors.

For a complete night out on the town, reserve a table at the ultra-happening **La Terra** (Baku Beach, Holetown; ☎ 246-432-1099; $$$$). Classical Italian plus fresh local ingredients equals Caribbean contemporary cuisine that deserves all the kudos. Downstairs, dance the night away at the Casbah. Since 1963, **Luigi's** (Dover Woods, St. Lawrence Gap, Christ Church; ☎ 246-428-9218; $), an open-air trattoria, has operated in a Greenland-white building built as a private house. Pizzas are offered as appetizers, along with more classic choices such as a half-dozen escargots or a Caesar salad. Many pastas are available in half-orders as starters.

Nico's Champagne Wine Bar & Restaurant (Derrick's, St. James; ☎ 246-432-6386; $), inspired by the wine bars of London, is set on a road that bisects some of Barbados's most expensive residential real estate. Housed in a 19th-century building that once served as headquarters for a thriving plantation, it does a big business from its air-conditioned bar area where a dozen wines are sold by the glass.

Enjoying spectacular water views

Dramatic lighting, alfresco dining on a terra-cotta terrace, and a cliffside setting overlooking the Caribbean (lit in the evenings) make **Carambola** (Derricks, St. James; ☎ 246-432-0832; $$$$) one of the island's most romantic. Carambola also serves some of the best food, with a dynamic menu of classic French and Caribbean cuisines — and a shot of Asian to add to the intrigue. One of the few Caribbean restaurants with a wine cellar, **Mango's by the Sea** (2 West End, Queen St., Speightstown, St. Peter; ☎ 246-422-0704; $$) is a romantic hideaway overlooking lapping waves. They buy the catch of the day directly from the fishermen's boats and employ a light touch with the seasonings. Two spectacular terraces offer one of the best settings to view the sunset with your favorite cocktail at **Mullins** (Mullins Bay, St. Peter; **246-422-1878**; $$$). Afterward, dine on the sophisticated menu in a friendly Caribbean atmosphere.

Hanging with the locals

The colorful **Angry Annie's** (First Street, Holetown, St. James; ☎ 246-432-2119; $$) serves up barbecued ribs and chicken, spicy curries, grilled fresh fish or juicy steaks, and the vegetarian favorite "Rasta pasta." When you tour the rugged east coast, plan to stop at **Bonito Beach Bar & Restaurant** (Coast Road, Bathsheba, St. Joseph; ☎ 246-433-9034; $) for a buffet lunch of wholesome West Indian home-cooking. Hidden behind lush foliage, **Brown Sugar** (Aquatic Gap, Bay Street, St. Michael; ☎ 246-426-7684; $$) is an alfresco restaurant in a turn-of-the-century Barbadian bungalow. From noon to 2:30, local businesspeople come for the three-course Planter's Buffet Luncheon — featuring dishes such as cou-cou and pepperpot stew. Owner-operators David and Darla Trotman live up to their promise that in **David's Place** (St. Lawrence Main Road, Worthing, Christ Church; ☎ 246-435-9755; $$) patrons sample "Bajan dining at its best." And **Tiny Ragamuffins** (1st Street, Holetown, St. James; ☎ 246-432-1295), the only restaurant on Barbados within an authentic chattel house (a small cottage in the traditional Bajan style), is funky, lively, and affordable. The menu offers seafood, perfectly broiled T-bone steaks, West Indian curries, and vegetarian dishes like Bajan stir-fried vegetables with noodles.

Looking for fun

The Boardwalk Grill (Baku Complex, Holetown, St. James; ☎ 246-432-2258) dishes out Caribbean fusion cuisine in a chic contemporary setting with lanterns glowing along the boardwalk. If hunger pangs strike while you're partying here, tapas and desserts are served here until 2 a.m. Owner-chef Larry Rogers and his wife Michelle turned a colorful old Bajan-style house into **Olives Bar & Bistro** (2nd Street,

Holetown, St. James; ☎ **246-432-2112; $$**). The street-level, air-conditioned dining room (where no smoking is allowed) spills out from its original coral-stone walls and scrubbed-pine floorboards into a pleasant garden. Mediterranean and Caribbean flavors enliven gourmet pizzas and salads.

Watching the sun go down

For comfort mixed with civility, linger over the excellent dinner on **The Terrace at Cobbler's Cove** (St. Peter; ☎ **246-422-2291; $$$$**). This idyllic restaurant has the elegance of an English country house. The food, however, is high art. An old coral stone house in the midst of tropical gardens at the water's edge has been reborn as **The Tides** (Holetown, St. James; ☎ **246-432-8356; $$$**), an innovative seafood restaurant touching on the best of Italian, French, Asian, and Caribbean cooking. Place yourself in the capable hands of French Chef Michel and his charming wife/hostess, Martine Gramaglia, who handle the kitchen and dining room of **Ile de France** (In the Settlers' Beach Hotel, Holetown, St. James (8 miles north of Bridgetown); ☎ **246-422-3245; $$**) with an enviable savoir-faire. Ingredients are either obtained fresh on Barbados or flown in from France or Martinique. At **Bellini's Trattoria** (Little Bay Hotel, St. Lawrence Gap, Christ Church; ☎ **246-435-7246; $$**), soft Italian music and waves gently lapping beneath the Mediterranean-style veranda set the stage for informal yet romantic dining. The cuisine is classic Northern Italian with a contemporary flair.

Settling into Barbados

Steeped in English tradition and a bit more straitlaced than some of its neighbors, Barbados has been giving the royal treatment to the wealthy and the famous for centuries. George Washington (and his younger brother) really did sleep here! And Barbados knows how to provide a rich experience for lovebirds.

The British influence remains quite strong, in part because Barbados is the favorite island retreat of most Brits and the retirement choice of many. Most hotels serve afternoon tea, cricket is the national pastime, and bar patrons are as likely to order a Pimm's Cup as a rum and Coke. Bajans, as islanders are known, partner British-style manners with a Caribbean friendliness and openness — a combination that makes travelers feel welcome and pampered.

Arriving in Barbados

Barbados is a sophisticated island, and handles arriving guests with grace and aplomb. You get the royal treatment from the moment you arrive. You won't find crinkly, sun-bleached tourist posters taped to the walls at the island's Grantley Adams International Airport; the thoroughly modern surroundings are clean and orderly, and the personnel smiling and helpful.

Airport renovations are underway, and by 2005, when the $70 million in improvements is completed, air-conditioning will be added to the customs, baggage claim, and departure lounge areas, and the airport's duty-free shopping area will double, to more than 10,000 square feet. In fact, the Barbados airport is one of the few we've encountered that has an **Arrivals Duty-Free Shop** (☎ 246-430-2150), so that you don't have to wait till you're in a hurry at the end of your trip to pick up some treasures.

Not to be outdone, the **Barbados Cruise Ship Terminal** was recently renovated to the tune of $6 million. Located on Bridgetown's waterfront, the terminal is now one of the Caribbean's finest.

Going through passport control and customs is often a snap. The neatly uniformed customs officials are crisply efficient and pleasant. If you're carrying valuables like expensive jewelry and camera equipment, don't forget to register those items with the customs officials as you're entering the country. Otherwise, you may find yourself paying an import duty on those items at the end of your stay.

The **Barbados Tourism Authority** operates welcome kiosks from 8 a.m. to 8 p.m. at both the airport, the cruise terminal, and in Bridgetown (☎ 246-428-5570, 246-426-1718, and 246-427-2623, respectively). And for those who arrive cash-poor, ATM machines are handily stationed at the kiosks.

About 500,000 people visit Barbados each year, and about half of them are cruise-ship passengers. Bridgetown's **Deep Water Harbour** is on the northwest side of Carlisle Bay, and as many as eight cruise ships can dock simultaneously at its cruise-ship terminal, whose interior features a faux island street scene with storefronts, brightly colored chattel houses, tropical flowers, benches, and pushcarts. Postal and banking facilities are also available at the terminal.

As soon as you clear customs and immigration, you can whip out your plastic at the port facility's 18 duty-free shops, 13 retailers, and dozens of vendors. You can also find car and bike rentals, a florist, dive shops, and a communications center with fax machines and telephones. Downtown Bridgetown is a half-mile (1 km) walk from the pier; a taxi costs about $3 each way.

Getting to your hotel

Presuming that your hotel knows your arrival time, a driver is usually there to greet you — holding a sign (discreetly, of course) for you at baggage claim. The resorts often provide free transport from and to the airport. Staying at one of the upscale resorts? The wheels sent to fetch you are elegant — Rolls Royce or BMW, anyone?

Airport taxis aren't metered, but drivers don't gouge here. A large sign at the airport announces the fixed rate for a taxi ride to each hotel or parish (district). You can readily pick out official taxis by the "Z" on their license plates. Rates are given in both Barbados and U.S. dollars: Count on about $28 to Speightstown, $20 to hotels on the west coast, and $10 to $13 to south coast locations.

Barbados is a good island on which to rent a car (see the next section for more details). To drive on the island, however, you need to purchase an international driver's license or Barbados driving permit, which you can pick up at a car-rental kiosk at the airport or a police station for $5.

Getting around Barbados

After you get to your hotel, you probably want to check out the island and its landscape. This section shares some sightseeing options.

Renting a car

Our favorite way to explore Barbados is by car. The island has good (though extremely narrow) roads, more than 800 miles of which are paved. The downside is that we have to remember to drive on the left, and most rental cars are tiny little putt-putts called mini mokes. For a little more money, you can rent a four-wheel-drive Jeep or a convertible, which is more our speed.

To rent a car you must have an international driver's license or Barbados driving permit, obtainable at the airport, police stations, and car-rental firms for $5 with a valid driver's license.

Oddly, none of the familiar major firms offer rentals on Barbados, but about 30 local agencies rent cars, Jeeps, or small open-air vehicles for $50 to $90 a day (or $250 to $325 a week), depending on the vehicle and whether it has air-conditioning. (We don't think air-conditioning is necessary.) The rental generally includes insurance. Rental companies provide pickup and delivery service, offer unlimited mileage, and accept major credit cards. Among the car-rental agencies in Barbados are the following: **Coconut Car Rentals** (St. Michael; ☎ **246-437-0297**); **Corbins Car Rentals** (St. Michael; ☎ **246-427-9531,** 246-426-8336, or 246- 426-8336); **Courtesy Rent-A-Car** (Grantley Adams International Airport; ☎ **246-431-4160**); **Drive-a-Matic** (St. James; ☎ **246-422-4000**); **National Car Rentals** (Lower Carlton, St. James; ☎ **246-422-0603**); P&S **Car Rentals** (Pleasant View, Cave Hill, St. Michael; ☎ **246-424-2052**); **Sunny Isle Motors** (Worthing; ☎ **246-435-7498**); and **Sunset Crest Rentals** (St. James; ☎ **246-432-2222**).

Taking a bus

Taking a bus in the Caribbean is *not* something we usually recommend, but Barbados is an exception among the islands. You can explore the island easily and cheaply by relying on a bus (☎ **246-436-6820**). The fare is 75 cents for any one destination. Public buses require exact change. Private coaches expect correct fare but are more flexible when it comes to making change. Blue buses with a yellow stripe are public; yellow buses with a blue stripe are private. Vans, white with a burgundy stripe, are also private. Just take whichever one comes along first, public or private; they are all equally nice.

Buses depart from Bridgetown several times a day between 6 a.m. and midnight. All travel about every 20 minutes along Highway 1 (St. James Road) and Highway 7 (South Coast Main Road), as well as inland routes, and are usually packed. Small signs posted on roadside poles — saying To CITY or OUT OF CITY, meaning the direction relative to Bridgetown — indicate the bus stops.

Flag down the bus with your hand, even if you're standing at the stop; drivers don't always stop automatically.

Hailing a taxi

Taxis aren't metered but operate according to fixed rates set by the government. They carry up to four passengers, and the fare may be shared. For short trips, the rate per mile should not exceed $1.50. Most taxi drivers are courteous and knowledgeable, and most narrate a tour at a fixed hourly rate of $17.50 for up to three people. Be sure to settle the rate before you start off and agree on whether the payment is to be in U.S. or Barbados dollars.

Fast Facts: Barbados

ATMs

About 50 automated teller machines (ATMs) are available 24 hours a day at bank branches, transportation centers, shopping centers, and other convenient spots throughout the island. ATMs dispense Barbados dollars, of course.

Banks

Major banks are the following: **Barbados National Bank** (☎ 246-431-5700); **Barclays Bank** (☎ 246-431-5151); the **Bank of Nova Scotia** (☎ 246- 431-3000); **Canadian Imperial Bank of Commerce** (☎ 246-426-0571); and **Royal Bank of Canada** (☎ 246-431-6700). All have main offices on Broad Street in Bridgetown, plus branches in Speightstown, Holetown, and various towns along the south coast. The Barbados National Bank has a branch at the airport, and Canadian Imperial Bank of Commerce has a branch at the cruise ship terminal.

Business Hours

Bridgetown offices and stores are open weekdays 8:30 a.m. to 5 p.m. and Saturdays 8:30 a.m. to 1 p.m. Out-of-town locations may stay open later. Some supermarkets are open daily 8 a.m. to 6 p.m. or later. Banks are open Monday to Thursday from 8 a.m. to 3 p.m. and Friday 8 a.m. to 5 p.m.

At the airport, the Barbados National Bank is open from 8 a.m. until the last plane leaves or arrives, seven days a week, even on holidays.

Credit Cards

Major credit cards and traveler's checks are widely accepted.

Currency Exchange

At press time, the Barbados dollar (Bds$1) was tied to the U.S. dollar at the rate of Bds$1.99 to US$1. U.S. dollars are readily accepted all over the island. Be sure that you know which currency you're dealing in when making a purchase. British pounds are not accepted; the currency exchange rate fluctuates daily and is posted at banks or online at www.xe.net/ucc/.

Departure Tax

At the airport, before leaving Barbados, each passenger must pay a departure tax of $12.50 (Bds$25), payable in either currency.

Doctors

Your hotel may have a list of doctors on call. The most often recommended are **Dr. J.D. Gibling** (☎ 246-432-1772) or **Dr. Ahmed Mohamad** (☎ 246-424-8236), both of whom pay house calls to patients unable or unwilling to leave their hotel rooms.

Electricity

Electric current on Barbados is 115/230 volts 50Hz. Hotels generally have adapters/ transformers for use by travelers from countries that operate on 220-volt current.

Emergencies

In an emergency, call ☎ 211. For an ambulance, call ☎ 511; in case of fire, call ☎ 311. To report a scuba diving accident, call **Divers' Alert Network (DAN)** at ☎ 246-684-8111 or 246-684-2948. The island also has a 24-hour hyperbaric chamber (Coast Guard Defence Force, St. Ann's Fort, Garrison, St. Michael; ☎ 246-427-8819; for nonemergencies, 246-436-6185).

Hospitals

If an accident or injury requires a hospital visit, you can choose from two modern facilities on Barbados: **Bayview Hospital,** St. Paul's Ave., Bayville, St. Michael (☎ 246- 436-5446) or **Queen Elizabeth Hospital,** Martindales Rd., St. Michael (☎ 246- 436-6450).

Information

The **Barbados Tourism Authority** is on Harbour Road in Bridgetown (☎ 246- 427-2623; Fax: 246-426-4080). Hours are 8:30 a.m. to 4:30 p.m. weekdays. Prior to your visit, contact the office of the **Barbados Tourism Authority** at 800 Second Avenue, 2nd Floor, New York, NY 10017 (☎ 888- BARBADOS; E-mail: btany@barbados. org; Internet: www.barbados.org). Another excellent resource is www. insandouts-barbados.com.

Language

The Queen's English is the official language and is spoken by everyone, everywhere. An amazing 98 percent literacy rate is a sign of the island's sophistication. The Bajan dialect is based on Afro-Caribbean rhythms tinged with an Irish or Scottish lilt.

Maps

You can pick up a free guide just about anywhere you travel across the island.

Pharmacies

Collins Pharmacy, Broad Street, Bridgetown (☎ 246-426-4515), open from 8 a.m. to 5 p.m.

Police

In an emergency, call ☎ 211; otherwise call ☎ 246-430-7100.

Post Office

The main post office, in Cheapside, Bridgetown, is open weekdays 7:30 a.m. to 5 p.m.; the Sherbourne Conference Center branch is open weekdays 8:15 a.m. to 4:30 p.m.; branches in each parish are open weekdays 8 a.m. to 3:15 p.m.

Safety

Although crime is not a major problem on Barbados, the U.S. State Department has reported an increase in crimes such as purse snatching, pickpocketing, armed robbery, and even sexual assault on women. Although Barbados is generally wealthy, poverty does exist here. Take normal precautions: Don't leave cash or valuables in your hotel room, beware of purse snatchers when walking, exercise caution when walking on the beach or visiting tourist attractions, and be wary of driving in isolated areas of Barbados.

When swimming, avoid stepping on black sea urchins (locally called "cobblers"), which have needle-sharp spines. They won't kill you, but their sting hurts terribly and prompts flu-like symptoms.

Beware of the little green apples that fall from the manchineel tree — they may look tempting, but they are poisonous to eat and toxic to the touch. Even taking shelter under the tree when it rains can give you blisters. Most manchineels are identified with signs. If you do come in contact with one, immediately wash your skin off with water, go to the nearest hotel, and have someone there phone for a physician.

Taxes

A 7.5 percent government tax is added to all hotel bills. A 15 percent VAT (value-added tax) is imposed on restaurant meals, admissions to attractions, and merchandise sales (other than dutyfree). Prices are often tax-inclusive; if not, the VAT is added to your bill.

Telephone

Direct-dialing to the U.S., Canada, and other countries is efficient, and the cost is reasonable, but always check with your hotel to see if a surcharge awaits on the final bill. To charge your overseas call on a major credit card without incurring a surcharge, dial ☎ 800-744-2000 from any phone.

All local calls are free if placed from private telephones. From pay phones, the charge is Bds25 cents for five minutes. Prepaid phone cards from Cable & Wireless (☎ 246-292-CARE), which can be used in pay phones throughout Barbados and other Caribbean islands, are sold at shops, tourist attractions, transportation centers, and other convenient outlets. For **MCI** dial ☎ 800-888-8000, for **Sprint** ☎ 800-877-4646, and for **AT&T** ☎ 800-872-2881.

For pre-paid Internet access while you're on the island, contact Sunbeach (☎ 246-430-1569, Internet: www.sunbeach.net) for its Insta-Net card.

Time Zone

Barbados operates on Atlantic Standard Time year-round (same as Eastern Daylight Time).

Tipping

A 10 percent service charge is usually added to hotel bills and restaurant checks in lieu of tipping. You can tip beyond the service charge to recognize extraordinary service. If no service charge is added, tip waiters 10 to 15 percent and maids $1 per room per day. Tip bellhops and airport porters $1 per bag. Taxi drivers expect a 10 percent tip.

Water

The water on the island is plentiful and pure, naturally filtered through 1,000 feet of pervious coral and safe to drink from the tap.

Weather Reports

The average temperature ranges between 80 to 85 degrees Farenheit (27 to 29 degrees Celsius) with an average annual rainfall of 60 inches. Call ☎ 246-976-2376 for current conditions.

Chapter 16

Honeymooning in Bermuda

By Echo & Kevin Garrett

- -

In This Chapter

▶ Finding the best honeymoon accommodations

▶ Discovering the fun and romance of Bermuda

▶ Uncovering all of the details

- -

*I*dyllic Bermuda's picturesque villages and pink beaches offer a safe and convenient isle with a distinctive British flair. It's long been popular with honeymooners from the East Coast. For many years, the tourist board successfully courted Ivy League schoolers and made Bermuda the cool place to hang during Spring Break. Then the moneyed set wound up spending their summer wedding honeymoons on Bermuda, too.

Bermuda's popularity with honeymooners has waned somewhat in the last few decades as the popularity of the Caribbean and Mexico has grown, thanks to their year-round tropical climates and the wider range of low-cost options. But this undeniably pretty place has its considerable charms and remains a reliable favorite, plus, it's a great choice if you're planning a destination wedding.

Figuring Out Where You Want to Stay

You can scarcely go wrong, choosing a place to stay on Bermuda. Most hotels and resorts offer access to lovely beaches. So the choice really depends more on what kind of amenities are important to you. We've selected our favorites from a wide variety of accommodations available on Bermuda to give you a taste of what's available.

Choosing Among Bermuda's Best Accommodations for Honeymooners

Bermuda offers a variety of accommodations: bed and breakfast inns, housekeeping cottages, clubs, cottage colonies, small hotels, and full-service resorts, though familiar U.S. chains aren't on this island. Special packages are available year-round.

Compare honeymoon, golf, and diving packages. The honeymoon package doesn't always give you the best deal.

Resorts that are members of the Bermuda Collection arrange for guests to dine at any of the other Collection properties including Cambridge Beaches, Stonington Beach Hotel, Pompano Beach Club, The Reefs, and Ariel Sands.

The rack rates listed in this section are in U.S. dollars and are for a standard double room during high season (mid-December to mid-April), unless otherwise noted. Lower rates are April-September, with the summer months being the priciest season and shoulder season.

Ariel Sands

$$$$ South Shore

The Ariel Sands, a 47-room cottage colony spilling down a manicured hillside overlooking a crescent beach, is owned by the island's Dill family, which includes actor Michael Douglas who ponied up $5 million for an extensive redo of the place. The designer took his inspiration from the classic film *That Touch of Mink* and the resort's 1940s hey-day using antique Chinese Chippendale furniture in rooms, soothing pastels with a few playful touches like clear pastic ottomans that look like beachballs, and simple natural beauty like shells. All rooms have porches, AC, TVs with cable, coffee machines, robes, safes, phones, radios, fridges, hairdryers, and breathtaking views of the ocean. Look for Douglas movie stills and family pictures in the bar where guests gather nightly. The clientele is a pleasant mix of Europeans and Americans, young honeymooners, and loyal returnees who spent their honeymoons here decades ago. The Nirvana Spa, though small, has a skilled staff who really knows how to pamper you. The food at the restaurant is delish, but we think the decor could still stand some more work. Don't go expecting a "wow" experience overall. Despite its glamorous owners, the Ariel Sands remains firmly rooted in the romance of yesteryear.

South Rd., Devonshire, Bermuda. ☎ *800-468-6610, 441-236-1010. Fax: 441-236-0087. E-mail:* ariel@ibl.bm. *Internet:* www.arielsands.com. *Rack rates: $240-$830 per couple per night including breakfast. AE, MC, V.*

Bermuda

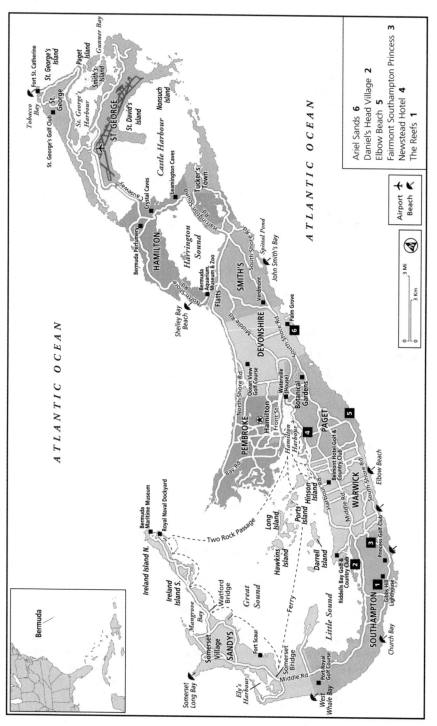

Ariel Sands **6**
Daniel's Head Village **2**
Elbow Beach **5**
Fairmont Southampton Princess **3**
Newstead Hotel **4**
The Reefs **1**

Airport ✈
Beach ⚓

ATLANTIC OCEAN

ATLANTIC OCEAN

Fort St. Catherine
St. George's Island
Paget Island
Smith's Island
Gunner Bay
Tobacco Bay
St. George's Golf Club
St. George
St. George's Harbour
ST. GEORGE
St. David's Island
Nonsuch Island
Castle Harbour
Kemasne
Crystal Caves
Leamington Caves
Tucker's Town
Bermuda Perfumery
HAMILTON
Harrington Sound
Harrington Rd.
South Shore Rd.
Spittal Pond
John Smith's Bay
North Shore Rd.
Bermuda Aquarium, Museum & Zoo
Flatts
Verdmont
SMITH'S
Shelley Bay Beach
Middle Rd.
DEVONSHIRE
Palm Grove
6
Ocean View Golf Course
North Shore Rd.
Waterville (House)
Botanical Gardens
South Shore Rd.
PAGET
Hamilton
Front St.
PEMBROKE
Hamilton Harbour
4
5
Bay Rd.
Belmont Hotel Golf & Country Club
Harbour Rd.
Hinson Island
WARWICK
Middle Rd.
South Shore Rd.
Elbow Beach
Bermuda Maritime Museum
Royal Naval Dockyard
Ireland Island N.
Two Rock Passage
Long Island
Ports Island
Darrell Island
Hawkins Island
Princess Golf Club
Riddells Bay Golf & Country Club
3
2
Ferry
Little Sound
1
Gibbs Hill Lighthouse
SOUTHAMPTON
Ireland Island S.
Great Sound
Watford Bridge
Mangrove Bay
Somerset Village
SANDYS
Fort Scaur
Somerset Bridge
Port Royal Golf Course
Middle Rd.
Church Bay
Somerset Long Bay
Ely's Harbour
West Whale Bay

Bermuda

0   3 MI
0   3 Km

Daniel's Head Village

$$ Daniel's Head, Sandys

We aren't usually bowled over by eco-resorts, but this one is so well-executed that we dub it the most exciting development on Bermuda in many years. A small collection of 16-by-16 "tent" cottages are built on stilts over the shallow teal waters of the ocean. Cutouts in the floors give you a window on what lies beneath, and each cottage has wrap-around windows as well as French doors opening to your private balcony. In other words, you're cocooned by Mother Nature and each other, but you also have a queen-size bed with soft linens and a private bath with large shower. The staff here is well-versed on Bermuda's unique flora and fauna and happily helps you immerse yourself. A pool, tennis courts, bikes, and a watersports center (but no noisy jet skis) round out the offerings. Most guests eat their three squares at the good onsite restaurant where the chef emphasizes organically grown fare. You're only a half-hour ferry ride away from Hamilton, though you may feel a world away.

4 Daniel's Head Lane, Sandys MABX. ☎ *888-468-6846, 877-418-1723, or 441-234-4272. Fax: 441-234-4270. E-mail:* info@danielsheadvillage.com. *Internet:* www.danielsheadvillage.com. *Rack rates: $130-$250 per cottage. Several packages are available for honeymooners. AE, MC, V.*

Elbow Beach

$$$$$ South Shore

If you're willing to break the bank, here's where we'd do it on Bermuda. From the time you roll up to this island fantasy — originally built in 1908 in traditional Bermudian pastel-painted limestone with white-tiered "cake-icing" roofs, and situated on a half-mile of the best beach on the island — you know that you're in for a dazzling time. This elegant European-style resort, on 55 breathtakingly landscaped acres, underwent a $55 million redo, and it looks like every dollar was thoughtfully spent. The room decor throughout the 250 accommodations, about half of which are in classic Bermudian cottage colonies, is tasteful island chic with every creature comfort you can imagine. Besides the gorgeous pool, Elbow Beach has five new plexipave tennis courts, a dive shop, guaranteed tee-times at a nearby golf course, and 24-hour room service. The villas, near the beach, offer the utmost in privacy despite being in the middle of the property. Combine all of this luxury with the kind of snap-to-service you expect in a grand hotel and you're in heaven.

60 South Shore Rd., Paget PG04. ☎ *800-223-7434, 441-236-35-35. Fax: 441-236-8043. E-mail:* elbowreservations@ibl.bm. *Internet:* www.elbowbch.com. *Rack rates: $455-$635, suites $1,200-$4,000. "Romance on the Isle" three-night package includes accommodations, champagne upon arrival, relaxing massage for two, candlelight dinner in room, use of moped, personal guided taxi tour, deluxe picnic lunch, Bermuda picture book, daily breakfast, and roundtrip airport transfers. Rates are $2,644 from April 11 through Oct. 31, 2001. AE, MC, V.*

Fairmont Southampton Princess
$$$$$ Southampton

Standing sentry on Bermuda's highest point and pretty-in-pink is the Grand Dame of resorts, surrounded by gardens and a golf course with sweeping views of the Great Sound, south shore, or golf course. The elegant lobby — all cool marble and chandeliers with soaring ceilings — sets the stage, and at nighttime it springs to life with jazz players and other entertainers. Frequent shuttles whisk guests down the hill to the private beach club, which has an indoor pool with whirlpool jets, an outdoor pool, tennis and golf pro shops, a fitness center with spa services, and more. The rooms are pleasant and well done in a classic English style. This resort is a classic, but some may find it too large for their tastes, and we wish it had more island charm.

101 South Shore Rd., Southampton SN02. ☎ **800-441-1414** *or 441-238-8000. Fax: 441-238-8968. E-mail:* southampton@fairmont.com. *Internet:* www.fairmont. com. *Rack rates : $369-$429, suites $839-$3,409. AE, DC, MC, V.*

Newstead Hotel
$$$ Harbour Road, Paget

Psssst. Here's Bermuda's best-kept secret. The management, which came here from Elbow Beach, brings high-service standards to this beautiful Colonial Bermudian manor house, which boasts terraced gardens overlooking the harbour and the city lights of Hamilton. You feel transported to another place and time at this hotel, which has been tastefully restored to its former glory. The owner has lovingly decorated the 38 individual rooms and six suites with Bermudian and European antiques. The suites have spacious, private terraces. The polished hardwood floors have that patina that only comes with age. Oriental rugs dampen any noise. At Newstead, couples can enjoy a fragrant welcome in a honeymoon suite strewn with rose petals or a sonorous entrance to the sound of Scottish pipers. The grounds are perfect for small weddings. Its new restaurant, the Rock Grill, provided us with one our tastiest dinners on our most recent visit. Shopping in Hamilton is a ten-minute ferry ride away. A Cybex gym, pool, spa, beauty salon, putting green, private dock with facilities for four yachts, and tennis are onsite.

27 Harbour Rd., Paget PG02. ☎ **800-468-4111** *or 441-236-6060. Fax: 441-236-7454. E-mail:* reservations@newsteadhotel.com. *Internet:* www.newstead hotel.com. *Rack rates: $295-$355; suites $375-$435. AE, MC, V.*

The Reefs
$$$$$ Southampton

Built around the ruins of a 1680s farmhouse on the southwest coast and built for romance, this friendly and dramatically-situated beach resort clings to a cliff overlooking its own private pink sand beach and the turquoise waters surrounding Bermuda. The onsite seaside restaurant, Coconuts, is *tres romantique*. The rates include spacious accommodations, breakfast, afternoon tea and dinner daily, and complimentary rum swizzle and in-room beverages on guests' arrival. A local daily newspaper and the weekly manager's party are also included. In-room amenities include a DVD player, microwave, TV, VCR, coffeemaker, refrigerator, bathrobes, hairdryer, in-room safe, iron and board, umbrella, and toiletries. The Reefs offers active guests two tennis courts including racquets and balls; a fitness center featuring stair climbers, bikes, treadmill, weights, and Cybex exercise equipment; complimentary beach towels and chairs; snorkeling equipment; kayaks with guided tours of the South Shore; a shuffleboard court; and croquet facilities. The welcoming staff makes you feel right at home; some have been with the resort since it opened its doors in 1947. This intimate hotel features 67 guest rooms, seven Cottage Suites (all have outdoor hot tubs on private patios), and one Cottage, each offering picturesque views of the ocean.

56 South Shore Rd., Southampton SN02. ☎ *441-238-0222. For reservations in the U.S. and Canada contact: Island Resorts Reservations, Ltd.* ☎ *800-742-2008. Fax: 441-238-8372. E-mail:* reefsbda@ibl.bm. *Internet:* www.TheReefs.com. *Rack rates: $298–$606. AE, MC, V.*

Enjoying Your Honeymoon in Bermuda

Strait-laced Bermuda gets extra points for its movie-set good looks. You two can find plenty of fun things to do and see here, and the island is undeniably romantic. However, everything on Bermuda is pricey, so don't expect any bargains unless you're willing to go during the winter months, which can be pretty chilly.

Bermuda is known for its golf and for wreck diving. Beyond that, the main happenings are exploring the island's historic towns, pretty-in-pink beaches, gardens, history, and watersports like sailing and fishing. Gone are the days when the nightlife on this island was cranking. You are hard-pressed to find live music except at a few hotels during the high season.

Bermuda's pink beaches — the surf pounding the pink coral reefs that surround the island — have enchanted beachgoers for years with their blush, which ranges in color from a champagne to strawberry sorbet. In many spots, you find the silvery blue and teal waters crystal clear — ideal for snorkeling hand-in-hand — with visibility exceeding 100 feet.

Exploring the depths

Explore a 499-foot Spanish luxury liner that went down in 1913, or dive a stacked wreck! More than 400 wrecks lurk beneath Bermuda's azure seas. Most major resorts have a dive operator, or you can try **Blue Water Divers Co. Ltd.** (☎ **441-234-1034;** Fax: 441-232-3670; Internet: www.divebermuda.com), the island's oldest operation.

Divers and those who've never been down under the deep blue enjoy **Bermuda Underwater Exploration Institute** (East Broadway, east of Hamilton; ☎ **441-292-7219;** Internet: www.buei.org; open Monday through Saturday, 9 a.m. to 4:30 p.m.). Take a few hours to discover the history of underwater exploration with the excellent exhibits. You also find one of the world's finest shell collections here.

Another good place to learn more about the local marine life is the small but well-executed **Bermuda Aquarium, Museum & Zoo** (☎ **441-293-2727;** $10 admission, open daily 9 a.m. to 5 p.m.). The North Rock Exhibit is a 140,000 gallon tank with a large man-made coral that features a variety of reef inhabitants including sharks. A new addition is a small area devoted to animals from the Caribbean.

Hitting the links

Bermuda has more golf courses per square mile than any other country in the world. The best courses are **Mid Ocean Club, Port Royal Golf Course,** and **Riddells Bay Golf & Country Club.** Reserve a tee-time from January to March at select courses up to two months in advance by calling ☎ **800-BERMUDA.**

Walking hand-in-hand

For a languid stroll through Bermuda, wander along the **Railway Trail,** a secluded 18-mile trail that runs the length of the island along the route of the former Bermuda Railway. Yes, this island once had a choo-choo. The path provides stunning backdrops of harbor and bay views, as well as colorful cottages and lush palmetto forests.

As you walk around the island, take note of Bermuda's moongates, which are made for lovers. Legend has it that couples who kiss under these coral and stone semi-circles are assured good fortune and happiness. Couples can find these amorous arches at most hotels and parks. A great spot for a picnic is in the elegant **Botanical Gardens,** showcasing more than 1,000 of the island's semi-tropical flora. A free tour commences every day, except on holidays, at 10:30 a.m. The Premier's Camden House, built around 1775, is the centerpiece and is open for viewing Tues and Friday, noon-2 p.m.

In Bermuda, even the flora and fauna pay tribute to romance. For example, the island's longtail bird flies across the ocean to mate in Bermuda every year. Fireworms do their thing in summer months, setting the sea aglow with a green bioluminescence. Island-grown jasmine, lily, and oleander make scintillating scents at the **Bermuda Perfumery** (North Shore and Harrington Sound roads, Bailey's Bay; ☎ 441-293-0627; open Monday through Saturday, 9:15 a.m. to 5 p.m. and from April through November Sunday 10 a.m. to 4 p.m.) where you can get a free tour. We especially like the tea garden.

Tour one of Bermuda's 110 underground wonderlands — the best is **Crystal Caves** (Bailey's Bay; ☎ 441-293-0640; admission $8.50), located near the Bermuda Perfumery.

Time travel in St. Georges

Reserve one afternoon for exploring **St. Georges,** Bermuda's historic former capital. The Old Town Tour starts every day at the town square at 10:30 a.m. and lasts an hour. You also find some interesting shops and a few tiny but intriguing museums there.

Pay the $5 to get yourself into all three small museums on the walking tour. The film on Bermuda's history gives a good overview.

Stop by **Ceramica Bermuda** (20 Duke of York Street East, St. Georges; ☎ 441-297-0901) for some of the few bargains on the island. We got a beautiful hand-painted pot from Spain for $14.

Another store worth checking out is the **Cracker Box** (York Street, St. Georges; ☎ 441-297-1205), which has the most beautiful shells for sale that we've seen in our travels, and the prices are reasonable.

Heading to the lighthouse

From the top of **Gibbs Hill Lighthouse** (Lighthouse Road, off South Shore Road, Southhampton; admission $2.50, open daily 9 a.m. to 4:30 p.m.), presiding 362 feet above the sea, lovers take in sweeping vistas of Bermuda's many islets. The second cast-iron lighthouse ever built, the structure also houses an interesting history of Bermuda's seafaring past. After the visit, couples can pause for some of the island's best tea at the Lighthouse Tea Room.

Indulging at a spa

Couples can recreate that special feeling time and time again after a couple's massage lesson from **BerSalon Spas of Bermuda.** Offered at either of their **Cambridge Beaches** (☎ 441-234-3636) or **Sonesta Beach Resort** (☎ 441-238-1226) locations, the Massage Duet features a certified instructor and an hour-long lesson for $105.

Dining in Bermuda

From simple and inexpensive to elegant and specialty dining, Bermuda has more than 150 restaurants. Although some restaurants vary, most open at 11 a.m. weekdays, noon Saturdays.

Creating special memories

Jackets are required but worth the trouble to dine at the 321-year-old landmark, **The Waterlot Inn** (Jew's Bay, Fairmont Southampton Princess; ☎ 441-238-2555; $$$$), right on the water. An elaborate wine list combined with dancing to the Joe Wylie Trio, plus a classically elegant menu, add up to an evening to remember.

Beachfront diners can experience the best of Bermuda — gourmet dining, spectacular sunsets, and gracious service — while playing footsie barefoot in the island's famous pink sands at **Coconuts at The Reefs** (at The Reefs, Southampton; ☎ 441-238-0222; $$$$). Reserve ahead and let them know that you're honeymooners. The in-crowd has discovered the lovely Mediterranean-style courtyard at **Fresco's Restaurant & Wine Bar** (Chancery Lane off Front Street and Reid Street in Hamilton; ☎ 441-295-5058; $$$), which has a terrific happy hour and Hamilton's widest selection of wines. The Mediterranean menu is worth sticking around for, too.

Looking for a local favorite

The bounty of Bermuda's water takes centerstage at the loft-like **Sea-horse Grill** (Elbow Beach; ☎ 441-236-3535; $$$$), where the award-winning chef turns out what has been crowned "new Bermudan cuisine."

For a Dark n' Stormy (Bermuda's signature drink featuring its famed black rum and ginger beer) on a balcony overlooking Hamilton Harbour, head to **The Pickled Onion** (53 Front Street, Hamilton; ☎ 441-295-2263; $$). Live music starts at 9:30 p.m. nightly and rocks till 1 a.m., but there's no cover charge.

The Newstead Hotel (Harbour Rd.; ☎ 441-236-6060; $$$), which has terraced tropical gardens overlooking the Harbour and Hamilton beyond, has become known for its sumptuous Sunday Brunch.

Settling in to Bermuda

Bermuda — with its sea-shell pink beaches, postcard-perfect pastel houses, and tidy English gardens, all just 650 miles east of North Carolina — offers nirvana for honeymooners seeking a genteel getaway close to home. Seen from the air, Bermuda resembles a fishhook. It actually consists of 181 named islands and islets. Abundant coral reefs and the resulting 400 offshore shipwrecks have earned this British colony the nickname "Isle of Devils" and made it a diver's paradise. Bermuda has captivated lovers for generations with its quirky history and quaint way of life on this small, prosperous island.

Arriving in Bermuda

Contrary to popular belief, Bermuda is not in the Caribbean. In fact it's almost 1,000 miles from the closest place in that body of water: Nassau, Bahamas. It's closer to North Carolina, Cape Hatteras, but once you see the teal blue waters surrounding Bermuda's pale pink beaches, you can understand why that misconception persists. You fly over the waters of the Atlantic for awhile to reach it. Your flight time is 1½ hours from Atlanta, 2 hours from New York City, 9½ hours from Los Angeles, 7½ hours from Chicago, and 6 hours from Dallas to neat-as-a-pin **Bermuda International Airport.**

You are quickly and efficiently processed through Customs and Immigration. After all, the small island — population 60,000 — is used to visitors, with more than half a million folks dropping in each year. Customs requires proof of citizenship, and a valid passport is the preferred document. However, a birth certificate with photographic identification is acceptable.

When entering this island, you are asked to declare any prescription drugs — even birth control bills — which must be in their original containers. You also need the original prescription from your doctor along with a note about why you take the medication. We know, we know . . . but that's the rule.

Getting to your accommodations

You don't have much choice on Bermuda. To get to where you're staying, you can either take a bus or a taxi. Only residents are allowed to have a car — one car per household because of environmental concerns — on this British island. There are no rental cars. Check with your hotel in advance because transportation may be included in your honeymoon package. The buses take a little longer (at least a 30 minute trip to most resorts), but depending on where you stay, you can save some money by taking the bus. But we suggest just paying the extra fare to have your own taxi.

Getting around Bermuda

Mopeds and scooters, bicycles, taxis, buses, ferries, and horse-drawn carriages are the way to go on Bermuda.

Scooter rentals are available at many resorts and other outlets throughout Bermuda. Rates vary according to size (single or double seats) and the duration of rental. One-day rental on a single seater runs about $35; for a double, $44. You get a helmet, locks, storage area, and lessons. No license is required, but you must be 16 years old to drive.

Remember to drive on the left — British-style. Wear your helmets or expect a ticket. Road rash — meaning wiping out or scraping against the rock walls lining the narrow road ways — is frighteningly common. If you do decide to rent a scooter or moped, exercise extreme caution and obey the strict speed limits (less than 20 miles per hour throughout the island; signs say 35, but that translates to 20 miles per hour in our lingo). We'd hate for you to spend some of your precious time together in Bermuda's hospital.

Hiring a taxi

All fares are on government-regulated meters, which should read $3.12 at the start of the journey, then $4.80 after the first mile. Each subsequent mile is $1.68. There are surcharges between midnight and 6 a.m. and on Sundays, as well as for packages and suitcases. Call ☎ **441-295-4141** or hail a cab with its yellow light on.

Going by ferry or bus

Ferries take a little longer to get from place to place, but they are more scenic. All the tourist board offices and hotels have ferry and bus schedules. Ask the concierge to help you figure out the best route.

Buses run from major hotels and islandwide into Hamilton from early morning until late a night. The system is divided into zones: $4 allows you to pass through all 14 zones, but you must have exact change. For information call ☎ **441-292-3854**.

Ferries ply between Hamilton and the central and western parishes (like our counties). Adult fares are $4 each way to the West End and $2.50 on the Paget/Warwick routes. Rental bikes can be taken on the West End ferry for an additional $4. For information call ☎ **441-295-4506**.

Fast Fact: Bermuda

ATMs

The Bank of Bermuda and the Bank of Butterfield have ATMs located island-wide for MasterCard, Visa, Cirrus, and Plus cash advances, most of which are available 24-hours-a-day.

Banks

Bank hours are generally Monday through Thursday from 9 a.m. to 3 p.m. and Friday 9 a.m. to 4:30 p.m. A handful have Saturday hours (9 a.m. to noon). Walk-up windows open at 8:30 a.m. on weekdays.

Credit Cards

Credit cards are widely accepted in Bermuda. VISA and MasterCard are the cards of choice at most local businesses, although American Express and, to a lesser extent, Diners Club are also popular.

Currency Exchange

The Bermuda Dollar (BD$) is divided into 100 cents and is pegged, through gold, to the U.S. dollar. The U.S. dollar is accepted by all merchants.

Doctors

Doctors in Bermuda are English-speaking. General physicians can be contacted at their offices Monday through Friday 9 a.m. through 5 p.m.

Electricity

110 volts; 60 cycles AC. Adapters are necessary for United Kingdom and European appliances.

Emergencies

For ambulance, fire, police and marine rescue dial ☎ **911.**

Hospitals

King Edward VII Memorial Hospital is Bermuda's first-class general hospital.

Information

Bermuda Department of Tourism, ☎ 1-800-BERMUDA; Internet: www. bermudatourism.com.

Language

English is the official language.

Maps

The Bermuda Department Tourism produces a pocket-size Handy Reference Map, a full-color reference map that includes roads, places of interest, accommodations, towns, golf courses, banks, Visitors' Service Bureau locations, gas stations, bus stops, and transportation information. For maps, brochures, weekly event updates, bus schedules, and more, visit Visitors Bureaus on Front Street (Hamilton), The Royal Naval Dockyard, Somerset Road (Sandy's Parish), King's Square (St. Georges), and Bermuda International Airport.

Newspapers/Magazines

Major daily U.S. and Canadian newspapers are normally available at the larger hotels and in leading drug stores on the afternoon of the day of publication. The Bermuda newspapers — *The Royal Gazette, The Mid-Ocean News,* and *Bermuda Sun* — carry both local and international news and stock reports.

Pharmacies

Pharmacies (listed under "Drug Stores" in the Yellow Pages) are located throughout the island, but pharmacists cannot dispense foreign prescriptions. In an emergency, a local doctor will have to see you and provide a prescription.

Post Office

The main post office (☎ 441-297-7893) is at 56 Church Street, Hamilton, and is open 8 a.m. to 5 p.m. Monday to Friday and 8 a.m. to noon on Saturday.

Safety

Bermuda has a low crime rate, and incidents of violent crime are infrequent. However, take normal common sense precautions.

Store Hours

9 a.m. to 5 p.m. Monday through Saturday. Closed on legal holidays. Some stores vary. Visitors from the U.S. may make duty-free purchases up to $400 after 48 hours. Most shops can pack your breakable purchases for travel or overseas shipping.

Tax

Hotel tax and service charge is 7.25 percent.

Telephone

Telephone charges may be reversed. Direct dialing is possible to and from Bermuda world-wide. AT&T Calling Cards are accepted. You dial direct to Bermuda, using 1 plus Bermuda's area code (441) followed by the 7 digit number.

Time Zone

Bermuda is on Atlantic Time, which places the islands one hour ahead of Eastern Standard Time.

Tipping

In cases where the gratuity is not included in the bill, 15 percent is the generally accepted amount for most services. A large number of guest houses add a percentage or set amount per person, per day in lieu of tips to the accommodations bill.

Water

Bermuda depends almost entirely upon rain-water for its water supply, which is caught on the white roofs and water catches and stored in individual underground tanks.

However, some of the larger hotels do operate desalination plants, there is a system of wells providing those who want it with semi-fresh water for sanitary purposes. The rain-water used for drinking, cooking, washing, and so on is fresh and pure, and there are seldom ill effects or upsets caused by drinking it. There are no factories to create air pollution, and as the island is so small, the prevailing winds carry any dust and impurities out to sea.

Weather and Surf Reports

Bermuda is a semitropical island about 650 miles (1046 kilometers) east of Cape Hatteras, North Carolina. The Gulf Stream, which flows between Bermuda and the North American continent, provides the island with two seasons, spring and summer, neither being too hot or too cold. Indeed, it has a year-round mild semitropical climate with temperatures ranging from 68 to 84 degrees. Relative humidity ranges from 71 to 84 percent. Average annual rainfall is 57.6 inches. Summer water temperatures reach 85°F. Dial 977 for the weather report.

Chapter 17

Honeymooning in Grand Cayman

By Echo & Kevin Garrett

● ●

In This Chapter

▶ Finding the best honeymoon accommodations

▶ Discovering the fun and romance of Grand Cayman

▶ Considering an island wedding

▶ Uncovering all the details

● ●

Grand Cayman is a curious place. Although tourism is huge here, and its famous Seven Mile Beach (like Aruba's hotel strip) features a lineup of every type of hotel and condo imaginable, the island still manages to exude a certain laid-back charm. Maybe that's because its residents by-and-large have the security of wealth — they're glad you're vacationing here, but nobody's desperate for your money. In fact, Grand Cayman's wealth isn't based just on tourism — it's built on banking.

Grand Cayman is a peaceful, safe, and upscale island that takes all the work out of your honeymoon if you just want to hang at the beach or swim with the fish. That's why the island has become a favorite with honeymooners looking to de-stress after the wedding. Be forewarned, though: The advice to take half as many clothes as you think you need and twice as much money definitely applies to Grand Cayman.

Despite its British ways, Grand Cayman has veered toward being too Americanized for some tastes. In recent years, many fast-food chains, cutesy little boutiques in restored buildings in George Town (the capital), and homogenized timeshares have increased the Florida-come-to-the Caribbean look. You can find local color, thanks to some of the quirky artists who live on the island, but you have to look for it.

The Cayman Islands don't have a predominance of mega all-inclusives. Traditionally, the islands have also lacked ultra deluxe, five-star resorts, but with **The Ritz-Carlton, Grand Cayman,** being built to the tune of $350 million, the tide is finally expected to turn. Until it opens in 2002, if you're looking to honeymoon in the lap of luxury, head to Barbados, Jamaica, St. Thomas, or Puerto Rico or one of the resorts in Chapter 36.

Figuring Out Where to Stay

As with Aruba, almost all 50 of Grand Cayman's hotels and condos are crowded along the island's famous Seven Mile Beach. From here, you have broad dining options; you can walk to town from many resorts.

Hard-core divers like to stay on the East End, near Grand Cayman's best diving. If you want to skip the crowds and Cayman Cowboys (as the dive operators who pack people in are derisively called), head to the much more secluded north side, which also offers good diving. The **Grand Caymanian Beach Club & Resort** (Safehaven/Crystal Harbor; ☎ 345-949-3100; Fax: 345-949-3161; Internet www.grandcaymanian.ky), an all-suite property, opened in March 2000. The Grand Caymanian is the only resort on the North Sound and is near both Stingray City and Rum Point.

Food is one of your bigger expenses when you vacation on Grand Cayman; restaurants here charge top dollar, compared with costs on other Caribbean islands. So that you don't have to eat out all the time, we recommend booking into a resort with a meal plan. But make sure that the resort has more than one good restaurant.

If you don't mind making your own meals on your honeymoon, you can save a bundle by renting a condo or guesthouse with a kitchen. You can easily spend as much on one dinner out in Grand Cayman as it would take to stock up enough groceries for a week. Two well-stocked grocery stores are **Hurley's Supermarket** (in Red Bay just beyond the intersection of Crewe Road and South Sound Road), which has 30,000 square feet with a bakery, deli, and sandwich and salad bar, and **Fosters Food Fair** (The Strand on Seven Mile Beach and at the Airport).

Remember that you can't bring in any fresh fruit or vegetables from outside the island. Also, request an advance list from management detailing what's already stocked in the kitchen, so you don't waste precious suitcase room on basics (such as spices). You must have a rental car to haul the groceries if you decide to prepare food on your own.

Choosing Among Grand Cayman's Best Accommodations for Honeymooners

Because Grand Cayman doesn't have a lot of rowdy nightlife, shopping, or even much sightseeing, you may spend much of your time around the property in which you are staying. Therefore, the amenities and what your room, pool, and particular stretch of beach are like are very important.

The rack rates we list are in U.S. dollars and are for a standard double room during high season (mid-December to mid-April), unless otherwise noted. Lower rates are often available during the off-season and shoulder season.

Please refer to the Introduction of *Honeymoon Vacations For Dummies* for an explanation of our price categories.

The Avalon

$$$$ **Seven Mile Beach**

The Avalon graces prime real estate on Seven Mile Beach and is one of the better condo options on Grand Cayman. We like the oversized tub and separate shower in the spacious baths, as well as the tropical decor of the roomy units. It also has daily maid service except on Tuesdays. The handsome property consists of 27 three-bedroom/three-bathroom units (15 of which can be rented). All are located right on the Caribbean. Only a short distance from restaurants and a five-minute drive from George Town, the Avalon has style that's disappointingly rare on Grand Cayman. Each condo has a fully equipped open kitchen and a large, screened lanai overlooking the glorious beach. Fitness buffs are bound to be pleased with the tennis court, fitness center, swimming pool, and hot tub.

West Bay Road (P.O. Box 31236), Grand Cayman, BWI. ☎ **345-945-4171.** *Fax: 345-945-4189. Rack rates: $650. Book through Four Seasons Villas for air discounts* ☎ **800-338-0474.** *AE, MC, V.*

Grand Cayman Marriott Beach Resort

$$$$$ **Seven Mile Beach**

The oversized adjoining rooms draw families to this five-story property (recently awarded Four Diamonds) just one mile from George Town — but the Grand Cayman Marriott is still a great place for honeymooners. The airy, marble lobby opens onto a plant-filled courtyard. Views are either of the ocean or the garden courtyard. Keep in mind that you can have an "ocean view" without being ocean front — our room's view gave us a mere sliver of the water. Double-check when making reservations if a view is important to you. All the rooms have large balconies, and most are perfectly angled to maximize the promised seaside view.

Grand Cayman Island

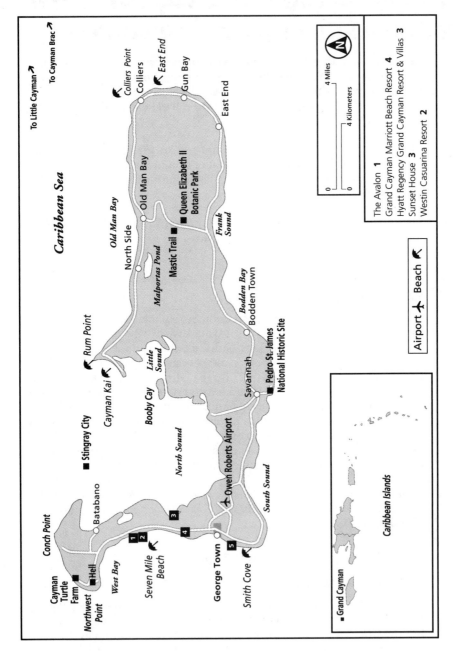

The Avalon 1
Grand Cayman Marriott Beach Resort 4
Hyatt Regency Grand Cayman Resort & Villas 3
Sunset House 3
Westin Casuarina Resort 2

Airport ✈   Beach ↙

Caribbean Sea

4 Miles

4 Kilometers

N

To Little Cayman ↗
To Cayman Brac ↗

Colliers Point
Colliers
East End ↙
Gun Bay
East End

Old Man Bay
North Side
Old Man Bay
Queen Elizabeth II
Botanic Park
Frank Sound
Mastic Trail ■
Malportas Pond

Rum Point ↙
Cayman Kai ↙
Stingray City ■
Little Sound
Booby Cay
Bodden Bay
Bodden Town
Savannah
Pedro St. James
National Historic Site

Conch Point
Batabano
North Sound
Owen Roberts Airport ✈
South Sound

Cayman Turtle Farm ■
Hell ■
West Bay
Northwest Point
Seven Mile Beach ↙
George Town
Smith Cove

Grand Cayman

Caribbean Islands

The resort offers a variety of wedding packages and settings. Couples may chose between the Turtle Courtyard, the Beach Front, or the Ballroom for their special day. The Marriott's "Simply Lovely" package for $1,000 includes the services of a wedding officer who completes the necessary applications, obtains a wedding license, and performs the wedding ceremony. Also included are a photographer, a photo album, and a witness to the ceremony. The "Turtledove Love" package for $1,125 includes all the amenities of the "Simply Lovely" package plus a bridal bouquet, groom's boutonniere, and bottle of champagne. For $1,500, the "Love Divine" package adds a five-course meal to the aforementioned services. A wedding cake, salon and spa services, themed receptions for groups, and chartered sunset sails are all available at extra cost.

Seven Mile Beach (P.O. Box 30371), Grand Cayman, BWI. ☎ *800-228-9290 or 345-949-0088. Fax: 345-949-0288. E-mail: marriott@candw.ky. Rack rates: $267-$394 double. AE, DISC, DC, MC, V.*

Hyatt Regency Grand Cayman Resort & Villas

$$$$$ **Seven Mile Beach**

Hugging one of the prime spots on famed Seven Mile Beach and housed in grand, low-slung British Colonial-style buildings amid beautifully landscaped gardens, this Hyatt Regency radiates elegance. We put it in our Top 10 for its great beach location, over-the-top watersports (the top-notch Red Sail Sports even caddies your gear for you), fantasy-inducing water oasis (seven pools, rooftop sundeck, a footbridge, and two swim-up gazebo bars), new full-service spa (the only one on Grand Cayman), two health clubs, and breathtaking Britannia Golf Club with a Jack Nicklaus-designed nine-hole course. Most of the accommodations here are across the street from the beach. But a covered walkway equipped with an elevator on either side over the road eliminates any concern about making it across with a stroller or wheelchair. The resort is quite large, with 289 units.

Its honeymoon package for $1,000 includes the help of an on-site wedding consultant, a marriage officer, the marriage license and documentation, plus a bridal bouquet, boutonniere, and wedding cake. A four day/three night honeymoon package is available from $1,050 (garden-view room) per couple or from $2,310 for eight days/seven nights, which includes an island-view room, a bottle of champagne, Britannia honeymoon breakfast for two delivered to your room, Jeep rental for one day, a sunset cruise aboard a 65-foot catamaran, and a couple's massage.

West Bay Road (P.O. Box 1588), Grand Cayman, BWI. ☎ *888-591-1234 or 345-949-1234. Fax: 345-949-8528. E-mail:* hyatt@candw.kyor. *Internet:* www.hyatt.com *or* www.britanniavillas.com. *Rack rates: $430-$510 double; $550 one-bedroom villa; $445-$565 two-bedroom villa. Additional fee for meal plans. AE, DC, MC, V.*

Sunset House

$$$ Seven Mile Beach

Low-key describes this diver's resort with 58 Spartan rooms on the iron-shore (sharp, hard, calcified black coral) south of George Town and about four miles from Seven Mile Beach. Some rooms have kitchenettes, and all have dataports and e-mail access. The congenial staff, a happening bar, a terrific seafood restaurant, and the full-service dive operation (including six dive boats) make this place extremely popular with scuba divers. Perhaps to make up for not being on the beach — a walk to a sandy beach is five minutes, and it's ten minutes to George Town — the hotel has two pools (one right by the sea), plus a whirlpool. Full dive services include free waterside lockers, two- and three-tank dives with its fleet of six dive boats, and use of the excellent Cathy Church's Underwater Photo Centre. (Church was inducted into the Women's Diving Hall of Fame in 2000 and is the best teacher on the island for underwater photography.) All-inclusive dive packages are the way to go here with great rates via Cayman Airways and American.

South Church Street (P.O. Box 479), Grand Cayman, BWI. ☎ *888-854-4767 or 345-949-7111. Fax: 345-949-7101. E-mail:* sunsethouse@sunsethouse.com. *Internet:* www.sunsethouse.com. *Rack rates: $165–$252 double; $720 double for three nights. Meal plans are available for an extra charge. AE, DISC, MC, V.*

Westin Casuarina Resort

$$$$$ Seven Mile Beach

Like the Hyatt, the low-slung Westin has 700 feet on palm-fringed Seven Mile Beach. A beautiful and large (343-room) British Caribbean-style resort, the Westin occupies one of the better stretches of Seven Mile Beach. The staff is cheerful and energetic. Like many other hotels on Grand Cayman, the Westin offers a plethora of watersports including the biggie, scuba diving, through Red Sail Sports. You can also find a challenging 18-hole golf course across the street, and a salon and a spa. Bright, airy rooms with private balconies face either the Caribbean or the lovely gardens. An elegant resort, the Westin is one of those places where the sea view is worth the extra money, so go for it. Two free-form pools with a happening swim-up bar are fun hangouts. If you love nightlife, you may not to love the Westin — it's the kind of place where everybody goes to bed early. Oh, but what a bed! If you haven't slept in Westin's new Heavenly Bed (yes, the company gave its specially designed and manufactured mattress a name), you are in for a treat. We've slept in a lot of hotel rooms, but the double-pillow topped mattresses with premium sheets here are amazing.

The Westin Causauarina Resort offers a honeymoon package that includes a bottle of chilled champagne upon arrival, room service for the first morning's breakfast, one day Jeep rental, round trip for two on the Rum Point Ferry to the legendary Rum Point, a full massage for two, a sunset cruise, and a 10 percent discount on clothing at Red Sail Sports Shops. Prices range from $1,336 to $3,040 (based on the date and view).

Seven Mile Beach Road (Box 30620), Grand Cayman, BWI. ☎ *800-WESTIN-1 or 345-945-3804. Internet:* www.westin.com. *Rack rates: $302-625 double. AE, MC, V.*

Enjoying Your Honeymoon in Grand Cayman

If Grand Cayman is your honeymoon pick, we assume that you love the water the way we do. And when it comes to activities centered around (and in) the sea, Grand Cayman makes a great choice.

Besides scuba diving, Grand Cayman is noted for other watersports like windsurfing and deep sea fishing, as well as for superb golf and decent shopping. In this section, we help make sure that you don't miss a thing Grand Cayman has to offer, and we take away any remaining stress factors. Hassle-free fun is what we're going for, and we're sure that's what you're seeking, too.

Heading for the sand and surf

Grand Cayman's **Seven Mile Beach** — one of the Caribbean's finer bands of sand — begins north of George Town, the capital. This famed stretch, which is actually only 5½ miles long (but who's counting?), boasts sparkling white sands edged by casuarina pines and a variety of palms. Toward the southern end, the landscape becomes quite rocky. Low-rise deluxe resorts, condos, and small hotels are strung along the beach, much like Aruba's immensely popular but crowded Palm Beach.

About the only time Seven Mile Beach gets crowded is when the cruise ships dock; no more than 6,000 passengers are allowed per day, but that's still a lot of folks. You also don't have to worry about vendors asking to braid your hair or inviting you to toss out the toll for cheap jewelry and tie-dyed T-shirts like in Jamaica or Puerto Rico. Panhandling is outlawed, so forget about being hassled. In fact, Grand Cayman has one of the lower crime rates in this hemisphere.

The rockier beaches on the east and north coasts, a good 20- to 30-minute drive, are protected by an offshore barrier reef and offer good snorkeling. They are much less congested, and the reefs here are in better shape than Seven Mile Beach, which has suffered from its popularity. On the southwest coast you can find small sandy beaches, but they're better for sunning than snorkeling because blankets of ribbon-like turtle grass have proliferated in the water.

Diving right in

First things first. Grand Cayman, ringed by glorious coral reefs teeming with marine life, has earned its reputation as a world-class diving destination. Underwater visibility often exceeds 100 feet in these crystalline teal waters and dive sites total over 130 — everything from wall dives and wreck dives to cave dives, coral garden dives, and shore dives. The island has won kudos from every diver's publication and is the Caribbean's premier dive spot.

If you've never tried scuba diving, Grand Cayman is a great place to start. You can take a "resort" or introductory course in the morning and make your virgin dive that afternoon. One resort course designed to teach the fundamentals of scuba to beginners who already know how to swim costs $99. It requires a full day: The morning is spent doing some classroom work and learning skills in the pool; the afternoon incorporates a one-tank dive. All necessary equipment is included. Contact **Bob Soto's Diving Ltd.** (☎ **800-BOB-SOTO** or 345-949-2022) or **Red Sail** (☎ **877-RED-SAIL** or 345-945-5966) at Treasure Island Resort. For more information on these companies, keep reading.

If you aren't in good physical shape, or if you have a great deal of anxiety about the prospect of being under the sea, we wouldn't recommend a resort course. Unless you're the type who catches on quickly, you may feel pushed, and we wouldn't want a bad initial experience to sour you on a great sport. If you have any sort of medical condition that may preclude you from diving, such as high blood pressure, frequent ear infections, or sinusitis, you need to clearance from a doctor on-island who specializes in dive medicine. The dive shop can give you a referral.

Although most dive operators on Grand Cayman are excellent, you may sometimes run into "cowboys." These "cattle boat" operators go out with disproportionate numbers of divers to instructors. Before you book, inquire about the maximum numbers of divers on a given trip. A better time is often found with a smaller group where you get more personalized service and help with the heavy gear (called valet service) — especially if you're a beginning diver. Plus, smaller groups create less stress and damage to the reef. Here are some recommended dive operators:

- **Ocean Frontiers** (P.O. Box 30433 SMB, East End, Grand Cayman; ☎ **800-544-6576** or 345-947-7500; Fax: 435-947-7600; E-mail: oceanf@candw.ky; Internet: www.oceanfrontiers.com)

- **Peter Milburn's Dive Cayman Ltd.** (P.O. Box 596 GT, Grand Cayman; ☎ **345-945-5770**; Fax: 345-945-5786; E-mail: pmilburn@candw.ky)

- **Bob Soto's Diving Ltd.** (P.O. Box 1801, Grand Cayman; ☎ **800-BOB-SOTO** or 345-949-2022; Fax: 345-949-8731; E-mail: bobsotos@candw.ky)

- **Red Sail Sports** (☎ 877-RED-SAIL or 345-945-5966; Internet: www. redsail.com) has locations at the **Hyatt Regency Grand Cayman** (☎ **345-949-8745**), **Westin Casuarina** (☎ **345-949-8732**), and the **Marriott Grand Cayman** (☎ **345-949-6343**).

- **FISHEYE** (☎ **800-887-8569**; Internet: www.divefisheye.com) has established a Web site that's a great resource on diving as well as for summer and fall bargains on dive vacation packages and specials. You can register online to receive its e-mail newsletter with late-breaking specials and updates.

Here's what you can generally expect to pay for dives:

- **Morning two-tank dive:** $70

- **Night dive:** $60 (including lights)

- **Stingray City dive:** $50

- **Stingray City snorkel:** $30

- **Resort course and dive:** $99

- **Open water check-out (with referral letter):** $85

- **Equipment rental (BCD and regulator):** $15; discount on weekly rentals

Snorkeling on Grand Cayman

If you are not a diver, snorkeling can allow you to see much of the same scenery thanks to the incredible clarity of the water. Popular spots where you can snorkel right off the beach include the West Bay Cemetery Reef, Smith's Cove, and Eden Rock. The snorkeling is excellent off the north coast. Many fish have taken to the Russian warship that was scuttled offshore from the now-defunct Buccaneer's Inn. (Look for the beautiful queen angelfish that make their home between two of the guns.)

All the dive operators listed in the previous section offer snorkeling trips, but one of our favorites is **Captain Marvin's Tropic Sea & Sea Tours** (☎ **800-550-6288,** ext. 3451 or 345-945-4590; Fax: 345-945-5673; E-mail: CAPTMVN@candw.ky).

Swimming with the stingrays

In the mid 1980s, when local fishers cleaned their catches and dumped the leftovers overboard, they noticed swarms of stingrays (which usually eat marine crabs) feeding on the debris, a phenomenon that quickly attracted local divers and marine zoologists. Today, between 30 and 50 relatively tame stingrays hover for daily handouts of squid from increasing hordes of snorkelers and scuba enthusiasts. If you book a tour to Stingray City, which is two miles east of Grand Cayman's northwestern tip, forget walking shoes — you need swimsuits. At this unusual underwater attraction (accessible via an easy dive in the 12-foot waters of North Sound or by snorkeling across the surface), you can see hordes of graceful creatures. (We're talking stingrays, not tourists.) **Treasure Island Divers** (☎ 800-872-7552 or 345-949-4456) charges divers $45 and snorkelers $25 to visit this unusual attraction. The trip starts Monday, Wednesday, Friday, and Sunday at 1:30 p.m.

During the summer, Captain Sterlin Ebanks of **Stingray City Tours** (call ☎ 345-949-9200, ext. 71, and ask for the "Summer Special") gives half off the three-hour Stingray City snorkel trip, which stops at Stingray City, Coral Garden, and the shallow barrier reef. For $17.85, you get snorkeling equipment, refreshments, and a free pickup from Seven Mile Beach. Trips depart daily at 10 a.m. and 1:30 p.m. You must reserve in advance and pay cash to get this price.

Staying dry in the underwater world

If you yearn for a peek under the sea but don't want to dive, you still have plenty of options. **Atlantis XI** on Goring Avenue (☎ 800-253-0493 or 345-949-7700) is a $3 million submersible that's 65 feet long, weighs 80 tons, and was built to carry 48 passengers. You can view the reefs and colorful tropical fish through the 26 two-foot-wide windows as the vessel cruises at a depth of 100 feet through a coral garden maze. Atlantis XI dives Monday through Saturday; reservations are recommended 24 hours in advance. *Atlantis Odyssey* features such high-tech extras as divers communicating with submarine passengers by wireless underwater phone. This 45-minute dive costs $82. *Atlantis Expedition* lets you see the famous Cayman Wall, lasts 55 minutes, and costs $72. *Seaworld Explorer,* which costs $35, is a semi-submarine that introduces viewers to the marine life of Grand Cayman.

Navigating the waves

The best-known waterskiing outfitter is **Red Sail Sports** in the Hyatt Regency Cayman on West Bay Road (☎ 345-945-5966). Water-skiing outings can be arranged for $75 per hour, with the cost divided among several skiers. Parasailing, which yields a great view of George Town, is offered for $50 per ride. Other outfitters are found at the **Westin Casuarina** (☎ 345-949-8732), **Rum Point** (☎ 345-947-9203), and the **Marriott Grand Cayman Beach Resort** (☎ 345-949-6343), charging comparable prices.

Jet skiing is allowed off Seven Mile Beach, where you can skip over the surf at more than 30mph. First get a quick lesson in operating the watercraft and a review of some safety tips. We personally don't like jet skis, and we'd like to see them eliminated from rental options, particularly in a spot known for its reefs. Many islands have banned jet skis because of the damage they wreak on the reefs, not to mention the noise they produce. Check with your resort's front desk for the nearest watersports operator offering jet skiing — if you must.

Some jet skiers ignore swimmers and divers in the area and come too close — we know that you won't be that careless.

If you prefer a gentler approach to the waves, you can glide quietly along the water enjoying the warm Cayman breezes from your rented sailboat. Anchor in a shallow spot and snorkel or swim to cool off. Red Sail Sports rents 16-foot catamarans for $28 per hour.

Living it up on dry land

The underwater delights are the main attraction on Grand Cayman, but sea-based exploration only scratches the surface of available activities on this island. Check out a few other options for your vacation pleasure.

Teeing off

The Links at SafeHaven (☎ 345-949-5988 for tee times) — Grand Cayman's only 18-hole championship course — is a Par 71, 6,605-yard course with panoramic views of the north coast. It bears a resemblance to the old Scottish coastal courses known as 'Links,' from which it takes its name. Call for prices and more information.

Grand Cayman offers an unusual golf experience at the **Britannia Golf Club** (☎ 345-949-8020), next to the Hyatt Regency on West Bay Road. The course, the first of its kind in the world, was designed by Jack Nicklaus. It incorporates an 18-hole executive setup designed for play with the Cayman ball, which goes about half the distance of a regulation ball.

The Britannia's greens fees run $50 to $80 in season, $40 to $65 off-season, depending on the configuration of the course you intend to play. Cart rentals go for $15 to $25; club rentals, $25. Hyatt guests receive a discounted rate and can reserve 48 hours in advance; the Britannia accepts reservations from everyone else no earlier than 24 hours ahead.

Exploring George Town

The good news on Grand Cayman is that you can feel safe walking anywhere on the island. The bad news? You won't have much to look at in your wanderings. The tiny capital of George Town can easily be explored in an afternoon. About the most exciting thing here is the post office on Edward Street where you can buy Cayman Islands' beautiful and highly collectible stamps.

Built in 1833, the **Cayman Islands National Museum** (☎ 345-949-8368) at Harbour Drive was used as a courthouse, a jail (now the gift shop), a post office, and a dance hall before reopening in 1990 as a museum. The museum is small but interesting, with good displays and videos that illustrate local geology, flora, fauna, and island history. Admission is $5 (open weekdays from 9 a.m. to 5 p.m. and Saturday from 10 a.m. to 4 p.m).

Pick up a walking-tour map of George Town at the museum gift shop before leaving.

Going to Hell and beyond

Hell really does exist on Grand Cayman — and we don't mean being caught on a dive boat on a rough day without Dramamine. On Grand Cayman, **Hell** is a surreal craggy landscape at the far northwest end of West Bay Beach Road about a half-hour from George Town. Once you've reached Hell, that's the end of the line — er, road, we mean. The area got that nickname in the 1930s thanks to the otherworldly rock formation of dolomite and limestone. Caymanians, always looking for a business opportunity, turned the natural sculpture into a tourist attraction. If you want to thrill your friends back home, the postmaster can stamp your postcard with "Hell, Grand Cayman" — a certain hit with those who envied your Caribbean honeymoon.

Spend 15 minutes tops in Hell. There's not much to do, and the biggest excitement is getting the postmarked proof that you've been there.

Ivan Farrington, the proprietor of the **Devil's Hangout Gift Shop,** dresses up like the demon himself. He cracks lots of jokes — "It's a hell of a town, isn't it? But it's hotter than hell here." — about the place while you buy your postcards. He can also tell you where to go when you leave.

The **Cayman Turtle Farm** (☎ **345-949-3894**), also on Northwest Point near Hell, is the only green sea turtle farm of its kind in the world. With some 250,000 visitors annually, Cayman Turtle Farm is the most popular land-based tourist attraction in the Cayman Islands. The turtle farm has a twofold purpose: to provide the local market with edible turtle meat and to replenish the waters with hatchling and yearling turtles. You can sample turtle dishes at the farm's snack bar and restaurant — if you can get past the endangered idea to take a taste. You can't bring turtle products back into the United States. The turtle farm is open daily from 8:30 a.m. to 5 p.m. Admission is $6 for adults.

Book the **Turtle Release Eco Tour** and you can participate in the program where you tag and release the endangered creatures after a tour of the Turtle Farm. It costs $125 including the rental of snorkel or dive gear. For more info, go to www.turtle.ky or www.divetech.com or contact **Divetech** (☎ **345-949-1700;** E-mail: divetech@candw.ky).

Enjoying the local history

At the end of a quiet, mango and mahogany tree-shaded road in Savannah, Grand Cayman, high atop a limestone bluff, lies one of the Caribbean's most spectacular historic restorations. The **Pedro St. James Historic Site** (Savannah, ☎ **345-947-3329**) is an historically accurate reconstruction of a 1780 Great House, which was the birthplace of democracy on the Cayman Islands and its first national landmark. The visitor's center offers a 20-minute film that gives a zippy overview of the Cayman Islands' 200-year history. The Pedro St. James Historic

Site is a 20-minute ride from George Town. Hours are 8:30 a.m. to 5 p.m. daily. Admission is $8.

The beautifully restored gardens on the grounds have become a popular place for weddings and vow renewals.

Hop in your rental car or onto the ferry at the Hyatt Regency dock and head to **Rum Point** on Grand Cayman's quiet North Side, a favorite destination for both residents and visitors. Experience island atmosphere the way it used to be (Rum Point was first documented on a 1773 map, and you can only speculate how it got its name!) in a scenic spot known for its clear, calm waters and tall pines. Sink into a hammock with a book, swim, snorkel, or try a glass-bottom boat trip. **The Wreck Bar & Grill** (☎ 345-947-9412), a Rum Point landmark, serves lunch and frosty drinks at picnic tables on the beach, and the **Rum Point Club Restaurant** (☎ 345-947-9412) is a romantic spot for a beachfront dinner.

Communing with wildlife

For a terrific walk, do it up royally at **Queen Elizabeth II Botanic Park** (☎ 345-947-9462 or 345-947-3558; for information call 345-947-7873; E-mail: guthrie@candw.ky) at Frank Sound Road on the North Side, about a 45-minute drive from George Town. The easy, short trail (less than a mile long — you only need an hour) slices through 60 acres of wetland, swamp, dry thicket, mahogany trees, orchids, and bromeliads.

Time your visit for early in the day when the animals are more active. You may see *hickatees,* the freshwater turtles found only on the Caymans and in Cuba. Occasionally the rare Grand Cayman parrot, or the anole lizard with its cobalt-blue throat pouch, can be spotted. Even rarer is the endangered blue iguana, but you can see 40 of them here. Your best chance to see animals in motion is from 8:30 to 10:30 a.m. on a sunny day.

The Queen Elizabeth II Botanic Park is open daily from 9 a.m. to 5:30 p.m.; guests are admitted until 4:30 p.m. Admission is CI$5 (US$6.25) for adults.

If you're more athletic and an eco-hound to boot, don't miss one of Grand Cayman's newer attractions: **the Mastic Trail** (west of Frank Sound Road, a 45-minute drive from George Town). This restored 200-year-old footpath winds through a 2-million-year-old woodland area leading to the North Sound. *Islands* magazine gave this site one of its top eco-preservation awards. Named for the majestic mastic tree, the rugged two-mile trail showcases the reserve's natural attractions, including a native mangrove swamp, traditional agriculture, and an ancient woodland area, home to the largest variety of native plant and animal life found in the Cayman Islands. The hike is not recommended for children under 6, the elderly, or persons with physical disabilities. Wear comfortable, sturdy shoes and carry water and insect repellent. For reservations, call ☎ 345-945-6588 Monday through Friday.

For $50 per person, you can take a guided tour of **Mastic Trail** that includes transportation and cold soft drinks. For more information and reservations, call ☎ **345-949-1996;** fax 345-949-7494, or write Mastic Trail, P.O. Box 31116 Seven Mile Beach, Grand Cayman. Two-and-a-half-hour guided tours, limited to eight participants, are offered Monday through Friday at 8:30 a.m. and at 3 p.m. and on Saturday at 8:30 a.m.

Longing for nightlife

Okay, okay. You gotta understand. Divers expend a lot of energy on their sport, plus some of them would rather see nature's nighttime light show on the coral reefs than hang out in a disco. That means if you're looking for a cranking nightlife, you're on the wrong island.

Barhopping is about as crazy as it gets here, particularly during happy hour (usually from 5 p.m. to 7 p.m.). Watching the sunset and trying to see the mysterious green flash that people say they see on the horizon right at the moment the sun sizzles into the sea is the big entertainment. For other options, look at the freebie magazine *What's Hot* or check the Friday edition of the *Caymanian Compass*. Here are the top choices:

- ✔ **Cracked Conch** (☎ 345-945-5217) on West Bay Road near Turtle Farm offers karaoke, classic dive films, and a great happy hour with hors d'oeuvres Tuesday through Friday evenings.

- ✔ **Lone Star Bar & Grill** (☎ 345-945-5175) on West Bay Road attracts sports nuts who can't live without ESPN. Mondays and Thursdays are fajita nights — an all-you-can-eat affair. Tuesday is all-you-can-eat lobster night — virtually unheard of in the Caribbean.

- ✔ **Sharkey's** (☎ 345-947-5366), in the Falls Shopping Centre, Seven Mile Beach, is a popular disco and bar filled with rock-and-roll memorabilia from the 1950s.

- ✔ **Coconuts Comedy Club** (☎ 345-945-4444) sets up shop at different venues along the main drag and draws comedy acts — some surprisingly well-known — from all over the world.

Dining in Grand Cayman

Dining out on Grand Cayman can put a serious dent in your budget, so consider whether some sort of meal plan at your hotel would make sense for you. One can easily blow $20 or more per person at breakfast. To cut costs, many people bring their own groceries from home or buy them on the island and cook for themselves in their condos. Despite the high prices and British influence, you won't have to spend money on fancy duds for dinner. Casual attire is suitable at most places.

Please refer to the Introduction of *Honeymoon Vacations For Dummies* for an explanation of our price categories.

Creating special memories

Conch is king at the casual **Almond Tree** (North Church St. between George Town and West Bay; ☎ 345-949-2893; $$$). The restaurant is surrounded by lush tropical trees and romantically lit with tiki torches at night. Set in a former plantation house built in the early 1900s, the New World-meets-Caribbean cuisine and setting at the **Grand Old House** (648 South Church St.; ☎ 345-949-9333; $$$$) lives up to its lofty name. A Web cam installed in the Grand Old House gazebo transmits wedding ceremonies on the big day via the Internet to those back home who can't attend the island shindig.

Located at the Caribbean Club in the heart of Seven Mile Beach, **Lantanas** (West Bay Rd., near the Strand Shopping Plaza; ☎ 345-945-5595; $$$) is a casual yet romantic restaurant decorated with painted wooden fish, potted plants, and teak furniture. **Ottmar's** (Grand Pavilion Commercial Centre, West Bay Rd.; ☎ 345-945-5879 or 345-916-2332; $$) is a romantic spot where you can listen to the whisper of a quartet playing Mozart and dine on delectable classic French cuisine.

One of the island's more memorable restaurants, **Ristorante Pappagallo** (Barkers, near the northern terminus of West Bay Road and Spanish Cove, eight miles north of George Town; ☎ 345-949-1119; $$$) lies on a 14-acre bird sanctuary overlooking a natural lagoon. **Garden Loggia Café** (at the Hyatt West Bay Rd.; ☎ 345-949-1234; $$$) has a beautifully landscaped courtyard and is one of our favorite breakfast spots. The don't-miss event is Sunday champagne brunch, which features a generous salad buffet, international cheeses, spicy lobster soup, seafood quiche, Belgian waffles, and custom-made omelets.

Enjoying a spectacular sunset

Cracked Conch by the Sea (857 Northwest Point Rd., near Turtle Bay Farm; ☎ 345-945-5217; $$$) is an island landmark with nautical antiques like scuba gear and shipwreck finds. The expansive terrace is a great place to sit and watch the sunset. Tip: The Sunday buffet is a divine array of island-style curries and jerk meats. Stunning sea views draw diners to **Hemingways** (West Bay Rd., on the beach in the Hyatt complex; ☎ 345-945-5700; $$$), a classy open-air restaurant that features a patio facing Seven Mile Beach. The portions are large, and the service is superb. One of the best new spots to drink in the sunset is **Reef Grill** (South of the Hyatt on Seven Mile Beach; 345-945-6358; $$$). Right on the water, this relaxed restaurant turns out excellent food in an upscale atmosphere.

Hanging with the locals

A 15-minute drive south of George Town, the **Crow's Nest** (104 S. Sound Rd. ☎ 345-949-9366; Fax: 345-949-6649) is tucked away in a rustic West

Indian Creole cottage that sits right on the beach and is shrouded by flowering shrubs. From here, you have a wonderful view of Sand Cay Island; bring your snorkeling gear in case you want to take a closer look after lunch. Another option is to go for dinner at **Miss Viveen's** (☎ 345-947-7435), a local about three miles from Gun Bay, who cooks Caymanian dishes for $6 to $10 a person. Call ahead to reserve a spot on her covered patio.

Settling into Grand Cayman

Despite its wealth and status as a British Overseas Dependent Territory — we know, even the designation sounds stuffy — Grand Cayman is relaxed and casual. In fact, Kevin says it reminds him of his tiny hometown in Georgia where you have to buy a car with an automatic transmission so you can have one hand free to wave to people.

The cost of living is about 20 percent higher in Grand Cayman than in the United States; one U.S. dollar is worth only about 80 Cayman cents. Nonetheless, many of the 38,000 islanders are wealthy, and they wear their millionaire status without any ostentation. If you run into any problem while on the island, the warm and friendly folks on Grand Cayman are happy to point you in the right direction.

Arriving in Grand Cayman

With more than 100 flights landing at Owen Roberts International Airport weekly — 70 direct flights from Miami alone — officials are adept at handling a continuous stream of visitors. This clean, modern airport with its good air-conditioning system is one of the more comfortable in the Caribbean. Even if you come in on a packed flight, you are likely to encounter few lines and may barely feel that you're entering a foreign country.

The airport (☎ 345-949-5252 for information) is centrally located for points east and west. After you clear customs and gather your luggage, head for the stacks of free tourist information and grab a copy of everything you see — especially useful is **Key to Cayman,** available at the airport, hotels, and shops. These giveaways often contain coupons for meals, attractions, and car rentals.

You'd better look like you can afford your honeymoon when you arrive on Grand Cayman. Otherwise, you may be questioned by customs officials to determine whether you've got the bank account to bankroll your fun on the island.

Getting to your hotel

Check with your hotel ahead of time to see if it offers free van pickup at the airport. All arriving flights are met by taxis, which line up neatly, awaiting an agent to assign them to deplaning passengers.

Taxis are usually vans (capable of transporting divers and all their accompanying gear) or Toyota Corollas. Taxi rates are fixed, and you can get fare information from the dispatcher at the curb. Drivers are generally charming and happy to share island lore. Typical one-way fares from the airport to Seven Mile Beach range from $11.50 to $20, depending, of course, on which end of the beach you travel to.

Taxis are also readily available from all resorts and from the taxi stand at the cruise ship dock in George Town. A sign with current rates is posted at the dock.

The island doesn't have a public bus system, but local minibuses run along main routes between 7 a.m. and 6 p.m. from George Town parallel to Seven Mile Beach. The fare is $2.

If you rented a condo but not a car and you need provisions, have **McCurley's Tours** (☎ **345-947-9626**) pick you up at the airport. The driver can take you by a grocery store en route.

If you rent a car, getting to your hotel from the airport should be easy on this flat island. The roads are well marked and in good shape, and your car rental agent can pencil in the route for you on the map. The major car rental companies all have offices in a plaza across from the airport terminal, where you can pick up and drop off vehicles.

Getting around Grand Cayman

Grand Cayman is one of the easiest islands in the Caribbean to navigate. The terrain is flat, and the easy-going locals are ready to help if by some weird happenstance you were to get lost. (We can't imagine such a thing happening here, but you never know.) For the most part, you can really walk to wherever you want to go.

You may want to tour the island for a day; you won't need more than that for a complete tour. For that day, rent a car — unless you find it important to pick up local history and color from one of the taxi drivers, who gladly serve as a guides. If you tour by taxi, though, the tab may exceed what you'd pay for a one-day car rental.

Walking around

If your accommodations are along Grand Cayman's Seven Mile Beach, your feet are enough to get you where you need to go. You can walk to the shopping centers, restaurants, and entertainment spots along West Bay Road. George Town is small enough to see on foot.

Riding a bicycle, moped, or motorcycle

Biking is popular on this flat, safe island where drivers tend to take it easy; bikes, mopeds, and motorcycles are good means to explore. When touring on a motor scooter or bicycle, don't forget to wear sunscreen. Also remember to drive on the left. Bicycles ($10 to $15 a day) and scooters ($25 to $30 a day) can be rented from **Bicycles Cayman** (☎ **345-949-5572**); **Cayman Cycle** (☎ **345-945-4021**); **Eagles Nest** (☎ **345-949-4866**), which specializes in renting Harley Davidson motorcycles; and **Soto Scooters** (☎ **345-945-4652**). Some resorts also offer free bicycles.

Renting a car

Grand Cayman is relatively flat and fairly easy to negotiate if you watch out for traffic. First you must obtain the $7 rental permit needed to drive any vehicle on the island. You can get a permit from either the rental agent or the central police station in George Town if you have a valid driver's license. You must have a credit card and be at least 21 years of age — 25 with some companies — to rent a car.

Rates range from $35 to $75 a day; remember to use coupons and ask about special promotions. Gas prices at press time were about $3.31 for an "imperial" gallon, which is slightly more than a U.S. gallon. Car rental companies include **Ace Hertz** (☎ **800-654-3131** or 345-949- 2280), **Budget** (☎ **800-472-3325** or 345-949-5605), **Cico Avis** (☎ **800- 331-1212** or 345-949-2468), **Coconut** (☎ **800-262-6687** or 345-949-4377), **Economy** (☎ **345-949-9550**), **Soto's 4x4** (☎ **345-945-2424**), and **Thrifty** (☎ **800- 367-2277** or 345-949-6640).

Most firms have a range of models, from compacts to Jeeps to mini-buses. Divers who are staying a bit farther afield and have gear to haul definitely need to rent a larger vehicle; we suggest a Jeep or van with plenty of sprawl room.

Everyone drives on the left side of the road, and the steering wheel is on the right, so when pulling out into traffic, look to your right. The car's setup may be slightly different in other ways, too. The local joke is to watch out for tourists with their windshield wipers on, because they're about to make a turn.

Once you get away from the airport, traffic thins out and driving is simple. You can't get lost, because Grand Cayman has only one main road — a route that offers a few little offshoots. George Town has several one-way streets marked with international signs. Ask the rental agent to show you what the signs look like. If you're behind a bus that stops to let off passengers, be sure to stop or else you may run over a fellow traveler: The exit doors swing out into traffic. Always watch for pedestrians; Grand Cayman attracts visitors from around the world, and you never know what the pedestrian rules are on their home turf.

Ask whether your speedometer is in kilometers per hour or miles per hour. They are often in kilometers, but the speed signs (circles with 25, 30, 40, or 50 on them) are posted in miles per hour.

Fast Facts: Grand Cayman

ATMs

Automatic Teller Machines are available universally on this bank-riddled island.

Banks

The principal banks are **Barclays Bank, Cayman National Bank, Royal Bank of Canada, Bank of Nova Scotia, Canadian Imperial Bank of Commerce,** and **Washington International Bank.**

Business Hours

Shops in George Town are open weekdays from 9 a.m. to 5 p.m. and Saturdays from 10 a.m. to 2 p.m.; in outer shopping plazas, shops are open daily from 10 a.m. to 5 p.m. Shops are usually closed Sundays except in hotels. Bank hours are Monday through Thursday 9 a.m. to 2:30 p.m. and Friday 9 a.m. to 1 p.m. and 2:30 to 4:30 p.m.

Climate

The average winter temperature is 60°F, summer 86°F. Temps seldom drop below 70°F or rise above 90°F. Annual average humidity is 83 percent.

Hurricane season is June to November, but the Cayman Islands have been fortunate in escaping serious damage or fatalities since the major strike in 1932. Rainy season is May through October.

Credit Cards

Major credit cards are widely accepted.

Currency Exchange

Although the U.S. dollar is accepted everywhere, you can save money if you go to the bank and exchange U.S. dollars for Cayman Island (CI) dollars, worth about US$1.25 at press time. The Cayman dollar is divided into a hundred cents

with coins of 1¢, 5¢, 10¢, and 25¢ and notes of $1, $5, $10, $25, $50, and $100 (no $20 bills). Prices are often quoted in Cayman dollars, so it's best to ask. All prices quoted in this book are in U.S. dollars, unless otherwise noted.

Doctors

Healthcare on the island is excellent. Ask your hotel concierge for a referral, or call **Cayman Medical and Surgical Centre**'s new 24-hour physician referral hotline at ☎ 345-949-8150.

Electricity

Electricity is the same in the Cayman Islands as in the United States (110-volt, 60 cycle).

Emergencies

For an ambulance, call ☎ **911** or **555.** For a hospital, call ☎ **911.**

Hospitals

The new $150 million **Cayman Islands Hospital** (☎ 345-949-8600) in George Town on Hospital Road has a state-of-the-art accident and emergency unit, staffed 24 hours a day. **George Town Hospital** (Hospital Road, George Town; ☎ 345-949-4234 or 555) has a two-man double-lock hyperbaric chamber; it's available on a 24-hour on-call basis by trained staff from the Cayman Islands Divers chapter of the British Sub Aqua Club, and it's supervised by a doctor trained to treat diving injuries.

Information

The main office of the **Department of Tourism** is in the Pavilion (Cricket Square and Elgin Avenue, P.O. Box 67; ☎ 345-949-0623 or 345-914-1270; Fax: 345-949-4053; Internet: www.caymanislands.ky). You can find information booths at the airport (☎ 345-949- 2635), at the Cruise Landing at Spotts when cruise ships are in port during rough seas, or in the kiosk at the cruise ship dock in George Town (☎ 345-949-8342). Grand Cayman also maintains an islands-wide tourist hot line (☎ 345-949-8989).

You can contact the **Tourist Information and Activities Service** (☎ 345-949-6598 or 345-945-6222) day or night for complete tourist information and free assistance in booking island transportation, tours, charters, cruises, and other activities.

Internet Access

Locally dial ☎ 976-4638 to connect at CI $.12 per minute. No log on or password is required. Internet access is available at the **Pirates Den, Dicken's Literary & Cyber Cafe Café** (Galleria Plaza, West Bay Road, ☎ 345-945-9195), and **CyberCOMP** in the AquaworldDuty Free Mall. Call ☎ 1-800-NET HELP or e-mail ipass@candw.ky for the visitor-only Internet technical support.

Language

English is the official language, and is spoken with a distinctive brogue that reflects Caymanians' Welsh, Scottish, and English heritage. For example, "three" is pronounced "tree"; "pepper" is "pep-ah"; and Cayman is "K-man."

Magazines/Newspapers

Dickens Literary & Internet is a great place to get international newspapers, check your e-mail, and surf the net. You can also get light snacks, bagels, and muffins here, as well as your morning cappuccino or fruit smoothie. The *Caymanian Compass* is published daily Monday to Friday, and the *Cayman Net News* is published on Tuesdays and Thursdays. The *Cayman Net News* is also available online at www.caymannetnews.com and is updated every Thursday.

Maps

You can pick up a good map at any tourist information kiosk or at the hotels.

Pharmacies

Island Pharmacy (☎ 345-949-8987), in West Shore Centre on Seven Mile Beach, is open daily.

Police

In an emergency, call ☎ **911.**

Post Office

Post offices are generally open weekdays from 8:30 a.m. to 3:30 p.m. and Saturday from 8:30 to 11:30 a.m. Beautiful stamps are available at the General Post Office in downtown George Town and at the philatelic office in West Shore Plaza. If you are addressing a letter to the Cayman Islands, include "BWI" (British West Indies) at the bottom of the envelope. Note that the islands don't use zip codes.

Safety

Grand Cayman doesn't suffer from the crime that plagues some other Caribbean islands. You can walk wherever you like. Nonetheless, don't tempt fate: Don't leave valuables in plain sight in rental cars, be sure to lock your hotel room when you leave, and don't leave valuables unattended on the beach.

Frankly, Caymanians are more concerned about you breaking the law than they are about islanders infringing on someone's property or person. Locals strictly observe and enforce laws that prohibit collecting or disturbing endangered animal, marine, and plant life and historical artifacts found throughout the islands and surrounding marine parks. Simply put, take only pictures, and please don't stand on the coral reefs because that kills them.

Penalties for importing drugs and firearms and possession of controlled substances include large fines and prison terms.

Poisonous plants on the island include the maiden plum, the lady hair, and the manchineel tree. If in doubt, don't touch. The leaves and apple-like fruit of the manchineel are poisonous to touch and should be avoided; even raindrops falling from them can cause painful blisters.

As for sharks, we were assured that they don't hang around the popular dive sites; they generally prefer deeper water. However, at Stingray City, an 8½-foot hammerhead swam right underneath Kevin.

Taxes

All accommodations add a 10 percent government tax, and you encounter a departure tax of $10 when you leave the island. Otherwise, there is no tax on goods or services. But most hotels and restaurants tack on a 10 to 15 percent service charge to your bill.

Telephone

For international dialing to the Cayman Islands, the area code is 345. To call outside, dial 0+1+area code and number. Phone service is supplied by Cable & Wireless (Cayman Islands). International direct dialling, telefax, telegram, and Connex Internet services are available 24 hours daily on all three islands.

Important long distance access numbers are **AT&T USA DIRECT** ☎ 800-872-2881; **MCI DIRECT** ☎ 800- 624-1000; and **U.S. SPRINT** ☎ 800-366-4663. Merely follow instructions on your hotel or condominium telephone for long distance dialling, dial the access number, and then proceed with your call. AT&T also offers a less expensive service at 1-800-CALL USA. Once connected to this service, you can use a credit card or US calling card, or you can make a collect call. You can call anywhere, anytime, through the cable and wireless system and local operators. To make local calls, dial the seven-digit number.

To place credit card calls, dial ☎ 110.

Time Zone

The islands are on Atlantic Standard Time, one hour ahead of Eastern Standard Time.

Tipping

At large hotels, a service charge is generally included and can be anywhere from 6 to 15 percent; smaller establishments and some villas and condos leave tipping up to you. Although tipping is customary at restaurants, note that some automatically include 15 percent on the bill, so check the tab carefully. Taxi drivers expect a 10 to 15 percent tip.

Water

Water is safe to drink, but please conserve for the island's sake.

Weather and Surf Reports

Check out the following Web sites: www.2gobeach.com/hurr.htm or www.weather.com.

Web Sites

Visit these very informative and helpful sites: www.caymanislands.ky or www.divecayman.ky. Find the latest news on www.caymannetnews.com.

Chapter 18

Honeymooning in Jamaica

By Echo & Kevin Garrett

· ·

In This Chapter

▶ Finding the best honeymoon accommodations

▶ Discovering the fun and romance of Jamaica

▶ Uncovering all the details

· ·

Based on the sheer breadth of its accommodations, Jamaica stands in a class by itself in the Caribbean and offers an almost endless array of choices for honeymooners.

 Jamaica's cultural life — its reggae music, distinctive art, and fiery cuisine — is as rich as most of its population is poor. But you may well feel a palpable racial tension and hostility, the legacy of slavery and colonization. We've never run into a problem, but at times we've had an uneasy feeling. We don't want you to be overly concerned about crime. Indeed, most of the potential trouble is concentrated in the capital of Kingston, which you won't find in our recommendations. We strongly suggest that you limit your adventures to those you can do with a guide recommended by your hotel — and stick close.

Bring your appetite for adventure and be prepared to dive into a whole different world. If you can get into the groove, you can have a wonderful time together.

Figuring Out Where to Stay

We've noticed that visitors' feelings about the Caribbean's fourth largest island are directly connected to where they stay, probably because most tourists tend to settle in and stick close to their resorts. So choosing the right place for your needs takes on major importance when you visit Jamaica.

Montego Bay, the most cosmopolitan of Jamaica's resort towns, is ground zero for the party crowd. Situated on the lush and hilly north-western coast, Mo Bay — as it's called by locals and those who've been on the island for more than five minutes — is the second largest city in Jamaica. Mo Bay is a sort of microcosm of Jamaica, in that it reflects the problem the entire island struggles with: how to put on a happy face for tourists when poverty and crime are tugging at your sleeve. Most visitors to Jamaica land at the Mo Bay airport, so this area gets the first shot at making an impression. Nonetheless, Mo Bay continues to be popular, because a seven-minute drive from the airport gets you to fine beaches, good shopping, and a pepper pot of locals and tourists mixing it up for a good time.

Negril is Mo Bay's younger, wilder, prettier sister. Sophisticated all-inclusive resorts here draw a better-heeled and less rowdy crowd from all over the globe to Negril's three well-protected bays: Long Bay, Bloody Bay (now called Negril Harbour), and Orange Bay. Negril has a dual personality. On the eastern fringe of Seven Mile Beach, which you pass on the road from Mo Bay as you enter town, you see most of the all-inclusives. Seven Mile Beach is action-packed with exhibitionists, watersport operators, vendors, and ganja peddlers all vying for attention. The quieter West End is a cluster of local restaurants, boutique hotels, and cottages tucked along the shaded limestone cliffs, which are honeycombed with caves.

Spring breakers have discovered Negril. About 3,000 college kids descend upon the tiny town during March.

We've lumped the following north coast resorts together — **Runaway Bay, Ocho Rios,** and **Port Antonio** — because distance, like time, doesn't mean a whole lot on Jamaica. If you travel from Mo Bay via car, van, or bus, Runaway Bay is the first of the major resort areas that you hit. Several major all-inclusives are in this area.

Better known is Ocho Rios, which is nicknamed Ochi. This north coast resort town, a good two-hour drive east of Montego Bay, is surrounded by the lush beauty that most people associate with the Caribbean. Ochi is a busy port town, but the brilliant greens of the surrounding hills hint at the glorious gardens, waterfalls, and other treasures to be seen if you know where to look.

Port Antonio is reflective of the Jamaica of yesteryear; small boutique resorts are the norm in and around Port Antonio. Unfortunately, 20 percent occupancy rates have also become the norm of late in Port Antonio. Several of the hotels in the area have suffered from a lack of guests and have fallen into disrepair. Many guidebooks still tout some of these places as "charming," but, frankly, they would send us screaming into the night. Stick with our recommendations.

Jamaica

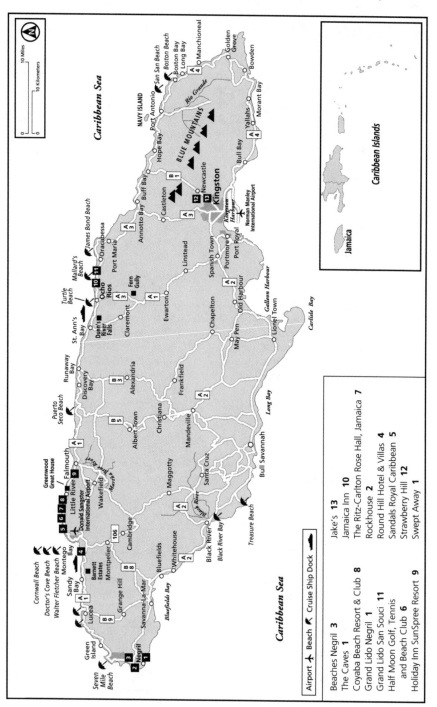

Caribbean Sea

Caribbean Sea

Caribbean Islands

Jamaica

Airport ✈ Beach ↙ Cruise Ship Dock ↙

Beaches Negril **3**
The Caves **1**
Coyaba Beach Resort & Club **8**
Grand Lido Negril **1**
Grand Lido San Souci **11**
Half Moon Golf, Tennis
  and Beach Club **6**
Holiday Inn SunSpree Resort **9**

Jake's **13**
Jamaica Inn **10**
The Ritz-Carlton Rose Hall, Jamaica **7**
Rockhouse **2**
Round Hill Hotel & Villas **4**
Sandals Royal Caribbean **5**
Strawberry Hill **12**
Swept Away **1**

Choosing Among Jamaica's Best Accommodations for Honeymooners

Jamaica is one of those islands where you should never go for the published rack rate. You can always do better. Packages and special deals abound. If you don't want to stick to the big all-inclusives, one of the best travel agencies specializing in great hotel deals is **Changes in L'Attitudes** (☎ **800-330-8272**). The company's Web site, www.changes.com, is fast-loading and informative, and it puts you in a good mood just surfing it.

Please refer to the Introduction of *Honeymoon Vacations For Dummies* for an explanation of our price categories.

Beaches Negril

$$$$$ Negril

Beaches welcomes everybody — singles, couples, and families with children of all ages — but it's hard to be all things to all vacationers. Beaches can marry you and take care of you on your honeymoon, but we'd recommend it only if you're on your second marriage and have kids in tow, or if you are planning a destination wedding and have several children in the wedding party. It's hard to feel romantic when the pools and restaurants are overflowing with tots and teens. On the plus side, this resort fronts an excellent beach and is beautifully laid out. The 225 rooms come in nine categories. They are all well air-conditioned and have ceiling fans, in-room safes, and king-size beds. Amenities include an amphitheater for nightly happenings, five restaurants, a beach bandstand, a disco, several bars, a beauty salon, two freshwater pools, three whirlpools, and a toddlers' pool. Available watersports are scuba diving, waterskiing, paddle boating, snorkeling, and windsurfing. The resort also offers tennis, beach volleyball, and board games.

If you want to avoid kids, but like the Beaches concept, head to the new Beaches Royal Plantation in Ocho Rios.

Norman Manley Blvd., Negril. ☎ *800-726-3257. Fax: 305-284-1336. E-mail: beachesnegril@cwjamaica.com. Internet: www.beaches.com. Rack rates: $600-$740 per couple. 2 BR Suite $1,725 per couple. Rates are all-inclusive. Children under age 2 are free; kids ages 2 to 15 stay for $70 a night. AE, MC, V.*

The Caves

$$$$$ Negril

Cloistered on ten acres of the cliffs near Negril Lighthouse on the edge of town, these colorful, wooden, thatched-roof cottages make the most of their fantastic location and cater to ultra-hip jet-setters. Our favorite cottage, Sunshine, has a roomy bed in an upstairs loft that's open to the Caribbean breezes. Hand-carved furniture, original art, outdoor showers, king-size beds with candles set all around, CD/cassette players, and a discreet staff make for a terrific experience. You won't find air-conditioning or a beach, but a web of grottos and stairs lead to a saltwater pool, sauna, hot tub, and sundecks overlooking the milky teal water below. You can climb down a ladder and slip into the sea for a swim over a coral reef with good snorkeling. Braver souls can take the plunge from Hopper's Hop (named for actor Dennis Hopper) where the aquamarine water below is 30 feet deep. At night, the dramatically lit sea caves below the resort are a fun place for snuggling. Aveda spa treatments are given in an open-air gazebo. Stellar, authentic Jamaican cuisine is served throughout the day at a casual thatched-roof hut that's the gathering place in the middle of the property.

Lighthouse Road, Negril. ☎ *800-OUTPOST or 305-531-8800. E-mail:* reservations@ islandoutpost.com. *Internet:* www.islandoutpost.com. *Rack rates: $375 one-bedroom unit; $825 two-bedroom/two-bathroom unit. No children under age 16. AE, MC, V.*

Coyaba Beach Resort & Club

$$$ Montego Bay

Coyaba is one of the best maintained resorts in Jamaica. Though only ten minutes from the Mo Bay airport, Coyaba feels far from the craziness of Montego Bay. Although families are welcome, the resort also manages to strike just the right note in the romance department. It features a private candlelit dinner for two, a two-hour horseback ride through the countryside, and a day's tour with a driver and picnic lunch. The 50 guest-rooms are located in plantation-style, tiled-roof, butter-yellow buildings. Besides air conditioning, guestrooms have ceiling fans, satellite TV, and French doors leading to oversized private balconies overlooking the well-manicured courtyard and the private white-sand beach edging the sea beyond. The 24 deluxe oceanview rooms — the most expensive — are large and have mahogany four-poster king-size beds, dining alcoves with windows, and sitting areas. Resort facilities include two stylishly decorated restaurants, a bar, a fitness gazebo, and a tennis court. (We especially like the free tennis clinics with visiting pros.) Coyaba also boasts a piano bar, volleyball, croquet, and bocce, as well as massage services.

The honeymoon package ($1,800 in the summer, $2,700 in the winter for eight days and seven nights per couple) is a standout.

Norman Manley Blvd., Little River (P.O. Box 88), Montego Bay. ☎ *800-237-3237 or 876-953-9150. Fax: 876-953-2244. E-mail:* coyaba@n5.com.jm. *Internet:* www. coyabajamaica.com. *Rack rates: $420 double. Meal plans available at additional cost. Three-night minimum stay required in winter. AE, MC, V.*

Grand Lido Negril

$$$$ Negril

Set on 22 acres, the Mediterranean-style property, another link in the SuperClubs chain, bowls over guests with a dramatic entrance. These luxurious digs all boast fine sea views and run parallel to the white-sand strand on famed Seven Mile Beach. The oceanview rooms that are closest to the water are on the nude beach side. You don't have to be in the buff to stay in these rooms, but you might get more of a view than you'd counted on. Room service operates 24 hours. The clubhouse offers Jacuzzis, music, and (get this) laser karaoke at the piano bar. A spa has been added that features air-conditioned treatment rooms encircling a plunge pool and two massage gazebos by the sea, as well as a full salon. Grand Lido has an extensive 24-hour, air-conditioned fitness center, perfectly positioned for a sweeping vista of Bloody Bay. An evening sail aboard the resort's classic 147-foot yacht, a wedding gift from Ari Onassis to Monaco's Princess Grace and Prince Rainier, is a must.

The so-called express check out that is supposed to save you time at the airport can wind up lopping off an hour and a half out of your last day.

Negril Bloody Bay (P.O. Box 88), Negril. ☎ *800-467-8737 in the U.S., 800-553-4320 in Canada, or 876-957-5010. Fax: 876-957-5517. E-mail:* glnsales@cwjamaica.com. *Internet:* www.superclubs.com. *Rack rates: $360-$590 per person double occupancy. Rates are all-inclusive. Children under 16 are not allowed. AE, MC, V.*

Grand Lido San Souci

$$$$$ Ocho Rios

Rooms at the Grand Lido San Souci are located in pretty-in-pink colonial buildings tucked into gentle hills covered with jungle-like, tropical growth. The setup yields a feeling of seclusion even when the resort is fully booked. If you want to splurge, go for the Roger Moore suite, which has a wide terrace on the top floor of the building overlooking the lovely main beach. Strolling musicians boost the romance factor. The air-conditioned gym with floor-to-ceiling glass walls overlooking the calm Caribbean boasts one of the best views we've seen reserved for the hard-body crowd, and Charlie's Spa is far ahead of the competition (indulge in the couples massage). The other notable attractions at this resort are the food and entertainment. When the dancing on the terrace starts at other resorts, we're sometimes tempted to run for cover and put in our earplugs. Not so here. Management finds appealing local talents who know how to get the crowd — which spans a wide age range, from mid-20s to late 50s — on its feet.

On Rte. A3 (P.O. Box 103), Ocho Rios. ☎ *800-467-8737 or 876-994-1353. Fax: 876-994-1544. E-mail:* sslido@cwjamaica.com. *Internet:* www.superclubs.com. *Rack rates: $355 one-bedroom, $530 penthouse per person double occupancy. Rates are all-inclusive. Children under 16 are not allowed. AE, DC, MC, V.*

Half Moon Golf, Tennis and Beach Club

$$$$$ **Montego Bay**

Seven miles east of Montego Bay (and a universe away), Half Moon sprawls over 400 acres with 418 guestrooms, suites, and villas. The resort has a jaw-dropping 52 swimming pools, 13 tennis courts, a croquet lawn, and an equestrian center, to name just a few of our favorite things. Its fantastic, mile-long crescent-shaped beach (hence the name Half Moon) draws a loyal following, which includes everyone from sitting U.S. presidents to royalty to movie stars. Its excellent sport facilities (the legendary golf course was designed by Robert Trent Jones, Sr.) add to the appeal. Queen Anne and Chippendale reproductions and Oriental rugs blend appealingly with bright Caribbean colors in the airy and luxurious villas — many of which have private pools. The oceanview rooms are older, but we think they're a steal, because you are just steps from one of our favorite palm-lined beaches. You get the same over-the-top service at this resort without some of the accompanying stuffiness of that grand dame, Round Hill, on the opposite side of town. One of Jamaica's most upscale shopping malls, with more than 40 stores, is on the grounds.

Rose Hall. ☎ *800-626-0592, 800-237-3237, or 876-953-2211. Fax: 876-953-2731. E-mail:* reservations@halfmoonclub.com. *Internet:* www.halfmoon.com. jm. *Rack rates: $195-$595 double. Weekly villa rates (sleeping up to eight) $19,650 and $20,580. Meal plans are available. Wedding and honeymoon packages available. AE, MC, V.*

Holiday Inn SunSpree Resort

$ **Montego Bay**

Holiday Inn SunSpree is Jamaica's second-largest resort, with 516 rooms. The friendly and efficient staff makes you feel like you're staying with an old family friend. (Just one caveat: Check-in can be slow at times.) Security is tight, and you don't have to worry about being hassled on the beach here or about walking around the property at any time. Housekeeping here is excellent, too. The busy complex boasts nightly entertainment, a sports bar with a big-screen TV, golf at nearby Ironshore Golf Course, an electronic gaming parlor, a disco, a fitness center with Nautilus equipment, four lighted tennis courts, a watersports center, a 12-person Jacuzzi, and basketball and volleyball courts. The restaurants have improved greatly in the last few years; you get a good variety of choices, as well as more traditional Jamaican favorites, in ample servings.

Montego Bay (P.O. Box 480), Rose Hall. ☎ *800-HOLIDAY or 876-953-2485. Fax: 876-953-2840. Rack rates: $80 double (room only); $150 double (all-inclusive). AE, MC, V.*

Jake's

$ Treasure Beach

The heliport is the only clue that Jake's has registered on the radar of the hip international jet set. Otherwise, you could easily imagine that you'd stumbled onto some hippie outpost circa 1960 when you first see this whimsical assemblage of ten cottages by the beach. If you want a rustic getaway — no phones, TV, or air-conditioning — Jake's is a good choice. Modern conveniences include coffeemakers, mini-bars, and CD players in each unit. Outdoor showers come with each room. Abalone, a romantic Moroccan-style adobe villa on the fringe of the property, would be our pick for a honeymoon hideout. Jake's is set on a tranquil beach on Jamaica's undeveloped south coast. The main entertainments here are taking a dip in the small shell-and-colored-sea-glass encrusted pool, snorkeling, fishing with the locals, and touring the nearby Black River savannah area and Lover's Leap. The excellent Jamaican chef attracts locals and guests to the open-air restaurant, which quickly acquires a party atmosphere as the evening wears on.

If you can't take the heat, pass on Jake's, which is in the arid part of Jamaica, where the mosquito nets, though lovely, aren't just decoration.

Treasure Beach, Calabash Bay P.A., Saint Elizabeth. ☎ *800-OUTPOST or 305-531-8800. Fax: 876-965-0552. E-mail:* jakes@cwjamaica.com. *Internet:* www.islandoutpost.com. *Rack rates: $75-$95 one-bedroom, $150 suite, $245 two-bedroom, $325 three-bedroom villa. AE, MC, V.*

Jamaica Inn

$$$$$ Ocho Rios

First opened in the early 1950s, it became known as a haven for famous guests seeking privacy in its spacious, airy rooms decorated with antiques. Churchill stayed here, as did T.S. Eliot. Noel Coward often tickled the ivories in the lounge, and movie stars like Marilyn Monroe and Elizabeth Taylor would drop by for an evening. Classically Caribbean, secluded, and yet conveniently located, the Jamaica Inn is only ten minutes away from the bustling port and has completed a number of upgrades to the property, following a carefully planned renovation, with all rooms and public areas having been thoroughly redecorated. The airy suites have private verandahs that are complete living rooms, boasting a spectacular view of the beach and the Caribbean. Niceties include Crabtree and Evelyn amenities, hairdryers, "natural" lighting in each bathroom, and cotton robes with the Jamaica Inn logo. And for guests who can't take a holiday from their workout, Jamaica Inn's exercise room features state-of-the-art Life Fitness equipment.

For those looking to tie the knot in elegant fashion, Jamaica Inn can arrange a wedding at one of the many romantic, private locations on the property.

Main St. (P.O. Box 1), Ocho Rios. ☎ ***800-837-4608*** *or 876-974-2514. Fax: 800-404-1841. Internet:* www.jamaicainn.com. *Rack rates: $450-$525 double (including all meals). AE, MC, V.*

The Ritz-Carlton Rose Hall, Jamaica

$$$$$ **Montego Bay**

Montego Bay's newest resort opened in August 2000. The resort occupies nearly 25 acres of remote beachfront property in the island's historic Rose Hall plantation area and features 428 guestrooms, including 51 Executive Suites and The Ritz-Carlton Suite. Its 18-hole championship golf course, the White Witch, is located just five minutes from the resort and boasts 16 holes with spectacular views of the Caribbean Sea. The open-air Club House Restaurant features a 1,700 square-foot veranda overlooking the White Witch course, ocean, and mountains. The resort also includes two tennis courts (one designed for exhibition play), a tennis pavilion with a retail shop and juice bar, and a variety of motorized and non-motorized watersports. The 8,000 square-foot Ritz-Carlton Spa offers a variety of unique signature services. A full-service Fitness Center and salon are also available. One complaint: This Ritz could be almost anywhere. While it has acres of plush carpeting and super-airconditioned buildings, Caribbean charm is in short supply.

1 Ritz-Carlton Dr., Rose Hall, St. James. ☎ ***876-953-2800.*** *Fax: 876-953-2501. Internet:* www.ritzcarlton.com. *Rack rates: $$400-$475 double; from $950 suite. AE, DC, MC, V.*

Rockhouse

$$ **Negril**

Rockhouse is a wonderful boutique hotel in Negril. The rooms (in timbers and stone with windows that allow uncluttered sea views) are perched on a dramatic cliff above the caves overlooking Pristine Cove. Some have romantic outdoor showers. The four-poster, queen-size beds, the dressers, and the bedside tables are all made of local woods. The cottages sit in tropical gardens created by the sure hand of a landscaper who knows how to get the most out of the wild environment. The rooms along the water have no air-conditioning, but the open-air design lets you make the most of the cooling sea breezes and ceiling fans. If you have to have air-conditioning, opt for a studio in the gardens. The best rooms are on the far end of the property, nearest the sea. The infinity pool built into the rocky cliff looks like it falls into the sea below. It's one of the most dramatic around. Plus, at night, the bar and excellent restaurant attract a young, fun clientele — hip but without pretense.

West End Rd. (P.O. Box 24), Negril. ☎ ***876-957-4373.*** *Fax: 876-957-4373. Internet:* www.rockhouse.com. *16 rooms, 12 villas. Rack rates: $139 for studios and $215 for villas. AE, MC, V.*

Round Hill Hotel & Villas

$$$$ **Montego Bay**

If you like the pomp and circumstance of colonial Jamaica with British-style service, Round Hill, occupying a 98-acre peninsula next to the sea and 10 miles west of Montego Bay, is the classic retreat. During high season, villas are reserved months — even years — in advance. Guests are chauffeured around the perfectly clipped property in golf carts. Comprised of 29 two- to four-bedroom villas (most with their own pools and all privately owned) and a 36-room, two-story hotel called Pineapple House, Round Hill draws an older, moneyed crowd that enjoys the white glove service. (You may opt for an all-inclusive plan here, but the staff steadily reminds you that tipping is not only allowed but expected. We found that annoying at times. Bring plenty of small bills.) When you rent a villa, you get your own housekeeper, gardener, and breakfast cook whose mission each day is to serve up your eggs exactly the way you want. Although the grounds and beach are lovely, you never know what you may get inside the villas. It all depends on the tastes of the owners. But when you dance under the stars on the terrace to the strains of the orchestra, or witness the moon settle — as if on cue — above the main Georgian-style building, or watch the lovely crescent beach below twinkle with tiki torches, you can understand how Round Hill enchanted Jackie and JFK, who spent part of their honeymoon here.

Rt. A1, Hanover Parish, Montego Bay. ☎ *800-972-2159 or 876-956-7050. Fax: 876-956-7505. E-mail:* resround@cwjamaica.com. *Internet:* www.rounhilljamaica.com. *Rack rates: Villa suites with pool $700; Pineapple House $240, double. A variety of packages are available, including one that lets bride and groom stay free if 15 or more rooms are booked for friends and relatives. The Round Hill Rendezvous ($4,950 low season, $8,150 high season for seven nights) is especially romantic. Inquire about meal plans and all-inclusive rates. AE, DC, MC, V.*

Sandals Royal Caribbean

$$$$$ **Montego Bay**

Okay, here's the crown jewel of the Sandals empire. Built around a Georgian-style great house on 17 acres near Montego Bay, this popular all-inclusive has all the bells and whistles. It is known for packing in folks determined to have a good time without ever having to leave the complex. Here you get continental breakfast in bed and afternoon tea. You have a choice of four restaurants — including the Bali Hai, which is on Sandals Cay, a private offshore island — plus four bars, three pools, three tennis courts, a good health club, all watersports, organized activities, and entertainment. This resort is suited to couples who want guaranteed, hassle-free fun in the sun. Shopaholics also enjoy the heavy concentration of stores in Montego Bay.

With a minimum five-night stay at any Sandals or Beaches property, your wedding is free of charge.

Mahoe Bay, North Coast Hwy. (Box 167), Montego Bay. ☎ 888-SANDALS or 876-953-2231. Fax: 876-953-2788. E-mail: sr.is@cwjamaica.com. *Internet:* www.sandals.com. *Rack rates: $520-$670 per couple a night. AE, MC, V.*

Strawberry Hill

$$$$ Irish Town, Blue Mountains

Who needs a beach when you've got panoramic views at 3,100 feet in the Blue Mountains? Built on the site of an eighteenth-century coffee plantation in nineteenth-century Jamaican style, Strawberry Hill is set amidst a gloriously restored botanical garden; the 12 white-washed, Georgian-style wooden cottages display carved fretwork, excellent Jamaican art, and plantation furnishings. Honeymooners flock to Birds Hill, a 1,500-square-foot house on the outpost of the property that has a private terrace perfect for breakfast and an outdoor Jacuzzi shrouded by lush tropical flowers. The living area features a large kitchen and living room. French doors lead to a spacious balcony that runs the cottage's entire length. The four-poster, canopied mahogany bed, hand-carved on the property, comes with a goose down comforter and heated mattress pad to ward off the mountain chill. (Honeymooners have asked to buy the beds so frequently that the resort now sells them.) Extras include CD players with a selection of CDs, coffee and tea makers, large writing desks, cordless telephones with answering machines, plush bathrobes, umbrellas, beach towels, hairdryers, refrigerators stocked with drinks, electronic safes, Aveda personal care products, and TV/VCRs.

Car transfers from Norman Manley International Airport to Strawberry Hill are $30 one way for two passengers. Helicopter transfers from the airport to Strawberry Hill are $600 one way for up to four passengers.

New Castle Rd., Irish Town, St. Andrew. ☎ 800-OUTPOST or 876-944-8400. Fax: 876-944-8401. E-mail: reservations@islandoutpost.com. *Internet:* www.islandoutpost.com. *Rack rates: $280-$595 for 12 Georgian-style cottages ranging from studios to three-bedroom suites.*

Swept Away

$$$$ Negril

A gorgeous, couples-only, all-inclusive resort, Swept Away has built an excellent reputation as a tranquil, romantic place for those active types more interested is sipping fresh carrot juice than a piña colada. Bodies beautiful abound at Swept Away, which occupies a prime half-mile stretch of Negril's famed Seven Mile Beach. The verandah suites, housed in 26 two-story villas, each with private, plant-shrouded terraces, make you feel secluded even when the resort is completely booked (which is most of the time). Rooms are tastefully decorated in minimalist style with Mexican tile floors, white canvas sailcloth upholstery, and clay lamp sconces. The centerpiece to this gem lies across the road: ten acres of an adult playground with an excellent health club, a lap pool, and ten tennis courts. It's one of the Caribbean's most extensive sports complexes. Nonguests can get a day pass.

Norman Manley Blvd., Long Bay (P.O. Box 77), Negril. ☎ *800-545-7937 in the U.S. and Canada, or 876-957-4061. Fax: 876-957-4060. Internet:* www.sweptaway.com. *Rates: $1,500–$1,875 per couple. Rates are for three nights and are all-inclusive, including airport transfers. AE, DC, MC, V.*

Enjoying Your Jamaican Honeymoon

Thanks to its varied coastline, Jamaica delivers many amazing sights, especially in its collection of beaches. The island boasts practically every imaginable watersport and some of the best golf courses in the West Indies, as well as outdoor activities like river rafting, mountain hiking, and serious biking. And of course around Montego Bay, Negril, and Ocho Rios, you can count on a party going on if you're so inclined. Disc jockeys set up huge speakers and blast throbbing rhythms of reggae, rock steady, and other Jamaican favorites. Jamaica's cultural and natural beauty are much more than skin-deep, but unfortunately, we only have room to scratch the surface.

Taking the plunge

Sadly, Jamaica's once glorious coral reefs have been heavily damaged by overfishing and careless boaters. Many of the reefs are dead. We don't really think scuba diving is worth the expense and time here (though some resorts include it as part of your package). You see few mature reef fish. Locals snatch sea fans and pretty shells out of the water to sell to tourists.

However, if you're determined to dive, you can. You need to show a C-card as evidence of your training and certification. The **Negril Scuba Centre** (Negril Beach Club Hotel and Hotel Sam Sara on Norman Manley Boulevard; ☎ **800-818-2963** or 876-957- 9641) is the most modern, best-equipped scuba facility in Negril. Beginner's dive lessons are offered daily, as well as multiple-dive packages for certified divers. Full scuba certifications and specialty courses are also available.

In Negril, the best area for snorkeling is off the cliffs in the West End. You can find dozens of shops along West End Road, where you can rent snorkeling equipment at fairly modest prices.

Runaway Bay and Ocho Rios offer decent snorkeling, too. Although some reefs are accessible from the shore, you can avoid the boats and beach activity if you take a short boat ride to the better reefs further off shore. Try **Resort Divers Shop,** Main Street, Turtle Beach (☎ **876-974-6632**). The skilled staff here can hook you up for dive trips or snorkeling. A boat leaving daily at 1 p.m. goes to Paradise Reef, where tropical fish are plentiful.

In Port Antonio, snorkel with **Lady Godiva's Dive Shop** at the Dragon Bay resort (☎ 876-993-8988). Lady Godiva offers two excursions daily to San San Bay, a colorful reef off Monkey Island, for $10 per person. Snorkeling equipment costs $9 for a full day's rental. Dive prices on the island range from $40-$60 per person.

Dolphin Cove (☎ 876-795-3708; Internet: www.dolphincovejamaica. com), which offers a Dolphin Encounter and Swimming with the Dolphins, opened May 2001. During the Dolphin Encounter ($69 per person), you can feed, pet, and interact with the dolphins. During the Swim with the Dolphins ($119 per person), you get to interact with the dolphins in waist-deep water, and have the dolphins push you in the water along the cove! Reservations are recommended and general admission for observers is $15.

Enjoying the water without getting wet

Jamaica is known for its plethora of waterfalls and rivers, great for exploring. You don't have to be a big water-buff to enjoy them. **Dunn's River Falls,** in Ocho Rios, are Jamaica's most photographed destination. Although you have to run the gauntlet of vendors hawking "I Survived the Falls" T-shirts, we still recommend the dramatically beautiful natural wonder. These 600-foot, icy cold waterfalls cascade over rock steps winding down to the Caribbean. They can be climbed, but to do so, you need to form a human chain, led by a guide (who expects a tip at the end). Don a swimsuit and take tennis shoes that you don't mind getting soaked. The rocks are very slippery, and the climb isn't suitable for those who are easily winded. If you want to do more than take a quick gander at the falls, set aside an hour or more for your visit. They're located off A-l, between St. Ann's and Ocho Rios. Call ☎ 876-974-2857 for information. Admission is $6. Open daily from 9 a.m. to 5 p.m.

Hitting the links

Golfers appreciate both the beauty and the challenges offered by Jamaica's courses, and the game has deep roots here. Some of the courses were established more than 100 years ago.

Caddies are mandatory throughout the island, and rates are $12 to $25, but for the price you get extra entertainment: They carry your golf bag and clubs balanced sideways on their heads.

Some of the best courses are in Mo Bay. The following are our favorites:

- ✔ **The Half Moon Golf, Tennis, and Beach Club,** 7 miles (11 km) east of Mo Bay (☎ 876-953-3105), has a Robert Trent Jones-designed 18-hole course, which is the home of the Red Stripe Pro Am. Greens fees are $55 for guests, $110 for nonguests.

✔ **Ironshore,** 3 miles (5 km) east of the airport (☎ **876-953-2800**), is an 18-hole, links-style course. The greens fee is $50.

✔ **Tryall Golf, Tennis, and Beach Club,** 15 miles (24 km) west of Mo Bay on North Coast Hwy. (☎ **876-956-5681**), has an 18-hole championship course on the site of a nineteenth-century sugar plantation. Greens fees run $40 to $60 for guests, $100 for nonguests.

✔ **Wyndham Rose Hall,** 4 miles (6½ km) east of the airport on North Coast Hwy. (☎ **876-953-2650**), hosts several invitational tournaments. Fees run $70 for guests, $80 for nonguests.

✔ **Ocho Rios has the Sandals Golf and Country Club,** 2 miles (3 km) east of Ocho Rios (☎ **876-975-0119**), whose adjacent 18-hole course is 700 feet above sea level. The greens fee is $70 for nonguests.

✔ **Breezes Golf and Beach Resort,** North Coast Hwy., Kingston (☎ **876-973-7319**), is an 18-hole course that has hosted many championship events. The greens fee is $80 for nonguests; guests play for free.

✔ **Grand Lido Braco,** in Runaway Bay, Trelawny, between Duncans and Rio Buena (☎ **876-954-0000**), is a 9-hole course with lush vegetation. Call for fee information.

✔ Great golf, rolling hills, and a "liquor mobile" go hand in hand at the 18-hole **Negril Hills Golf Club,** east of Negril on Sheffield Rd. (☎ **876-957-4638**). The greens fee is $58.

Looking for some nightlife

Jamaica supports a lively community of musicians. Reggae, popularized by the late Bob Marley and the Wailers and performed today by Ziggy Marley, Jimmy Tosh (the late Peter Tosh's son), Gregory Isaacs, Third World, Jimmy Cliff, and many others, is its most famous contribution to the music world.

For the most part, the liveliest late-night happenings throughout Jamaica are in the major resort hotels. Some of the all-inclusives offer a dinner and disco pass from about $95. Pick up a copy of *The Daily Gleaner, The Jamaica Observer,* or *The Star* (available at newsstands throughout the island) for listings on who's playing when and where.

The principal club in Ocho Rios is **Jamaica'N Me Crazy,** Renaissance Jamaica Grande, Main St. (☎ **876-974-2201**). The place usually hosts a packed crowd. The place to be in Mo Bay on Friday night after 10 p.m. is Pier 1, Howard Cooke Blvd., opposite the straw market (☎ **876-952-2452**). **Margueritaville** (☎ **876-952-4777**) on the hip strip has also steadily become ground zero for the party crowd. It's a giant sports bar that turns into a music and dance scene late in the evenings. In Negril, you find the best music and an eclectic crowd of locals and in-the-know tourists at **Alfred's Ocean Palace,** Norman Manley Blvd.

(☎ 876-957-4735). It has a dance area set up on a beach and a stage for live reggae (Tuesday, Wednesday, and weekend nights). On Mondays and Thursdays, there's live jazz.

Dining in Jamaica

On Jamaica, most guests simply take an all-inclusive plan and never venture out to a restaurant. The availability of good food at the all-inclusives, combined with the perception that going outside the gates of a resort isn't necessarily a good idea, has effectively put a chill over the dining scene in Jamaica. We're sorry to see this happen, because some of our absolute best dining experiences in the Caribbean have been on Jamaica. But the truth is that many restaurants are hurting for business. Prices have gone up, which means tourists are even less likely to take in the local charm. It's a vicious cycle. So we're not naming many places, recognizing that you'll likely stick close to your digs.

If you plan to stay at an all-inclusive, reserve at least one night off-property to experience something new. Also, make reservations a day or so in advance; because business has been off, restaurants' hours may be irregular, so calling ahead is a must. During high season, you should make reservations shortly after you arrive in order to secure your spot at popular restaurants.

Most restaurants outside the resorts in Mo Bay and Ocho Rios provide complimentary transportation. Ask when you make your reservations. Otherwise, a taxi ride can get mighty expensive.

Soaking up the best views

Jamaica's finest restaurant, **Norma's on the Wharf** (10 minutes west of Mo Bay in Reading; ☎ 876-979-2745; $$$$), a historical dockside beauty, is the creation of Norma Shirley, Jamaica's most famous chef, who launched Jamaican nouvelle cuisine. Heaven is at a table for two on the edge of the balcony at the Italian **Evita's** (Mantalent Inn, Eden Bower Rd, Ocho Rios; ☎ 876-974-2333; $$$), housed in an 1860s ginger-bread house suspended high above Mallard's Bay. You feel like characters in a romantic flick at sunset when the lights of Ocho Rios glitter like diamonds below. The spectacular setting alone would merit a trek up the mountain to **Strawberry Hill** (Irish Town; ☎ 876-944-8400; $$$$), which draws a sophisticated crowd of Kingston's intellegensia and the music world. Book a table right at sunset and watch the twinkling lights of Kingston below.

Creating special memories

Jamaican-born chef Wilbert Mathison prepares beautiful meals that match the romantic setting of the dining terrace at **Jamaica Inn** (North

Coast Highway, just east of Ocho Rios; ☎ 876-974-2514; $$$$). After dinner, couples dance under the starlight and the warm glow of lamp-lights, or they slip off to the loggia — an open gallery — where the sound of the waves competes with the quartet who softly plays reggae classics. Housed in a handsomely restored Methodist nineteenth-century mansion, **Toscanini** (Harmony Hall, P.O. Box 192, four miles east of Ocho Rios on the Oracabessa main road; ☎ 876-975-4785; $$$$) is expertly run by a young couple, Emanuele and Lella Giulivi, and her brother Pierluigi (P.G.), all from Parma, Italy. An excellent but pricey wine list pushes this wonderful surprise — great Italian food — to a level rarely attained in the Caribbean.

For great service and good food, stop in at **Kuyaba on the Beach** (Norman Manley Blvd., Negril; ☎ 876-957-4318; $$), a thatch-roofed, brightly colored restaurant where the menu features a mix of kingfish steak, grilled lamb with sautéed mushrooms, and several pasta dishes. By day, you can snag a chaise lounge and hang out at the small beach. It's become especially popular with Europeans, who seem to have a knack for finding good value when it comes to dining.

Looking for a local favorite

Owner-character Cosmo Brown rules his **Cosmo's Seafood Restaurant and Bar** (Norman Manley Blvd., Negril; ☎ 876-957-4330; $$) on East End beach, specializing in all manner of seafood. He's a wizard with conch (which can be chewy and tasteless in unskilled hands), whether stewed, curried, or in a soup. The blue-canopied, open-air **Ocho Rios Village Jerk Centre** (Da-Costa Drive; ☎ 876-974-2549; $) doles out frosty Red Stripe beer and Tings (a local lime-flavored soft drink) with our favorite fiery jerk pork, chicken, or seafood. You can see locals hanging out, playing dominoes, and talking politics (a popular topic in Jamaica) here.

Hanging at a hotspot

If we've had a long day of traveling, we head to the **Pork Pit** (Gloucester Avenue, a half-mile past the brewery and Walter Fletcher Beach, Montego Bay; ☎ 876-952-1046; $) where we were first introduced to fiery jerk pork on the casual picnic benches open to the sea breezes. **The Ruins** (Turtle River, DaCosta Drive, Ocho Rios; ☎ 876-795-1421; $$$) now features two restaurants and a café, all centered around a 40-foot lime-stone waterfall surrounded by tropical gardens. The main restaurant, Cascades, offers a variety of sumptuous, healthy-lifestyle dishes complimented with the perfect atmosphere, accented with music and intimate lighting, while the Roadside Diner features the best of Jamaican and Asian dishes in a modern, vibrant and colorful setting. The River-side Café offers full bar service, a coffee bar with a variety of pastries and snacks, and Internet stations and an outside deck overlooking a river.

Settling into Jamaica

Jamaica is undeniably a ravishing beauty, boasting mountains that soar to 7,500 feet (higher than any in the eastern half of North America) and 160 rivers laced with cascading waterfalls, not to mention fabulous white-and-black sand beaches as well as tropical rain forests. If we squint our eyes, the flat southern coast reminds us of the African savanna. And if we ignore the palm trees, Jamaica's rolling green hills look like the south of England. No wonder Jamaica has carved out a niche for itself with honeymooners looking for a tropical paradise.

While we're comfortable with this island's promise of excitement and expression, many visitors find Jamaica a shock to their systems. Although it's wildly vibrant and beautiful, Jamaica can also be plain wild. Much of its population is extremely impoverished, and things that we take for granted are sometimes not available in Jamaica.

Arriving in Jamaica

When you come to Jamaica, you most likely fly into **Donald Sangster International Airport** (☎ 876-952-3124), about two miles east of Montego Bay. It's the most efficient point of entry for those heading to Ocho Rios, Runaway Bay, Negril, or, of course, Mo Bay, where virtually all the major resorts are located.

 Norman Manley International Airport (☎ 876-924-8235) in Kingston is best for visitors headed to Strawberry Hill in Irish Town in the Blue Mountains or the small resorts in Port Antonio.

Landing in Mo Bay

The Mo Bay airport is the product of upgrades over the last several years, but you still deplane on the tarmac and walk in the heat to the terminal. Once inside, you walk down a wide, overly air-conditioned hallway and join the throngs waiting to go through Customs and Immigration. The lines move efficiently, except during the summer when hordes of Jamaican nationals come home for vacation. You should see a Jamaica Tourist Board counter where you can grab some material about the island to peruse while you wait your turn in line. (You can also find coupons for attractions, rental cars, and more inside the free magazines.)

Immediately after you go through Customs and Immigration, you see a currency exchange office, where you can get Jamaican dollars. If you're carrying U.S. currency, we suggest holding onto it; U.S. money is widely accepted and even preferred by many. But if you want or need to get local currency, you can expect a slightly better rate of exchange here than at your hotel or the banks.

If you checked luggage, you may have to wait for it . . . and wait and wait. We find that collecting luggage takes at least 15 minutes or so and sometimes as much as 45 minutes. Once you get your luggage, keep a close eye on it, because theft can be a problem.

Landing in Kingston

 Security is extremely tight at the Kingston airport. We advise honeymooners to avoid flying into or out of that airport if possible. Our last trip, we were both pulled aside by security after passing through three checks. We were patted down bodily, which was not a fun way to end a romantic rendezvous.

The airport lies about 11 miles southeast of the capital city. When you exit customs in Kingston, you see a taxi information booth on the left, and beyond that, a counter for **Island Car Rentals,** the most reputable local rental agency, and the **JUTA** (Jamaica Union of Travelers Association) taxi office. Again, keep an eye on your luggage at all times.

Getting around Jamaica

If you have a ride arranged, look for a driver holding a sign with your name or your resort's name, or go to the kiosk for your particular resort.

The all-inclusives, like Sandals, have their own large buses and vans. SuperClubs arrivals are contracted out, so you may be on a bus or a van. The attendant for the properties has a list of all the arrivals due in at the same time as you, and you won't roll until everyone has been accounted for. Baggage handlers should hoist your luggage onto the bus or into the van. Tip them $1 per bag and watch to be sure that all your property makes it on. This process for all passengers can take another 20 to 30 minutes.

 If for some reason you need to arrange your own transport or pick up a rental car, deal only with official representatives. Don't accept help with your luggage from anyone whom you can't identify as an airport baggage handler, and don't accept a ride from someone who approaches you. Don't wander beyond the ground transportation dispatch area.

If you want to skip the notoriously wild drive to the resorts outside of Montego Bay, you could catch a flight on **Air Jamaica Express.** Reservations are handled by **Air Jamaica** (☎ **800-523-5585;** Internet: www. airjamaica.com; 876-952-4300 in Mo Bay; 876-922-4661 in Kingston; 876-957-4210 in Negril; and 876-974-2566 in Ocho Rios). We suggest you reserve before you leave home through a travel agent or through Air Jamaica to secure a seat, because the planes are small. Be sure to reconfirm your departing flight a full 72 hours in advance.

Taking a taxi

We strongly urge you to get into only special taxis and buses operated by **JUTA, the Jamaica Union of Travelers Association** (☎ 876-952-0813; Fax: 876-952-5355). All such vehicles have the union's emblem on the side. The prices are controlled, and any local JUTA office can supply a list of rates. These vehicles are clean, air-conditioned, and up to the standards you expect in the U.S. or Europe. Only taxis with red license plates, issued by the Jamaica Tourist Board, with the initials PPV (public passenger vehicle) are properly insured and licensed to carry fee-paying passengers.

Have the restaurant or resort that you're visiting call a cab for you in advance. A typical one-way fare from Montego Bay to Ocho Rios is $50 to $60. Drivers may negotiate sometimes, especially if you agree to let them come back and pick you up for the return trip.

Catching a bus

You can take a bus to Negril or Ocho Rios. The fare is $20 a person for the two-hour trip to Negril's Seven Mile Beach area; $25 for the hotels along the West End's cliffs. We recommend **Tour Wise** (☎ 876-979-1027), which has a desk in the transportation hall at the Montego Bay airport just outside the passenger arrival hall, or **Caribic Vacations** (☎ 876-953-9874) in Montego Bay. The bus drops you off at your final destination.

Negril is a mere 60 miles from the Montego Bay airport. We always heard that Negril was a wild spot for free spirits. The spot got crazy for us early in our trip. Our bus ride from Montego Bay was a white-knuckle adventure, as we whizzed along the scenic coast, passing slower traffic on curves and up hills. Apparently, our driver embraced the notion that if you're the biggest on the road, you automatically have the right of way. Thanks to continual road "improvements," you can count on at least a two-hour trip — especially if the cows decide to come out into traffic for a rousing game of chicken with the buses and cars.

Traveling the roadways in Jamaica can be a religious experience. For half the trip to Negril, the woman in front of us was looking out the window, clawing her husband's arm and muttering repeatedly, "Oh, my God, oh, my God, Tom. Tom, we're passing again." At the halfway point, we stopped for a bathroom break. Tom got back on the bus and handed his wife two Red Stripe beers. "Here," he said. "Drink these and stop looking out the window."

You may be tempted to ride the local buses, because they're cheap (a few dollars for most places) and offer frequent service between Kingston, Mo Bay, and other major destinations. However, resist the temptation. Local buses are so slow, stiflingly hot, and rife with pick-pockets that even the locals aren't using them much anymore. Tourists rarely attempt to use this form of transportation — with good reason.

Schedule information (although the buses rarely follow one) and route information are available at bus stops (usually near the main markets) or from the bus driver.

Renting a car

We don't recommend it, especially if you're a first-timer on Jamaica. Here are some of the reasons why:

- ✔ Bad roads
- ✔ Bad drivers
- ✔ Bad characters
- ✔ Bad directions
- ✔ Bad vibes

Jamaica beckons, with its considerable charms, but for the reasons we already mentioned, we don't recommend renting a car to explore it. Accidents and petty theft make damage to the rental car highly probable, and even if you're used to the British style of driving on the left, you still practically need the driving skills of James Bond to stay out of trouble. Avis pulled its offices out of Jamaica entirely in 1998.

If you still want to rent wheels after all our Heads Ups, here are the major agencies. **Budget International** (☎ **800-472-3325** or 876-952-3838 at the Montego Bay Airport, or 876-924-8762 in Kingston) is a good choice; with Budget, a daily collision-damage waiver costs another $15 and is mandatory. Other U.S.-based operators on Jamaica include **Dollar International** (☎ **800-800-4000** in the U.S.); **Hertz International** (☎ **800-654-3001** in the U.S. or 876-952-4250); **Thrifty Car Rental** (☎ **876-952-5825** or 876-952-5826); and **Kernwel International** (☎ **800-678-0678**).

A few tour operators offer good fly-drive packages that include rental cars. If you are determined to have your own wheels, consider that route to conserve funds.

Exploring on foot

If you want to explore the resort towns on foot, you should be fine if you stick to the main drags where you find shopping and restaurants. Use common street sense, and you can walk around the following places without a problem:

- ✔ Mo Bay's hip strip, where you find lots of restaurants, clubs, shopping, and beaches
- ✔ Ochi's shopping district, near where the cruise ships unload their passengers
- ✔ Negril's Seven Mile Beach or West End

These areas are well populated by tourists. Just don't stop to talk to strangers or pull out money to buy anything on the street. Jamaica reminds us of New York City. You're fine on most streets, as long as you project confidence and keep moving. But take a wrong turn, and you can quickly get into trouble.

If you do venture to Kingston, we don't recommend walking the streets. The U.S. State Department has a traveler's advisory issued for that city.

Wherever you are, be aware of your surroundings at all times and don't walk around alone — especially if you're a woman. Jamaican men apparently have heard about the book and movie *How Stella Got Her Groove Back* (the story of an author who falls in love with a young Jamaican man while she's on vacation). You'll get lots of offers if you're walking unaccompanied. Just say no, firmly but politely, and stride on.

Hopping on a bicycle, moped, or motorcycle

Most hotels' concierge or tour desks can arrange the rental of bicycles, mopeds, and motorcycles. Daily rates run from about $45 for a moped to $70 (helmets and locks included) for a Honda 550. Deposits of $100 to $300 or more are required.

 However, we highly recommend that you don't rent a moped or motorcycle. Jamaica has the third highest accident rate in the world, and you don't want the hassle-factor of fending off aggressive vendors and drug dealers at traffic lights. If you ignore our advice, at least check on your medical insurance before you leave and have proper identification handy in case you land at a healthcare facility.

Fast Facts: Jamaica

ATMs

Few ATM machines in Jamaica accept U.S. bank cards, although cash advances can be made using credit cards. Currency from the machines, of course, is Jamaican dollars.

Banks

You can find branches of the **Bank of Nova Scotia** at the following addresses throughout the island: Sam Sharpe Square, Montego Bay (☎ 876-952-4440); Main St., Ocho Rios (☎ 876-974-2081); Negril Square, Negril (☎ 876-957-3040); 35 King St., Kingston (☎ 876-922-1420).

Banks islandwide are open Monday to Thursday from 9 a.m. to 2 p.m. and Friday from 9 a.m. to 4 p.m. A few are open on Saturday morning. Be

aware, however, that the banks don't have computers, and you're likely to encounter at least a half-hour wait in line. Many hotels and resorts offer currency exchange.

Credit Cards

Major credit cards are widely accepted. MasterCard and VISA are the most popular, followed by American Express. Some places also accept Discover and Diners Club.

Currency Exchange

The unit of currency on Jamaica is the Jamaican dollar, represented by the same symbol as the U.S. dollar ($). Both U.S. and Jamaican currencies are widely accepted. Always clarify which currency is being quoted. There is no fixed rate of exchange for the Jamaican dollar. At press time, the exchange rate was about $48 Jamaican to $1 U.S.

Jamaican currency is issued in banknotes of J$10, J$20, J$50, J$100, and J$500. Coins are available in denominations of 5¢, 10¢, 25¢, 50¢, J$1, and J$5. We recommend carrying small change in Jamaican or U.S. dollars for tips, beach fees, and other incidentals.

Bank of Jamaica exchange bureaus are located at both international airports (Montego Bay and Kingston), at cruise ship terminals, and in most hotels. Immigration cards, needed for bank transactions and currency exchange, are given to visitors at the airport arrivals desks. It is illegal to exchange currency outside of the banking system.

Customs

We can't emphasize strongly enough that you'd have to be crazy to use or try to transport illegal drugs in Jamaica. On almost every trip we see at least a few people pulled aside by customs officials. Drug-sniffing police dogs are stationed at the airport, and on one recent trip we went through three checkpoints where the Jamaican officials were hand-checking carry-ons.

Doctors

Hotels have doctors on call. If you need any particular medicine or treatment, bring evidence, such as a letter from your own physician.

Electricity

Most places have the standard 110 volts AC (60 cycles), same as the United States. However, a few establishments operate on 220 volts AC (50 cycles). If your hotel is on a different current from your U.S.-made appliance, ask for a transformer and adapter.

Emergencies

To report a fire or call an ambulance, dial ☎ **110.** For the police and air rescue, dial ☎ **119.**

Hospitals

For dire situations, seek help in Puerto Rico or Miami. **St. Ann's Bay Hospital,** St. Ann's Bay

(☎ 876-972-0150) has a hyperbaric chamber for scuba diving emergencies. In Kingston, the **University Hospital** is at Mona (☎ 876-927-1620); in Montego Bay, the **Cornwall Regional Hospital** is at Mount Salem (☎ 876-952-5100 or 876-952-6683); and in Port Antonio, the **Port Antonio General Hospital** is at Naylor's Hill (☎ 876-993-2646). Negril only has minor-emergency clinics.

Information

You find the **Jamaica Tourist Board** offices at the international airports and at 2 St. Lucia Ave., Kingston (☎ 876-929-9200); Cornwall Beach, St. James, Montego Bay (☎ 876-952-4425); Shop no. 29, Coral Seas Plaza, Negril, Westmoreland (☎ 876-957-4243); in the Ocean Village Shopping Centre, Ocho Rios, St. Ann (☎ 876-974-2582); in City Centre Plaza, Port Antonio (☎ 876-993-3051); and in Hendriks Building, 2 High St., Black River (☎ 876-965-2074). Before you visit, you can contact the Jamaica Tourist Board at 801 Second Avenue, 20th Floor, New York, NY 10017 (☎ 800-233-4582 or 212-856-9727; Fax: 212-856-9655).

Language

The official language of Jamaica is English. However, among themselves islanders usually speak patois, a distinctive and lyrical blend of English, Spanish, and myriad African languages. An example of patois is *"me diyah"* ("I'm here;" pronounced *mee de-ya*). If someone asks how your vacation is going, just say *"irie"* (pronounced *eye-ree*), which means "great."

Nudity

Nude bathing is allowed at a number of hotels, clubs, and beaches (especially in Negril), but only where signs indicate that swimsuits are optional. Elsewhere, English sensibilities prevail, and the law does not even allow topless sunbathing.

Maps

Good maps are widely available at the airport, tourist information offices, and resorts.

Newspapers and Magazines

Resort gift shops carry a decent selection, including *USA Today,* and many resorts offer *The New York Times* via fax at no charge. However, serious news junkies will find the cover price on foreign magazines and newspapers extremely inflated.

Pharmacies

In Montego Bay, **Rosehall Village Pharmacy,** Shop 22, Half Moon Bay (☎ 876-953-2399; Fax: 876-953-2287; open 9 a.m. to 7 p.m.); in Ocho Rios, **Great House Pharmacy,** Brown's Plaza (☎ 876-974-2352); and in Kingston, **Moodie's Pharmacy,** in the New Kingston Shopping Centre (☎ 876-926-4174). Prescriptions are accepted by local pharmacies only if they're issued by a Jamaican doctor.

Police

For the police and air rescue, dial ☎ **119**. In Negril, dial ☎ 876-957-4268.

Post Office

Jamaica issues gorgeous stamps. The Montego Bay post office (☎ 876-952-7389) is at 122 Barnett Street and is open weekdays 8 a.m. to 5 p.m. As you leave Negril Square, the post office is on the Lighthouse Road.

Safety

Most hotels, resorts, and even some villas have private security guards. However, beaches are public, so if you go for a stroll, you can expect to be approached by people selling everything from wood carvings and shells to drugs and sex to tours of the "real Jamaica." Safeguard your valuables and never leave them unattended on a beach. Likewise, never leave luggage or other valuables in a car or in the trunk. The U.S. State Department has issued a travel advisory about crime rates in Kingston, so don't go walking around alone at night. Caution is also advisable in many north coast tourist areas, especially remote houses and isolated villas that can't afford security.

Drugs (including marijuana) are illegal, and imprisonment is the penalty for possession.

Also, you may well be buying ganja from a police informant, many of whom target tourists so that they aren't turning on their hometown buddies. Don't smoke pot openly in public, no matter who you see doing it. You may be the one who gets caught. Above all, don't even consider bringing marijuana back into the United States. Drug-sniffing dogs are stationed at the Jamaican airports, and they will check your luggage. U.S. Customs agents pay keen attention to all those arriving from Jamaica, and they easily catch and arrest those who try to take that sort of souvenir home.

Shopping Hours

Hours vary widely, but as a general rule most establishments are open Monday to Friday from 8:30 a.m. to 4:30 or 5 p.m. Some shops are open on Saturday until noon.

Taxes

Jamaica now charges a general consumption tax of 15 percent on all goods and services, which includes car rentals and telephone calls. Additionally, the government imposes a 6.25 percent tax on hotel rooms. You also encounter a J$1,000 ($27 U.S.) departure tax at the airport, payable in either Jamaican dollars or in its equivalent in U.S. dollars. Don't count on getting the cash at the airport, because few ATMs accept U.S. bank cards, and the machines are often out of money or service.

Telephone

To call direct from the United States, dial the area code 876, then the local number. Likewise to call the U.S., you simply dial the area code and number. But the best idea is to call collect. Otherwise, you pay about $3 a minute plus hefty surcharges, including the 15 percent general consumption tax. To make on-island calls, simply dial the six-digit phone number. Coin-operated phones are rare. If you need to make many calls outside of your hotel, purchase a World-Talk card at the post office or other outlets advertising it. Local and international calls made with these cards are cheaper than operator-assisted calls.

Time Zone

Jamaica is on Eastern Standard Time year-round; it doesn't observe daylight saving time. So, when the United States is on daylight saving time, it's 6 a.m. in Miami when it's 5 a.m. in Mo Bay.

Tipping

Tipping is customary. Generally, hotels and restaurants expect 10 or 15 percent, and the same goes for tour guides and drivers. Some places add a service charge to the bill. Tipping is not allowed in the all-inclusive hotels. But on our last day, we discreetly tip those staff members who went out of their way to make our stay pleasant.

Water

Water is safe to drink island-wide, because it's filtered and chlorinated. But, as always, you're more prudent to drink bottled water if it's available. Negril has had problems with water shortages.

Weather and Surf Reports

The local newspaper is the most reliable source.

Chapter 19

Honeymooning in Puerto Rico

By Echo & Kevin Garrett

● ●

In This Chapter

▶ Finding the best honeymoon accommodations

▶ Discovering the fun and romance of Puerto Rico

▶ Uncovering all of the details

● ●

Sparkling high-rises, soft-sand beaches, stunning nature reserves — you find it all in Puerto Rico. You want glitzy casinos? No problemo. How about charming seaside villages with modest country inns? Ditto. Want history? You can stay in an old convent. The range of accommodations on Puerto Rico is impressive.

Figuring Out Where to Stay

Puerto Rico is big — 100 miles long by 35 miles wide — and you have tons of lodging choices on this island. All-inclusive packages haven't quite taken hold on Puerto Rico, and we're glad. It's not the kind of island where you want to just stay at one resort the whole time.

 Most hotels in Puerto Rico operate on the European Plan (or EP), although larger establishments offer other meal plans. Dining at the hotel properties is often exorbitant. Be prepared for sticker shock the first time you order breakfast. Our breakfast bill at one resort was almost $50 for two for what was essentially a continental breakfast.

Think of **San Juan** as two towns: one old, one new. Old San Juan is seven square blocks of living history, a World Heritage Site graced with sixteenth-, seventeenth-, and eighteenth-century buildings and fortifications in which people go about twenty-first-century daily life. Of all the Caribbean capitals, it's our favorite because of its beauty, its thriving art scene, and — thank goodness — the absence of tacky T-shirt shops clogging every corner. One of our favorite hotels in all of the Caribbean — the intimate and chic El Convento — is found here, too.

Most of our hotel picks, though, are in **Condado** or **Isla Verde,** both just a short hop from the airport. These neighborhoods, which cater primarily to the gambling crowd and to cruise passengers in port for a day or so, are strung along the Atlantic shore due east of Old San Juan's peninsula. This area reminds us of Waikiki Beach in Hawaii. Most of the big hotels here have casinos — gambling is big in San Juan. Don't expect the frenzy of Las Vegas, though. For one reason, liquor isn't served free of charge for gamblers in casinos here.

Outside San Juan, particularly on the east coast, you can find self-contained luxury resorts that cover hundreds of acres. In the west, southwest, and south — as well as on the islands of Vieques and Culebra — lodging is primarily in smaller inns, villas, and condominiums for short-term rentals.

Choosing Among Puerto Rico's Best Accommodations for Honeymooners

In hotels outside of San Juan, rates don't often include airport transfers. Be sure to ask when you book.

The rack rates listed in this section are in U.S. dollars and are for a standard double room during high season (mid-December to mid-April), unless otherwise noted. Lower rates are often available during the off-season and shoulder season.

Please refer to the Introduction of *Honeymoon Vacations For Dummies* for an explanation of our price categories.

Copamarina Beach Resort

$$$ Guanica

Copamarina, on the south coast, is a dream come true if you are looking for a quiet getaway with an understated elegant atmosphere. The resort is in nature's thrall, but there's nothing rustic about the luxurious Copamarina. The spotless rooms have small, private balconies and patios with water views. The restaurants are run by two gold-medal-winning chefs who have elevated the dining here to world-class status. The resort offers well-equipped watersports, and the excellent PADI dive center here also rents kayaks, paddle boats, and snorkel gear for use in the shallow, exceptionally calm waters off the good beach, which has plenty of palms for shade. Scuba packages are available, or you can arrange a snorkeling excursion to Gilligan's Island, an offshore key ($3 for the ride). Copamarina also has two bars, two tennis courts, and volleyball. Bicycles are available for rental.

Puerto Rico

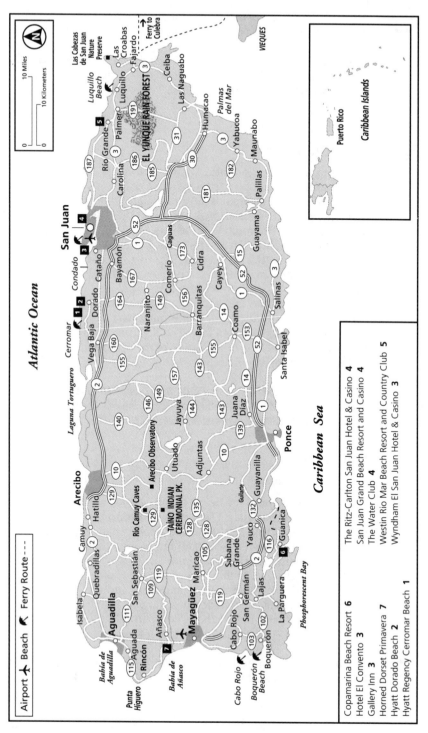

Airport ✈   Beach 🏄   Ferry Route - - -

Atlantic Ocean

Caribbean Sea

Caribbean Islands

Puerto Rico

VIEQUES

Copamarina Beach Resort **6**
Hotel El Convento **3**
Gallery Inn **3**
Horned Dorset Primavera **7**
Hyatt Dorado Beach **2**
Hyatt Regency Cerromar Beach **1**

The Ritz-Carlton San Juan Hotel & Casino **4**
San Juan Grand Beach Resort and Casino **4**
The Water Club **4**
Westin Rio Mar Beach Resort and Country Club **5**
Wyndham El San Juan Hotel & Casino **3**

Honeymooners may want to consider the resort's two new 2,600 square-foot villas with wrap-around verandahs and hammocks for enjoying the water views ($1,000 a night), opening to the tropical gardens and the adjoining forest. Furnishings are imported from Ecuador.

Route 333, km 6.5, Cana Gorda (P.O. Box 805), Guanica, PR 00653. ☎ *800-468-4553 (direct to hotel) or 787-821-0505. Fax: 787-821-0070. Internet:* www.copamarina. com. *Rack rates: $200-$290. AE, MC, V. EP.*

Hotel El Convento

$$$$ Old San Juan

Hotel El Convento is an intimate, elegant hotel in the heart of Old San Juan that transports guests to the days of Spain's conquest of the New World. The 59 rooms are unique and delightful, with mahogany antiques and hand-crafted Spanish furnishings and tiles. Bright paint and stencils adorn the walls. The rooftop plunge pool and hot tub have glorious views of dramatic Old San Juan and its harbor. Our favorite room lets you step out onto the rooftop terrace and in to the bubbling hot tub. In the evenings, savor a martini and appetizers at the El Picoteo Tapas Bar in the hotel — artsy and above the fray— before heading out for a late dinner at one of the city's many ultra-hip restaurants. You get three restaurants, two bars, in-room safes, mini-bars, an exercise room, shops, a library, and parking (for a fee). The discreet service is excellent. Hotel El Convento is the kind of place where the staff remembers you by name and honors room requests.

100 Cristo Street, Old San Juan, PR 00901. ☎ *800-468-2779 or 787-723-9020. Fax: 787-721-2877. E-mail:* elconvento@aol.com. *Internet:* www.elconvento.com. *Rack rates: $195-$380 double; suites $550-$1,200. AE, DISC, DC, MC, V.*

Gallery Inn

$$$ Old San Juan

Once you step behind the heavy doors of this unassuming entrance, you feel a part of Old San Juan. Owners Jan D'Esopo and Manuco Gandia have skillfully molded this rambling, classically Spanish house — one of the city's oldest residences — into an inn of bohemian opulence. The lush, sunlit courtyard gardens, where the owner's pet macaws and cockatoos call to each other, invite lingering. From the rooftop deck, the grand view is of the El Morro and San Cristobal forts and the Atlantic Ocean. The winding stairs take you to balconies; a music room with a Steinway grand piano; or a private nook where you can talk. Request a room with a whirlpool bath. There's no TV to distract you from one another.

The inn has no sign, so tell your taxi driver it's on the corner of Calles Norzagaray and San Justo.

204-206 Calle Norzagaray, Old San Juan, PR 00901. ☎ *787-722-1808. Fax 787-724-7360. Rack rates: $195-$300 double, includes continental breakfast. AE, MC, V. CP.*

Horned Dorset Primavera

$$$$ Rincón

A handsome Spanish colonial-style resort, the Horned Dorset Primavera is tucked away amid lush landscaping overlooking the sea and a small secluded beach. The resort is geared to the high-powered and couples who truly want to escape the frenetic pace fueled by cell phones and pagers. The only sounds that you may hear as you lounge on the long, secluded beach are the crash of the surf and an occasional squawk from Pompidou, the enormous guacamayo (parrot) in the lounge.

The Horned Dorset is constructing 22 luxury villa suites, which should be ready in 2002. Each of the 1,400 square-foot, Caribbean-style villas features over-size master bedrooms, with wet bars and seaview terraces. Existing suites have balconies and are exquisitely furnished with antiques, including ultra-comfy mahogany four-poster beds, dressers, and nightstands. Casa Escondida, where you find the most exclusive accommodations, has eight rooms — four with their own plunge pools and hot tubs — and is designed as a turn-of-the-century Puerto Rican hacienda, with tile or wood floors, mahogany furnishings, terraces overlooking the ocean, and black marble baths. The rooms have no radios, TVs, or phones. (Children under 12 are not permitted.)

The excellent staff handles weddings with aplomb.

Route 429, km 3 (P.O. Box 1132), Rincón, PR 00677. ☎ *800-633-1857, 787-823-4030, or 787-823-4050. Fax: 787-725-6068. Internet:* www.horneddorset.com. *Rack rates: $280-$800 double. AE, MC, V. EP, MAP.*

Hacienda Tamarindo

$$ Vieques

Owners Burr and Linda Vail left Vermont, with their prized collection of art and antiques in tow, to build this extraordinary hotel, which has a huge tamarind tree right in the middle and sweeping Caribbean views from its windswept hilltop location. Rooms are individually decorated but have such details as mahogany-louvered doors and terra-cotta tile floors. Some rooms have terraces, and half the rooms have air-conditioning. Those that aren't air-conditioned face the trade winds. A full breakfast is served on the second-floor terrace. You can walk down the hill to the Inn on the Blue Horizon for dinner. Box lunches are available on request. (Children under 12 are not permitted.)

Route 996, km 4.5 (P.O. Box 1569), Vieques, PR 00765. ☎ *787-741-8525. Fax: 787-741-3215. Rack rate: $140 double. AE, MC, V. CP.*

Hyatt Regency Cerromar Beach Resort & Casino and Hyatt Dorado Beach

$$$ Dorado

Located on a 1,000-acre estate 22 miles west of San Juan, the Hyatts are a deluxe operation that aims to please — and succeeds. Guests can use the facilities of either property, so you feel like you get two resorts for the price of one. Recreational options here are the best on the island: two 18-hole golf courses designed by Robert Trent Jones, Sr.; a clubhouse; two pools (one Olympic-size); a spa and fitness center with aerobics classes; eight tennis courts; oceanside inline skating and jogging trails; a windsurfing school; and a private beach with watersports. Dining options range from four formal restaurants to the casual beach bar to theme nights.

 If you're torn between the two properties, keep in mind that the Dorado has nicer rooms and a better beach and appeals to an older crowd, while the Cerromar has a better pool, a younger clientele, and a renowned children's program.

Ask about the Honeymoon Romance Package.

Route 693, km 10.8 (P.O. Box 1351), Dorado, PR 00646. ☎ 800-55-HYATT or 787-796-1234. Fax: 787-796-2022 or 787-796-6560. Rack rates: $205-$1,785. AE, DISC, DC, MC, V. EP, MAP optional.

San Juan Grand Beach Resort and Casino

$$$$ Isla Verde

In place of the former Sands Hotel stands the sparkling San Juan Grand, which opened under new management in late 1998 after $12 million in renovations. The 16-story monolith sits on one of the city's most popular beaches. The theme of understated luxury carries from the large cream-and-brown-tiled lobby (with its blue sky ceiling motif) to the spacious rooms, decorated in somber brown and green hues. Suites of the Plaza Club (which has 24-hour snacks on hand and a private concierge) overlook the pool area, but the views from the standard rooms — either over the ocean or toward the city and the San Jose Lagoon — are almost as nice. Off the lobby is a mammoth casino overlooking tropical gardens and the pool area. Besides five restaurants, you get two bars, in-room safes, no-smoking rooms, a pool, a hot tub, an exercise room, a spa, boating, a beach, shops, and the casino.

187 Avenue (P.O. Box 6676), Isla Verde, PR 00914. ☎ 800-544-3008 or 787-791-6100. Fax: 787-255-2510. Rack rates: $325-$475 double. AE, DISC, MC, V. EP.

The Ritz-Carlton San Juan Hotel, Spa & Casino

$$$$$ Isla Verde

The Ritz-Carlton is one of the most spectacular deluxe hotels in Puerto Rico. This beachfront hotel lies only five minutes from the international airport on eight acres of prime oceanview property. (Don't worry: The hotel's excellent construction means that you won't notice plane noise.) The preferred accommodations are in the upper floor Ritz-Carlton Club, which has the added benefit of a private lounge and personal concierge staff, accessed by a key-activated elevator. A total of 46 guestrooms and suites are available in this private club. The 12,000 square-foot spa here, the largest and most sophisticated of its kind on Puerto Rico, offers panoramic ocean views. The elegant marble and stone bilevel building is also the setting for yoga, aerobics, aqua-aerobics, and other fitness activities. Upstairs are 11 treatment rooms that offer facials, massages, manicures, pedicures, hydrotherapy, and body wraps, among other treatments. The three-night honeymoon package ($1,250) includes two Swedish massages, welcome drinks, daily tea for two, use of the fitness center, a daily $100 food and beverage credit for two, daily continental breakfast, and a deluxe oceanview room.

Waits for room service can be lengthy. Coffee makers are available in the room only upon request.

6961 Avenue of the Governors, Isla Verde, San Juan, PR 00979. ☎ *800-241-3333, 888-451-9868 or 787-253-1700. Fax: 787-253-0700. Internet:* www.ritzcarlton. com. *Rack rates: $400-$475 double; from $950 suite. AE, DC, MC, V.*

The Water Club

$$$$ Isla Verde

Formerly known as the Colony San Juan, this 84-room boutique hotel facing one of Puerto Rico's most happening beaches features playfully sexy rooms with custom-designed beds perfectly positioned for ocean views. This chic hotel's corridors play soothing surround-sounds of gently breaking waves. The open-air tenth floor features a Brazilian bar with the Caribbean's only roof-top fireplace, perfect for watching the sunset. The resort also offers a spacious deck, pool, fitness club, and massage-treatment center. The Water Club's main bar has become the new hangout for those in the know. The three-night romance/honeymoon package gives you a luxury oceanview room, champagne on arrival, chocolates, and daily breakfast in bed for $399 a night per couple.

Tartak Street #2, Isla Verde. Internet: waterclubsanjuan.com ☎ *888-265-6669. Fax 787-728-3610. E-mail:* info@waterclubsanjuan.com. *Rack rates: $205-$475 double. AE, MC, V.*

Westin Rio Mar Beach Resort and Country Club

$$$$ Rio Grande

The Westin Rio Mar represents Puerto Rico's first resort to be built from scratch in 15 years. It opened in August 1996 and marked Westin's first foray into the Caribbean. The seven-story hotel is situated on 481 lush acres hemmed in by a one-mile beach on the island's northeast coast and the Caribbean National Forest. Guestrooms come in six categories, all including private balconies or patios, voice mail, electronic security locks, in-room safes, 24-hour room service, ice, cable TV, and mini-bars. A concierge level has added amenities on the seventh floor. Facilities at the $178-million property include 11 restaurants and lounges, a Las Vegas-style casino, a 35,000 square-foot clubhouse, 13 tennis courts and a tennis clubhouse, a fitness center and spa, and a business center. Activities include 36 holes of golf (at Tom and George Fazio's Rio Mar Ocean Course, and at River Course by Greg Norman) and watersports (especially scuba diving and deep sea fishing). A thoroughbred track is also nearby.

Avoid suites 5099 and 5101 — the balconies overlook the hotel's noisy airconditioning ducts.

Ask about the excellent honeymoon packages.

6000 Rio Mar Blvd. (P.O. Box 6100), Rio Grande, PR 00745. ☎ 800-WESTIN-1 or 787-888-6000. Fax: 787-888-6600. Internet: www.westinriomar.com. *Rack rates: $205-$475 double. AE, DISC, DC, MC, V. EP, MAP.*

Wyndham El San Juan Hotel & Casino

$$$$ Isla Verde

When the Rat Pack was in town, they stayed in this opulent resort, sprawled on one of Puerto Rico's finest beaches. The eye-popping grand lobby, splendorous with carved mahogany ceilings and a chandelier as big as an old Cadillac, sets the stage for a continual fiesta. In one corner is a 12-piece Cuban band. Off to the side is a snazzy casino. A Las Vegas-style showroom is within earshot, as is San Juan's hottest disco. And that's not even the whole scene! An $80-million redo has brought this terrific resort one of our favorite pools — it's Olympic-size; has whirlpools, a waterfall, and a swim-up bar; and fronts the 700-foot beach. The hotel's 56 new suites are roomy and feature showers for two and Jacuzzi tubs in spacious bathrooms, as well as handsome Caribbean furnishings. The suites also have a more private pool in a gated area. All rooms have VCRs, CD players, mini-bars, three multi-line phones, fax/modem, and voice mail. Excellent shopping is available onsite, as well as eight bars and six fine dining options — from southwestern to northern Italian to Chinese — including some of San Juan's finest restaurants.

Avenue Isla Verde (P.O. Box 2872), Isla Verde, San Juan, PR 00902. ☎ 800-468-2818, 800-WYNDHAM, or 787-791-1000. Fax: 787-791-0390. Rack rates: $395-$545 double. AE, CB, DC, MC, V. EP, MAP.

Enjoying Your Honeymoon in Puerto Rico

From the glorious art scene of the beautifully restored Spanish Colonial city of Old San Juan to dramatic rain forests, gargantuan caves, 18 golf courses, and beaches boasting activities from whale watching to surfing, Puerto Rico is like the most lavish buffets on the cruise ships that make San Juan the Caribbean's busiest port. If you can't find something you like on Puerto Rico, you aren't really hungry for a good time.

Spending a day at the beach

Much of the action on Puerto Rico revolves around its excellent beaches, which are well appreciated by locals as well as tourists. On some Caribbean islands, you see only a handful of islanders on any given day at the beach. Puerto Ricans relish their sand and surf, flocking to the waterfront to enjoy the warmth and beauty of the place they call home. With almost 300 miles of shoreline, you see everything from blanket-to-blanket beach fiestas on city beaches to white-sand crescents so far removed that the locals haven't even given them names.

The continental shelf, which surrounds Puerto Rico on three sides, gives this island an abundance of coral reefs, caves, sea walls, and trenches ideal for scuba diving and snorkeling.

By law, all Puerto Rican *playas* (beaches) are open to the public. The government runs 13 *balnearios* (public beaches), which have dressing rooms, lifeguards, guarded parking, police, and in some cases, cafeterias, gazebos, picnic tables, playgrounds, and camping facilities. Admission is free, but parking is $2. Most *balnearios* are open from 9 a.m. to 5 p.m. Tuesday through Sunday. When a holiday falls on a Monday, they are open on the holiday and closed the following day. For more information, contact the **Department of Recreation and Sports** (☎ 787-722-1551 or 787-724-2500).

Puerto Ricans love the beach. So if you plan to hit the sand on the weekend or a holiday, go early to beat traffic and stake a good spot.

Diving in Puerto Rican waters

You probably won't find Puerto Rico at the top of a diver's list of favorite spots among the Caribbean islands. For one thing, all the fishing in its waters means that you won't see many larger fish. However, both hard and soft corals are still abundant and in good to great shape at many sites. The island's many caves, mangrove swamps that serve as fish nurseries, and two bioluminescent bays for night dives all offer rich prospects for diving adventure.

Snorkeling and scuba diving instruction and equipment rentals are available at **Boquerón Dive Shop** (Main St., Boquerón; ☎ 787-851-2155); **Caribbean School of Aquatics** (San Juan Bay Marina; ☎ 787-728-6606); **Taíno Divers** (Rincón; ☎ 787-823-6429; Internet: www.tainodivers.com); **Descheco Dive Shop** (Rincón; ☎ 888-823-0390 or 787-823-0390); and **Dive Copamarina** (Copamarina Beach Resort, Route

333, Km 6.5, Guánica; ☎ **787-821-6009**). Advanced divers who are comfortable with boat dives should try **Parguera Divers Training Center** (Posada Par La Mar, Route 304, La Parguera; ☎ **787-899-4171**).

Sailing away

Virtually all the resort hotels on San Juan's Condado and Isla Verde strips rent paddleboats, Sunfish, Windsurfers, and kayaks. The waves here can be strong, but the constant wind makes for good sailing. In San Juan, contact the **Condado Plaza Hotel and Casino Watersports Center** (999 Avenue Ashford; ☎ **787-721-1000**, ext. 1361) or the **Wyndham El San Juan Hotel & Casino Watersports Center** (Avenue Isla Verde; ☎ **787-791-1000**). Boating and sailing trips of all kinds are offered by **Caribbean School of Aquatics** (San Juan Bay Marina; ☎ **787-728-6606**) and **Castillo Watersports** (ESJ Towers, Isla Verde; ☎ **787-791-6195** or 787-725-7970).

Outside of San Juan, **Iguana Water Sports** (Westin Rio Mar Beach Resort and Country Club, 6000 Rio Mar Blvd., Rio Grande; ☎ **787-888-6000**) has a particularly good selection of small boats. Sailing instruction is available at the **Palmas Sailing Center** (Doral Resort at Palmas del Mar, Route 906, Humacao; ☎ **787-852-6000**). **East Wind II Catamaran** (Fajardo; ☎ **787-860-3434**) can fix you up with a catamaran.

Heading to the greens

For golf lovers, Puerto Rico is paradise. In recent years, the island has hosted the LPGA tour and the Hyatt PGA Matchplay Challenge. You can pick from 18 courses on the island, 14 of which are championship links designed by the best-known names: Greg Norman; Robert Trent Jones, Sr.; George Fazio; Arthur Hills; Gary Player; and, of course, home-island hero Chi Chi Rodriguez. Call ahead for details on reserving tee times. Hours vary, and several hotel courses limit their players to guests only (or at least give preference to guests). Greens fees start at about $25 and go up as high as $114.

The island's newest courses are **Dorado del Mar** (☎ **787-796-3065**) and **Flamboyan at the Doral Resort at Palmas del Mar** (Route 906, Humacao; ☎ **787-852-6000**). The Flamboyan is classic, elegant, and beautiful. The view from the twelfth hole is breathtaking, and the thirteenth hole is a showstopper. If you can't get a tee time on this course, try the property's older but revitalized Gary Player-designed Palmas course, or book time at the immense driving range.

Just 19 miles from San Juan, the **Westin Rio Mar Beach Resort and Country Club** (6000 Rio Mar Blvd., Rio Grande; ☎ **787-888-6000**) has two world-class courses. Greg Norman designed the River Course, while George Fazio designed the famous Ocean Course. Both are sandwiched between the ocean and the foot of El Yunque, the only tropical rain forest in the U.S. National Forest system.

Four attractive Robert Trent Jones-designed 18-hole courses are shared by the Hyatt Dorado Beach and the **Hyatt Regency Cerromar Beach** hotels (Route 693, Km 10.8 and Km 11.8, Dorado; ☎ **787-796-1234,** ext. 3238 or 3016). Some of Chi Chi's favorite holes are on these courses.

Hiking the island

Trails lace the 28,000 acres of the Caribbean National Forest known as **El Yunque,** which is 45 minutes from San Juan (El Portal Tropical Forest Center, Highway 3 then right on Route 191; ☎ **787-888-1810** or 787-888-1880). El Portal Tropical Forest Center features displays that explain El Yunque and tropical forests around the world. A theater holds shows in English and Spanish. The visitor's center for the forest is open daily from 7:30 a.m. to 5 p.m. (6 p.m. on weekends). El Portal has a $3 entry fee.

For more information, you can contact the **Department of Natural Resources** (☎ **787-724-3724**) and the **U.S. Forest Service** (☎ **787-766-5335**). We suggest planning a full day of exploring this magnificent preserve; if you have kids along, you can find plenty of easy trails for them to tackle.

Most San Juan hotels have a tour desk that can make arrangements for you to hike the forests. All-day tours ($25 to $45) can include a trip to Ponce, a day at El Comandante Racetrack, or a combined tour of the city of Ponce and E1 Yunque rain forest. Leading tour operators include **Gray Line of Puerto Rico** (☎ **787-727-8080**), **Normandie Tours, Inc.** (☎ **787-722-6308**), **Rico Suntours** (☎ **787-722-2080** or 787-722-6090), **Tropix Wellness Tours** (☎ **787-268-2173**), and **United Tour Guides** (☎ **787-725-7605** or 787-723-5578).

Exploring Old San Juan

Designated a U.S. National Historic Zone in 1950, the crown jewel of Puerto Rico is Old San Juan, the most beautiful city in the Caribbean. The original city, founded in 1521, contains carefully preserved examples of sixteenth- and seventeenth-century Spanish colonial architecture and is the oldest capital city under the U.S. flag. UNESCO has designated the El Morro and Fort San Cristobal fortresses as World Heritage Sites; each is also a National Historic Site. You can take a tour or wander on your own. Here are the some of the sites you don't want to miss:

✔ **Fuerte San Filipe del Morro:** An imposing fortress built by the Spaniards between 1540 and 1783, El Morro is a labyrinth of dungeons, ramps, barracks, turrets, towers, and tunnels. Calle

Norzagaray; ☎ 787-729-6960. Admission is $2. Open daily from 9 a.m. to 5 p.m.

✔ **Museo de Arte y Historia de San Juan:** A bustling marketplace in 1855, this handsome building is now the modern San Juan Museum of Art and History. Calla Norzagaray at Calle MacArthur; ☎ 787-724-1875. Admission is free. Open Tuesday through Sunday from 10 a.m. to 4 p.m.

✔ **Museo Pablo Casals:** The Pablo Casals Museum contains memorabilia of the famed cellist, who made his home in Puerto Rico for the last 16 years of his life. 101 Calle San Sebastian, Plaza de San Jose; ☎ 787-723-9185. Admission is $1. Open Tuesday through Saturday from 9:30 a.m. to 5:30 p.m.

✔ **San Cristobal:** This eighteenth-century fortress guarded the city from land attacks. Even larger than El Morro, San Cristobal was known in the seventeenth and eighteenth centuries as the Gibraltar of the West Indies. Calle Norzagaray; ☎ 787-729-6960. Admission is $2. Open daily 9 a.m. to 5 p.m.

Living la vida loca

Wherever you find Sanjuaneros (San Juan's residents), you find a party going on. Puerto Ricans love social life, and tops on their lists are dancing and dressing up.

Like New York, the whirling club scene of San Juan can be tough to keep up with. **Que Pasa,** the official visitor's guide, has current listings of the happenings in San Juan and out on the island. Also, pick up a copy of the **San Juan Star, Quick City Guide,** or **Bienvenidos,** and check with the local tourist offices and the concierge at your hotel to find out what's doing.

Fridays and Saturdays are big nights in San Juan, so dress to party. Bars are usually casual, but if you go out in jeans, sneakers, and a T-shirt, you'll probably be refused entry at most nightclubs or discos, unless you look like a model. You have to be stylish in this town.

Old San Juan's cobblestone streets are closed to auto traffic on Friday and Saturday nights, making the area perfect for a romantic stroll. If you want more action, walk to **Calle San Sebastian,** lined with trendy bars and restaurants where you see lines of people waiting to get through the doors.

Outside of San Juan, nightlife is hard to come by beyond the resorts. If you stay at an upscale hotel, ask the concierge if he or she can reserve a good table at the most happening spots; otherwise, you may be left standing outside the gilded doors.

Remember: The hottest action doesn't start until around 10 p.m.

The place to see and be seen is the lobby of the **El San Juan Hotel & Casino,** where you can find couples doing the merengue to live Latin bands. (A ten-member Cuban band was rocking when we were there last.) The hotel's **Babylon** (☎ **787-791-2781**) is the hot ticket for Puerto Ricans, but the dress is decidedly upscale, so make sure you look the part.

By law, all casinos are in hotels, primarily in San Juan, dress for the larger casinos tends to be on the formal side, and the atmosphere is refined. The law permits casinos to operate from noon to 4 a.m., but individual casinos set their own hours within that time frame. In addition to slot machines, typical games include blackjack, roulette, craps, Caribbean stud poker (a five-card stud game), and pai gow poker (a combination of American poker and the ancient Chinese game of pai gow, which employs cards and dice). Hotels that house casinos have live entertainment most weekends, restaurants, and bars; players can usually buy drinks in the casino. The minimum age is 18.

Dining in Puerto Rico

If eating well is a key part of your vacation, get ready to love Puerto Rico. Old San Juan is known as a haven for cutting-edge chefs who win rave reviews from food enthusiasts.

If you want to splurge on one of Puerto Rico's many chic restaurants, remember that this is an island where appearance matters. Puerto Ricans love to dress up and dine out, and the scene at the over-the-top weekend extravaganza that happens at their beloved El San Juan every week, which has numerous terrific restaurants, has trained the locals to expect great cuisine from the hotels. Pack your finest resort wear. You won't be shut out of a restaurant because you don't look the part, but the right dress and approach helps to determine how you're treated. Wherever you go, make reservations during the busy season (mid-November through April).

Creating special memories

We were lured into **Chef Marisoll** (202 Calle Cristo; ☎ **787-725-7454; $$$$**) by the dramatic arrangement of tables in a palm-studded courtyard overhung with ornate balconies; more tables were tucked into high-ceilinged rooms on either side. Eye-catching art decorates the walls and your plate. Head straight through the outside passage of **Amadeus** (106 Calle San Sebastian; ☎ **787-722-8635; $$$**) to the romantic dining room in the back of the restaurant, where you find printed tablecloths, candles, and exposed brick. The best Italian restaurant in Old San Juan, **Il Perugino** (105 Calle Cristo; ☎ 787-722-5481; $$$$), a small, intimate eatery set in a 200-year-old townhouse, stresses attentive service and delicious Italian cuisine. The **Horned Dorset Primavera** (Route 429, Km 3, Rincón; ☎ 787-823-4030 or 787-823-4050; $$$$), tucked away on the west coast of the island in the posh Horned Dorset Primavera hotel, is where foodies head when they want to get out of Old San Juan. A five-course, prix-fixe menu is available for $56 per person.

Knowing a hot spot

Parrot Club (363 Calle Fortaleza; ☎ 787-725-7370; $$$), the red-hot restaurant (and beautiful people's second home) in Old San Juan, is a crowded bistro and bar serving Nuevo Latino cuisine. The gorgeous setting elevates the experience further — the restaurant is housed in a circa-1902 building that once served as a hair-tonic factory, in a neighborhood known as SOFO (South of Fortaleza Street).

Discovering unusual cuisine

To enter the fantastical setting of **Back Street Hong Kong** (In the El San Juan Hotel & Casino, Isla Verde Ave.; ☎ 787-791-1000; $$$$), you walk down a re-creation of a backwater street in Hong Kong. Disassembled from its original home at the 1964 New York World's Fair, the set was rebuilt here according to the original design. At the **Butterfly People Café** (Calle Fortaleza 152; ☎ 787-723-2432; $$), next to the world's largest gallery devoted to butterflies, you can dine on the second floor of a restored mansion and overlook a courtyard.

Looking for a late-night hangout

A wide selection of beers combined with live Spanish guitar-playing and a namesake pizza make **El Patio de Sam** (102 Calle San Sebastian, across from the Iglesia de San José; ☎ 787-723-1149; $$) a popular spot with locals and tourists alike.

Finding a local favorite

At **Ajili-Mójili** (1052 Av. Ashford (at the corner of Calle Joffre); ☎ 787-725-9195; $$$), Chef Mariano Ortiz elevates *comida criolla*, the starchy, sometimes greasy cuisine that developed on the island a century ago, to an art form. Wash it down with an ice-cold bottle of Medalla, the local beer. **La Bombonera** (259 Calle San Francisco; ☎ 787-722-0658; $), a landmark restaurant, with its ornate street-side facade, was established in 1902 and is known for its strong Puerto Rican coffee and excellent pastries. It's a favorite Sunday-morning gathering place.

Settling into Puerto Rico

You can scarcely ask for an island easier and cheaper to get to in the Caribbean than Puerto Rico, which is the gateway island to the region. You know that you're not in Kansas anymore — though still in a U.S. territory — from the moment you touch down on this island, which is about half the size of New Jersey and two hours by plane from Miami, Florida. You feel at least 1,000 miles away (which you are!) when you hear Spanish being spoken all around you.

Arriving in Puerto Rico

The **Luis Muñoz Marin International Airport** (☎ 787-791-4670), east of downtown San Juan, is one of the easiest and cheapest destinations to reach in the Caribbean. It's also the Caribbean's premier airport — clean, safe, spacious, and modern. It reminds us somewhat of the Miami airport with its tropical flair. It is the Caribbean hub for American Airlines, which has nonstop flights from New York, Newark, Miami, and many other North American cities. American has 82 daily departures, serving 21 Caribbean destinations. Several other major airlines also serve the Caribbean from this airport. Delta has increased its presence here, too. That means it's also the busiest Caribbean airport, so expect bustling crowds.

If you are a U.S. citizen or resident, you don't have to go through Customs and Immigration at the airport, because Puerto Rico is a U.S. territory. Just follow the signs to ground transportation. U.S. citizens do not need a passport to visit Puerto Rico.

As soon as you arrive in Puerto Rico, grab several of the island's terrific materials for tourists. You can find a wealth of information (and great coupons that you want in hand if you rent a car). One of the better discount programs is the **Fun and Savings Program** ($15 per person), which offers up to $3,400 worth of savings for everything from restaurants, car rentals, hotels, shows, sightseeing tours, and more. You can sign up for it at the airport, or you can find information at hotels. For information, call ☎ **800-866-7827** or 787-723-3135 or check the island's excellent Web site at www.prtourism.com.

Getting around Puerto Rico

Your preferred method of transportation in Puerto Rico may depend on how much time and money you want to spend. **Bracero Limousine Ltd.** (☎ **787-253-1133**) offers minivan transport from the airport to various neighborhoods of San Juan for prices that are lower than for similar routings offered by taxis. Whenever eight to ten passengers can be accumulated, the fare for transport (with luggage) to any hotel in Isla Verde is $2.50 per person; to Condado, $3 per person; and to Old San Juan, $3.50 per person.

Renting a car

If you stay in San Juan, you can get around on foot or by bus, taxi, and hotel shuttle, but if you venture out on the island, you should definitely rent a car.

Roads in Puerto Rico are generally good and well-marked, until you get out in the more rural areas. There, many exits just read *salida* (which means "exit"), with no indication of what town you're accessing. Some car-rental agencies give you a free island map when you pick up your car, but these maps lack detail and are usually out of date. Be sure to get a good map (see the "Fast Facts: Puerto Rico" section later in this chapter) — one that's as detailed and up to date as possible.

A valid driver's license from your country of origin can be used in Puerto Rico for three months. All major U.S. car rental agencies are represented on the island, including the following:

- ✔ **Avis** (☎ **800-874-3556** or 787-791-2500)
- ✔ **Budget** (☎ **800-527-0700** or 787-791-3685)
- ✔ **Dollar** (☎ **800-800-4000** or 787-791-5500)
- ✔ **Hertz** (☎ **800-654-3030** or 787-791-0840)
- ✔ **National** (☎ **787-791-1805**)
- ✔ **Thrifty** (☎ **787-253-2525**)

Local rental companies, sometimes less expensive, include:

- ✔ **L & M Car Rental** (☎ **800-654-3030** or 787-791-1160)
- ✔ **Tropical** (☎ **877-791-2820** or 787-791-2820)

Rental rates can start as low as $30 per day (plus insurance), with unlimited mileage. Discounts are offered for long-term rentals, and insurance can be waived for those who rent with American Express or certain gold credit cards. (Be sure to check with your credit card company before renting.) Look for discount coupons in tourist magazines. Some discounts are offered for AAA membership or 72-hour advance bookings.

Most car rentals have shuttle service to or from the airport and the pickup point.

You may go loco with all the mixed signage: Speed limits are posted in miles per hour, but distances are listed in kilometers. Gas is sold per liter and priced accordingly. Note that many service stations in the central mountains don't take credit cards.

Hiring a taxi

Taxi Turisticos, which are painted white and bear the company's logo on the doors, is the major company in the tourist areas. It charges set rates based on zones, so your cost depends on your destination. These taxis run from the airport or the cruise ship piers to Isla Verde, Condado/ Ocean Park, and Old San Juan, with rates ranging from $6 to $16.

Metered cabs authorized by the **Public Service Commission (☎ 787-756-1919)** have a minimum charge of $3 and an initial $1 to get rolling. After that, you're charged 10 cents for every additional ⅟₁₃ mile or every 45 seconds of waiting time. You also pay 50 cents for every suitcase. Be sure that the driver starts the meter. You can also call **Major Taxicabs (☎ 787-723-2460)** in San Juan and **Ponce Taxi (☎ 787-840-0088)** in Ponce.

Taxis are lined up outside the entrances to most hotels, and if not, a staff member can almost always call one for you. But if you would like to arrange a taxi on your own, call the **Rochdale Radio Taxi (☎ 787-721-1900)**.

Walking

If you stay in one of the major tourist areas, you can easily tool around on foot — especially in Old San Juan, which is a walking city. If you get tired, you can always hop on Old San Juan's free trolley (which is described later in this section).

You can go on a self-guided walking tour; look for tour outlines in a copy of *Que Pasa,* available at all tourist offices and hotels. If you want to go deeper, hire a tour guide from **Colonial Adventure** (201 Recinto Sur; **☎ 787-729-0114**). The company offers a variety of informative walking tours; rates range from $16 to $22 per person.

Taking a bus

The **Metropolitan Bus Authority (☎ 787-729-1512)** operates *guaguas* (buses) that thread through San Juan. The fare is 25 cents on a regular bus and 50 cents on a Metrobus. Buses are comfortably air-conditioned, but sometimes they are crowded and don't always run on schedule. We'd only use them if our funds were exceptionally tight.

Publicos (public cars), with yellow license plates ending in "P" or "PD," scoot to towns throughout the island, stopping in each town's main plaza. These 17-passenger vans operate primarily during the day, with routes and fares fixed by the Public Service Commission. In San Juan, the main terminals are at the airport and at Plaza Colón on the water-front in Old San Juan. Information about *publico* routes between San Juan and Mayagüez is available from **Linea Sultana,** Calle Esteban González 898, Urbanización Santa Rita, Rio Piedras (**☎ 787-765-9377**). Information about *publico* routes between San Juan and Ponce is avail-able from **Choferes Unidos de Ponce,** Terminal de Carros Publicos, Calle Vive in Ponce (**☎ 787-764-0540**) or **Linea Boricua (☎ 787-765-1908)**.

Trying a trolley

If your feet fail you in Old San Juan, climb aboard the free open-air trolleys that rumble and roller-coast through the narrow streets. Departures are from the Covadonga parking lot in the southeastern corner of the city. The trolleys cover two routes: up to Plaza de Armas, and a northern route to El Morro. Passengers can get on and off at any stop.

Ferrying around

The **Ferry de Cataño** (☎ 787-788-1155) crosses San Juan Bay between Old San Juan (Pier 2) and costs a mere 50 cents one-way. It runs every half hour from 6 a.m. to 10 p.m. The 400-passenger ferries of the **Fajardo Port Authority** (☎ 787-863-0705), which carry cargo as well as passengers, make the 90-minute trip between Fajardo and Vieques three times daily ($2 one-way). They make the 90-minute run from Fajardo to Culebra twice a day on weekdays and twice (with three runs from Culebra to Fajardo) on weekends ($2.50 one-way).

Fast Facts: Puerto Rico

ATMs

These machines are called ATH on Puerto Rico, but they operate the same as ATMs and are widely available on the island. You find one at the airport near Gate 4.

Banks

Most major U.S., Canadian, and European banks have branches in San Juan and are open weekdays from 8:30 a.m. to 2:30 p.m. and Saturday from 9:45 a.m. to noon.

Credit Cards

All major credit cards are widely accepted on the island. But gasoline cards from the U.S. typically aren't accepted on the island.

Currency Exchange

Puerto Rico, as a commonwealth of the United States, uses the U.S. dollar as its official currency. International travelers can find foreign exchange offices in San Juan. A good one is the Caribbean Exchange (201 Calle Tetuan; ☎ 787-722-8222).

Departure Tax

Airport departure tax is included in the price of your ticket.

Doctors

Puerto Rico has an excellent healthcare system. Ask your hotel for a referral if necessary.

Electricity

Puerto Rico uses a 110-volt AC (60-cycle) electrical system, the same as in North America. European guests who have traveling appliances that use other systems can call ahead to confirm that their hotel has adapters and converters.

Emergencies

Ambulance, police, and fire: ☎ **911.**

Hospitals

If you need hospital care, contact one of the following: **Ashford Presbyterian Community Hospital** (1451 Av. Ashford, Condado, San Juan; ☎ 787-721-2160); **Bella Vista Hospital** (Cerro las Mesas, Mayagüez; ☎ 787-834-6000 or 787-834-2350); the clinic **Eastern Medical Associates** (267 Av. Valero, Fajardo; ☎ 787-863-0669), and **San Juan Health Centre** (200 Av. de Diego, San Juan; ☎ 787-725-0202).

Information

Contact the **Puerto Rico Tourism Company** (P.O. Box 902-3960, Old San Juan Station, San Juan,

PR 00902-3960; ☎ 800-223-6530 from the United States, or 787-721-2400; Internet: www.prtourism.com).

Language

Puerto Rico's official languages are Spanish and English. Although English is widely spoken, you may want to take a Spanish phrase book with you, especially if you plan to travel beyond San Juan.

Maps

On Puerto Rico, the **Puerto Rico Tourism Company** (Paseo de la Princesa, Old San Juan, PR 00901; ☎ 787-721-2400) is an excellent source for maps and printed tourist materials. Be sure to pick up a free copy of *Qué Pasa* and *Bienvenidos,* the official visitors' guide.

Newspapers/Magazines

Getting publications from all over the world is easy on this island. You find excellent news-stands at the airport. The *San Juan Star* comes out daily in English and Spanish.

Pharmacies

The most common and easily found pharmacies are **Puerto Rico Drug Company** (157 Call San Francisco, Old San Juan; ☎ 787-725-2202) and **Walgreens** (1330 Av. Ashford, Condado, San Juan; ☎ 787-725-1510). Walgreens operates more than 30 pharmacies on the island. Condado has one that is open 24 hours a day (☎ 787-725-1510).

Police

For assistance with a police emergency, ☎ **911.**

Post Office

Post offices in major Puerto Rican cities offer Express Mail next-day service to the U.S. mainland and to Puerto Rican destinations.

Major post office branches are located at 153 Calle Fortaleza in Old San Juan, 163 Avendia Fernandez Juncos in San Juan, 60 Calle McKinley in Mayagüez, and 102 Calle Garrido Morales in Fajardo. Post offices are open weekdays from 7:30 a.m. to 4:30 p.m. and Saturday from 8 a.m. to noon.

Safety

San Juan, like any other big city, has its share of crime, so guard your wallet or purse on the city streets. Puerto Rico's beaches are open to the public, and muggings can occur at night even on the beaches of the posh Condado and Isla Verde tourist hotels. Although you certainly can, and should, explore the city and its beaches, use common sense. Don't leave anything unattended on the beach. Leave your valuables in the hotel safe, and stick to the fenced-in beach areas of your hotel. Always lock your car and stash valu-ables and luggage out of sight. Avoid deserted beaches at night. Surfers have had several problems with gear being stolen from rental cars.

Store Hours

Street shops are open Monday through Satur-day from 9 a.m. to 6 p.m. (9 a.m. to 9 p.m. during Christmas holidays). Mall stores tend to stay open later, until 8 or 9 p.m. in most cases.

Taxes

Some hotels automatically add a 10 to 15 per-cent service charge to your bill. Check ahead to confirm whether this charge is built into the room rate or is tacked on at checkout. Some smaller hotels might charge extra (as much as $5 per day) for the use of air-conditioning, called an "energy tax." The government tax on rooms is 9 percent (11 percent in hotels with casinos and 7 percent on *paradores*). As with service charges, you need to confirm whether or not the tax is built into the room rate.

Telephone

Puerto Rico's area code is 787 — for North Americans, dialing Puerto Rico is the same as dialing another state in the U.S. or a Canadian province. When making a call on the island, just dial the seven-digit number.

Time Zone

Puerto Rico is in Atlantic Standard Time, one hour ahead of Eastern Standard Time and the same as Eastern Daylight Time. For the current time of day, call ☎ 787-728-9696.

Tipping

Tips are expected, and appreciated, by restaurant waitstaff (15 to 18 percent if a service charge isn't included), hotel porters ($1 per bag), maids ($1 to $2 per day), and taxi drivers (10 to 15 percent).

Water

Tap water is generally fine on the island; just avoid drinking it after storms (when the drinking-water supply might become mixed with sewage).

Thoroughly wash or peel produce that you buy in markets before eating it.

Weather Reports

Log on to the Caribbean Weather Man at www. caribwx.com/cyclone.html or listen to Radio WOSO (1030 AM), an English-speaking radio station.

Chapter 20

Honeymooning in St. Lucia

By Echo & Kevin Garrett

● ●

In This Chapter

▶ Finding the best honeymoon accommodations

▶ Discovering the fun and romance of St. Lucia

▶ Uncovering all the details

● ●

*A*hhhh, St. Lucia. An often-overlooked gem, the island yields one surprise after another: a steamy volcano, secluded waterfalls, dramatic mountain vistas, lush rain forests, even private mineral baths used by Napoleon's muse Josephine, who grew up on one of the island's plantations. It has for years been a favorite of honeymooners.

But the crowning glory of St. Lucia (pronounced *loo-sha*) is the Pitons, postcard-perfect twin volcanic peaks rising majestically out of the sea. To the east, the Atlantic Ocean crashes against the coast; to the west lie the serene beauty of the Caribbean and the island's best beaches.

On St. Lucia, you have a wide range of accommodations from which to choose: from small, inexpensive guest houses to romantic villas to pampering spas to corporate all-inclusives to swank boutique hideaways. The cool thing is that none are the monolithic high-rises that look so out of place on other Caribbean islands.

 Not everyone shares our sensibilities, of course. Some people love to escape civilization, while others break into hives at the thought of a resort without a swim-up bar, a hairdryer, or a television. (We'll never forget being at one of our ultimate-fantasy favorites — Anse Chastanet — and hearing a couple complain that the tree frogs were too loud). If you, too, prefer the hum of electronics to the peeping of frogs, please note that not all the resorts described in this chapter have air-conditioning and televisions, and not all are right on the beach, so read our write-ups carefully.

Figuring Out Where to Stay

Virtually all of St. Lucia's lodgings are along the calm Caribbean coast, either around Soufrière to the south or between Castries and Cap Estate in the north. You find the densest concentration of the all-inclusives, sprawling resorts, and guest houses hugging the coastline between Castries and Gros Islet.

We know it's tempting — and easy — to simply ensconce yourself in a beach chair and hole up at your all-inclusive resort (especially if Castries was your first impression of St. Lucia), but if you neglect touring the island, you miss one of the most beautiful places in the Caribbean. Covered with banana plantations, lush rainforests, and one stunning vista after another, St. Lucia is well worth the extra money for a day tour.

Choosing Among St. Lucia's Best Accommodations for Honeymooners

Out of the past seven couples who have gotten married who are friends of ours, six chose St. Lucia for their honeymoon, and the majority picked Anse Chastanet. But we'd be hard-pressed to choose from among these excellent choices. Like Jamaica, St. Lucia's lodging scene is increasingly dominated by all-inclusives. Several also offer terrific wedding and honeymoon packages; many offer specialty packages, too, for eco travelers and those looking to de-stress at a spa.

The rack rates that appear for each accommodation are in U.S. dollars, and they represent the price range for a standard double room during high season (mid-December to mid-April), unless otherwise noted. Lower rates are often available during the off-season summer months and the shoulder seasons of late spring and fall.

Please refer to the Introduction of *Honeymoon Vacations For Dummies* for an explanations of our price categories.

Anse Chastanet

$$$$$$$ **Soufrière**

Lovers can commune with nature and each other in this lush, private 500-acre estate that's 1½ miles from Soufrière up the worst road on the island. It's a magical place — one of our top five most romantic picks — and features 59 whimsically designed rooms. Each has louvered wooden walls, an ultra-private balcony with chaise lounges, terra-cotta tile floors, crisp madras cotton fabrics, island furniture of hand-crafted mahogany, teak, or purple heart, and a spacious bath. Great diving and guided snorkeling — a PADI/SSI Platinum five-star dive operation is onsite — is another of the draws. You also have Bike St. Lucia (mountain bike rides), a mini-spa that specializes in couples' massage, two restaurants and bars, tennis courts, but no pool. You won't miss the pool since the calm sea waters gently lap the sheltered shore.

St. Lucia

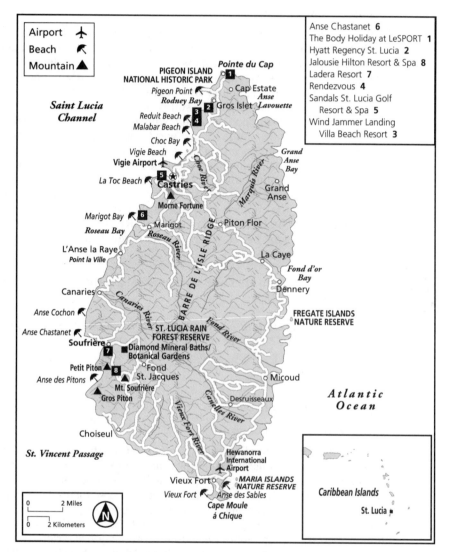

Airport ✈		Anse Chastanet **6**
Beach ✓		The Body Holiday at LeSPORT **1**
Mountain ▲		Hyatt Regency St. Lucia **2**

Anse Chastanet isn't for everybody. We don't recommend it to anyone who has trouble getting around (you need to be fit enough to climb the 100 steps from the volcanic sand beach up to the restaurant and the many, many steps to the hillside suites beyond). Also, the rooms don't have air conditioning, phones, or TVs.

P.O. Box 7000, Soufrière. ☎ ***800-223-1108,*** *reservations for divers 888-GO-LUCIA or 758-459-7000. Fax: 758-459-7700. E-mail:* ansechastanet@candw.lc. *Internet:* www.ansechastanet.com. *Rack rates: $520-$695 double. AE, DC, MC, V. Eco, romance and dive packages available.*

The Body Holiday at LeSPORT

$$$-$$$$ **Cap Estate**

Although we're not usually bowled over by all-inclusives, we love The Body Holiday at LeSPORT, an ultra all-inclusive secluded on St. Lucia's northern tip. The airy, bright rooms in the new wing are elegant in the French colonial style to which many aspire, but few attain. Each room has a balcony or terrace; deluxe rooms are on the ocean or have a view of it. Two adjoining one-bedroom suites have a hand-stenciled ginger-bread motif on the walls, cool blue-and-white fabrics, white marble floors, huge double balconies, and stocked wet bars. In between relaxing spa treatments, active types can get a great workout: archery, tai chi, golf, biking, fencing, tennis, volleyball, hikes, mountain climbing, and yoga are all available. Even scuba diving PADI certification and water-skiing are included in the rates. A personal trainer can help you devise a plan if you're addled by the choices, and, best of all, stress management is part of the package. The Body Holiday at LeSPORT is known for its lavish Moorish-themed spa, Oasis, where guests receive two complimentary treatments a day.

Alert the staff that you are honeymooners and ask that your schedule be matched accordingly.

Cariblue Beach, Cap Estate (P.O. Box 437), Castries. ☎ *800-544-2883, 0181-780-0800 in the UK. Fax: 305-672-5861 or 758-450-0368. E-mail:* tropichol@aol.com. *Internet:* www.lesport.com.lc. *Rack rates: $195-$390. Rates are all-inclusive. AE, DC, MC, V.*

Hyatt Regency St. Lucia

$$$$ **Pigeon Island Causeway**

Located six miles north of Castries (15 minutes from the airport) and over-looking Rodney Bay, this latest offering from Hyatt Resorts carefully blends all the ingredients to create a top-notch Caribbean escape. While this resort features Hyatt's signature design elements — lushly landscaped, elaborate water features, and beach/poolside concierges — it has taste-fully incorporated St. Lucia's British colonial character throughout the four-story resort. Plantation-style antique reproduction and rattan furnishings and native art showcase the island's local culture. Each of the 284 air-conditioned guest rooms features oversize balconies with panoramic Caribbean or bay views. For true water lovers, it has lagoon swim-up rooms. Other draws are its 4,000 square-foot spa with private outdoor treatment rooms, golf, tennis, and 1,000 feet of excellent sandy beach.

Gros Islet. ☎ *800-55-HYATT or 758-451-1234. Fax: 758-450-9450. Internet:* www.hyatt.com. *Rack rates: $275-$345. Honeymoon and wedding packages available. AE, DC, MC, V.*

Jalousie Hilton Resort & Spa

$$$$$ **Jalousie Bay, Soufrière**

This Edenic 325-acre resort overlooking Jalousie Bay, snuggled between St. Lucia's signature twin landmarks, the Pitons, occupies one of the most breathtaking locations in the Caribbean. The resort, designated a rain-forest nature sanctuary by the St. Lucia Naturalist's Society, was built on the remains of an eighteenth-century sugar plantation. It has 102 bright and air-conditioned, 550 square-foot cottages with huge bathrooms and private plunge pools. (Hint: the Sugar Mill rooms, which cost less, are amply sized and closer to the beach and pool area. You just don't get your own plunge pool.) The beach and main pool area are a good five-minute walk from the cottages. Amenities include a full-service spa featuring indigenous treatments, a PADI dive center, a three-hole golf course, a well-equipped fitness center, all kinds of water sports, a marina, and four restaurants, bars, and tennis courts. Oh, and did we mention basketball, biking, racquetball, and squash? How about the shops, night-club, airport shuttle, Jeep rental, and helipad — for $75 you can skip the 45-minute drive from the airport?

5 miles from Soufrière on Anse des Pitons (P.O. Box 251), Soufrière. ☎ *800-445-8667, 888-744-5256 (direct to hotel), or 758-459-7666. Fax: 758-459-7667. E-mail:* jhr_sales&mkt@candw.lc. *Internet:* www.jalousie-hilton.com. *Rack rates: $475 Sugar Mill Room; $500 Villa; $600 Villa Suite. Honeymoon, tennis, scuba, cook-ing, and more packages available. AE, DISC, DC, MC, V.*

Ladera Resort

$$$$$ **Soufrière**

Peaceful and remote, Ladera boasts one of the Caribbean's most coveted locations, and its eagle's-eye view of the Pitons lures rock stars, TV celebs, corporate VIPs, and honeymooners seeking solitude. To make sure that you don't miss the view — as if this were a possibility — each suite and villa comes with a completely open west wall. The best part: You can soak in your own private plunge pool or your villa's pool fed by a waterfall while the sun sinks behind the Pitons. Each suite and villa, cooled by ceiling fans and the tropical breezes, is a little different, built of stone, island woods, and tiles. All are decorated with an artful blend of local crafts, wicker, four-poster beds, and nineteenth-century French antiques. Free snorkeling equipment, a breakfast buffet, and daily shuttle service throughout the day to Soufrière and tranquil Anse Chastanet's beach are all part of the rates.

Above the Pitons, 2 miles south of town (P.O. Box 225), Soufrière. ☎ *800-738-4752 or 758-459-7323. Fax: 800-404-1841 or 758-459-5156. E-mail:* Ladera@candw.lc. *Internet:* www.Ladera-StLucia.com. *Rack rates: high season: suites from $345; luxury villa with pool $725. Rates include breakfast and transfers to Hewanorra with a three-night stay; from George F. Charles Airport with a four-night stay. Romance and wedding packages are available. AE, MC, V.*

Rendezvous

$$$ Malabar Beach

Rendezvous, a 100-room, couples-only resort, has evolved over the past 30 years into a collection of low-slung buildings housing 100 rooms spread over seven acres of landscaped tropical gardens. There's much to do if you desire, but the activities must be sought out. Windsurfing, kneeboarding, kayaking, scuba diving and island tours are a few of the options. The largely European clientele appears content to loll for hours on the wide, nutmeg-colored beach and read book after book. The beach chairs and hammocks, coupled with the attentive but unobtrusive staff, are irresistible. Usually warning flags are up, because dangerous rip tides tend to develop in the surf here.

Rendezvous is on the site of an old coconut plantation fronting two miles of beach, with the far end of the beach starting literally at the end of the Vigie Airport runway. Fortunately, by the end of the first day we scarcely noticed the infrequent noise of the small aircraft.

P.O. Box 190, Castries. ☎ *800-544-2883 or 758-452-4211. Fax: 758-452-7419. Internet:* www.rendezvous.com.1c. *Rack rates: $350-$386 double; $440-$481 ocean-front suite. Rates are per couple and all-inclusive. AE, MC, V.*

Sandals St. Lucia Golf Resort & Spa

$$$$$ Castries

Sandals St. Lucia is secluded on 155-acres, 15 minutes from the Castries airport, and is extremely popular with young couples drawn by the Sandals formula for delivering a reliably fun vacation experience at an all-inclusive price. Guests have a blast — thanks to the young, energetic, and fun-loving staff. The list of facilities and amenities is almost endless: an 18-hole golf course, floodlit tennis courts, an outstanding fitness center, and nightly entertainment. The fine-dining restaurant, La Toc, stands out, but the food here in general is far above what you may expect at an all-inclusive. The gargantuan, 5,000 square-foot pool — the resort boasts that it's the biggest in the Caribbean, but we didn't have our measuring tape — has a waterfall, swim-up bar, and bridges for strolling.

La Toc Rd. (P.O. Box 399), Castries. ☎ *800-223-6510 or 758-452-3081. Fax: 758-453-7089. E-mail:* sandals@candw.1c. *Internet:* www.sandals.com. *Rack rates: $300-$385 per person; suites $420-$695 per person. Note: three-night minimum. AE, D, DC, MC, V. Guests also have privileges at nearby Sandals Halcyon St. Lucia (P.O. Box GM910, Castries;* ☎ *758-453-0222; Fax: 758-451-8435; E-mail:* sandalshc@candw.1c; *Rack rates: $280-$330) and vice versa. But the spa gives this one the edge.*

Windjammer Landing Villa Beach Resort

$$$ Labrelotte

Honeymooners flock to this sun-kissed resort village with sweeping views of one of St. Lucia's most beautiful bays, though the water isn't the teal blue some expect of the Caribbean. The secluded beach has some rocks and scattered shells, so bring water shoes. Electric carts zip you around the steep hill between the villas, the main activity area, and two hillside pools connected by a waterfall on this 55-acre property. Well-organized water sports feature scuba instruction, Sunfish sailing, and kayaking. You also have shopping excursions, tennis courts, a fitness center, and four bars to keep you busy. The service here is friendly with only occasional stumbles, like failure to give wake-up calls, which can be a problem if you need to catch an early flight at the other end of the island.

This resort also markets itself to families, so during times when school vacation is on, you may find your dream spot overrun with tykes.

*Labrelotte Bay (P.O. Box 1504), Castries. ☎ **800-958-7376** or 758-452-0913. Fax: 758-452-9454. Internet:* www.WLV-Resort.com. *Rack rates: $150-$450 villa with 1-4 bedrooms. AE, DC, MC, V.*

Enjoying Your St. Lucian Honeymoon

St. Lucia has much more to offer than beach and water play. It's rougher around the edges than neighboring prim and proper Barbados, and you can see more of the *real* Caribbean here than on any of the other islands in this book. St. Lucia is much more akin in spirit to Jamaica, which has an equally colorful past. We've found the people of St. Lucia to be eager to help and eager to show you their island. Although they are poor, we haven't felt hustled or hassled, except right in Soufrière.

Because St. Lucia was formed by volcanic action, its natural beaches range in color from dark gold to almost black, and they tend to be small crescents tucked into lush coves. You find few wide, white sand beaches here — unless they are man-made like Jalousie Hilton's. All the beaches are public, and many on the west coast are flanked by a hotel where you can rent watersports equipment.

Unfortunately, the beaches — particularly around Castries — that are not directly in front of a hotel are often strewn with trash. The government has not done a good job of educating the population on how detrimental litter can be to the tourist trade. A few secluded beaches are accessible only by water, but your hotel can arrange boat trips. Don't swim along the windward (east) coast; the views are spectacular, but the Atlantic waters are rough.

Diving and snorkeling

Snorkelers and divers alike adore **Anse Chastanet Reef,** near the Pitons, which drops off from 20 feet to nearly 140 feet in a stunning coral wall. You literally walk right off the beach and start swimming until you're smack in the middle of one of the top snorkeling sites we've seen, with abundant colorful fish. Much of St. Lucia's coastal waters have been declared a national marine park, which protects the coral reefs and marine life by strictly controlling what fishermen, boaters, and divers can do in these waters. For instance, you can't drop anchor anywhere you want, which is extremely damaging to the reefs. Collecting fish, spearing fish, touching corals — all of those things are prohibited.

At the point of Anse Chastanet (see the hotel review earlier in this chapter), a plateau named **Fairy Land** slopes gently from 40 to 60 feet. Strong currents sweep the corals and sponges clean here, making it ideal for an underwater photo-op. Although the diving isn't challenging here, even those who've been all over the Caribbean agree that Anse Chastanet's corals are some of the better preserved, and the marine life excellent. Note to the obnoxious guides from Sandals: Cool it with feeding the fish! Everything was beautiful until you came on the scene.

Anse Chastanet reef has a mystery: "The Thing," St. Lucia's own "Loch-Ness-monster-on-vacation," which is seen regularly but only on night dives.

Many operators can arrange snorkeling and diving for you. One-tank dives start at about $50. Snorkeling trips run about $30, including gear rental. Gear and trips off shore are often included at your hotel, or you pay $10 for a day rental.

SCUBA St. Lucia (☎ 758-459-7000 at Anse Chastanet; or at Rex St. Lucian, Rodney Bay, ☎ 758-459-7755) is run by a couple from California, who spearheaded the drive to get St. Lucia's Marine Park established. A SSI Platinum/PADI facility, SCUBA St. Lucia runs two of the island's longest established and first five-star PADI Centers. Eco-lovers enjoy **Dive Fair Helen** (☎ 758-450-1640 or 758-451-7716), owned and run by a St. Lucian environmentalist with more than ten years experience in marine research. It offers a comprehensive range of PADI Courses with an emphasis on marine preservation.

Sailing away

Rodney Bay and **Marigot Bay** are centers for bareboat or crewed yacht charters. Their marinas offer safe anchorage, shower facilities, restaurants, groceries, and maintenance for yachts sailing the eastern Caribbean. Try one of these operators:

- ✔ **Destination St. Lucia Ltd.,** Rodney Bay (☎ 758-453-8531), runs bareboat yacht charters; vessels range in length from 38 to 51 feet.

- ✔ **Sunsail Stevens,** Rodney Bay (☎ 758-452-8648), is one of the oldest companies in the Caribbean and offers a variety of crewed or bareboat charters.

- ✔ **The Moorings Yacht Charters,** Marigot Bay (☎ 758-451-4357 or 800-535-7289), charters bareboat or crewed yachts ranging from a 39-foot Beneteau to a 60-foot Morgan.

Teeing off

The scenery's half the fun on St. Lucia. You won't find serious golf here, but head to **St. Lucia Golf and Country Club** (Cap Estate; ☎ **758-450-8523**; Fax: 758-450-0647; Internet: www.stluciagolf.com), the island's only public course, if you get the urge. Set at the island's northern tip, it boasts panoramic views of both the Atlantic and Caribbean. The clubhouse has a bar, and there's a pro shop where you can rent clubs and arrange for lessons. An $85 package includes 18 holes, a cart, and clubs. Reservations are essential.

Taking a hike

The island is laced with trails, but it's a jungle out there, so don't set off on your own. Besides, you have to get permission to hike in the parks. For a $10 fee, you get permission and a naturalist guide. For rain forest hikes or to hike Gros Piton, contact the **Forest and Land Department** (☎ **758-450-2231** or 758-450-2078).

An extremely poisonous snake — the *fer de lance* — hides in heavy brush. Encounters with the reptile are rare, but you probably won't live to tell the tale should you have one.

Here are a few tips before you set off: Don't wear open-toed shoes, and hiking boots are too heavy to schlep with you to the Caribbean. We'd go with either sneakers or, if you can find them, river-rafting shoes — they're waterproof, lightweight, and have plenty of grip. You'll thank us, especially if you attempt climbing the Pitons. If you go during rainy season (June to November), when brief but heavy showers regularly occur, take a lightweight windbreaker to help you stay dry.

Taking a driving tour

No matter where you stay on the island, a trip to **Soufrière** and its surrounding attractions is essential. To get here from Castries, follow the Coast Road, making sure to stop at a few of our not-to-be missed suggestions for quintessential island experiences along the way. Plan to spend the entire day to drive there and back. The drive itself is about an hour and a half each way if you don't stop, but you have quite a bit to see and do along the way. If you prefer hiring a guide to do the driving, you can do so through your hotel. Expect to pay about $80 for the day's tour, excluding tip.

Don't forget to bring your camera and plenty of film, and if you're planning on stopping at Soufrière Estate, and think you may want to take a dip in the Mineral Baths, bring (or wear) your bathing suit.

Driving to Morne Fortune from Castries takes you past some of the handful of surviving **French Victorian private homes** with delicately carved fretwork. Morne Fortune, whose name means "Hill of Good Luck," serves as a dramatic backdrop for Castries. You also pass the stately **Government House,** on Government House Road, the official residence of the governor-general of St. Lucia and one of the best examples of this type of architecture.

A few miles south of Castries along the coast road, you find **Marigot Bay,** one of the Caribbean's prettiest natural harbors. In 1778, a British admiral sailed into this secluded bay-within-a-bay, covered his ships with palm fronds, and hid from the French behind the dense cover of mangroves. It's a favorite hangout of the yachting crowd, and you find a handful of small inns and restaurants here, including J.J.'s Paradise. A 24-hour ferry connects the bay's two shores.

Continuing on the twisting, turning road to Soufrière, you see vendors selling freshly gathered coconuts. If you're with a guide, ask him or her to stop at a spot where you can also get a sample of the delicious cassava bread sold along this route. For $2 you get a hunk of warm bread made from the cassava root (an important food staple in the Caribbean and starchy like a potato) and sweetened with roasted coconut and honey. You can wash it down with fresh coconut milk, which looks nasty, tastes fine, and is a healthy, natural drink.

Exploring Soufrière

The oldest town in St. Lucia, the picturesque fishing village of Soufrière was founded by the French in 1746 and named for the nearby volcano and sulfur springs. Its harbor is the deepest on the island, accommodating smaller cruise ships that tie up at the wharf or at moorings in the bay. This quiet scene makes the already stunning Pitons picture-postcard perfect.

The **Soufrière Tourist Information Centre** on Bay Street (☎ 758-459-7200), across from the waterfront, provides information about area attractions, but there's really not much to do in this little village. You can take some lovely photos of the Pitons from the beach just beyond the seaside cemetery dating to 1743 where cockscomb and other flowers grow wild over the graves.

Nor is the village a shopper's spot, but check out the **Batik Studio** (☎ 758-459-7232) in Hummingbird Beach Resort on the bayfront north of the wharf, which has superb batik sarongs, scarves, and wall panels designed and created on site by Hummingbird's owner Joan Alexander. Hummingbird makes a pleasant stop for breakfast or lunch, too. The other half of the town is pedestrian concrete buildings like Castries.

A five-minute drive from the village along the inland road to Fond St. Jacques takes you to **Soufrière Estate** (☎ 758-452-4759 or 758-454-7565), a 2,000-acre land grant made in 1713 by Louis XIV to three

Devaux brothers from Normandy in recognition of their service to France. Here you can see how crops such as copra and cocoa are harvested and processed, and tour a mini-zoo. Admission is $2.75, and hours are Monday to Saturday, 10 a.m. to 5 p.m., Sunday and holidays, 10 a.m. to 3 p.m.

Also at the Estate are the **Mineral Baths at Diamond Falls** and one of our favorite botanical gardens in the Caribbean. One of the original owners' descendants lovingly created this enchanted garden, which makes us think of Eden. You pay an attendant at the private pool $10 EC (for a dip in the outside pool, $7 EC). You're limited to 30 minutes. Water bubbling up from sulfur springs streams downhill in rivulets to become Diamond Waterfall, easily reachable via the winding path through the gardens. A small, pleasant gift shop sells $2 rum punches and ice cream bars — both handy for cooling off.

Allow at least an hour to stroll through the gardens. If you're on a guided tour, talk to the guide before hand and insist that your group be allowed time to enjoy this place. We saw many groups being herded in and out like dutiful sheep — in under 30 minutes.

La Soufrière Drive-in Volcano is unique in the Caribbean and is worth seeing, but don't plan more than 15 minutes or so for this stop. It's extremely smelly from the sulphur. To get here, continue south of town on the road to Vieux Fort. You see small signs for the volcano. If you park on the far side, drive beyond where everyone else stops, away from the crowds, where you see a small road off to the right. If you take that gravel road, it drops you out near **Ladera's Dasheene Restaurant and Bar** (☎ **800-738-4752** or 758-459-7323), one of the island's best resorts and restaurants, where you can have lunch. Ask the guide at the volcano if you are uncertain. Since the island's so rural, some roads simply aren't marked.

On the same road to Vieux Fort, you also see **Morne Coubaril Estate,** Soufrière (☎ **758-489-7340;** Fax: 758-459-5759; E-mail: coubaril@candw. lc), a 250-acre coconut and cocoa plantation established in 1713. It's definitely worth a stop. Guides escort you along a mule carriage pathway and quietly explain 18th-century plantation life. It's a leisurely-paced tour, but we liked not being rushed, and if you're genuinely interested, the polite young guides are more than happy to share details about the island's fascinating history. Admission is $6, and hours are daily 9 a.m. to 4 p.m.

Looking for some nightlife

Your best bet in St. Lucia is the legendary **Gros Islet Jump Up.** Every Friday night, starting at about 9 p.m., the sleepy fishing village of Gros Islet, just a mile north of Rodney Bay, erupts into a huge street party. Nothing else compares in the Caribbean for consistency.

Gros Islet Jump Up is crowded and rowdy, so stick close together. Visitors to the island should consider going early and leaving early: Otherwise, women may well find themselves being groped as the night heats up. Leave your wallet and purse at the hotel; hide your money, and don't wear nice jewelry.

The same advice goes for **J.J.'s Friday Night Jam** (☎ 758-451-4076), in Marigot Bay, the southside answer to Gros Islet. **La Shala Club** (☎ 758-450-0022) in Rodney Bay is a disco where the music ranges from salsa and zouk to love songs. Also in Rodney Bay, **Indies** (☎ 758-452-0727) is a late-night dance hall where the action doesn't even start until 11 p.m. Dress is casual but no hats, sandals, shorts, or sleeveless shirts are allowed. There's shuttle bus service to and from most major hotels. For a chance to hang out with the locals, try **The Late Lime** (☎ 758-452-0761) on Reduit Beach in Rodney Bay, a particular favorite of St. Lucians. It's air-conditioned and intimate, with a DJ or local entertainment every night but Tuesday.

Dining in St. Lucia

St. Lucia certainly doesn't top our list for sophisticated dining options in the Caribbean, but dining out here gives you a great chance to experience the best of what island life has to offer: breathtaking sea views, down-to-earth people, and simple, but tasty food. So even if you stay at an all-inclusive, do yourself a favor and check out some of our favorites.

Like most businesses on the island, virtually all restaurants are shuttered on Sundays, except for those at the hotels. During high season, the best places are often full, and during low season restaurant owners can be somewhat whimsical about opening their doors. Even the fanciest places are elegant-casual — a nice sundress for women and slacks with a collared sport shirt for men are fine for "limin'," or hanging out and relaxing.

Creating special memories

Coal Pot (Vigie Cove Marina; ☎ 758-452-5566; $$$$) has been in business more than 40 years. Expertly prepared New World cuisine with a French flair. We recommend saving a trip to the Coal Pot for evening when the candlelight and stars transform this tiny restaurant. Asian-fusion **TAO** (Cariblue Beach; ☎ 800-544-2883 or 758-450-8551; $$$$) is stylish and hip. The décor is a black-and-white theme with eye-catching Asian antiques punctuating the stark, open room. Over-size plates and giant pepper-mills purchased in South Beach adorn the tables. Here's one of the most romantic restaurants in the Caribbean: **Dasheene** (Ladera Resort, 2 miles south of Soufrière; ☎ 800-738-4752 or 758-459-7323; $$$$). This glorious, open-air restaurant has such killer views that you may feel as if you've walked onto a movie set.

Soaking up the views

One of our most romantic dinners in the Caribbean was at **Piton** (at Anse Chastanet, Soufrière; ☎ **800-223-1108** or 758-459-7000; $$$$$), a stunner. Hand-carved railings serve as the only walls in this intimate outdoor restaurant, clinging to a hill overlooking the small volcanic beach. Request the tiny table for two at the far end of the narrow passage for the most privacy. To reach **Café Paradis** (Marigot Beach Club; ☎ **758-451-4974**; $$$) take the ferryboat, which runs about every ten minutes all day and into the evening from the Moorings across picturesque Marigot Bay.

Looking for local color

A lovely, open-air dining spot, **Froggie Jack's Restaurant & Cocktail Bar** (Vigie Marina; ☎ **758-458-1900**; $$$), which sits amidst a tropical garden, offers pleasant views of Vigie Harbor across to the Morne, just five minutes from downtown Castries. Each dinner is prepared to order, and you're served free appetizers while you wait. If you want to tour this little fishing village, **Hummingbird** (on the waterfront just north of the wharf, Soufrière; ☎ **758-459-7232** or 758-7232-7492; $$), with the majestic Pitons and sailboats bobbing in the harbor as a backdrop, makes a good lunch stop.

Since returning to his native St. Lucia almost 20 years ago, Chef Edward Harry has held court nightly at the **Green Parrot** (Red Tape Lane, Castries; ☎ **758-452-339**; $$$$), which commands jaw-dropping panoramic views of the city from its perch on Morne Fortune high above Castries Harbor. Chef Harry puts on quite a show, and we aren't just talking about the food. He's liable to burst into song and join the limbo sessions and belly dancers on Wednesday nights and line dancing on Saturdays. Executive Chef Swain Louis, St. Lucia's Chef of the Year in 1998, presides over **Café Panache** (Derek Walcott Square; ☎ **758-452-7373** or 758-453-1199; $$$$$), housed in the 100-year-old family home of the island's first Nobel Prize winner for economics, Sir Arthur Lewis. On the ground floor, the bistro offers an all-day buffet with a daily-changing selection of local and international dishes. Every Friday, the buffet is St. Lucian favorites.

Blink and you may miss **Camilla's** (7 Bridge St., Soufrière; ☎ **758-459-5379**; $), a pink confection on the second floor of one of the quaint gingerbread Victorian buildings in Soufrière. If it's a hot night, try to snag one of the two balcony tables overlooking the busy street, a block from the waterfront. For some odd reason the owners of **Capone's** (across from the Rex St. Lucian; ☎ **758-452-0284**; $$) thought a campy take on Chicago's Italian family would play well in the tropics. Odder still, they were right. Capone's became a hit for its homemade pasta dishes and traditional Italian fare like osso buco and roasted chicken. A player piano cranks out tunes, while waiters dressed like mobsters hustle across the black-and-white tile floor, serving rum drinks with names like Valentine's Day Massacre and Mafia Mai Tai.

Settling in to St. Lucia

St. Lucia is the island time forgot. As you drive along the roads, you see people walking everywhere, some toting machetes for whacking the dense tropical undergrowth that springs up seemingly overnight. Islanders are predominantly of African descent, and two-thirds of the population is between the ages of 17 to 35.

Tourism is still relatively new to St. Lucia. Although the country is poor, you don't get that grasping feeling like you may encounter on Jamaica nor the aloofness that we've run across on Barbados. St. Lucia has a low-key pace with a small-town friendliness.

In this section, we let you know what to expect and how to get around. We also give you a rundown of facts to make your stay simpler. In fact, that's what a romantic interlude in St. Lucia does for us. It helps us breathe again and remember to keep life simple.

Arriving in St. Lucia

Your first encounter with St. Lucia can vary greatly depending on which airport you fly into. Jets and large aircraft from Europe and the U.S., as well as puddle jumpers from Barbados and other nearby islands, fly into **Hewanorra International Airport** (☎ 758-454-8686), on the southern tip of the island just outside of Vieux Fort, St. Lucia's second largest city. British air carriers predominate in St. Lucia, and it doesn't take Sherlock Holmes to deduce just from the planes arriving at the airport that U.S. visitors aren't the main business here. On the northwest coast, tiny **George F.L. Charles Airport** (☎ 758-452-1156) — formerly known as Vigie Airport — in the capital of Castries, right beside the beach on the Caribbean side, is just a short airstrip for inter-island aircraft, charters, and propeller-driven planes.

In either case, once you deplane, you step into a bare-bones facility, but you move pretty quickly through customs and passport control.

Getting around St. Lucia

Once you get off the plane, follow the signs inside to get to the baggage claim. After you've left customs, you're practically there. Once outside, you find a swarm of friendly locals and cabs lined up at the curb. If airport transfers are included in your hotel package, look for a driver holding a sign with your name or the name of your hotel on it. If you don't immediately see anyone, ask the attendant who matches passengers with taxis. A uniformed official should ask you where you're headed and consult a pad crammed with information on arriving passengers.

Be patient because rounding up your driver may take a few minutes, and you may share your taxi or van with other arriving passengers.

The drive from Hewanorra to Castries takes about 1½ hours; to Soufrière, expect about 45 minutes to an hour's ride along St. Lucia's dramatic west coast (the Caribbean side). You drive past many banana plantations, lush rain forests, and tiny villages before you get to either main hotel area. But both rides are pretty — and an adventure. (Actually, the winding route to Soufrière reminds us of Mr. Toad's Wild Ride at Disney.) Both roads have been greatly improved in the last few years, but potholes do appear with regularity during rainy season.

If you fly into George F.L. Charles Airport, you're a mere 5 to 20 minutes from the hotels in and around Castries. Typically, either your hotel sends a car or van to pick you up, or you can simply grab a cab.

Hailing a taxi

The taxi fare between Hewanorra and Castries is about $50; between George F.L. Charles Airport and nearby resorts, your fare runs $15 to $25. Be sure to agree on the fare and the currency before you get in the cab. Taxis are expensive and unmetered, but most belong to a taxi cooperative called **National Taxi Council** (☎ 758-452-6067). Stick to the standard fares mentioned above.

You can tip 10 percent to 15 percent of the fare. If the hotel provided transport, we still tip the driver.

Renting a car

If you rent a car, you have to get a local license, which you can obtain from the immigration officer at either airport when you arrive or from the major rental car companies' agents. You must show a valid license. The license, which costs $20, is valid for three months. All rental companies offer unlimited mileage. Without a coupon, expect to spend about $30 to $75 a day. During high season make sure to call ahead and reserve. The most commonly rented car on the island is the Toyota Corolla. Request a 4-wheel drive if you plan on touring the island, because only half the roads on the island are paved. And don't forget air-conditioning.

The west coast road from Cap Estate in the north down to Vieux Fort in the south is the route you take to Soufrière. It's a beautiful ride, but heart-stopping at times. Watch for mudslides and rocks during the rainy season (August to November). In the towns, many of the roads are one-way, so you have to do a bit of zigging and zagging.

Here are some of the operators:

- ✔ **Avis Rent-A-Car:** Hewanorra Airport, ☎ **758-454-6325**; George F.L. Charles Airport, ☎ **758-452-2046**

- ✔ **Budget:** ☎ **800-527-0700**; Hewanorra Airport, ☎ **758-454-5311**; Castries, ☎ **758-452-0233**

- ✔ **Cool Breeze Jeep Rental:** Soufrière, ☎ **758-459-7729**

- ✔ **Cost Less Rent-a-Car:** Gros Islet, ☎ **758-450-3416**; PAGER ☎ **758-481-7376**

- ✔ **Hertz/Sun-Fun Car Rentals, Ltd.:** ☎ **800-654-3001**; Castries, ☎ **758-452-0680**; George Charles Airport, ☎ **758-451-7351**; Hewanorra Airport, ☎ **758-454-9636**; after hours 758-452-0742

- ✔ **Holiday & Business Car Rental Gros Islet:** ☎ **758-452-0872**; after hours 758-453-2613

- ✔ **St. Lucia National Car Rental Gros Islet:** ☎ **758-450-8500**; Le Sport, ☎ **758-450-9406**; George Charles Airport, ☎ **758-452-3050**; Pointe Seraphine, ☎ **758-453-0085**; Hewanorra Airport, ☎ **758-454-6699**

Walking around

Although St. Lucia yields some of the best hikes in the Caribbean, we don't suggest that you walk to most destinations on the island. The terrain is fairly rugged, the roads narrow, and at many junctures, you don't have much of a place to step out of the way of oncoming traffic.

Taking a bus

St. Lucia's public bus system consists of privately owned and operated minivans, primarily used by locals. The mini-buses, identifiable by an "H" on their license plates, are a fun and colorful way to get around, plus they're reliable, insured, and, best of all, inexpensive. A local trip is $1.25, while more distant trips can run up to $6.00. The easiest route for someone new to the island is the route that takes you from Castries to Gros Islet. You may, however, be packed in tightly with locals carrying produce to market. You can get a current schedule from your hotel's front desk.

Reserve this mode of travel for quick trips only — preferably during the light of day. If you want to make a run to the market or the shopping center at Point Seraphine, for example, catching a bus is a quick and cheap way to go. However, only easygoing or cash-strapped travelers should attempt St. Lucia's bus system after dark or for long trips. The bus stops aren't well-lit, and the buses themselves aren't that comfortable. On top of that, drivers usually won't budge until they've loaded up with passengers, which can means waiting in the heat.

Boarding a boat

A great way to tour the island is to take a boat to Soufrière. It's a quick, scenic trip, and several operators offer a combination sail/land-based tour that hits the high points around Soufrière. You don't feel rushed, and we think this option offers the best of both worlds at a reasonable price. Contact the **Soufrière Water Taxi Association** (☎ 758-454-5420). Rates are standard, and their members also provide watchman services while boat owners are ashore.

Hopping a ferry

The **Rodney Bay Ferry** (☎ 758-452-0087) in Gros Islet makes the trip between the marina and the shopping complex daily on the hour from 9 a.m. to 4 p.m. A round-trip is $8. Ferry service to Pigeon Island from Rodney Bay (adjacent to The Lime Restaurant) is available twice daily for $40 round-trip, including the entrance fee to Pigeon Island and snacks; snorkel equipment can be rented for $12.

Choppering around

Looking for a thrill or just in a hurry? If you've got $100 burning a hole in your Bermuda shorts, your helicopter awaits to whisk you from Hewanorra to Castries. That trip takes 15 minutes, (saving you more than an hour in a car). For the ten-minute flight to Soufrière, you pay $85 per person. There are helipads at Pointe Seraphine and the Jalousie Hilton. Contact **St. Lucia Helicopters,** Pointe Seraphine (☎ **758-453-6950;** Fax: 758-452-1553).

Fast Facts: St. Lucia

ATMs

ATMs are available 24 hours a day at all bank branches. **National Commercial Bank of St. Lucia** has ATMs at the airport. You can get cash from ATMs using major credit cards or bank cards, but it will be in Eastern Caribbean currency — not U.S. dollars.

Banks

Barclays Bank has branches at Jeremie St., Castries ☎ 758-452-3305; Hewanorra Airport ☎ 758-454-6255 and Soufrière ☎ 758-459-7255. **National Commercial Bank of St. Lucia** has branches at Pointe Seraphine, Castries

☎ 758-452-4787; Hewanorra Airport ☎ 758-454-7780; and Soufrière ☎ 758-459-7450.

Business Hours

Most stores are open weekdays 8:30 a.m. to 12:30 p.m. and 1:30 to 4:30 p.m., Saturdays 8 a.m. to 12:30 p.m. **Gablewoods Mall** shops are open Monday to Saturday 9 a.m. to 7 p.m., and **Pointe Seraphine** shops are open weekdays 9 a.m. to 5 p.m., Saturdays 9 a.m. to 2 p.m.

Banks are usually open Monday to Thursday 8 a.m. to 3 p.m.; Friday 8 a.m. to 5 p.m.

Credit Cards

Major credit cards (American Express, Master-Card, and Visa) are readily accepted.

Currency Exchange

The Eastern Caribbean (EC) dollar is the official currency, but U.S. dollars are accepted everywhere. At press time, the exchange rate was $1 to $2.70 EC at banks. The exchange rate at hotels and stores was about U.S. $1 to $2.50 EC. The British pound is also readily accepted. The conversion rate varies daily and is available from any bank.

In the markets, you usually get change back in the local currency if you make a purchase. You really don't need to exchange money, unless you want pocket change for soda machines or as a collectible, because the coins are cool looking. Traveler's checks are readily accepted, but you need your passport to cash them.

Departure Tax

$20 cash, which is paid at the airport.

Doctors

Hotels have doctors on call.

Emergencies

In case of fire call ☎ **911,** for an ambulance or the police call ☎ **999.**

Hospitals

St. Jude's Hospital (Viex Fort, ☎ 758-454-6041); **Tapion Hospital** (La Toc Road, Castries, ☎ 758-459-2000); and **Victoria Hospital** (Hospital Road, Castries, ☎ 758-452-2421 or 758-453-7059).

Information

The main office of the **St. Lucia Tourist Board** (☎ 758-452-4094; Fax: 758-453-1121) is at Vide Boutielle in Castries (just north of George Charles Airport). The office is open weekdays 8 a.m. to 4:30 p.m. The information desk at George F.L. Charles Airport (Vigie, Castries ☎ 758-452-2596) is open from 8 a.m. until the last flight; the information desk at Hewanorra International Airport (Vieux Fort, ☎ 758-454-6644) is open from 7 a.m. until the last flight.

Language

Couldn't be simpler: English. The everyday language of the people is Patois, a French Creole language. If you can't stand not knowing what folks around you are saying, pick up a copy of *A Visitor's Guide to St. Lucia Patois,* a small paperback book sold in local bookstores for $4.

Maps

Available in the back of free guides.

Newspapers/Magazines

Sunshine Bookshop (☎ 758-452-3222) in the Gablewoods Mall, Castries, has newspapers, books, and magazines. *The New York Times* by fax is available at the larger resorts, and local papers are *The Star, One Caribbean,* and *The Weekend Voice* (out on Saturdays); *The Voice* (out on Tuesdays and Thursdays); and *The Mirror* (out on Saturday). Tourists should pick up the complimentary glossy *Visions,* which is printed annually.

Pharmacies

Try **Clarke's Drugstore** (☎ 758-452-2727) on Bridge St. in Castries, or one of the several locations of **M&C's Drugstore:** Bridge St., ☎ 758-452-2811, ext. 2115; Gablewoods Shopping Mall, ☎ 758-451-7808; J.Q.'s Mall, Rodney Bay, ☎ 758-458-0178; or J.Q.'s Plaza, Vieux Fort, ☎ 758-454-3760. Pharmacy hours are Monday through Thursday from 8 a.m. to 4:30 p.m.; Friday 8 a.m. to 5:30 p.m.; and Saturday 8 a.m. to 1 p.m. All are closed Sunday.

Police

In an emergency call ☎ **999,** or the **Marine Police Unit** at ☎ 758-453-0770 or 758-452-2595.

Post Office

Your hotel's front desk can help with letters and postcards. It costs 35 cents U.S. (95 cents EC) to mail a post card back to the U.S.

Safety

We've always felt pretty safe on St. Lucia, but pickpockets are a problem at the street parties and in town. Don't flash cash in the markets. Don't pick up hitchhikers — even though the locals do so all the time; there's no need to take unnecessary risks. Lock up your valuables in the hotel safe, and leave unnecessary valuables like fancy jewelry and watches at home.

Taxes

The government room tax is 8 percent; hotels sting you for an additional 10 percent service charge for room, food, and beverages.

Telephone

To call St. Lucia from the U.S., dial 1, then the area code and the seven-digit local number. Different hotels have different primary carriers. Always read the instructions usually printed by the phone or in the directory you find in your room before attempting a call to the U.S. If you can't find directions, call the hotel operator. If you dial direct, you dial 1 plus the area code and the number, but expect to pay $5 a minute and perhaps a hefty hotel surcharge. We strongly recommend using a phone card. On the island, you have to dial all seven digits of the local number to make a local call.

Time Zone

Atlantic Standard time year-round, which places it one hour ahead of New York and Miami. However, when the U.S. is on Daylight Savings Time, St. Lucia's clocks are in sync with Eastern Daylight Time.

Tipping

The standard is 10 percent to 15 percent, and on St. Lucia the tips generally aren't included in the bill. Tip $1 per day for maids, $1 per bag for bellhops.

Water

The water's fine to drink, but bottled water is readily available at hotels and supermarkets. Don't drink water from streams, even though it may look inviting. You may wind up with parasites if you give into the temptation. Take bottled water on hikes.

Weather

You find local weather reports on HTS Channel 4 and DBS Channels 2 and 10.

Chapter 21

Honeymooning in the United States Virgin Islands

By Echo & Kevin Garrett

● ●

In This Chapter

▶ Finding the best honeymoon accommodations

▶ Discovering the fun and romance of the United States Virgin Islands

▶ Uncovering all the details

● ●

The U.S. Virgin Islands (USVIs) have a little bit of everything a romantic duo could want, from secluded beaches to fun nightlife to island-hopping options. It's one of the easiest introductions to the Caribbean, and in this chapter we touch on everything you need to know to make your honeymoon go smoothly from where to stay, to where to go and how to get there.

In the USVIs, you can find as many different kinds of accommodations as swimsuit fashions. Like Puerto Rico and Jamaica, the USVIs have everything from gorgeous villas to simple guesthouses. The islands also have familiar chains — from the Best Western to more upscale choices like Marriott, Westin, and The Ritz-Carlton.

You may encounter a full house with popular properties like the exclusive Caneel Bay Resort and the award-winning eco-friendly campgrounds, both on St. John, and The Ritz-Carlton, St. Thomas, during the busy winter season. The much-in-demand campgrounds often stay booked as much as a year in advance.

Highly developed St. Thomas supports a mind-boggling number of rooms, many of them timeshares. If you like atmospheric bed-and-breakfast inns, you can find a few on St. Thomas and St. Croix. Eco-hounds delight in St. John.

Figuring Out Where to Stay

You can expect the densest concentration of hotels and timeshares east and north of Charlotte Amalie, the capital of St. Thomas. Several smaller properties are in this area — ideal if you plan to get out and mingle with the locals — because you are within walking distance of Frenchtown. If you just want a clean room to return to after a day of exploring or beach-bumming, consider staying in town, where you can find inexpensive lodgings that meet your standards of convenience and tidiness.

Not all of our picks are on a beach, but all have access to some of the best beaches in the Caribbean. We alert you in our reviews if a place isn't on a beach.

The USVI-based Internet site www.caribbeanchannel.com recently announced the launch of two new Web pages featuring information about "Hotels & Resorts" and "Inns & Small Hotels" in the territory and throughout the Caribbean.

Choosing Among the USVIs' Best Accommodations for Honeymooners

The rack rates listed in this section are in U.S. dollars and are for a standard double room during high season (mid-December to mid-April), unless otherwise noted. Lower rates are often available during the off-season and shoulder season.

Please refer to the Introduction of *Honeymoon Vacations For Dummies* for an explanation of our price categories.

Bolongo Bay Beach Club & Villas
$$$$ South Shore, St. Thomas

Bolongo Bay, a straightforward, 75-room, beachfront resort, is a good choice if you want a no-fuss, no-muss honeymoon. It also includes the 20-room Bolongo Villas next door and the six-room Bolongo Bayside Inn across the street. The best part is Bolongo's beautiful white-sand, palm-encircled beach. The resort opened in 1974 but has stayed fresh. It has a nice feel and is family-owned and operated by Dick and Joyce Doumeng, long-time hoteliers on St. Thomas. All rooms — whether they're one of the mini-suites or a one- or two-bedroom unit — have efficiency kitchens and balconies and are just steps from a 1,000-foot strand of white sand. The resort offers a choice of all-inclusive or semi-inclusive plans, which means you can pay less if you opt for fewer activities. The all-inclusive rate covers all meals and drinks, use of the tennis courts, and many watersports activities — including an all-day sail and half-day snorkel

St. Thomas

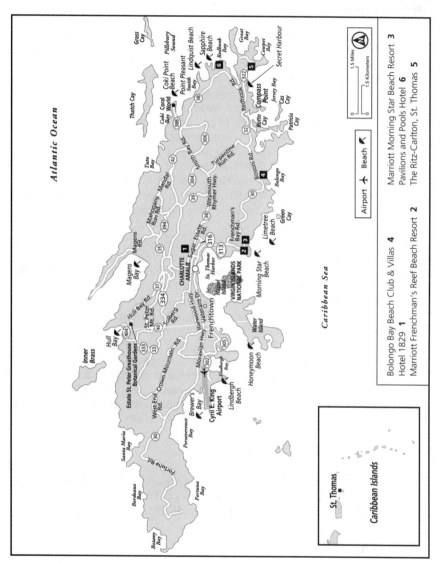

Atlantic Ocean

Grass Cay
Pillsbury Sound
Lindquist Beach
Sapphire Beach
Coki Point Beach
Point Pleasant
Smith Bay
Coki Coral Bay World
Thatch Cay
Great Bay
Redhook Bay
Compass Point
Cowpet Bay
Secret Harbour
Jersey Bay
Cas Cay
Botto Cay
Patricia Cay
Redhook
Tutu Bay
Mandel Rd.
Mahogany Run Rd.
Smith Bay Rd.
Turpentine Run Rd.
Weymouth Rhymer Hwy.
Bovoni Rd.
Bolongo Bay
Green Cay
Limetree Beach
Frenchman's Bay Rd.
Magens Rd.
Magens Bay
CHARLOTTE AMALIE
Sugar Estate Rd.
St. Thomas Harbour
Hassel Island
VIRGIN ISLANDS NATIONAL PARK
Morning Star Beach
Caribbean Sea
St. Peter Mt. Rd.
Solberg Rd.
Harwood Hwy.
Veterans Dr.
Frenchtown
Water Island
Hull Bay Rd.
Hull Bay
Estate St. Peter Greathouse Botanical Gardens
West-End Rd.
Crown Mountain Rd.
Moravian Hwy.
Brewer's Bay
Cyril E. King Airport
Lindbergh Bay
Lindbergh Beach
Honeymoon Beach
Inner Brass
Santa Maria Bay
Perseverence Bay
Bordeaux Bay
Fortuna Bay
Fortuna Ru
Botany Bay

1.5 Miles
1.5 Kilometers

Airport ✈   Beach ⤡

Bolongo Bay Beach Club & Villas **4**
Hotel 1829 **1**
Marriott Frenchman's Reef Beach Resort **2**
Marriott Morning Star Beach Resort **3**
Pavilions and Pools Hotel **6**
The Ritz-Carlton, St. Thomas **5**

St. Thomas
Caribbean Islands

trip on one of the resort's yachts. The all-inclusive plan requires a minimum three-night stay. There are two restaurants and bars, three pools (including one with a swim-up bar), two tennis courts, a large health club with free weights and lots of gear, a dive shop, and a dock. Snorkeling, windsurfing, boating, and jet skiing are available at an extra charge.

7150 Bolongo, St. Thomas, USVI 00802. ☎ ***800-524-4746*** *or 340-775-1800 (both direct to the hotel). Fax: 340-775-3208. E-mail:* bolongobeach@worldnet.att.net. *Internet:* www.bolongo.com. *Rack rates: $325–$460. AE, DISC, DC, MC, V.*

The Buccaneer

$$$$ East End, St. Croix

On the grounds of a former 340-acre sugar plantation, this gracious family-owned and operated resort boasts three sandy beaches (one has some nice small shells); one of our favorite swimming pools in the Caribbean; an 18-hole golf course with sweeping sea views; a championship tennis facility with eight courts; four restaurants; shops; spa services and a fitness center; a hiking/nature trail; and lots of activities. A palm tree-lined drive leads to an imposing pink Danish Colonial structure atop a hill. Shops, restaurants, and other guest quarters dot the rolling, manicured lawns. The ambience and decor are Mediterranean-meets-Caribbean, with tile floors, four-poster beds, massive wardrobes of pale wood, pastel fabrics, spacious marble baths, and local works of art. Manager Elizabeth Armstrong, whose Dutch family owns this elegant place, is an excellent hotelier who makes guests feel welcome.

Many couples marry at this elegant property. Couples who exchange vows can announce their marriage on the Web and share their Caribbean wedding photos with far-flung friends and family via a World Wide Wedding Album on the hotel's Web site. Inclusion in the World Wide Wedding Album is available to couples for $50 as an optional extra to the resort's "Elope to Paradise" wedding package ($475 plus accommodations), which includes the services of a photographer and a non-denominational minister, a West Indian wedding cake, a bride's bouquet and groom's boutonniere of roses or tropical flowers, and a bottle of champagne and other extras. The "Jump the Broom" package ($475 plus accommodations) offers all of the "Elope to Paradise" features plus an African-based wedding tradition wherein both the bride and groom leap over a brightly decorated broom, symbolizing the coming together of man and woman in one house.

Ask about the honeymoon packages.

Rte. 82 (P.O. Box 25200), Gallows Bay, St. Croix, USVI 00824. ☎ 800-255-3881 or 340-773-2100. Fax: 340-773-6665. Internet: www.thebuccaneer.com. *Rack rates: $250-$600. Rates include full breakfast. AE, DISC, DC, MC, V. EP.*

Caneel Bay Resort

$$$$$ Caneel Bay, St. John

A private boat fetches you from the dock at St. Thomas and ferries you to another time and place. Built by Laurance Rockefeller in 1952 on a 170-acre peninsula, Caneel Bay, now well-run by Rosewood Hotels & Resorts, remains a cherished retreat of the old-money set. With seven spectacular (and we don't use that word lightly) beaches and some of St. John's better restaurants, this resort may hold you in its glorious grasp, making you hesitate to venture outside the confines of paradise. The reasonably priced rooms near the tennis courts are actually more spacious than the higher-price, beachfront rooms. Air-conditioning is a recent addition, but you really don't need it in these peaceful rooms open to tropical breezes.

St. Croix

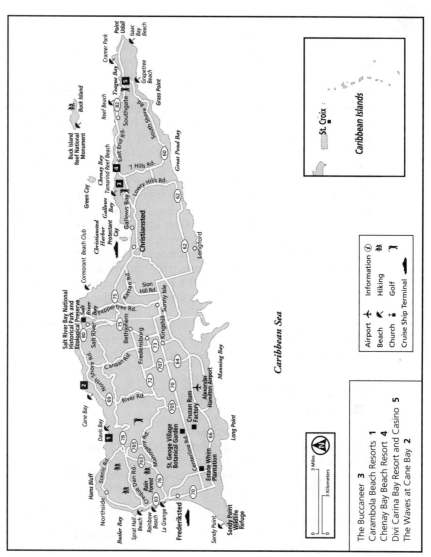

Cottage 7, which Rockefeller favored, stays continually booked. The attentive staff makes sure that you take full advantage of the three restaurants, 11 tennis courts, dive shop, windsurfing, boating, and children's program. Of the luxury digs in the USVIs, this one is our pick, edging out The Ritz-Carlton because Caneel Bay puts you more in touch with the Caribbean experience.

Rte. 20 (P.O. Box 720), Cruz Bay, St. John, USVI 00831. ☎ **800-928-8889** *or 340-776-6111. Fax: 340-693-8280. Internet:* www.caneelbay.com. *Rack rates: $400-$750 double; $950 cottage. AE, MC, V. EP.*

Carambola Beach Resorts
$$$$ **North Shore, St. Croix**

This resort was originally built by the Rockefellers. It boasts a marvelously set-apart locale, a great beach, and rustic chic appeal. However, over the years, it's been treated as a stepchild and is still trying to sort out its audience. The 26 two-story, red-roof villas (including one that's wheelchair-accessible) are connected by lovely, lush arcades strung along the seaside. They have terra-cotta floors, ceramic lamps, and mahogany ceilings and furnishings. We enjoyed the rocking chairs on screened-in porches, and we loved being lulled to sleep by the sound of surf at night. Each room has a huge bath (shower only). Golfers can enjoy the 18-hole, award-winning championship golf course designed by Robert Trent Jones. The large pools and hammocks strategically strung between the ancient seagrapes invite lounging. The two-bedroom suite, with its three-foot-thick plantation walls and large patio, is ideal for families. The onsite picnics offered by the Carambola Beach Club open-air restaurant have a sophisticated, contemporary menu. However, when we were there, the service wasn't perfect. The resort staff seemed befuddled by the few arrivals trying to check in. The restaurants have improved, thanks to a new chef. We call this hotel a diamond in the rough. If you can get a good package deal and are willing to put up with less than stellar service, go for it.

Rte. 80 (P.O. Box 3031), Kingshill, St. Croix, USVI 00851. ☎ **888-316-9648** *or 340-778-3800. Fax: 340-778-1682. Internet:* www.sunterra.com. *Rack rates: $275-$370 for one- to two-bedroom cottage. AE, DISC, DC, MC, V.*

Chenay Bay Beach Resort
$$$ **East End, St. Croix**

The sheltered, calm beach location, combined with complimentary tennis and watersports equipment (including kayaks), make this casual resort a real find. Set on 30 acres of a former sugar plantation, the spacious but basic cottages have ceramic-tile floors, bright peach or yellow walls, front porches, rattan furnishings, and kitchenettes with microwaves and coffeemakers. A nice touch: hammocks for two strung at the waters edge. Gravel paths connect the terraced gray-and-white wood cottages with the shore, where you find a large L-shape pool, a picnic area, and a casual restaurant.

The resort offers a "Honeymoon in Paradise" package ($300) that gets you tropical flowers and champagne upon arrival; cottage accommodations with a king-size bed; a secluded beach picnic; dinner for two, including wine, at Chenay's King Conch's Coconut Hut; a one-day rental car, passes to Whim Plantation Museum and St. George Botanical Gardens; a day trip to Buck Island Underwater National Park for snorkeling; one round-trip shuttle ride to Christiansted; and a honeymoon gift.

Rte. 82 (P.O. Box 24600), Christiansted, St. Croix, USVI 00824. ☎ **800-548-4457** *or 340-773-2918. Fax: 340-773-6665. E-mail:* chenaybay1@worldnet.att.net. *Internet:* www.chenaybay.com. *Rack rates: $236-$380 cottage. AE, MC, V. EP.*

St. John

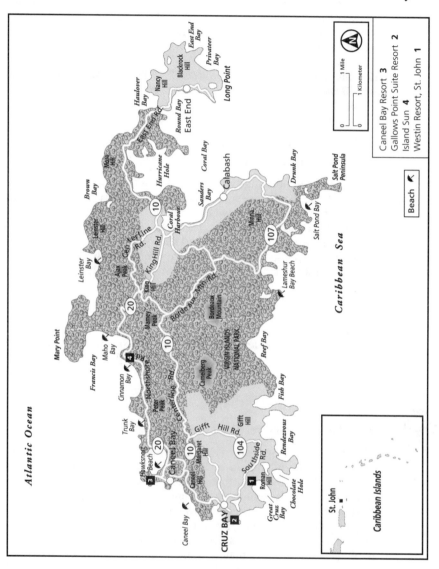

Divi Carina Bay Resort and Casino
$$$$ Christiansted, St. Croix

The Divi Carina, located off the scenic Southshore Road, on the southeast end of St. Croix, is the island's newest resort. Guests find a high standard of personalized service and attention to detail. The distinct decor merges the flair of today's European design with the comfort of casual chic. Ideal for those guests with multiple expectations from their trip, Divi Carina offers a comprehensive array of amenities: a good beach, a selection of dining options, lighted tennis courts, and varied watersports. All the rooms have air-conditioning, satellite TV, VCR, telephone with dataport and voice mail system, in-room safes, wet bar, mini-refrigerator, and plush robes. Divi Carina Bay is also the home of the USVIs' first casino. The 10,000-square-foot casino features 275 slot machines and 12 gaming tables.

25 Estate Turner Hole, St. Croix, USVI 00822. ☎ *888-464-3484 or 340-773-9700. Fax: 340-773-6802. Internet:* www.divicarina.com. *Rack rates: $225-$400 double. AE, MC, V.*

Gallows Point Suite Resort
$$$ Cruz Bay, St. John

These soft-gray buildings with peaked roofs and shuttered windows are clustered on a peninsula south of the Cruz Bay ferry dock. If you want to stay on St. John but don't want a villa or the more expensive Westin or Caneel Bay, Gallows Point is a great value. The garden apartments have kitchens and sky-lighted, plant-filled showers that are big enough for frolicking. The upper-level apartments have loft bedrooms and better views. Only the first-floor units are air-conditioned. The harborside villas get better trade winds, but they're also noisier. The entranceway is bridged by Ellington's restaurant, which serves good contemporary cuisine. Ask about the generous homeymoon packages.

Gallows Point (P.O. Box 58), Cruz Bay, St. John, USVI 00831. ☎ *800-323-7229 or 340-776-6434. Fax: 340-776-6520. Internet:* www.gallowspointresort.com. *Rack rates: $160-$380 apartment. AE, DC, MC, V.*

Hotel 1829
$$ Charlotte Amalie, St. Thomas

What a find. This Spanish-style, family-owned inn built by a French sea captain for his bride has sprawled to six levels interlaced with lovely gardens. The inn, now a National Historic Site, boasts fabulous views of Charlotte Amalie, which is second only to Old San Juan as the Caribbean's most beautiful city. You won't have elevators to rely on, but if you don't mind the stairs and narrow pathways, you find rooms with character-adding elements like old brick walls and antique Colonial furnishings. Some visitors may find the rooms too small, but to us, the setting makes up for it. A new museum at the top of the property shows colonial life on St. Thomas amidst riotous gardens. The second-floor botanical gardens and open-air champagne bar make a romantic spot for sunset viewing before you indulge in dinner at the gourmet Hotel 1829 restaurant. Hotel 1829 counts phones and VCRs in its list of in-room amenities. There's a tiny, tiny pool for cooling off, and the shops of Charlotte Amalie are just a stroll down the steep hill away.

This is not a good pick if you are physically challenged in any way.

Kongens Gade (P.O. Box 1567), St. Thomas, USVI 00804. ☎ *800-524-2002 or 340-776-1829. Fax: 340-776-4313. Internet:* www.hotel1829.com. *Rack rates: $90-$180 double. Rates include continental breakfast. AE, DISC, MC, V.*

Island Sun

$$$$ Estate Catherineberg, St. John

Sitting high atop St. John in the heart of the national park, Island Sun offers some of the Caribbean's most exquisite, breathtaking views. Island Sun is set among a small group of private homes, 800 feet above Cinnamon Bay. Nestled among lush tropical flowers and fragrant bay trees, each home has four bedrooms that feature king-size beds and private baths. Each home also has a deck or balcony, a fully equipped kitchen, ceiling fans, 25-foot swimming pool, hot tub, secluded outdoor shower, grill, telescope, washer/dryer, telephone, fax, TV, VCR, stereo, and a stock of games, books, videos, and CDs. Of the villas we've seen on St. John, this one was our favorite.

Estate Catherineberg, P.O. Box 272, St. John, USVI 00831. ☎ *340-776-6094. Fax: 340-693-8455. Rack rates: $5,900 per week. AE, MC, V.*

Marriott Frenchman's Reef Beach Resort

$$$$ South Shore, St. Thomas

Sprawling, luxurious, and on a prime harbor promontory east of Charlotte Amalie, this full-service 408-room superhotel and its smaller neighbor, Morning Star, were renovated extensively in 1998. Each of the 88 suites has a glorious ocean or harbor view; 21 are loft-style, with a spiral staircase that takes you to your bed where you can watch the cruise ships roll in and out. The rooms also have ice-makers, a nice touch, but they can be noisy in the middle of the night. Guests at either resort can work out at the Reef Health Club & Spa, which offers state-of-the-art cardiovascular and strength training equipment, therapeutic massages, and skin care therapies. Dining is alfresco on American or gourmet Caribbean fare, or oceanfront at the Tavern on the Beach; there's also a lavish buffet, served overlooking the sparkling lights of Charlotte Amalie and the harbor. Live entertainment and dancing, scheduled activities for all ages, and a shuttle boat to town make having fun easy.

Marriott Frenchman's Reef and Morning Star Beach Resort help couples who are interested in tying the knot in America's Caribbean by offering a new "Virtual Wedding" package. Couples who book one of the resort's four "Weddings in Paradise" packages can now share their special day with friends and family by broadcasting the event over the Internet.

Estate Bakkeroe (P.O. Box 7100), St. Thomas, USVI 00801. ☎ *800-367-5683 or 340-776-8500. Fax: 340-715-6191. Internet:* www.marriott.vi. *Rack rates: $350-$395 double. AE, DISC, DC, MC, V.*

Marriott Morning Star Beach Resort
$$$$ Flamboyant Point, St. Thomas

Both the public areas and the plush accommodations here are among the most outstanding on the island. The resort stands on the landscaped flatlands near the beach of Marriott's well-known Frenchman's Reef. The rooms are elegantly turned out in Caribbean chic in buildings nestled surfside along the fine white sand of Morning Star Beach. Each of the five buildings contains between 16 and 24 units, all having rattan furniture and views of the garden, the beach, or the lights of Charlotte Amalie. Guests can enjoy the amenities, restaurants, and attractions of the larger hotel nearby yet escape to the privacy of this more exclusive enclave. For honeymooners, we pick this one over the other. Guests can take advantage of two giant swimming pools, four tennis courts, watersports — including parasailing — a dive shop, a Jacuzzi, and one of the island's finer private beaches.

At Frenchman's Reef Beach Resort, Flamboyant Point, Charlotte Amalie, P.O. Box 7100, St. Thomas, USVI 00801. ☎ *800-524-2000 or 340-776-8500. Fax: 340-776-3054. Internet:* www.marriott.vi. *Rack rates: $350-$450 double; for MAP (two meals daily), add $73 per person per night. AE, DC, MC, V.*

Pavilions and Pools Hotel
$$$ Estate Smith Bay, St. Thomas

Popular with honeymooners, this resort, seven miles east of Charlotte Amalie, is a string of tastefully rebuilt and furnished condominium units. After check-in, you follow a wooden pathway to your villa, where you enter your own private world complete with a private swimming pool encircled by a deck and plenty of tropical greenery. Each villa has floor-to-ceiling glass doors, an individually styled bedroom, and a roomy outdoor shower. The resort adjoins Sapphire Bay, which boasts one of the island's best beaches and watersports concessions. A small bar and barbecue area sit against a wall on the reception terrace, where the hotel hosts rum parties and cookouts. Informal, simple meals are served nightly, and occasionally a musician or singer entertains. Free snorkeling gear is offered. Honeymoon packages are available.

6400 Estate Smith Bay, St. Thomas, USVI 00802. ☎ *800-524-2001 or 340-775-6110. Fax: 340-775-6110. Internet:* www.pavilionsandpools.com. *Rack rates: $250-$275 double. Rates include continental breakfast in winter only. AE, MC, V. CP.*

The Ritz-Carlton, St. Thomas
$$$$ Charlotte Amalie, St. Thomas

When you walk into the grand welcoming area here, with all the crystal, marble, and finery, you may think you've suddenly landed in Venice — for good reason. This grand property was originally built by an Italian hotel company. The guestrooms, in six buildings that fan out from the main villa, are spacious and tropically furnished. Each has a good view of the bay facing St. John. The Ritz has given the place its own special brand of treatment, and the results show in this deluxe Caribbean property. The few complaints that we've heard whispered by other guests indicate that you don't quite capture the Caribbean rhythm here. The atmosphere is a little too buttoned up. The marvelous suites at the end of the property with the best views, though, do give in to the prime Caribbean setting and get into the groove with plantation-style furnishings and wooden hurricane windows that crank open to let in the tropical breezes. A multilingual staff and 24-hour room service enhance the sophisticated atmosphere. The exercise room is on the small side, and the air-conditioning definitely wasn't working when we last visited.

The resort offers generous and surprisingly well priced honeymoon packages which include treats like a sunset cruise.

6900 Great Bay Estate, St. Thomas, USVI 00802. ☎ *800-241-3333 or 340-775-3333. Fax: 340-775-4444. Internet:* www.ritzcarlton.com. *Rack rates: $325-$575 double. AE, DISC, DC, MC, V.*

The Waves at Cane Bay
$$ East End, St. Croix

Lapping waves lull you to sleep at this isolated inn well-run by Suzanne and Kevin Ryan, avid divers who tapped this spot as their dream. Although the beach is rocky, Cane Bay Beach is next door, and the world-famous Cane Bay Reef is just 100 yards offshore (divers take note). You can also sunbathe on a small patch of sand beside the unusual pool, carved from the coral along the shore. Waves crash dramatically over its side, creating a foamy whirlpool on blustery days. Two peach and mint-green buildings house enormous balconied, light-drenched guestrooms done in soothing creams and accented with homey touches like well-worn books and shells collected by the Ryans' children. All the rooms have kitchens or kitchenettes and ceiling fans, but not all have air-conditioning.

Rte. 80 (P.O. Box 1749), Kingsbill, St. Croix, USVI 00851. ☎ *800-545-0603 or 340-778-1805. Fax: 340-778-4945. Internet:* www.canebaystcroix.com. *Rack rates: $140-$195 double. AE, MC, V.*

Westin Resort, St. John
$$$$$ Great Cruz Bay, St. John

Spread out over 47 acres adjacent to Great Cruz Bay, the Westin is one of two luxe choices on St. John. It has lushly planted gardens, a large pool, and a good beach where you can swim or sail. If you want to get out and about, taxi jaunts into Cruz Bay are a breeze. The rooms recently underwent the Starwood treatment, meaning that they were redone in Caribbean chic. Ultra-comfy beds (we've tried to duplicate the set-up at home), which have deservedly become the signature of these hotels, have been installed. Many rooms have excellent views of the Caribbean, and all have computer ports for those who just have to keep in touch with the world. As we've noted at several corporate resorts, the staff, especially in the restaurants, can use some additional training in service with a smile. Guests at the Westin Vacation Club, a condominium complex located across the street, enjoy all the hotel amenities. At your disposal are three restaurants, a masseuse, six tennis courts, an exercise room, a beach, a dive shop, snorkeling, windsurfing, boating, fishing, and shops.

Physically challenged guests may find the grounds too sprawling and hilly for their comfort.

Rte. 104 (P.O. Box 8310), Great Cruz Bay, St. John, USVI 00831. ☎ ***800-808-5020** or 340-693-8000. Fax: 340-693-4500. E-mail:* stjon@westin.com. *Internet:* www.westin.com. *Rack rates: from $440 double. AE, DISC, DC, MC, V.*

Enjoying the U.S. Virgin Islands

Billed as an "American Caribbean," the U.S. Virgin Islands (USVIs) deliver a vacation experience as rich and rewarding as any Caribbean getaway. Each lively island in the USVIs, though certainly showing its connection to the United States, has its own exotic flavor. You're sure to feel the warm welcome of the culturally diverse people who make their homes in the islands, 1,000 miles south of the southernmost tip of the U.S. mainland.

St. Thomas, which has one of the Caribbean's loveliest harbor cities, Charlotte Amalie, is the best known of the three main islands. It's the second busiest cruise port in the Caribbean. Cruise shippers love the shopping just off the waterfront in the old colonial harbor city.

Just a short ferry ride away from St. Thomas lies our favorite of the trio of USVIs: St. John. Two-thirds national park, this beautiful little island has a funky, collegial feel to it. The close runner-up for us is St. Croix, which has been overlooked by many tourists. It has two historic towns with beautiful Dutch architecture to explore, and it's a rural island with many working farms where you can get a good sense of the old Caribbean.

All three islands have fantastic beaches. Each is so different from the others that we strongly recommend splitting your time between at least two. If you have a longer honeymoon planned, hit all three.

Soaking up some water fun

On St. Thomas

Dive sites around St. Thomas feature wrecks such as the **Cartanser Sr.,** a 35-foot-deep, beautifully encrusted, World War II cargo ship, and the **General Rogers,** a 65-foot-deep Coast Guard cutter with a gigantic resident barracuda. Reef dives offer hidden caves and archways at Cow and Calf Rocks, coral-covered pinnacles at Frenchcap, and tunnels where you can explore undersea from the Caribbean to the Atlantic at Thatch Cay, Grass Cay, and Congo Cay. Many resorts and charter yachts offer dive packages. A one-tank dive starts at $40; two-tank dives are $55 or more. There are plenty of snorkeling possibilities, too. Nick Aquilar's *At-A-Glance Snorkeler's Guide To St. Thomas,* available at local souvenir shops, describes 15 idyllic spots in detail.

Aqua Action (6501 Red Hook Plaza; ☎ **340-775-6285**) is a full-service, PADI, five-star dive shop that offers all levels of instruction at Secret Harbour Beach Resort. Owner Carl Moore, a certified instructor for the Handicap Scuba Association, teaches scuba to physically disabled visitors. **Chris Sawyer Diving Center** (☎ **800-882-2965** or 340-775-7320), at Compass Point Marina, is a PADI five-star outfit that specializes in dives to the 310-foot-long RMS Rhyne in the BVIs. (Don't forget your passport and your C-card if you take this trip.) This center also has a NAUI certification center that offers instruction up to "dive master."

Caribbean Parasail and Watersports (6501 Red Hook Plaza; ☎ **340-775-9360**) makes parasailing pickups from every beachfront resort on St. Thomas. It also rents such water toys as jet skis, kayaks, and floating battery-powered chairs.

Try your luck clipping through the seas around St. Thomas on a surfboard with a sail. Most beachfront resorts rent windsurf gear and offer one-hour lessons for about $50. One of the island's best known independent outfits is **West Indies Windsurfing** (Vessup Beach, No. 9 Nazareth; ☎ **340-775-6530**).

On St. Croix

St. Croix has several excellent dive sites. At **Buck Island National Reef Monument,** a short boat ride from Christiansted or Green Cay Marina, you can see lots of barracuda and stoplight parrot fish, which live up to their name. You can dive right off the beach at **Cane Bay,** which has a spectacular drop-off. **Frederiksted Pier** is home to a colony of small seahorses, creatures seldom seen in the waters off the Virgin Islands. At **Green Cay,** just outside Green Cay Marina in the East End, you see colorful fish swimming around the reefs and rocks. Two exceptional North Shore sites are **North Star** and **Salt River,** which you can reach only by boat. You can float downward through a canyon filled with colorful fish and coral.

The island's dive shops take you out for one- or two-tank dives. Plan to pay about $50 for a one-tank dive and $70 for a two-tank dive, including equipment and an underwater tour. **Anchor Dive Center** (Salt River Marina, Rte. 801; ☎ **800-532-3483** or 340-778-1522) explores the wall at Salt River Canyon from its base at Salt River Marina. It also provides PADI certification. **Dive St. Croix** (☎ **800-523-3483** or 340-773-3434) takes divers to 35 different sites from its base on the Christiansted Wharf. It's the only operation that runs dives to Buck Island. **V.I. Divers**

Ltd. (☎ **800-544-5911** or 340-773-6045) is near the water in the Pan Am Pavilion. It's a PADI five-star training facility and takes divers to their choice of 28 sites.

St. Croix's trade winds make windsurfing a breeze. You can also check in with Kevin and Suzanne Ryan, who operate a good dive operation from their hotel, The Waves at Cane Bay. Most hotels rent windsurf and other watersports equipment to non-guests. **St. Croix Watersports** (Hotel on the Cay; ☎ **340-773-7060**) offers Windsurfer rentals, sales, and rides; parasailing; and a wide range of watersports equipment, such as jet skis and kayaks.

On St. John

While just about every beach on St. John has nice snorkeling, we favor **Cinnamon Bay** and **Waterlemon Cay** at Leinster Bay. Otherwise, you need a boat to head out to the more remote snorkeling locations and the best scuba spots. Sign on with any of the island's watersports operators to take you to hot spots between St. John and St. Thomas, including the tunnels at **Thatch Cay,** the ledges at **Congo Cay,** and the wreck of the **General Rogers.** Dive off St. John at **Stephens Cay,** a short boat ride out of Cruz Bay, where fish swim around the reefs as you float downward. At **Devers Bay,** on St. John's south shore, fish dart about in colorful schools.

Count on paying $55 for a one-tank dive and $75 for a two-tank dive. Rates include equipment and a tour. **Cruz Bay Watersports** (☎ **340-776-6234**) has three locations: Cruz Bay; the Westin Resort; and Palm Plaza Shopping Center. Owners Marcus and Patty Johnston offer regular reef, wreck, and night dives and USVI and BVI snorkel tours. **Low Key Watersports** (☎ **340-693-8999**) at Wharfside Village offers PADI certification and resort courses, one- and two-tank dives, and specialty courses.

St. John's steady breezes and expert instruction make learning to windsurf a snap. Try **Cinnamon Bay Campground** (Rte. 20; ☎ **340-776- 6330**), where rentals are available for $12 to $15 per hour. Lessons are available right at the waterfront; just look for the windsurf boards and gear stacked up on the beach. The cost for a one-hour lesson is about $40.

Enjoying the waves

The USVIs were built on boating and sailing is an integral part of the experience of being in these lovely isles.

On St. Thomas

With well more than 100 vessels to choose from, St. Thomas is the charter boat mecca of the USVIs. You can go through a broker to book a private sailing vessel with a crew, or you can contact a charter company directly.

Island Yachts (6100 Red Hook Quarter, 18B; ☎ 800-524-2019 or 340-775-6666) is a charter boat company in Red Hook. **Nauti Nymph** (6501 Red Hook Plaza, Suite 201; ☎ 800-734-7345 or 340-775-5066) has a large selection of powerboats for rent. Rates range from $215 to $350 a day and include snorkel gear.

Fish dart, birds sing, and iguanas lounge in the dense mangrove swamps deep within a marine sanctuary on St. Thomas's southeast shore. **Virgin Islands Ecotours** (2 Estate Nadir on Rte. 32; ☎ 340-779-2155) offers 2½-hour, guided trips on two-man sit-atop ocean kayaks; there are stops for swimming and snorkeling. Many of the resorts on St. Thomas's eastern end have kayaks, too.

On St. Croix

You can sail to Buck Island aboard one of the island's charter boats. Most leave from the Christiansted waterfront or Green Cay Marina. The captain stops to allow you to snorkel at the eastern end of the island before dropping anchor off a gorgeous beach for a swim, a hike, and lunch. **Big Beard's Adventure Tours** (☎ 340-773-4482) takes you on a catamaran, the *Renegade,* from the Christiansted Waterfront to Buck Island for snorkeling before dropping anchor at a private beach for a barbecue lunch. **Buck Island Charters'** (☎ 340-773-3161) trimaran *Teroro II* leaves Green Cay Marina for full- or half-day sails. Bring your own lunch.

On St. John

For a speedy trip in St. John to offshore cays and remote beaches, a power boat is a necessity. If you're boatless, book with one of the island's agents. Most day sails include lunch, beverages, and at least one stop to snorkel. **Connections** (Cruz Bay, a block up from the ferry dock and catty-corner from Chase Manhattan Bank; ☎ 340-776-6922) pairs you with sailboats that suit you. **Ocean Runner** (☎ 340-693-8809), on the waterfront in Cruz Bay, rents one- and two-engine boats for fast trips around the island's seas. **Proper Yachts** (☎ 340-776-6256) books day sails and longer charters on its luxury yachts that depart from Caneel Bay Resort.

Poke around and explore St. John's crystal bays in a sea kayak. **Arawak Expeditions'** (☎ 800-238-8687 or 340-693-8312) professional guides use kayaks to ply coastal waters. Prices start at $40 for a half-day trip.

Hitting the links

The USVIs offer several great options for practicing your swing.

On St. Thomas

When we were last in the BVIs, we met a group of fellows who were sailing around the isles but decided to take a break in the midst of their pirate adventure. They chartered helicopters to take them over to

St. Thomas's **The Mahogany Run Golf Course** (Rte. 42; ☎ 340-777-5000). The course, favored by former U.S. President Clinton for his vacation, is open daily and often hosts informal tournaments on weekends. A spectacular view of the BVIs and the challenging three-hole "Devil's Triangle" attracts avid golfers to this Tom Fazio-designed, par-70, 18-hole course.

On St. Croix

St. Croix's courses welcome you with spectacular vistas and well-kept greens. Check with your hotel or the tourist board to determine when major celebrity tournaments will be held; there's often an opportunity to play with the pros. **The Buccaneer** (off Rte. 82 at Teague Bay; ☎ 340-773-2100) is an 18-hole course conveniently close to (east of) Christiansted. **The Reef Golf Course** (☎ 340-778-5638), in the northeastern part of the island, has nine holes. The spectacular course at **Carambola Beach Resort** (Rte. 80; ☎ 340-778-5638), in the remote and rural northwest valley, was designed by Robert Trent Jones.

Taking a hike

Get a ground-level view of all the flora, fauna, and other attractions by strapping on your most comfortable shoes and setting out to explore. (St. Thomas doesn't rate high scores for cool hiking sites.)

On St. Croix

Although you can set off by yourself on a hike through a rain forest or along a shore, a guide points out what's important and tells you why. The nonprofit **St. Croix Environmental Association** (Arawak Bldg., Suite 3, Gallows Bay, 00820; ☎ 340-773-1989) offers hikes through several of the island's ecological treasures, including Estate Mt. Washington, Estate Caledonia in the rain forest, and Salt River. The hikes take nearly two hours and cost $25 per person.

On St. John

Although it's fun to go hiking with a Virgin Islands National Park guide, don't be afraid to strike out on your own. We found the trails easy to follow and more fun on our own. However, unless you're just wild about hiking, you can cover the most interesting trails in a day. To find a hike that suits your ability, stop by the park's visitors center in Cruz Bay and pick up the free trail guide. The guides detail points of interest, dangers, trail lengths, and estimated hiking times.

Although the park staff recommends pants to protect against thorns and insects, most people hike in shorts because pants are too hot. Wear sturdy shoes or hiking boots even if you hike to the beach. Don't forget to bring water and insect repellent, and coat yourself in waterproof sunscreen.

The **Virgin Islands National Park** (☎ 340-776-6201) maintains more than 20 trails on the north and south shores and offers guided hikes along popular routes. A full-day trip to **Reef Bay** is a must; it's an easy hike through lush and dry forest, past the ruins of an old plantation, and to a sugar factory adjacent to the beach. Take the public Vitran bus to the trailhead where you meet a ranger who serves as your guide. The park provides a boat ride back to Cruz Bay for $14.50 to save you the walk back up the mountain. The schedule changes; call for times and reservations, which are essential.

Reef Bay Trail is one of the most interesting hikes on St. John, but unless you are a rugged individualist who wants a physical challenge (and that describes a lot of people who stay on St. John), you may get the most out of the trip if you join a hike led by a park service ranger. A ranger can identify the trees and plants, fill you in on the history of the Reef Bay Plantation, and tell you about the petroglyphs on the rocks at the bottom of the trail.

Exploring the USVIs

These islands each have something very different, but all share a rich history. Here we hit the absolute high points.

St. Thomas

St. Thomas is only 13 miles (21 km) long and less than 4 miles (6.5 km) wide, but it's an extremely hilly island. Even an 8- or 10-mile (13- or 16-km) trip can take several hours in a vehicle. Don't let that discourage you, though, because the ridge of mountains that runs from east to west through the middle and separates the Caribbean and Atlantic sides of the island has spectacular vistas and is a lot of fun to explore.

When exploring Charlotte Amalie, look beyond the pricey shops, T-shirt vendors, and crowds for a glimpse of the island's history. Here our some of the must-see spots:

- **Government House:** Built as an elegant residence in 1867, today Government House serves as the governor's office with the first floor open to the public. The staircases are made of native mahogany, as are the plaques hand-lettered in gold with the names of past governors. Brochures detailing the history of the building are available, but you may have to ask for them. (Government Hill; ☎ 340-774-0001. Admission is free. Open weekdays from 8 a.m. to 5 p.m.)

- **Coral World Marine Park & Underwater Observatory:** This is the best marine park in the Caribbean. It houses the Predator Tank, one of the world's largest coral reef tanks, and an aquarium with more than 20 portholes providing close-up views of Caribbean sealife. Our favorite exhibit was of the seahorses in different stages of development. Outside are several outdoor pools where you can touch starfish, pet a baby shark, feed stingrays, and view endangered sea turtles. (Coki Point, turn north off Rte. 38 at sign approximately 20 minutes from Charlotte Amalie; ☎ **340-775-1555;** Internet www.coralworldvi.com. Admission is $18; $9 for children 3 to 12. Open daily from 9 a.m. to 5 p.m.)

✔ **Frenchtown:** If you want to check out local bars and good restaurants, head here. Turn south off Waterfront Hwy. at the U.S. Post Office.

✔ **Mountain Top:** Stop here for a banana daiquiri and spectacular views from the observation deck more than 1,500 feet above sea level. There are also shops that sell everything from Caribbean art to nautical antiques, ship models, and T-shirts. Head north off Rte. 33; look for signs.

✔ **Paradise Point Tramway:** Fly skyward in a gondola, similar to a ski lift, 700 feet up the hill to Paradise Point, an overlook with breathtaking views of Charlotte Amalie and the harbor. There are several shops, a bar, and a restaurant. A one-mile long nature trail leads to spectacular sights of St. Croix to the south. Wear sturdy shoes. (Rte. 30 at Havensight; ☎ **340-774-9809.** Admission is $12 round trip; $6 for ages 6 to 12; ages 5 and under free. Open daily from 7:30 a.m. to 4:30 p.m.)

St. Croix

Christiansted is a historic, Danish-style town that has always served as St. Croix's commercial center. Spend the morning, when it's still cool, exploring the historic sites here. This two-hour endeavor doesn't tax your walking shoes and leaves you with energy to poke around the town's eclectic shops. Break for lunch at an open-air restaurant before spending as much time as you like shopping.

An easy drive (roads are flat and well marked) to St. Croix's eastern end takes you through some choice real estate. Ruins of old sugar estates dot the landscape. You can make the entire loop on the road that circles the island in about an hour, a good way to end the day. If you want to spend a full day exploring, you find some nice beaches and easy walks, with places to stop for lunch.

You can't get lost on St. Croix. All the streets lead gently downhill to the water. Still, if you want some friendly advice, stop by the **Visitor's Center** (53A Company St.; ☎ **340-773-0495**) weekdays between 8 a.m. and 5 p.m. for maps and brochures.

Be sure to check out some of these sites on your trip to St. Croix:

✔ **Danish Customs House:** Built in 1830 on foundations that date from 1734, the Danish Customs House (near Ft. Christiansvaern) originally served as both a customs house and a post office. In 1926, it became the Christiansted Library, and it has been a National Park Service office since 1972.

✔ **Government House:** One of the town's most elegant structures, the Government House was built as a home for a Danish merchant in 1747. Today it houses USVI government offices. If the building is open, slip into the peaceful inner courtyard to admire the pools and gardens. (King St.; ☎ 340-713-9807.)

✔ **Estate Whim Plantation Museum:** This lovingly restored estate, with a windmill, cook house, and other buildings, gives you a sense of what life was like on St. Croix's sugar plantations in the 1800s. The oval-shaped great house has high ceilings and antique furniture, decor, and utensils. The apothecary exhibit is the largest in all the West Indies. Now you can buy beautiful island antiques at this impressive museum shop. (Rte. 70, Frederiksted; ☎ 340-772-0598. Admission $6. Open Tuesday through Saturday from 10 a.m. to 4 p.m.)

✔ **Fredriksted:** The town is noted less for its Danish than for its Victorian architecture, which dates from after the slave uprising and the great fire of 1878. One long cruise ship pier juts into the sparkling sea. The former Customs House, now **The Visitor's Center** (Waterfront; ☎ 340-772-0357), right on the pier, was built in the late 1700s; the two-story gallery was added in the 1800s. Today, you can stop in weekdays from 8 a.m. to 5 p.m. and pick up brochures or view the exhibits on St. Croix. (Waterfront; ☎ 340-772-2021. Admission is free.)

✔ **St. Croix Leap:** This workshop sits in the heart of the rain forest, about a 15-minute drive from Frederiksted. It sells a wide range of articles, including mirrors, tables, bread boards, and mahogany jewelry boxes crafted by local artisans. (Rte. 76; ☎ 340-772-0421.)

✔ **St. George Village Botanical Gardens:** At this 17-acre estate, you find lush, fragrant flora amid the ruins of a nineteenth-century sugarcane plantation village. There are miniature versions of each ecosystem on St. Croix, from a semiarid cactus grove to a verdant rain forest. (Turn north off Rte. 70 at the sign; Kingshill; ☎ 340-692-2874. Admission $5. Open Monday through Saturday from 9 a.m. to 4 p.m.; closed holidays.)

St. John

Few residents remember the route numbers, which were instituted about five years ago, so have your map in hand if you stop to ask for directions. Bring along a swimsuit for stops at some of the most beautiful beaches in the world. Be advised that the roads are narrow and sometimes steep, so don't expect to get anywhere in a hurry.

You find lunch spots at **Cinnamon Bay** and in **Coral Bay,** or you can do what the locals do — picnic. The grocery stores in **Cruz Bay** sell Styrofoam coolers for this purpose. If you plan to do a lot of touring, rent a car; taxis are reluctant to go anywhere until they have a full load of passengers. Although you may be tempted by an open-air Suzuki or Jeep, a conventional car can get you just about everywhere on the paved roads, and you can also lock up your valuables. You may be able to share a van or open-air vehicle (called a safari bus) with other passengers on a tour of scenic mountain trails, secret coves, and eerie bush-covered ruins. Don't miss these favorite spots:

✔ **Annaberg Plantation:** In the eighteenth century, sugar plantations dotted the steep hills of the USVIs. Slaves and free Danes and Dutchmen harvested the cane that was used to create sugar, molasses, and rum for export. Built in the 1780s, the partially restored plantation at Leinster Bay was once an important sugar mill. Though there are no official visiting hours, the National Park Service has regular tours. Occasionally you find a living-history demonstration — someone making johnnycake or weaving baskets. For information on tours and demonstrations, contact the St. John National Park Service Visitor's Center. (Leinster Bay Rd; ☎ 340-776-6201. Admission $4.)

✔ **Bordeaux Mountain:** St. John's highest peak rises to 1,277 feet. Centerline Road passes near enough to the top to offer breathtaking views. Drive nearly to the end of the dirt road for spectacular views at Picture Point and for the trailhead of the hike downhill to Lameshur. Get a trail map from the park service before you start. (Rte. 70.)

✔ **Catherineberg Ruins:** This is a fine example of an eighteenth-century sugar and rum factory. In the 1733 slave revolt, Catherineberg served as headquarters for Amina warriors, a tribe of Africans captured into slavery. (Rte. 70.)

Living it up in the USVIs

On any given night, you find steel pan orchestras, rock-and-roll bands, piano music, jazz, disco, and karaoke. Pick up a copy of the free, bright yellow *St. Thomas This Week* magazine when you arrive. (You see it at the airport, in stores, and in hotel lobbies.) The back pages list who's playing where. The Thursday edition of the *Daily News* carries complete listings for the upcoming weekend.

St. Thomas

Of the trio, St. Thomas has the most happening nightlife. Here's where to go:

✔ **Iggies:** Sing along karaoke style to the sounds of the surf or the latest hits at this beachside lounge. There's often a DJ on weekends, when a buffet barbecue precedes the 9 p.m. music fest. Dance inside, or kick up your heels under the stars. (50 Estate Bolongo; ☎ 340-775-1800.)

✔ **Andiamo at the Martini Café:** You find a piano bar nightly at this spot. (70 Honduras, Frenchtown; ☎ 340-776-7916.)

✔ **Agave Terrace:** Island-style steel pan bands play here on Tuesday, Thursday, and Saturday. (Point Pleasant Resort, Smith Bay; ☎ 340-775-4142.)

St. Croix

Christiansted has a lively and casual club scene near the waterfront, including the following spots:

✔ **Cormorant:** On Thursday night during the winter season, this club at 4126 La Grande Princesse dishes up a West Indian buffet with a small local band. (☎ 340-778-8920.)

✔ **Hotel on the Cay:** This spot has a West Indian buffet on Tuesday night in the winter season that features a broken-bottle dancer (a dancer who braves a carpet of broken bottles) and mocko jumbie characters (stilt-walkers in wild costumes). (Protestant Cay; ☎ 340-773-2035.)

✔ **Indies:** Easy jazz flows from the courtyard bar on Saturday evenings. (55-56 Company St.; ☎ 340-692-9440.)

✔ **2 Plus 2 Disco:** DJs spin a great mix of calypso, soul, disco, and reggae; there's live music on weekends. (17 La Grande Princesse; ☎ 340-773-3710.)

St. John

St. John isn't the place to go for glitter and all-night partying. Still, after-hours Cruz Bay can be a lively little village in which to dine, drink, and dance. Notices posted on the bulletin board outside the Connections telephone center (up the street from the ferry dock in Cruz Bay) or listings in the island's two small newspapers (the *St. John Times* and *Tradewinds*) keep you apprised of special events, comedy nights, movies, and the like. Take a gander at the following spots for some nightlife:

✔ **Ellington's:** After a sunset drink at this spot up the hill from Cruz Bay, you can stroll here and there in town; much is clustered around the small waterfront park. (Gallows Point Suite Resort; ☎ 340-693-8490.)

✔ **Fred's:** There's calypso and reggae on Wednesday and Friday. (Cruz Bay; ☎ 340-776-6363.)

✔ **Skinny Legs Bar and Restaurant:** Check out the action at this happening place at Coral Bay on the far side of the island. (Rte. 107; ☎ 340-779-4982.)

Dining in the USVIs

You can find good restaurants on St. Thomas, St. John, and St. Croix, whether you're looking for simple and cheap local food or a more sophisticated dining experience with experimental dishes whipped out by professional chefs. The USVIs' dining scene attracts some of the best chefs and waitstaffs the U.S. has to offer because these beautiful islands offer plenty in return.

Dining in the USVIs is relaxed and informal; few restaurants require a jacket and tie. But while shorts and a tank top may not get you tossed out of a better restaurant, you may find yourself seated at a dark corner table. Men should wear slacks and a shirt with buttons. Women should wear a nice sundress or pants outfit in the evenings.

When you visit one of the U.S. Virgin Islands, you're likely to stay put, perhaps popping over to one of the other islands for a day or so. We arranged our dining favorites to reflect the ways you're most likely to experience the USVIs.

Looking for romance

Craig & Sally's (22 Estate Honduras, St. Thomas; ☎ **340-777-9949; $$$**), a long-time favorite, has a daily changing menu with only a few staples, such as eggplant cheesecake with pinenut-garlic bread crumb crust as a starter. Boasting an extensive wine list with a dozen wines offered by the glass, this Frenchtown classic relies on the wine selections of husband Craig while Chef Sally Darash concentrates her skills in the kitchen.

From the moment we stepped into this cloud-kissing spot, we knew we were in for a treat. Reserve a table at **Asolare** (Caneel Hill, St. John; ☎ **340-779-4747; $$$**), which means "leisurely passing the time," on a night when you can linger and linger and linger. If you've ever imagined supping in a tree house, you'll feel right at home at **Le Chateau de Bordeaux** (Junction 10, Centerline Rd., St. John; ☎ **340-776-6611; $$$**), a rustic spot graced with wrought-iron chandeliers, fine lace table-cloths, and Victorian antiques. The innovative preparations appeal equally to the eye and palate. Before dinner, have a drink in the cozy, darkly atmospheric bar, which prompts you to wonder who has lingered in **Hotel 1829** (Kongens Gade, at the east end of Main St, Charlotte Amalie, St. Thomas; ☎ **340-776-1829; $$$**).

Perched high above a steep and heavily forested hillside on the eastern tip of St. Thomas, **Agavé Terrace** (Point Pleasant Resort, Smith Bay, St. Thomas; ☎ **340-775-4142; $$$**) offers a sweeping panorama of St. John and the BVIs at night. The young couple who owns it has gleaned six gold medals in Caribbean cooking competitions. Come early and have a drink at the Lookout Lounge. After you wind your way through the historic Bluebeard's Castle, you find one of our treasures, **Banana Tree Grille** (Bluebeard's Castle, Charlotte Amalie, St. Thomas; ☎ **340-776-4050; $$$**), an open-air, cheery spot clinging to the hillside and sporting one of the best views of this harborfront city. When you call for reservations, ask for a table as far to the edge of the multilevel terrace as possible.

Celebrating your love

Victor's New Hide-Out (Sub Base, Frenchtown, St. Thomas; ☎ 340-776-9379; $$$) is sandwiched between Nisky Shopping Center and the airport and overlooks Water Island. Its colorful owner, Victor Sydney, hailing from the tiny Caribbean island of Montserrat, has attracted celebrities for decades with his Caribbean cooking. Tiny lights add a soft glow to **Indies'** (55-56 Company St., St. Croix; ☎ 340-692-9440; $$$) open-air courtyard where palms gently rustle overhead in the tropic breeze. The Caribbean has infused and inspired the daily-changing menu of owners/chefs Eric Zolner and Steve Hendren, who make the most of St. Croix's freshest fish, fruit, and vegetables. Great for a Friday or Saturday evening under the stars when the strains of live jazz relax. For several years, **Kendricks** (2132 Company St., St. Croix; ☎ 340-773-9199; $$$$), handsomely bedecked with island antiques, has been known as the island's most in-tune restaurant. The French Contem-porary food merited a write-up in *Bon Appetit,* plus you have a view of Christiansted Harbor.

Looking for a local favorite

Chef Aaron Willis conjures up such tasty appetizers as conch fritters and chowder at the laidback **Fish Trap Cruz Bay** (St. John,, next to Our Lady of Mount Carmel Church; ☎ 340-693-9994; $$). The chef/owner at **Café Wahoo** (Piccola Marina, Red Hook, St. Thomas; ☎ 340-775-6350; $$$$) gets first pick from the fishermen who bring their catches across the dock of Red Hook's American Yacht Harbor. **Harvey's** (11B Company St; ☎ 340-773-3433; $) has been turned into a shrine to home-island basketball hero Tim Duncan of the San Antonio Spurs. If you've got a jones for great local fare, this place can sate you with goat stew and tender whelks (similar to mussels) in butter, served with heaping helpings of rice, fungi, and vegetables. Locals also congregate at **La Tapa** (across from Scotia Bank on an unnamed street that heads inland from Red Hook ferry dock in Cruz Bay, St. John; ☎ 340-693-7755; $$) to feast on tasty bites and sip sangria. From the street-side tables you can watch the world go by. "Tapas hours" are held Monday through Friday from 3:30 p.m. to 6:30 p.m. **Villa Morales** (Plot 82C, off Rte. 70, Estate Whim, St. Croix; ☎ 340-772-0556; $), a family-run spot, is known for its well-prepared Cruzan and Spanish dishes and the dancing in the cavernous back room. Meanwhile, the **Lime Inn** (Downtown Cruz Bay, St. John, east of Chase Manhattan Bank; ☎ 340-776-6425; $$$) offers gargantuan and excellent seafood salads in a congenial atmosphere with fantastic service.

Settling into the USVIs

Whether you come by air or by sea, the United States Virgin Islands (USVIs) are among the easier destinations to connect with in the Caribbean. Many airlines have direct flights to both St. Thomas and St. Croix, and many cruise ships have these islands in their schedules.

Most visitors arrive on St. Thomas, and then either take a ferry to St. John or a plane to St. Croix, if either is their final destination.

Arriving in St. Thomas

If you fly to the 32-square-mile island of St. Thomas, you land at its western end at **Cyril E. King Airport** (☎ **340-774-5100**), a modest but busy airport that serves flights continuing on to St. Croix as well as the British Virgin Islands.

One advantage to visiting the USVIs is the abundance of nonstop and connecting flights that can whisk you away to the beach in three to four hours from most eastern United States departures — especially since you won't be slowed by going through U.S. Customs. You breeze right through to pick up your luggage and follow the signs to ground transportation. Pick up a copy of the excellent *What To Do: St. Thomas & St. John,* a terrific tourist magazine, which contains several coupons and all the latest happenings on the islands.

Getting around the USVIs

This section shows you how to get around the islands.

Renting a car

If you want to explore much, especially on St. Thomas and St. Croix, we recommend renting a car. On St. John, a car is a good idea if you stay in a villa some distance from Cruz Bay. Otherwise, we suggest hiring a driver for a day or two of touring.

Any U.S. driver's license is good for 90 days on the USVIs, as are valid driver's licenses from other countries. The minimum age for drivers is 18, although many agencies won't rent to anyone under the age of 25.

Driving is on the left side of the road (although your steering wheel will be on the left side of the car). The law requires everyone in a car to wear seat belts. Many of the roads are narrow, and the islands are dotted with hills, so there's ample reason to put safety first. Even at a sedate speed of 20 miles per hour, driving can be an adventure. For example, you may find yourself in a stick-shift Jeep slogging behind a slow tourist-packed safari bus at a steep hairpin turn. Give a little beep at blind turns; there are some lu-lus on St. John.

Note that the general speed limit on these islands is only 25 to 35 miles per hour, which seems fast enough for you on most roads. If you don't think you need to lock up your valuables, a Jeep or open-air Suzuki with four-wheel-drive makes it easier to navigate pot-holed dirt side roads and to get up slick hills when it rains. We consider four-wheel-drive a necessity on St. John. All main roads are paved. Expect to pay top prices for gasoline.

Driving on St. Thomas

Traffic on St. Thomas sometimes crawls along like a sea turtle on dry land, especially in Charlotte Amalie at rush hour (from 7 to 9 a.m. and 4:30 to 6 p.m.). Cars often line up bumper-to-bumper along the waterfront.

If you need to get from an East End resort to the airport during these times, use the alternate route (starting from the East End, Route 38 to 42 to 40 to 33) that goes up the mountain and then drops you back onto Veteran's Highway. If you plan to explore by car, be sure to pick up the 2000 Road Map St. Thomas - St. John that includes the route numbers and the names of the roads that are used by locals. It's available anywhere you find maps and guidebooks.

You can rent a car on St. Thomas from the following companies:

- ✔ **Budget** (☎ **800-626-4516** or 340-776-5774)
- ✔ **Cowpet Rent-a-Car** (☎ **340-775-7376**)
- ✔ **Dependable Car Rental** (☎ **800-522-3076** or 340-774-2253)
- ✔ **Discount** (☎ **340-776-4858**)
- ✔ **Sun Island Car Rental** (☎ **340-774-3333**)

Driving on St. Croix

Unlike St. Thomas and St. John, where narrow roads wind through hillsides, St. Croix is relatively flat, and it even has a four-lane highway. The speed limit on the Melvin H. Evans Highway is 55 miles per hour and ranges from 35 to 40 miles per hour elsewhere. Roads are often unmarked, but locals are friendly on this rural island and can put you back on the right route.

Occasionally, all the rental companies run out of cars at once. To avoid disappointment, make your reservations early. Call one of the following:

- ✔ **Avis** (☎ **800-331-1084** or 340-778-9355)
- ✔ **Budget** (☎ **888-227-3359** or 340-778-9636)
- ✔ **Olympic** (☎ **888-878-4227** or 340-773-2208)
- ✔ **Thrifty** (☎ **800-367-2277** or 340-773-7200)

Driving on St. John

Use caution on St. John. The terrain is extremely hilly, the roads winding, and the blind curves numerous. You may suddenly come upon a huge safari bus careening around a corner, or a couple of hikers strolling along the side of the road. The major roads are well paved, but if you get off a specific route, dirt roads filled with potholes are common. For such driving, a four-wheel-drive vehicle is your best bet.

At the height of the winter season, it may be tough to find a car. Reserve well in advance to ensure that you get the vehicle of your choice. Call one of the following:

- ✓ **Cool Breeze** (☎ **340-776-6588**)
- ✓ **Delbert Hill Taxi Rental Service** (☎ **340-776-6637**)
- ✓ **Denzil Clyne** (☎ **340-776-6715**)
- ✓ **St. John Car Rental** (☎ **340-776-6103**)
- ✓ **Spencer's Jeep** (☎ **888-776-6628** or 340-693-8784)

Hiring a taxi

USVI taxis don't have meters, but you needn't worry about fare-gouging if you check a list of standard rates to popular destinations. Drivers are required by law to carry the rate lists, and the lists are often posted in hotel and airport lobbies and printed in free tourist periodicals, such as *St. Thomas This Week* and *St. Croix This Week*. Settle on the fare before you start out. Fares are per person, not per destination, but drivers taking multiple fares (which often happens, especially from the airport) charge you a lower rate than if you're in the cab alone.

On St. Thomas, taxis of all shapes and sizes are available at various ferry, shopping, resort, and airport areas, and they also respond to phone calls. Try one of the following:

- ✓ **Islander Taxi** (☎ **340-774-4077**)
- ✓ **The VI Taxi Association** (☎ **340-774-4550**)
- ✓ **East End Taxi** (☎ **340-775-6974**)

Taxi stands are located in Charlotte Amalie across from Emancipation Garden (in front of Little Switzerland, behind the post office) and along the waterfront. But you probably won't have to look for a stand, because taxis are plentiful and routinely cruise the streets, looking for fares. Walking down Main Street, you are asked regularly: "Back to ship?"

On St. Croix, taxis (generally station wagons or minivans) are a phone call away from most hotels and are available in downtown Christiansted, at the Alexander Hamilton Airport, and at the Frederiksted pier during cruise ship arrivals. Try the **St. Croix Taxi Association** (☎ **340-778-1088**) at the airport and **Antilles Taxi Service** (☎ **340-773-5020**) or **Cruxan Taxi and Tours** (☎ **340-773-6388**) in Christiansted.

On St. John, taxis meet the ferries arriving in Cruz Bay. Most drivers use vans or open-air safari buses. You find them congregated at the dock and at hotel parking lots. You can also hail them anywhere on the road. You may travel with other tourists en route to their destinations. On this tiny island, you may find it difficult to get taxis to respond to a phone call. If you need one to pick you up at your rental villa, ask the villa manager for suggestions on whom to call or arrange a ride in advance. If the person doesn't show up within 15 minutes of the appointed time, put in a call. Drivers on St. John can be somewhat unreliable.

Taking public transportation

St. Thomas's 20 deluxe, mainland-size buses make public transportation a comfortable but slow way to get from east and west to Charlotte Amalie and back. (Service to the north is limited.) Buses run about every 30 minutes from stops that are clearly marked with VITRAN signs. Fares are $1 between outlying areas and town and 75 cents in town.

Privately owned taxi vans crisscross St. Croix regularly, providing reliable service between Frederiksted and Christiansted along Route 70. This inexpensive ($1.50 one way) mode of transportation is favored by locals, but the many stops on the 20-mile (32-km) drive between the two main towns make the ride slow. The public VITRAN buses aren't the quickest way to get around the island, but they're comfortable and affordable. The fare is $1 between Christiansted to Frederiksted or to places in between.

On St. John, modern VITRAN buses run from the Cruz Bay ferry dock through Coral Bay to the far eastern end of the island at Salt Pond, making numerous stops in between. The fare is $1 to any point.

Boarding a ferry

If you're heading to St. John, you fly into St. Thomas and take a taxi to either the dock at Charlotte Amalie or Red Hook, where you catch a ferry to Cruz Bay, St. John. The ferry from Charlotte Amalie makes the 45-minute trip several times a day and costs $7 a person.

Red Hook is a funky little community where you can grab a soda and fish patty from a vendor while you wait. The ferry runs at 6:30 and 7:30 a.m., then on the hour starting at 8 a.m. until midnight. The 20-minute trip costs $3 per person. We recommend getting a seat on top and toward the front where you can take in the view.

 Ferries are also a great way to travel around the islands; you can pick up service between St. Thomas and St. John and their neighbors, the BVIs. You need to present proof of citizenship upon entering the BVIs; a passport is best, but a birth certificate or voter's registration card with a photo ID will suffice.

Ferries to Cruz Bay, St. John, leave St. Thomas from either the Charlotte Amalie waterfront west of the U.S. Coast Guard dock or from Red Hook. From Charlotte Amalie, ferries depart at 9 and 11 a.m. and 1,

3, 4, and 5:30 p.m. (To Charlotte Amalie from Cruz Bay, they leave at 7:15, 9:15, and 11:15 a.m. and at 1:15, 2:15, and 3:45 p.m.) The one-way fare for the 45-minute ride is $7 for adults, $3 for children. From Red Hook, the ferries to Cruz Bay leave at 6:30 and 7:30 a.m. Starting at 8 a.m., they leave hourly until midnight. (Returning from Cruz Bay, they leave hourly starting at 6 a.m. until 11 p.m.) The 15- to 20-minute ferry ride is $3 one-way for adults, $1 for children under 12. Schedules vary; for the most up-to-date departure times, contact your hotel travel desk or check in with the ferry services.

There's daily service between either Charlotte Amalie or Red Hook on St. Thomas, and West End or Road Town on Tortola (BVI), by either **Smith's Ferry** (☎ **340-775-7292**) or **Native Son, Inc.** (☎ **340-774-8685**). Smith's Ferry also runs to Virgin Gorda (BVI). The times and days the ferries run change, so it's best to call for schedules after you're on the islands. The fare is $22 one-way or $40 round-trip. The trip from Charlotte Amalie to West End takes between 45 minutes and an hour. To Road Town, the trip takes up to 1½ hours. From Red Hook to Road Town, the trip is only half an hour. The twice-weekly, 2½ hour trip from Charlotte Amalie to Virgin Gorda costs $28 one-way and $40 round-trip. There's also daily service between Cruz Bay, St. John, and West End, Tortola, aboard the **Sundance** (☎ **340-776-6597**). The half-hour one-way trip costs $21.

Reefer (☎ **340-776-8500**, ext. 445) is the name of both brightly colored 26-passenger skiffs that run between the Charlotte Amalie waterfront and Marriott Frenchman's Reef Beach Resort daily every hour from 9 a.m. to 4 p.m., returning from the Reef from 9:30 a.m. until 4:30 p.m. A ride on a skiff costs about the same as a taxi fare. Plus, you get a great view of the harbor as you travel. The fare is $4 each way, and the trip takes about 15 minutes.

Flying from island to island

If your final destination is not St. Thomas, the following are some common carriers who fly to other nearby islands:

- ✔ **American Eagle** (☎ **340-778-2000**) offers frequent flights daily from St. Thomas to St. Croix's Henry E. Rohlsen Airport.

- ✔ **LIAT** (☎ **340-774-2313**) has service from St. Thomas and St. Croix to Caribbean islands to the south.

- ✔ **Cape Air** (☎ **800-352-0714**; Internet: www.flycapeair.com) offers hourly air service to St. Croix and Tortola (BVI).

- ✔ **The Seaborne Seaplane** (☎ **340-773-6442**), which you catch from a terminal on the waterfront across from Charlotte Amalie's main drag, also flies between St. Thomas and St. Croix several times daily. A round-trip ticket to St. Croix costs $120 and to Tortola costs $80. **Seaborne Seaplane Adventures** (☎ **340-777-1227**) offers narrated "flightseeing" tours of the USVIs and the BVIs from its Havensight base on St. Thomas. The 40-minute "Round-the-Island" tour is $94 per person.

Make reservations for the seaplane and check your luggage early. It has a strict weight limit of 40 pounds of luggage per passenger. Your luggage may be on the next flight if you don't check in early; we learned that the hard way. We found the plane really handy and fun, though. The 20-minute flight to St. Croix is pretty, and you're dropped off right at the dock, a five-minute walk from Christiansted. If you do get caught waiting for your luggage, you can wander around and look at the neat little shops or grab a bite at one of the waterfront restaurants there.

Choppering around

Air Center Helicopters (☎ **340-775-7335**), on the Charlotte Amalie waterfront (next to Tortola Wharf) on St. Thomas, has 25-minute island tours priced at $125 per trip per person (two-person minimum).

Fast Facts: USVIs

ATMs

On St. Thomas, the branch of **First Bank** (☎ 340-776-9494) near Market Square and the waterfront locations (☎ 340-693-2777) and **Chase Manhattan Bank** (☎ 340-775-7777) have automatic teller machines. On St. Croix, contact **Banco Popular** (☎ 340-693-2777) or **Chase Manhattan Bank** (☎ 340-775-7777) for information on branch and ATM locations. On St. John, **Chase Manhattan Bank** (☎ 340-775-7777) has the island's only ATM machine.

Banks

Bank hours are generally Monday through Thursday from 9 a.m. to 3 p.m. and Friday 9 a.m. to 5 p.m. A handful have Saturday hours (9 a.m. to noon). Walk-up windows open at 8:30 a.m. on weekdays.

Credit Cards

Credit cards are widely accepted in the USVIs. VISA and MasterCard are the cards of choice at most local businesses, although American Express and, to a lesser extent, Diners Club are also popular.

Currency Exchange

The U.S. dollar is used throughout the territory, as well as in the neighboring BVIs. All major credit cards and traveler's checks are generally accepted.

Doctors

On St. Croix, a good local doctor is **Dr. Frank Bishop,** Sunny Isle Medical Center (☎ 340-778-0069). On St. Thomas, **Doctors-on-Duty** (Vitraco Park; ☎ 340-776-7996) in Charlotte Amalie is a reliable medical facility. On St. John, contact **St. John Myrah Keating Smith Community Health Clinic** (28 Sussanaberg; ☎ 340-693-8900).

Emergencies

On all USVIs, call ☎ **911** for ambulance, fire, and police.

Hospitals

St. Thomas Hospital (☎ 340-776-8311) has a recompression chamber. On St. Croix, outside Christiansted there's the **Gov. Juan F. Luis Hospital and Health Center** (6 Diamond Ruby, north of Sunny Isle Shopping Center on Rte. 79; ☎ 340-778-6311). You can also try the **Frederiksted Health Center** (516 Strand St.; ☎ 340-772-1992). On St. John, visit the **Myrah Keating Smith Community Health Center** (Rte. 10, about 7 minutes east of Cruz Bay; ☎ 340-693-8900).

Information

Before you visit the island, contact the **USVI Division of Tourism** at #1 Tolbod Gade, St. Thomas, VI 00802 (☎ 800-372-USVI or 212-332-2222; Fax: 212-332-2223; Internet: www.usvi.net).

On St. Thomas, the **USVI Division of Tourism** has an office in Charlotte Amalie (Box 6400, Charlotte Amalie 00804; ☎ 800-372-8784 or 340-774-8784). You also find a visitors center in downtown Charlotte Amalie and a cruise ship welcome center at Havensight Mall. The National Park Service has a visitors center across the harbor from the ferry dock at Red Hook.

On St. Croix, the **USVI Division of Tourism** has offices at 53A Company Street in Christiansted (P.O. Box 4538, Christiansted 00822; ☎ 340-773-0495) and on the pier in Frederiksted (Strand St., Frederiksted 00840; ☎ 340-772-0357).

On St. John, there's a branch of the **USVI Department of Tourism** (P.O. Box 200, Cruz Bay 00830; ☎ 340-776-6450) in the compound between Sparky's and the U.S. Post Office in Cruz Bay. The **National Park Service** (P.O. Box 710, 00831; ☎ 340-776-6201) also has a visitors center at the Creek in Cruz Bay.

Language

English is the official language, though island residents often speak it with a lilting Creole accent, so you may not recognize certain words at first.

Maps

If you plan to do extensive touring of the island, purchase The Official Road Map of the U.S. Virgin Islands, available at island bookstores and free at the Christiansted office of the Department of Tourism.

St. Thomas This Week, distributed free by the visitors center and usually on cruise ships stopping on St. Thomas, contains a great two-page map with a clear, easy-to-follow street plan of Charlotte Amalie, plus the locations of important landmarks and all of Charlotte Amalie's leading shops.

The **St. John Tourist Office** (☎ 340-776-6450) is located near the Battery, a 1735 fort that is a short walk from where the ferry from St. Thomas docks. You find plenty of travel information here, including a free map of Cruz Bay and the entire island that pinpoints all the main attractions. Hours are Monday through Friday from 8 a.m. to noon and 1 to 5 p.m.

St. Croix This Week, which is distributed free to cruise ship passengers and air passengers, has detailed maps of Christiansted, Frederiksted, and the entire island, pinpointing individual attractions, hotels, shops, and restaurants.

Newspapers/Magazines

Copies of U.S. mainland newspapers, such as *The New York Times, USA Today*, and *The Miami Herald*, arrive daily in St. Thomas and are sold at hotels and newsstands. *St Thomas Daily News* covers local, national, and international events. Pick up *Virgin Islands Playground* and *St. Thomas This Week;* both are packed with visitor information and are distributed free all over the island.

Newspapers such as *The Miami Herald* are flown into St. Croix, which also has its own newspaper, *St. Croix Avis.* Your best source for local information is *St. Croix This Week,* which is distributed free by the tourist offices.

On St. John, copies of U.S. mainland newspapers arrive daily and are for sale at Mongoose Junction, Caneel Bay, and the Hyatt. The latest copies of *Time* and *Newsweek* are also for sale. Complimentary copies of *What to Do: St. Thomas/St. John* contain many helpful hints, although this publication is a commercial mouthpiece. It is the official guidebook of the St. Thomas and

St. John Hotel Association and is available at the tourist office and at various hotels.

Pharmacies

On St. Thomas, **Havensight Pharmacy** (☎ 340-776-1235) in the Havensight Mall is open daily from 9 a.m. to 9 p.m. **Kmart** (☎ 340-777-3854) operates a pharmacy inside the Tutu Park Mall; it's open from 8 a.m. to 9 p.m. **Sunrise Pharmacy** (☎ 340-775-6600), in Red Hook, is open daily from 9 a.m. to 7 p.m.

On St. Croix, although most drugstores are open daily from 8 a.m. to 8 p.m., off-season hours may vary; call ahead to confirm times. **Kmart** (☎ 340-692-2622) operates a pharmacy at its Sunshine Mall store. **People's Drug Store, Inc.,** has two branches: on the Christiansted Wharf (☎ 340-778-7355) and at the Sunny Isle Shopping Center (☎ 340-778-5537), just a few miles west of Christiansted on Route 70. In Frederiksted, try **D&D Apothecary Hall** (501 Queen St.; ☎ 340-772-1890).

On St. John, the **St. John Drug Center** (☎ 340-776-6353) is in the Boulon shopping center, up Centerline Road in Cruz Bay. It's open Monday through Saturday from 9 a.m. to 5 p.m.

Post Office

Hours may vary slightly from branch to branch and island to island, but they are generally 7:30 or 8 a.m. to 4 or 5:30 p.m. weekdays and 7:30 or 8 a.m. to noon or 2:30 p.m. Saturday.

The main U.S. Post Office on St. Thomas is near the hospital, with branches in Charlotte Amalie, Frenchtown, Havensight, and Tutu Mall. There's a post office at Christiansted, Frederiksted, Gallows Bay, and Sunny Isle on St. Croix, and one at Cruz Bay on St. John.

Safety

Vacationers tend to assume that normal precautions aren't necessary in paradise. They are. Though there isn't quite as much crime here as in large U.S. mainland cities, it does exist. To be safe, stick to well-lighted streets at night, and use the same kind of street sense that you would in any unfamiliar territory. (Don't wander the back alleys of Charlotte Amalie after five rum punches, for example.)

If you plan to carry things around, rent a car — not a Jeep — and lock possessions in the trunk. Keep your rental car locked wherever you park. Don't leave cameras, purses, and other valuables lying on the beach while you snorkel for an hour (or even for a minute), whether you're on the deserted beaches of St. John or the more crowded Magens and Coki beaches on St. Thomas. St. Croix has several remote beaches outside of Frederiksted and on the Fast End; it's best to visit them with a group rather than on your own.

Shops

In St. Thomas, stores on Main Street in Charlotte Amalie are open weekdays and Saturday from 9 a.m. to 5 p.m. Shop hours at Havensight Mall (next to the cruise ships dock) are the same, though some sometimes stay open until 9 p.m. on Friday, depending on how many cruise ships are at the dock. You may also find some shops open on Sunday if a lot of cruise ships are in port. Hotel shops are usually open evenings, as well.

St. Croix shop hours are usually Monday through Saturday 9 a.m. to 5 p.m., but you find some shops in Christiansted open in the evening. On St. John, store hours run from 9 or 10 a.m. to 5 or 6 p.m. Wharfside Village and Mongoose Junction shops in Cruz Bay are often open into the evening.

Telephone

The area code for all of the USVIs is 340, and you can dial direct to and from the mainland as well as to and from Australia, Canada, New Zealand, and the United Kingdom. Local calls from a public phone cost 25¢ for five minutes.

On St. John, the place to go for telephone or message needs is **Connections** (Cruz Bay; ☎ 340-776-6922; Coral Bay; ☎ 340-779-4994).

Time Zone

The USVIs are on Atlantic Time, which places the islands one hour ahead of Eastern Standard Time. However, during daylight saving time, the USVIs and the East Coast are on the same clock.

Tipping

Many hotels add a 10 to 15 percent service charge to cover the room maid and other staff. However, some hotels may use part of that money to fund their operations, passing on only a portion of it to the staff. Check with your maid or bellman to determine the hotel's policy. If you discover you need to tip, give bellmen and porters 50 cents to $1 per bag and maids $1 or $2 per day. Special errands or requests of hotel staff always require an additional tip. At restaurants, bartenders and waiters expect a 10 to 15 percent tip, but always check your tab to see whether or not service is included. Taxi - drivers get a 15 percent tip.

Water

There is ample water for showers and bathing in the Virgin Islands, but please conserve. Many visitors drink the local tap water with no harmful aftereffects. To be prudent, especially if you have a delicate stomach, stick with bottled water.

Weather and Surf Reports

All three islands receive both cable and commercial TV stations. Radio weather reports can be heard at 8:30 a.m. and 7:30 p.m. on 99.5 FM.

Part V
Mexico

"Oooo! Back up Robert. There must be a half dozen Lightening Whelks here."

In this part . . .

Salsa, sizzle, and gorgeous stretches of sand — not to mention some of the friendliest people in the world — all that and *mas, mas* more await if you decide to head for Mexico on your honeymoon. However, getting a handle on our neighbor south of the border is harder than making that initial decision to go there.

You've got enough on your (wedding) plate right now, so let us ease you through the differences between the various beach resorts. We tell you the best places to lay your heads in your chosen destination; the top ways to spend your days and nights when you get there; and, finally, the practicalities.

Chapter 22

Honeymooning in Mexico

By Echo & Kevin Garrett

● ●

In This Chapter

▶ Decidging which area is best for you

▶ Reviewing Mexico's top resort areas

● ●

Contemplating taking the plunge — or the post-plunge — in Mexico? Your best bet is one of the coastal resorts, where beautiful beaches, plenty of sun, and great seafood are a given. That said, not all south-of-the-border getaways are created equal. If you're trying to decide which to choose, these snapshots should help you focus on the Mexican resort that may best suit you.

Cancún

You won't have to worry about culture shock in this most gringo-ized of the resort towns, where many fast food franchises and upscale hotel chains say "Made in the U.S.A."

Don't expect many honeymoon bargains in Cancún (pronounced *kan-KOON*). Prices are comparable to — or higher than — those at home.

But there's a reason for the astounding success of Mexico's Numero Uno tourist destination: Superb white-sand beaches on an azure Caribbean sea, and fun, fun, fun. You'll emerge from your room to oceans of splashy pursuits, including all the latest water toys; miles of air-conditioned malls; sophisticated seaside restaurants; and wild all-night bars and discos, as well as plenty of places where you can dance cheek-to-cheek. Side trips to the ruins of the Yucatan peninsula complete this action-packed getaway picture. If you're up for endless diversion, rather than seeking the real Mexico, it doesn't get better than this.

Cozumel

Geographically speaking, Cozumel is close to Cancún but in nearly every other way, it's a universe apart. For one thing, you don't have to worry about blowing your post-nuptial budget here. Cozumel (pronounced *KOH-zoo-mel*) has plenty of kicked-back beachside lodgings, although digs for serious pampering are available, too. At mealtimes, your options span the spectrum from inexpensive mom-and-pop — make that *madre-y-padre* — places to more upscale, romantic marine-view dining rooms.

During the day, the dazzling Caribbean Sea is your playground, and you've got ringside seats at the best underwater show in Mexico. When you're ready to come up for air, you can explore the island's many solitary beaches on the southeast shore and the rugged west coast. But at night it's far quieter here than it is in Cancún — and in most of the other resort towns, for that matter. Cozumel is ideal for lovers of underwater action and those who don't mind doing a lot of gazing into each other's eyes after dark.

Acapulco

An oldie but a goodie. The southernmost of the Pacific Coast resorts, Acapulco (pronounced *ah-kah-PULL-koh*) has long been in the visitor-pleasing business, and it shows. Although Old Acapulco, or downtown, has lost the sheen of its glamorous Hollywood heyday, you can still see traditional holidays being celebrated at the main plaza and buy love potions at the municipal market.

Cancún may have almost as many discos, but in Acapulco, Mexico City escapees, rather than gringos, set a spicier Latin tone. Mexicans also like to party late, so no matter what time you retire your dancing shoes, you can find something to eat. Prefer more private evenings? Acapulco may have the largest number of romantic bay-view eateries in the country. Acapulco is better for night owls than for water birds, but with a nice choice of price ranges and lots of local atmosphere.

Ixtapa/Zihuatanejo

Double your pleasure, double your fun: Ixtapa/Zihuatanejo (pronounced *eeks-TAH-pah/zee-wah-teh-NAY-hoe*) has something for everyone. Although they're neighbors, these two Pacific Coast resort have distinct personalities. Zihuatanejo is the introvert. Great beaches and an excellent dive center keep many couples firmly rooted to this side of the hilly divide between the two towns.

Created, like Cancún, by the Mexican government in the 1970s — although not nearly as overgrown or glitzy as its Caribbean counterpart — Ixtapa is the outgoing new kid on the block, with designer golf courses, a modern marina, high-rise hotels, and fashionable restaurants laid out along creamy, wide Playa Palmar. Ixtapa has more nightlife here than there is in Zihua (which isn't saying much), but, for after-dark action, Ixtapa doesn't hold a candle (or strobe-light) to Acapulco or Cancun. A honeymoon here is not ideal for action junkies, but the diving's good, and oh, those starry, starry nights . . .

Puerto Vallarta

You've got the complete crowd-pleaser here, a resort that rolls up the greatest variety of Mexican experiences — and price ranges — into a single, sparkly package. Poised against a backdrop of lush jungle and the foothills of the Sierra Madre, the largest bay on Mexico's Pacific Coast draws everyone from hippies to international yachters, who like to dock at the tony Marina Vallarta complex.

Puerto Vallarta (pronounced *pwer-toh vah-YAHR-tuh*) has grown considerably over the years, but still has cobblestone streets and sure-footed donkeys to trot along them. You can dine at some of the best restaurants outside of Mexico City, and although nightlife may not be as wild as in places like Cancún or Acapulco, you won't have any problem finding a place to boogie. Pretty much all types of couples — active or kicked-back — enjoy Puerto Vallarta.

Los Cabos

Of the three very different destinations that Los Cabos (pronounced *lohs KAH-bohs,* which means literally, "The Capes") encompasses, the one most people are talking about when they say they're going to "Cabo" is the town of Cabo San Lucas, party central for Californians. But Cabo San Lucas has a much more sedate sibling, San Jose del Cabo, a sleepy Mexican town that pretty much shuts down after dark. The two are connected by the Corridor, a long stretch of highway lined — at discreet distances, naturally — with gorgeous resorts, magnificent golf courses (some of the best in Mexico), and sophisticated restaurants.

After Cancún, San Jose del Cabo is the costliest of the Mexican beach resorts, and the most Americanized. Why honeymoon here? Stunning desert-meets-the-sea scenery, including the Playa de Amor (Beach of Love — need we say more?). And of course, there's that gigantic beach bash at Cabo San Lucas, which starts at midday and rages until it's time for your huevos rancheros the next morning. It helps if you're extroverts, but money can buy you some great secluded getaways here.

Chapter 23

Mexico's Top Accommodations for Honeymooners

By Echo & Kevin Garrett

● ●

In This Chapter

▶ Figuring out where to stay

▶ Finding the best rates

● ●

*W*ant a once-in-a-lifetime blowout? An idyll that won't leave you biting your nails over the checkbook? A chance to work off every last pre-wedding jitter? Whatever you're looking for in a honeymoon, Mexico has got your number (times dos). Read on to find the south-of-the-border lodgings that best suit your notion of the perfect post-nuptials retreat.

When it comes to deciding where to spend your nights, Mexico spoils you with its choices. Bed and breakfasts haven't really caught on there, but otherwise you've got just about everything you may be looking for in lodgings: large, glitzy resorts, tony boutique hotels, non-stop all-inclusives, low-key places with lots of local color, and so on. The types represented in this chapter vary widely but have one thing in common: They were selected because of their honeymoon-enhancing potential.

Keeping Costs in Mind

Honeymoon promotions don't always get transmitted to U.S. reservation numbers. In some cases, you need to phone the hotel directly to get details. It's an expensive call — but it may save you lots of money in the long run.

Don't forget to ask about all kinds of packages — romance may not be in the computer under that name, but plenty of extended stay or advance booking discounts are available, as are deals that throw in meals, activities, or spa treatments. As far as prices go, we've noted

high season rack rates as well as, where available, honeymoon packages. This way, you can compare what kind of deal you get if you
decide to go for the latter — and, in the case of Mexico, you're usually
smart to do so.

Unless money is no object, don't even think about trying to piggyback
your honeymoon with the Christmas holiday. In Mexico rates sometimes skyrocket as much as 50 percent between December 22 and
January 3.

Choosing Among Mexico's Best Accommodations for Honeymooners

Please refer to the Introduction of *Honeymoon Vacations For Dummies*,
1st Edition, for an explanation of our price categories.

Cancún

Blue Bay Village
$$$ East/West Hotel Zone

At this all-grownup all-inclusive — no kids under 16 allowed — you get a
two-fer. You can eat and drink your way through this tropical garden
resort, where rooms are arranged in the main building or a series of red-
tile-roofed low-rises, and then cross the bay to Blue Bay Club and Marina
Resort and start all over again; the resort has six bars and seven restau-
rants in all, Chinese and Italian included. Choose from an activities menu
of windsurfing, kayaking, snorkeling, tennis, and poolside scuba lessons.
When it's time for a siesta, settle down in your colorful room, which some-
how manages to make orange, red, green, blue, and salmon look harmo-
nious (but request a room with an oceanview room or you'll be staring at
a wall). The "Crazy Bunch," as the staff call themselves, strut and sing on
stage nightly. If you don't like the act, you can always duck out to one of
the nearby bars; you'll be staying in one of the liveliest sections of Cancún.

Paseo Kukulkán, km 3.5. ☎ *800-BLUE-BAY or 98-83-0344. Fax: 98-83-0904. E-mail:*
Cancun@bluebayresorts.com. *Internet:* www.bluebayresorts.com.
Rack rates: $290 (garden view) to $310 (ocean view) per room, including all meals,
drinks, and activities (prove that you married within the last two months, and you
get upgraded to an oceanview room and free flowers). AE, MC, V.

Caesar Park Beach & Golf Resort
$$$$$ North/South Hotel Zone

Occupying 250 lush beachside acres, this busy place is Cancún's
largest hotel — and has the activities to match. You can ramble along a

Isla Cancún (Zona Hotelera)

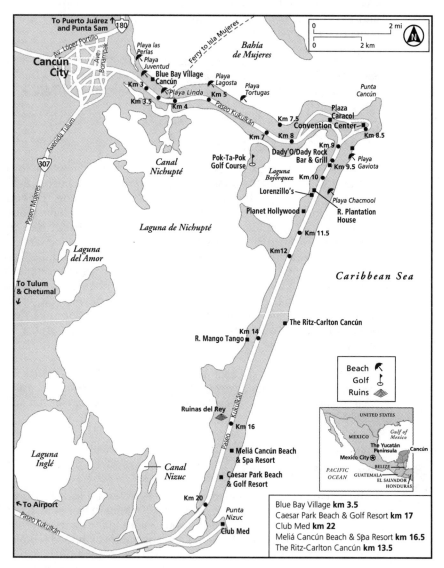

700-yard-long beach, plunge into any one of seven cascading swimming pools or two hot tubs, play 18 holes of golf or a few rounds of tennis (at night, if you like, too), indulge in myriad watersports at one of the best concessions around, or get pampered in the fitness center. Of the three restaurants that can provide the juice for all this, the best is Spices, which mixes Mexican, Argentinean, and Italian cuisine under one roof. Standard rooms in the main building, done in earth tones with contemporary wicker and hardwood furniture, are decent sized, but the Royal Beach Club rooms, in separate low-rise villas, are larger and include extra amenities like in-room coffee makers, free Continental breakfast, and cocktail hour. Although it's Westin managed, this sprawling resort was built with Japanese yen; you may encounter many Japanese lovebirds who've crossed several continents to have a mariachi wedding here.

Paseo Kukulkán, km 17, Retorno Lacandones. ☎ ***800-228-3000*** *or 98-81-8000. Fax: 98-81-8082. Rack rates: $300 standard double; $380-$430 Royal Beach Club double. Contact the hotel directly regarding honeymoon packages. AE, DC, MC, V.*

Club Med
$$ North/South Hotel Zone

Mexico's first all-inclusive resort, Club Med is none the worse for wear, and still offers you the most for your hard-earned pesos. Set on a secluded peninsula at the far southern tip of the hotel zone, this country-clubbish, adults-only property is far from the malls. You have more than enough to keep you busy here, however: volleyball, basketball, tennis, waterskiing, windsurfing, kayaking, snorkeling, and sailing, and, if you pay extra, scuba diving, deep-sea fishing, and horseback riding. Or check out one of the newest residents, Elvis, an alligator who likes snoozing in the lagoon. Activities — well away from Elvis — are very spread out, so that even when the resort is booked solid, it never feels crowded. Average-sized guest rooms, which look onto the lagoon, gardens, or ocean, are in two- and three-story buildings; ask for one on the lowest floor if you don't like stairs.

Paseo Kukulkán, km 22 at Punta Nizac. ☎ ***800-258-2633*** *or 98-818200. Fax: 98-818280. Rack rates: $143 per person, per night standard double (including all meals, wine or beer at meals, and most activities). AE, MC, V. No children under 18 accepted.*

Meliá Cancún Beach & Spa Resort
$$$$ North/South Hotel Zone

Hotel in a jungle? No, jungle in a hotel — or at least it feels terribly tropical in the Meliá's atrium lobby, with its 8,500 square feet of lush gardens and streams (an understandably popular setting for Cancun weddings). The waterfalls cascading down the entrance of this stepped temple-style property — with 700 rooms — topped with glass pyramids, also add to the feeling you're in Mayan territory. You can sacrifice yourself to a snake-shaped pool (the second-largest in Cancún), laze on a sundeck, hit a few tennis balls around, or play the executive golf course; five restaurants (including two for fine dining and one with light spa cuisine) can keep you well fortified. At Cancún's only spa with European-type services, you can get pampered from head-to-toe in a private cubicle lit with candles.

The Meliá Cancun can arrange a "wedding by the sea" for $900 that includes the judge's fee, wedding certificate, administration fees, wedding cake for eight guests, one boutonniere, a bottle of sparkling wine, decorations and set-up, and the bride's floral bouquet. For more information, contact the food and beverage assistant or the public relations manager (☎ **011-52-98-81-11-00,** ext. 6032; Fax: 011-52-98-81-11-80).

Ask about the honeymoon packages.

Paseo Kukulkán, km 16.5. ☎ ***800-33-MELIA*** *or 98-85-1160. Fax: 98-85-1263. Internet:* www.solmelia.com. *Rack rates: $290 standard lagoon view to $320 ocean view. AE, DC, MC, V.*

The Ritz-Carlton Cancún
$$$$$ **North/South Hotel Zone**

No need to pack that tiara and tuxedo for putting on the ritz — not when it's the Ritz-Carlton Cancún. Sure, the chandeliered lobby with its polished marble floors seems more suited to presidential inauguration ball attire than to flip flops and beach coverups. That's okay. You can enjoy all the advantages of this primo Cancun property — rooms with plush wall-to-wall carpeting, fresh flowers, thick terry robes, and private balconies overlooking the sparkling, 1,200-foot-long beach; an on-call masseuse; 24-hour room service; a Cigar Lounge with every kind of serious smoke you can imagine, including Cubans; a "tequilier" who has more than 120 types to taste-test — without ever having to say you're sorry for having sand between your toes. Book a beachside massage for two or don some fancy duds to take a turn at the hotel's Club Grill, where intimate dining nooks encourage dancing cheek-to-cheek (the food's terrific, too).

Retorno del Rey, off Paseo Kulkukán, km 13.5. ☎ ***800-241-3333*** *or 98-85-0808. Fax: 98-85-1015. Rack rates: $348 standard oceanview room to $459 executive ocean-front suite. Honeymoon package: four days and three nights, including dinner for two in the Club Grill, two 30-minute aromatherapy messages on the beach, and private airport transfers; from $1,677 for a deluxe oceanview room to $2,055 for an executive oceanfront suite. AE, DC, MC, V.*

Cozumel

Fiesta Americana Dive Resort
$$$ **Southern Hotel Zone**

Your room won't sit right on the beach if you bunk at this far southern hotel — the smallish stretch of shore is just across the highway, reachable by pedestrian bridge — but you get a good deal, and you are near some of the best reefs in Cozumel. You can book a cheery, tropical-decor room in the main building, fronted by a pool with a swim up bar, or (more romantic) one of the 14 *casitas* suites. Built in 1997 behind the hotel, these latter are arranged in two-story thatched buildings landscaped to look like they're in the middle of a jungle; all are extra spacious, with casual-elegant blond-wood furniture and balconies. Playing Jacques Cousteau is the main draw — this place has a super dive center — but when you're ready to come up for air, you can hit a few balls around the

Cozumel

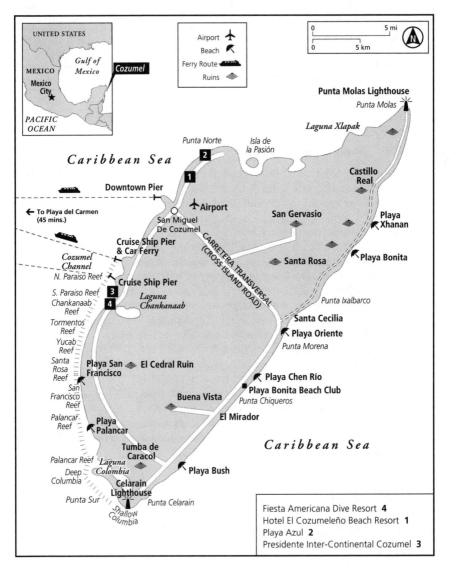

UNITED STATES

Gulf of Mexico

Cozumel

MEXICO

Mexico City

PACIFIC OCEAN

Airport ✈
Beach 🏄
Ferry Route ⛴
Ruins ◈

0   5 mi
0   5 km

Punta Molas Lighthouse
Punta Molas

Laguna Xlapak

Punta Norte

Isla de la Pasión

Caribbean Sea

2

1

Castillo Real

Downtown Pier

← To Playa del Carmen (45 mins.)

Airport

San Miguel De Cozumel

San Gervasio

Playa Xhanan

Cruise Ship Pier & Car Ferry

CARRETERA TRANSVERSAL (CROSS ISLAND ROAD)

Cozumel Channel

Santa Rosa

Playa Bonita

N. Paraíso Reef

Cruise Ship Pier

3

Laguna Chankanaab

Punta Ixalbarco

S. Paraíso Reef

Chankanaab Reef

4

Santa Cecilia

Tormentos Reef

Playa Oriente

Yucab Reef

Punta Morena

Santa Rosa Reef

Playa San Francisco

El Cedral Ruin

Playa Chen Río

San Francisco Reef

Playa Bonita Beach Club

Buena Vista

Punta Chiqueros

Palancar Reef

El Mirador

Playa Palancar

Caribbean Sea

Tumba de Caracol

Palancar Reef

Laguna Colombia

Playa Bush

Deep Columbia

Celarain Lighthouse

Punta Sur

Punta Celarain

Shallow Columbia

Fiesta Americana Dive Resort **4**
Hotel El Cozumeleño Beach Resort **1**
Playa Azul **2**
Presidente Inter-Continental Cozumel **3**

tennis court, sweat it out at the health club, or chow down at one of the three restaurants, ranging from casual to sophisticated. They offer three and seven-night packages, including an oceanview room, daily buffet breakfast, dinner at the Miramar Restaurant on the beach, a fruit basket, and one bottle of domestic wine.

Carretera Chankanaab, km 7.5. ☎ *800-FIESTA-1 in the U.S., or 987-2-2622. Fax: 987-2-2666. Internet:* www.fiestamexico.com. *Rack rates: $151 standard double; $177 casitas; from January 2 to the 26th, the three-night rate is $650 per* *room, and from January 27 through December 21, the three-night package is $582 per room. The seven-night package is $708 per room and is valid until April 14. Taxes and service charges are included. AE, MC, V.*

Hotel El Cozumeleño Beach Resort

$$$$ Northern Hotel Zone

If you want your honeymoon tied up in a tidy package — and don't want to pay a bundle for that bundle — you may like this moderately priced all-inclusive, situated on one of the prettiest beaches in Cozumel and only 5 minutes by cab from the island's only town, San Miguel. Guest rooms, which all face the Caribbean, are extra roomy and nicely furnished in contemporary style (but you need to book a deluxe one if you want a king-size rather than two double beds). During the day, you can snorkel, sunbathe, or relax under a shady *palapa,* soak in a hot tub, or swim in the free-form pool (the seashore is a bit rocky), play tennis, or hit some balls around the 19-hole miniature golf course, gratis — windsurfing or diving cost extra. Come sunset, the social scene moves inside to the marble lobby, which has cozy pockets of chairs and couches. A spirited live show of some sort or another kicks off shortly after dinner. Not enough to keep you going? You can rent a car or moped or book a tour from the lobby.

Carretera Santa Pilar, km 4.5. ☎ 800-437-3923 or 987-2-0050. Fax: 987-2-0381. Rack rates: $114 per person, deluxe room (includes three meals, domestic drinks, room service, taxes and tips, all non-motorized water sports). Honeymoon packages: Three night packages begin at $768 per couple and include deluxe accommodations, bottle of domestic champagne, two T-shirts, roses in room, and one 12-photo album. AE, MC, V.

Playa Azul

$$-$$$ Northern Hotel Zone

This small (40 unit) hotel isn't fancy, but it's got every tropical amenity you'd want: a white sandy beach replete with *palapa* bar, watersports instructors, a seaview pool with cushioned lounge chairs, and a private dock for dive boats. When you're ready to take a break from old Sol, play a round of pool in the lounge, hit some paddleballs around, watch a video, or cut loose altogether by renting a scooter or car at the front desk. The tile-floor rooms are simple but extra-clean and spacious, with large baths (shower only, though); most have balconies or terraces. Book a room with an ocean view and king-size bed; they come with comfy sitting areas. Enjoy balmy breezes on the patio of the main Mexican/seafood restaurant or — from 7 a.m. to 11 a.m. — order room service. The management is very friendly, and the service is personalized. Honeymooners get particularly royal treatment, with three new suites with hot tubs and a variety of wedding packages and offers designed for them. In addition to its wedding packages, Playa Azul offers a boat ride and picnic at the deserted beach of Isla de la Pasión (The Isle of Passion) for $120, including picnic basket, bottle of wine, tax, and tips.

Km 4 Carretera a San Juan. ☎ **987-2-0199** *or 987-2-0043. Fax: 987-2-0110. E-mail:* playazul@cozumel.cxm.com.mx. *Internet:* www.playa-azul.com. *Rack rates: Rooms $150, oceanfront suites $200; Honeymoon Package: $659 for seven nights in oceanfront suite, daily full breakfast, tropical fruit basket and domestic wine upon arrival, one candlelight lobster dinner with domestic Chardonnay on your balcony, all taxes and tips. MC, V.*

Presidente Inter-Continental Cozumel

$$$$ Southern Hotel Zone

One of the largest (253 rooms on 100 acres) and most elegant resort complexes on the island, the Presidente is great for active couples, though you can mingle with families and groups, too. Veterans as well as novice scuba divers like to stay here for the professional diving classes, scuba excursions, and fine snorkeling (possibly the best on the island directly from a hotel), but you've got tennis, sailing, and windsurfing to keep your adrenalin up, too. The crescent-shaped beach is one of the most beautiful in Cozumel — and the large pool with a hot tub isn't too shabby, either. You can rent a motor bike when you're ready to hit the road (though there's not all that much reason to). Restaurants include the elegant Arrecife, where you can dine on Mediterranean fare to a soft music backdrop, and the more casual poolside El Caribeño; the food at both is supervised by the one-time executive chef at New York's famed Russian Tea Room. All the rooms are attractive, with vivid Mexican textiles, marble floors, and white cedar furniture, but the deluxe oceanview or beachfront units are far superior to the others.

Carretera a Chankanaab, km 6.5. ☎ **800-327-0200** *or 987-2-0322. Fax: 987-2-1360. E-mail:* cozumel@interconti.com. *Internet:* www.interconti.com. *Rack rates: $260 standard double; $350-$385 deluxe. Honeymoon package: Deluxe king or beachfront room, bottle of champagne, daily breakfasts for two, floral arrangements, candlelight dinner, all tips. $598 for two nights, $1,510 for six nights. AE, DC, MC, V.*

Acapulco

Acapulco Princess

$$$$ Acapulco Diamante

Maybe it's pyramid power, emanating from the stunning triangular guest tower at the center of this resort; otherwise, it's hard to explain how this sprawling 480-acre property — arguably the biggest in Mexico — manages to feel at once friendly and intimate. If golf is your game, you can play 36 holes on the superb courses of the Princess and its sister property, Pierre Marques. Besides the five freeform pools, there are 11 tennis courts and a fitness center. When you're tired, you can sun yourselves on a beautiful, wide beach (the water's a bit too rough for swimming). You are far from the Costera action if you stay here, but seven high-quality restaurants (including the Hacienda for fine dining), an onsite disco, and a slew of tony

Acapulco Bay Area

Beach 🏖	Acapulco Princess **5**
Bus Station 🚏	Copacabana **3**
Golf ⛳	Elcano Hotel **2**
	Hyatt Regency Acapulco **4**
	Qualton Club **1**
	Westin Las Brisas **5**

boutiques should keep you more than satisfied. The standard rooms are casually elegant; if the sight of a golf course, gorgeous as the Princess's is, doesn't thrill you, go for a deluxe oceanview room or one of the corner Pacific Premier rooms (these give you a full-on water view and extra space).

El Revolcadero Beach, just west of the airport, Box 1351. ☎ *800-441-1414 or 74-69-1000. Fax: 74-69-1016. Internet:* www.cphotels.ca. *Rack rates: $225 double, $250 deluxe ocean view, $325 PacificPremier. AE, DC, DISC, MC, V.*

Copacabana

$$ The Costera

Although the rates are very low, you won't stint on style or comfort here. This slightly off-the-main-drag hotel has surprisingly attractive rooms, done in vibrant colors with rattan furniture; all have small balconies with ocean views. The public areas are a restful, sea-foam green; even the building, with its dramatically curving wings, has more style than your typical high-rise. The hotel's beach is fairly small and crowded, but the pool is large and has a swim-up bar as well as an adjacent taco stand. Other features include a 24-hour doctor (hope you won't need one, but it's always nice to know), a copious breakfast buffet, and two balcony-level hot tubs. All-inclusive packages are available through wholesalers such as Apple Vacations.

Tabachines 2, a block (toward the beach) from the Costera, across from the Convention Center. ☎ *800-562-0197 or 74-84-3260 and 84-3155 in Mexico. Fax: 74-84-6268. E-mail:* copacabana@infosel.net.mx. *Rack rates: $78 double. AE, MC, V.*

Elcano Hotel

$$ The Costera

Couples with a strong sense of style and nostalgia adore the 1950s-era (but completely refurbished) Elcano, in the thick of the Costera action, but with the feel of a Mediterranean retreat. Classical music wafts through the lobby (at night it comes live from the lobby bar), and the rooms have uncluttered art deco lines. Under ordinary circumstances you'd probably be satisfied with even the smallest rooms (called studio suites), but for this occasion it's worth shelling out a bit extra for a gleaming wooden deck, overlooking the hotel's good beach and huge pool; the latter has four hot tubs and piped-in underwater music. The beachside Bambuco restaurant is a perpetual favorite. In high season, it's complemented by the more formal Victoria, attached to an intimate bar where you can be serenaded by romantic guitar music.

On Elcano Beach, Costera Miguel Alemán 75, just west of the Convention Center. ☎ *74-84-1950. Fax: 74-84-2230. E-mail:* ika@delta.acabtu.com.mx. *Internet:* acapulco-travel.web.com.mx/hotels/elcano. *Rack rates: $130 studio, $140 junior suite, $310 honeymoon suite. Honeymoon package: $443 includes two* *nights in the honeymoon suite, one dinner in your room with national wine, flowers, tax, and tips included ($123 each night extra); in effect except holiday weekends and Christmas and Easter weeks. AE, DC, MC V.*

Hyatt Regency Acapulco
$$$ The Costera

A longtime Costera landmark — it marks the beginning of Acapulco's main hotel strip at its eastern end — the high-rise Hyatt has become competitive with pricier Acapulco Diamante properties since it completed a multimillion-dollar face-lift in 1997. A gleaming marble lobby hosts a dimly lit piano lounge where you can swirl to live marimba music at night and where, during the day, an arcade of tony boutiques wears a come-hither-with-your-plastic look. The attractive accommodations are done in rich turquoise and terra-cotta; suites offer two separate rooms, not just a little sitting area. Some of the seafood dishes at the atmospheric beachside El Pescador restaurant have an Asian influence; the indoor Zapata, Villa y Compania restaurant features the largest selection of tequila (114 kinds) in Acapulco — and a live burro. Also unique is the Glatt kosher restaurant that opens near the pool during high season.

Costera Miguel Alemán 1. ☎ 800-233-1234 or 74-69-1234. Fax: 74-84-3087. Internet: www.hyatt.com. *Rack rates: $185 double (ocean view). DC, DISC, MC, V.*

The Qualton Club
$$ The Costera

The assorted couples, families, and groups of friends who frequent this all-inclusive resort on Acapulco's main drag have two common goals: Eat and drink as much as possible and take advantage of every activity (including non-motorized water sports, beach volleyball, poolside scuba lessons, aerobics, nightly shows, and an on-premises disco). As a result, you won't find much tranquillity except maybe in La Cava Restaurant, the Qualton Club's fine dining spot (reservations required), and in your room. All the bedrooms are blandly attractive, but those in the taller tower are larger and have tubs as well as showers. If you snag a corner room with a wraparound balcony, you've hit the jackpot (a few units in the smaller tower have no balconies at all). Should you somehow manage to get bored here, the Gran Plaza shopping mall is right across the Costera.

Costera Miguel Alemán no. 159, just east of Papagayo Park. ☎ 74-86-8210. Fax: 74-86-8324. E-mail qualton@acanet.com.mx. *Internet:* www.qualton.com. *Rack rates: $77 per person double (includes all meals and activities). AE, MC, V.*

Westin Las Brisas
$$$$ Acapulco Diamante

Welcome to honeymoon central — jokingly called "the baby factory" by employees — a super-romantic retreat perched on a hibiscus-and-bougainvillea-bedecked hillside in Acapulco's posh Las Brisas neighborhood. Accommodations are all in separate bay-view *casitas* (little houses), many of which have their own private pools (but no TVs). No need to leave your room until noon: A continental breakfast, including a decanter of hot coffee, is delivered to your door every morning. Because the property is so spread out — 110 acres, total — you need to phone for a Jeep to take you to the front lobby; to the property's restaurants (which include Bella Vista, a fine dining room with a superb view); and to the La Concha Beach Club, about 10 minutes away. The Beach Club doesn't actually have a beach, but makes up for it with a freshwater pool and two fantastic saltwater pools, one deep enough for diving practice. If you're allergic to pink, Las Brisas is not for you: Everything bears that color (there's even a Pink Shop on the property). The place is showing its age a bit — it was 40 years old in 1997 — but service is as top-notch as ever.

Carretera Escénica s/n, Las Brisas, Box 281. ☎ 800-223-6800 or 74-84-1580. Fax: 74-84-2269. E-mail: lasbrisas@infosel.net.mx. *Rack rates: $240 shared pool casita to $360 private pool casita (low season), $315-$415 (high season). Romantically Las Brisas Packages: $1,259 three nights, four days to $2,439 seven nights, eight days, low season; includes private pool casita, bottle of domestic champage, one dinner for two at the Bellavista restaurant with wine, complimentary tennis, Jeep with gas, unlimited mileage, and complimentary water sports. $20 daily service charge covers all tips. AE, DC, MC, V.*

Ixtapa/Zihuatanejo

Krystal Ixtapa
$$$ Ixtapa

You'd have to work really hard to get bored at the Krystal. This link in the Mexican-owned chain (the seven classical columns found in each hotel represent the members of the de la Parra family) is huge, with plenty of room for racquetball and tennis courts, a pool with a waterfall and water slide, and more. The hotel's top two restaurants are Il Mortero, serving gourmet Mexican food, and the super-romantic Bogart's. Christine, the best disco in town — okay, pretty much the only one — is on the property. Don't dance? Catch a film in the open-air movie theater or listen to live Latin music in the lobby. Rooms — you remember those? — are pleasant and light; they're arranged around a central atrium in a high-rise that was recently renovated, so everything is fresh and sparkly.

Blvd. Ixtapa s/n. ☎ 800-231-9860 or 755-3-0333. Fax: 755-3-0216. E-mail: kixtapa@krystal.com.mx. *Internet:* www.wotw.com/krystal. *Rack rates: $190 deluxe room. AE, DC, MC, V.*

La Casa Que Canta
$$$$$ Zihuatanejo/Beaches

The "The House that Sings" may be playing your song. This little colony of thatched-roof villas looks as though it grew, organically, from its cliffside aerie. The Mexican design is pseudo-rustic — thatched roofs, quaint cobblestone paths, brightly colored tiles, vibrant folk art furnishings — but it all comes together to create a totally elegant picture. With only 24 suites and no children under 16 allowed, La Casa Que Canta is a wonderfully exclusive and serene getaway, and details like the flower petals strewn on the bed multiply the romance factor. You won't be directly on the beach — the superb Playa la Ropa is a short walk from here — but two gorgeous pools more than compensate (make that three if you book the suite with its own pool). And wherever you are — lazing on your private terrace, dining at the excellent restaurant or tapas bar — you have picture-postcard views of Zihuatanejo Bay.

Camino Escenico, Playa la Ropa s/n. ☎ *800-525-4800 or 755-4-7030. Fax: 755-4-7040. Rack rates: $315 terrace room, $355 suite, $525 master private pool suit (in summer, suites $275, master pool private suite $400). AE, DC, MC, V.*

Presidente Inter-Continental Ixtapa
$$$ Ixtapa

The only all-inclusive hotel in Ixtapa's hotel zone, the Presidente has it all: bicycle tours, tennis, golf, dancing lessons, diving clinics, snorkeling, language and cooking classes — even the greens fees for the Marina Ixtapa Golf Club are part of the deal. With its legion of restaurants and menus, including 24-hour room service, unlimited name-brand drinks (ordinarily you get only the domestic stuff), and nightly entertainment (everything from comedy shows to casino night to karaoke), it's hard to figure how this appealing, reasonably priced place breaks even. Rooms in the high-rise building, which cost only slightly more, are farther away from the sound of day- and nighttime activities than those arrayed, pueblo-style, around the gardens. Feeling guilty about your self-indulgence? The hotel even runs a program to save and release baby sea turtles.

Blvd. Ixtapa s/n. ☎ ***800-327-0200** or 755-3-0018. Fax: 755-3-2312. Rack rates: $250 standard room, $300 deluxe room (rate covers all meals and drinks, including imports, and activities for two people). Sunny Moon packages: $485 for two nights, $1,285 for six nights, includes deluxe room, all activities, plus champagne and flowers in the room and a honeymoon gift. AE, MC, V.*

Villa del Sol
$$$$$ Zihuatanejo/Beaches

At this intimate beachside hotel you find dozens of different ways to kick back, including lounging in a hammock or hot tub on the deck of your folk art-filled guest suite, getting a margarita delivered to your poolside lounge chair, hitting a few tennis balls around, or enjoying a magnificent buffet in the *palapa* restaurant. You can also amble directly from your room to one of the finest beaches in Zihuatanejo, with calm waters and lots of sports concessionaires. Well-heeled couples, many from Europe,

Ixtapa & Zihuatanejo Area

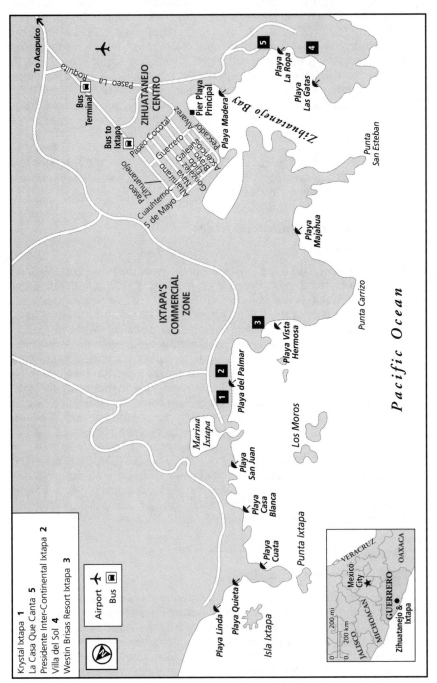

gather at this posh property, the only member in Mexico of both the Relais & Chateaux and Small Luxury Hotels of the World; as you can imagine, service and attention to detail is superb. Amenities increase with the room rates, from just phones in the standard minisuites to private plunge pools, minibars, TVs, stereo CD players, and fax machines in the new oceanside suites. No matter where you stay, you get a tray with croissants and coffee outside your door each morning. The bartender, Orlando, for whom the hotel's friendly watering hole is named, gets your drink order down by your third bar visit.

Camino Escenico, Playa la Ropa s/n. ☎ **888-389-2645,** *755-4-2239, or 755-4-3239. Fax: 755-4-2758 or 755-4-4066. E-mail:* villasol@iwm.com.mx. *Rack rates: $375 standard mini-suite to $800 beach suite with ocean view. Mandatory MAP (breakfast and dinner plan) included in the rates. Low season $220 to $500, meal plan optional. No children under 14 in winter. AE, MC, V.*

Westin Brisas Resort Ixtapa
$$$$-$$$$$ Ixtapa

Created by one of Mexico's leading architects, the Westin Brisas Ixtapa is a dazzler. The only major hotel in Ixtapa that's not on the main drag, the dramatic terra-cotta building terraces down the side of a jungly cliff to the secluded Vista Hermosa beach below, sheltered from the elements by craggy rocks. Each level of the flower-decked resort reveals another pleasure center — say, one of the four swimming pools, connected to each other by waterfalls, or the night-lit tennis courts. The beach boasts one of the best watersports concessions anywhere — and because this place is so out-of-the-way, you don't have to worry about braving the crowds. The standard rooms are stylish, if a bit small, but you can always hang out in a hammock on your huge and oh-so-private bay-view terrace, or book a junior or fiesta suite (the former has a hot tub, the latter its own pool on the balcony). Start your day with a lavish breakfast buffet at the Bellavista restaurant — the tortilla-and-cheese casserole is incredible — and end it with an ultra-romantic Italian dinner at Portofino.

Playa Vista Hermosa. ☎ **800-WESTIN-1** *or 755-3-2121. Fax: 755-3-0751 or 755-3-1038. Internet:* www.westin.com. *Rack rates: $200 standard double, $224 Royal Beach Club, $360 junior suite, $460 fiesta suite. Call the hotel directly regarding honeymoon packages. AE, MC, V.*

Puerto Vallarta

Camino Real
$$$$ South of Town

The finest in Mexican design makes a stay at the Camino Real memorable, from the whitewashed stucco walls of the main building and extra-large matromonial hammocks on your room's terrace, to the blue-glass chandelier of the beachside buffet restaurant and the domed ceiling of La Perla, the hotel's excellent fine-dining room (try the margarita scallops with mild poblano chiles if they're on the menu). This early Puerto Vallarta hotel pioneer snagged one of the best secluded beaches in town, a long white stretch of sand with a dramatic mountain backdrop and (usually) calm, swimmable waters. The shopping arcade has a good art gallery, and if you're both aesthetes and athletes, you can enjoy looking at the mural by Puerto Vallarta's famed naif painter, Manuel Lepe, while sweating it out at the health club (true, the art is better than the equipment). Surrounded by lush jungle foliage, the 250-room property offers spacious guestrooms and suites, all with spectacular ocean views. Go for the Camino Real Club rooms in the newer of the two towers — they're larger, with balconies and extra amenities. Deluxe Club Rooms gild the lily with a hot tub, and two duplex suites with private plunge pools.

Playa Las Estacas s/n, at km 3.2 of Hwy. 200. ☎ *800-722-6466 or 322-1-5000. Fax: 322-1-6000. E-mail:* pvr@caminoreal.com. *Internet:* www.caminoreal. com/puertovallarta/ *or* www.pvr-caminoreal.com *for reservations. Rack rates: $294 standard deluxe double ($140 low season); Club Room $384 ($200); Club Room with hot tub $432 ($220). Ask about the honeymoon packages. AE, DC, MC, V.*

Hotel Playa Conchas Chinas
$$ South of Town

Many artistic types enjoy the seclusion, Old Mexico charm, and reasonable rates of Playa Conchas Chinas, which clings to the rocks above the beach for which it's named. A rabbit warren of halls and stairways leads to rooms quaintly decorated with Talavera tiles and leaded glass lamps (but with newly redone kitchens). Each has a balcony overlooking the beach below, a small and not overly smooth stretch of sand, but wonderfully secluded. If you go for the deluxe studio, you get your own hot tub on the terrace. You can relax around the pool, kick back a few at the restaurant/bar at the water's edge, or join the crowd at the nearby El Set restaurant, a terrific (and popular) place to watch the sunset. It's a beautiful, if longish, stroll north along the beach into town. Now if only you didn't have to climb all those stairs to your room when you returned . . .

Mismaloya Hwy. 200, km 2.5. ☎ *and fax: 322-1-5770 or 322-1-5230 or 322-1-5763. E-mail:* hconchas@pvnet.com.mx. *Rack rates: $86 standard double; $92 deluxe studio. MC, V.*

Krystal Vallarta
$$$ Hotel Zone

This hotel has it all: A great beach with wonderful watersports, top-notch tennis and racket ball, a hopping pool scene — and even a bull-ring for (bloodless) fights. Plus, it's got personality to spare. It's built to resemble

Puerto Vallarta

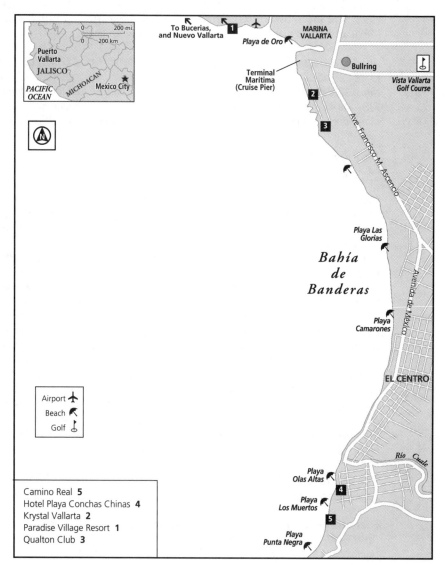

0   200 mi.
0   200 km

Puerto Vallarta
JALISCO
PACIFIC OCEAN
MICHOACAN
Mexico City

To Bucerias, and Nuevo Vallarta
Playa de Oro
MARINA VALLARTA
Terminal Marítima (Cruise Pier)
Bullring
Vista Vallarta Golf Course
Ave. Francisco M. Ascencio
Playa Las Glorias
Bahía de Banderas
Avenida de México
Playa Camarones
EL CENTRO
Río Cuale
Playa Olas Altas
Playa Los Muertos
Playa Punta Negra

Airport ✈
Beach ☂
Golf ⛳

Camino Real **5**
Hotel Playa Conchas Chinas **4**
Krystal Vallarta **2**
Paradise Village Resort **1**
Qualton Club **3**

a Mexican village, with a series of low-slung Spanish-style buildings and individual villas connected by little streets, surrounded by lush vegetation, and dotted with waterfalls, bridges, and fountains. The grounds are huge. If — say, after a night at Christine, the hotel's superhot disco — you don't feel like walking back to your room, carts are provided to scoot you around. All the units are different, but you can depend on lovely Old World details, such as brick walls, beamed ceilings, or a rough-hewn Spanish Colonial-style armoire (which hides a cable TV, of course). The world-class restaurants include Kamakura, featuring exquisitely presented Japanese food; Tango, an Argentinian steakhouse; and the ultra-romantic Bogart's. Need still more fireworks? On Tuesdays and Saturdays in high season, Mexican fiestas end with a dazzling light show.

Av. de la Garza s/n. ☎ *800-231-9860 or 322-4-0202. Fax: 322-4-0222. E-mail:* krystalmex@iserve.net.mx. *Internet:* www.wotw.com/krystal. *Rack rates: $220 standard deluxe; $240 one-bedroom villa with shared terrace and pool; $290 one-bedroom villa with private pool, terrace, and dining room. Rates include buffet breakfast for two. Ask about the honeymoon packages. AE, DC, MC, V.*

Paradise Village Resort
$$$ Nuevo Vallarta

Nuevo Vallarta, a marina, golf, and condo complex carved out of a mangrove swamp some 3½ miles north of Puerto Vallarta, has miles of superb, quiet beaches — and resorts like Paradise Village to keep you occupied when you tire of wiggling your toes in the sand. Shades of Indiana Jones: You can climb a Mayan temple and exit through a crocodile's jaws into a huge lagoon swimming pool. And hold on to your sunglasses — the frisky spider monkeys like to grab them (they're in a small zoo next to the tennis courts). Whether it's deep-sea fishing, horseback riding on the beach, or hopping aboard a banana boat, you're bound for adventure here. And when you're ready to return to civilization, hydromassages, herbal wraps, and loofa salt scrubs can help you face another day in the jungle. Plenty of eateries help you keep your strength up, and there's a grocery store on the premises. True, most of the activities cost extra, but you'd pay for them anywhere else, and here the price of your suite (the only type of accommodation here) won't break the bank to begin with, and you can save by buying food to keep in your room. All the units have balconies and kitchens, and some have hot tubs. The decor is Miami Beach pastel, with a Latin dash.

The Paradise Village Resort is a time-share property. Avoid the "friendly" reps who want to have breakfast or lunch with you or give you a free tour.

Paseo de los Cocoteros 1, Nuevo Vallarta, Nayarit C.P. 63730. ☎ *800-995-5714 or 329-7-0770. Fax: 329-7-0551. Internet:* www.paradisevillage.com. *Rack rates: Junior suite $150 (marina view); $185 (ocean view). AE, MC, V.*

Qualton Club
$$$ Hotel Zone

It's exhilarating just sitting around the lobby of the Qualton Club, watching the young international crowd buzzing around this activity hive. Although it's a pretty typical all-inclusive, it's got far better health facilities than most. You may even lose weight if you take advantage of the good tennis courts, top-of-the-line cardio machines, and relentless aerobics, step, and yoga classes — and ignore the unlimited quantities of food and drink. There's nightly entertainment on the premises as well as outings to discos, which waive the cover charge for hotel guests. Rooms, in a 14-story high-rise, are bright and cheerful, with light-wood furnishings; their most outstanding feature is a sweeping bay view from the balconies. If you want to shell out a bit extra, you can get your own hot tub on the terrace.

Av. Francisco Ascencío, km 2.5. ☎ *322-4-4446. Fax: 322-4-4447. E-mail:* qualton@pvnet.com.mx. *Internet:* www.qualton.com. *Rack rates: $140 per person based on double occupancy, including all meals and activities. AE, MC, V.*

Los Cabos

Casa del Mar Golf Resort & Spa
$$$$ The Corridor

Frazzled with wedding stress? You'll be totally soothed by this heavenly hacienda, where fine Mexican art and gardens full of fresh-cut flowers deck the hallways and rooms are arranged around a central courtyard. And what rooms they are, with cool marble floors, restful earth-tone furnishings, and hot tub baths positioned so you can see past your balcony to the dazzlingly blue Pacific. Plunge into one of six freshwater pools, sip something cool, and then tee off at the championship golf course designed by Robert Trent Jones II. At the state-of-the-art spa, you can cavort together under a waterfall in a gigantic hot tub or sign up for a moonlight massage for two. Also relaxing: the ultra-romantic fine dining room, with flickering candlelight, more fresh flowers, and, of course, a sea view; the seafood is excellent, too. Luxury like this doesn't come cheap — but compared to the rest of the resorts on the exclusive Corridor section of Los Cabos, Casa del Mar is a good deal.

Transpeninsular Hwy., km 19.5. ☎ *800-221-8808 or 114-4-0030 to 114-4-0033. (*☎ *800-393-0400 for golf reservations from the U.S.) Fax: 114-4-0034. E-mail:* casamar@cabonet.mex. *Internet:* www.mexico.online.com/casamar.html. *Rack rates: $275 standard double low season, $325 high season, luxury suite $350 low season, $375 high season. AE, MC, V.*

Las Ventanas al Paraíso
$$$$$ The Corridor

Scope it out. At the "Windows to Paradise" you get your own personal telescope — perfect for watching the whales migrate in winter or for stargazing any time of the year. You can also tee off at a stunning desert-meets-sea golf course designed by Robert Trent Jones, or perch on an underwater stool in one of the largest infinity-edge pools in the world. Attendants bearing chilled hand towels, spritzers filled with designer water, baskets of paperback books, and little bowls of chocolate sorbet ensure your poolside comfort. You can also belly up to the ceviche and tequila bar, or, when you're ready for something more substantial, toast

Los Cabos

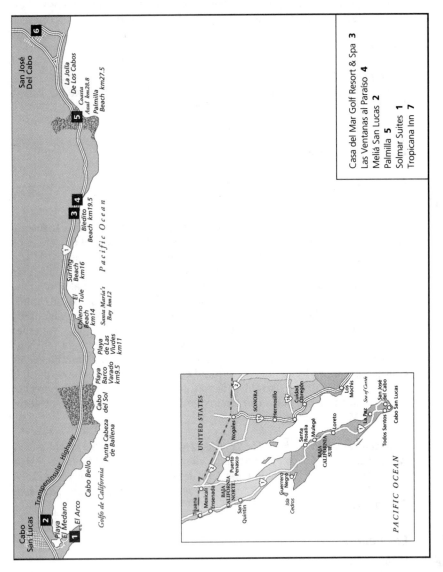

Casa del Mar Golf Resort & Spa **3**
Las Ventanas al Paraíso **4**
Meliá San Lucas **2**
Palmilla **5**
Solmar Suites **1**
Tropicana Inn **7**

each other at the lovely Sea Grill restaurant. The spa is state of the art, but if you don't want to mingle with the other guests, order a massage on your terrace. Each beautiful, Mexican-art-filled suite has its own water-jet tub, so there's no need to leave your quarters for a pre- or post-treatment soak. And on cool evenings, a hand-painted beehive fireplace provides an additional afterglow.

Transpeninsular Hwy., km 19.5. ☎ ***888-525-0483*** *or 114-40-300. Fax: 114-40-301. E-mail:* rosewood@gte.net. *Internet:* www.rosewood-hotels.com. **Rack** *rates: $275 Gardenview Junior Suite (low season — June 1 to Oct. 15), $475 (rest of the year) to $900 one-bedroom luxury suite (low season), $1,080 (high season). AE, DC, DISC, MC, V.*

Meliá San Lucas
$$$$ Cabo San Lucas

If you don't want to miss even a minute of the party, you've come to the right place. But you can also linger over a cold drink in the tiled lobby, which has smashing vistas of El Arco, Cabos's famous rock arch, enjoy live entertainment at night, or just relax by the poolside *palapa* bar when you're ready to wind down. Three restaurants let you decide whether you're feeling haute-y or casual. Two tennis courts await when you want drydock action, and a car rental agent/travel agency can get you on the move, too.

The Meliá Cabo Real Beach & Golf Resort features a three-night, four-day honeymoon package that includes an oceanview room, sparkling wine in the room upon arrival, daily buffet breakfast, a romantic dinner in the hotel restaurant of your choice, and a relaxing "moon and stars" massage. Through April 22, 2001, the package costs $832. April 23 through December 22, 2001, the package runs $766. A civil wedding ceremony can be arranged through the hotel at an additional charge. To make wedding and reception arrangements at the resort, contact the chief concierge or the conference services manager (☎ **011-52-114-40-000,** ext. 1831; Fax: 011-52-114-40-192).

The Meliá Los Cabos All-Suites Oceanfront Spa & Golf Resort offers a three-night, four-day package that includes and oceanview studio suite, one romantic dinner for two (on the beach or in the room), and one bottle of wine with dinner. The price is $335 per person, per package. Tax and service charge are not included. To make wedding arrangements at the resort, contact the group sales manager (☎ **011-52-114-4-02-02;** Fax: 011-52-114-4-00-85; E-mail: grupos.melia.cabos@solmelia.com).

*Playa Medano. ☎ **800-336-3542** or 114-3-1000. Fax: 114-3-0418. Rack rates: $245 double; suites from $444. AE, MC, V.*

Palmilla
$$$$$ The Corridor

Not only does this pretty Spanish-style property occupy 900 acres on its own private point, which boasts spectacular scenery and one of the best swimming beaches in Los Cabos, but it also has its own little white chapel — ideal for fulfilling that wedding-by-the-sea fantasy, if you can afford to fly all the guests into the resort's private airstrip (okay, they can arrive at the airport and taxi in, but it's $2,000 for permission to get married on the property alone). Built in 1956 by the son of a Mexican president as a sportsfishing retreat — which would explain the private airstrip — the Palmilla has expanded its activity roster to include a Jack

Nicklaus signature golf course, a fitness center, an infinity pool with a swim-up bar, volleyball and tennis courts, and a croquet lawn. Fresh juice, croissants, and coffee are delivered to your room every morning. (We suggest booking one of the elegant new suites.) Each room has telephones, dataport, voice mail, television, and VCR. In the evening, after drinks at the open-air Bar Neptuno, enjoy American, Continental, or Mexican fare at the elegant La Paloma.

Transpeninsular Hwy., km 24.5. ☎ *800-637-2226 or 114-2-0582. Fax: 114-2-0583. Internet:* www.palmillaresort.com. *Rack rates: Doubles from $200 (low season) to $375 (high season), suites start at $320 (low season), $550 (high season), plus 15 percent service charge automatically added to the bill; three-night minimum on weekends, no Saturday arrivals or departures. AE, MC, V.*

Presidente Inter-Continental
$$$$ San José del Cabo

San José del Cabo is the quietest of the three destinations that comprise Los Cabos, but you'd never know it if you stay at this beachside all-inclusive. The relentless activities include tennis, snorkeling, dive classes in the huge pool, Spanish lessons, volleyball, shopping tours, free golf and golf clinics at the nearby nine-hole Los Cabos Golf and Tennis Club, whale-watching excursions (in season), and more; at night, you can be serenaded by mariachis at a Mexican fiesta or get your bootie moving at Bones disco. You can also find several quiet areas to escape to, including the fresh water estuary/bird sanctuary next door (but get a room at this end of the hotel and you may literally be up with the birds). The accommodations are attractive, with vibrant pink and turquoise touches; even the standard ones are roomy (and 24-hour room service means you don't have to leave your room if you don't want to). The food in the hotel's three restaurants is a cut above the usual all-inclusive fare; you can end a meal of mushroom-corn quesadillas and grilled banana stuffed with lobster with the local Damiana liqueur, purported to be an aphrodesiac.

Paseo San José, next to the San José estuary. ☎ *800-327-0200 or 114-2-0038. Fax: 113-2-0232. Internet:* www.interconti.com. *Rack rates: $470 standard garden-view double, $525 deluxe room; rates include all meals, soft and alcoholic drinks, and nonmotorized sports for two people. Sunnymoon packages: $530 for two nights, $1,426 for six nights, includes deluxe room, all activities, plus champagne and flowers in the room and a honeymoon gift. AE, DC, MC, V.*

Solmar Suites
$$$ Cabo San Lucas

Just a long stroll (or cheap cab ride) from the action, this friendly, low-glitz property is ideal if you want to hedge your bets. You may want to stay put for long periods: You're at the very tip of the Baja peninsula, and the hotel is set against dark cliffs, so the scenery is spectacular. True, the ocean is too rough for swimming, but when you get your fill of the sand, you can always jump into one of the three pools (two with swim-up bars) or the hot tub, which is where everyone gathers anyway. You can't go wrong with one of the standard rooms (termed "junior suites"). They're comfortably furnished and roomy, have coffeemakers with free coffee, and sit directly on the sand. The more expensive studio or deluxe units are set back on a hillside; one of the pools is in this area, but you're farther from the beach.

Av. Solmar 1 (at the end of Blvd. Marina). ☎ *800-344-3349 or 114-3-3535. Fax: 114-3-04-10. E-mail:* caboreal@aol.com. *Internet:* www.solmar.com. *Rack rates: $152 junior suite (no honeymoon packages, but you can expect a free bottle of champagne if you announce your newlywed status; summer packages include fourth night free and complimentary dinners on the last three nights for $139 per night). AE, MC, V.*

Tropicana Inn
$ San José del Cabo

You may be in the center of town, but you feel as though you're a world apart. The rooms, which have nice folk art details, surround a bougainvillea-decked courtyard with a pool, swim-up *palapa* bar, and Spanish-style fountain; this enclave is so pretty that you won't miss not being on the beach. You get an in-room percolator and complimentary continental breakfast by the pool. Sit in the vine-draped courtyard of the Tropicana's restaurant and enjoy specialties ranging from seafood to Italian, then go next door to the sports bar — San Jose's hottest night spot. One major drawback: All the rooms have two double beds.

Blvd. Mijares 30, 1 block south of Mijares Plaza. ☎ *114-2-1580 or 114-2-0907. Fax: 114-2-1590 or 925-939-2725 in the U.S. Rack rates: $80 double, including tax. AE, MC, V.*

Chapter 24

Enjoying Your Mexican Honeymoon

By Echo & Kevin Garrett

· ·

In This Chapter

▶ Finding fun in Mexico

▶ Discovering the best places to dine

▶ Planning romantic adventures

· ·

Here's where you contemplate how to spend your time (outside of the hotel room, natch) once you get where you're going in Mexico. What follows is a resort-by-resort rundown of the top beaches, activities, and eateries.

Carrying On in Cancún

Cancún's powdery white sand beaches and startlingly blue-green waters attract more visitors than any other destination in Mexico — but that's not all there is to this Caribbean paradise. Endless ways to play in the water and side trips to places such as abandoned Mayan cities can keep you hopping during the day, and at night — *¡Ay caramba!*

Having fun on land and at sea

Cancún's got plenty of first-class aquatic concessions (if you don't have a great one at your hotel, the front desk should be able to direct you to one nearby). You can also check out one of the several water sports companies operating from Cancún's myriad marinas, such as **AquaWorld** (Paseo Kukulkán, km 15.2; ☎ **98-85-2288;** Internet: www.aquaworld.com.mx) or **Aqua Fun** (Paseo Kukulkán, km 16.2; ☎ **98-85-3260**). Expect to pay around $35 a half hour for a speedboat, $22 an hour for paddleboats, and $14 an hour for kayak. There's a per person, per half hour fee of approximately $39 for water skiing, $25 for jet skiing, and $39 for Waverunners. Prices vary from place to place, so shop around if you're peso-pinching.

Parasailing into the sunset

Book the Skyrider, and for $70, you and your honey get strapped into a contraption that looks like a double-seated beach chair and soar above the crowds together. The view is magnificent, the ride is exhilarating, and you don't even have to get wet — when you're through pretending to be a seagull, you land back on the boat deck. Although it's brought to you by **AquaWorld** (☎ 98-85-2288), the ride can be booked through most travel agencies in town.

Exploring the deep blue sea

The coral reefs in this area are teeming with sea life and are considered to be the best for diving in Mexico. A lot of the resorts have classes for beginners that start out in the hotel pool. If you want to get certified, **AquaWorld** (☎ 98-85-2288) offers PADI certification courses, which take four or five days and cost $300 (advanced certification) or $345 (open water certification). One-tank dives run $50 and twilight dives, $55. A four-hour resort course with a one-tank dive is $80. **Scuba Cancún** (☎ 98-83-1011) and **Aqua Tours** (☎ 98-83-0400) also specialize in certification, resort courses, and diving excursions, at similar prices.

Catching a wave

You can matriculate from **Windsurfer Sailing School** (Club International, next to the Calinda Beach Hotel, Paseo Kukulkán, km 4.5; ☎ 98-84-3212), or just rent equipment ($12 per hour, $25 for the day). Classes, which cost $50, are held in Bahía de Mujeres. AquaWorld, which operates from the lagoon side of the hotel zone, also offers windsurfing with or without lessons ($22 per class or $16.50 an hour without instruction).

Braving a bullfight

Introduced centuries ago by Spanish viceroys, bullfighting is about as Mexican now as a shot of tequila with lime and salt. And when in Rome (or Cancún). *Corridas* (bullfights) take place every Wednesday at 3:30 p.m. year-round. You can buy tickets at a travel agency or at the **Plaza de Toros** where the bullfights take place (Avenida Bonampak and Sayil, downtown; ☎ 98-84-8372) for the same price: $31.

Remember, if you go to a bullfight, that's exactly what you're going to see. Stay away if you're an animal lover, or hate the sight of blood.

Hitting the links

The most exclusive place to tee off in Cancún is at the **Caesar Park Hotel** (Paseo Kukulkán, km 17; ☎ 98-81-8000), where the 18-hole championship, par-72 course is landscaped around the Ruinas del Rey archaeological site. There are 72 sand traps for you to shoot your way out of. Greens fees ($80 for hotel guests, $100 for outsiders) include electric carts; no caddies are available. The older but no less magnificent 18-hole, par-72 **Pok-Ta-Pok** (Paseo Kukulkán, km 6.5; ☎ 98-83-0871) course, designed by Robert Trent Jones, overlooks the lagoon near the Holiday Inn Express hotel; two of the greens skirt the edge of the water. Greens fees run $100, including carts; caddies are another $20.

Getting submersible

For an hour and 20 minutes, the glass-bottomed submarine **Nautibus** (☎ 98-83-3552) glides over and around a coral reef dense with tropical fish. From 9:30 a.m. to 2 p.m., it departs every hour and a half from the Playa Linda pier (price: $25). **AquaWorld** (☎ 98-85-2288) sends you off in a slick glass-bottomed boat to tiny Paradise Island, a slip of land off Punta Nizac just large enough to hold a restaurant, rest rooms, showers, and lockers. You can pay for just the air-conditioned underwater sightseeing trip ($28), or the trip plus lunch on the island ($39), or — if you decide at the last minute to get wet after all — get snorkeling thrown in for a total of $50. Rates include guides, instruction, and equipment. Boats leave every hour from 9 a.m. to 3 p.m. from the AquaWorld pier.

Ruin-ing a day at Tulum

Tulum, a walled fortress some 80 miles south of Cancún, wasn't the most important of the Mayan settlements, but it may well be the most scenic. You can visit about a dozen structures, including the Temple of the Upside Down God, famous for a stone carving of a "diving" god. Excursions to Tulum are usually combined with a visit to Xel-Há (pronounced *shell-HAH*), a national park some eight miles to the north. The lure here is swimming or snorkeling in the warm, calm waters of the lagoons and canals, but you can also amble down one of several walking paths or visit a small museum. Trips booked through travel agencies depart at 8 a.m. and return at 4:30 p.m.; the price ($60) includes lunch at Xel-Há (snorkeling equipment is extra).

Xcaping to Xcaret

A 250-acre ecological park, **Xcaret** (pronounced *ISH-car-et*), 50 miles south of Cancún, was built around natural grottoes, pools, and some small Mayan ruins. It's overdeveloped and often crowded, but the beaches are lovely and (for an extra $60) you can swim with some dolphins. Other pluses include subterranean rivers for snorkeling, fresh- and saltwater pools, an aquarium, an aviary, stables, a museum, restaurants, and a Mayan-themed light-and-sound show. Travel agency tours, which cost approximately $70, include the evening show and, usually, lunch. Departure is at 8 a.m. with an 8 p.m. return. You can go on your own by taking the bus (marked "Xcaret," it's the only bus here) that leaves frequently from the Xcaret Terminal (Playa Caracol, across Paseo Kukulkán from Plaza Caracol; $3 a person). The park entrance fee of $30 includes the evening show.

Swinging into the jungle

Play Tarzan and Jane at the **Sian Ka'an Biosphere Reserve,** 1.3 million acres of tropical forest, salt marsh, savannah, and coral reef where jaguars, spider monkeys, manatees, and more than 340 types of birds cavort. Some 22 archaeological sites have been charted within the reserve, too. A six-hour, biologist-guided tour ($90) sponsored by the nonprofit Amigos de Sian Ka'an — book it through the **Ecologos Travel Agency** (☎ 98-84-9580), the only company authorized to conduct tours from Cancún — gives you an in-depth explanation of the reserve before setting you off in motor launches that wind through the mangroves and channels. Tours start at 7 a.m. and end around 7:30 p.m.

Venturing to Isla Mujeres

Less than an hour's boat ride from Cancún, little Isla Mujeres *(moo-hair-ace)* is the quintessential kicked-back fishing village. Among the many things to do here, you can spend the morning snorkeling at Garrafón National Park, have lunch at a beachfront restaurant, shop, visit a turtle farm, wander the rest of the waterfront where the fishing boats come in, or rent bikes. Here are a few ways to get to Isla Mujeres from Cancún:

✔ **Caribbean Express** and **Caribbean Miss** ferries which depart from Puerto Juárez, north of Cancún, reachable via the number 8 bus from Avenida Tulum in downtown Cancún. Ferries depart every half hour from 7 a.m. to 7:30 p.m; the cost is about $3 one-way.

✔ Water taxis depart to Isla Mujeres from the **Club Nautico at Playa Caracol** (☎ 98-86-0777) several times a day starting from 9 a.m., with the last boat returning at 5 p.m; the cost is $10 each way.

✔ **Isla Mujeres shuttle** over from Playa Tortuga (☎ 98-83-3448) four times a day from 9:15 a.m. to 3:45 p.m. and return from 10 a.m. to 5 p.m. for approximately $18 each way. Call for exact schedules.

Drinking in a sunset

The sunsets over Nichupte Lagoon are the best on the island. You get a front row seat for the show if you have a drink at **La Valentina** (Blvd. Kukulcan, km 15; ☎ 98-85-0257), a barefoot elegant room that sits at water level; the soaring, thatch-roof **Lorenzillo's** (Blvd. Kukulcan, km 10; ☎ 98-83-1254), perched on its own peninsula; and the **Plantation House** (Blvd. Kukulcan, km. 10.5; ☎ 98-83-1433), where the formal Caribbean colonial decor — not to mention the stunning vistas — make you feel like the king and queen of the world.

Dancing to a Latin beat

It's a replay of *That 70s Show* every night in Cancún, where disco never died: Dance clubs have the latest in sound-and-light effects and everyone dresses to impress. Cover charges range from $10 to $20, although there are free nights, especially for women.

At **Azucar** (Camino Real Hotel, Punta Cancún; ☎ 98-83-0441), a bona fide Cuban dance club, you can swing your hips to merengue, Mexican boleros, and more, courtesy of sizzling bands from Cuba, Jamaica, and the Dominican Republic, until 4:30 a.m. Also spicing up the scene is **Liquid** (km 9 Paseo Kukulkan in the Party Center; ☎ **98-83-1302**) is a sleek, sophisticated, slightly more intimate club with techno pop and alternative music.

The most popular clubs change every minute, but the following should still be here when you arrive. At **La Boom** (Paseo Kukulkán, km 3.5; ☎ **98-83-1152**) you can choose between a video bar with live music, a split-level flashing-light section, and a special room above it for more mature couples (read: anyone over 25) who want to dance without the ear-splitting music. At the top of the charts is **Dady O** (Paseo Kukulkán, km 9.5; ☎ **98-83-3333**), with lines so long you're reminded of clubbing in New York or Los Angeles. The nondescript exterior gives no hint of the high-tech special effects, including a "third dimension" laser show.

When Mexicans do the town, they do it late. Don't even think about arriving at a bar before 10 p.m. or at a disco before 11:30 p.m. And dress to impress. Most Cancún discos have a dress code: Men aren't allowed to wear tennis shoes, sandals, baseball caps, or tank tops, but women can pretty much get away with anything as long as they're not barefoot. Don't count on squeaking in, either; there's always a checker at the door eyeballing the waiting crowd.

Dining in Cancún

Cancún Island's extended hotel zone has by far the most dining choices — which is to be expected, as that's where most of the people who come to Cancún stay. The east/west section of the hotel strip tends toward trendy party places, although some sedate dining rooms are left over from earlier days. From there, you can literally go in two directions: If you want fancy gourmet food in a luxurious setting, head south for the lower section of the hotel zone, and if you're interested in more traditional fare in low-key surroundings, go inland to Old Cancún.

Creating special memories

Snuggle up in a draped, Mata Hari-style dining alcove at **Bogart's** (Krystal Hotel, Paseo Kukulkán, km 7.5; ☎ **98-83-1133**; $$$-$$$$), where the theme is Casablanca but the food is upscale Continental. Swirling ceiling fans, gleaming wood floors, and an elegantly attired clientele — some of whom may look familiar from films — make **Celebrity** (Casa Turquesa Hotel, Paseo Kukulkán, km 13.5; ☎ **98-85-2924**; $$$$) feel like an Old Havana hideaway. The specialty is seafood, but the chef is Swiss. The classiest dining room on the island, and arguably the best, the **Club Grill** (Ritz-Carlton Hotel, Retorno del Rey, off Paseo Kukulkán, km 13.5; ☎ **98-85-0808**; $$$$) oozes elegant Old World charm. After a dinner of peppered scallops in tequila, take a turn on the dance floor. Besides the excellent wine cellar at **La Habichuela** (Margaritas 25; ☎ **98-84-3158**; $$), you can enjoy delicious Mexican dishes like *cocobichuela* — curried lobster and shrimp in a coconut sauce — on the vine-draped patio of a classic Mayan mansion that flickers with candlelight.

Be sure to make reservations at all of these places.

Finding a local favorite

Seafood lovers fall hook, line, and sinker for the low-key, rustic **El Pescador** (Calle Tulipanes 28, off Av. Tulum; ☎ 98-84-2673; $-$$); for a taste of everything, try the *zarzuela* combination plate. At **Hacienda El Mortero** (Krystal Hotel, Paseo Kukulkán, km 7.5; ☎ 98-83-1133; $$-$$$) you are served by waiters dressed in *charro* (Mexican cowboy) costumes and seranaded by strolling mariachis. Classic Mexican dishes come with hot, hand-patted tortillas — just like back on the hacienda. An authentic Yucatecan restaurant in a town awash in international cuisine, the large, colorful **Los Almendros** (Av. Bonampak and calle Sayil, across the street from the bullring; ☎ 98-87-1332; $) takes you back to Cancún's ancestral roots with traditional dishes such as lime soup or chicken píbil baked in banana leaves. Take a culinary tour of the states of Oaxaca, Michoacan, and Jalisco at the three-tier, folk-art-bedecked **Maria Bonita** (Camino Real Hotel, Punta Cancún, Paseo Kukulkán; ☎ 98-83-1730; $$-$$$), which is named after a famous Mexican love song. For authentic but creative Mexican cooking, follow the townies to **Rosa Mexicano** (Claveles 4; ☎ 98-84-6313; $-$$), which is decorated with colorful piñatas and *papel picado* (paper cutout) streamers. A guitar trio spins out romantic ballads nightly.

Looking for action

You'll recognize **Périco's** (Calle Yaxchilán 71; ☎ 98-84-3152; $$) by the horse-and-buggy on the roof and the waiters out front dressed like bad boys from Pancho Villa's army; revolution is the theme, and rowdiness is the means. Illuminated by bulbs from Mexican movie marquees and old chandeliers from bordellos, the more romantic **La Farandula** (Paseo Kukulkán and Calle Cenzontle, across from Fat Tuesday's; ☎ 98-83-0160; $$-$$$) pays tribute to Mexico's silver screen idols. The menu is 100 percent Mexican and the music mixes mambo, cha-cha, danzón, and salsa with its cheek-to-cheek numbers. **Mango Tango** (Paseo Kukulkán, km 14.2; ☎ 98-85-0303; $$$) puts on a lively Caribbean revue at 7 and 9:30 p.m.; the show is included in the price of any dinner. If you like reggae and jerk chicken, you can't lose with this one.

Cozying Up in Cozumel

Balmy, carefree Cozumel is a typical Caribbean port — except that many of its main attractions are under water. But although Cozumel is one of the world's top five diving spots, submerging is not all that Cozumel has to offer. Miles of sugar-spun beaches, sportsfishing galore, ancient Mayan ruins, appealing waterfront restaurants, and an unpretentious, friendly capital with Mayan roots are great lures, too.

Having fun on land and at sea

Cozumel has two distinct coastlines. The beaches on the west coast, or leeward, side of Cozumel face — and are protected by — the mainland; as a result, the waters are calm and good for swimming. But the island's east, or windward, side is ruggedly beautiful, with higher winds, sand dunes, and lots of craggy limestone outcroppings dotting the shore; it's virtually undeveloped because of the less-than-benign ocean.

In general, be extremely careful about swimming on the east coast. The combination of open sea, dangerous undertows, and no lifeguards is potentially lethal.

Exploring the deep blue sea

If you're like most people, you came to Cozumel to take the plunge (or, in your case, the post-plunge plunge). Why not? You've got amazingly colorful underwater scenery viewed through crystal clear waters — sometimes with a visibility of as much as 200 feet. The **Palancar Reef** system, three miles off the west coast of Cozumel, is the world's second largest reef colony — it's about 1,500 miles long, and outranked only by Australia's Great Barrier Reef. More than 30 recorded reefs, reaching depths of 50 to 80 feet, lie near Cozumel. The range of dive trips is exhaustive — and potentially exhausting. Day dives, night dives, wall dives, and open-ocean dives all are options, and they branch off into subdivisions such as photo, sunken ship, or ecological dives. It'd be impossible to list all the prices, but here's a rough idea of what you can expect to pay for the basics:

- ✔ **Courses:** A four-hour resort course for beginners costs about $60; a refresher course is $55; an advanced course, $250; open-water training dives, $165; four- to five-day PADI certification course, $350. Be sure to buy dive insurance, which you can get through any dive shop for about $1 a day.

- ✔ **Dives:** Several shops can arrange half-day, two-tank expeditions with lunch for $50. A two-tank morning dive (no lunch) also costs $50, but if you decide to tack on an afternoon dive, one tank runs $9 extra, and two tanks add $30 more. A one-tank night dive generally runs about $35.

- ✔ **Gear:** The going rate for scuba gear rental is $5 for a tank, $6 for a regulator, $7.50 for a buoyancy compensator, $5 for mask and fins, $5 for a wet suit, and $33 for a 35mm underwater camera.

Always check out credentials, safety standards, and equipment, and only dive with diving pros. Avoid the *piratas* (pirates) — salesmen selling dive trips on the ferry pier or on the streets at cut-rate prices. They rarely represent reputable dive operations. Your safety is worth far more than the few pesos you may save.

Snorkeling

Diving may be king in Cozumel, but you don't have to go all the way under to enjoy the scenery. Among the best snorkeling spots are the shallow waters of Chankanaab Park and Playa San Francisco; the docks at the Presidente Inter-Continental Cozumel, La Ceiba, and Club Cozumel Caribe hotels are also good. Snorkel rentals, available at most hotels and beaches along the west coast, run about $8 a day. Travel agencies can arrange five-hour snorkeling trips, which include three separate reefs and lunch, for about $40. Many dive shops offer two-hour afternoon excursions for around $25.

Getting hooked

Before diving overshadowed all the island's other nautical activities, Cozumel was known as one of the country's premier sportsfishing resorts. Charter boats vary in size and price, starting from the small, modest *ballenera*, which goes for $100 for four hours (half day) for two. The going rate, though, for most charter boats is $300 a half day for up to six people, $350 for a full day — which includes a captain and crew, fishing gear, bait, a license, and lunch if you're on a full-day charter. Reliable charter companies include **Aquarius Fishing and Tours** (Calle 3 Sur at Avenida Salas; ☎ 987-2-1092); **Club Nautico de Cozumel** (Puerto de Abrigo on Avenida Rafael Melgar; ☎ 987-2-1024); and **Dive Cozumel** (Avenida Salas at Avenida 5 Sur; ☎ 800-253-2701 in the U.S., or 987-2-1842).

Tip 10 to15 percent of the total price of your charter, depending on the service received. Give the money to the captain, who splits it with the mate.

Catching a wave

You can windsurf under the tutelage of a master: Raul de Lille and his partner Nilo Dzib, both Olympic champions, offer classes ($80 for two hours) and equipment rental (short board for $20 an hour, long board for $30 an hour) at the **Sol Cabañas del Caribe** hotel beach (Carretera Santa Pilar, km 4.5; ☎ 987-2-6185).

Skimming the surface

Other ways to play on the water in Cozumel include jet skiing ($45 for two for a half hour), parasailing ($45 per person for the ten-minute ride), kayaking ($15 an hour for two), or pedal boating ($15 an hour for two). The best places to secure water toys, all on the activity-friendly western side of the island, include the **Presidente Inter-Continental Cozumel** (Carretera a Chankanaab, km 6.5; ☎ 987-2-0322), **Plaza Las Glorias** (Av. Rafael Melgar, km 1.5; ☎ 987-2-2000), the **Fiesta Americana** (Carretera a Chankanaab, km 7.5; ☎ 987-2-2622), and **Sol Cabañas del Caribe** (Carretera Santa Pilar, km 4.5; ☎ 987-2-6185) hotels. Concessions on Playa San Francisco also rent a full array of gear.

Venturing to the best sites

The island is dotted with archaeological sites built by the Maya — more than 35 of them. Most are inaccessible, but you can visit the well preserved ruins of San Gervasio, once the largest Mayan settlement on the island.

Guides on site charge $10 to take up to six people around the site. You're better off getting a copy of **San Gervasio,** a booklet sold at San Miguel bookshops for about $2, and doing the tour on your own.

From town, you can reach San Gervasio by Avenida Benito Juárez, the cross-island road; the turnoff to the ruins is to the left a few miles past the airport. You pay a $1 road fee at the gate, and then drive about four miles to reach the ruins. Entrance to the site, open daily from 8 a.m. to 5 p.m., is $1.25. Alternatively, taxi drivers stationed along the water-front in San Miguel can drive you there, wait while you tour (it should only take about ½ hour), and drive you back to town for about $25.

The long, wide beach at **Chankanaab Park** (Carretera Sur km 9) — one of the most beautiful in Cozumel — has a natural aquarium: a lagoon created from a sinkhole. You can't swim in the fragile lagoon, but you can snorkel in the open sea (equipment rental is available on site). Don't want to get wet? Stroll the lovely botanical gardens surrounding the lagoon or explore the archaeological park, where long pathways are lined with replicas of Mayan and Olmec artifacts. Open daily from 8 a.m. to 5 p.m; admission about $3.

Amble along the **Malecón.** The seaport promenade is always picturesque, and it's fun to watch the huge cruise ships come in (you may not want to wait around for the crowds to descend, however).

Ascend 127 steps to the top of the **Punta Celerain Lighthouse** if you want to gaze at the sea from a spectacular perch. It's located at the extreme southern point of the island, past the small El Cedral ruins, an atmospheric landscape of sand dunes, jungle, and mist. If you want company — besides the lighthouse keeper, Sr. Garcia, who opens the door for you — come on Sunday, when the Garcia family serves up fish and beer for visitors at mid-day.

Swimming with the dolphins

It's said that these mammals give out good vibes. The **Dolphin Discover at Chankanaab National Marine Park** is open daily for swims at 9 a.m., 11 a.m., 1 p.m., and 3 p.m. The price, including a 30-minute educational film and 30-minute swim, is $119 per person.

Living it up in Cozumel

Drink in some local atmosphere. The patio of **Las Palmeras** (Av. Rafael Melgar, on the plaza; ☎ 987-2-0532) isn't serene, but the giant mango, banana, or strawberry daiquiris are killer, so you won't care; the sea-breezes and views of the ferry dock multiply the romance factor, too. The **Cafe del Puerto** (see the following section) usually opens an hour before sunset, so even if you don't want to eat here, you can enjoy the gorgeous light show. The tony bar at the **Arrecife** (Presidente-Intercontinental Hotel, Carretera a Chankanaab, km 6.5; ☎ **987-2-0322**), open only in high season, can be depended on for some kind of soothing live music.

Dining in Cozumel

For a low-key island, Cozumel has a surprisingly diverse dining scene. You've got a choice of divers' dives, hoity-toity places for the snob-inclined, candle-lit hideaways, and simple thatched huts oozing island atmosphere. The town of San Miguel is the oldest part of the island and the one closest to the cruise piers, so it stands to reason that it's got the most restaurants — and the best mix of prices, ambience, and local color. The hotels along the northern and southern hotel zones are fine for peso-stretching breakfast and lunch buffets, but for dinner, cab it over to San Miguel.

Creating special memories

The quintessential seaport restaurant, **Café del Puerto** (Av. Rafael Melgar number 3, across the street and to the left of the pier; ☎ **987-2-0316; $$$-$$$$**) has soft music playing in the background; an old-fashioned spiral staircase leads to the elegant room where you can dine on prime rib or shrimp brochette with pineapple. Super romantic in a Gilligan's Island kind of way, **La Cabaña del Pescador** (Carretera Pilar, km 4.5, across the street from the Plaza Azul hotel; no phone; **$$$**) serves only lobster in an intimate, low-lit dining room hung with nets and other marine-o-bilia.

Finding a local favorite

The homey **Comida Casera Toñita** (Av. Salas number 256, between *calles* 10 and 15 North, San Miguel; ☎ **987-2-0401; $**) lets you know you're in the Yucatan, serving delicious victuals to a classical music backdrop in a converted family residence. The Yucatecan specials at **El Moro** (75 Bis Norte 124, between *calles* 2 and 4 Norte, San Miguel; ☎ **987-2-3029; $-$$**) are terrific, and a jumbo margarita can render you oblivious to the tacky orange-on-orange color scheme. Some dishes are so traditional at the modest, folk-art adorned **La Choza** (Av. Salas 198 and Av. 10., San Miguel; ☎ **987-2-0958; $$.**) that you'd be hard-pressed to find them in any other restaurants in Mexico. Marimba music fills the air most evenings.

Craving Italian

For some reason, Italian restaurants seem to thrive in Cozumel. The decor is tropical at the family-run **La Cuchina Italiano** (Av. 10 between Av. 1 and Salas, San Miguel; ☎ **987-2-5230; $$**), but such fresh-made dishes as fettuccine with seafood in white wine are pure Italy. Dine on a pretty patio or watch the waterfront action from the open air-dining room; either way, the creatively topped pies and Italian specialties at **Guido's** (Av. Rafael Melgar between calles 6 and 8 Norte, San Miguel; ☎ 987-2-0946; $-$$) taste good. Many people claim that **Prima** (Av. Salas number 109; ☎ 987-2-4242; $-$$), with its small, daily-changing menu, is the cream of the Italian crop; the second-floor covered terrace is atmospheric.

Acting Up in Acapulco

Acapulco. The name alone, a Latin beat between an "ah" and an "oh," has the sound of excitement. In addition to miles of white sand beaches where you can worship the twin gods of sun and water sports, glittery all night discos and dazzling bay-view restaurants are at your beck and call.

Having fun on land and at sea

Gorgeous Acapulco Bay has weathered years of tourism well, but we won't lie to you: Its beaches are not all pristine, especially along the Costera Miguel Aleman — just call it the Costera — the main tourist drag.

A few people get sucked into Acapulco's deadly riptides and undertows every year. Pay serious attention to the warning flags posted on the beaches. Red or black flags mean stay out of the water altogether, yellow suggests you use caution, and white or green says go ahead, have a good time. Don't even think about swimming on any of the beaches that front the open sea.

Skimming the surface

The beaches along the Costera, and especially the ones behind hotels such as the Qualton Club, the Acapulco Plaza, the Continental Plaza, La Palapa, and the Hyatt, have the most water sports concessions. You typically find **banana boats** ($3 per person for about ten minutes); **parasails** ($15 for about eight minutes); **Waverunners** ($35 for two people for a half hour); water skis (anywhere from $30 to $60 an hour — shop around for the best deals on this one); and jet skis ($50 per hour). Parasailing is especially big — at any given moment, look up and you're likely to see someone soaring in a parachute above Acapulco Bay. You also find some concessions on Caletilla Beach, Puerto Marques Bay, and Coyuco Lagoon near Pie de la Cuesta, although they are not as well stocked as the ones along the Costera.

Hitting the links

The Costera doesn't have any great golf courses, but for a cheap and easy game, there's the public nine-hole **Club de Golf** (Avenida Costera

Miguel Alemán s/n, near the Convention Center; ☎ 74-84-0781 or 84-0782) near the Convention Center. Greens fees are about $20 for one goaround the course, or $35 if you want to play an 18-hole game. The top-notch greens lie to the east, at the sister hotels **Acapulco Princess** (El Revolcadero Beach, just west of the airport; ☎ 74-69-7000) and **Pierre Marques** (☎ 74-66-1000). Greens fees at either 18-hole course run $60 for hotel guests, including carts, and $80 for outsiders.

If you don't stay at the hotel, you need to phone on the same day to find out if you can play. Guests get the first crack at reserving tee times.

Farther east and equally prestigious is the 18-hole course at the **Mayan Palace Golf Club at the Vidafel Mayan Palace** (Geranios 22, Fracc. Copacabana, Playa Revocadero; ☎ 74-66-1924). The $75 greens fee includes a cart; a caddie runs you another $15.

Gaping at the cliff divers

You can't say you've been to Acapulco if you haven't seen the cliff divers at **La Quebrada,** daredevils who plunge into 15 feet of water from a spotlighted ledge on a cliff 134 feet above the pounding surf. The graceful plunge is breathtaking, but the ritual surrounding the dive is as interesting as the act. The divers mill around, looking as though they're trying to steel their nerves, and then cross themselves at a small chapel on the top of the cliff.

La Quebrada is uphill from Avenida Lopez, which is three blocks west of the *zócalo*; the best way to get there is by cab. Shows take place daily at 1, 7:30, 8:30, 9:30, and 10:30 p.m; admission to the viewing platform is about $1.25, and you're expected to tip — 50 cents is fine — when the dripping divers file by afterward to greet you.

Scaling the Fortress

The 18th-century **San Diego Fortress** on the Costera Miguel Alemán, east of the Zócalo, is worth visiting not only for its excellent Acapulco Historical Museum, but also for the fantastic views it affords of the entire bay.) The museum is open Monday through Saturday from 9:30 a.m. to 6:30 p.m; admission is $2.

Strolling the Zócalo

Acapulco's town square is its cultural heart, the place where locals gather on benches to gossip, listen to music at the bandstand, and celebrate religious holidays at the church of Nuestra Señora de la Soledad, a striking art deco structure with Moorish-looking blue and yellow domes. The Costera turns into the *malecón* (seaside promenade) here; it's fun to hang around and scope out the fishing boats and sightseeing yachts. When your feet start hurting, there are plenty of sidewalk cafes to repair to.

Catching a bullfight

Bullfights are held at a ring near Caletilla Beach and start at 5:30 p.m. on 14 Sundays during the winter season. Tickets bought through travel agencies cost around $40 and include transportation to and from your hotel. You won't see the best bullfights in the country here — you've got to go to Mexico City for that — but this spectacle is played out by aspiring young matadors.

Don't go if you have a weak stomach or want to stage a protest; the sport is taken seriously here.

Drinking in a sunset

Catch the sunset at **Playa la Angosta,** an often-deserted cove just around the bend from La Quebrada, where the cliff divers perform. It's the only beach near Acapulco with an unobstructed horizon. If you want to watch the spectacle from a ringside seat with the locals, walk east up the cliffside boulevard from the beach to Sinofia del Sol Amphitheater.

Living it up in Acapulco

Acapulco's discos may be the glitziest in Mexico, with all the latest in high-tech sound-and-light effects, and its patrons may possibly be the best dressed. With the exception of **Discobeach** (keep reading for more information), these shrines to the '70s don't allow entry to anyone wearing tank tops, shorts, or sandals. Covers change year-round, but can go as high as $20; they're often lower (or nonexistent) for women. Doors open at around 10:30 p.m., but don't bother going until almost midnight unless you're trying to advertise just how uncool you are. Closing hours? Whenever the last weary dancers straggle out, sometimes as late as 8 a.m. Phone to make reservations in the high season.

Andromeda (Costera Miguel Alemán, at the corner of Fragata Yucatán; ☎ 74-84-8815) attracts throngs of duded-up 20-somethings to its fortress-like building. Inside, the place looks like a bathosphere; accordingly, a mermaid and merman perform in a giant fishtank after midnight. **Baby O** (Costera Miguel Alemán 22; ☎ 74-84-7474) has been around for a while, but stays packed even during the week. **Discobeach** (Condesa Beach; ☎ 74-84-7064) — surprise, surprise — is on the sand. The house drink? Sex on the Beach, of course. Don't bother turning up if you're over 30. **Extravaganzza** (Costera Miguel Alemán s/n, next to El Ranchero Restaurant and near the Naval Base; ☎ 74-84-7154 and 74-84-7156) pulls in an older crowd (Gen X and up) for the knockout views of Acapulco Bay from the floor-to-ceiling windows and for the latest in special effects. When you tire of hearing loss, head upstairs to the **Sibony Bar** for some champagne and caviar. **Palladium** (Carretera Escénica s/n, near Las Brisas; ☎ 74-81-0330) features the ultimate in high-tech sound-and-light systems and amazing bay views to boot. More romantic than the others along the Costera, **Salon Q** (Costera

Miguel Alemán number 3111, near Oceanic 2000; ☎ **74-81-0114**) is popular with Mexican couples, who sit at intimate tables and listen to the sizzling salsa sounds or dance to slower "tropical" tunes.

Dining in Acapulco

Whether you want a pull-out-the-stops romantic hideaway, a see-and-be-seen scene where the food is almost secondary, or a down-home dive, you are spoiled for choice in Acapulco. Because Acapulco relies on Mexico City residents for much of its business, it's accustomed to catering to some of the most sophisticated palates in the country (think New York or San Francisco foodies with Latino leanings). The Costera has the most restaurants, but you may want to splurge on one of the glitzy Acapulco Diamante dining rooms or head downtown for some local color.

Creating special memories

Palm trees swaying, a gentle breeze wafting over to your beachfront table — it doesn't get much better than **Bambuco** (Hotel Elcano, Costera Miguel Alemán 75, The Costera; ☎ **74-84-1950**; $$-$$$). Seafood rules, but the meat dishes are well done (if you want them that way) too. At **Casa Nova** (Carretera Escénica number 5256, across from the Westin Las Brisas, Acapulco Diamante; ☎ **74-84-6815**; $$$$), the food is Italian and the service is impeccable; the prices are off the scale — but so are the decor and the dramatic bay views. A striking blue-and-white room overlooking the water prepares you for the gorgeous presentations at **El Olvido** (Costera Miguel Alemán, Plaza Marbella; ☎ **74-81-0214** or 81-0240; $$$), where Mexican dishes get a delicious nouvelle twist. A converted villa, **Madeiras** (Carretera Escénica 33, Acapulco Diamante; ☎ **74- 84-4378**; $$$) dazzles with both its Acapulco Bay vistas and its prix-fixe menu, divided between international or updated Mexican fare. If it weren't for its (sigh — yet another) amazing Acapulco Bay overlook, the trendy Asian/international menu at **Spicey** (Carretera Escénica s/n, Marina Las Brisas, Acapulco Diamante; ☎ **74-81-1380** or 74-81-0470; $$$) may make you think you were in New York or L.A. A lovely hillside hacienda awash with tropical plants, **Su Casa/La Margarita** (Av. Anahuac 110, Lomas de Costa Azul, The Costera; ☎ **74-84-4350** or 84-1261; $$-$$$) lets you choose between creative Mexican and Continental dishes in two different dining rooms. Wherever you eat, you gaze out over the bay. A re-creation of a 17th-century Venetian estate, **Villa Fiore** (Av. del Prado 6, The Costera; ☎ **74-84-2040**; $$-$$$) may not be on — or even look out on — the water, but candlelight, a lush garden, and delicious northern Italian dishes on a reasonably priced set menu more than compensate.

Finding a local favorite

The namesake specialty at **El Cabrito** (Costera Miguel Alemán 1480, opposite the Hard Rock Café, The Costera; ☎ **74-84-7711**; $) is roasted goat, but there are plenty of other regional specialties less reminiscent of a petting zoo at this low-key local favorite. Ideal for a post-disco nosh (it hardly every closes), **El Zorrito** (Costera Miguel Alemán at Anton de Alaminos, The Costera; ☎ 74-85-3735; $) is a good place to try pozole or any number of standard Mexican dishes, such as huevos rancheros or Tampico-style beef steak. A cheerful bargain in the Las Brisas area, the large, open-front Los Rancheros (Carretera Escénica s/n, Las Brisas, across from Fantasy disco, Acapulco Diamante; ☎ 74-84-1908; $$) serves food that's all over the Mexican map. If you head for the unassuming seafood house, **Mariscos Pipos** (Almirante Breton 3, Downtown/Old Acapulco; ☎ 74-82-2237; $$), you join the many fish-savvy folks from Mexico City who make it their first dining stop when they arrive in Acapulco. It's slightly gringoized, but the food at **Zapata, Villa y Compania** (Hyatt Regency Acapulco, Costera Miguel Alemán 1, The Costera; ☎ 74-69-1234; $$) is super tasty, and you may get a kick out of the pseudo-revolutionary atmosphere — not to mention the 114 types of tequila.

Playing Around in Puerto Vallarta

Puerto Vallarta is no longer the sleepy fishing village of 1963, when Liz and Dick's doings on the set of *The Night of the Iguana* drew the international press corps here, but its cobblestone streets, sparkling marina, and backdrop of mountains and jungle against the huge Bay of Banderas still make it a wonderfully romantic getaway. If you're here for only a week, your biggest problem may be fitting in a host of dry-dock activities while setting aside sufficient stretches of kick-back beach time.

Having fun on land and at sea

Not all of Puerto Vallarta's creamy stretches of sand are isolated these days, but if you make an effort, you can still find some genuine getaways.

Catching a wave

Scope out the hotel zone beaches if you want to amuse yourself with water toys like jet skis (about $30 per half hour), water skis ($35 per half hour), parasails ($25 for a ten-minute ride), or banana boats ($5 per person for a 15-minute ride). Concessions come and go, but you can surely find some in front of the Sheraton, Fiesta Americana, and Krystal hotels. You can also locate outfitters on Playa de los Muertos, especially around the Playa Los Arcos Hotel, but you may have to share the waves with far more people.

Sailing away

The folks at **Sail Vallarta** (Club de Tenis Puesta del Sol, Local 7-B, Marina Vallarta; ☎ 322-1-0096 or 322-1-0097; E-mail: sail@puerto.net.mx) can set you on course with a skipper and crew. Prices for a day charter range from $50 to $65 per person, or $400 to $600 for the boat.

Also at Marina Vallarta, **Island Sailing International** (Isla Iguana, Hotel Plaza Iguana; ☎ 322-1-0880) offers lessons as well as rentals. For $200, you can get American Sailing Association certification after completing a 12-hour course.

Plumbing the depths

Good visibility — up to 130 feet in summer — plus lots of underwater action makes Puerto Vallarta an ideal place to take the plunge. Great spots for diving and snorkeling include the Marietas Islands, Los Morros Islands, south of the Marietas, and Los Arcos, an underwater preserve just north of Mismaloya beach. Reliable dive operators include **Chico's** (downtown, 772 Díaz Ordaz, near Carlos O' Brien's; ☎ 322-2-1895; E-mail: chicos@tag.acnet.net; Internet: www. chicos-diveshop.com), with branches at the Marriott, Vidafel, Vila del Palmar, Camino Real, and Continental Plaza hotels; and **Vallarta Adventure** (Marina Vallarta, Edificio Marina Golf, Local 13-B; ☎ 322-1-0657 or 322-1-0658; E-mail: adventure@tag01.acnet.net; Internet: www.vallarta-adventures.com). Two-tank dives run around $80 to $120, depending on the destination; rates include lunch. Both Chico's and Vallarta Adventure offer night dives and three-day PADI certification courses.

Biking or hiking

Bike Mex (downtown at Guerrero 361; ☎ 322-3-1680; E-mail: bikemex@ zonavirtual.com.mx; Internet: www.vivamexico.com) runs a series of full- and half-day bike trips for all levels of cyclers. The terrain covered ranges from jungle to small town and beaches; swimming is often involved. Prices, which include top-quality equipment, snacks, and experienced English-speaking guides, begin at $44 for a four-hour trip. If you just want to tool around on your own, you can rent all types of two-wheelers at **B-B-Bobby's Bikes** (downtown, Miramar 399 at Iturbide; ☎ 322-2-3848 or 322-3-0008; E-mail: bbikespv@acnet.net); $35 nets you a bike, a helmet, gloves, and a water bottle for the day. Tours are available, too.

Bike Mex (see the previous paragraph) transforms itself into **Hike Mex** for a series of all-terrain trekking tours that generally require a bit of bush-whacking. The cost — beginning at $30 for a four-hour hike — includes transportation to the hiking area, lunch (or snacks), and bottled water. **Open Air Expeditions** (Guerrero 339, downtown; ☎ 322-2-3110; E-mail: openair@zonavirtual.com.mx; Internet: www. vivamexico.com) offers a similar menu of hiking adventures; a three-hour river-trail walk goes for about $35, for example.

Hitting the links

If you stay in one of the major luxury hotels in Puerto Vallarta, you can probably tee off at the 18-hole, Joe Finger-designed **Marina Vallarta Golf Course** (Marina Vallarta; ☎ 322-1-0701 or 322-1-0171). It's private, but playing privileges are a common perk. The $80 greens fees at this excellent par-71 course include a cart. Located just north of Nuevo Vallarta, the 18-hole **Los Flamingos Golf Course** (☎ **329-8-0606**), designed by Percy Clifford, is somewhat less challenging, but it's also less exclusive; everyone who can shell out $35 for greens fees can play. Carts cost $25, and a caddie runs you another $14.

Flying away

You get a bird's-eye view of the coastline, jungle, and farmland if you sign on with **Hot Air Balloon Tours** (Av. Moreles 36 at Corona, downtown; ☎ **322-3-2002**). In high season, there are two daily ascents, weather permitting, one at 7 a.m., the other at 5 p.m. The price ($120 to $140 per person) includes celebratory champagne at the end of the flight.

Strolling the Malecón

A faithfully observed ritual in Puerto Vallarta is strolling up and down the Malecón, the seaside promenade that extends about 16 blocks from just north of the Cuale river to 31 de Octubre street. At the open-air Aquiles Serdan Amphitheater (better known as Los Arcos) on the southern end, artists labor over seascapes they're hoping you'll buy; you may catch anything from a folk-dancing performance or Hai Kwan Do demonstration to a classical piano concert here. Farther to the north, at the main Plaza de Armas (also called the Zócalo), the municipal band entertains in the kiosk on Thursday and Saturday evenings at 6 p.m. The Malecón is also an outdoor gallery of sculptures, including the Friendship Fountain, in which three dolphins cavort; an image of Triton with a friendly sea nymph; and Puerto Vallarta's signature seahorse.

Lots of the Malecón sights make for great photo ops, but two favorites are the lovers gazing out to sea and a group of huge bronze chairs by Guadalajara artist Alejandro Colunga, which feature two giant ears as a backrest.

Drinking in a sunset cruise

Departing at 5:30 p.m. and returning at 7:30 p.m., sunset cruises usually stay fairly close to shore in the main tourist areas — the better to see the shore lights begin to twinkle along with the stars. The price of $20 usually includes an open bar, an hors d'oeuvre buffet, and dance music. Going a bit farther to Los Arcos and returning at 9 p.m., the Marigalante cruise includes spectacular fireworks; it's $30 if you just want snacks with the open bar, $48 if you need something more substantial to anchor all that booze. The ultra-romantic Rhythms of the Night cruise, departing at 6 p.m. and returning at 11, transports you to Caleta Beach, where director John Huston built a home. There's no electricity here, so you dine by candlelight on the terrace of his lushly landscaped estate, overlooking the bay, and then watch pre-Hispanic dances performed by torchlight in a natural amphitheater. Cost: $50 per person. Book directly through **Vallarta Adventure** (see "Plumbing the depths," earlier in this section) or through a travel agent, which can also book the other cruises.

Dining in Puerto Vallarta

Puerto Vallarta is one of the most cosmopolitan restaurant towns in Mexico, thanks in part to an influx of American and European visitors, some of whom stayed on to become chefs. You can be as conservative or as adventurous in your eating as you want — you can get everything from schnitzel to sushi as well as Mexican here — and as down home or as dressed up as you like. There are decent places to eat in most Puerto Vallarta neighborhoods, but the greatest concentration of good restaurants by far is downtown. With some notable exceptions in both cases, the area around the malecón tends to have the rowdier and more touristy eateries, while the section south of the Río Cuale, and especially Basilio Badillo, known as Restaurant Row, is a gourmet mecca.

Creating special memories

Serious gastronomes love the adventurous pairings of local Mexican recipes with nouvelle French recipes at the **Café des Artistes** (Guadalupe Sánchez 740, Downtown/North; ☎ 322-2-3228; $$$$.). The main dining room is gorgeous but a bit formal; grab a table on the terrace if you want to relax. An Old World, Viennese-style bistro, **Café Maximilian** (Olas Altas 380-B, Playa de los Muertos, Downtown/South; ☎ 322-3-0760; $$$-$$$$) creates an elegant atmosphere for gemütlich dishes like Wiener schnitzel with sautéed potatoes. The mix-it-up international menu is as stylish as the decor at **Le Bistro** (Río Cuale Island 161, Downtown/South; ☎ 322-2-0283; $$$), where you can watch palm fronds sway on the Río Cuale while you dine under swirling ceiling fans.

Finding a local favorite

Expect lines in high season at the homey **Café de la Olla** (Basilio Badillo 168, between Olas Altas and Pino Suárez, Downtown/South; ☎ 322-2-1626; $), where everything's served with fresh-made tortillas, and the margaritas are killer. An open-fronted Mexican *fonda* (small economical restaurant), **La Paz** (Condominiums Marina Rey, local l 01A, entrance to Marina Vallarta; ☎ 322-1-0313; $-$$) is a rare slice of authentic Mexican life in the generally touristy Marina. At **La Palapa** (Pulpito 103, Downtown/South; ☎ 322-2-5225; $$-$$$) you can wiggle your toes in the sand of Playa de los Muertos while downing delicious nouvelle-style Mexican specialties such as smoked marlin enchiladas. Right next door, the palapa-roof **El Dorado** (Pulpito 102, Downtown/South; ☎ 322-2-1511; $$) draws business types, expatriates, and visitors alike for great beachside Mexican breakfasts and seafood lunches.

Swinging into the jungle

Puerto Vallarta's "jungle" restaurants — casual open air-eateries around or south of Mismaloya Beach — are as touristy as all get-out, but loads of fun (don't forget your bathing suit). **Chino's Paradise** (off Hwy. 200, km 6.5; ☎ 322-3-3012; $$) has five open-air terraces that look out on huge boulders, a swift-flowing river, and a waterfall; a marimba band usually plays from 1 to 3 p.m. At **El Eden** (off Hwy. 200, km 6.5; no phone; $), the former film set of the Arnold Schwarzenegger machofest, *Predator,* you can look out on folks dropping from a rope swing into the river below — or try it yourself (but not after drinking too many margaritas, please). The food at **Chico's Paradise** (km 20, just beyond Boca de Tomatlán; ☎ 322-2-0747; $$) is a cut above the rest, and the setting is especially spectacular. Settle in under the huge palapa roof and enjoy shrimp smothered in garlic butter, served with fresh, hot tortillas — you can watch them being made — or just order some nachos and a potent Coco Loco.

Getting Ixciting in Ixtapa/Zihuatanejo

Although Ixtapa, a newcomer on the beach vacation scene, isn't as fast paced as larger, more developed resorts like Acapulco or Cancún, and Zihuatanejo isn't nearly as sleepy as it once was, together they have plenty to offer both those seeking sun-and-fun and those looking to kick back.

Having fun on land and at sea

The two towns are only four miles apart, so it's simple to shuttle back and forth between them — giving you the best of both worlds.

Exploring the depths

Ixtapa/Zihuatanejo is a diver's dream. Water visibility often reaches more than 100 feet, especially from December through May, and the temperature is always comfortably warm. Moreover, the convergence of the Humboldt Current and the Equatorial Counter Current in this area has resulted in an incredibly rich sea life. You never know what you may see — huge schools of Mexican yellow goatfish, giant manta rays, sea horses, maybe even a humpback whale. You're unlikely to recover any lost Spanish treasure, but you may spot a 400-year-old anchor or other artifacts from the conquistador days.

Take the plunge at the **Zihuatanejo Scuba Center** (Cuauhtemoc 3; ☎ and fax **755-4-2147**; E-mail: divemexico@mail.com; Internet: www.divemexico.com). For $70, you can learn the basics in a hotel pool and then take an afternoon dive. Already certified? You pay $70 for two deep-sea dives ($10 less if you brought your own equipment). Certification courses are available, too.

If snorkeling is more your speed, **Zihuatanejo's Playa Las Gatas, Isla Ixtapa's Playa Varadero,** and **Playa Hermosa** in front of the Westin Brisas Ixtapa are excellent spots for snorkeling. All offer equipment rentals at anywhere from $5 to $15 a day.

Catching a wave

Walk along **Playa la Ropa** in Zihuatanejo and **Playa del Palmar** in Ixtapa for the best water sports pickings; **Playa Las Gatas** in Zihuatanejo is a runner-up, and **Isla Ixtapa** also has a few concessionaires. You also find parasailing (about $20 for a 15-minute ride), water-skiing and Wave-runners (about $30 per half hour), jet skis ($25 per half hour), and banana boat rides ($5 for a 20-minute trip). You can also hire small sailboats, sailboards, and sea kayaks at these aquatics booths.

Sailing away

The 67-foot *Tristar* trimaran, operated by **Yate del Sol** (☎ 755-4-2694 or 4-8270) from the Puerto Mio marina in Zihuatanejo, alternates between day cruises to Isla Ixtapa ($49) and ones to Playa Manzanillo ($59); the price includes hotel transfers, lunch, and an open bar (snorkeling gear is $5 extra). On the return trip, the Tristar anchors in front of Playa la Ropa; if you like, you can take a flying (parachute) leap from the company's 2400-square-foot spinnaker. Reserve through the company or via a travel agent.

Hitting the links

Ixtapa's hotel zone is sandwiched by two excellent golf courses. The first one you encounter en route from Zihuatanejo is the 18-hole **Ixtapa Golf Club** (☎ 755-3-1410), designed by Robert Trent Jones, Jr. Parts were set aside as a wildlife preserve, so you may spot flamingos on the 5th hole. Greens fees: $45 ($30 after 3 p.m.), $20 for a cart. **The Marina Ixtapa Golf Club** (at the far end of the hotel zone; ☎ 755-3-1410), an 18-hole Robert Von Hagge creation considered one of the most challenging in Mexico, is known for its meandering canals and its rolling dunes-style topography, as well as for its proximity to the restaurants and shops of the tony Marina complex. (And, yes, there are crocs in this course's waters, too.) Greens fees: $55 ($30 after 4 p.m.), including cart.

Don't even think about trying to recover a ball from water traps at Ixtapa Golf Course. Zoologists from Mexico City are regularly called out to the club to relocate oversized crocodiles.

Taking in the sites

Amble along the beachside **Paseo del Pescador** to get a real feel for this area; it's clear, watching the small fishing boats, that the economy of the sea that sustains Zihuatanejo has continued uninterrupted for centuries. Near Guerrero, at the east end of the street, the **Museo de Arqueologia de la Costa Grande** lets you glimpse at the cultures that occupied the coastal stretch from Acapulco to Ixtapa/Zihuatanejo before the Spanish arrived. Displays are modest and marked only in Spanish; you can cover the museum (open Tuesday through Sunday, 10 a.m. to 5 p.m.; admission $1) in about half an hour.

Drinking in a sunset

In Ixtapa, the best spots to watch Ol Sol descend are at opposite ends of town: the lobby bar at the Westin Brisas Ixtapa and the Bar El Faro, at the top of the pseudo-lighthouse in the Marina Ixtapa complex. Because of the curve of the bay, sunset views are blocked in many parts of Zihuatanejo. Not affected are the Sunset Bar, at the Catalina & Sotovento hotels on Playa la Ropa, and Restaurant Gaviota, at the end of the same beach.

Living it up in Ixtapa/Zihuatanejo

In Ixtapa, you can usually catch live sounds of the tropical persuasion at the lobby lounges at the **Westin, Sheraton, Dorado Pacifico,** and **Krystal** hotels. No cover — just keep ordering those piña coladas. In Zihua, live Mexican bolero or salsa sizzle at **El Canto de la Sirena,** a friendly local club near the main bus terminal, just south of the road to Ixtapa and the airport (you have to cab it here, but it shouldn't run more than $4 from Ixtapa and Zihuatanejo beaches). Closer to the center of town, at Pedro Ascencío and Agustín Ramírez, is **El Rincon de Agustín Ramírez,** a cozy guitar bar dedicated to a musician who wrote in, and about, the state of Guerrero.

Dining in Ixtapa/Zihuatanejo

What Ixtapa/Zihuatanejo lack in sightseeing options, they make up for in restaurant-hopping possibilities. You can change scenes — and cuisines — practically every night of an extended stay. You want water views? You got 'em. In Ixtapa they tend to be clean and serene, whether from a table side at the Marina Ixtapa or from the cliffs above Vista Hermosa. In downtown Zihuatanejo, more people come into the picture: Dine along Paseo del Pescador, and you get a great snapshot of village and tourist life at no extra charge. The restaurants on Zihuatanejo's Playa Madera and Playa la Ropa run the gamut from places that deliver ceviche and Corona to your lounge chair to upscale, romantic hideaways.

Creating special memories

A bit of Northern Italy in Southern Mexico, **Beccofino** (Marina Ixtapa, near the lighthouse; ☎ 755-3-1770; $$$) serves creative seafood and pasta in a sparkling marina setting. It doesn't get much more exotic than the Casablanca-themed **Bogart's** (Krystal Ixtapa hotel, Blvd. Ixtapa; ☎ 755-3-0303; $$$$), where you dine on Continental specialties in white-draped, cushioned nooks. A romantic garden, a lively bar, and a great Mexican/international menu all make **Coconuts** a contender (Agustín Ramírez 1, Downtown Zihuatanejo; ☎ 755-4-2518; $$$). **Kau-kan** (Playa Madera, below the Hotel Brisas del Mar, Zihuatanejo/Beaches; ☎ 755-4-8446; $$-$$$) defines casual elegance, with its three-tier dining room basking in the glow of candles and fairy lights on the beach and its superb seafood. Perched on a lush cliffside above Hermosa Beach,

Villa de la Selva (Paseo de la Roca, Ixtapa; ☎ 755-3-0362 and 3-0462; $$$$) feeds your spirit with its stunning sea views — and your body with its rich Continental dishes.

Finding a local favorite

A prime seafront location and well-prepared, reasonably priced Mexican seafood have kept the crowds coming to **Casa Elvira** since 1956 (Paseo del Pescador, near the town pier, Downtown Zihuatanejo; ☎ 755-4-2061; $-$$). The name means "Hell and Glory," but the regional specialties at **El Infierno y La Gloria** (La Puerta shopping center, Ixtapa; ☎ 755-3-0272; $$) are heavenly. Although "from the pier to your plate" could be the logo at the nautical-decor **Garrabos** (Álvarez 52, Downtown Zihuatanejo; ☎ 755-4-2977 or 4-2191; $$), you also find plenty of delicious dishes that don't involve fish. Mouth-wateringly creative seafood tacos (conch with cactus and fish mole, for example) and a relaxing, dockside perch lure locals and visitors alike to **La Sirena Gorda** (Paseo del Pescador 20-A, Downtown Zihuatanejo; ☎ 755-4-2687; $). Ask anyone: **Tamales Any y Atoles** (Calle Ejido at the corner of Vincente Guerrero, Downtown Zihuatanejo; ☎ 755-4-7373; $) has the best down-home Mexican food in town, with namesake tamales that you definitely would write home about.

Laughing It Up in Los Cabos

A singular destination but also a triple threat, Los Cabos boasts jaw-dropping desert-meets-sea scenery and three distinct areas in which to revel in it — sometimes literally. There's the low-key town of San José del Cabo, party-hearty Cabo San Lucas, and the glitzy row of resorts and golf courses called the Corridor that connects the two. That gives you plenty of places to get in the mood — whatever that mood may be.

Having fun on land and at sea

With their dramatic dark outcroppings of rock, startling growth of cactus along the shore, and astonishing palate of blues as the Pacific merges with the Sea of Cortez, Los Cabos's beaches are among the most spectacular in Mexico. Unfortunately, however, because of the lack of public transportation and the impossibility of hailing cabs along the Corridor, the only way to visit some of the best ones is by renting a car.

 The beaches that are not fronted by hotels don't fly water safety flags and don't have lifeguards. Swim only at the beaches that are considered safe — otherwise you're risking your life.

Catching a wave

For one-stop water sports shopping, **Medano Beach** can't be beat. If it floats, bobs, or zips around on the sea, you can rent it here.

Wave-runners and jet skis cost about $35 per half hour to $60 per hour, waterskiing starts at roughly $40 a half hour, Hobie Cats run around $30 an hour, a Windsurfer is about $15 an hour, and you pay approximately $30 for a ten-minute parasailing experience. You can hop on a banana boat for about $6 per person. In the Corridor, you can rent equipment at both Bahia Chileno (including kayaks and canoes) and Palmilla beaches. The town beach in San José del Cabo also has several sports concessionaires. Prices at other Los Cabos beaches are comparable to those on Medano.

Plumbing the depths

Marine flora and fauna from both the Sea of Cortez and the Pacific Ocean proliferate off the coast of Los Cabos, resulting in a unique underwater show. Visibility, which ranges from about 30 to 50 feet in the winter months, reaches over 100 feet from April to October. The water gets warmed up to an average of 80°F by the end of the summer and stays warm through December and into January.

Two of the most reliable dive operators in Cabo are **Amigos del Mar** (Cabo San Lucas marina; ☎ **800-344-3349** in the U.S., or 114-3-0505) and **Cabo Acuadeportes** (Medano Beach, near the Hacienda Hotel, and Bahia Chileno Beach at the Hotel Cabo San Lucas; ☎ **114-3-0117**). In San José, contact **Tourcabos** (Plaza Garuffi, Local 10, Paseo San José and Blvd. Las Palmas; ☎ **114-2-4040**; E-mail: tourcabos@1cabonet.com.mx).

The companies mentioned in the previous paragraph, as well as several others in both towns and along the Corridor, also offer snorkeling tours to Playa de Amor, Playa Santa María, Playa Bahia Chileno, and Playa Barco Vardaro. A two-hour cruise to sites around El Arco typically runs around $30, and a four-hour trip to Playa Santa María costs $55; both rates include gear. Snorkeling equipment alone, available on Palmilla, Chileno Bay, and Medano beaches, rents for around $15.

Getting hooked

Once known as "Marlin Alley," Los Cabos was an exclusive fishing ground for the wealthy in the 1940s and '50s. Although those strictly seeking seclusion have moved to the more low-key East Cape, Los Cabos is still one of the hottest angling destinations in the world, hosting annual competitions with some of the largest purses around.

Angling excursions run the gamut from three-hour trips in a two-person *panga* (motorized skiff) to all-day trips in a deluxe cabin cruiser that holds eight plus the captain and mate. Typical prices for a full-day trip range from $150 for a "super *panga*" for two people and $340 for a 28-foot single-engine cruiser for four to $430 for a 33-foot twin-engine cruiser for six. Among the many reliable companies in Los Cabos, we recommend **Victor's Sportsfishing** (Palmilla Beach, the Corridor; ☎ **800-521-2281**, 114-2-1092, or 114-2-0155); **Pisces Fleet** (Blvd. Marina and Madero in Cabo San Lucas; ☎ **114-3-1288**; E-mail: pisces@1cabonet.com); and

Solmar (Solmar Hotel, Blvd. Marina and Av. Solmar; ☎ **800-344-3340,** 114-3-0646, or 114-3-4542; E-mail: CaboResort@aol.com; Internet: www.solmar.com).

Hitting the links

Los Cabos is Mexico's top golf destination, and it's easy to see why. In the past decade, large swaths of the Corridor have been put in the hand of some of the game's prime designers — and of course, nature took its course on these courses, too. Expect club rentals to cost you $40; greens fees (those quoted are for high season) include a cart, practice balls, and bottled water.

In summer, you won't have a problem getting a prime tee time, but in winter, it's always best to phone ahead to reserve, especially if you're not staying at one of the hotels that has privileges at the course you want to play; the best slots are often reserved for the guests.

At the 18-hole, Jack Nicklaus designed **Palmilla Golf Club** (Palmilla Hotel, Hwy. 100, km 27.5; ☎ **800-386-2465** or 114-4-5250), the back "Mountain" nine holes play around small lakes, while the front "Arroyo" are a bit more prickly, having 400-year-old Cordon cactus as hazards. Greens fees: $180 from Thursday to Saturday, $165 the rest of the week. Just a long-shot away (well, practically), Jack Nicklaus's par-72 **Cabo Real** (Playa Barco Vardaro; ☎ **800-386-2465** or 114-3-3990) has been described as Mexico's answer to Pebble Beach and is rated among the world's top 100 courses by *Golf Digest* magazine. Greens fees: $175 Sunday to Wednesday, $190 Thursday to Saturday. The 18-hole **Cabo Real** course (Hwy. 100, km 19.5; ☎ **114-4-0040;** E-mail: caborealgolf@cabonet.net.mx) was designed by Robert Trent Jones, Jr., and every hole looks out on the Sea of Cortez; the 14th, which sits on a mesa, is especially impressive. Greens fees: $165. Just outside the town of Cabo, the 18-hole **Cabo San Lucas Country Club** (Hwy. 100, km 3.5; ☎ **800-854-2314** or 114-3-4653) is par for a Corridor course. It was designed by a top golf architect — in this case, Roy Dye; it's got stunning views; and it's part of a large community (a gated residential one). Greens fees: $121, with cart.

Drinking in the sunset

Typical of the flotilla of big boats that you can set sail are the 42-foot catamaran *Pez Gato* (☎ **114-3-3797**), the 100-foot catamaran *Kaleidoscope* (☎ **114-8-7318**), and the *Encore* (☎ **114-3-4050**), a 60-foot ocean-racing yacht. For something slightly more exotic, board the *Sunderland* (☎ **114-3-4050**), a 110-foot-long sailing vessel dating back to the 1880s that's decked out to look like a pirate ship. Most of the cruises, bookable through a travel agent, hotel desk, or by calling the company directly, depart around 5 and last two hours; they include unlimited soda, beer, and domestic brand liquor.

It's not possible to see the sun go down everywhere in Los Cabos — only places facing the Pacific get a ringside view — but on the Corridor, you can catch the nightly light show from **Da Giorgio II,** at the Misiones del Cabo hotel (Hwy. 100, km 5; ☎ 113-3-3988) and at **Pitahayas at Cabo del Sol** (see "Dining in Los Cabos," later in this chapter). In Cabo, the more casual **Whale Watcher Bar at the Hotel Finisterra** (Blvd. Marina s/n, almost at the end; ☎ 114-3-3333) or the cocktail lounge at the **Hotel Solmar Suites** (Av. Solmar 1, at the end of Boulevard Marina; ☎ 14-3-3535) are equally fine options.

Looking for romance

Relax to some soothing music. For some quiet sounds during or after dinner, try **Edith's** (Medano Beach at Paseo del Pescador; ☎ 114-3-0801), which also offers a terrific view of El Arco. Tucked away behind the northeast side of the Plaza Las Glorias hotel, **Sancho Panza Wine Bar Cafe** (on the marina, just up from KFC; ☎ 114-3-3212) has soft lighting, the best selection of wine in town, and Latin jazz trios during the week (call ahead for the schedule). You won't go wrong if you come for dinner, either.

Living it up in Cabo

If you want to go in for the Cabo San Lucas melee, here are some spots to try. Just be prepared for . . . well, anything. **Cabo Wabo Cantina** (Guerrero at Lázaro Cárdenas; ☎ 114-3-1188), owned by rock musician Sammy Haggar, banks not only on its owners' occasional appearances, but also on good acoustics and a hopping dance floor. Cabo Waco even makes its own tequila. **Giggling Marlin** (Lázaro Cárdenas at Zaragoza, across from the marina; ☎ 114-3-1516) is not for the prudish or faint of heart; the club's most infamous feature is the fish scale on which singles or couples get strung up by the heels.

Dining in Los Cabos

Although you won't lack for restaurants no matter where in Los Cabos you bed down, you may have a harder time locating an inexpensive meal in the tony Corridor than in other parts of town. San José is best for authentic Mexican cooking at reasonable prices. Cabo San Lucas has the best selection of eateries of the three, everything from romantic dining rooms to down-home taco stands.

Unlike other beach towns, where the tax is always included in the final tab, in Los Cabos it's sometimes extra. If you see "no incluye el I.V.A" on the menu, expect 10 percent to be tacked onto your bill. Here, as everywhere else in Mexico, tips are not ordinarily added in, but if the words "propina incluida" or "servicio incluida" appear on your bill, then you know that service has already been covered. If it hasn't, the standard in nice restaurants is 15 percent.

Creating special memories

Just down the block from rowdy Medano beach, **Casa Rafael's** (Calle Playa el Medano at Camino Pescador, Cabo San Lucas; ☎ 114-3-0739;

$$$$) seems a world away, what with the candlelight, the European antiques, and the sophisticated international cuisine. A lovely ocean-side setting and innovative Pan-Asian cuisine make **Pitahayas** (Cabo del Sol Resort, Hwy. 1, km 10, The Corridor; ☎ 114-3-2157; $$$-$$$$) worth both the drive and the splurge. Sit on the colorfully decked-out patio of **Peacock's** (Paseo del Pescador s/n, next to the Meliá Hotel entry to Playa Medano, Cabo San Lucas; ☎ 114-3-1858; $$$-$$$$) for creatively prepared and beautifully presented seafood (the rack of lamb and duck are super too).

Finding a local favorite

Set in an 18th-century hacienda on San José's town plaza, **Damiana** (Plaza Mijares, Blvd. Mijares at Zaragoza, San José; ☎ 114-2-0499; $$-$$$) serves both gringo-friendly dishes and south-of-the-border specialties. At **Mi Casa** (Av. Cabo San Lucas between Serdán and Lázaro Cárdenas, Cabo San Lucas; ☎ 114-3-1933; $$-$$$) you can sit in a pretty courtyard, surrounded by vivid fuchsia flowers, and take a culinary tour of Mexico. Sit by a burbling fountain and watch an eclectic array of dishes — seafood, steak, and Continental — emerge from the colorfully tiled open kitchen of the **Tropicana Inn Bar & Grill** (Blvd. Mijares 30, San José; ☎ 113-2-1580; $$).

You get super fresh fish at **Pescaderia El Mercado del Mar** (Mauricio Castro 1110 (just off Hwy. 1), San José; ☎ 114-2-3266; $$), a casual terrace restaurant that's connected to a seafood market and has its own smoker. For Baja-style fish tacos, head for the tiny, family-run **Tacos Chidos** (Zapata s/n, between Hidalgo and Guerrero, Cabo San Lucas; ☎ 114-3-0551; $); the beef and pork versions are tasty, too.

Chapter 25

Making Plans and Settling In

By Echo & Kevin Garrett

● ●

In This Chapter

▶ Making your way to Mexico

▶ Knowing what to expect when you arrive

▶ Watching out for your health and safety

● ●

*I*n this chapter, we get down to the nitty gritty of how to make your honeymoon in Mexico happen. We lay out what you can expect when you get there — everything from *dinero* matters to the weather.

Getting to Mexico

It's no good deciding that you want to go to a particular beach resort in Mexico, only to discover that getting there requires changing planes six times and costs you an arm and a leg to boot. Flight patterns — and prices — are a major factor in deciding where you go honeymoon in Mexico. Check routes, times, and prices closely before making your final decision about your destination.

The following is a list of the major carriers to Mexico:

✔ **AeroMéxico** (☎ 800-237-6639; Internet: www.aeromexico.com) makes daily nonstop flights from Los Angeles to Puerto Vallarta and from Atlanta to Cozumel. It also offers nonstop flights from New York's JFK twice a week to Cancún.

✔ **AeroCalifornia** (☎ 800-237-6225) makes daily direct flights from Los Angeles to Cabo San Lucas.

✔ **Alaska Airlines** (☎ 800-426-0333; Internet: www.alaskaair.com) makes direct flights from Los Angeles, San Diego, San Jose, San Francisco, Seattle, Vancouver, Anchorage, and Fairbanks to Los Cabos, Ixtapa/Zihuatanejo, and Puerto Vallarta. Daily flights to Los Cabos and Puerto Vallarta, less frequent to Ixtapa/Zihuatanejo.

✔ **America West** (☎ 800-363-2597; Internet: www.americawest.com) makes direct nonstop flights from Phoenix to Ixtapa/Zihuatanejo (once a week low season; twice a week high season), Los Cabos (daily), Acapulco (once a week low season; four times in high season), and Puerto Vallarta (four times a week).

✔ **American Airlines** (☎ 800-433-7300; Internet: www.americanair. com) makes daily direct flights from Dallas/Fort Worth to Puerto Vallarta (in high season), Acapulco (six days a week in low season), and Cancún, and daily nonstops from Miami to Cancún. In high season, nonstop service from Chicago to Acapulco on weekends.

✔ **Continental** (☎ 800-231-0856; Internet: www.flycontinental. com) makes daily direct flights from Newark, N.J., to Cancún, and from Houston to Cozumel, Cancún, Ixtapa/Zihuatanejo, Puerto Vallarta, Los Cabos, and Acapulco.

✔ **Delta Airlines** (☎ 800-221-1212; Internet: www.delta-air.com) makes nonstop flights daily from Atlanta to Cancún.

✔ **Mexicana** (☎ 800-531-7921; Internet: www.mexicana.com) makes direct flights from Los Angeles to Los Cabos (daily, nonstop), Cancún (most days of the week, nonstop), Puerto Vallarta (most days of the week, nonstop), and Ixtapa/Zihuatanejo (seasonal).

✔ **Northwest** (☎ 800-225-2525; Internet: www.nwa.com) makes direct flights to Cancún from Minneapolis (once a week low season, daily high season), Memphis (daily), and Detroit (once a week high season); to Cozumel from Minneapolis (once a week in high season); to Puerto Vallarta from Detroit and Minneapolis (for both, once a week during high season); to Acapulco from Minneapolis (once a week, high season); to Ixtapa/Zihuatanejo from Minneapolis and Detroit (for both, once a week during high season).

✔ **US Airways** (☎ 800-428-4322; Internet: www.usairways.com) makes nonstop flights daily from Charlotte, N.C., to Cancún and once a week from Philadelphia to Cancún.

Entering Mexico

You need a birth certificate or a valid passport to enter Mexico. If you rely on a birth certificate, make sure that it's an original, not a photo copy, and that it's an official, government-issued birth certificate from a city, county, or state agency, as opposed to one issued by the hospital or a church; the certificate should have a raised seal on it. A birth certificate must be accompanied by a current photo ID (such as a driver's license).

Children traveling without both parents or guardian need a notarized letter from the absent parent or guardian authorizing the trip (good to know if you plan to bring the kids).

Knowing what to bring

To enter Mexico, visitors need a *tarjeta de turista* (tourist permit), which is free and available through airlines, Mexican government tourism offices, Mexican consulates, or at the border customs office when crossing by land. The card is only good for one entry and for 180 days.

On the plane, you're issued a form to fill out, asking for your address in Mexico, the purpose of your visit, and so on.

Understanding customs regulations

The belongings of all incoming travelers (except for diplomatic personnel) are subject to spot check using a "traffic light" system. Customs declaration forms must be filled out by domestic or foreign travelers. The form is then passed through a machine — a red light indicates possessions to be spot checked; a green light means a search is not conducted. This method is already used in Mexico City's airport and is already implemented throughout all of Mexico's international airports.

All travelers to Mexico are allowed to bring in clothing, photographic and sports equipment, and a portable computer, for their personal use, as well as two liters of spirits or wine, 400 cigarettes, and 50 cigars.

Your declaration document, when stamped, turns into your tourist card. Hang on to it carefully — you may even want to make a copy of it, to be kept in a separate place, when you reach your hotel; it is collected by the airline ticket clerk.

Staying Healthy

You don't need any special immunizations to travel in Mexico. Of course, it never hurts — okay, only for a second — to get a tetanus booster if you haven't had one in a long time (tetanus shots are effective for ten years).

Immunization and other health information is available from the non-profit **International Association of Medical Assistance to Travellers,** 417 Center St., Lewiston, NY 14092 (☎ **716-754-4883;** Internet: www. sentex.net/~iamat). Membership, which also entitles you to a list of approved English-speaking physicians in Mexico, is free, although donations are gratefully accepted.

If you don't have any preexisting condition, but are still worried about getting sick away from home, it's a good idea to buy medical travel insurance (see Chapter 7 for more information).

There's a lot of hysteria about health disasters awaiting the unwary tourist to Mexico — largely the result of decades of bad jokes about "Montezuma's revenge." However, most health problems tourists encounter in Mexico are self-induced. If you take in too much sun, too many margaritas, and too many enchiladas within 24 hours of your arrival, don't blame the water if you get sick.

La Turista, or traveler's diarrhea, can involve fever, nausea, and vomiting as well as the runs. To help prevent La Turista, do the following:

- ✔ Get enough sleep.

- ✔ Don't overdo the sun.

- ✔ Drink only purified water. In addition to drinking bottled water, that means sticking with tea, coffee, and other beverages made with boiled water. Avoid ice, which may be made with nonpurified water; however, in most resort restaurants and hotels, both water and ice are perfectly safe.

- ✔ Drink plenty of bottled water to avoid dehydration.

- ✔ Choose your food carefully. Avoid street food (as in vendors with little carts), salads, uncooked vegetables, unpasteurized milk or milk products, and undercooked meat, fish, or shellfish.

- ✔ Wash your hands often.

If you get sick, don't panic. Medical services are generally good in Mexico. Most major hotels have English-speaking doctors on 24-hour call, or know how to contact one for you. Even the smaller hotels should be able to find someone to treat you quickly

Renting a Car in Mexico

You don't need to rent a car in Mexico. Macho drivers — and there are many, many of them on the road — disdain such things as traffic lights, stop signs, speed limits, and anyone who gets in their way. In addition, there are no cattle guards and few barbed-wire fences to contain farm animals. If you hit a cow, goat, or other cash-producing creature, you can expect to pay a hefty sum to compensate its owner. Moreover, Napoleonic code dictates that you're guilty before proven innocent in case of an accident — which means that if you're on a federal road or the pileup is sufficiently serious, you can be thrown in jail along with the other driver while blame is being assigned. Finally, in most of the resorts, buses and cabs are plentiful, and far cheaper, so there's absolutely no reason to subject yourself to this kind of road stress.

If you want to take a side trip from one of the beach towns, you can either book a package tour through your hotel's tour desk or a tour operator recommended by your hotel, or take a first class bus; they're cushy and air-conditioned and not particularly expensive. Trains on the other hand, have gotten not only run down, but increasingly dangerous. Don't get on the wrong track by riding the rails.

Note: We'd rather just say don't rent a car period. We simply wouldn't recommend it for anyone at this juncture.

Also, you can't fall back on your U.S. credit card insurance once you're out of the country. Mexican insurance, which adds about $20 to the rental car price per day, is mandatory. You wouldn't want to be without it, anyway. If you get into an accident, your insurance company representative is your ticket out of the pokey, should it come to that.

Playing It Safe

For the most part, you needn't worry about bodily harm in the Mexican beach resorts. The crime rate in Mexico isn't nearly as high as it is in the United States, and it's only logical that towns where tourism is the cash cow do everything possible to protect that resource, including ensuring the security of their visitors. Tourist police patrol the main drags in most of the resorts.

On the other hand, tourists are prime targets for pickpockets wherever they go, and that holds true in Mexico. You're especially vulnerable when you're in crowded places like markets. Expensive jewelry (don't wear it!) and big cameras make you particularly attractive to thieves.

Carry any credit cards and cash you need in a money bag strapped securely to your person. Use your hotel safe to stash your jewelry, passport, tourist card, extra credit cards, cash, and return plane tickets. Don't forget to lock the door to your patio when you leave your hotel room to go down to the beach.

Use common sense and don't do anything you wouldn't do at home — like wandering off into dark alleys or unpopulated streets late at night. Strolling along dark, deserted beaches, especially if you've been drinking, is not the smartest plan, either.

Fast Facts: Mexico

ATMs

Some ATMs belong to Cirrus, Plus, and NYCE systems that enable travelers to access their accounts while in Mexico. However, people depending on ATMs for all their travel money may experience difficulty traveling off the beaten path where ATMs are not available.

Banks

Bank hours are generally Monday through Thursday from 9 a.m. to 3 p.m. and Friday 9 a.m. to 5 p.m. A handful have Saturday hours (9 a.m. to noon). Plan to purchase pesos ahead of weekends and Mexican holidays when banks are closed. Banks don't cash personal checks.

Credit Cards

Major credit cards (primarily MasterCard and Visa) are welcome at many establishments. However, most American Express offices cash personal checks for cardholders at their offices located throughout Mexico. Travelers' checks can be cashed into pesos in many establishments, with proper identification. But it may be difficult to use them in small towns or any place without banking facilities nearby.

Currency Exchange

Mexican coins come in denominations of 5, 10, 20, and 50 centavos and 1, 2, 5, 10, and 20 pesos; bills come in denominations of 20, 50, 100, 200, and 500 pesos.

Enter Mexico with at least the equivalent of $100 U.S. in pesos obtained at your bank or an international airport. Once in Mexico, currency can be exchanged at banks or *casas de cambio* (exchange houses).

Acceptance of U.S. dollars is not uncommon, although change may arrive in pesos. Always travel with at least enough pesos to cover travel for the day since gas stations only accept pesos, as do most market or craft vendors. Check www.xe.net/currency for the exchange rate before you go.

Doctors

English-speaking doctors are usually on call at most hotels.

Electricity

The voltage in Mexico is 110, same as in the United States. If you have three-pronged appliances, however, you need an adapter. The outlets in most hotel rooms have only two slots, and in some older hotels, the plugs with one larger prong won't fit.

Embassies and Consular Services

The U.S. Embassy is located in Mexico City at Paseo de la Reforma 305 (☎ 5209-9100).

It is open weekdays 9 a.m. to 2 p.m. and 3 to 5 p.m. and closed for U.S. and Mexican holidays; however, a duty officer is always on call. The Canadian Embassy is located at Schiller 529 (☎ 5724-7900). It is open weekdays 9 a.m. to 1 p.m. and 2 to 5 p.m. and closed for Canadian and Mexican holidays. There are Consular Offices or Consular Agencies in most main tourist and business cities. A complete list of U.S. and international embassies and consulates is on the Internet at www.safemexico.com.

Emergencies

For a major medical emergency, jet evacuation services are available, including Air Ambulance America of Mexico (from Mexico dial ☎ 001-880-222-3564) and Air Evac (offices in Mexico City and San Diego call ☎ 619-278-3822). A 24-hour tourist helpline is at ☎ 800-903-9200.

Information

The Mexico Hotline (☎ 800-44-MEXICO; Internet: www.visitmexico.com) is a good source for general information, including brochures and answers to the most commonly asked questions. A fax machine nets you the Fax-Me Mexico line operated by the Mexican Ministry of Tourism (☎ 541-385-9282), which has information on more than 100 topics, from general tips about food to specific information about various destinations, including all the beach resorts. The best Web site by far for both general and specific information about Mexico is www.mexonline.com. For more information about Puerto Vallarta, call ☎ 888-384-6822 or 52-322-4-11-75; Fax: 52-322-4-09-15; Internet: www.puertovallarta.net.

Language

Spanish is the official language. English is spoken in resort areas, but locals greatly appreciate even a minimal effort to speak their language.

Laws

The drug laws here are, in a word, harsh. Unless you want to start your new life together in an unpleasant, confined space — and not likely in the same one, either — don't even think about buying or possessing illegal drugs in Mexico.

You can smoke Cuban cigars while in Mexico, but be advised that it is illegal to bring them back to the United States with you.

Maps

Widely available at hotels and from tour operators.

Newspapers/Magazines

English-language newspapers are widely sold in major cities.

Pharmacies

Mexico has an abundant number of pharmacies (*farmacias*) that dispense prescription drugs (often without prescriptions) at a fraction of the cost back home.

Post Office

Don't use the mail for anything important. Courier services such as Mexpost (which is a branch of the Mexican Post Office), Federal Express, DHL, UPS, and others operate throughout Mexico. Mail acceptance services such as Mail Boxes Etc. are also available. In addition, Internet centers or cyber cafes are increasingly found throughout the country.

Safety

Normal travel safety precautions are always necessary — the same ones used traveling anywhere in the world: Carry money inside clothing; keep your eye on your possessions at all times; don't leave valuables in plain view in vehicles; don't be alone on empty beaches; and don't buy or use illegal drugs. For bus travel use only buses that run on toll highways during daylight hours. Consult www.safemexico.com and the U.S. State Department site at www.travel.state. gov/mexico.html for safety and travel tips.

Taxes

The 15 percent IVA tax on goods and services in Mexico (10 percent in Cancún, Cozumel, and Los Cabos) is usually included in the posted price.

Telephones

Most public telephones require debit phone cards, which can be purchased at newsstands or convenience stores. For calls beyond Mexico, calling collect saves considerably on the cost of the call. Calling long distance from hotels is very expensive.

Public phones marked "Ladatel" are the best to use for long-distance calls. In addition there are special streetside businesses set up for long-distance calling; they are usually marked "Caseta de Larga Distancia" (long-distance telephone booth). Casetas have several private booths and a clerk who makes and times the call, directs you to a booth, and collects the money. Caseta offices usually offer fax service, and some have Internet service. They are also located at most bus stations in major tourist or business locales. These, along with Ladatel phones, are the least expensive way to phone home or even within Mexico. Avoid coin-operated wall phones that are prohibitively expensive.

Also accessible is toll-free calling assistance provided by major U.S. telephone companies, such as AT&T, Sprint, MCI, and Bell Canada to their card holders.

Dial 090 to make a long-distance call from Mexico or an international call from a public phone. To dial the U.S. directly, dial 001 plus the area code plus the phone number. To dial directly within Mexico, dial 01 plus the area code plus the phone number. To call Mexico, the number and area code must be preceded by 011 plus the country code, which for Mexico is 52, plus the area code and number.

Time Zones

Los Cabos is on Mountain Standard Time, but the other beach resorts are all on Central Standard Time. Mexico observes Daylight Savings Time.

Tipping

Most service employees in Mexico count on tips to survive — especially restaurant wait staff and bellhops. Tip 50 cents to $1 a bag. Leave 10 to 20 percent depending on the level of service during your meal. It isn't customary to tip taxi drivers unless they have given you a tour.

Water

Bottled water is readily available at local pharmacies, corner groceries, and at many hotels. Luxury hotels often have purified tap water.

Part VI
Walt Disney World and Orlando

The 5th Wave   By Rich Tennant

"The hotel said they were giving us the 'Indiana Jones' suite."

In this part . . .

Disneymoon? Why not? You've been sharing dreams with Minnie and Mickey, Cinderella and Prince Charming, even Chip 'n' Dale for years. Perhaps it's only natural that you want to begin your own fairy tale in their backyard.

You won't be alone. Every year, thousands of couples spend their first days as husband and wife in Orlando, walking hand in hand through Walt Disney World, wishing at enchanted fountains, toasting each other with champagne and bubble baths. Walt's kingdom even has a state-of-the-art, nondenominational wedding chapel for those who want to say their vows within eyesight of a fantasy castle. P.S. The glass slippers are optional.

Chapter 26

Disney World's and Orlando's Top Accommodations

By David Swanson

- -

In This Chapter

▶ Choosing the best area to stay

▶ Finding the perfect accommodations

- -

*Y*ou know the scene: the alley-side of a sidewalk trattoria, illuminated by a full moon. The characters are benevolent waiters, a pair of mismatched canine lovers. Add a little wine, a little song, and a long string of spaghetti. Get the point? Lady, her tramp, and the creativity of Walt Disney probably have been a part of your romantic imaginings since you were a child. And Walt Disney World, in central Florida, is where these fantasies are lived out, larger than life, 365 days a year.

 You can exchange vows or celebrate newly-wedded bliss virtually anywhere in Uncle Walt's empire. Cinderella Castle and Disney's Grand Floridian Resort and Spa are the backdrop for thousands of storybook beginnings. The well-oiled Disney machine can deliver on almost any flight of fancy you dream up — as simple as chocolate covered strawberries before bed, or as grand as a gleaming white coach and horses — just come with a ready wallet. But Disney's major competitor, Universal Orlando, has grown to encompass two theme parks, a nighttime entertainment complex, and a pair of hot new hotels. Wooing wedding-and-honeymoon guests is part of their agenda, too.

If you're still a kid or love being around them, Orlando is a great place to visit. If you're the other sort, you may want to find a more suitable honeymoon destination. The per capita kid population of Orlando is nearly double anywhere else on the planet. All of the kids are wired — and you and yours may soon be, too, because you're about to find Mickey to the left of you; Minnie to the right of you; Cat in the Hat and the Hulk coaster in between.

Walt Disney World is scattered across 30,500 acres — about twice the size of Manhattan Island. When you add Universal Studios, SeaWorld, and the lesser knowns (70-something at last count) — well, you have so many tourist attractions to choose from that it can be difficult to decide what to do. You can't do it all in a week, or even two. And roller coasters aren't the only things that make heads spin at WDW — so do all the choices.

There's no shortage of activities and attractions to keep your days and nights filled. Of course, theme parks top the agenda — Disney has four major parks that require a full day to tour, plus a handful of smaller enticements; Universal has a pair of big parks; and SeaWorld has added a noteworthy (and romantic) new attraction, Discovery Cove, heralding a swim with a dolphin. Orlando's also-rans are numerous, but more suited to repeat visitors and families than couples looking for a special escape. But, there's more to Orlando than theme parks. Superb golf (99 holes of championship tees in WDW alone), a wealth of watersports, shopping, and nightclubs can be part of the agenda.

Is cost a concern? A budget honeymoon is not hard to accomplish in Orlando, though carefree gestures and spur-of-the-moment notions can hide behind careful planning ahead of your trip. Your best bet is to stay at one of the **"All-Star" resorts** on Disney property or, for better value, lodge off Mickey's turf at a neighboring hotel and explore Orlando in a rental car. By staying off-property you have better access to a range of less expensive dining and entertainment. And wherever you land, by organizing an itinerary before you arrive, you can buy the amount of pricey theme park admissions that you need, rather than resorting to less cost-effective "all-inclusive" options. With stealth preparation, you can keep your honeymoon to under $250 per day for two (including lodging, dining, sightseeing and admissions; excluding airfare and souvenirs).

The sky's the limit? Disney is more than happy to show you how to blow the bank on a stupendous honeymoon, replete with gold-plated frills. For the full-court treatment, check in to Disney's best hotel, the **Grand Floridian,** where theme parks may take a back seat to several superb restaurants, a sumptuous spa, and a smashing new beachside pool. Or, investigate one of the deluxe suites available at WDW's other resorts (especially the lavish Presidential Suites at the Wilderness Lodge and the Yacht Club Resort — the berths Michael Eisner (the CEO of Disney) stays at when he needs face time with the head mouse). And don't forget that a handful of accommodations off-property compete, perk-for-perk, quite admirably with Disney's finest.

Of course, many of us aim for something in between these extremes, and here the choices are endless. Because Orlando is one of the largest hotel markets in the world — more than 100,000 rooms and counting — the competition keeps room rates reasonable for most of the year, but you're excused for being a little overwhelmed by the options.

To help you narrow the vast choices, we weeded out dozens of hotels that don't meet at least one of our two basic criteria for this book: romance-inducing or good value.

Figuring Out Where You Want to Stay

You have two basic choices to deal with up front: stay on Disney property, or honeymoon off-property. Obviously, the main advantage of staying off-property is budgetary. But if you don't want a mouse ruling your days, nights, and everything in between, you also may seriously consider lodging in environs where the Disney experience is turned down a few notches.

 Although many of the off-property hotels advertise free transportation to the major theme parks, it may be one scheduled bus in the morning, and a return trip in the afternoon, putting a crimp in your touring plans (the Disney transportation system provides buses, boats, and Monorails between their resorts and parks every 15 to 25 minutes). When making reservation inquiries, find out exactly how comprehensive the hotel's service is to the attractions you want to visit. If you really hope to conquer the World during your honeymoon, or if your visit is limited to a few days, you may find some of the savings of staying off-property eaten up by renting a car.

Walt Disney World: Mickey at your doorstep

The empire, **Walt Disney World,** its big and little parks, resorts, restaurants, and assorted trimmings aren't in Orlando. They sprawl southwest of the city, off I-4. Disney's resorts, theme parks, and entertainment areas are linked by a huge transportation system, free to guests (parking at the parks is also free; $6 for non-guests). But stay here and learn that convenience has a price. The accommodations are up to double the rates in neighboring Kissimmee. On the other hand, WDW has almost anything you may need in a compressed area, and staying at the Disney resorts has one other tangible benefit: early admission to the theme parks, before the unwashed masses swarm in. In sum, no other part of Orlando can match this landing zone for nonstop fun, pulsating clubs, candlelight dinners, and your favorite, fuzzy characters. It really is where dreams come true . . . for a little while and a price.

Lake Buena Vista: The World within reach

The area termed **Lake Buena Vista** is an ill-defined zone, some of which is actually on Disney's land; the rest is a next-door neighbor that sprang up around one of the World's three main entrances. Lake Buena Vista is where the so-called "official" (yet not Disney-owned or -managed) hotels are located, as well as a number of resorts with no connection to WDW.

The area is close (a five-minute drive) to Downtown Disney and Pleasure Island, which are some of the best places to shop or take in the nightlife. The "official" hotels are somewhat overpriced, but their just-off-property prices are more modest, and the pace is substantially calmer. The Disney theme parks and SeaWorld are a 10 to 15 minute drive, while Universal is a little farther.

Kissimmee: Canoodle behind the bargains

The burg of **Kissimmee** runs along U.S. 192 and is actually closer to WDW than Orlando is, and a cheaper base than other areas. But some find the 15-mile-long, two-block-wide strip of low-budget motels, souvenir shops, and fast-food joints a turn-off. Still, fervid honeymooners may be so consumed with each other that they overlook the black-velvet Elvises on the walls (okay, we may be overstating the tack-factor a bit, here). Kissimmee has a lot of inexpensive restaurants — fast fooderies, buffeterias, and all-you-can-eateries, which help stretch your dollars. The Disney parks are a 5 to 10 minute drive from the intersection known as "Maingate," SeaWorld is 15 to 20 minutes, and Universal requires a 20 to 30 minute commute.

International Drive: Touristo central

On **International Drive,** a ten-mile stretch of road northeast of the Disney parks, are SeaWorld and Universal, as well as a wealth of smaller attractions (like Ripley's Believe it or Not and miniature golf), lodging, restaurants, and shops. Owing to sheer quantity, bed bargains are common. The north end is cluttered with T-shirt shacks and burger barns; the south is less developed. In between the land is a bit more open and green, with semi-private spots for hand-holding, but take notice that traffic in the central portion of I-Drive can be a bear. Universal and SeaWorld are a 5 to 15 minute drive (a few hotels are within walking distance of these parks); the Disney parks are 15 to 25 minutes.

Disney avails little in the way of discounts or other incentives. But if you plan to tour much of Orlando outside The Wonderful World, it pays to check in with the **Orlando/Orange County Convention and Visitors Bureau.** They maintain a walk-in location at 8723 International Drive, open daily 8 a.m. to 7 p.m., and some attraction tickets are sold at a discount. They can mail a comprehensive visitor info packet on request; call ☎ **407-363-5872,** or visit their Web site at www.orlandoinfo.com.

Note: We list rack rates for a standard (non-suite) room — that is, the regular season price you pay without discounts. Be sure to add 11 percent local tax to these rates. Discounts are not hard to find during low season, most commonly the non-holiday periods between November and mid-February. The Disney Resorts charge higher rates during the Christmas holidays and for a few weeks leading up to Easter.

Finding a Honeymoon Hotel in Disney World

Although more than 25,000 rooms exist in WDW alone, we list only half in this book — the ones that are either certifiably passion fostering, or a good value. Disney offers other accommodations worth checking out, from a pleasant, clean campground to villas with full kitchens.

Phone numbers for the Disney resort listings are as follows: Disney's main reservation line ☎ **407-934-7639** followed by the front desk for the specific hotel. There is one Web site for all the Disney hotels, www. asp.disney.go.com/disneyworld/db/seetheworld/resorts/ index.asp, or call Disney's central reservation number for brochures ☎ **407-934-7639**.

The company maintains a separate number and Web site for wedding- and honeymoon-related packages — ☎ **800-370-6009**; Internet: www.disneyhoneymoons.com.

The rack rates listed in this chapter are in U.S. dollars and are for a standard double room during high season (mid-December to mid-April), unless otherwise noted.

Please refer to the Introduction of *Honeymoon Vacations For Dummies* for an explanation of our price categories.

Disney's All-Star Sports, Music and Movie Resorts

$$ **Walt Disney World**

If you insist on staying on Disney property and are on a tight budget — an iffy combo, even in low season — you can't beat the All-Star rates. This trio of huge, motel-like properties caters to lots of families, rooms are Disney's smallest (260 square feet), and dining options are limited to less-than-romantic food courts. But you can request a king-size bed, and then console your mate with the notion that you are positioned within reach of the Mickey Magic. Then scoot off to more romantic corners of the World. A cheap room at WDW is nothing to sniff at, and you still get the other perks offered to Disney Resorts guests: free parking and transportation, early admission privileges, and so on. Note, however, that no theme parks or full-service restaurants are next door, so plan on spending more time on the (frequent) Disney bus system to and from the All-Stars than with our other recommendations.

Disney's Parks

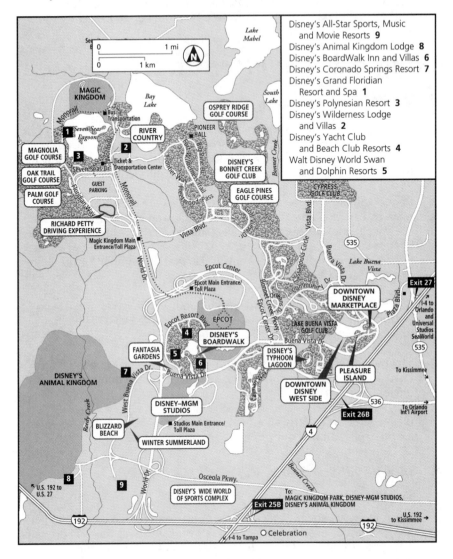

Disney's All-Star Sports, Music
and Movie Resorts **9**
Disney's Animal Kingdom Lodge **8**
Disney's BoardWalk Inn and Villas **6**
Disney's Coronado Springs Resort **7**
Disney's Grand Floridian
Resort and Spa **1**
Disney's Polynesian Resort **3**
Disney's Wilderness Lodge
and Villas **2**
Disney's Yacht Club
and Beach Club Resorts **4**
Walt Disney World Swan
and Dolphin Resorts **5**

The three 1,920-room resorts are colorful and theme-oriented, accented by huge icons. One is dedicated to sports lovers and has three-story football symbols adorning one building (huge helmets protect stairwells from the rain); other sports themes are baseball, basketball, tennis, and surfing. The All-Star Music tributes jazz, country, and rock (nope — lush operas aren't a part of Disney's musical world), while the All-Star Movies has Goliath-sized dalmations and Love Bugs. Each of the complexes has a large theme pool.

Buena Vista Dr. ☎ *407-934-7639* or *407-939-5000 (Sports), 407-939-6000 (Music), 407-939-7000 (Movies). Fax: 407-939-7333 (Sports), 407-939-7222 (Music), 407-939-7111 (Movies). 1,920 units at each resort. Rack rates: $77-$99 double. AE, DC, DISC, MC, V.*

Disney's Animal Kingdom Lodge

$$$$ **Walt Disney World**

Disney's newest and perhaps most innovative resort, isinspired by both the wildlife viewing and local culture experienced at African safari lodges. Of course, Disney does this on a huge scale (about 100 times the size of most game lodges), but the effect is still pretty striking. The key selling point is 33 acres of naturalistic savannah brimming with free-roaming animals like giraffe and sacred ibis.

The soaring lobby has a mud fireplace and a bridge spanning its width. Behind the hotel is an elevated *kopje*, or rock outcrop, that provides a panorama of animals and streams. The room wings extend from the lobby in a giant, six-story, horseshoe-shaped structure that encircles the savannah. The guest rooms are adorned in jewel tones and feature hand-carved furnishings that embellish the safari theme; although most rooms overlook the savannah, note that the cheapest ones have a pool or parking lot view. Regular suites have a parlor, wet bar, generous marble bathrooms, and concierge service, while the Royal Assante Suite is a palatial 2,115 square feet, with fireplace, vaulted thatch ceiling, hot tubs, and an extended balcony.

The swimming pool is designed to look like an oasis, and at night, lighting effects and a campfire creates a romantic aura. Use the Zahanti Fitness Center for $12 per day (massage treatments available), and shop in the Zawadi Marketplace for authentic African crafts. The lodge has three restaurants, featuring dazzling multicultural dining and a winelist showcasing South-African varieties. Although the Animal Kingdom park is nearby, a bus is still necessary to reach this and the other theme parks.

2901 Osceola Pkwy. ☎ 407-934-7639 or 407-938-3000. Fax: 407-938-7102. 1,293 units. Rack rates: $199-$435 double, $600-$2,140 suite. AE, DC, DISC, MC, V.

Disney's BoardWalk Inn and Villas

$$$$$ **Walt Disney World**

More than any other Disney resort, the BoardWalk appeals to couples looking for a sliver of yesterday. Night owls appreciate the entertainment options, the location (within walking distance of both Epcot and the Disney-MGM Studios) is in the center of WDW, and the family element is more subdued than at most other Disney resorts.

Buying a Disney honeymoon package

Although the various components and prices evolve regularly, you can purchase anything from a basic honeymoon to a lavish, anything-goes package. Disney's Honeymoon Escape — the least expensive sold by the Mouse — starts at $1,138 per couple for a three-night stay at one of the All-Star resorts and includes the following:

✔ An Ultimate Park-Hopper ticket — unlimited in-and-out privileges at the Disney theme parks during your stay

✔ Personalized pre-arrival planning — a Disney rep calls before your honeymoon to help arrange meal reservations, flowers, and so on

✔ A pair of commemorative trading pins

✔ A pair of his-and-her commemorative watches

✔ Choice of one of three special options: a professional photo session; a couples-only massage treatment; or dinner at one of Disney's fine dining venues, including a bottle of wine

Before signing up for a package, evaluate it against the cost of purchasing the various elements individually to make sure that you assemble exactly the honeymoon you want. Although most of the items in cluded in the packages are difficult to value individually, if you do the math, this (and other Disney packages) is not a good deal — particularly considering that the hotel room by itself is priced less than $100 a night. Besides, if commemorative watches aren't your style, why pay for them?

A 1920s-era seaside resort is the theme, and the hotel overlooks a village green on one side and a lagoon on the other. The bed-and-breakfast style rooms (mismatched furniture and the like) are larger than in the moderate-priced Disney resorts, with rich cherry wood furnishings, two queen-size beds, a mid-size bathroom, a balcony or patio, and a ceiling fan. There's a concierge level for added amenities like snacks and a cocktail hour, plus reservations assistance. Villas are available, but preferable accommodations for honeymooners are the sweet, two-story Garden Suites, which overlook a tiny private garden (some even have views of the nightly Epcot fireworks).

Other amenities include three pools (one with a wooden roller-coaster slide), a free daily newspaper, a health club (extra $12 per day), and recreational options like tennis, bass fishing, and surry rental. The property lines a quarter-mile long boardwalk that offers shops, several good restaurants, and street performers, which means there's plenty to do after the sun goes down. A couple dozen other dining options are within strolling distance at the neighboring Yacht/Beach and Swan/Dolphin hotels. Note that rooms overlooking the boardwalk have the best views, but can be a little noisier at night thanks to the action below. Transportation is via boat or on foot to Epcot and the Disney-MGM Studios, and on frequent buses to other corners of the World.

2201 N. Epcot Resorts Blvd. ☎ 407-934-7639 or 407-939-5100. Fax: 407-939-5150. 910 units. Rack rates: $279-$460 double, Garden Suites $535-$590, other suites $1,035-$1,820. AE, DC, DISC, MC, V.

Disney's Coronado Springs Resort

$$$ Walt Disney World

Though the rooms aren't cheap, Coronado Springs is one of Disney's three moderately priced hotels, and it offers good value amid an American Southwest theme. It has a slightly upscale feel, thanks in part to the 95,000-square-foot convention center on the premises, but nametag types aren't the only ones using the resort. Unlike the All-Stars, a porter escorts you and your bags to the room. Rooms are housed in four- and five-story hacienda-style buildings with terra cotta tile roofs and palm shaded courtyards. Some face the 15-acre Golden Lake (the better views are more expensive). The room layouts are all pretty much the same, but the decor varies slightly between each of three sections of the resort; amenities include in-room coffeemakers, hairdryers, and modem ports. Ninety-nine rooms are specially designed for travelers with disabilities.

Couples that like to splash about delight in the Mayan temple theme main pool. Dining options include the Pepper Market food court and the Maya Grill, both of which predominantly serve Mexican food. The only real drawback to staying at Coronado Springs is that you may feel a bit isolated: The Animal Kingdom and Blizzard Beach are less than five minutes away, but otherwise dining and shopping is a bit of a trek using the Disney transportation system.

1000 Buena Vista Dr. ☎ 407-934-7639 or 407-939-1000. Fax: 407-939-1003. 1,967 units. Rack rates: $129-$164 double, $258-$940 suite. AE, DC, DISC, MC, V.

Disney's Grand Floridian Resort and Spa

$$$$$ Walt Disney World

You won't find a more luxurious Orlando address than this 40-acre Great Gatsby-era fantasy located on the shores of the Seven Seas Lagoon and modeled after Floridian coastal resorts. As pricey as it is plush, the Grand Floidian is WDW's upper-crust flagship and a great choice for couples who aren't on a tight budget. The opulent, five-story domed lobby hosts afternoon teas accompanied by live piano; in the evening an orchestra plays big-band tunes. A birdcage elevator serves the second floor where excellent restaurants are located.

The guest rooms are luxurious in their detail, using warm Victorian wood trim and floral wallpaper with Disney elements discretely interwoven. Yet the Grand Floridian is not so prim and proper as to be intimidating — terry-cloth robes and whirlpools are standard equipment. If the sky's the limit, book the two-bedroom Roosevelt Suite — appointed with hardwood floors (bring your own bear skin), a white piano, ten-foot ceilings, and five private balconies, one of which looks out over Cinderella Castle. For Disney fanatics, the Walt and Roy O. Disney suites reflect and tribute the company's founding brothers. Honeymoon rooms on the Royal Palm Club level are to themselves and more reasonably priced. Each has a king-size bed, sitting area, and small whirlpool tub. Better still — they're off limits to kids, have their own concierge desk, and offer a complete buffet five times a day (mind-altering beverages included).

The Grand Floridian has Disney's best selection of dining options, ranging from a straightforward food court to the posh Victoria & Albert, with three restaurants in between. There is also a sumptuous spa facility, fitness center, and the new pool is Disney's classiest, with a zero-entry edge that melts into the sand beach that surrounds it, and featuring cabanas with computer hook-ups. The Palm, Magnolia, and nine-hole Oak Trail golf courses are virtually across the street. The resort is located on the Monorail line that serves Magic Kingdom and Epcot, as well as dining at the Polynesian and Contemporary resorts. Frequent bus service connects the resort to the other parks and Downtown Disney. If you're planning a Disney wedding, note that the wedding pavilion is located next door.

4401 Floridian Way. ☎ *407-934-7639 or 407-824-3000. Fax: 407-824-3186. 901 units. Rack rates: $314-$600 double, $810-$1,960 suite. AE, DC, DISC, MC, V.*

Disney's Polynesian Resort

$$$$$ Walt Disney World

Opened just a few months after the Magic Kingdom in 1971, and after a late-90s spruce-up, the Polynesian is still a great place to stay. It offers the convenience of Monorail access to the Magic Kingdom, Epcot, and the dining at two neighboring resorts, combined with the privacy of spread-out accommodations that seem more off the beaten path than they really are. The resort does a good job of creating a lush island ambiance — the lobby is a virtual rainforest of tropical plants.

The standard rooms are among the largest on Disney property, and most have balconies or patios — a number overlook the Seven Seas Lagoon with Cinderella Castle sparkling in the distance. Mini canopies hang above the beds, and bamboo and rattan furnishings build on the island feel. Some rooms also have concierge amenities. Watersports are plentiful down on the lake, and you can lounge on the white-sand beach (though swimming is not allowed in the lake); the newly revamped tropical pool has a slide and waterfall wrapped around the flanks of a volcano. The Polynesian also has Disney's best child care facility, the Neverland Club, a cool babysitting service that allows parents to have a night on the town. 45 holes of golf are just across the street, and the Monorail buzzes through the lobby every few minutes to whisk you to Magic Kingdom, Epcot, or nearby resorts; there's also boat service to Magic Kingdom, plus buses to other corners of the World.

1600 Seven Seas Dr. ☎ *407-934-7639 or 407-824-2000. Fax: 407-824-3174. 853 units. Rack rates: $289-$490 double, $640-$2,015 suite. AE, DC, DISC, MC, V.*

Disney's Wilderness Lodge and Villas

$$$$ Walt Disney World

Here's an option for those who like the real outdoors but would rather stay indoors than rough it in a tent. The Wilderness Lodge is patterened after a rustic national park lodge, with a soaring eight-story lobby comprised of immense timber beams and a towering stone fireplace. A hot spring bubbles inside the lobby, and its stream meanders outside to a waterfall that leads to the boulder-lined swimming pool, seemingly excavated from the rocks. Another hot spring serves as the hot tub, and nearby is a geyser that erupts every hour. The main restaurant, Artist Point, is styled with subtle Frank Lloyd Wright accents.

The rooms are modest in size for a resort of this price, but they have appealing, Mission-style decor. Many have bunk beds (though these probably aren't preferable for honeymooners); all have patios or balconies overlooking the lake, woods, or a nearby meadow. A concierge floor is available. But for the most romantic rooms, check into one of the Presidential suites, named Yosemite and Yellowstone. A new building next door offers condo-style villas — that are quieter and more private, and more expensive — as well as the resort's fitness center and massage rooms.

 In relation to occupancy, this resort is perhaps Disney's most popular, particularly for families with children (the Cubs Den is a cool, western-themed activity center for kids age 4 to 12). But pleasant trails lead into the surrounding forest where the moppet factor is almost nil; horseback riding is nearby. The Magic Kingdom is reached via short boat ride, the other theme parks are via bus; getting to other resort dining options is a little more involved.

901 W. Timberline Dr. ☎ 407-934-7639 or 407-824-3200. Fax: 407-824-3232. 728 units. Rack rates: $189-$385 double, $620-$790 suite. AE, DC, DISC, MC, V.

Disney's Yacht Club and Beach Club Resorts

$$$$$ Walt Disney World

This pair of five-story resorts — joined at the shoulder, but with separate front desks and entrances — goes for the New England ambiance. They are situated on a 25-acre lake across from the BoardWalk complex. Yacht is vaguely more sophisticated, resembling a turn-of-the-century boating club, with dark hues of blue, red, and brown, while Beach has the feel of a seaside beach resort and a softer color scheme. Honey-mooners tilt slightly in favor of the Yacht, which draws fewer Mouseketeers in favor of conventioneers, plus it has a concierege level. The room decor here is nautical, with bathroom mirrors framed in brass portholes and head-boards shaped like a ship's wheel. On the Beach side, the Nantucket-style setting is charming, but if you like a balcony, be sure to ask for a room with a "full" one (many of the rooms have balconies that aren't even big enough for a chair). There is a variety of suites at both hotels; including a Presidential Suite on the Yacht side that is decorated in Chinoiserie, including Ming vases.

Both hotels share Disney's most dazzling pool, Stormalong Bay, though its network of channels, grottos, and whirlpools is filled with kids at most hours (check out the spiffy slide through the fallen mast of a shipwreck); each side also has a "quiet" pool. There's a well-appointed Ship Shape Health Club ($12 per day), croquet, volleyball, tennis, and marina. Several good eateries (including the Mouse's best steakhouse and an ice cream parlor) plus others and evening entertainment are a short walk away at the BoardWalk and Swan/Dolphin. Epcot and the Disney-MGM Studios are reached via bus or boatride, while buses connect guests to the other parks.

Epcot Resorts Blvd. ☎ *407-934-7639 or 407-934-7000 (Yacht), 407-934-8000. Fax: 407-934-3450 (Yacht), 407-934-3850 (Beach). 630 units (Yacht) and 583 units (Beach). Rack rates: $279-$500 double, $490-$1,625 suite. AE, DC, DISC, MC, V.*

Walt Disney World Swan and Dolphin Resorts

$$$$$ Walt Disney World

Though not technically Disney-managed, these monolithic sibling resorts are connected by a canopied walkway, were designed (architect: Michael Graves) and built at the same time, and share an over-the-top personality that is either a visual treat or a Vegas-meets-Florida-on-acid nightmare, depending on your personal outlook. Located next to the BoardWalk and Yacht/Beach resorts, they are managed by Westin and Sheraton but offer pretty much all the benefits availed by the real Disney hotels (free transportation, early theme park admission, and so on) — the staff is even Disney trained. They cater primarily to the convention crowd and are a bit overpriced, but deals crop up between nametag invasions, and the resorts are, well . . . memorable.

The 12-story Swan is the smaller, marginally more intimate of the duo, while the 27-story, pyramidal Dolphin towers over every other point within WDW. The rooms are well appointed if a tad snug for the price, and about half have small balconies. The hotels share a vast tropical pool with waterfalls and a slide, plus a near-Olympic size lap pool, a health club and exercise room, volleyball and tennis courts, a wealth of restaurants and, in addition to 24-hour room service, one of the only 24-hour eateries in WDW. Epcot and the Disney-MGM Studios are a ten-minute boat ride or walk; the other kingdoms are ten minutes away by bus. Disney's Fantasia Gardens miniature golf is just across the street.

Epcot Resorts Blvd. ☎ *800-227-1500 or 407-934-3000 (Swan), 407-934-4000 (Dolphin). Fax: 407-934-4499 (Swan) and 407-934-4710 (Dolphin). Internet:* www. swandolphin.com. *758 units (Swan) and 1,509 units (Dolphin). Rack rates: $310-$490 double, $585-$3,100 suite. AE, CB, DC, DISC, JCB, MC, V.*

Choosing a Honeymoon Hotel in Orlando

The magic factor is still present at a number of non-Disney accommodations — but for the most part, you need to supply the pixie dust. As a reminder, locations are categorized as follows: **Lake Buena Vista** includes the hotels located near the Downtown Disney entrance to WDW; **Kissimmee** represents hotels located on (or just off) U.S. 192, which runs east-west, immediately south of WDW; and **International Drive** covers the hotels located on or near this north-south corridor that starts northeast of Lake Buena Vista and contin-ues north to the Universal area.

The rack rates listed in this chapter are in U.S. dollars and are for a standard double room during high season (mid-December to mid-April), unless otherwise noted.

Please refer to the Introduction of *Honeymoon Vacations For Dummies* for an explanation of our price categories.

Celebration Hotel

$$$ **Kissimmee**

Located in the Disney-run housing development of Celebration, this hotel has a three-story wood frame design straight out of 1920s Florida. The lobby sets the tone with walnut hardwood floors, paddle ceiling fans, historic Orlando photos, and rustic bird cages — on each floor is a bowl of fresh fruit next to the elevator. All the rooms have ceiling fans, safes, hairdryers, and make-up mirrors. Most have views of the lake. There's a pool, hot tub, and a fitness center, and a short walk takes you to several good, moderately-priced restaurants as well as shops. An 18-hole golf course is nearby. The Romantic Celebrations package includes breakfast daily (in-room or at the Plantation Restaurant), a bottle of champagne, and free valet parking. Celebration is an offbeat, but appealing hideout offering free transportation to the Disney parks.

700 Bloom St., Celebration. ☎ *888-499-3800 or 407-566-6000. Fax: 407-566-1844. Internet:* www.celebrationhotel.com. *115 units. Rack rates: $155-$295 double, $360-$470 suite. The Romantic Celebrations package is $199 per night. AE, DC, DISC, MC, V.*

Doubletree Guest Suites

$$$ **Lake Buena Vista**

Doubletree Guest Suites, a seven-story, all-suite hotel, is as good a choice for couples who want a little extra room as it is for families. As an "Official"

WDW hotel — located on Mickey's turf — the Doubletree is about a half-mile from Downtown Disney. But unlike some of the other official hotels, staying here does avail early-admission into the parks (or you're allowed to practice sleeping in together), and the hotel has a shuttle to the four main parks. Each unit has a tiny kitchen with a microwave, coffeemaker, refrigerator, and wet bar that allows you to save on meals, if you choose. The resort has a pool and whirlpool, tennis courts, and a basic restaurant. Doubletree is a good place to rumple the covers, and there's a romance package which includes bubbly, a board game (yes, you read correctly!), breakfast, and an upgrade to an executive or lanai suite.

2305 Hotel Plaza Blvd., Lake Buena Vista. ☎ *800-222-8733 or 407-934-1000. Fax: 407-934-1015. 229 units. Internet:* www.doubletreeguestsuites.com. *Rack rates: $149-$199 double. Romance package: $158-$198 per night. AE, CB, DC, DISC, MC, V.*

Hard Rock Hotel

$$$$ **International Drive**

The latest addition to Orlando's theme-sleep empire is a California mission-style resort (think: "Hotel California") — a co-venture of Universal, Hard Rock Café, and Loews Hotels. The hotel is a hip, surprisingly beautiful hybrid of the Eagles album cover with that ambiance that makes the noisy Hard Rock restaurants popular. Encompassing a relatively compact 19 acres, the resort apes L.A. lovingly, with towering palms, pink stucco, and a sprawling pool (with underwater speakers, natch). Yes, rock 'n roll (and accompanying videos) blares away in every corner of the resort, 24 hours a day — great if you're the type who likes to have the radio tuned to an 80s rock station from dawn to dusk, and beyond. Others who like to switch stations here and there may feel boxed in.

The rooms are stylish and modern, in the fashion of the trendy W Hotels, with sleek white funishings, a minibar, coffeemaker, bathroom scale, and black-and-whote rock star photos. Very comfortable, and the piped-in music system has a volume control! The Hard Rock is home to two restaurants, two eye-popping bars, a business center, and a health club. And, of course, a retail store selling theme merchandise. As with the restaurants, classic rock memorabilia is showcased in the public areas throughout. The entrances to Universal, Islands of Adventure, and CityWalk are a five- to ten-minute walk, and your card key allows you charging privileges throughout Universal Orlando. If it was hard-rockin' music that brought you together, and a Mickey-free ambiance is what you're after, this may be just the spot to celebrate "I Did." Bonus: Stay here and you get to bypass the lines when touring Universal/Islands.

5800 Universal Blvd., Orlando. ☎ *800-232-7827 or 407-503-ROCK. Fax: 407-503-ROLL. Internet:* www.universalorlando.com. *650 rooms. Rack rates: $185-$345 double, $345-$1,500 suite. AE, DISC, MC, V.*

Orlando Hotel Neighborhoods

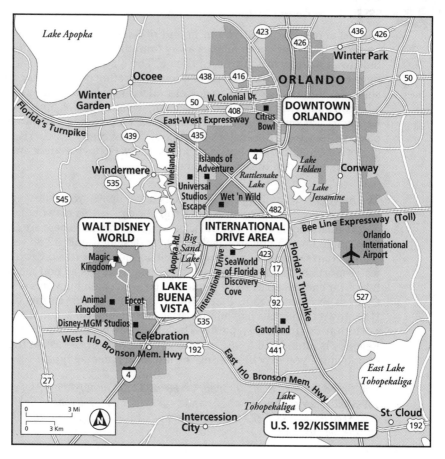

Hawthorn Suites

$$ International Drive

One of Orlando's better all-suite properties and located less than a mile from SeaWorld, Hawthorne Suites is a five-story complex surrounding an appealing pool. Individual units are a tad dark, but nicely furnished with green carpets and bedspreads. One-bedroom models have sitting areas, dining rooms, kitchens, a stereo system and VCR, and either two doubles or a king. There's a small exercise room and a pool area; rates include a continental breakfast. The Get Acquainted package promises two nights in a pool-view suite with a bottle of vino, cheese, and crackers; other packages throw in admission to SeaWorld.

6435 Westwood Blvd., Orlando. ☎ *800-527-1133 or 407-351-6600. Fax: 407-351-1977. E-mail:* hawthorno@aol.com. *Internet:* www.hawthorn.com. *150 units. Rack rates: $89-$165 double. Two-night Get Acquainted package: $179. AE, CB, DC, DISC, MC, V.*

Hyatt Regency Grand Cypress Resort

$$$$ Lake Buena Vista

A 1,500-acre resort destination in and of itself, a stay here offers the opportunity to park your fannies away from the crowds in a lush, super hideaway with a Florida tropics theme. The airy, 18-story tower has a huge atrium at its apex, with three wings projecting outward. The rooms sport a southern decor and are decorated with wicker furniture; all have a balcony and view of the lake, garden, or swimming pool. Spring for the Regency Club level and get cushy amenities, or, better, buy the Romance package and treat yourselves to chocolate covered strawberries and champagne nightly, and breakfast in bed daily. Honeymooners are automatically upgraded to Deluxe rooms.

The half-acre swimming pool is an oasis of channels, waterfalls, lagoons, slides, and grottos, all spanned by a rope bridge — this may be the most spectacular pool in central Florida. Other sports facilities here are equally tops, including 45 holes of Jack Nicklaus-designed golf, 12 all-weather tennis courts, horseback riding at a full service Equestrian Center, and watersports on the lake. Hemingway's restaurant has a good menu and tables far enough apart to be semi-private; at the ajoining Villas of Grand Cypress is the elegant Black Swan, another great eating choice. Downtown Disney is a five-minute drive, and the resort offers free transportation to the Disney parks. The only drawback is that the Hyatt Regency is often filled to the brim with convetioneers — ask at the time of booking if you may be sharing the site with nametag types.

One Grand Cypress Blvd., Orlando. ☎ *800-233-1234 or 407-239-1234. Fax: 407-239-3800. Internet:* www.hyattgrandcypress.com. *750 rooms. Rack rates: $209-$540 double, $395-$2,240 suite. Romance package: $245-$370. AE, CB, DISC, DC, CB, MC, V.*

Peabody Orlando

$$$$$ International Drive

Welcome to the digs of the famous Marching Mallards. Their home is just a waddle away from the thick of all the action I-Drive has to offer, including a plethora of secondary attractions, shopping, and restaurants. The real, live ducks troop to their luxury fountain each morning — no kidding! — through the lobby on a red carpet, accompanied by John Philip Sousa marching music. You don't have to be a guest to enjoy the fun — daily at 10:50 a.m. and 5 p.m. — but beware that these pampered pets have mean tempers.

Real guests are coddled just as royally at this posh, 27-story luxury landing. Located across the street from the local convention center, the Peabody is a spin-off of the classic Memphis original; as such, it caters to many business travelers, but honeymooners can expect red carpet treatment as well. The guest rooms, even the standard ones, are lavishly furnished and decorated in neutral tones of beige, brown, and rust. The suites are fabulous (and five times the size of standards), and the Peabody Club, a concierege level, occupies the top three floors. The hotel's ambiance, which extends to its two top-rated restaurants (plus a 24-hour diner) isn't duplicated anywhere else in Orlando. Combos play jazz and blues in the atrium lobby bar nightly, and al fresco jazz concerts take place on the fourth-floor recreation level in the spring and fall. Afternoon English tea is hosted here on weekdays, and sporting events are aired in the cozy Mallards Lounge. There's an Olympic-size lap pool, an expansive athletic club, lighted tennis courts with pro instructors, and massage therapists. And for those honeymooning later in life, the hotel offers steep discounts — over 50 percent off rack prices — to guests over 50. A "Romance Romance" package includes Executive room accommodations, dinner at Capriccio's, breakfast at the B-Line Diner, Champagne on arrival, complimentary valet parking, and use of the athletic club.

9801 International Dr., Orlando. ☎ *800-732-3639 or 407-352-4000. Fax: 407-351-0073. Internet:* www.peabodyorlando.com. *891 units. Rack rates: $360-$450 double, $530-$1,350 suite. Romance Romance package: $499 per night. AE, CB, DC, DISC, JCB, MC, V.*

Portofino Bay Hotel

$$$$ **International Drive**

This 1999 arrival is styled after the Mediterranean seaside village of Portofino, Italy. If you've been to or seen pictures of the real Portofino and how it drapes over the steep coast, you may wonder how they pulled the illusion off in flat Florida, but the design and detail are pretty remarkable in delivering the illusion, especially at night. Portofino has many lavish touches, such as Murano crystal chandaliers in the lobby, a brick piazza, and bocci ball courts. The Loew's-run property was the first onsite hotel for Universal Orlando, and they opted to go after the luxury market from the start.

The rooms are bright and airy, with high beds, plush duvets, and epic bathrooms; the deluxe rooms are slightly larger and boast a CD/video system, and there are also butlered villas. The latter takes the "concierge level" concept to a new high, with 24-hour butler service, complimentary breakfast, and evening cocktails and hors d'oeuvres served in-room. The Presidente Suite has walk-in closets, a garden tub, and a private terrace. The hotel features three pools — one with a Mediterranean beach theme, another is stately and surrounded by olive and citrus trees and cabanas. There is a full-service spa, fitness center, and eight dining venues, ranging from sidewalk trattorias to over-the-top dining rooms. Regular boat service shuttles you via canals to nearby Universal, Islands of Adventure, and CityWalk, and your card key allows you charging privileges throughout Universal Orlando. If you plan to spend a good chunk of your honeymoon at the non-Disney parks, Portofino is a smart choice — guests who stay here can bypass the line at all Universal/Islands attractions.

5601 Universal Blvd. ☎ ***800-232-7827*** *or 407-503-1000. Fax: 407-503-1010. Internet:* www.universalorlando.com. *750 rooms. Rack rates: $240-$450 double, $325-$2,005 suite. AE, DISC, MC, V.*

Radisson Resort Parkway

$$$ Kissimmee

This eight-story hotel is one of the few Kissimmee lodgings that truly deserves to call itself a resort, with a Disney-close location near the intersection of I-4 and U.S. 192. Most rooms have two double beds, but a number of kings are available, as well as 20 suites. Pool and garden views are the norm, as are minibars, in-room safes, hairdryers, coffeemakers, and marble/granite bathrooms. The interiors were undergoing a remodel at press time, but don't expect much more than standard mass-market decor after they finish the upgrade. A better attraction is the hotel's verdant grounds — 20 acres in all — and the larger of the two free-form swimming pools is extensive, with a waterfall and a slide enveloped by lush greenery. Tennis, volleyball, and a small exercise room are also available. Theme park transportation is free: four shuttles daily to Magic Kingdom, one to Universal and SeaWorld.

2900 Parkway Blvd., Kissimmee. ☎ ***800-634-4774*** *or 407-396-7000. Fax: 407-396-6792. E-mail:* reservations@radissonparkway.com. *Internet:* www.radisson.com/kissimmeefl. *718 units. Rack rates: $129-$169 double. AE, CB, DISC, DC, MC, V.*

The Villas of Grand Cypress

$$$$ Lake Buena Vista

Meet the sister hotel to the Hyatt Regency Grand Cypress (see the review earlier in this chapter), another resort close to but shielded from the theme park action. The separately managed Villas are a short drive from the larger hotel, but the Villas offers a level of privacy not found in most of Orlando's big resorts, plus great views of the canals and golf courses that wind through the 1,500-acre Grand Cypress property — and a fleet of resident ducks (come prepared with crackers or bread crumbs). The two big draws are the top-of-the-line Equestrian center (riding lessons and packages available) and the 45 holes of Jack Nicklaus-designed courses and a golf academy.

The Medeterranean-style villas, which house everything from 650-square-foot junior suites to four-bedroom affairs, have patios or balconies and Roman tubs. The one-bedroom and larger villas have full kitchens, or dining is available in the elegant Black Swan, which has a view of the ninth green. In-room spa services are available, and the perks include nightly bed turndown, valet assistance, and 24-hour room service. There is a free shuttle to the Hyatt Regency (where you can use the facilities), and the $10-a-day resort fee includes transportation to the Disney parks, health club, nine-hole pitch and putt, and driving range. The Romance package includes daily breakfast and one dinner for two at the Black Swan with a bottle of house wine.

1 N. Jacaranda, Lake Buena Vista. ☎ *800-835-7377 or 407-239-4700. Fax: 407-239-7219. Internet:* www.grandcypress.com. *146 units. Rack rates: $215-$450 double, $315-$1,800 one- to four-bedroom villas. Honeymoon package: $330-$480 per night. AE, CB, DISC, DC, MC, V.*

Chapter 27

Filling Your Dance Card

By David Swanson

• •

In This Chapter

▶ Choosing your thrills, chills, and spills

▶ Having fun after dark

▶ Topping off the fuel tanks — the food front

• •

*E*ven you diehard honeymooners have to spend some time out of the room. So, this chapter is where we introduce you to Orlando's theme parks, clubs, and romantic restaurants. Of course, you have to share air space at these places. Central Florida teems with sweaty bodies, especially during summer and holidays. And all of them are hell-bent on riding the same rides, dancing in the same discos, and eating in the same restaurants (at the same time) as you. Here's our take on what's worth your time.

Holding Hands at the Disney Theme Parks

The Disney theme parks — the Magic Kingdom, Epcot, Disney-MGM Studios, and Animal Kingdom — are consensus favorites. Universal Studios Florida, Islands of Adventure (the other Universal park), and SeaWorld complete the A-Team roster. Each of these is a member of the $50 set. That's about what it costs adults (kids age 3 to 9 are $40), including tax, for a one-day, one-park admission. Discounts to these seven major parks are few and far between, and if these don't empty your wallets, plenty of smaller amusements exist to finish the job. Multi-day passes are available and may save a few bucks here and there.

Still, even the frugal couple typically spends $75 to $100 per person per day on admissions, souvenirs, food, and other incidentals. That doesn't include the allowances for your hotel, airfare, rental cars, and the $6 charge for parking at the major parks (though parking is free is you are staying at a WDW hotel). If you don't abide by your budget, dreams can turn into nightmares.

If you want more information, get a copy of *Walt Disney World and Orlando For Dummies*, by Jim & Cynthia Tunstall, published by Hungry Minds, Inc., call WDW central at ☎ **407-824-4321,** or pay a visit to the Mickster's site on the Web at http://disney.go.com-DisneyWorld-index.html.

The Magic Kingdom

Symbolized by Cinderella Castle, the Magic Kingdom dates to 1971 and is the first (and still the most popular) of Disney's Florida parks. A virtual replica of Disneyland in Anaheim, California, the Magic Kingdom has become a cultural institution — something of a rite of passage, which accounts for its top-dog popularity in the battle against newer parks with higher-tech rides. As is the case with every park we talk about in this chapter, there isn't space for a lot of detail on individual rides, shows, shops, and restaurants.

Epcot

Uncle Walt saw Epcot as a high-tech city with 20,000 residents (the word is short for Experimental Prototype Community of Tomorrow). After he died, the concept was changed to a kind of permanent world's fair that showcases technology and international harmony, but for some reason the acronym stuck when the park opened in 1982. Today, Epcot is equal parts amusement park and museum, with a healthy dose of shopportunities.

Epcot has plenty of interactive, hands-on experiences, so seeing the exhibits here is best at a slower pace. Allow a full day, and be sure to stick around for the nightly fireworks show, **IllumiNations,** at 9 p.m. Also note that international dining is a big part of the Epcot experience — remember to make reservations for prime seating times.

The Disney-MGM Studios

Disney's ad writers tout the Disney-MGM theme park as "the Hollywood that never was and always will be." There is a lot of charm walking along the recreated Hollywood streets of the 1930s, and through studio backlots that replicate New York street scenes for movie backdrops. But don't come to the Disney-MGM Studios to see real movies in production — little of note gets shot here. But that hardly detracts from the appeal of the park, which offers some terrific shows, a few modest attempts to explain how movies are made, and three awesome thrill rides. In sum, anyone who loves movies or the golden age of Hollywood can enjoy this combination theme park and working studio.

Indulge in the honeymoon spa treatment

Disney operates two polished spa facilities that offer half- and full-day treatment programs. The better known of the two is the **Grand Floridian Spa and Health Club** (adjacent to the Grand Floridian Resort), a luxurious facility that even has its own line of ruby-red grapefruit-infused products. The spa is open from 8 a.m. to 8 p.m. daily. A couples massage with two therapists runs $206, or you can spring for the Grand Romantic Evening, which throws in candles and aromatherapy oils for $242. An instructional massage for couples is also available, costing $298 for a three-hour session. For reservations, which are strongly advised, call ☎ **407-824-2332**.

The state-of-the-art **Spa at the Disney Institute**, located next to Downtown Disney, also offers massage therapy, plus skin treatments, seaweed programs, and a half-day men's program (that includes a sports hydro-massage, men's facial, and manicure). Some of the Institute's prices are a little lower, and the menu of services is slightly different; there is also a comprehensive health and fitness club. For reservations call ☎ **407-827-4455**.

A third full-service WDW spa is located at the **Wyndham Palace Resort**, next to Downtown Disney; the spa is as appealing as the Disney facilities, and the resort offers some great spa-related packages. Call ☎ **800-981-1472** or 407-827-2727 for more information. Several other Disney resorts also have massage rooms for a more limited selection of treatments, including the **Animal Kingdom Lodge, Contemporary Resort, Yacht and Beach Club, Coronado Springs,** and the **Swan** and **Dolphin** resorts.

Animal Kingdom

The newest kid on the Disney theme-park block opened in 1998 and offers plenty of fun, especially if you like animals or have an interest in the environment. Rides take a back seat to the critters, and they can make it worth the price of admission, if you like a cheetah here, an elephant over there, white rhinos, black rhinos, lowland gorillas, 7,000-pound hippos, bongos (the antelopes, not the drums), and (gasp!) naked mole rats.

Although the Animal Kingdom has several thrill rides (with more on the way), Animal Kingdom is unlike any other theme park — it's a unique hybrid of zoo, educational experience, arboretum, ride emporium, cultural odyssey, and crafts bazaar. The animals may be hidden from view for lengthy periods in some of the naturalistic enclosures, but when the great apes come out to play — well, you may feel as though suddenly transported to the remote highlands of the Congo. As such, it's worth lingering and looking, rather than rushing to the next adventure.

Everything else in Disney's world

Walt Disney World offers an amazing roster of activities beyond the big four parks, most of which cost a stack of bills to enjoy.

- ✔ **Blizzard Beach:** Blizzard Beach (☎ 407-560-3400) is the most spectacular of Disney's three water parks. The loopy theme has something to do with a freak snowstorm that invaded a little patch of central Florida. Blizzard Beach is usually open from 10 a.m. until shortly before dusk. Admission is included with most WDW ticket packages. But if you purchase single admissions, the price is $31.75 (including tax).

- ✔ **Typhoon Lagoon:** Typhoon Lagoon (☎ 407-560-4141) is more-or-less the equal of Blizzard Beach, but the slides aren't quite as tall, fast, or numerous (there are 10 here, compared to 17 at Blizzard Beach). Despite that, there's plenty of fun to be had, plus several unique attractions. Typhoon Lagoon is almost as popular as Blizzard Beach, so arriving soon after the park opens (which is usually at 10 a.m.) is strongly advised. Admission is a part of most WDW ticket packages; otherwise admission is $31.75.

- ✔ **River Country:** Disney's original themed water park, River Country (☎ 407-824-4321) is styled after an old-fashioned swimming hole, with tire swings, a 330,000-gallon swimming pool, and several moderate slides. There's a lot less to do than at Disney's other two water parks, but if lazing about for an afternoon of sun and soaking sounds appealing, you can have low-key fun here — plus the crowds are usually thinner and the price slightly cheaper (admission is $16.91). River Country is typically open 10 a.m. until dusk, but in winter months the park is not always open daily. Check for hours before heading over, as it's also a convoluted trip using the WDW transportation system.

- ✔ **Golf (full-scale):** 99 holes of championship golf sprawls across WDW land, including five regulation par-72 courses and a 9-hole, par-36 walking course. All are open to the public and offer driving ranges, pro shops, locker rooms, snack bars or restaurants, and PGA-staffed teaching and training programs. For tee times and reservations, call ☎ 407-824-2270 up to seven days in advance (Disney resort guests can reserve up to 30 days in advance). Greens fees average $120 to 160, with late afternoon twilight rates about half that price (the 9-hole Oak Trail Course is $42).

- ✔ **Disney's Wide World of Sports:** A 200-acre mega-complex that includes a 7,500-seat baseball stadium, two Little League fields, six basketball courts, 12 lighted tennis courts, a track-and-field complex, a golf driving range, six sand volleyball courts, and more. The **Atlanta Braves** use the stadium for Spring Training starting early March (call ☎ 407-939-1500 for schedules). Ongoing activities include the **NFL Experience** which has drills testing, punting, passing, and receiving skills (admission $9).

✔ **Richard Petty Driving Experience:** If you think Test Track is for sissies, the **Richard Petty Driving Experience** (☎ 800-237-3889 or 407-939-0130) offers the opportunity to zip down the track at up to 145 miles per hour. There's only one hitch: You ride shotgun while your mate cools his or her jets back at the starting gate. Want something more sedate? How about **horseback riding** along Bay Lake? Disney offers 45-minute, wrangler-led trail rides at a walk, leaving from the Fort Wilderness Resort and Campground, ☎ **407-939-7529. Bass fishing** is offered on several WDW lakes, ☎ **407-939-7529,** and **watersports** like wakeboarding, parasailing, and water-skiing are available from the Contemporary Resort marina; call ☎ **407-939-0754.**

Finding "The World" Is Not Enough

While Mickey is still the big cheese, he's not the only heavyweight today, with players like Universal Orlando and SeaWorld also on the scene. In fact, there's enough *off* Disney property to craft a perfectly enjoyable honeymoon without stepping foot in the mouse house (for that matter, you may save a few bucks, as well).

Universal Orlando, located nine miles northeast of WDW and just off I-4, is the biggest bundle of competition for Disney. The 840-acre property has two full-scale theme parks, **Universal Studios** and **Islands of Adventure,** a 30-acre nighttime dining and entertainment complex called **CityWalk** (see the review later in this chapter), plus two snazzy resorts, with a third on the way. You can also stay at one of 19 other Universal-affiliated hotels and still partake in an early-admission program to Universal/Islands (similar to Disney's Surprise Morning program). On nearby International Drive, Universal also owns **Wet 'n Wild,** a water park. Multi-day ticket packages encompassing all of these attractions, plus **SeaWorld,** are available, while **Universal Studios Vacations** (☎ 800-224-3838; Internet: www.universalorlando.com) sells travel packages that include accommodations, car rental, airfare, and theme park tickets.

Universal Studios

Most folks don't know movie studios well enough to know which produces what, but Universal and Disney-MGM make sure their patrons leave well informed. They flaunt their movies and franchises like a relentless barrage of previews leading up to a movie. The products on offer? *E.T., Men in Black,* and *Terminator.* Universal is a spin-off of the Universal Studios in Hollywood, with one notable caveat: Like Disney-MGM, Universal Orlando pretends to be both a working studio and a theme park, but a noteworthy production has not been shot here in quite a while. Still, you find at least a half-dozen themed attractions at Universal that are as good as any created on Disney soil, adding up to a enjoyable day's entertainment. The park is divided into six themed areas, which we list here in counter-clockwise order. Admission is $50.88, or you can purchase a multi-day ticket. Parking is $6.

Two shows are scheduled at Universal (check the map you received at the entrance for times). At **Beetlejuice's Rock 'n Roll Graveyard Review,** your favorite horror stars, like Frankenstein and Dracula, are brought together for a hammy rock musical. The **Wild, Wild, Wild West Stunt Show** is a lively demonstration of pratfalls from gunfights to falls from three-story buildings.

Islands of Adventure

It's no secret that Universal is trying to cut into Disney's magic formula for printing money, and in 1999 they upped the ante with the debut of Islands of Adventure. The state-of-the-art park has a fanciful theme that may be best compared to — dare we even think it? — the Magic Kingdom, but with several aggressive rides that keep young adults begging for more. Roller coasters thunder overhead, restaurants are camouflaged to match their surroundings, and the theming — from Seuss Landing to Jurassic Park — is as lush and imaginative as anything on Disney's land. As with the other big parks, a one-day ticket is $50.88, but multi-day tickets are also available. Parking is $6.

 Universal's two parks are almost as busy as Disney's. Prepare yourself for lines by late morning — 30 minutes is common for the best thrills, and an hour or more is routine at peak times. Insanity? Perhaps, but most people love it!

SeaWorld

SeaWorld is one of Orlando's most pleasant touring experiences. A modern, lush marine park, SeaWorld focuses more on discovery than thrill rides — though it offers two of the area's best: Kraken and Journey to Atlantis — so lines are a rarity. The more-than 200 acres of educational fun stars Shamu and his troupe of balletic killer whales, polar bears, sea lions, manatees, penguins, dolphins, sharks, and so on.

SeaWorld is located on SeaWorld Drive, four miles northeast of Down-town Disney and five miles south of Universal Orlando. The park is open 365 days a year, generally 9 a.m. to 7 p.m. (later in summer or during holidays). Admission is $50.88 for adults; parking is $6. If you're considering a visit to SeaWorld's new sibling, **Discovery Cove,** note that admission includes a week's worth of visits to SeaWorld, too. Also note that SeaWorld participates in the Universal/Islands/Wet 'n Wild multi-day pass. For more information call ☎ **800-327-2424** or 407-351-3600, or check out SeaWorld's Web site at www.seaworld.com.

The price is high, but for $349 — $698 for two — SeaWorld's **Trainer for a Day** program is an enriching way to spend eight hours. The program starts at 9 a.m., and you get to encourage dolphins through hoops, slosh around with 15-pound buckets of slimy fish, and stuff vitamins into salmon entrees. The price includes a T-shirt, disposal underwater camera, and a gourmet picnic lunch. The program is done by reservation only, and just three individuals participate daily. Call ☎ 407-370-1382 for more information.

SeaWorld has three types of attractions: rides, scheduled shows, and walk-through exhibits. Pick up a show schedule as you enter, but note that the suggested itinerary thoughtfully provided by SeaWorld is designed to make sure that you see every show *and* that you stay until the park closes.

Discovery Cove

Discovery Cove, a one-of-a-kind attraction that opened in 2000, is a by-reservation, all-inclusive marine-themed park. Only 1,000 guests are admitted daily, and, at over $200 per person, Discovery Cove is by far Orlando's priciest park — though the price includes a decent lunch, plus a seven-day pass valid at SeaWorld. The fringe benefits include swimming with stingrays and thousands of tropical fish in a realistic coral reef/lagoon setting, and getting a close look at sharks and barracudas (you're separated by underwater plexiglass panels). And because attendance is limited, the park is never swarming with people or lines. The main hook, however, is a chance to swim with one of several dolphins in a lagoon. Discovery Cove is a steep ticket, but it's a memorable way to conclude an Orlando visit.

Compared to the other theme parks, Discovery Cove encompasses a relatively small area (which is one big reason that attendance is capped) — when 1,000 people are here, it won't feel like an intimate experience. But most days, the park is a very relaxed, subtle experience, and, compared to most of busy Orlando, it's almost a hideaway for couples in love.

Other activities

Need a break from all-day, expensive theme parks? Orlando and the surrounding areas have a second tier of parks that average half the price and take just a few hours to see. Winter Park, the appealing upscale community just north of downtown Orlando, is worth an afternoon of leisurely strolling, shopping, and museum touring. At the same time, don't forget to take advantage of what you are already paying for: the hotel pool.

Wet 'n Wild

A fixture since 1977, Wet 'n Wild is the country's most popular water park. The park was acquired by Universal Orlando in 1999, and free shuttles from the Universal-affiliated hotels make the trek to the park daily. While it doesn't have the charm or theming of the Disney water parks, the 25-acre Wet 'n Wild makes up for its shortcomings with a bevy of ferocious slides and other heart-palpitating inducements, not to mention the flumes, a lazy river, a wave pool, and a picnic area. The **Hydra Fighter** is a wild swing controlled by your water cannon; **Fuji Flyer** is a pulse-pounding water toboggan through 450 feet of banked curves; and **The Surge** is one of the longest, fastest, multi-passenger tube rides in the Southeast.

Wet 'n Wild is located at 6200 International Drive, on the other side of I-4 from Universal. Admission is $31.75 (reduced admission is available after 3 p.m.); parking is $5. Tube, towel, and locker rental is $9, plus a $4 refundable deposit. The park is open daily, 9 a.m. to 6 p.m., or as late as 10 p.m. in summer (☎ **800-992-9453** or 407-351-9453; Internet: www.wetnwild.com).

Gatorland

Gatorland got a 22-year head start on Disney, and today it stands as a page from yesterday's Florida — a family-owned and -operated roadside tourist pit-stop. Its namesakes put on shows like the **Gator Jumparoo,** a loony crowd-pleaser in which ten-footers pathetically lunge out of the water to snag a Tyson chicken reject. There's also alligator wrestling and a gift shop where you can drop hard-earned cash on gator leather goods. It's a pretty amusing place to camp for a couple hours en route to the airport.

Gatorland is located at 14501 S. Orange Blossom Trail, Orlando, about three miles east of Downtown Disney. Admission is $17.93; parking is free. Hours are 9 a.m. to dusk daily. ☎ **800-393-5297** or 407-855-5496.

Winter Park Scenic Boat Tour

After visiting the Morse Museum, you may want to relax on the peaceful Winter Park Scenic Boat that has been operating since 1938. The one-hour narrated cruises showcase Winter Park's beautiful lakes and canals, Rollins College, the Kraft Azalea Gardens, and a number of historic lakefront mansions.

The boat tour launches from 312 East Morse Blvd. in Winter Park, every hour on the hour. The tour is priced $7, and it runs daily from 10 a.m. to 4 p.m. ☎ **407-644-4056.**

Golf

More than 125 golf courses are located within a 45-minute drive of downtown Orlando — some of them designed by Arnold Palmer, Jack Nicklaus, Tom Fazio, Pete Dye, Robert Trent Jones, and others. *Golf* magazine recognized the 45 holes designed by Nicklaus at the **Grand Cypress Resort** as among the best in the nation. For general golf information, check with **Golfpac** (☎ **800-327-0878** or 407-260-2288; Internet: www.golfpacinc.com) or **Tee Times USA** (☎ **800-374-8633;** Internet: www.teetimesusa.com). These companies package golf vacations with accommodations and other features, and they pre-arrange tee times at more than 40 Orlando-area courses.

Living It Up when the Sun Goes Down

Orlando's action used to rise and set with the sun, literally — but that's hardly the case today. Here's a tip of the hat to those of you who still have the pizzazz for a nighttime adventure after a busy day at the theme parks.

Enjoying Disney and the BoardWalk

What? A corner of the World that doesn't require a pricey ticket? Don't worry, the head Mouseketeer always finds multiple ways to extract a wad of greenbacks during your visit to Downtown Disney — a mammoth shopping, dining, and entertainment complex — or the BoardWalk, a more low-key entertainment area lining the BoardWalk Resort. For additional information on any Disney nighttime offerings, call the WDW general info number, ☎ **407-824-4321.**

Downtown Disney

Downtown Disney has two sections that wrap around a lake. Pleasure Island (see the following section), a 24-screen **AMC Movie Theater** (for show times call ☎ **407-298-4488**), and the Planet Hollywood restaurant anchor the complex at its center.

On one side is the **Marketplace,** which has shops including World of Disney (the largest Disney merchandise shop on the planet), a LEGO store, and smaller shops selling everything from resort apparel to character art. Among the restaurants are the Rainforest Café, a Wolfgang Puck pizzeria, and a McDonald's.

After dusk, the action gravitates more to the newer, more built-up **West Side,** which houses a Virgin Megastore (a terrific pit-stop for CDs and videos), a cigar store, a guitar shop, and a place specializing in western duds. There's also a House of Blues restaurant and concert venue that draws big name acts to Orlando (for schedules and tickets call ☎ **407-934-2583**) and two huge restaurants, Wolfgang Puck Café and Bongo's Cuban Café (watch out for the steep drink prices).

Most of the shops open by 10 a.m., and they all stay open until well after dark. Parking is free, but it gets pretty tight by dusk — if you stay in Mickeyville, use the free WDW transportation. All the Disney resorts have regular bus transportation to Downtown Disney that runs until past midnight. Dining is discussed under the dining section later in this chapter, while the following three attractions are part of the Downtown Disney complex and require admission.

Pleasure Island

Paradise Island is a six-acre, gated nightclub-themed park offering an island of after-dark entertainment. A total of eight nightclubs are featured here, providing something for virtually everyone. They include **Mannequins,** a high-energy disco with a big, rotating dance floor and contemporary club music played loud enough to wake the dead; **BET Soundstage,** which offers traditional R&B and hip-hop and an expansive dance floor; **8Trax,** a 1970s-style club where 50 TV screens air videos above the dance floor; **Wildhorse Saloon,** which attracts country connoisseurs with prime booty-scootin' tunes; the **Pleasure Island Jazz Company,** which features live blues and jazz acts; and the **Rock 'n Roll Beach Club,** where live bands perform cover songs. Two nonmusical venues worth noting include the **Comedy Warehouse,** which has scheduled, 45-minute standup performances throughout the evening, and the **Adventurers Club,** a hilarious mock English gentleman's club with a cast of characters subtly (and not so subtly) interacting with guests. A fireworks show erupts in the street connecting the clubs, nightly at midnight.

Admission to Pleasure Island is $21, but the fee is included in some of the Disney multi-day ticket packages. Alcohol is served throughout Pleasure Island, but note that you must be 21 to enter Mannequins or the BET Soundstage — the staff is dead serious about it. Although Pleasure Island is open during the day for shopping and dining, the clubs open at 7 p.m. and stay hopping until well after midnight.

DisneyQuest

One rung down the amusement park food chain, DisneyQuest isn't exactly a theme park but an elaborate, five-story virtual video arcade, located at Downtown Disney West Side. Going in the door, adults may look at it as kid stuff, but when they get a gander at the electronic wizardry, many bite the hook as hard as their youngsters (teens and younger kids are the predominant audience). What it lacks in intimacy, it makes up in high-tech adventure, with games like **Aladdin's Magic Carpet Ride,** which has you straddling the saddle of a motorcycle-like seat and flying through the 3-D Cave of Wonders. Best thing is, you won't be juggling a pocket full of quarters to enjoy DisneyQuest — your admission covers everything except for snacks, drinks, and a few select premium attractions.

DisneyQuest is open daily 10:30 a.m. to midnight; admission is $30.74, but the fee is included in some of the Disney multi-day ticket packages.

Cirque du Soleil

Lions and tigers and bears? Nope, but you won't feel cheated. Disney's partnership with the famed Montreal-based, no-animals circus Cirque du Soleil is an expensive 90-minute excursion, but many visitors rank it as the highlight of their Disney World visit.

Cirque du Soleil, which is pronounced *sairk doo so-lay,* means "circus of the sun." Cirque created the show **La Nouba** specifically for Down-town Disney. There's no story or dialogue, but non-stop energy pours from the high-tech stage, with a hypnotic score provided by a live orchestra/band. At times it seems all 64 performers are on view simultaneously, especially during the intricately choreographed trampoline routine. Trapeze artists, high-wire walkers, airborne gymnasts, a sexy Russian who has a way with long red scarves, a posing strongman, mimes, and two zany clowns cement a spectacular evening's entertainment.

The schedule evolves, but at press time, La Nouba is performed twice each evening, Thursday through Monday. Tickets are $71.02, and reservations ahead of your visit can ensure the best seats. Call ☎ 407-939-7600.

The BoardWalk

If the pace of Downtown Disney is a bit too rambunctious for proper hand-holding, try the BoardWalk. It's a prime (not to mention free) place for strolls, bicycling, and people watching, located at Disney's same-named resort, between Epcot and the Disney-MGM Studios. Along the outdoor boardwalk are street performers, surrey (bike) rentals, and souvenir shopping, all wrapping around a pacific lagoon. Indoors is the **ESPN Club,** a sports bar with 71 TV monitors; **Atlantic Dance** with live retro swing and Latin music ($3 cover charge); while **Jellyrolls** offers dueling pianos in a rustic saloon-style setting. You also find a good selection of restaurants (see the restaurant listings later in this chapter) here and at the adjacent resorts.

The only hitch is that none of the Disney resorts (with the exception of the neighboring Yacht/Beach and Swan/Dolphin) have transportation to the BoardWalk. You can use your rental car, take a pricey taxi, or use WDW transportation to a connection point — either the Disney-MGM Studios, where you can catch a boat to the BoardWalk during park hours, or to Downtown Disney, which has buses to the BoardWalk Resort until after midnight. The BoardWalk is also a short walk from the secondary, rear entrance to Epcot.

Discovering something Grand

Rent the Love Boat, Disney-style. The **Grand** is a stately 44-foot yacht, based at the Grand Floridian's marina. It cruises the Seven Seas Lagoon and Bay Lake days or evenings and is available for couples or groups up to 15; catering is also an option. The $300-per-hour price tag includes a captain and deckhand, and on select nights, one of the most exclusive seats in the house for the Magic Kingdom fireworks show. Or, just troll the lakes and ask the crew to turn a blind eye while you and yours take advantage of the boat's three bedrooms and two bathrooms with showers. Call ☎ 407-824-2621 for more information.

Exploring Universal's CityWalk

CityWalk is Universal's answer to Disney's Pleasure Island — a something-for-everyone nighttime entertainment zone. The complex is a very slick package, with two levels of clubs, shops, and restaurants located between Universal Studios and Islands of Adventure.

The world's largest **Hard Rock Café** is here, as well as **Hard Rock Live Orlando,** a state-of-the-art, 2,200-capacity live performance hall that hosts top-name music artists (for schedules and tickets call ☎ **407-351-5483**). The **Down Beat Jazz Hall of Fame** has a collection of jazz memorabilia, while the adjoining **Thelonious Monk Institute of Jazz** provides live jazz by nationally-known acts, against a backdrop of sushi and tapas. Get back into the track at **the groove,** a high-tech visual effects club with specialty bars and customized audio systems where you can shake, shake, shake all night long. **Latin Quarter** has dancing to live salsa bands (the acoustics are atrocious), while the **Motown Café** spins motor city's greatest. **Bob Marley — A Tribute to Freedom** honors the late, great star in a Jamaican-style tin-roofed shack, while **Jimmy Buffett's Margaritaville** is Orlando's home to parrotheads — it has a volcano that erupts margaritas (nope, we're not kidding). There's also a 16-screen movie theatre, shops, and a variety of restaurants, including the local venue for **Emeril's.**

There's no admission fee to explore CityWalk, but the various clubs extract a cover charge when attendance is up (the cover charge goes up and down accordingly). Or buy the Key to the Clubs ticket for $8.43; it gets you in everywhere without a cover — it isn't necessarily a great deal on slow nights, or if you just plan to attend two or three clubs. Drink prices range from average to pricey. CityWalk (☎ **407-363-8000;** Internet: www.universalorlando.com) is located in the same complex as Universal Studios Florida and Islands of Adventure; parking is $6.

Dining in Disney World and Orlando

Hungry yet? Stomach growling like a cornered wildcat? Look no further. Orlando is home to almost 4,000 restaurants — there is something to please almost everyone, even the most finicky palate. Although the city is not exactly the culinary capital of the universe — many spots are part of national franchises, or have all the impersonal qualities of a chain restaurant — plenty of good or very good meals can be found. Many of the theme park dining rooms offer passable food at sky-high prices, so we weeded out most of these and instead feature places that are swooningly romantic, serve quality comestibles, or offer (relative) intimacy and good value.

All restaurants located inside the theme parks require park admission. If you're set to eat in one of them, do so on a day when you tour the park (unless you purchased unlimited-admission passes).

Three of the four Disney parks serve alcohol at their sit-down restaurants, but the Magic Kingdom serves no booze before (or after) its time. All WDW restaurants are exclusively non-smoking; a few dining venues beyond Disney turf offer smoking/non-smoking seating.

You get reservations for all WDW venues (except Victoria & Albert's) through **Disney Dining** (☎ **407-939-3463**). Actually, you don't actually secure reservations — you get "priority seating" assignments. In general, priority seating works without too many hitches, but instead of a table waiting for you when you arrive at the appointed time, you must get in a line for the next available seating — usually one becomes available within five minutes or so. For the most popular restaurants (like California Grill, Victoria & Albert's, Jiko's), note that priority seating slots often fill up weeks in advance — and we can't stress highly enough to book special meals *ahead* of your arrival in Orlando. If you're a diabetic, a vegetarian, a struggling dieter, or you need to keep kosher, don't wring your hands; Chef Mickey can tailor menus to guest needs (advise by phone when making priority seating arrangements).

For listings within WDW and Universal Orlando, the location refers to the resort or theme park where the venue is located. Outside WDW and Universal Orlando, we use the location categories Lake Buena Vista, Kissimmee, and International Drive. A few choice spots don't fit these categories and are listed as being located in Orlando.

Please refer to the Introduction of *Honeymoon Vacations For Dummies* for an explanation of our price categories.

Creating special moments

Although every night of your honeymoon should be a special occasion, there should be at least one evening where money's no object. These are our favorites.

Victoria & Albert's (Grand Floridian Resort; ☎ **407-824-1089**; $$$$$) is Disney's number one pick for an ultra-romantic, candlelight dinner. Royal Doulton china, Sambonet silver, soft harp music, and personalized menus are just the start of a memorable experience. The food is impeccable, and with just 18 tables, it's hard to beat it for intimacy. It's also the most expensive restaurant in central Florida — expect to pony up $100-plus per person with wine, tax, and tip. Next door is **Citricos** (Grand Floridian Resort; ☎ **407-824-3000**; $$$$$), which serves extravagant creations like Florida lobster ratatouille with lamb loin. For dessert? How about chocolate ravioli with licorice ice cream? The lush decor is full of sunny citrus hues; the ambiance is cheerful, not stuffy. Let them know you're on a honeymoon and they may toss in a glass of champagne.

For some, nothing says "love" better than perfectly-seared beef. If that describes you or yours, head straight to **Shula's** (Dolphin Resort;

☎ 407-939-3463; $$$$$), a chain run by Miami Dolphins coach Don Shula. The ambiance is testosterone-heavy, but they serve mega-portioned NY sirloin, porterhouse, filet mignon, and Floridian-style seafood faultlessly prepared, and with the prices to prove it.

The restaurant **Dux** at the Peabody Orlando hotel (9801 International Dr., International Drive; ☎ 407-345-4540; $$$$$) honors the ducks that splash away in the hotel's fountain. The tables are elegant, the Italian-accented menu changes seasonally. You may find dumplings stuffed with portobello mushrooms, chevre, and scallions; lamb chops in Hunan barbecue sauce; or grilled grouper in spices — you won't, however, find the titular feathered creatures on the menu.

Another formal, local favorite is **Maison et Jardin** (430 Wymore Rd., Orlando; ☎ 407-862-4410; $$$$$), located 17 miles north of Orlando's convention center, in Altamonte Springs. Old World elegance blends with entrees like beef Wellington or medallions of elk (venison, if you will) with raspberry sauce for some enchanted evening (ask to sit in the Gazebo Room).

Christini's (4600 Dr. Phillips Blvd., Orlando; ☎ 407-345-8770; $$$$$) gives you secluded booths, dim lights, and strolling musicians (violin and accordion) that compliment a Northern Italian venue where you can count on good service and, maybe, a peek at show-biz celebs from nearby Universaland. The wine list is epic.

Two Epcot venues deserve mention — if you're lucky, the moppet factor will be at a minimum. **Chefs de France** (Epcot; ☎ 407-939-3463; $$$) is the joint venture of three high-profile French chefs: Paul Bocuse, Roger Verge, and Gaston LeNotre. Though the chefs stop by only once in a blue moon, the kitchen does prepare well-above-average theme park dinners in a bistro setting. On the other side of the Epcot lagoon, in the Mexico pavilion, is the **San Angel Inn** (Epcot; ☎ 407-939-3463; $$$). The food is expensive for Mexican dishes, but how many other restaurants have a riverside cantina setting, a smoldering volcano in the distance, and a twilight ambiance (at lunch, too)?

Searching for fabulous food

If great food is the priority, here's where you can find it (but don't overlook the **California Grill,** which we tell you about in the next section).

Marty Dorf, the designer behind most of Disney's best-looking restaurants, created the whimsical carny-meets-seafood ambiance for the **Flying Fish Café** (BoardWalk Resort; ☎ 407-939-3463; $$$$), but the food is equally inspired, prepared from a bustling open kitchen. Try tuna encrusted with pepper and coriander, or roasted red snapper wrapped in a paper-thin potato wrapper. WDW's newest addition is **Jiko's — the Cooking Place** (Animal Kingdom Lodge; ☎ 407-939-3463; $$$$), which serves a vibrant melange of international flavors, like sea bass and asparagus puree steamed in a banana leaf, and roasted papaya stuffed with beef. The restaurant showcases the largest South African wine list in the country (many bottles are delicious). The gorgeous room features iridescent tile work and flying sculptures hanging overhead.

Downtown Disney has several tasty dining options, but **Wolfgang Puck Café** (Disney's West Side; ☎ 407-938-9653; $$$$-$$$$$) leads the way. The restaurant is actually three separate venues: the main room upstairs, a somewhat scaled down and less expensive menu downstairs, and a sushi bar-cum-lounge. Puck's pizzas are what gained him fame, and though they're still delicious (and not too pricey), they're overshadowed by the cutting-edge taste sensations that merge comforting Euro classics like wiener schnitzel with winning Asian spices and preparations. Another celebrity chef has an Orlando presence, but **Emeril's** (CityWalk; ☎ 407-224-2424; $$$$$) attaches his name to the Universal end of things with memorable nouveau Cajun-Creole. Don't miss those lamb chops.

Restaurants exist beyond the theme parks that are worth seeking out. **Le Coq au Vin** (4800 South Orange Ave., Orlando; ☎ 407-851-6980; $$$) is the local favorite for French bistro cuisine. The menu changes often but may have braised rabbit or grilled salmon. For an intimate evening, ask for table number 4 — it's in a corner where there's a fair measure of privacy but still a good view of everything. Another winner for its continental menu is **Chatham's Place** (7575 Dr. Philips Blvd., Orlando; ☎ 407-345-2992; $$$$), where a fine wine list and live music to help set the tone.

Dining with a view

Two spots take the cake when it comes to top-floor panoramas. And yet, amazingly, unlike many spots where you pay through the nose for a view only to be saddled with mediocre dining, the **California Grill** (Contemporary Resort; ☎ 407-824-1576; $$$$$) proffers food so good, the vivid scene — of the Magic Kingdom and Seven Seas Lagoon — takes a back seat. The menu is contemporary Californian, with flat-breads (pizza to most of us), sushi, and dazzling market-inspired entrees. The sunsets are often memorable, but note that securing a table for the summer fireworks shows requires finesse. The California Grill is probably Disney's best all-around dining experience.

Arthur's 27 (1900 Lake Buena Vista Dr., Lake Buena Vista; ☎ 407-827-2727; $$$$$), located on the 27th-floor of the Wyndham Palace, comes with a vista (Disney's fireworks and sunsets) that may take your breath away. It has the mellow mood of a supper club out of a 1940s Bogart film (less the clouds of cigarette smoke). Reservations are a must, yet the independent minds running Arthur's say you only can request (not reserve) special tables. So, request number 1 for a window seat; ask for table number 2 on the Epcot side to see the IllumiNations fireworks show.

Cinderella's Royal Table (Inside Cinderella's Castle, Magic Kingdom; ☎ 407-939-3463; $$$) offers the chance to dine in that big glittering castle that sits at the hub of the Magic Kingdom. Ceaselessly popular, book a table well in advance. Most tables are filled with wide-eyed pre-teens, anxiously awaiting a tableside visit by Cindy herself. The food is average at best, and way overpriced. But if a Fantasyland view is your cup of tea, Cinderella's Royal Table is *the* place to dine.

Another unique theme park perspective is provided at **Coral Reef** (Epcot; ☎ 407-939-3463; $$$$), a venue that faces the immense, 27-foot-deep aquarium at the Living Seas Pavilion — enormous fish, sharks, and rays glide by. Alas, the "water-driven" menu reads well, but the preparations are disappointing (lunch is a slightly better value). Still, the show is pretty spectacular, and the room is beautifully designed, with rippling water effects echoing off the ceiling.

Well worth the long drive north from themeparkville, **Enzo's on the Lake** (Orlando; ☎ 407-834-9872; $$$$) is a Mediterranean-style villa on Lake Fairy, in Longwood. It's a wonderful place for sunsets, and the atmosphere is festive and frenetic, like an Italian family reunion. The menu showcases veal, chicken, beef, and marine cuisine in an exquisite array of sauces.

Getting the best of all worlds

Usually, fine, romantic feasting means breaking out the gold card. But thankfully a few places offer dining value with warm ambiance and tasty menus that equal good dining in a good setting for a good value.

Artist Point (Wilderness Lodge; ☎ 407-824-3200; $$$) is one of Disney's most beautiful restaurants — a soaring, wood-lined dining room with Craftsman and Frank Lloyd Wright accents. The Pacific Northwest-style menu features Penn Cove mussels, game and cedar plank roasted salmon, plus a wine list heralding Oregon and Washington vintners. The tables along the back wall are cozier than most; window seats overlook the pool.

The dazzling new **Boma** (Animal Kingdom Lodge; ☎ 407-939-3463; $$) is a great place to set your palate on fire with nouveau pan-African cuisine; stuff yourself silly from a lonnggg buffet; and enjoy the ambiance of a vibrant room and spectacular new resort. The spice-happy food isn't for the unadventurous, but Boma provides a nifty food safari, and at $20 per person for dinner, it's an excellent value.

With its mishmash Euro farmhouse decor and scampering children, **Spoodles** (BoardWalk Resort; ☎ 407-939-3463; $$) is not the most idyllic trysting location, but the Mediterranean menu of tapas and flavorful entrees may certainly satisfy your heart. Tapas are also the headliner at **Café Tu Tu Tango** (8625 International Dr.; ☎ 407-248-2222; $), which looks like an artist's loft in Barcelona — there's usually at least one working painter or sculptor here. Latin music keeps the mood festive, but there's a quieter area to the left of the restaurant, and the menu of appetizer-size items is great for light meals. Just down the street is **Bahama Breeze** (8849 International Dr.; ☎ **407-248-2499; $$**).

Located in the Disney hamlet of Celebration, **Café d'Antonio** (Kissimmee; ☎ **407-566-2233; $$**) is great for people watching and Italian specialties, like delicious *zuppa di pesce* (fish soup). The local chain **Pebbles** (12551 Florida 535, Lake Buena Vista (and elsewhere); ☎ **407-827-1111; $**) is short on intimacy, but it's well-run, friendly, and moderately priced. Duck, lamb, and pasta dishes as well as tapas and homemade soup headline four locations.

Chapter 28

Making Plans and Settling In

By David Swanson

• •

In This Chapter

▶ Finding your way to Orlando

▶ Getting around once you arrive

▶ Knowing all the details

• •

*Y*ou know it. We know it. The airlines and highway builders know it. Getting there isn't half the fun. But the journey doesn't have to cause a divorce.

We begin this chapter by getting you there, then help you decide the best time to come, and finally, how to get around.

Getting to Orlando

In the last handful of years, air travel has become pretty annoying. Many airports and airlines limit carry-on bags, forcing you to arrive earlier than ever, and making you deal with steadily worsening lines. As if that weren't enough aggravation, flights more frequently are delayed to await connectors and ensure the plane is full. Translation — expect your trip to be longer than necessary.

Arriving by plane

Orlando International Airport, ☎ 407-825-2001, handles more than 27 million passengers a year. Most major carriers fly here. Regulars include the following:

- ✔ **Air Canada: ☎ 800-776-3000;** Internet: www.aircanada.com
- ✔ **America West Airlines: ☎ 800-235-9292;** Internet: www.americawest.com
- ✔ **American Airlines: ☎ 800-433-7300;** Internet: http://aav3.aavacations.com/

- ✔ **British Airways:** ☎ **800-247-9297** in the U.S.; ☎ **0345-222-111** in Britain; Internet: www.britishairways.com

- ✔ **Canadian Airlines:** ☎ **800-426-7000;** Internet: www.cdair.com

- ✔ **Continental:** ☎ **800-525-0280;** Internet: www.continental.com

- ✔ **Delta:** ☎ **800-221-1212;** Internet: www.delta-air.com

- ✔ **Northwest:** ☎ **800-225-2525;** Internet: www.nwa.com

- ✔ **Southwest:** ☎ **800-435-9792;** Internet: www.iflyswa.com

- ✔ **United Airlines:** ☎ **800-241-6522;** Internet: www.wual.com

- ✔ **US Airways:** ☎ **800-428-4322;** Internet: www.usairways.com

- ✔ **Virgin Atlantic:** ☎ **800-862-8621** in the U.S.; ☎ **0239-747-747** in Britain; Internet: www.fly.virgin.com

Here are samples of non-stop flying times (less connections and other delays) from some major cities to Orlando International Airport: New York and Philadelphia, 2½ hours; Chicago, Dallas, and Detroit, 3 hours; Los Angeles and San Francisco, 5 hours; and London, 7 to 8 hours.

Arriving by train or bus

Amtrak (☎ **800-872-7245;** Internet: www.amtrak.com) has stations in Orlando, Winter Park, and Kissimmee. **Greyhound** (☎ **800-231-2222;** Internet: www.greyhound.com) has terminals in Orlando, Kissimmee, Sanford, and St. Cloud.

Arriving by car

The major road from the north is I-4. You also can connect with it from I-95 in Daytona Beach. If you use I-75, you can connect with Florida's Turnpike, a toll road, at Wildwood. If you don't mind towns and traffic, U.S. 441, 27, and 17 arrive from the north and west.

Whether you rent a car or drive your own, be ready for weekday rush hours, 7 to 9 a.m. and 4 to 6 p.m., which are brutal along the I-4, between downtown Orlando and WDW. The "heart" of International Drive — between Wet 'n Wild and the Convention Center — crawls at a snail's pace at seemingly any hour.

Getting Around

The good news: Most streets are on the grid system. North-south addresses start at Central and east-west at Orange Avenue. The bad news: These are named rather than numbered streets, so interior addresses aren't that easy to find — read, ask for directions from the source or your front desk. However, most of the attractions are easy to find. International Drive has an exit off I-4 on the north end; take the Sand Lake Road exit for its mid section; use S.R. 536 for the southern end. Universal Studios is off I-4 south of Orlando. SeaWorld is on International Drive. To get to Disney from I-4, exit on S.R. 536, Osceola Parkway, or U.S. 192 and go west.

If you plan to rent a car, most national rental car companies have offices at or very near the airport. These include the following:

- **Alamo:** ☎ **800-327-9633;** Internet: www.goalamo.com
- **Avis:** ☎ **800-331-1212;** Internet: www.avis.com
- **Budget:** ☎ **800-527-0700;** Internet: www.budgetrentacar.com
- **Dollar:** ☎ **800-800-4000;** Internet: www.dollar.com
- **Enterprise:** ☎ **800-325-8007;** Internet: www.enterprise.com
- **Hertz:** ☎ **800-654-3131;** Internet: www.hertz.com
- **National:** ☎ **800-227-7368;** Internet: www.nationalcar.com
- **Rent-A-Wreck:** ☎ **800-535-1391;** Internet: www.rent-a-wreck.com
- **Thrifty:** ☎ **800-367-2277;** Internet: www.thrifty.com

Saving Money with a Package Deal

 You can save money and a quantity of aggravation by choosing a package plan that satisfies all or some of your needs, from airfare and rooms to meals and ground transportation. We're not talking about escorted tours here. Packages are the various elements of a vacation, purchased in bulk by an intermediary who then bundles them together for you. In theory, packages can shave a few dollars — maybe a few hundred — off the cost of your honeymoon. However, not all packages are created equal. Be sure to evaluate the cost of the individual elements purchased separately, and don't pony up for extras you don't want.

Here are a few package tour operators worth contacting:

- **Walt Disney World:** ☎ **800-828-0228;** Internet: http://disney.go.com/disneyworld/intro.html
- **Universal Studios Vacations:** ☎ **800-224-3838;** Internet: www.usevacations.com
- **American Airlines Vacations:** ☎ **800-321-2121;** Internet: http://aav1.aavacations.com/
- **Delta Dream Vacations:** ☎ **800-872-7786;** Internet: http://deltavacations.com/disney.html
- **US Airways Vacations:** ☎ **800-455-0123;** Internet: http://www.usairwaysvacations.com

Fast Facts: Disney World and Orlando

AAA

American Automobile Association members can contact their local offices for maps and optimum driving directions or call ☎ 800-222-4357 and asked to be transferred to the office nearest you. Other auto clubs also have service agreements with AAA. You can find information at www.aaa.com.

American Express

Call ☎ 800-297-3429 or go to www.americanexpress.com/travel to reach the card company's Travel Service offices nationally. In Orlando, call ☎ 407-843-0004. American Express is the official card of Walt Disney World; it has windows at each of the four WDW theme parks, and using the card in conjunction with your Disney resort room key avails a few nice discounts (check at the front desk for details).

ATMs

Machines honoring Cirrus, Honor, Plus, and other systems are common in all of Orlando's theme parks. They're also at many banks, shopping centers, and convenience stores.

Camera Repair

Try **Photo Time** (☎ 407-352-1818) on International Drive.

Credit Cards

American Express, MasterCard, and VISA are accepted pretty much everywhere throughout Orlando's hotels, restaurants, and theme parks. Discover and Diners Club are accepted at most, but not all venues.

Customs

Every visitor 21 years of age or older may bring in to the U.S., free of duty, the following: one liter of wine or liquor; 200 cigarettes or 100 cigars (but no cigars from Cuba) or 3 pounds of smoking tobacco; and $100 worth of gifts. These exemptions are offered to travelers who spend at least 72 hours in the United States and who haven't claimed the same exemptions within the preceding six months. You can't bring food (particularly cheese, fruit, cooked meats, and canned goods) and plants (vegetables, seeds, tropical plants, and so on) into the country. Foreign tourists may bring in or take out up to $10,000 in U.S. or foreign currency with no formalities; you must declare larger sums to Customs upon leaving.

Doctors

For minor problems, local walk-in clinics cost considerably less than signing in at an emergency-room counter. **Centra-Care**, operated by a local hospital, is a reputable clinic with 13 locations throughout Orlando. For more information, including the nearest location, call ☎ 407-660-8118. If you want a direct feed to a doctor, try **Ask-A-Nurse.** They ask if you have insurance, but that's for information purposes only (so they can track who uses the system). Ask-A-Nurse is a free service open to everyone. In Kissimmee, call ☎ 407-870-1700; in Orlando call ☎ 407-897-1700.

Emergencies

All of Florida uses ☎ **911** as the emergency number for police, fire departments, ambulances, and other critical needs. There's also a 24-hour, toll-free number for the **Poison Control Center**, ☎ 800-282-3171. Call ☎ 407-238-2000 for in-room, 24-hour medical service at Disney resort properties. For less urgent requests, call ☎ 800-647-9284, a number sponsored by the **Florida Tourism Industry Marketing Corporation,** the state tourism promotion board. With operators speaking more than 100 languages, this service can provide general directions and help with lost travel papers and credit cards, medical emergencies, accidents, money transfers, airline confirmation, and much more.

Hospitals

Sand Lake Hospital, 9400 Turkey Lake Rd. (☎ 407-351-8550), is about two miles south of Sand Lake Road. From the WDW area, take I-4 east to Exit 29, turn left onto Sand Lake Road, and make a left on Turkey Lake Road. The hospital is two miles on your right. **Celebration Health** (☎ 407-764-4000), located in the Disney-owned town Celebration, is at 400 Celebration Place. From I-4, take Exit 25A. At the first traffic light, turn right onto Celebration Avenue. At the first stop sign, take another right.

Information

To receive local telephone information, call ☎ 411. The other most common sources of information are **Walt Disney World**, P.O. Box 10000, Lake Buena Vista, FL 32830-1000 (☎ 407-934-7639; Internet: http://disney. go.com/DisneyWorld/intro.html), and the **Orlando/Orange County Convention & Visitors Bureau,** 8723 International Dr., Suite 101, Orlando, FL 32819 (☎ 407-363-5871; Internet: www.go2orlando.com).

Internet Access and Cyber Cafes

Have a laptop? To check your e-mail, all you need is a data port, e-mail address, or free-mail account. You have to pay local and long-distance charges (expect up to 95 cents a minute, plus up to a $7 connect fee). Some places offer a flat, 24-hour fee, and some hotels without in-room connections have business centers where you can connect for an hourly fee.

In the Universal Orlando theme parks, you find AOL kiosks — compact stations located throughout the parks where you can check and send e-mail. They're free but ask you to spend five minutes or less.

In Mickeyville, the kiosks at the Epcot "Innovations" attraction let you send and receive e-mail. **DisneyQuest** at Downtown Disney West Side offers Internet access in the Wired Wonderland Café, where you can send postcards and play games in five-minute blocks (*Note:* You can't check free-mail accounts here).

Liquor Laws

Orlando's liquor laws are pretty straightforward. Florida law requires revelers to be 21 before they consume alcohol.

Mail

If you want to receive mail on your vacation and you aren't sure of your address, you can have your mail sent to you, in your name, in care of General Delivery at the main post office of the city or region where you expect to stay. Orlando's main post office (☎ 800-275-8777) is located at 1040 Post Office Blvd. Lake Buena Vista's main post office (☎ 800-275-8777) is at 12133 S. Apopka-Vineland Rd. You must pick up your mail in person and produce proof of identity (driver's license, passport, and so on).

Maps

AAA (see "AAA," earlier in this appendix) and other auto clubs usually provide maps for members. You can also find them in bookstores and libraries in your hometown. Most rental car companies provide reasonably detailed maps as hand-outs at the time of pick-up.

Newspapers/Magazines

Check out the Sunday travel section in your hometown paper (or the one in the biggest city nearby) for bargains, ideas, and tips. After you land in O-Town, you can find a lot of bargains in the *Orlando Sentinel* (online at www. orlandosentinel.com) throughout the week. The paper's Friday *Calendar* section is a gold mine for current local information particularly on the area's nightclub goings-on. The free *Orlando Weekly,* available in some International Drive restaurants and at many other non-tourist spots outside WDW and Universal, is another good source for nightclubbing and other entertainment info. And, though rarely spotted within WDW, don't overlook all of those handout (free) coupon books and throwaway magazines in restaurant and hotel lobbies. Everyone you run into in Orlando wants to give you a discount coupon — just make sure that there isn't a timeshare tour attached to it.

Pharmacies

Walgreen's drugstore, 1003 W. Vine St. (Hwy. 192), just east of Bermuda Avenue (☎ 407-847-5252), operates a 24-hour pharmacy. There's also an **Eckerd** drugstore at 7324 International Dr. (☎ 407-345-0491) and 1205 W. Vine. (☎ 407-847-5174) that's open 24 hours a day.

Police

In any emergency, call ☎ **911**. If you have a cellular phone and need help, dial ☎ ***FHP** for the Florida Highway Patrol. Otherwise, call the Orlando police non-emergency line at ☎ 407-246-2414 or the Orange County Sheriff's Office at ☎ 407-649-8400.

Restrooms

Foreign visitors often complain that public toilets are hard to find, but Orlando isn't any worse than most U.S. cities. True, there aren't any public restrooms on the streets, but you can usually find one in a bar, restaurant, hotel, museum, department store, convenience store, attraction, fast food barn, or service station — and it'll probably be clean. In particular, Mobil service stations have made a public pledge to provide spic-and-span bathrooms, most decorated with homey touches. Note, however, that restaurants and bars in resorts or heavily visited areas may reserve their rest rooms for the use of their patrons. Within the theme parks, rest rooms are clearly marked on the park maps.

Safety

Don't let the Fantasyland aura allow you to lower your guard. Metro Orlando has a crime rate comparable to most other major U.S. cities. Stay alert and remain aware of your immediate surroundings. Keeping your valuables in a safe-deposit box (inquire at your hotel's front desk) is a good idea, although nowadays most hotels are equipped with in-room safes. Keep a close eye on your valuables when you're in public places, such as restaurants, theaters, or even airport terminals. Renting a locker is always preferable to leaving your valuables in the trunk of your car, even in the theme park lots. Be cautious and avoid carrying large amounts of cash in a backpack or fanny pack, which thieves can easily access while you stand in line for a ride or show. If you rent a car, carefully read the safety instructions that the rental company provides. Never stop in a dark area.

Smoking

If you smoke, you most likely know to expect a diminishing playground. Restaurant space and hotel rooms for smokers are fast evaporating. On Disney turf, you will not find smoking sections in restaurants, and tobacco is no longer sold on the property. (Hey, don't get too worked up about it — gum is also absent from store shelves here.) In the theme parks, designated smoking zones are marked. Outside WDW, smoke-free sections are found in some, but not all restaurants.

Special Diets

Some local restaurants can arrange for special meals, including kosher, if you call in advance. Disney (☎ 407-939-3463) excels at this.

Taxes

Expect to add 11 or 12 percent to room rates; and 6 to 7 percent on most everything else — except groceries and health supplies or medical services.

Taxis

Yellow Cab (☎ 407-699-9999) and **Ace Metro** (☎ 407-855-0564) are among those cabs serving the area. But for day-to-day travel, cabs are expensive unless your group has five or more people. Rates are $2 for the first ⅔-mile, $1.75 per mile thereafter. Example: The trip from the airport to WDW is about $47 plus tip; to the I-Drive area is a bit less; Kissimmee can be slightly higher.

Telephone

Local calls within the 407 area code require ten-digit dialing, even if you're trying to get the store right across the street. You must dial 407 plus the local number. In some cases, there is a toll within the 407 area code (for instance, when calling from WDW to Kissimmee). If you make a long-distance call, it's just like anywhere else in the U.S.: dial 1 (or 0 for an operator-assisted call), followed by the area code and seven-digit number.

Time Zone

Orlando is on Eastern Standard Time. That means, when both of Mickey's gloved hands are on 12 noon in Orlando, it's 7 a.m. in Honolulu, 8 a.m. in Anchorage, 9 a.m. in Vancouver and Los

Angeles, 11 a.m. in Winnipeg and New Orleans, and 6 p.m. in London.

Transit Info

Lynx (☎ 407-841-8240; Internet: www.golynx.com) bus stops are marked with a paw print. The buses serve Disney, Universal, and International Drive ($1 for adults, 25 cents for kids and seniors; $10 for an unlimited weekly pass), but they're not particularly tourist-oriented.

Weather

Call ☎ 321-255-0212 to get forecasts from the National Weather Service. When the phone picks up, punch in 412 from a touch-tone phone to get the Orlando forecast. Also, check with The Weather Channel if you have cable television or go to its Web site at www.weatherchannel.com.

Part VII
Cruises

The 5th Wave   By Rich Tennant

©RICHTENNANT

"Oh look! Isn't that Raoul, the ship steward you refused to tip after he fished your watch out of the pool?"

In this part . . .

A cruise is a perfect honeymoon choice. Why? Among other things, a cruise is a dream vacation that's virtually all-inclusive. You pay once and your accommodations, food, entertainment, onboard daytime activities, and nighttime entertainment are all taken care of.

Of course, plenty of opportunity arises on cruise ships for romance — with that romance, in our opinion, elevated by the rolling of the seas. You can stroll hand-in-hand on a moonlit deck, get an expert massage in the spa (some ships even offer massage sessions for two), watch movies in your cabin, enjoy a Jacuzzi for two, take breakfast (or even dinner) in bed, and do whatever you want on your private balcony (if you can afford a cabin with this amenity).

On a cruise you get privacy, pampering and fun. What could be a better choice for your dream honeymoon?

Chapter 29

Honeymooning on the High Seas

By Fran Wenograd Golden

• •

In This Chapter

▶ Answering common cruise questions

▶ Considering the different types of ships

▶ Deciding where to go

▶ Planning your day

• •

*I*magine strolling the promenade deck with your new spouse, sipping champagne as the ocean breeze whispers to you softly. Cruising to a romantic destination tops many couples list of post-wedding wishes.

Each year thousands of honeymooners make that dream a reality, most of them first-time cruisers. Cruise Lines International Association (CLIA), the marketing group for the cruise industry, in fact is reporting as much as a 25 percent increase in couples choosing honeymoons and other romance vacations (like weddings) on ships.

And what's not to like? Being at sea is romantic. You pretty much pay upfront. And cruising is one of the easiest and most relaxing vacations you can choose.

Plus, you're pretty likely to be happy with the experience. According to CLIA, some 80 percent of the seven million or so people, including honeymooners, who will cruise this year are likely to want to cruise again.

Overcoming Cruise Anxiety

If you haven't taken a cruise before, you may have a million and one misconceptions about cruising that make you hesitate to honeymoon onboard. You may be thinking any of the following, for example: *I'll get sick. I'll get fat. I'll be bored. One word, "Titanic."* In this section, we do our best to cast out misconceptions like these.

Is it too expensive?

Buying a cruise is like buying a car: You never really pay the list (or brochure) price. In fact, most people pay 25 to 50 percent less. And when you consider everything included in the cruise price — cabin, meals, activities, parties, entertainment, and the option of airfare and transfers — you may find that a cruise is actually a cost-conscious vacation choice.

Table 29-1 gives you an idea of how the per person price of an average cruise vacation compares with that of a land-based vacation.

Table 29-1	Cost Comparison by Land and by Sea	
Expense	**Caribbean Cruise (7 nights)**	**Bahamas Resort (7 nights)**
Cruise fare	$1,400	N/A
Room	Included	$700
Airfare	Included (purchased through the line)	$400
Ground transfers	Included	Included
Meals and snacks	Included	$350
Beverages (Alcohol)	$100	$150
Sports activities	Included	
Entertainment	Included	$55 or more
Tips	$63	$80
TOTAL	$1,560	$1,740 or more

What if we get seasick?

No promises here, but most ships are well-stabilized, and popular cruising areas tend to be in calmer waters, particularly in the Caribbean and Alaska's Inside Passage.

Unless you're particularly prone to seasickness, you probably don't need to worry much. But if you are, you can get medications, both over-the-counter and by prescription, that can help. Some people also have had success in curbing seasickness by using ginger capsules (available at health-food stores) or with wristbands (available at most pharmacies).

What if we feel stuck?

Ships are big these days, and the newest ones are bigger than big. It can take days to explore all the diverse spaces they offer, which include tiered atriums and rooms with lots of windows, as well as plenty of open deck space. You won't feel claustrophobic or trapped on a big ship any more than you would at a resort hotel.

Will we be bored?

Not likely. As one cruise-line executive explained, activities offered on cruise ships vary "from the sublime to the ridiculous," and they really do include something for everyone. Intellectuals can attend a lecture. Sports nuts can shoot hoops or play golf (on simulated or mini courses). Intellectuals who are also sports nuts may even be able to find a sporting lecture.

Most ships offer so much to do that you can't possibly do it all.

What's there to see?

Cruise ships visit some 1,800 ports around the world. You can literally take a cruise to Casablanca or a slow boat to China, if you so choose. And ships even go places you can't get to any other way, like the private islands some cruise lines operate in the Bahamas.

Depending on the port of call, you can explore ancient ruins, bicycle down a 10,000-foot volcano, visit museums, take a helicopter or small-plane flight-seeing tour, explore miles of beaches, eat native foods, or look for shopping bargains.

The ships give you a choice of exploring in a group or — for an extra charge — on your own.

Will the ship be crowded?

Big ships have a lot of people (there are fewer on small ships) and many things to do, but you are not forced to mingle or participate. If you want to sit and read a book, snuggle in a quiet deck chair, or watch movies all day in bed in your cabin, you can feel totally comfortable in doing so.

Realize, however, that cruising is by nature a group travel experience. If you want to sit by yourselves at dinner, rather than with other passengers, for instance, you can make a special request to do so (on many ships, you can also choose to dine alone in your cabin).

Avoiding human contact altogether on a cruise ship is difficult. And on the bigger ships, crowds can be a problem.

Are the ships safe?

The *Titanic* happened a long time ago, and a gazillion things have changed since then as far as safety is concerned. Ships today have plenty of lifeboats for everyone (crew included), they have radar to help spot those pesky icebergs (which aren't found in popular cruising areas like the Caribbean, anyway), and they follow so many safety regulations that it sets your head spinning to contemplate them all. As a result, there have been relatively few deaths involving North American-based cruise ships in the last 30 years.

Rather than icebergs, the biggest safety concern even on the newest ships today is fire. In 1994, the International Maritime Organization updated its *Safety of Life at Sea* (SOLAS) standards for fire safety. The rules require most ships to have smoke detectors and low-level emergency lighting for escape routes. Sprinklers are also recommended, but some pre-2004 ships — thanks to grandfather clauses — are not required to install them until 2005. Having sprinklers is not a guarantee of safety (too many other factors come into play). Still, if you want to know whether the ship is so equipped, you can ask the cruise line in advance of your trip.

What will we wear?

Most ships have only two formal nights during a one-week sailing. On these nights, men can wear a suit (preferably dark) or tuxedo (most lines can rent you one if you don't own your own). Women can wear anything from a simple cocktail dress to a glitzy ball gown and feel totally appropriate. If you don't want to dress up at all, some ships also offer casual dining options (you avoid the formal hubbub by eating in a venue other than the main dining room on formal nights).

In addition to the formal nights, most lines have one or two semiformal nights during a one-week sailing, meaning that men should wear jackets and women should wear any sort of nice dress or pants suit, and the rest of the nights are casual nights, where the only rule is no shorts.

Casual attire and bathing suits are the norm during the day (although bathing suits are sometimes banned in restaurants).

If dressing up is not your thing at all, check out small ship lines, which tend to be more casual.

Finding the Right Ship

To assure that your cruise vacation meets your honeymoon dreams, you must give careful consideration to what kind of ship you want to cruise on.

 Making the right choice on the ship is even more important than price. What kind of a bargain is it, for example, if you want a quiet time and find yourself on a rowdy party cruise? Your fantasy vacation may be another person's nightmare (and vice versa).

Cruise ships come in many shapes and sizes and offer a wide range of environments and amenities. Here are the basics:

- ✔ **Big:** Large ships offer nearly all the amenities you'd expect to find at a big land-based resort, including Broadway-style shows, a large casino (except on Disney ships, which do not have casinos), lots of bars and lounges, a big sunning deck and pool area with a Caribbean band playing in the background, a big health spa and gym, constant activities like contests and games, and fun, fun, fun. These ships are for people who like Vegas glitz and don't mind cruising on a ship with lots of families and people who want to party. And who don't mind being part of a crowd.

- ✔ **Classic-style:** If your tastes include some of those listed under the "Big" ship category, but you like things a little less glitzy, you may want to consider more of a classic-style ship. These ships offer good service and a variety of food and entertainment offerings, as well as a choice of activities (although probably not as much as on the bigger ships). There is probably a small gym and spa, and there may or may not be a disco and casino. Show productions may be held in a show lounge or theatre. These vessels especially appeal to people who like things old and traditional, appreciate history, and think vintage is cool.

- ✔ **Small:** Those looking for a more low-key vacation and who are into "soft adventure" should consider a small ship. These vessels go to interesting places, with the destination being as important as the onboard offerings. They are best for people who can entertain themselves over drinks with maybe some music in the background, and are a good option for people who dislike crowds and enjoy casual elegance.

- ✔ **Sailing:** If your idea of a cruise is climbing the rigging like Errol Flynn, you're into sailing, and you really like the sea, choose one of the sailing ships. Casual is the word on these vessels, and there won't be crowds or anything remotely like Las Vegas onboard. Instead you get a chance to meet new people, entertain yourselves (which shouldn't be difficult on your honeymoon anyway), and go-with-the-wind to new places.

Choosing the Perfect Honeymoon Location

After you choose the type of ship you want, you need to decide where you want to cruise. Here's a guide to our picks of honeymoon-appropriate destinations to get you started. When you have an idea of where you may want to go and on what type of ship, flip to Chapter 30 for cruise line specifics.

Sailing the Caribbean

White sand beaches, swaying palms, clear turquoise-blue waters — that's what the Caribbean is all about. Plus there are rainforests, historical sites, and an undersea world to explore. And those seeking adventure of a different sort can check out the truly wild bar scenes.

- ✔ **The experience is great for:** Sunworshippers and funseekers.

- ✔ **What to see and do:** Beaches, palm trees, rain forests, watersports, hiking, local history and culture tours (including Mayan ruins in Mexico), bars and casinos, and duty-free shopping.

- ✔ **Cruise season:** Year-round.

- ✔ **Typical one-week itinerary:** Roundtrip from Miami or Port Everglades (Fort Lauderdale) to three or four islands in the Eastern Caribbean or Western Caribbean (including Cozumel and sometimes Key West, Florida); or roundtrip from San Juan, Puerto Rico, visiting several islands in the Southern Caribbean.

Adventuring to Alaska

Think picture postcard. Alaska is glaciers, whales, icebergs, moose, bears eagles, towering mountains, and rain-forested fjords. Mother Nature's the thing in this vast landscape. Cruise passengers also get a chance to learn about Native American culture and the general heartiness of the locals.

- ✔ **The experience is great for:** Those into the great outdoors for whom spotting a whale means a whale of a good time.

- ✔ **What to see and do:** Mountains, glaciers, fjords, wildlife, forests, Alaska history and culture tours, kayaking, mountain biking, salmon fishing, flightseeing, and dogsledding.

- ✔ **Cruise season:** May to September.

- ✔ **Typical one-week itinerary:** Roundtrip from Vancouver, British Columbia, or one-way between Vancouver and Seward (near

Anchorage), Alaska, with stops at several port towns and glacier areas.

Romancing on the Mexican Riviera

Particularly for those from the West Coast, the Mexican Riviera is a good alternative to the Caribbean for those seeking sand, sun, water-sports, and a fun-in-the-sun party scene.

- ✔ **The experience is great for:** West Coast-based sunworshippers and funseekers — the flight to L.A. is cheaper than flying to Florida for a Caribbean cruise.

- ✔ **What to see and do:** Beaches, scenery, watersports, local culture, and deep-sea fishing.

- ✔ **Cruise season:** Year-round.

- ✔ **Typical one-week itinerary:** From Los Angeles with calls at Puerto Vallarta, Mazatlán, and Cabo San Lucas.

Heading to Hawaii

Aloha to cruise passengers means a chance to explore several of the fabulous Hawaiian Islands and their natural and manmade treasures.

- ✔ **The experience is great for:** Those who want to see and experience all the Hawaiian islands (not just one).

- ✔ **What to see and do:** Beaches, gorgeous scenery (including volcanic peaks, rugged coastlines, waterfalls, and lush forests), watersports, island culture and history, hiking, bird watching, and shopping for loud Hawaiian shirts.

- ✔ **Cruise season:** Year-round.

- ✔ **Typical one-week itinerary:** Roundtrip from Honolulu or Maui, visiting four islands.

Cruising in Costa Rica or Belize

The name means "Rich Coast" in Spanish, and that's what you find, an unspoiled place rich in lush rain forests, beaches, mountains and wildlife.

- ✔ **The experience is great for:** Nature lovers with a sense of adventure.

- ✔ **What to see and do:** Lush rain forests, isolated beaches, wildlife, excellent scuba and snorkeling, and ancient ruins.

- ✔ **Cruise season:** January to April.

✔ **Typical one-week itinerary:** (For Costa Rica) from Puerto Caldera, exploring the Pacific Coast of Costa Rica; (for Belize) from Cancun (Mexico), visiting Roatan, Honduras, and several tiny islands in Belize.

Exploring the Greek Islands or Italian and French Rivieras

Looking for a little more than fun-in-the-sun? In the Med, in addition to incredible scenery, you find medieval ramparts, amazing archeological site, and some of the best museums in the world. History literally awaits at every turn.

✔ **The cruise is great for:** Those who can afford to honeymoon in Europe and want some ancient history and lively European culture with their fun-in-the-sun.

✔ **What to see and do:** Scenery, historic sites, interesting architecture, local culture, quaint villages, rugged shorelines, beaches, watersports, and shopping.

✔ **Cruise season:** April to October.

✔ **Typical one-week itinerary:** (Greek Isles) from Piraeus, Greece or a port in Italy, visiting several Greek Islands as well as a port or two in Turkey; (Italian and French Rivieras), from Nice or Cannes (France) or Venice or Rome (Italy), to ports in France and Italy as well as Monte Carlo (Monaco).

Voyaging to Tahiti

A visit here is truly a visit to paradise. We're talking volcanic peaks rising from clear blue lagoons, unpopulated beaches, and a pleasingly laid back atmosphere.

✔ **The experience is great for:** Sunworshippers with big bucks; those who can afford to go to one of the most beautiful places in the world.

✔ **What to see and do:** Scenery, beaches, watersports, local culture, hiking, and shopping for black pearls.

✔ **Cruise season:** Year-round.

✔ **Typical one-week itinerary:** Roundtrip from Papeete, with port calls at several islands including Bora Bora and Moorea.

Going transatlantic

Head to sea and go somewhere like they did in the old days, when getting on a ship was for transportation purposes. These cruises take you

to or from the U.S. and Europe, with several lazy days to relax while
you are at sea.

✔ **The experience is great for:** Those who can appreciate being on
the ocean for days and want to travel to Europe the traditional
way.

✔ **What to see and do:** Look at the sea on your way to Europe,
onboard activities.

✔ **Cruise season:** April to December.

✔ **Typical one-week itinerary:** Six-day crossing from New York to
Southampton, England or the reverse, and fly back.

Deciding How Long to Go

To get the most out of your honeymoon cruise vacation, we suggest
a seven-night itinerary. Usually, ships leave on a Saturday or Sunday
afternoon and return early the following Saturday or Sunday, giving you
plenty of time to do everything on the ship and still get home in time to
go back to work on Monday.

If you're a little wary of booking a full-week cruise your first time out, a
three- or four-night getaway cruise can still give you a nice taste of the
cruise experience. These shorter cruise lengths also allow you to combine a week's vacation with land-based options — say, a visit to Disney.
Of course, the cruise lines have thought of this and offer an array of
pre- and post-cruise land packages.

And, of course, if you both have all the time in the world on your hands,
longer cruises of ten days, two weeks, or more are also available.

Knowing What to Expect On Board

On a cruise, you are already in a romantic environment, *and* you get to
visit some of the most romantic places you can find. Use the information
and recommendations in this chapter to help you enjoy your cruise
vacation and make it extra-special for your honeymoon.

The cruise ship has gyms to work out in, spas to relax in, pools to
swim in (or just sun by), stores to shop in, contests to play, games to
win, movies to watch, musicians to hear, and lectures to attend (you
may even find a cooking class to take). You can play bingo or get your
scuba-diving certification.

You can participate in crazy pool games that involve things like finding
out how many Ping-Pong balls your bathing suit holds or attend an art
auction. There really is something for everyone on a cruise ship.

You can always also just choose to relax in a deck chair where you can rub each other with suntan lotion, or in your cabin where you can have a pillow fight and watch movies. It's your special vacation. Do what you like best!

Check out the daily program in your cabin each evening for details on the next day's shipboard activities, entertainment offerings, meal times, featured movies, items on sale in the gift shop (including ship logo-wear), featured drinks (of the alcoholic variety), and hours the ship is expected to remain in port, as well as the dress code for the night.

Dining on a cruise

Food is a big part of the cruise experience, and no matter what ship you choose, there's bound to be plenty of it. Most lines have adapted their menus to include low-fat and vegetarian choices, but they still serve plenty of filet mignon, lobster, pastas, and just about everything else you can imagine.

Some people may not want to eat a five-course meal in a formal setting every night. Many cruise lines have created casual dining options, such as cafes and pizzerias. At breakfast and lunch you usually have a choice of dining room service or a more casual buffet, and you may have that choice at dinner as well.

Although some ships still offer midnight buffets, a new trend is to have at least one eating venue on board open on a 24-hour basis. If you get the munchies but don't feel like getting out of bed, most ships usually provide 24-hour room service — although the selections may be limited.

While all food at meals, including room service, is free, some ships charge extra for gourmet ice cream as a snack. There may also be a service fee (usually $5 to $20) for dinner in the fancy alternative restaurant.

If you order something in the dining room that you don't like, it's perfectly okay to send it back and ask for another selection. And if you can't choose between two dishes, feel free to order both. The staff — and chefs — want you to be happy.

Sitting at the captain's table

Ship captains invite VIPs to sit at their table. As a honeymooner, you may qualify as a VIP.

If you'd like an invite, write a brief letter to the line — via your travel agent — including a brief biography (no, we're not kidding). Make sure to mention your important event.

If you do get an invite (which is delivered to your cabin after you're on the ship), dress up, even if it's on one of the ship's informal nights. Men should wear a jacket and tie, women a dress or nice pants suit.

The captain usually provides wine for the table, and there may be a special menu.

Staying in shape

With all that eating, you're probably wondering how much weight you may gain. They — the ominous naysayers — say the average person gains five pounds during a one-week cruise. But we say you don't have to gain any if you're careful.

In addition to your (ah-hem) honeymoon workout, you can burn calories in the ship's gym, which, especially on newer ships, tend to be spacious and popular places, often with ocean views, and equipped with weights, treadmills, stair-climbers, and bikes. Most ships also offer exercise classes, and if you're not into the group thing, you can jog on the Promenade Deck or other designated jogging area, or burn calories walking up and down the stairs (climbing 12 stories works wonders for your calves). Many bigger ships also have personal trainers available. And when you're done working out, you can reward yourself with a massage or sauna at the ship's spa or have your hair or nails done at the ship's beauty parlor.

Cruising the nightlife

Nighttime is one of the liveliest times on a cruise ship. After your five-course meal you can, depending on the ship, head off to a lounge to dance to your old-time favorites, pulse to the beat in the disco, try your luck in a glitzy casino, sip drinks at a piano bar, check out the stogies at a cigar bar, hear lounge-lizard or comedy acts, see a Las Vegas- or Broadway-style review, or enjoy a feature film in a movie theatre. No additional admission is charged for you to attend any of the entertainment events — but you do have to pay for your drinks.

If you're in a port at night, you can also partake of the local nightlife. Ask the ship's tour staff for recommendations.

High rolling at the casino

If your ship has a casino (most do), it is open whenever the ship is at sea but not in port (due to local regulations). Ship-board casinos are usually smaller than their land-based counterparts, but they feature the same kind of games. A typical casino offers roulette wheels, craps, black jack, and poker (including Caribbean Stud Poker) tables. Slot machines are typically quarter and dollar (some with progressive jackpots).

Going ashore

When the ship gets into port, you have three choices: Go on a shore excursion organized by the cruise line, go it alone, or stay on the ship.

Shore excursions are designed to help you make the most of your limited time at each port of call, but they are also a money-making area for the cruise line. The offerings can add a hefty sum to your vacation costs, ranging from about $25 for a bus tour to $250 or more for an elaborate private sailing or flight-seeing trip. Whether you choose to take a shore excursion is a matter of both personal preference and pocketbook concerns.

Some are worth the money. We especially like the active offerings such as snorkeling, mountain biking, golf, and kayaking. And tours that go beyond the port city are sometimes more economical than taking a cab.

Some other excursions aren't worth the money, however. A tour may consist, for instance, of a bus ride past the local sights with hokey commentary and an obligatory stop at a souvenir stand. Rather than join the masses on the bus tour it may be more fun and romantic to go off exploring on your own, to find a secluded beach or park, or just walk hand-in-hand through the town.

When making the decision on shore excursions, consider the following:

✔ How easy is it to find a cab, and how reliable are they if you find one?

✔ What's within walking distance of the ship and what's not?

✔ How much does it cost to see the attractions we want to see?

✔ Are any reservations required (for restaurants or activities?

✔ Are there things we want to do that are not on the organized tours? And if we take a tour is there time for us to do those things?

You should feel free to ask questions of the shore excursion desk on the ship even if you're not taking one of the ship's tours. They have maps and plenty of other information available, and they can help you make reservations for restaurants or activities such as golf.

If you do decide to go off on your own, make sure that you return to the ship at the required time. If you miss the boat, you may have to pay your own way to the next port.

Some lines let you book shore excursions in advance, and if that's the case with your cruise, you may want to take advantage of the offer, as popular excursions tend to sell out.

Chapter 30

Finding the Ideal Honeymoon Cruise

By Fran Wenograd Golden

• •

In This Chapter

▶ Discovering the best cruise ships for honeymooners

▶ Knowing where the cruise lines sail

▶ Finding a special honeymoon package

• •

*T*he ship lines we discuss in this chapter were chosen as the best of the lot in terms of romance, onboard offerings, and itineraries. At the top of the reviews we specify which ships in the fleet of each cruise line are best for honeymooners (they are often the newest ships), and which destinations those ships visit are best for honeymooners (we don't necessarily mention every destination the vessels visit). We also note what types of ships are in the fleet (big, small, and so on).

As you look through our reviews of each ship, you see that we tell you the size of each vessel. The size of ships is often described not in length but in Gross Registered Tons, a way to determine size that takes into account interior space used to produce revenue on each vessel. One GRT equals 100 cubic feet of enclosed, revenue-generating space. A big ship, sometimes called a *megaship,* is 70,000 GRTs and up.

We also factor in demographics with an eye towards making sure you aren't the only ones in your age group on the ship.

We highly recommend that you book (if you can afford it) a cabin with a verandah, and we also specify, in the reviews, the availability of these offerings.

For more information on choosing a cabin and shipboard dining, turn to Chapters 29 and 31.

The rates listed in the reviews that follow are per person, double occupancy, for a seven-day (meaning seven nights on the ship) cruise. Double the number to see the total cost for the two of you.

The rates we list are rack rates, which means that they are the maximum price. You can expect to save up to 60 percent off these prices by booking early. See more on ways to save in Chapter 31.

Inside means no windows; outside means with windows. Because most people like natural light, outside cabins are more expensive. Suites are the biggest cabins on the ship.

The cruise lines offer a variety of honeymoon packages, typically sold as add-ons (you pay for the package in addition to the cruise fare), but sometimes the honeymoon package is complimentary. Even if you don't book a package, you should let the line know that you're a honeymooner (they are likely to do something special for you).

American Hawaii Cruises/ United States Lines

1380 Port of New Orleans Place, Robin St. Wharf, New Orleans, LA 70130-1890. (The company is moving to Sunrise, Florida, in early 2002.) ☎ *800-513-5022 (American Hawaii);* ☎ *877-330-6600 (United States Lines). Internet:* www.cruisehawaii. com *and* www.unitedstateslines.com. *Rack rates: $1,335-$2,185 inside, $1,535-$2,799 outside, $2,635-$3,435 suite.*

> ✔ **Honeymooners' destinations:** Hawaii (Oahu, Kauai, Maui, and the Big Island)
>
> ✔ **Honeymooners' choice:** *Independence* (built 1951, 818 passengers, 30,090 GRTs); *Patriot* (built in 1983, 1,214 passengers, 33,930 GRTs)
>
> ✔ **Ship style:** Classic

American Hawaii operates the classic twin-funneled ocean liner *Independence,* which for quite some time was the only game in town when it came to cruising around the Hawaiian Islands (a big plus of these cruises being that you get to visit four islands). Late last year, the line got competition from its own new sister line, United States Lines (they share the same owner), which launched the *Patriot* on a similar Hawaiian Islands route.

The *Independence* has an old oceanliner ambiance combined with a strong Hawaiian theme in its decor, furnishings, and collection of artifacts and entertainment offerings. It tends to attract mostly older couples, but also some families and honeymooners. The *Patriot* is a slightly larger, traditional-style ship that was previously operated by Holland America Line as the *Nieuw Amsterdam*. For its new incarnation, the vessel has been slightly Hawaiian-ized decor-wise, and is geared towards a slightly younger demographic than the *Independence* (although most passengers still tend towards 50 and up). A *kumu* (traditional Hawaiian teacher and storyteller) sails with both ships.

The staff on the vessels is mostly American and both friendly and professional, and the ambiance casual. The ships don't have casinos, nor do they have discos per se (although late-night dancing with a D.J. is offered). Meals include local ingredients such as fresh mahi-mahi. The *Independence* does not offer 24-hour room service, but the *Patriot* does.

Cabins on the *Independence* come in some 50 different configurations (a far cry from new ships with their modular units). They are comfortably done up in Hawaiian fabrics, with very small bathrooms. Not all the cabins can be configured with double beds, so make sure to ask. Six large suites have outside (but not inside) access. Only the owner's suites have TVs, and they also offer VCRs, hairdryers, and bathtubs. None of the cabins have verandahs. Cabins on the *Patriot* are more standardized and feature a contemporary resort decor. Interior cabins are small, but outside cabins are quite comfy. Superior oceanview cabins include a sitting area, window, bathtub, and shower (make sure to ask for a queen-size bed). The ship's large Parlor Suites have a king-size bed, sofa bed, sitting area, picture window, fridge, and bath with a tub. Again, none of the cabins have verandahs.

American Hawaii Lines offers a number of specials for honeymooners. The **Aloha Package** includes a Hawaiian pineapple filled with assorted cheeses and tropical fruit, sweets, an etched farewell bottle of red wine, and a Memories of Paradise photo album. Cost: $99. The **Romance Package** adds a bottle of champagne, a tropical flower arrangement, and two bathrobes embroidered with the cruise line's emblem. Cost: $199. An **Ultimate Luxury Package** includes all of the above plus two body massages, two hors d oeuvres platters (delivered to the cabin), and an 8-by-10 photo with a keepsake frame. Cost: $499.

Carnival Cruise Lines

3655 NW 87th Ave., Miami, FL 33178-2428. ☎ *800-CARNIVAL. Internet:* www.carnival.com. *Rates racks: $1,349-$1,859 inside, $1489-$2,399 outside, $2,399-$3,199 suite.*

> ✔ **Honeymooners' destinations:** Eastern Caribbean, Western Caribbean, Southern Caribbean, Mexican Riviera, and Alaska

✔ **Honeymooners' choice:** *Destiny* (built in 1996, 2,642 passengers, 101,000 GRTs); *Spirit* (built in 2001, 2,124 passengers, 84,000 GRTs); *Triumph* (built in 1999, 2,766 passengers, 102,353 GRTs); *Victory* (built in 2000, 2,766 passengers, 102,353 GRTs); *Paradise* and *Elation* (both built in 1998, 2,040 passengers, 70,367 GRTs)

✔ **Ship style:** Big

Carnival was named the top line for honeymoons by both *Brides* and *Modern Bride* magazines, and it's easy to see why. Carnival is the Big Kahuna of the industry, its modern fleet boasting big ships that are bold, innovative, and expert at delivering non-stop action and fun. You get all the resort amenities you can imagine, offered at a reasonable price.

The ships attract the same crowd found in Las Vegas and at Florida's megaresorts, with a decor that is eclectic and definitely glitzy (think theme park on water). The food is well-prepared and bountiful, and the dining rooms offer several seating times for added flexibility. The ships have midnight buffets and 24-hour pizzerias as well as alternative casual dining at night. The new *Spirit* even offers a supper club where, on a reservations-only basis, you can enjoy live entertainment while you dine. Service is not as refined as on smaller or fancier ships, but then that's not the point here. The entertainment is splendiferous, with each ship boasting a dozen dancers, a 12-piece orchestra, comedians, jugglers, and numerous live bands, as well as big (and in some cases, giant) casinos. All the ships also have large spa and gym areas.

If you're on a really tight budget, the *Destiny* offers a special category of cabins called Night Owl. These 11 cabins are offered at a really low price (less than half of what you'd pay for comparable rooms) but come with a caveat: They are located above the disco and consequently are not very conducive to sleeping until the disco shuts in the wee hours. It's a perfect deal only if you plan to be up all night, too.

Standard cabins are modular units that are nearly identical, and a decent number of cabins offer verandahs (especially on the *Spirit*). All ocean-view accommodations come with bathrobes (to use on the cruise), and on the *Destiny, Triumph,* and *Victory*, all cabins have hairdryers as well. Suites add VCRs, whirlpool tubs, sitting areas, refrigerators, and bars.

The *Paradise* is a totally smoke-free cruise ship (shipyard workers weren't even allowed to smoke while building her). You have to sign a contract before you get on vowing not to smoke, and if you are caught smoking on the ship you are dropped off at the next port, forfeit your cruise fare, have to pay your own way home, and face a fine of $250 for each infraction (to pay for new curtains, bedding, and the like). They're serious about this, folks.

Newlyweds receive a **"Happy Honeymoon"** cake in the dining room, and they are the guests of honor at the **Couples & Lovers party** where complimentary champagne is served. Cost: Free!

The Carnival Spirit has a wedding chapel where you can get married at sea by a designated crew member (not the captain) on Alaska sailings (permission to offer weddings at sea on other itineraries was pending at press time).

Celebrity Cruises

1050 Caribbean way, Miami, FL 33132. ☎ *800-437-3111. Internet:* www. celebritycruises.com. *Rack rates: $1,499–$2,079 inside, $1,899–$3,129, outside, $3,029–$9,599 suites.*

- ✔ **Honeymooners' destinations:** Eastern Caribbean, Western Caribbean, Southern Caribbean, and Alaska

- ✔ **Honeymooners' choice:** *Century* (built in 1995, 1,750 passengers, 70,606 GRTs); *Galaxy* and *Mercury* (built in 1996/1997, 1,870 passengers, 77,713 GRTs); *Infinity* and *Millennium* (built in 2000/2001, 1,950 passengers, 91,000 GRTs)

- ✔ **Ship style:** Big

Celebrity has an impressive sense of style, pays careful attention to detail, and offers exceptional service — a luxury product offered at an affordable price. The Celebrity Fleet is among the newest in the industry, and renowned designers worked on the interiors of the vessels (and it shows). These ships offer just the right amount of drama — including an impressive art collection — without resorting to glitz. The ships feature an array of cushy public rooms that include cigar clubs, champagne bars, coffee bars, and martini bars. The entertainment is usually good, and in some cases, it's extraordinary (especially the featured acts). The cuisine is extra-special and is meticulously guided by Michel Roux, Celebrity's famous culinary consultant and one of the top French chefs in Britain.

The cabins on Celebrity ships are all good-sized and well-organized — there's really no bad cabin — and they provide plenty of storage space. All cabins come with safes, refrigerators, and hairdryers, and a good number have verandahs. Upper-category cabins also have VCRs. Suites come with complimentary butler service, verandahs, bathtubs, sitting areas, bathrobes, and lots of other extras, and some have verandahs. The penthouse suites are among the largest at sea (on the *Millennium* and *Infinity* they are nearly 3,000 square feet) and boast separate sleeping, living, and dining areas as well as very large balconies with hot tubs.

 The **Honeymoon Package** include breakfast in bed featuring champagne, two keepsake champagne flutes, a flower arrangement, a red rose, two Celebrity Cruises bathrobes, and a box of pralines. Cost: $134.

Costa Cruise Lines

200 South Park Rd., Hollywood, FL 33021. ☎ ***800-33-COSTA.*** *Internet:* www. costacruises.com. *Rack rates: $1,209–$3,240 inside, $1,409–$3850 outside, $2,459–$4,800 suites. Higher rates are for Greek Isles cruises and include roundtrip airfare to Europe.*

- ✔ **Honeymooners' destinations:** Greek Isles, Eastern Caribbean, and Western Caribbean

- ✔ **Honeymooners' choice:** *CostaVictoria* (built in 1996, 1,928 passengers, 76,000 GRTs); *CostaClassica* (built in 1991, 1,308 passengers, 53,000 GRTs); and *CostaAtlantica* (built in 2000, 2,680 passengers, 84,000 GRTs)

- ✔ **Ship style:** Big, Classic

The origins of Costa Cruise Lines (which date back to 1860 and the olive-oil business) are in Italy, and it shows from the Italian food, sleek Italian design, and Italian-speaking crew (although they're not all from Italy), to the mostly Italian entertainers and the onboard activities, which include toga parties. The Costa ships aren't designed strictly for an American audience, and therein lies the charm.

The food is flavorful, plentiful, and presented with theatrical flare. Alternative venues include pizza cafes and patisseries.

All cabins have hairdryers and safes, and most have minibars (in suites only on the *CostaClassica*). Suites come with butler service, whirlpool baths, queen-size beds, and bathrobes (to use on the cruise), and 10 suites on the *CostaClassica* and 58 on the *CostaAtlantica* have private verandahs. The *CostaClassica,* which recently underwent a major facelift, is considerably smaller than the other two vessels.

The honeymoon package includes a chilled bottle of sparkling Italian wine, fresh flowers, a keepsake portrait taken by the ship's photographer, an 8-by-10 silver frame to hold the photo, a certificate suitable for framing, an invitation to a cocktail party for honeymooners hosted by the ship's captain, his and hers Costa robes to take home, and a red rose. Cost: $99.

Cunard Line

6100 Blue Lagoon Dr., Suite 400, Miami, FL 33126. ☎ ***800-5CUNARD.*** *Internet:* www. cunard.com. *Rack rates: (for six-day crossing) $2,170-$2,850 inside, $3,020-$9,040 outside, $14,060-$25,440 suites.*

✔ **Honeymooners' destinations:** Transatlantic

✔ **Honeymooners' choice:** *Queen Elizabeth II* (built in 1969, 1,500 passengers, 70,327 GRTs)

✔ **Ship style:** Classic

Cunard, the British-bred grande dame of the cruise industry, comes with an impressive pedigree, including the famous ships *Mauritania, Queen Mary,* and *Queen Elizabeth.*

The atmosphere aboard the line's current flagship, the famous *Queen Elizabeth II,* is rather traditional British and a bit formal (royals have walked these decks). The *QE2* is the only ship today continuing the tradition of scheduled transatlantic crossings, and she does so with an old-fashioned class system (the *QE2* has four classes). The class system means that you sleep and dine on decks assigned to your class. The ship has been called a "City at Sea" for good reason, and amenities are aplenty. Service is ever-so-polite, delivered by very attentive white-gloved staff.

The food is high quality and presented at single seatings. The British among the passengers — and there can be many — take high tea quite seriously (pinkies out, please). Entertainment includes big-name guest performers, and activities include big-name guest lecturers. Cabins come in a variety of shapes and sizes ranging from small to large, with the best, and most expensive, in the Queen's Grill category. Some cabins have bathtubs and walk-in closets. Top suites have sitting areas, bathtubs, refrigerators, and butler service, as well as a host of other amenities, and some have private verandahs.

 Cunard offers six-day transatlantic crossings from late April to December (in the later months the seas can be rough) between New York and Southampton, England. You can return by air, with the cost of one-way, economy-class air included in the cruise fare.

Disney Cruise Line

210 Celebration Place, Suite 400, Celebration, FL 34747-1000. ☎ *888-325-2500. Internet:* www.disneycruise.com. *Rack rates: $829-$1,599 inside, $1,099-$2,600 outside, $2,999-$4,299 suites.*

✔ **Honeymooners' destinations:** Eastern Caribbean, Western Caribbean, and Bahamas

✔ **Honeymooners' choice:** *Disney Magic* and *Disney Wonder* (built in 1998/1999, 1,760 passengers, 83,000 GRTs)

✔ **Ship style:** Big and Classic

The *Disney Magic* and *Disney Wonder* are great ships, reflecting a beautiful mix of old and new, designed to appeal to both first-timers (especially fans of Disney's vacation resorts) and the megaship crowd looking for a little something different. Disney set out to reinvent the wheel with these ships, and among the innovations is an adults-only nighttime entertainment area, and a unique rotation dining system where you get to eat in a different dining room (and very different environment) every night. The adults-only **Palo** restaurant, available on a reservations-only basis (you're advised to book a table when you first get on board), serves Northern Italian cuisine, and it's one of the best dining options at sea.

Obviously, because we're talking Disney, these ships get a number of kid passengers. But also wanting to cater to couples, the ships offer an adults-only pool area (separate from the family pool) and ban kids from the gym and spa. Also, at Disney's wonderful private island, Castaway Cay, there's an adults-only beach, aptly named Serenity Bay.

Entertainment is what you'd expect of Disney, with lavish stage shows and fun treats such as an adults-only improv comedy club and, for the sports minded, an ESPN sports bar. Be warned if you're a party-hearty type, however, that there is a rather quiet pace on these ships at night; there is no casino, and a fair number of people go to bed with their kids before midnight.

The ships' cabins are larger than the industry average, and most come with separate compartments for the toilet and bath/shower. They all have safes, hairdryers, bathrobes, and refrigerators, and some have balconies. The suites come with all of the above as well as concierge service, VCRs, and whirlpool tubs; the suites are downright huge and are some of the nicest at sea.

Cruises on the *Disney Wonder* are for three or four days and are usually sold together with a land vacation at Walt Disney World to create a one-week vacation experience.

The honeymoon package on the Disney line, **Romantic Escape at Sea,** includes a bottle of champagne, two champagne flutes, cheese and crackers, a silk rose, a half-hour aromatherapy body massage (one per person), and priority seating at Palo, the reservations-only restaurant. Cost: $179. The **Romantic Escape Option** is geared to guests who book a land and cruise package (including a stay at Walt Disney World). It includes an exclusive Disney's Fairy tale Honeymoons Pin (one per person), Disney Fairy Tale Honeymoons His and Her limited edition watches, a choice of dinner at a selected specialty restaurant within the Walt Disney World Resort (with wine or champagne), a couples-only spa treatment, a professional honeymoon photography session at the Disney Theme Park of the guests' choice, and onboard the ship, the same features as the Romantic Escape at Sea. Cost: $609.

Princess Cruises

24305 Town Center Drive, Santa Clarita, CA 91355-4999. ☎ ***800-PRINCESS.*** *Internet:* www.princess.com. *Rack rates: $1,289-$1,969 inside, $1,499-$3,149 outside, $2,399-$5,079 suites.*

- ✔ **Honeymooners' destinations:** Eastern Caribbean, Western Caribbean, Southern Caribbean, Alaska, and Mexican Riviera

- ✔ **Honeymooners' choice:** *Golden Princess* and *Grand Princess* (built in 2001/1998, 2,600 passengers each, 109,000 GRTs); *Dawn Princess, Ocean Princess, Sea Princess,* and *Sun Princess* (built in 1997/2000/1998/1995, 1,950 passengers, 77,000 GRTs)

- ✔ **Ship style:** Big

These real life "love boats" (made famous in the TV show) are among the best run ships on the high seas, offering passengers a good range of choices in accommodations, dining, and entertainment. Even though the Princess megaships offer megaresort facilities, Princess still also preserves the kind of intimate spaces that you can find on smaller vessels. The decor tends to be stylish and moderately upscale, but presented in a conservative way (without the glitz).

The entertainment includes elaborate stage shows and excellent cabaret acts, and the ships offer a wealth of activities including PADI (Professional Association of Diving Instructors) scuba certification classes and computer-simulated golf. The food has been upgraded, but is still pretty mass-market. Princess recently introduced a nice option that lets guests dine restaurant-style, when and where they want, rather than having to commit to set dining room seating. Service on Princess ships is gracious and relaxed.

The *Grand Princess* debuted in 1998 as the largest ship afloat (Royal Caribbean's *Voyager of the Seas* took that title away in 1999). And both the *Grand Princess* and its new sister ship, *Golden Princess,* have wedding chapels where you can actually get married by the captain at sea, just like on *The Love Boat.* Cabins on the *Dawn, Ocean, Sea,* and *Sun Princesses* are well designed and offer bathrobes, fruit baskets, and chocolates on the pillow at night. A good number of cabins have verandahs. Suites and mini-suites also have whirlpool bathtubs, separate sitting areas, and butler service. The larger *Grand Princess* and *Golden Princess* have a whopping 710 cabins with verandahs, and three levels of suites (mini, suite, and very fancy Grand Suite, the latter with a hot tub).

The honeymoon package includes a bottle of champagne, two long-stemmed roses, two Princess Cruises engraved souvenir champagne glasses, a framed formal portrait, chocolate-dipped strawberries, and a personalized honeymoon card from the Captain. Cost: $99. A deluxe package adds on to the regular package with a champagne breakfast in bed, two terry cloth bathrobes, a visit to the spa for a massage or facial, an invite to the bridge, and a choice of *canapes* or *petits fours* delivered to you cabin. Cost: $299.

Radisson Seven Seas Cruises

600 Corporate Dr., Suite 410, Fort Lauderdale, FL 33334. ☎ *800-285-1835. Internet:* www.rssc.com. *Rack rates: No inside, $2,795-$5,495 outside, $6,695-$10,095 suites.*

> ✔ **Honeymooners' destinations:** Tahiti
>
> ✔ **Honeymooners' choice:** *Paul Gauguin* (built in 1997, 320 passengers, 18,800 GRTs)
>
> ✔ **Ship style:** Small

Operated by a division of Radisson Hotels, Radisson Seven Seas Cruise ships include the French-flagged *Paul Gauguin,* a luxurious yet casual ship featuring modern French decor and Polynesian artwork.

The *Paul Gauguin* vessel is extraordinary in terms of service, amenities, cabins, and cuisine. Seating in the dining rooms, which include a reservations-only French restaurant and an outside grill, is on an open-seating basis. Wine with meals is complimentary. All the cabins are suite-sized and have outside views (mostly large windows, but also some portholes) and sitting areas, and more than half have private verandahs. They come with VCRs, refrigerator/bars (with complimentary soft drinks and booze), safes, bathtubs, bathrobes, fresh flowers, hairdryers, and in most, queen-size beds. In addition, seven even larger suites are available.

The line assumes that most passengers are happy entertaining themselves, so organized activities are limited. At night cabaret and production shows are staged, and at some ports, local entertainers come on board. The gym and spa are tiny, but there's plenty of opportunity to jog, bike, or enjoy watersports on the islands the ship calls at. Port calls include a visit to a private *motu* (a small island attached to a reef). The *Paul Gauguin* also has its own retractable marina.

Honeymooners receive an in-cabin gift and bottle of champagne, a Polynesian "blessing" ceremony, a cocktail party, and a photograph. Cost: Free!

Royal Caribbean International

1050 Caribbean Way, Miami, FL 33132. ☎ *800-ALL-HERE. Internet:* www.royalcaribbean.com. *Rack rates: $1,249-$2,199 inside, $1,799-$3,149 outside, $3,829-$9,379 suites.*

✔ **Honeymooners' destinations:** Eastern Caribbean, Southern Caribbean, Western Caribbean, Greek Isles, Italy, France, Mexican Riviera, and Alaska

✔ **Honeymooners' choice:** *Adventure of the Seas* (built in 2001, 3,114 passsengers, 138,000 GRTs), *Enchantment of the Seas* (built in 1997, 1,950 passengers, 73,817 GRTs), *Explorer of the Seas* (built in 2000, 3,114 passengers, 138,000 GRTs), *Grandeur of the Seas* (built in 1996, 1,950 passengers, 73,817 GRTs), *Radiance of the Seas* (built in 2001, 2,100 passengers, 90,000 GRTs), *Rhapsody of the Seas* (built in 1997, 2000 passengers, 78,491 GRTs), *Vision of the Seas* (built in 1998, 2,000 passengers, 78,491 GRTs), *Voyager of the Seas* (built in 1999, 3,114 passengers, 138,000 GRTs)

✔ **Ship style:** Big

What kind of cruise line would put a full-sized skating rink (complete with Zamboni machine) on a cruise ship? Royal Caribbean! In 1999 the megacruise line (it's number two only to Carnival) introduced the *Voyager of the Seas,* the largest ship afloat, with such unique shipboard features as an ice skating rink and a rock-climbing wall. In 2000, the successful vessel got a sister, *Explorer of the Seas,* and in 2001, a new sibling set sail called *Adventure of the Seas.* Some of the same features (including the rock climbing wall) can be found on the new and smaller (but still darned big) *Radiance of the Seas,* which also adds the unique cruise ship feature of a billiards room.

The trend-setting Royal Caribbean line sells a reasonably priced, mass-market oriented cruise experience. The ships have enough activities to please almost everyone, except maybe those who hate crowds. The fleet is all well-run and the product consistent, with a veritable army of service employees paying close attention to day-to-day details. The classy, contemporary decor on these vessels doesn't bang you on the head with glitz like, say, top competitor Carnival. The ships have spacious public rooms and areas, including elaborate health clubs, spas, swimming pools (some with retractable roofs), and open sun deck areas. Food on Royal Caribbean is mass-market rather than gourmet. However, Royal Caribbean spends big bucks on entertainment, and you can see it in the line's savvy, high-tech show productions.

The line has its own island, CocoCay (Little Stirrup Cay) in The Bahamas, and an isolated beach in Haiti called Labadee. Both give passengers a venue for fun in the sun, complete with watersports and all the trimmings.

Cabins on the *Enchantment, Grandeur, Rhapsody,* and *Vision* are similarly functional and have interactive TVs, and some have verandahs. Suites include sitting areas, bathtubs, and VCRs; the suites come in various sizes, the best being the apartment-sized Royal Suites with such amenities as a grand piano.

The *Voyager of the Seas, Explorer of the Seas,* and *Adventure of the Seas* add a new concept: interior cabins with a view of the ship's Promenade. The suites on these ships are similar to those on the other ships, but they're a bit bigger and there are more of them. They also have the added amenity of minibars. The *Radiance* has more cabins with verandahs than the other ships, and all the cabins have minibars and hairdryers.

The **Deluxe Romance Package** includes champagne, a champagne breakfast for two in your cabin, an after-dinner dessert tray, and a photo in a silver frame. Cost: $99. The **Luxury Romance Package** includes champagne, two velour bathrobes (embroidered with the Royal Caribbean International emblem), a massage or facial for both the bride and groom, a champagne breakfast for two in your cabin, pre-dinner canapés and goodnight sweets, and a photo in a silver-plated frame. Cost: $499.

The *Voyager, Explorer,* and new *Adventure* all have wedding chapels, but weddings are only conducted when the ships are in port, not at sea.

Star Clippers

4101 Salzedo St., Coral Gables, FL 33146. ☎ *800-442-0553. Internet:* www. starclippers.com. *Rack rates: $1,345-$1,675 inside, $1,545-$3,795 outside, $3,465-$4,795 suites.*

- ✔ **Honeymooners' destinations:** Caribbean (from St. Maarten or Barbados), Greek Isles, Italy, and France
- ✔ **Honeymooners' choice:** *Star Clipper* (built in 1992/1991, 172 passengers, 2,298 GRTs); *Star Flyer* (built in 1992/1991, 172 passengers, 2,298 GRTs); and *Royal Clipper* (built in 2000, 228 passengers, 5,000 GRTs)
- ✔ **Ship style:** Small ship

The twins *Star Flyer* and *Star Clipper,* and the new *Royal Clipper,* are modern replicas of the big, 19th-century clipper sailing ships (or *barkentines*) that once circled the globe. Their tall, square rigs carry enormous sails; the ships themselves offer a particular thrill for history buffs. The atmosphere on board these ships is akin to being on a private yacht rather than a mainstream cruise ship. It's casual and friendly. Dining is open seating, with the food good, but not great.

Despite stabilizers, movement of these small ships may be troublesome to those who get seasick.

Activities on the ships tend toward the nautical, such as visiting the bridge, watching the crew handle the sails, and taking classes in skills such as knot-tying. The vessels each have two pools, and massages are offered in a spare cabin or in a cabana on deck. PADI-approved

(Professional Association of Diving Instructors) scuba diving instruction is offered, and water-skiing and snorkeling are also available. Local entertainment is sometimes brought on at night, and the ships also have a piano player and a makeshift disco in the Tropical Bar.

All the cabins have marble bathrooms, and the deluxe cabins have whirlpool bathtubs and minibars. They also have TVs which show in-house movies only. The *Royal Clipper* has 14 suites with verandahs and two owner's suites, which come without verandahs but are located at the extreme stern of the ship. The owner's suites also feature butler service, and room service.

The honeymoon package includes a bottle of wine, a fruit basket, and a special signed certificate by the captain. Cost: Free! We think the best cabins for honeymooners are the two near the aft swimming pool on the Sun Deck. You can literally walk out the door for a swim.

Windjammer Barefoot Cruises

1759 Bay Rd., Miami Beach, FL 33119-0120. ☎ *800-327-2601. Internet:* www. windjammer.com. *Rack rates: no inside, $1,000–$1,100 outside, $1,225–$1,525 suites. (Pricing is for a five-day cruise. Port charges are not included and are an additional $90.)*

> ✔ **Honeymooners' destinations:** Eastern Caribbean (from St. Thomas) and Southern Caribbean (from St. Lucia or Aruba)
>
> ✔ **Honeymooners' choice:** *Legacy* (built in 1959, 120 passengers, 1,165 GRTs)
>
> ✔ **Ship style:** Small

The Windjammer experience is very different than a megaship experience, and the line is very proud of that fact. These ships are about sailing, soft adventure, making friends, and barefoot fun — you don't need to pack much more than T-shirts, shorts, and a bathing suit or two. The fleet is made up of classic sailing vessels and one motorized vessel, and the small size of the ships allows them to anchor in out-of-the-way Caribbean harbors that bigger ships can't get near. The pricing is inexpensive, but then again, the amenities are minimal.

The going can be bumpy at times, so those who get seasick are forewarned.

On Windjammer vessels, basically anything goes — activities aren't set in stone. Guests can help hoist the sails if they want to, but they don't have to. Relaxing, checking out the gorgeous scenery, and telling stories are the favorite pastimes. Windjammer has a reputation for attracting party-hearty types, but we've found the tone of any given Windjammer cruise is really set by the passengers aboard (kids can even be found on some sailings). The *Legacy* is the only ship in the Windjammer fleet with suites (and we don't recommend that you book a smaller cabin). The top Burke's Berth suites come with sitting areas, entertainment centers, bars, and picture windows. Bathtubs, TVs, and room service are not available.

The honeymoon package includes a bottle of champagne, a special welcome-aboard gift basket with "barefoot honeymoon" T-shirts, and an offer to take an anniversary cruise for half fare. Cost: Free!

You can stowaway on the ship the night before your sailing for $55 each, much less than the cost of a hotel room. Plus you get dinner and free rum swizzlers.

Windstar Cruises

300 Elliott Ave. W., Seattle, WA 98119. ☎ *800-258-7245.* *Internet:* www.windstarcruises.com. *Rack rates: no inside, $4,000–$5,399 outside, $6,198 suites.*

- ✔ **Honeymooners' destinations:** Caribbean (from St. Thomas and Barbados), Costa Rica, Belize, Greek Isles, Italy, and France
- ✔ **Honeymooners' choice:** *Wind Song, Wind Spirit, Wind Star* (built in 1987/1986/1988, 148 passengers, 5,350 GRTs); *Wind Surf* (built in 1990, 312 passengers, 14,745 GRTs)
- ✔ **Ship style:** Small

Nothing rustic here. The *Wind Star, Wind Spirit, Wind Song,* and *Wind Surf* ships may have tens of thousands of square feet of Dacron flying from their masts (four on the *Star, Spirit,* and *Song* and five on the *Surf*), but they operate as smoothly as the very best modern yachts, owing to the million-dollar computers that control not only the sails but also the stabilizers, ensuring a pretty smooth ride. Like the best yachts, these ships feature incredible cuisine (served open seating) and oversized accommodations. And they are casually elegant (no need to bring a tux or even a suit for that matter). There's no set regime, and most passengers are perfectly happy entertaining themselves — definitely not your mega-ship crowd. All the cabins are large and outside, and they have VCRs, CD players, teakwood bathrooms, hairdryers, safes, and minibars. The *Wind Surf* is the only ship in the fleet with suites.

A watersports platform at the stern provides for a variety of activities when the ships are in port. Nighttime entertainment is low key, with a pianist and sometimes a vocalist, and most people prefer to take movies from the video library to watch in their cabins. These ships also have small casinos. The larger *Wind Surf* has an expanded spa and gym (these offerings are tiny on the other ships).

The line offers a Honeymooners cocktail party hosted by the captain for all honeymooners, and the Honeymooners Package comes with champagne and caviar. Cost: $195.

Chapter 31

Making Plans and Settling In

By Fran Wenograd Golden

● ●

In This Chapter

▶ Arranging your honeymoon cruise

▶ Knowing what to expect on arrival and departure

▶ Getting married on a ship

● ●

Cruise fares include accommodations; as many as six meals a day (for those who can eat that much); a plethora of onboard activities, including sports; resort-style offerings, such as swimming pools and gyms; admission to Las Vegas-style shows, piano bars, discos, and other nighttime entertainment; and stops at interesting ports of call. All in all, it adds up to a good vacation value.

Planning Your Honeymoon Cruise

You can usually get a good deal, and sometimes a great deal, on a cruise vacation, with savings of up to 60 percent, but more commonly 25 to 40 percent, by booking in advance. These rates are also referred to as *early-bird discounts*.

The early-bird pricing is perfect for honeymooners who generally plan their vacations six to 12 months in advance anyway. Booking early also ensures that you have your first choice of cabin (the best cabins and cheapest cabins both tend to sell out first).

Cruise lines usually announce their itineraries about a year in advance. Some popular dates fill up fast, but generally, you can have a good choice of accommodations and still have a stab at the best rates by booking six months in advance.

If you're worried about booking early because you think a better price may come along later, remember that most cruise lines have a policy that if they do later offer a rate below the early bird rate, which is rare, they make good and give you the lower rate — although you or your travel agent may have to point it out to them.

Booking air transport through the cruise line

The cruise lines offer to handle your flight arrangements in what is called an *air add-on*. As a general rule, booking your air travel through the cruise line is the best idea. Why? First of all, as big customers of the airlines, the cruise lines tend to get very good (if not the best) discounted airfare rates, which they pass on to their customers.

Booking airfares with the cruise line also allows the line to keep track of you. If your plane is late, for example, they may even hold the boat. And most cruise lines include transfers from the airport to the ship, saving you the hassle of getting a cab. If you do book on your own, you may still be able to get the transfers separately — inquire with your travel agent or with the cruise line.

The only time it may pay to book your own airfare is if you use frequent-flyer miles to get the flight for free, or if you are fussy about which carrier you fly or route you take (you're more or less at the mercy of the cruise line to make these choices if you take its airfare offers, and you may even end up on a chartered aircraft).

Some lines offer special deviation programs, which allow you to request specific airlines and routing for an extra fee — as honeymooners you may prefer this route and seek a non-stop flight, for instance, to avoid changing planes and other hassles. These requests should be made at the time of your initial deposit.

After the air tickets issued by the cruise line, you usually aren't allowed to make changes.

Occasionally airfare is included in the cruise package rate, and if that's the case, and you choose not to use that airfare, you are refunded the air portion.

Staying at a hotel before or after the cruise

Just as with air travel add-ons, the cruise lines negotiate special deals with hotels at port cities. If you can, arrive at the departure city a day ahead of time, take advantage of the reduced hotel rates, and visit some local attractions. That way, you don't have to sweat it if your flight runs late — running to catch a boat at anytime, let alone on your honeymoon, is no fun. You can take advantage of these same deals if you want to extend your honeymoon a day or two after your cruise.

Knowing what's not included in the fare

When you get a quote for a cruise, make sure that you know what's included. Is the agent quoting a cruise-only fare, or a fare that includes airfare, transfers, port charges, taxes, and other fees? These charges, if not included, can add substantially to your honeymoon costs. If you're comparing quotes on two different cruises, make sure that you're comparing apples and apples and not apples and oranges.

It's also important to know what's *not* included in that fare. These items can add substantially to your overall vacation bill. Although, of course, all these purchases are optional (not mandatory).

To help figure out how much extra money to bring, consider these typical onboard costs:

- ✔ **Soda:** $1.50
- ✔ **Mixed drinks:** $3.25 to $5 (with tip)
- ✔ **Beer:** $2.95 domestic, $3.95 imported (with tip)
- ✔ **Wine at dinner (per bottle):** $10 to $300
- ✔ **Alternative dining service charge:** $5 to $20 per person
- ✔ **Beauty services (shampoo and haircut):** $52 to $70 (women); $29 (men)
- ✔ **Cruise-line logo souvenirs:** $3 to $50
- ✔ **Dry cleaning (per item):** $2.50 to $7.50
- ✔ **Massage (50-minute session):** $89 to $109
- ✔ **Phone calls (per minute):** $7.95 to $16.95
- ✔ **E-Mail (per minute):** 50 cents to $1
- ✔ **Photos:** $6.95 to $7.95 (for a 5-by-7)
- ✔ **Crew tips (per passenger, per week):** $63 to $70
- ✔ **Shore excursions:** $25 to $250 per person, per tour

Cruise folks we've talked to advise that passengers set aside spending money of between $40 and $ $50 a day per person, for a week-long cruise (not including tips). But you can plan for more or less based on your specific wants and needs.

Choosing a cabin

One of your biggest decisions once you choose the ship you want to sail on is what type of cabin you desire. Ask yourselves if you can be comfortable in a slightly cramped space without a window, or if you require a suite with a verandah.

Obviously, price is a factor here. But as honeymooners you may want to spend more time in your cabin than the average passengers, and in that case we recommend that you book the biggest cabin you can afford. Keep in mind that lower-end cabins can be quite tight for two, and on most ships, lower-end means inside cabins (they have no window or porthole). If you can afford a cabin or suite with a verandah, splurge, as those verandahs can be very romantic spots for dining, lounging, and more. But ask how big the verandah is — is there room for two lounge chairs? A table? — as some are quite small. And keep in mind that many verandahs are not really private (your neighbors may be able to peak in).

If you chose a cabin with a window, make sure that the view is not obstructed by lifeboats and the like. You can determine where your cabin is by looking at a diagram of the ship (included in the cruise brochure).

Usually the higher on the ship the cabin is located, the more expensive it is. But upper decks also tend to be rockier in rough seas than the middle or lower parts of the ship (a factor to consider if you are prone to seasickness).

The cruise line's brochures list cabin sizes in terms of square feet. As a rough guide, 120 to 150 square feet is low-end and cramped, 180 square feet is mid-range and the minimum for people with claustrophobia, and 250 square feet and up is suite-sized.

If noise bothers you, try to pick a cabin away from the engine room and nowhere near the disco, gym, or children's play area. Keep in mind that the most-expensive and least-expensive cabins on any given ship tend to sell out first. If you're on a tight budget, or you want a suite, book early!

Choosing a meal time

While open, restaurant-style seating tends to be the rule on small ships, most big-ship dining rooms aren't large enough to accommodate all the passengers at the same time at dinner. Consequently, dining times and tables are typically assigned; you eat at the same time and the same table every night.

Recently there has been a move towards more flexibility with meal hours (Princess, for example, has an option where you dine restaurant-style, when and with whom you want). Still, many ships still offer set hours, with early seating around 6 or 6:30 p.m., and a late seating around 8 or

8:30 p.m. If you're on a ship with set meal times, we recommend that you take the later seating, which allows time for a nap or late spa appointment before dinner. A hipper crowd is usually found at the late seating (families with kids and older folks tend to dine earlier).

You also need to consider whether you want to sit alone or make new friends. You can request, on most ships, to be at a table for 2, 4, 8, 10, or 12. The actual table assignment, assuming one is required, is not usually given until you arrive at the ship. If you are not happy with your assignment and/or your tablemates, let the maitre d' know, and he or she can find you another table (greasing his or her palm helps).

Most ships offer smoke-free dining rooms, but if not, you should request, in advance, seating in the smoking or non-smoking section — an particularly important factor in Europe, where smoking is still quite popular.

 The cruise line should also be informed at the time you make your reservations about any special dietary requests you have. Some lines offer Kosher menus and all have vegetarian, low-fat, low-salt, or sugar-free options.

Using a Travel Agent

Booking a cruise vacation can be tough because of the number of factors to consider. To ensure that you get what you paid for, book through an experienced travel agent. The agent can help make sure that you choose a cruise that suits your needs, help you decide whether you want to combine your cruise with a land tour, and help you find the best deal on the cruise itself and airfare.

A good agent can also save you time. You don't have to hassle with calling cruise lines for brochures; agencies have them in stock. Cruise lines rely on agents to sell their product, and may even refer you to an agent if you call to book direct.

To find a good agent, ask your friends and relatives who they use. Look for a cruise-only agency or an agent who specializes in cruises. Cruise specialists are in frequent contact with the cruise lines and are alerted by the lines about the latest and greatest deals and special offers. Some agencies even buy blocks of space that they sell at a special price.

As a rule, you can find an experienced agent by contacting the **Cruise Lines International Association (CLIA)** (☎ **212-921-0066;** Internet: www. cruising.org) or the **National Association of Cruise Oriented Agencies** (☎ **305-663-5626;** Internet: www.nacoa.com www.nacoaonline.com). At both Web sites you can search for members in your area.

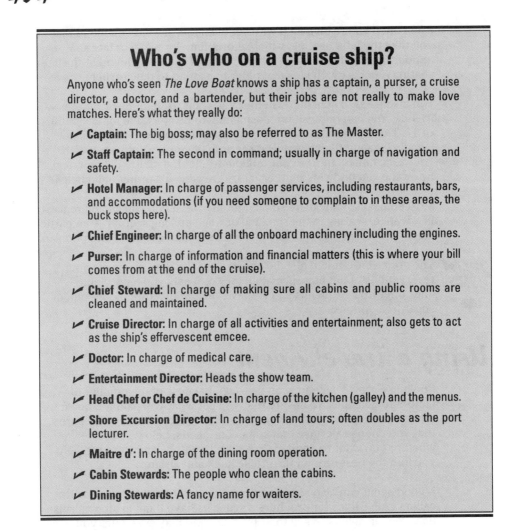

Who's who on a cruise ship?

Anyone who's seen *The Love Boat* knows a ship has a captain, a purser, a cruise director, a doctor, and a bartender, but their jobs are not really to make love matches. Here's what they really do:

- ✔ **Captain:** The big boss; may also be referred to as The Master.
- ✔ **Staff Captain:** The second in command; usually in charge of navigation and safety.
- ✔ **Hotel Manager:** In charge of passenger services, including restaurants, bars, and accommodations (if you need someone to complain to in these areas, the buck stops here).
- ✔ **Chief Engineer:** In charge of all the onboard machinery including the engines.
- ✔ **Purser:** In charge of information and financial matters (this is where your bill comes from at the end of the cruise).
- ✔ **Chief Steward:** In charge of making sure all cabins and public rooms are cleaned and maintained.
- ✔ **Cruise Director:** In charge of all activities and entertainment; also gets to act as the ship's effervescent emcee.
- ✔ **Doctor:** In charge of medical care.
- ✔ **Entertainment Director:** Heads the show team.
- ✔ **Head Chef or Chef de Cuisine:** In charge of the kitchen (galley) and the menus.
- ✔ **Shore Excursion Director:** In charge of land tours; often doubles as the port lecturer.
- ✔ **Maitre d':** In charge of the dining room operation.
- ✔ **Cabin Stewards:** The people who clean the cabins.
- ✔ **Dining Stewards:** A fancy name for waiters.

Preparing for Your Honeymoon Cruise

About one month before your cruise, and no later than one week before, you should receive your cruise documents, including your airline tickets (if you purchased them from the cruise line), a boarding document with your cabin and sometimes dining choices on it, boarding forms to fill out, luggage tags, and your prearranged bus transfer vouchers and hotel vouchers (if applicable).

You should also receive information about shore excursions and additional material detailing things you need to know before you sail — read all of it carefully. Make sure that your cabin category and dining preferences are as you requested and that your airline flight and arrival times are what you were told. If you discover a problem, call your agent immediately. Make sure that there is enough time so you can arrive at the port no later than an hour before departure time.

Before you leave for the airport, tag your bags with the tags provided by the cruise line, and fill in your boarding cards. Doing so saves time when you arrive at the ship.

Managing your money

You have already paid the lion's share of your cruise vacation. But you need a credit card or traveler's checks to establish credit for onboard expenses. Some, but not all ships take a personal check.

If you want to pay in cash or by traveler's check, you must leave a deposit, usually $250 for a one-week sailing.

On most ships, after you establish credit, you get a shipboard credit card. You can charge everything, including gift shop purchases, on the card (the only place cash is accepted is in the casino).

Cash is needed for taxis, drinks, small purchases, and tips for guides in port. You also may need cash for crew tips at the end of the cruise (although many lines now offer the option of putting tips right on your shipboard account). Some (but not all) ships have onboard ATMs.

We suggest that you keep careful track of your onboard expenses to avoid any unpleasant surprises at the end of your cruise.

Packing practically

The cruise documents you receive prior to you departure should advise you of the number of casual, informal, and formal nights on your cruise so that you can pack accordingly. Make sure to pack your cruise documents in your carry-on luggage, as you need to show them when you get to the pier.

Remembering your passports

If you leave from a U.S. port, you don't need a passport, but you do need Proof of Citizenship in the form of an official copy of your birth certificate (a driver's license is not enough identification). If you depart from a foreign port, a passport is mandatory. (See Chapter 7 for more passport information.)

Arriving at the Port

If you booked air and transfers through the cruise line, you are met at the airport by a cruise line representative, and you and your luggage (usually separately) are transferred by bus to the pier (or your hotel if you booked a pre-cruise hotel stay).

If you booked air travel on your own, you must claim your bags and arrange your own transportation to the hotel or ship.

Embarking

Check-in is usually two to three hours before sailing. You may encounter crowds at the terminal. If you arrive early, the ship may be disembarking passengers from the previous sailing. Expect to wait in line. Despite the best efforts of the cruise line, the scene at the pier may be zoo-like.

You have up until a half hour — one hour on some ships — before departure to board, but the advantages to boarding earlier are well worth the effort. For instance, you get first dibs on prime dining room tables (if you haven't been assigned a table in advance) and spa treatment times. Plus, if you get on early enough, you can eat lunch on the ship (lunch may be served until 3 p.m. or even 4 p.m. the first day).

At check-in on most ships you establish your shipboard credit account and get an ID card to use when you get off the ship at the ports (it's important to remember to carry this card or you'll have trouble getting back on). In some cases your shipboard credit card, ID card, and room key are one and the same.

After you clear the check-in area, you are asked, and in some cases forced, to pose for the ship's photographer. Your photo is later displayed at the ship's photography shop. You are under no obligation to buy it.

Going onboard

As you exit the gangplank, a crew member escorts you to your cabin. No tip is required for this service.

Either immediately or a short time later, your steward — the person responsible for the upkeep of your cabin — stops by to introduce him- or herself. Remember to alert the steward immediately if the beds are not configured to your liking or if there is any other problem you see. If the cabin itself is not what you thought you booked, go right to the hotel manager with your complaint.

Your room should also be outfitted with a "do not disturb" sign (especially important for honeymooners), order forms for room service breakfast (if offered), and forms and bags for dry cleaning and laundry services.

You may want to try the TV, safe, and other gadgets out to see how they work, check out the bathroom, and so on. The loud whoosh of the toilet is normal (most ships use a vacuum system).

There may be bottles of water provided in your cabin (although the water on most ships is perfectly drinkable). Just because the bottles are there doesn't mean they are free. If you don't know, ask before you open them.

Your luggage probably won't have arrived yet, but if it has, go ahead and unpack. If not, after you've exhausted your tour of your room, we recommend that you check out the rest of the ship.

Don't forget to take your shipboard credit card (in case you want to buy a drink) and key with you.

Begin your tour on the top deck and work your way down, checking out the main public rooms. That way, you can stop at the beginning of your tour, at the "welcome aboard" buffet, which is usually set up in the casual dining area, near the pool deck.

If you plan to use the spa services, stop by and make appointments so that you can get your preferred times (the best times go fast, and some popular treatments sell out).

Note that the ship's casino and shops are always closed when the ship is in port. While in the port the swimming pool(s) may be covered with a tarp. Don't worry. They are filled with either fresh or salt water after the ship sets sail.

Participating in the lifeboat/ safety drill

In your cabin — either waiting on your bed or in the closet or a drawer — are bright orange life jackets. Ships are required by law to conduct safety drills the first day out. Most do it either right before the ship sails or shortly thereafter. Attendance is mandatory.

A notice on the back of your cabin door lists the procedures and advises where your assigned muster station is located and how to get there. Directions to the muster station in the hallway are also provided.

Setting sail

Most people like to be out on deck as the ship sails, waving at those seeing the ship off on shore and at other ships as you pass by in the harbor.

There is often live music on the pool deck (on Princess ships they first play a pre-recorded version of *The Love Boat* theme song) and a lively party atmosphere. Some lines offer complimentary champagne toasts, but most charge for the drinks.

> # What happens if your bags get lost?
>
> Before you start to panic, keep in mind that on big ships, some 4,000 bags need to be loaded and distributed. But if you're hours into the sailing and getting concerned, don't hesitate to call the guest-relations desk (or purser's office). If your luggage really does get lost, the cruise line customer-relations folks are supposed to spring into immediate action. They, not you, should contact the airline and ground operators to see what's what. They should also provide you with any toiletries and even clothing you need in the meantime.

Departing for Home

On the last evening of your cruise, you receive a preliminary bill for your shipboard expenses. If you plan to settle your account with a credit card, you don't have to do anything but make sure that all the charges are correct. If there is a problem, report it to the purser's office (where you may encounter long lines).

 If you plan to pay by cash or traveler's checks, you are asked to settle your account either during the day or night before you leave the ship — report to the purser's office to do so.

Tipping tips

Tipping an area some people stress about and you don't have to. Typically, the cruise lines leave tipping suggestions in the cabins and recently some lines including Carnival have been experimenting with adding tips automatically to your shipboard account. You can move the amounts up or down, but keep in mind that to not tip is considered bad form. For each passenger you usually tip your cabin steward and waiter each a minimum of about $3.50 per day, and your bus boy $1.50 to $2. That totals up to about $63 for a seven-night cruise (you don't have to include disembarkation day). On some ships you are also encouraged to tip the dining room's headwaiter and maitre d'. Those lines that automatically add tips to your shipboard account usually set the daily amount at about $10 per person, or $70 for a one-week cruise. Tips are typically paid at the end of the cruise, . Many lines now let you put tips on your charge card, although some still encourage tips in cash. In the latter cases, envelopes are provided to hand to the appropriate crew member (on some ships, particularly in Europe, tips are pooled and you just get one envelope).

Bar bills automatically include a 15 percent tip, but if the wine steward, for instance, has served you exceptionally well you can slip him or her a bill too. If you have spa or beauty treatments, you can tip that person at the time of the service (you can charge it on your shipboard charge account).

Don't tip the captain or other officers. They are salaried employees, and tipping then is gauche, if not embarrassing, for all involved. However, the porters at the pier may expect a tip.

If a staff member is particularly great, a written letter to a superior is always good form and may earn that person an "employee of the month" honor and maybe even a bonus.

Packing up

With thousands of suitcases to deal with, big ships require guests to pack the night before departure. You are asked to leave your bags in the hallway before you retire for the night (or usually by midnight). The bags are picked up overnight and removed from the ship before passengers are allowed to disembark. You won't see them again until the cruise terminal. Make sure that your bags are tagged with the luggage tags given to you by the cruise line so that they end up in the right place. If you don't leave your bags in the hall, you have to carry them off the ship yourself.

When packing, remember to leave out any clothes and toiletries you need for the next day, and don't pack your valuables, breakables, travel documents, or medication. Make sure that everything you keep out fits in your overnight bag.

If you party too late and end up putting you bags out after the other bags on your deck have already been collected, advise the purser's office so that they can send someone to get your bags.

Exiting the ship

You know your honeymoon cruise is over when the loud speaker announcements start blaring early in the morning.

You can't get off the ship until the ship is cleared by Customs and other authorities — a process that usually takes 90 minutes. On the bigger ships it takes around two hours to get everyone off. Those with earlier flights are allowed to leave first. Everyone wants to leave the ship at the same time, but unless you have an early number, you shouldn't rush. Grab a book and head up to the deck, catch a movie or other ship offering, or find another way to occupy yourselves. Clogging the hallways doesn't help anyone get off faster.

If things drag on and you're concerned about missing your flight, tell a crew member.

If you booked your air through the cruise line, and are heading right home, collect your bags — porters should be around to help — and proceed to the buses to the airport. If you booked your own air travel, you're on your own.

Getting through Customs

The U.S. Customs Service has streamlined its entry procedures for cruise passengers, using computer-tracking systems to target certain passengers for inspections, based on information from law enforcement and other databases. Ships are also required to submit a "big spender" list from the onboard gift shop.

Random inspections of passengers not based on database information are rare. But if your things are inspected, you may have to show the officer all the goods you have purchased. It also pays to have your receipts handy so that you can show how much you paid for the items — otherwise, inspectors value your purchases based on U.S. prices.

If you disagree with a Customs determination, you can contest it later, in writing.

Planning a Wedding at Sea

Shipboard weddings are offered at most U.S. ports as well as in Vancouver, Canada, San Juan, and St. Thomas. Island weddings are offered at a variety of Caribbean locales.

A prerequisite for either a shipboard or island wedding booked through a cruise line is that you must book a cruise at least for yourselves. Your guests can come aboard the ship at the port for a few hours, or cruise with you (or meet you at the island).

The cruise lines typically provide a licensed officiate, such as a Notary Public, or you can have the ceremony conducted by clergy that you arrange for.

Princess Cruise introduced the first cruise ship wedding chapel in 1998 on the *Grand Princess*. And on that ship, and sister ship *Golden Princess*, you can get married at sea, with the ceremony conducted by the ship's captain. Obviously, in that case, your guests have to cruise with you, although for those who can't, **Princess** recently introduced a new feature on the *Golden Princess*, a Wedding Cam that allows your friends back home to view the nuptials on the Internet. **Carnival's** new *Spirit* also has a wedding chapel, and weddings at sea are offered on Alaska sailings (permission is pending to offer the weddings in the Caribbean as well). **Royal Caribbean's** *Voyager of the Seas, Explorer of*

the Seas, and new *Adventurer of the Seas* also have wedding chapels, but weddings are only conducted there when the ships are in port.

Whether you choose to get married shipboard or on one of the islands, you can book your entire wedding, including the ceremony, reception, and honeymoon, through the cruise lines. The lines have special departments set up to help you plan your special event (or they refer you to their wedding consultant). The idea is one-stop shopping.

The costs of a wedding arranged by the cruise lines are very reasonable when compared to land-based offerings. Basic packages range from $550 to $1,400 not including the cruise fare, and generally include the ceremony, a bottle of champagne, flowers for the bride and groom, recorded music, a small cake, photography services, and some sort of keepsake. Extras are available. License fees typically add an extra $150.

If there is no onboard chapel, the weddings generally take place either on the ship's deck or in a lounge area. On the islands, ceremonies are offered in romantic spots with garden gazebos or beachfront settings.

Follow the ship's rules in scheduling the time of your ceremony. Shipboard ceremonies are typically in the early afternoon, and island weddings are performed during the limited time the ship is in port.

If you're planning a cruise wedding, we suggest that you keep the following in mind:

- Book your wedding and honeymoon cruise well in advance (6 to 12 months) to get the best rates.

- Arrive at the port a day or two before your wedding (you don't want delayed flights to cause you heartache).

- Hand carry (don't check as baggage) your wedding dress and any other essential items.

- Ask the cruise line for a wedding coordinator and a special escort on your wedding day to make that sure things run smoothly.

- If your wedding party and guests are sailing with you, ask about a group rate.

- Make sure that your non-sailing guests are off the ship at the required hour.

Requirements such as blood tests and physical examinations for marriage licenses are determined by the state or country where the wedding takes place.

Part VIII
Paris

The 5th Wave   By Rich Tennant

"I know it's a wedding present from your niece, I just don't know why you had to wear it to the Louvre."

In this part . . .

*P*aris is tops when it comes to romantic fantasy. What better place to celebrate your love? All you have to do is get here, and the city will take care of the rest. Paris offers fabulous dining, exquisite art, and the opportunity for romantic walks and stealing cozy kisses.

Here we break Paris down to make your trip as simple as possible. We give you the best bets for spending your days and nights. We tell you the best places for honeymooners to stay — and for every budget. A honeymoon in Paris is truly magical.

Chapter 32

Top Accommodations for Honeymooners in Paris

By Reid Bramblett

● ●

In This Chapter

▶ Knowing what to expect

▶ Deciding which area stay in

▶ Finding romantic accommodations

● ●

*P*aris is the City of Light — the world capital of romance, birthplace of bohemians and impressionists, muse to Hemingway and the Lost Generation, and the high temple of haute cuisine. You can overdose on art at the Louvre, cruise past 18th-century palaces on the Seine, write poetry at a sidewalk cafe table, dance in the colored glow of Nôtre Dame's stained glass, dine stupendously in a tiny bistro, or steal long kisses atop the Eiffel Tower. Paris strikes a lively balance between the vibrant, modern metropolis of today and the majestic, historic city of yesterday. It's this balance that keeps Paris intriguing, keeps it attractive, keeps an army of faithful admirers coming back year after year, and makes it one of the most romantic cities on Earth.

No matter how tempting it may be, don't try to pack in too much. Paris is a cultural carousel, and attempting to see all its museums, churches, monuments, and other attractions may leave you panting from exhaustion, frustrated — and with no time left over for each other. Pace yourself. For example, on the day you tour the Louvre, plan on doing nothing else in particular. When you are tired of the museum, head out the door to stroll the Tuileries gardens or along the Seine, drinking in the ambiance of the city and each other's company.

Figuring Out Where to Stay

The Seine River divides Paris between the **Right Bank** *(Rive Droite)* to the north and the **Left Bank** *(Rive Gauche)* to the south. Paris began on the **Ile de la Cité,** an island in the Seine that is still the center of the city and home to **Nôtre-Dame cathedral.** It's also connected to the nearby posh residential island of **Ile Saint-Louis.** Traditionally, the Right Bank is considered more upscale, with Paris's main boulevards, such as the Champs-Elysées, and museums such as the Louvre. The Left Bank is the old Bohemian half of Paris with the Latin Quarter around the university.

Paris is divided into 20 districts called *arrondissements.* These districts start with the first **arrondissement** (which includes the Louvre neighborhood and the tip of the Ile de la Cité) and then spiral out from there. At the end of each address in this chapter, you see a number followed by an "e" (or in the case of 1, an "er"), such as 8e or 5e. That number refers to the *arrondissement.* A Parisian address, spoken or written, isn't complete unless the neighborhood name or *arrondissement* is included. The last two digits of a zip code also indicate the *arrondissement,* so an address listed as "Paris 75003" is in the third *arrondissement.* (Most of these districts also correspond with traditional, named neighborhoods.)

Among the major *arrondissements* (for tourism) on the Right Bank is the **3e.** Called **Le Marais,** this up-and-coming neighborhood manages to remain genuinely Parisian amid the swirl of tourism in the city center. The **4e** includes most of the Ile de la Cité, Ile St-Louis, the Beaubourg pedestrian zone, and the **Pompidou** modern art center.

The **8e** — a natural extension westward of the 1er — is Paris's most posh area, consisting of ritzy hotels, fashion boutiques, fine restaurants, and upscale town houses. It centers along the grandest boulevard in a city famous for them: the **Champs-Elysées.** Although the sidewalks of this historic shopping promenade were recently cleaned up and widened, the Champs-Elysées has become merely a shadow of its former elegant self; it's no more than a string of international chain stores and movie theaters.

The Champs-Elysées beelines east-west from the **Place de la Concorde** — an oval plaza at the western end of the Louvre complex where French royalty met the business end of a guillotine during the Revolution — to the **Arc de Triomphe.** The Arc is one of the world's greatest triumphal arches, a monument to France's unknown soldier and to the gods of car-insurance premiums (surrounding the Arc is a five-lane traffic circle where, it seems, anything goes).

In the northerly reaches of the Right Bank lies **Montemarte,** still echoing with the ghosts of Bohemian Paris, topped by the fairy-tale gleaming white basilica of **Sacre Coeur,** and tramped by tourists. The neighborhood is so distinct and (despite the tour buses) charming.

Left Bank *arrondissements* include the **5e,** the famous old **Latin Quarter,** named for the language spoken by the university students who gave it its once colorful, bohemian atmosphere.

The adjacent **6e** has been lucky enough to retain some of its counter-culture charm. The students of Paris's Fine Arts School help liven up things here, especially in the now highly fashionable but still somewhat artsy **St-Germain-des-Prés** neighborhood of cafes, brasseries, and restaurants. The **7e,** tucked into a wide arc of the Seine, intrudes a bit on the St-Germain neighborhood, but its major features are the **Musée d'Orsay,** the **Eiffel Tower,** and the **Rodin Museum.**

Choosing Among Paris's Best Accommodations for Honeymooners

Please refer to the Introduction of *Honeymoon Vacations For Dummies* for an explanation of our price categories.

Hôtel d'Angleterre

$$ Saint-Germain (6e)

Spend your honeymoon under the high-beamed ceilings of this 18th-century Breton-style inn and live a bit of U.S. history — when this was the British Embassy in 1783, it was the spot where the English finally signed the papers recognizing American independence. Some rooms have exposed stone walls and four-poster canopy beds, and all boast period furnishings, carved-wood closet doors, and silk wall hangings. Splurge for your nuptials on a deluxe suite with double marble sinks and a more regal decor (the "apartments," with two bedrooms, are really meant more for families). The homey common lounge has a piano; there's room service until 8 p.m., and the hotel has a small lush courtyard where you can breakfast in summer.

44 rue Jacob (off rue Bonaparte). ☎ *01-42-60-34-72. Fax: 01-42-60-16-93. E-mail:* anglotel@wanadoo.fr. *Métro: St-Germain-des-Prés. Rack rates: 800F (122E, $114) standard double; 1,100F-1,350F (168-206E, $157-$193) deluxe double; 1,700F (259E, $243) apartments. AE, DC, MC, V.*

Hôtel de la Bretonnerie

$ Marais (4e)

The Sagots keep a cozy, friendly hotel where each room is done in a classic French style but with a unique decor, from Empire divans or Louis XIII chairs to Napoleon III tables. The nicest are the so-called "chambres de caractère," like numbers 25 and 37 with their canopy beds, or country-style number 21 with heavy-beamed ceilings and floral-print walls. Numbers 1, 2, and 3 are cozy duplexes defined by beamed ceilings and huge, curtained windows (number 2 is the best — on a corner with windows on both sides). Junior suite number 5 has a large honeymoon-perfect bed. "Classique" rooms are smaller, but still have nice touches, like the four-poster and beams in numbers 14 and 29. You can sleep in and take breakfast in your room, or dine under the stony barrel vault of the 17th-century basement.

Paris

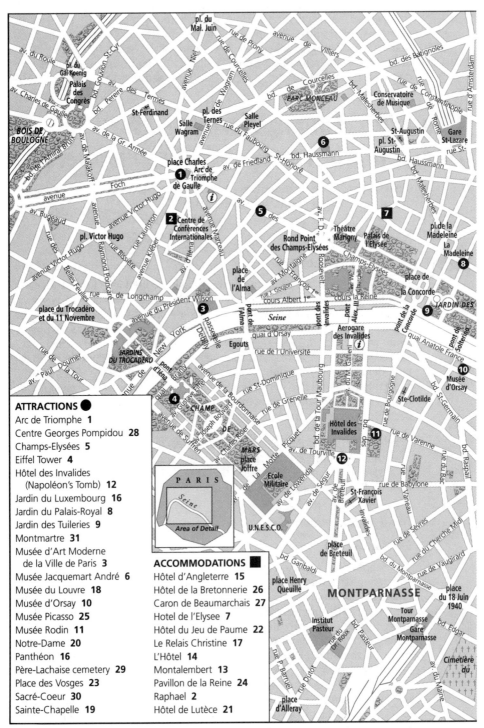

ATTRACTIONS ●
Arc de Triomphe **1**
Centre Georges Pompidou **28**
Champs-Elysées **5**
Eiffel Tower **4**
Hôtel des Invalides
  (Napoléon's Tomb) **12**
Jardin du Luxembourg **16**
Jardin du Palais-Royal **8**
Jardin des Tuileries **9**
Montmartre **31**
Musée d'Art Moderne
  de la Ville de Paris **3**
Musée Jacquemart André **6**
Musée du Louvre **18**
Musée d'Orsay **10**
Musée Picasso **25**
Musée Rodin **11**
Notre-Dame **20**
Panthéon **16**
Père-Lachaise cemetery **29**
Place des Vosges **23**
Sacré-Coeur **30**
Sainte-Chapelle **19**

ACCOMMODATIONS ■
Hôtel d'Angleterre **15**
Hôtel de la Bretonnerie **26**
Caron de Beaumarchais **27**
Hotel de l'Elysee **7**
Hôtel du Jeu de Paume **22**
Le Relais Christine **17**
L'Hôtel **14**
Montalembert **13**
Pavillon de la Reine **24**
Raphael **2**
Hôtel de Lutèce **21**

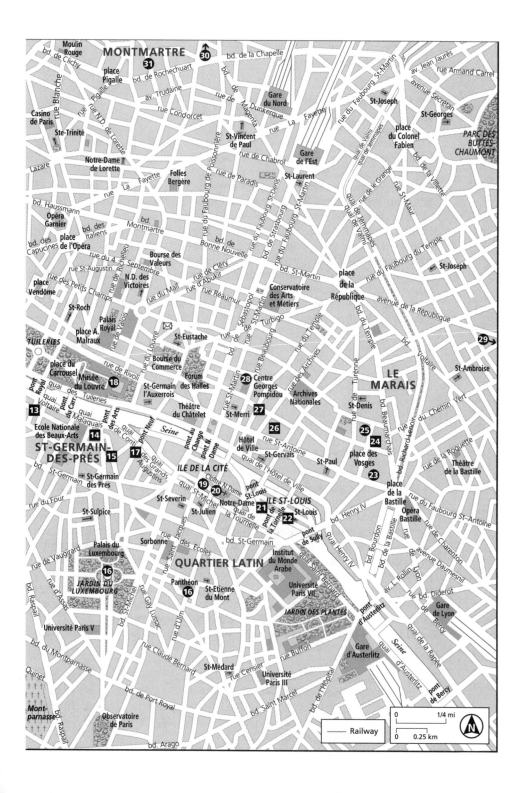

22 rue Saint-Croix-de-la-Bretonnerie (between rue des Archives and rue Vieille-du-Temple). ☎ *01-48-87-77-63. Fax: 01-42-77-26-78. Internet:* www.bretonnerie.com. *Métro: Hôtel de Ville. Rack rates: 680F (103E, $97) chambres classiques; 870F (132E, $124) chambre de caractère; 1,100F (168E, $157) duplex or junior suite. MC, V.*

Caron de Beaumarchais

$ The Marais (4e)

The reception area of Étienne and son Alain Bigeard's small Marais hotel looks like a salon of 200 years past, with its Louis XVI fireplace, spinet, wafting classical music, antique card table in one corner, and garden statuette in the other. The rooms are smallish, but nicely outfitted as befits an 18th-century Marais townhouse — beamed ceilings and a touch of gold about the carved filigree on curving chair backs and mirror frames. Rooms in the front are largest, expect on the top floor where the sloping roof cuts into rooms 60 and 61 (but they do get the best Parisian rooftop views). Those overlooking the garden are also smallish, but set up to feel cozy rather than confining. If you want a small balcony with table and chairs, book a room on the 2nd, 5th, or 6th floors (the hotel notes such room preferences, though can't guarantee them). For such genteel style, the price is hard to beat.

12 rue Vieille-du-Temple (off rue de Rivoli). ☎ *01-42-72-34-12. Fax: 01-42-72-34-63. Internet:* www.carondebeaumarchais.com. *Métro: Hôtel de Ville. Rack rates: 790F (120E, $113) small doubles on back; 870F (133E, $124) larger doubles on front. AE, DC, MC, V.*

Hotel de l'Elysee

$$ Champs-Elysées (8e)

A small, exceeding friendly inn, the Hotel de l'Elysee has been overhauled in Restoration style, and while the rooms are individually styled, each may contain wallpaper of stamped 18th-century etchings, built-in closets, half-testers or embroidered velvet headboards, or stuccoed ceilings (the last most prevalent in the suites). The unofficial honeymoon hideaway here is quirky number 60, a little mansard suite with wood beams criss-crossing the space, a bed coving, and skylights set into the low, sloping ceilings that provide peek-a-boo vistas of Parisian rooftops, including a perfectly framed view of the Eiffel Tower. All 5th and 6th floor rooms enjoy at least rooftop views, the former from small balconies (numbers 50 to 53 even glimpse the Eiffel). If number 60 is taken, you may enjoy number 31; it's smallish, but has a canopy bed and windows on two sides opening onto balconies.

12 rue des Saussaies (off rue Faubourg St-Honoré at place Beauvau, two blocks north of Champs-Elysées). ☎ *01-42-65-29-25. Fax: 01-42-65-64-28. Internet:* www.france-hotel-guide.com/75008efsh.htm. *Métro: Champs-Elysées-Clemenceau or Miromesnil. Rack rates: 820F-1,380F (124E-197E, $117-$197) double; 1,500F (227E, $214) suite. AE, DC, MC, V.*

Hôtel du Jeu de Paume

$$$ Ile Saint-Louis (4e)

Built in 1634 as a Jeu de Paume court (a precursor of tennis), Hôtel du Jeu de Paume is a successful marriage of 17th-century wood beams and plaster with 20th-century burnished steel and glass. The impressive, airy, three-story ancient wood skeleton incorporates public lounges, an indoor breakfast terrace, a hanging corridor, and a glass elevator, all to marvelous effect. Most accommodations are on the cozy side of medium, but the simplicity of the stylishly modern decor under hewn beams (on the ground and second floors, but not the first) keeps them from feeling cramped. The three standard duplexes with spiral stairs are a bit small, but don't cost any more than a double. For true newlywed bliss, however, check into one of the two junior suites, duplexes with a lounge below and bedroom above, two baths, and one with a private terrace overlooking the small stone garden rimmed with flowers and where guests can breakfast in fine weather.

54 rue Saint-Louis-en-L'Ile. ☎ *01-43-26-14-18. Fax: 01-40-46-02-76. Internet:* www. JeudePaumehotel.com. *Métro: Pont-Marie. Rack rates: 1,280F-1,365F (194E-207E, $183-$195) double; 1,600F (244E, $229) duplex; 2,500F-2,750F (379E-417E, $357-$393) suite. AE, DC, MC, V.*

Le Relais Christine

$$$$$ Saint Germain (6e)

As you pass through the cobbled courtyard and enter the early 17th-century building, you feel less like you're checking into a hotel and more like the baron and baroness arriving at your own country manor house, with its cozy wood-paneled, honesty bar-lounge and antique painted beams in the foyer. Most of the mid-size rooms are done in a contemporary relaxed style, but a few splash out with grand, repro-Louis XIII decor. All are refurbished every five years, and include extra amenities like mini-stereos, VCRs, and modem jacks. For your honeymoon, splurge on a junior or regular suite for the added space and the marble bathrooms sporting (usually) double sinks. Most suites are duplexed, with sitting areas downstairs and a small lofted bedchamber and walk-in closet. Numbers 14 and 15, are special: laid out side-by-side, with a high-beamed ceiling in the bedroom and a bright sitting room that opens directly onto a small grassy garden. The basement breakfast/dining room is installed under the low, rough vaulting of the kitchen of a 13th-century abbey formerly located here and founded by Saint Louis himself.

3 rue Christine (off rue Dauphine, near the Pont Neuf). ☎ *800-525-4800 in the U.S. or 01-40-51-60-80 in Paris. Fax: 01-40-51-60-81. E-mail:* relaisch@club-internet. fr. *Internet:* www.relais-christine.com. *Métro: Odéon or St-Michel. Rack rates: 2,300F (351E, $329) double; 3,200F (488E, $457) junior suite or duplex; 3,900F (595E, $557) deluxe duplex; 4,500F (686E, $643) suite. AE, DC, MC, V.*

L'Hôtel

$$$ Saint Germain (6e)

The flop house where Oscar Wilde died in 1900 is no more (his room is now the deluxe number 16). Today L'Hôtel is definitely upscale, completely overhauled in summer 2000 by top French designer Jacques Garcia. The luxurious (but not large) rooms open onto a round, central, skylit courtyard about 20 feet across, and everything is done in good taste, with rich draperies and carved marbles in deep burgundies, gold, green, and black. Each room has a distinct style, from Louis XV and Empire to art nouveau, Russian Tsar, or Buddhist India. The luxurious appointments include CD stereos, fax machines, some half-tester beds, stucco work fringing the hand painted walls, and marble baths (which feature old fashioned half tubs with elaborate chrome hand-held nozzles; deluxe rooms come with double sinks and separate shower stalls). Deluxe room 54 is *très romantique* with dusty pink fabric on the ceiling and draping down the walls, and a small balcony with a cast-iron table and chairs overlooking a courtyard of Parisian rooftops (suite 62 on the top floor also has a balcony). In the basement is a tiny but deep swimming pool that looks as if it came straight out of the nearby Cluny ancient Roman baths.

13 rue des Beaux-Arts (between rue Bonaparte and rue de Seine, one block from the Quai Malaquais). ☎ *01-44-41-99-00. Fax: 01-43-25-64-81. Internet:* www. l-hotel.com. *Métro: St-Germain-des-Prés. Rack rates: 2,100F-2,250F (320E-343E, $300-$321) double; 3,900F (595E, $557) deluxe double or suite; 4,500F (686E, $643) apartment. AE, DC, MC, V.*

Montalembert

$$$$ Saint-Germain (7e)

If the excessive 17th-century styling of most refined Parisian hotels is too much for your 21st-century sensibilities, try the Montalembert, a thoroughly contemporary setting that hides business amenities, like in-room fax and modem hook-ups and VCRs, behind its classy hotel decor. The guest rooms were set to be completely remodeled in summer 2001, just after this guide was researched. The rooms should retain the modern look — let's hope along as clean, simple, and elegant lines as before the renovation. Suites come with separate sitting rooms, CD players, and larger baths than the standard rooms. However, for optimum romance skip the suites and book junior suite number 81. It may only consist of one large room (with a huge bath), but its small terrace has the best Eiffel Tower view of any hotel in town. The three mansard doubles also have dreamy views of Parisian rooftops but, alas, no Eiffel.

3 rue de Montelembert (off rue de Bac, behind the church of St Thomas d'Aquin). ☎ *800-628-8929 in the U.S. or 01-45-49-68-01 in Paris. Fax: 01-45-49-69-49. Internet:* www.montalembert.com. *Métro: rue de Bac. Rack rates: 2,033F-2,230F (310E-340E, $290-$319) standard double; 2,230-2,427F (340-370E, $319-$347) superior* *double; 2,623-2,820F (400E-430E, $375-$403) deluxe double; 3,149F-3,542F (480E-540E, $450-$506) junior suite; 3,477F-4,920F (530E-750E, $497-$703) suite. AE, DC, MC, V.*

Pavillon de la Reine

$$$$ The Marais (3e)

Shop-lined, arcaded place des Vogues has lately regained its 17th-century status as one of Paris's most elegant squares, and the "Queen's Pavilion" lives up to its place at the head of the square. You enter via a cobblestone courtyard where the walls spill with ivy and window boxes burst with bright flowers. The tapestries and oil portraits in the paneled lobby evoke a modest castle, while the rooms are done in a more modern, but still elegant, fashion. No two are the same, but for a good idea just picture post-modern iron bed frames, antique dressers, and plush contemporary chairs against walls of dusty vermilion or rough-hewn oak beams against creamy plaster. Most of the suites are arranged so that the sitting room is on the street while the bedroom overlooks a quiet, plant-filled inner court. There's a wood-paneled bar and lounge with a stone fireplace, and a vaulted basement breakfast room. The service is impeccable. The highest rates are only applied during trade fairs (in May, June, September, and October).

28Place des Vogues. ☎ 800-525-4800 in the U.S. or 01-40-29-19-19 in Paris. Fax: 01-40-29-19-20. Internet: www.pavillion-de-la-reine.com. Métro: St-Paul or Bastille. Rack rates: 2,250F (343E, $321) double; 2,450F-2,700F (373E-412E, $350-$386) deluxe double or duplex; 2,950F-3,500F (450E-534E, $421-$500) junior suite or deluxe duplex; 4,300F (656E, $614) suite. AE, DC, MC, V.

Raphael

$$$$$ Arc de Triomphe (16e)

Located in a 1925 townhouse, Raphael is the clubbiest Parisian hotel, from the dark wood and Aubusson carpets of the entry hall to plush velvet chairs in the "English Bar." It's been host to Katherine Hepburn, Marlon Brando, and presidents from Kennedy to Bush, Sr. (Eisenhower even made it his headquarters after the liberation of Paris). Most rooms are done in Louis XVI style, with marble tables and fireplaces, gilded flourishes on the hardwood wardrobes, and two-tone 18th-century-style scenes painted in niches above the doorways. The "chambres de salon" rooms have huge armoires and a sitting room separate from the bedroom, while the "chambres de boudoir" feature a lighter decor, roomy baths with separate tub and Jacuzzi shower, and small sitting rooms. Even the simplest rooms, "chambres de charme," are oversized and posh, similar in decor to the boudoir but without the separate sitting room. The junior suites have a bedroom set off from the sitting area by a filagreed wood screen hung with theatrically swooping curtains. They can also link two adjacent "boudoir" rooms to make a small apartment, removing the bed to make a salon. There is a honeymoon suite with views of the Arc de Triomphe, but if money is no object, book the "Appartement de Paris." One of Paris's finest lodgings, the "Paris" is a three-story wonderland of opulence, from the hand-painted tiles in the Jacuzzi and genuine Louis XV-era Chinese paneling in the bed- and sitting rooms (some taken from a castle in the Ardennes; others copies) to private access via a spiral wooden staircase onto the choicest section of the roof terrace, with its excellent 360-degree views of Paris, including the nearby Arc and the Eiffel Tower. No matter what room you take, you can arrange to dine — breakfast, buffet lunch, or dinner — up on the public section of the terrace for the best dining with a view the city has to offer (roughly May to September).

17 av. Kleber (at av. des Portugais). ☎ *01-53-64-32-00. Fax: 01-53-64-32-01. Internet:* www.raphael-hotel.com. *Métro: Kleber. Rack rates: 2,500F (379E, $357) "chambres de charme" double; 3,010F (456E, $430) "chambre boudoir" deluxe double; 3,980F (603E, $569) alcove junior suite; 3,980F-5,150F (603E-780E, $569-$736) "chambre salons" suites; 6,500F-9,500F (985E-1,439E, $929-$1,357) apartments; 18,000F (2,727E, $2,571) "Le Penthouse" suite. AE, DC, MC, V.*

Hôtel de Lutèce

$ Ile Saint-Louis (4e)

The refined Lutèce is one of the best buys in central Paris; you get three times the hotel at ⅓ the price of many comparable inns. It occupies a converted 17th-century house accented with rustic details, such as wood-beam ceilings and terra-cotta floors, and the comfy rooms are large (as are the baths) for such a central, chic neighborhood. The street is lined with restaurants and shops, and it's just a five-minute stroll from Nôtre Dame. It doesn't have any suites or special honeymoon rooms per se, but with its antique character, ideal location, and excellent rates, the Lutèce makes a perfect budget romantic getaway anytime.

65 rue Saint-Louis-en-L'Ile (on the main drag of the island). ☎ *01-43-26-23-52. Fax: 01-43-29-60-25. Métro: Pont-Marie. Rack rates: 900F (136E, $129) double. AE, MC, V.*

Chapter 33

Enjoying Your Parisian Honeymoon

By Reid Bramblett

● ●

In This Chapter

▶ Experiencing the best of Paris

▶ Celebrating your romance

▶ Finding the top Parisian restaurants

● ●

*P*aris has dozens of museums and hundreds of churches and monuments. Half the joy of a Parisian honeymoon is simply wandering the streets in the City of Light, but this chapter tells you about the must see sights.

Paris's best buy is the **Carte Musées et Monuments,** a pass that lets you into 70 Parisian sights for free (the only notable exceptions are the Eiffel and Montparnasse towers and the Marmottan museum). It costs 85F (13E, $12) for a one-day pass — the cost of the Louvre and Musée d'Orsay alone. You can also get three-day (170F, 26E, $24) or five-day (255F, 39E, $36) versions. The biggest benefit, though, is that you don't have to wait in line! You just saunter up to a separate window and they wave you through, like visiting royalty. You can buy the pass at any train station, tourist office, main Métro stations, or participating sight. For more info, visit the Association interMusées Web site at www.intermusees.com.

Appreciating Fine Art

A former royal palace, the **Louvre** (☎ 01-40-20-53-17; Internet: www.louvre.fr; Métro: Palais-Royal-Musée du Louvre) opened to the public as an art gallery when the French Revolution struck. The museum has 195,000 square feet of galleries, five million visitors annually, and over 30,000 works on display spanning three millennia. If time permits, take in the Louvre over several visits. You enter via the giant glass pyramid in the courtyard between the qaui du Louvre and rue de Rivoli. The Louvre is open Thursday to Sunday 9 a.m. to 6 p.m., Wednesday 9 a.m. to 9:45 p.m., Monday 9 a.m. to 6 p.m., plus main galleries until 9:45 p.m.

In 1986, Paris consolidated most of its collections of French art, from 1848 to World War I, in the most unlikely of spots: a converted train station now called the **Musée d'Orsay,** 1 rue Bellechasse or 62 rue de Lille (☎ **01-40-49-48-14;** Internet: www.musee-orsay.fr; Métro: Solférino, RER: Musée-d'Orsay). Although the Orsay has earlier works by the likes of Ingres and Delacroix, its biggest draw is undoubtedly those crowd-pleasing impressionists. You can easily spend a full day at "M'O." The museum is open Tuesday to Saturday 10 a.m. to 6 p.m. (until 9:45 p.m. Thursday), Sunday 9 a.m. to 6p.m. June 20 to September 20, it opens at 9 a.m.

The **Rodin Museum,** 77 rue de Varenne, (☎ **01-44-18-61-10;** Métro: Varenne), is terribly romantic, both for its statue-studded gardens surrounding the small villa that was once his studio (the *Thinker* is surrounded by gigantic pink roses), and for the touching, often sultry, sculptures inside, including *The Kiss, The Three Shades, The Hand of God,* and *Iris.* Wander the English gardens out back to find Rodin's *The Gate of Hell, The Burghers of Calais,* and *Balzac.* The Rodin Museum is open Tuesday to Sunday 9:30 a.m. to 5:45 p.m. (until 4:45 p.m. October to March).

When Picasso left some $50 million in French inheritance taxes when he died, the state instead accepted 203 paintings, 177 sculptures, and thousands of sketches and engravings and with them set up the **Musée Picasso,** 5 rue de Thorigny, (☎ **01-42-71-25-21;** Métro: St-Paul or Filles du Calvaire). One of the most representative collections of Picasso's works in the world, the offerings span his entire career. The museum is open Wednesday to Monday 9:30 a.m. to 6 p.m. (closes 5:30 p.m. October to March).

The Centre Georges **Pompidou,** Place Georges Pompidou (☎ **01-44-78-12-33;** Internet: www.cnac-gp.fr; Métro: Rambuteaux), is Paris's odd, colorful homage to 20th-century creativity. Aside from the gallery of modern art — featuring the works of Matisse, Chagall, Kadinsky, Bonnard, Ernst, Pollock, Calder, and Henry Moore — there are exhibits on industrial design, music research, photography, and the history of film. The cafeteria on the top floor has some fantastic views. Even if you don't want to go inside, come by to shake your head at the wildly colorful and controversial transparent inside-out architecture — which was outrageously avant-garde in the 70s but by 1998 had deteriorated so badly they had to shut it down for repairs that are just now ending — and to enjoy Paris's best street performers on the sloping square out front. The Pompidou is open Monday and Wednesday to Friday noon to 10 p.m., Saturday and Sunday 10 a.m. to 10 p.m.

Visiting the Best Attractions

The **Eiffel Tower,** Champs-de-Mars(☎ **01-44-11-23-23;** Internet: www. eiffel-tower.com; Métro: Trocadéro, Ecole-Militaire, or Bir-Hakeim; RER: Champ-de-Mars-Tour Eiffel), rises 1,056 feet above the banks of the Seine in all its steel girder glory. The quintessential Parisian symbol, the Eiffel Tower was built merely as a temporary exhibit for the Exhibition of 1899, but its usefulness as a transmitter of telegraph, radio, and TV signals saved it from demolition. It was the tallest manmade structure in the world until the Chrysler Building stole the title in 1930. The restaurants and bars on the first level are pricey, but not bad. The vista from the second level is an intimate bird's eye view of Paris; from the fourth level, you can see the entire city spread out below and, on a good day, as far out as 42 miles. Visibility is usually best near sunset. It opens July to August daily 9 a.m. to midnight, September to June daily 9:30 a.m. to 11 p.m. (in winter, the stairs stay open only until 6:30 p.m.).

The **Champs-Elysèes,** the grandest boulevard in a city famed for them, has sadly been inundated by fast food chains and movie houses. But even the modernization of these "Elysian Fields" can't detract from the drama of approaching the **Arc de Triomphe** at the avenue's end (☎ **01-55-37-73-77;** Métro: Charles-de-Gaulle-Étoile). The world's largest triumphal arch stands mighty at the center of place Charles-de-Gaulle (the world's craziest traffic circle). Napoléon ordered the Roman-style arch to honor his brilliant military victories and the rapid growth of his ill-fated Empire, but it wasn't finished until 1836 — 22 years after Napoléon's defeat at Waterloo. Take the pedestrian under-pass to visit the eternal flame honoring France's unknown soldier that burns at its base, then ride the elevator to the top (daily 10 a.m. to 10:30 p.m. — 9:30 a.m. to 11 p.m. May to September); the Arc crests the tallest rise of Paris's center, and the low-profile panoramas over the rooftops and monuments of the City of Lights are fantastic.

On the Ile de la Cité, an island in the Seine at the very center of Paris, rises **Nôtre Dame Cathedral** (☎ **01-42-34-56-10;** Métro: Cité). "Our Lady of Paris" is the heart and soul of the city, a monument to Paris's past slung in the cradle of its origins (the island is where the first Celtic village of the Parisii existed before the Romans). The 12th- to 14th-century cathedral is a study in Gothic beauty and gargoyles, at once solid, with squat, square facade towers, and graceful, with flying buttresses all around the sides and apse. The Cathedral has been remodeled, embellished, ransacked, and restored so often that it's a wonder the church still has any architectural integrity at all (during the Revolution, it was even stripped of its religion and re-christened the Temple of Reason). The lines to get in are long (and Quasimodo's a no-show), but while you wait to get in, you can admire the Bible stories played out in intricate stone relief around the three great portals on the facade. Much of the facade was (poorly) restored once in the 18th century and then again (as well as can be done) in the 19th. If you're keen to see some medieval originals, the upper tier of the central portal is ancient, and much of the sculpture on the right-hand portal has also survived from 1165 to 1175.

In the high, airy Gothic interior, the choir section has a gorgeously carved and painted stone screen from the early/mid-14th century on its outer flanks and 18th-century wooden choir stalls along the inside. The main draw, though, are the three enormous rose windows, especially the 69-foot diameter north window (left transept), which has retained almost all of its original 13th-century stained glass. Save Nôtre Dame for a sunny day and the best light effects. No visit to Nôtre Dame is complete without tackling the 387 steps up the north tower to examine those grotesque, amusing, or sometimes downright frightening gargoyles. From up here, you also get fine views of the city. You should also walk around the outside of the building. Those famous flying buttresses at the very back, holding up the apse with 50-foot spans of stone strength, are particularly impressive. Cross the Seine to admire the entire effect from the Left Bank. Nôtre Dame is open daily 8 a.m. to 6:45 p.m., or 7:30 p.m. weekends except on Sunday, open for mass only 9:30 a.m. to 2 p.m.

Two blocks from Nôtre Dame but still on the Ile de la Cité is one of Paris's most precious jewels and romantic spots, the tiny Gothic chapel of **Sainte-Chapelle,** 4 bd. du Palais (☎ **01-53-73-78-50;** Internet: www.monuments-france.fr; Métro: Cité), built in 1246 to house the Crown of Thorns. Almost entirely hidden by the bulk of the Palace of Justice surrounding it, the chapel's interior is a sculpture of light and color. The thin bits of stone that hold the tall stained-glass windows and brace the roof seem to dissolve in the diffuse and dappled brightness glowing through the 13th-century windows. It's open April to September daily 9:30 a.m. to 6:30 p.m., October to March daily 10 a.m. to 5 p.m.

Taking a Romantic Garden Stroll

Paris is not just a city of boulevards and museums; it also offers a remarkable amount of green space — aside from strolls along the quais of the Seine River (so evocative they are now protected as an UNESCO World Heritage site), Paris numbers nearly 400 parks, gardens, and shady squares within the city itself.

The meticulously planned, statue lined promenades, perfectly placed fountains, and regimentally planted trees of the **Tuileries** (Métro: Tuileries or Concorde) running along the Seine between the Louvre and the place de la Concorde were laid out by 17th-century architect Le Nôtre. At the place de la Concorde end are two excellent small art galleries. The **Jeu de Paume** (☎ **01-47-03-12-50)** hosts temporary exhibits, while the wonderful **Orangerie** (☎ **01-42-97-48-16)** is one of Paris' best secret romantic spots: Impressionist works hang in the rooms upstairs while in the basement hides Monet's grandest project and most beautiful memorial: two specially-built oval rooms each set with 360-degrees of continuous Waterlilies. The Jeu de Paume hours vary with exhibits; the Orangerie opens Wednesday to Monday 9:45 a.m. to 5:15 p.m. Alas, the Tuileries is to be avoided after dusk.

The **Jardin de Luxembourg** (Métro: Odéon or RER: Luxembourg) sits behind the Italianate Senate building in the upper reaches of the Latin Quarter. It features the fantastic Medicis Fountain, built for Marie de Medici in 1612, lots of strolling families, and a huge apple and pear orchard called the Verger de Luxembourg tucked into one corner.

The 1640 **Jardin des Plantes** (Métro: Gare de L'Austerlitz) consists mainly of fenced-off gardens and a natural history museum (a quirky 19th-century holdover: one huge room filled by a frozen stampede of extinct and exotic animal skeletons). But its secret is the *Jardin Alpin,* which initially looks like any old regimented Paris garden. However, halfway down the Jardin is a tunnel ducking under the main path, which pops you out into a miniature valley largely hidden from the main part of the park by profuse bushes up at ground level. In the microclimate of this secluded vale thrive over 2,000 species of mountain plants (from the Alps, Pyrenees, Caucasus, Rockies, Himalayas, and others) arranged lushly around a small stream that winds through the miniature wonderland past tiny waterfalls. There are plenty of benches in nooks for smooching in relative privacy. It's open April to September only, Monday to Friday 8 a.m. to 11 p.m. and 1:30 to 5 p.m.

The **Parc André Citroën** (Métro: Balard or Bd. Victor) is a sort of avant-garde urban park, with lots of small gardens on odd themes — the five senses, movement, and wildflowers, for example — all tied together by water: rushing, pooling, falling, jetting, and just generally creating a relaxing babbling-brook backdrop to the whole park. **Parc de Bercy** (Métro: Bercy), in one of the latest of Paris's redeveloping neighborhoods, also features themed gardens, but with more traditional themes — aromatic, roses, orchards, a "philosophers' garden" and, of course, a *jardin romantique* — all set amid abandoned wine warehouses.

The **Bois de Vincennes** (Métro: Château de Vincennes) at the city's eastern edge incorporates small lakes, a château, a flower garden, two out-of-place but interesting monuments — a Tibetan Buddhist temple and a museum of African and Oceanic art and culture — and terrific Parisian panoramas from the Parc de Belleville. You can also get city vistas from the faux temple in Baron Haussmann's 19th-century, Romantic-era **Parc de Buttes-Chaumont** (Métro: Buttes-Chaumont).

By far Paris's largest greensward is the vast, forest-like **Bois de Boulogne** (Métro: porte Maillot, porte Dauphine, av. H. Martin, or porte d'Auteuil) bounding the city's western edge. There's much to explore here, but unfortunately much of the park has been given over to prostitutes these days (definitely don't wander here after dark). But the pretty Pre Catalan; the rose bushes, irises, and peacocks strutting in the revamped English gardens of the Bagatelle; and the Shakespeare Garden (filled with plants, flowers, and trees mentioned in his plays) all remain very pleasant indeed.

Exploring Montmartre

One thing's for sure — La Bohème it ain't anymore. Although inundated by tourists these days, Montmartre, Paris's classic bohemian artists' neighborhood crowning a hill at the city's northern edge (the 18e), still has an intriguing village flavor and remains one of the best Parisian areas to wander. Take the Métro to Abbesses and work your way uphill to the **Basilique du Sacré-Coeur** (there's a funicular to save you the steep stairs; cost: one Métro ticket), a frosty white neo-Byzantine basilica built from 1876 to 1919 and towering over the city. Climb the dome for a vista that on clear days extends 35 miles.

Some of Montmartre's quirkiest sights include a pair of **windmills,** visible from rue Lepic and rue Girardon, and Paris's only **vineyard,** on rue des Saules. Next door to the latter, at rue Saint-Vincent 12, is the **Montmartre Museum** (☎ 01-46-06-61-11), dedicated to the neighborhood in a house that was at times occupied by van Gogh, Renoir, and Utrillo. Pay your respects to the writers Stendhal and Dumas, the composers Offenbach and Berlioz, and the painter Degas at their graves in the **Cimitère de Montmartre** on avenue Rachel. Finish the evening at 22 rue des Saules in **Au Lapin Agile** (☎ 01-46-06-85-87) — in Picasso and Utrillo's day called Café des Assassins — Paris's foremost spot for folk music. The cover, including first drink, is a steep 130F ($21.65).

For a racy interlude before heading into bohemian Montmartre, get off the Métro one stop early at Pigalle. Here you're on the northwest edge of **Paris's red light district,** centered on the sex shop-lined boulevard de Clichy, which is more depraved than cheeky these days but still features hangers-on like the Moulin Rouge at number 87 (☎ 01-53-09-82-82; Internet: www.moulinrouge.com) with its pre-packaged, over-priced can-can shows; and the surprisingly quasi-tasteful **Museum of Erotic Art** at number 72 (☎ 01-42-58-28-73; Internet: www.eroticmuseum.net), which is open daily 10 a.m. to 2 a.m.

Picturing the Perfect Parisian Panorama

The most famous and highest panoramas in Paris are, of course, from the second and third stories of the **Eiffel Tower.** The problem with that and many other vistas in Paris is that they are marred by the **Montparnasse Tower** (☎ 01-45-38-52-56; Métro: Montparnasse-Bienvenue), a modern skyscraper jutting indecorously from the Lost Generation's Parisian hillside. Luckily, you can kill two birds with one stone: Get the Montparnasse out of your postcard view by riding its elevator to the roof, and in doing so enjoy the second-highest views (690 feet) in Paris. From here there's a great close-up of the Eiffel lined up straight down the Champs de Mars park, the perfect backdrop to a picture of the newlyweds smooching.

Out on the edge of Paris is a weird modern office-building complex known as **La Défense,** the centerpiece of which is the hollow cube-shaped skyscraper **Grande Arche de la Défense** (☎ 01-49-07-27-57; Internet: www.grandarche.com; Métro: Esplanade de la Défense). It was built to line up perfectly along av. de la Grande Armee, through the Arc de Triomphe, and down the Champs-Elysées to place de la Concorde, the Tuileries gardens, and the Louvre. Ride the elevator 363 feet to the top (open daily 10 a.m. to 7 p.m.).

Less obvious viewpoints include the roof terrace of the **Institute du Monde Arabe** (Métro: Jussieu; open Tuesday to Sunday 10 a.m. to 6 p.m.) on quai Saint-Bernard at the pont de Sully, with a fantastic view of the backside of Nôtre Dame and all those flying buttresses. The top floor of Magasin 2 of **La Samartaine** department store (Métro: Pont-Neuf or Châtelet-Les-Halles) takes in the Left Bank and the Eiffel beyond.

And don't forget the spots already mentioned in earlier in this chapter: the **cafeteria of the Pompidou,** the top of the **Arc de Triomphe,** the towers of **Nôtre Dame,** the **Parc de Belleville** in the Bois de Vincennes, and the temple in the **Parc des Buttes-Chaumont.**

Cruising the Seine

Is there anything more romantic than slipping down the current of one of the world's great rivers past 18th-century palaces? Well, perhaps killing the canned P.A. sightseeing commentary and getting rid of all the other camera-clicking tourists would help the romantic mood. But if it's mood you're after, you can always do it on a more refined dinner cruise (keep reading for more information on those).

The classic Bateaux-Mouches float down the Seine is offered by several companies, the biggest being **Bateaux Parisiens** (☎ 01-44-11-33-44; Internet: www.bateauxparisiens.com), which departs from quai de Montebello at Nôtre-Dame or from pont d'Iena at the foot of the Eiffel Tower; and **Les Vedette du Pont-Neuf** (☎ 01-46-33-98-38), which leaves from Pont Neuf on the Ile de la Cité. Vessels depart every half hour 10:30 a.m. to noon, 1:30 to 8 p.m., and 9 to 11 p.m. (fewer in winter). Regular 90-minute trips with multilingual commentary cost 50F (8E, $7).

After dark, the boats sweep both banks with mega-powered floodlights — illuminating everything very well, but sort of spoiling the romance. These tend to be touristy too, unless you opt for one of the more refined and romantic luncheon or dinner cruises, which are considerably more expensive — 350F to 780F (53E to 118E, $50 to

$111) for jacket-and-tie dinners, and the food is only so-so. The setting, however, can't be beat.

A cheaper, and less contrived, alternative to the day-time tour is the **Batobus** (☎ 01-44-11-33-99), a kind of water taxi (no piped-in commentary) that stops every 25 minutes at five major points of interest: Hôtel de Ville, Nôtre Dame, the Louvre, the Eiffel Tower, the Musée d'Orsay, and Saint-Germain-des-Prés. A day ticket costs 65F (10E, $9) per person. Batobus runs April 15 to November 1, 10 a.m. to 7 p.m. (to 9 p.m. June to August).

Living the Cafe Life

The Paris cafe is a sort of public extension of the living room, where intellectuals debate, executives make deals, politicians hold court, lovers meet, and poets dream. You can sit all day over a single cup of coffee or order a light meal or flute of champagne.

You can ensconce yourself indoors or stand at the bar, but most people choose to sit outside — in a glassed-in porch in winter or on the sidewalk in summer — because one of the cafe's biggest attractions is the people-watching. Many Parisian cafes are legendary, immortalized by historical circumstances and Hemingway novels.

Of the thousands of cafes — from simple, tiny locals' joints to cavernous glittering belle époque bastions — here are some classics. **Les Deux Magots** (☎ 01-45-48-55-25), 6 place St-Germain-des-Prés, established in 1885, was the haunt of Picasso, Hemingway, and Sartre. Sartre wrote a whole trilogy holed up at a table in **Café de Flore** (☎ 01-45-48-55-26), 172 bd St-Germain, a Left Bank cafe frequented by Camus and Picasso and featured in Gore Vidal novels.

The Champs-Elysées may no longer be Paris's hot spot, but **Fouquet's** (☎ 01-47-23-70-60) at number 99 is still going strong based on its reputation, good food, and favorable reviews by Chaplin, Churchill, FDR, and Jackie Onassis. Henry Miller took his morning porridge at **La Couple** (☎ 01-43-20-14-20), 102 bd. du Montparnasse, a brassiere that also hosted the likes of Josephine Baker, John Dos Passos, Dalí, and F. Scott Fitzgerald.

Finally, you can make a pilgrimage to the art nouveau interiors of the new **La Rotonde** (☎ 01-43-26-68-84), 105 bd. du Montparnasse, risen like a phoenix from the ashes of its namesake that once stood here. In *The Sun Also Rises,* Hemingway writes of the original, "No matter what cafe in Montparnasse you ask a taxi driver to bring you to . . . they always take you to the Rotonde."

Dining in Paris

Paris is perhaps the world capital of dining, its cuisine a delicate balance of flavors, sauces, and ingredients blended with a studied technique.

Some people may be intimidated by the idea of sitting down to what many — certainly the French themselves — consider the most refined food on the planet. Don't sweat it. The only people with a need to impress anyone are the chef and kitchen staff. Have your waiter suggest some dishes, let the sommelier pick a wine; then just sit back and enjoy the flavors.

Be careful — ordering wine by the bottle can jack up the cost of your meal in no time.

Sparing no expense

For tradition and a cuisine so scrupulously haute it belongs in a museum, you can do no better than Jean-Claude Vrinat's **Taillevent,** 15 rue Lamennais (☎ **01-44-95-15-01;** Métro: George-V; $$$$), named after the 14th-century alchemist who wrote France's first cookbook.

Alain Ducasse is one of the few chefs ever to garner six Michelin stars at once (spread across three restaurants), so he doesn't need to bother naming his ludicrously expensive but excellent Paris dining room — in an early 20th-century townhouse decorated with a subdued Art Nouveau clubby elegance — anything but **Alain Ducasse,** 59 av. Raymond Poincaré (☎ **01-47-27-12-27;** Métro: Victor-Hugo; $$$$).

The best view of any Parisian restaurant belongs to fancy **La Tour d'Argent,** 15-17 quai de la Tournelle (☎ **01-43-54-23-31;** Métro: Maubert-Mutualité or Pont-Marie; $$$$), a penthouse with a vista of the Seine and the lit apse of Nôtre-Dame.

If it's star-gazing of a different type you're after, two of Paris most trendy restaurants of the moment are **Man Ray,** 34 rue Marbeuf (☎ **01-56-88-36-36;** Métro: Roosevelt; $$$$), co-owned by a Paris nightclub impresario, Sean Penn, and Johnny Depp, with a varied menu that borrows heavily from Asian and Mediterranean kitchens; and the French-Pacific Rim fusion cuisine at funky **Buddha Bar,** 8 rue Boissy d'Anglais (☎ **01-53-05-90-00;** Métro: Concorde; $$$$), last year's hottest ticket and still a prime see-and-be-seen joint.

Relaxing at a baby bistro

About 15 years ago, a tired haute scene and French recession teamed up to inspire top chefs to branch out into what have become known as baby bistros: small, relaxed eateries whose menus are designed by the biggest names in the business but whose prices are up to 75 percent below what you pay in these chefs' flagship restaurants.

Renowned chef Guy Savoy spun off several successful little spots, including the popular **La Butte Chaillot,** 110 bis av. Kléber (☎ **01-47-27-88-88;** Métro: Trocadéro; $$$), with terrace dining, and **Les Bookinistes,** 53 quai des Grand Augustins (☎ **01-43-25-45-94;** Métro: Saint-Michel; $$), a contemporary dining room on the Seine with a constantly changing menu that hints at a Mediterranean touch.

Alain Ducasse got into the game with **Le Relais du Parc,** 57 av. Raymond Poincaré (☎ **01-44-05-66-10;** Métro: Victor-Hugo; $$$), and a Mediterranean-influenced menu.

Hot cook Michel Rostang may not have shown much imagination in naming all three of his babies **Le Bistrot d'à Côté** — one at 10 rue Gustave-Flaubert (☎ **01-42-67-05-81;** Métro: Courcelles; $$$); another at 16 av. Villiers (☎ **01-47-63-25-61;** Métro: Villiers; $$$); and the other, the seafood-oriented **Le Bistrot, Côté Mer** 16 bd. St-Germain (☎ **01-43-54-59-10;** Métro: Maubert-Mutualité; $$) — but he put plenty of thought into the French menus and traditional bistro ambience.

Breaking bread at a bourgeoisie bistro

Seeing the success of the baby bistros, many young and up-and-coming chefs decided to forgo the fancy restaurant part and start right off with a small, informal, relatively inexpensive trendy bistro. Perhaps the best is **L'Epi Dupin,** 11 rue de Dupin (☎ **01-42-22-64-56;** Métro: Sèvers Babylone; $$), with fine modern bistro cuisine in an antique French setting of hewn beams and stone walls.

Another cutting-edge boîte, **Le Bambouche,** 15 rue de Babylone (☎ **01-45-49-14-40;** Métro: Sèvers-Babylone; $$), is a good place to get your fix of escargots or frogs' legs (don't worry: they serve plenty of less, ahem, "traditional" dishes as well).

Finding a bargain

The **Restaurant Perraudin,** 157 rue St-Jacques (☎ **01-46-33-15-75;** Métro: Cluny; RER: Luxembourg; $), fills up early (no reservations) with hungry travelers and locals after the inexpensive classic bistro fare in a convivial, wood-beamed atmosphere.

In the 17th century, army sergeants would shanghai young conscripts by getting them drunk at the **La Taverne du Sergent Recruteur,** 41 rue St-Louis-en-L'Ile (☎ **01-43-54-75-42;** Métro: Pont-Marie; $$), where today's only danger is overindulging on the ample fixed-price menus and bottomless bottles of wine.

Paris' most lauded cheap meal is the remarkable 49F ($8.15) menu at **Le Petit Gravouche,** 15 rue Sainte-Croix-de-la-Brentonnaire (☎ 01-48-87-74-26; Métro: Hôtel-de-Ville; $), so work-a-day simple and utterly plain that you'd never believe this old school bistro, and its low prices, are known around the world.

Discovering a local favorite

A *brasserie* is somewhere between a cafe and a restaurant, with great low prices and a cuisine usually based on the Franco-Germanic cooking of the Alsace region — lots of choucroute (sauerkraut, usually served with sausages or salamis). They're also good for off-hours dining, tending to stay open continuously from noon to 1 a.m.

The first, and still the best, *brasserie* is **Bofinger,** 5-7 rue de la Bastille (☎ 01-42-72-87-82; Métro: Bastille; $$), opened in 1864 and sporting a restored 1919 Art Deco decor. Service can be whirlwind. You can get French comfort food at the century-old **Brasserie Balzar,** 49 rue des Écoles (☎ 01-43-54-13-67; Métro: Odeon or Cluny-La Sorbonne; $$), once frequented by Sartre, Camus, and James Thurber. Or sit amid Hemingway memories and a delightful mirror-and-sepia-toned decor at the famed 1880 **Brassiere Lipp,** 151 bd. St-Germain (☎ 01-45-48-53-91; Métro: St-Germain-des-Prés; $$), popular with Parisian businesspeople at lunch, so come around noon to secure a table.

Savoring regional cuisine

The Basque from the southwest corner of France (and northeast section of Spain) are renowned both for their unique, non-Indo-European language and for practicing some of the best cooking and most refined cuisine in all of France. Jean-Guy Loustau serves perhaps Paris's best Basque at **Au Bascou,** 38 rue Réaumur (☎ 01-42-72-69-25; Métro: Artes et Metiers; $$) in a simple and softly lit rustic interior. Lower-rent Basque cooking like grandma used to make can be had at the friendly little **Auberge de la Jarente,** 7 rue de Jarente (☎ 01-42-77-49-35; Métro: Saint-Paul; $).

Tiny **Campagne et Provence,** 25 Quai de la Tournelle (☎ 01-43-54-05-17; Métro: Maubert-Mutualité; $$$), serves some of Paris's choicest Provençal cuisine (go for either seafood or game) at reasonable prices. You get a bit more Provençal food for your franc with the fixed-price menus at **Chez Toutoune,** 5 rue de Pontoise (☎ 01-43-26-56-81; Métro: Maubert-Mutualité; $$$), but the atmosphere isn't as romantic.

To sample the cooking of the wild Auvergne region, head to quirky **Chantairelle,** 17 rue Laplace (☎ 01-46-33-18-59; Métro: Cardinale Lemoine or RER: Luxembourg; $$) with its piped-in bird song and boutique of regional products; book ahead for a table on the pretty little flagstone garden out back.

Creating magic by moonlight

Right in the chaotic heart of Paris is a quiet retreat surrounded by the arcaded courtyard of the Royal Palace, where tucked into one corner, and with tables out on the terrace in warm weather, hides the **Restaurant du Palais Royal,** 110 Galerie de Valois in the Jardin du Palais Royal (☎ **01-40-20-00-27;** Métro: Palais-Royal; $$$). And don't forget the patio seating at **Chanteraille,** recommended in the previous section.

Even more romantic are two restaurants within the Bois de Boulogne. Indulge in Franco-Asian cuisine sitting out on the lawn at **Le Pre Catalan,** on route de Suresnes (☎ **01-45-24-55-58;** Métro: Porte-Maillot then bus 144; $$$), or fine traditional French dishes at **Le Grande Cascade,** on Allée de Longchamp (☎ **01-45-27-33-51;** Métro: Porte-Maillot then bus 144; $$$), a Belle Époque restaurant at the base of a waterfall.

Chapter 34

Making Plans and Settling In

By Reid Bramblett

● ●

In This Chapter

▶ Arranging your transportation

▶ Finding the best ways to get around Paris

▶ Knowing all the details

● ●

*Y*our dream Paris honeymoon is planned, the perfect hotel picked out, and you're raring to go — customs regulations and getting tourist information, for example? Can you plug in your hairdryer? What about changing money and using your credit cards? Is it safe to drink the water? Unexciting as these things are, they're an integral part of getting ready for a trip. We tell you everything you need to know in this chapter.

Getting to Paris

You can go with one of the U.S.-based airlines, but you may find better deals by flying transatlantic with a European national carrier — Virgin Atlantic, British Airways, or Air France, for example. However, don't rule out the other European airlines, which often offer cheap fares (though sometimes involving a transfer in the major hub of their home country).

Air France (☎ 800-2-FRANCE; Internet: www.airfranceholidays.com) offers a Paris Honeymoon Package that includes airfare, six nights with breakfast in bed, a Seine river cruise, a nighttime tour of the city, shows, and various little romantic touches starting around $1,800 for two. Budget specialist **New Frontiers (☎ 800-366-6387;** Internet: www.newfrontiers.com) can give you a bubbly-themed tour: the best of Paris (four nights, including a museum pass and Seine cruise) and the Champagne region (three nights, including a visit to the Moët & Chandon champagne caverns), plus airfare *and* four days of car rental, for about the best price around, from $2,200 for two.

Two other French specialist operators who can put together special honeymoon packages for you are **The French Experience** (☎ 212-986-3800; Internet: www.frenchexperience.com) and **Jet Vacations** (☎ 800-JET-0999; Internet: www.jetvacations.com), whose pick-and-choose, "create your own package" style gives you the best of both worlds — the convenience of a package tour but with a freedom of choice normally associated only with independent travel.

Getting Around Paris

After you arrive safely in Paris, you should start exploring. How you get around depends on how much ground you need to cover in a given time frame, but you can use several modes of transportation before your trip is over. This section gives you pointers on how to master the public transportation system, how to find a cab when you need one most, and what to watch out for while walking.

Probably your best introduction to Paris, and the way the city is laid out, is the view from the tower at Nôtre-Dame. The magnificent cathedral is visible from many parts of the city, and a visit helps you get oriented. You also realize that the Seine is actually Paris's most important "street."

Getting around by Métro

The best way to get around Paris is to walk, but for longer distances the Métro, or subway, is best.

The Métro is fast, safe, and easy to navigate. A dozen stations also enjoyed a recent centenary makeover as well; based on themes, the newly designed stations include Bonne Nouvelle, which now resembles a film set and displays film screens showing various old movies. Operated by the RATP (*Régie Autonome des Transports Parisiens*), as are city buses, the Métro has a total of 16 lines and more than 360 stations, making it likely that one is near your destination. The Métro is connected to the *Réseau Express Régional* (RER), which connects downtown Paris with its airports and suburbs. Subway trains run from 5:30 a.m. to 1 a.m., and you often witness people running down streets at about 12:50 a.m. trying to catch the last train. After that, the RATP operates **Noctambuses** that run on the hour from 1:30 a.m. to 5:30 a.m. from Châtelet-Hôtel de Ville, but they don't cover every *arrondissement*. Check the maps at the entrance to Métro stations to determine if a Noctambus services your destination. You recognize the bus by its yellow and black owl symbol. Noctambus tickets cost 30F ($4.30). Métro and the RER tickets cost 8F ($1.15) to any point within the first 20 *arrondissements* of Paris, and slightly more if you travel to an outlying suburb (the exact cost depends on where your particular destination is).

A ten-ticket *carnet* (booklet) good for the Métro and on buses is a good deal for 55F ($7.90) because a single ticket costs 8F ($1.15). *Carnets* are on sale at all Métro stations as well as *tabacs* (cafés and kiosks that sell tobacco products). You also see ads for the **Paris Visite** card, which starts at 55F ($7.90) a day. It does offer free or reduced entry to some attractions in addition to unlimited travel, but make sure that the attractions that interest you are included on the list.

At the turnstile entrances to the station, insert your ticket in the turnstile, pass through the entrance, and take your ticket out of the machine. You must keep your ticket until you exit the train platform, at which point an inspector may ask to see your ticket again. If you fail to produce it, you are subject to a steep fine. When you ride the RER, you must keep your ticket because you have to insert it in a turnstile when you exit the station.

Some older Métro stations are marked by elegant art nouveau gateways reading Métropolitain; others are marked by big yellow M signs. Every Métro stop has maps of the system, which are also available at ticket booths. Once you decide which line you need, make sure you are going in the right direction: On Métro line 1, "Direction: Esplanade de la Defense" indicates a westbound train, "Direction: Château de Vincennes" is eastbound. To change train lines, look for the correspondence signs; blue signs reading *sortie* mark exits.

Near the exits is usually a *plan du quartier,* a very detailed pictorial map of the streets and buildings surrounding the station, with all exits marked. Consult the *plan du quartier* before you climb the stairs, especially at very large stations; you may want to use a different exit to reach the other side of a busy street or wind up closer to your destination.

For more information on the city's public transportation, stop in at the **Services Touristiques de la RATP,** at place de la Madeleine, 1er (☎ **01-40-06-71-45;** Internet: www.ratp.fr; Métro: Madeleine), or call ☎ **08-36-68-41-14** for information in English.

Getting around by bus

The bus system is convenient and can be an inexpensive way to sightsee without wearing out your feet. Each bus shelter has a route map, which you want to check carefully. Because of the number of one-way streets, the bus may make different stops depending on its direction. Métro tickets are valid for bus travel, or you can buy your ticket from the conductor, but you can't buy *carnets* on board. Tickets must be punched in a machine inside the bus and retained until the end of the ride.

Some bus routes are great for sightseeing because they take a scenic route and pass many attractions. Try these bus routes for easy jump-on, jump-off sightseeing itineraries: **Bus 69:** Eiffel Tower, Invalides, Louvre, Hôtel de Ville, Place des Vosges, Bastille, Père Lachaise Cemetery. **Bus 80:** Department stores on bd. Haussmann, Champs-Elysées, Ave. Montaigne haute-couture shopping, Eiffel Tower. **Bus 96:** St-Germain-des-Prés, Musée de Cluny, Hôtel de Ville, place des Vosges.

Getting around by taxi

Parisian taxis are expensive, and you need to know a few things before you hail one.

Look for the blue taxi sign denoting a taxi stand; although you can hail taxis in the street (look for a taxi with a white light on; an orange light means the cab is occupied), most drivers refuse to pick you up if you are in the general vicinity of a taxi stand.

For one to three people, the drop rate in Paris proper is 13F ($1.90); the rate per kilometer is 3.45F (49 cents) from 7 a.m. to 7 p.m.; otherwise, 5.70F (81 cents). You pay supplements from taxi ranks at train stations and at the Air France shuttle-bus terminals of 5F (75 cents), 6F (90 cents) for luggage, and, if the driver agrees to do so, 10F ($1.45) for transporting a fourth person. Common practice is to tip your driver 2F to 3F (30 to 45 cents), except on longer journeys when the fare exceeds 100F ($14.30); in these cases, a 5 to 10 percent tip is appropriate.

Check the meter carefully, especially if you are coming in from an airport; rip-offs are very common. If you feel that you may have been overcharged, demand a receipt (which drivers are obligated to provide) and contact the **Préfecture of Police** (☎ **01-55-76-20-00**).

Getting around by car

The streets are narrow, parking is next to impossible, and nerve, skill, ruthlessness, and a knowledgeable copilot are required if you insist on driving in Paris. We *strongly* recommend that you do not.

A few tips: Get an excellent street map and ride with another person; traffic moves so lightning-fast that you don't have time to think at intersections. For the most part, you must pay to park in Paris. Depending on the neighborhood, expect to pay 5F to 15F (75 cents to $2.15) an hour for a maximum of two hours. Place coins in the nearest meter, which issues you a ticket to place on your windshield. You can also buy parking cards at the nearest *tabac* for meters that accept only cards. Parking is free on Sundays, holidays, and for the entire month of August.

Drivers and all passengers must wear seat belts. Drivers are supposed to yield to the car on the right, except where signs indicate otherwise, as at traffic circles.

 Watch for the *gendarmes* (police officers), who lack patience and who consistently contradict the traffic lights. Horn blowing is frowned upon except in emergencies. Flash your headlights instead.

Getting around by bicycle

City planners have been trying to encourage more cycling by setting aside 62 miles of bicycle lanes throughout Paris. The main routes run north-south from the Bassin de La Villette along the Canal St-Martin through the Left Bank and east-west from Château de Vincennes to the Bois de Boulogne and its miles of bike lanes. For more information and a bike map, pick up the *Plan Vert* from the tourist office. In addition, the banks of the Seine are closed to cars and open to pedestrians and cyclists each Sunday from March to November 10 a.m. to 5 p.m. It might not make much of a dent in the air quality, but bicycling is a fun and healthy way to spend a Sunday afternoon.

To rent a bicycle, contact **Paris-Vélo,** 2 rue du Fer-à-Moulin, 5e (☎ **01-43-37-59-22;** Métro: St-Marcel). The price is 80F ($11.45) a day, 60F ($8.60) a half-day. A steep deposit is required.

Getting around on foot

Paris is one of the prettiest cities in the world for strolling, and getting around on foot is probably the best way to really appreciate the city's character. The best walking neighborhoods are St-Germain-des-Prés on the Left Bank and the Marais on the Right Bank, both of which are filled with romantic little courtyards, wonderful boutiques, and congenial cafés and watering holes. The quais of the Seine, as well as its bridges, are also lovely, especially at sunset when the sun fills the sky with a pink glow that's reflected on the water.

 A word to the wise: Take special care when crossing streets, even when you have the right of way. The number one rule of the road in France is that whoever is coming from the right side has the right of way. Drivers often make right turns without looking, even when faced with pedestrians at crosswalks. And don't *ever* attempt to cross a traffic circle if you're not on a crosswalk. The larger roundabouts, such as the one at the Arc de Triomphe, have pedestrian tunnels.

Fast Facts: Paris

American Express

The full service office at 11 rue Scribe (☎ 01-47-77-78-75) is open Monday to Friday 9 a.m. to 6:30 p.m. The currency desk only is open Saturday 9 a.m. to 6:30 p.m.

ATM

ATMs are widely available; there is a bank on many a Paris coner. If you'd like to print out a list of ATMs that accept MasterCard or Visa cards before you leave home, ask your bank, or print out lists from the following sites: www.visa. com/pd/atm or www.mastercard. com/atm.

Business Hours

The grands magasins (department stores) are open Monday through Saturday 9:30 a.m. to 7 p.m.; smaller shops close for lunch and reopen around 2 p.m., but this is rarer than it used to be. Many stores stay open until 7 p.m. in summer; others are closed on Monday, especially in the morning. Large offices remain open all day, but some close for lunch. Banks are normally open weekdays at 9 a.m. to noon and 1 or 1:30 to 4:30 p.m. Some banks are also open on Saturday morning. Some currency-exchange booths are open very long hours; see "Currency Exchange," in this list.

Credit Cards

Visa, MasterCard, American Express, and Diner's Club cards are all accepted in Paris, but not at all establishments.

Currency Exchange

Banks and *bureaux de change* (exchange offices) almost always offer better exhange rates than hotel, restaurants, and shops, which should be used only in emergencies. For good rates, without fee or commissions, and quick service, try the **Comptoir de Chang Opéra**, 9 rue Scribe, 9e (☎ 01-47-42-20-96; Métro: Opéra; RER: Auber). It is open weekdays 9 a.m. to 6 p.m., Saturday 9:30 a.m. to 4 p.m. The bureaux de change at all train stations (except Gare de Montparnasse) are open daily; those at 63 av. de Champs-Elysees, 83 Métro: Franklin-D-Roosevelt), and 140 av. des Champs-Elysées, 8e (Métro Charles- de-Gaulle-Étoile), keep long hours.

Customs

Non-EU nationals can bring into France duty-free 200 cigarettes or 100 cigarillos or 50 cigars or 250 grams of smoking tobacoo; 2 liters of wine and 1 liter of alcohol over 38.80 proof; 50 grams of perfume, one-quarter liter of toilet water; 500 grams of coffee, and 100 grams of tea. Travelers ages 15 and over can also bring in 1,200F ($171.45) in other goods; for those 14 and under, the limit is 600F ($85.75). EU citizens may bring any amount of goods into France as long as it is for their personal use and not for resale.

Returning U.S. citizens who have been away for 48 hours or more are allowed to bring back, once every 30 days, $400 worth of merchandise duty-free. You are charged a flat rate of 10 percent duty on the next $1,000 worth of purchases; on gifts, the duty free limit is $100. You can't bring fresh foodstuffs into the United States; tinned foods, howeve,r are allowed.

Doctors and Hospitals

SOS Médicins (☎ 01-47-07-77-77) recommends physicians. **SOS Dentaire** (☎ 01-43-37-51-00) can locate a dentist for you. The U.S. embassy can also provide a list of doctors. Both the **American Hospital of Paris**, 63 bd. Victor-Hugo in Neuilly-sur-Seine (☎ 01-46-41-25-25; Metro: Porte Maillot), and the **Franco-British Hospital**, 3 rue Barbes in Levallois-Perret (☎ 01-46-39-22-22; Metro: Anatole France), staff English-speaking physicians.

Electricity

The French electrical system runs on 220 volts. Adapters are needed to convert the voltage and fit sockets, and are cheaper at home than they are in Paris. Many hotels have two-pin (in some cases, three-pin) sockets for electric razors. It's a good idea to ask at your hotel before plugging in any electrical appliance.

Embassy and Consulate

The **U.S. Embassy** (☎ 01-43-12-22-22; Internet: www.amb-usa.fr) is at 2 av. Gabriel, 75008 Paris. The **U.S. consulate** is at 2 rue Saint-Florentin, 75382 Paris (☎ 08-36-70-14-88 or 01-43-12-48-76), open Monday to Friday 9 a.m. to 3 p.m.

Emergency

Dial ☎ **17** for the police. To report a fire, call ☎ **18**. If you need an ambulance, call the paramedics at the *Sapeurs-Pompiers* (fire department) at ☎ **18** or ☎ **15** for SAMU (Service d'Aide Medicale d'Urgence), a private ambulance company.

Money

The French unit of currency until 2002 is the French franc (F), which is divided into 100 *centimes*. Roughly, $1 equals 7F, or 1F equals 14 cents. As of January 2002, the Euro single European currency (valid in most of Western Europe save the U.K. and Switzerland) will be introduced; the franc will be withdrawn from circulation by July 2002. The Euro, which already exists as the official currency for bank transactions (just not as hard cash until 2002) has fluctuated wildly, but seems most comfortable a few cents shy of the dollar at $1 = 1.07E (or 1E = 94 cents). The franc-to-Euro rate is a fixed 1F = 0.15E (or 1E = 6.60F).

Pharmacies

One pharmacy in each neighborhood remains open all night. One to try is the 24-hour **Pharmacie Dhéry**, 84 av. des Champs-Elysées, 8e (☎ 01-45-62-02-41), in the Galerie des Champs-Elysées shopping center. Or check the door of the nearest pharmacy; it should list the pharmacies open at night.

Taxes

France charges a Value-Added Tax (VAT) of 14 to 17.1 percent on goods and services — it's like a sales tax that's already included in the price.

Citizens of non-EU countries can, as they leave the country, get back most of the tax on purchases (but not services) if you spend more than 1,200F ($171) in a single store. Look for a "Tax Free Shopping for Tourists" sign posted in participating stores. Ask the storekeeper for the necessary forms, save all your receipts, and, if possible, keep the purchases in their original packages. Save all your receipts and VAT forms from each EU country to process all of them at the "Tax Refund" desk in the airport of the last country you visit before flying home (allow an extra 30 minutes or so at the airport to process forms).

Taxis

Although you can hail a taxi on the street, cabs in Paris are scarce, and it may be easier to hire one at a stand. Check the meter when you board to be sure you're not also paying the previous passenger's fare, and if your taxi lacks a meter, settle the cost of the trip before setting out. You can also call a cab to pick you up, but fares are higher because the meter begins running when the driver receives the assignment. Try ☎ 01-45-85-85-85, 01-42-03-50-50, or 01-49-36-10-10.

Telephone

The minimum charge for a local call is 2F (30 cents). Coin-operated phones take 1F, 2F, and 5F coins, but you're more likely to use a phone that requires a *télécarte* (phone card) sold at post offices and tabacs (newsstands/tobacco shops) for 40F ($6) or 96F ($14). Just insert the *télécarte* and dial. For directory assistance, dial ☎ 12.

France's country code is 33. Calling anywhere within the country's borders requires dialing a ten-digit phone number (it already includes the city code) even if you are calling another number from within Paris. To call Paris from the United States, dial 011-33, and then drop the initial zero of the French number and just dial the remaining nine digits. To charge your call to a calling card or call collect, dial AT&T at ☎ 0-800-99-0011; MCI at ☎ 0-800-99-0019; or Sprint at ☎ 0-800-99-0087. To call the United States direct from Paris, dial 00 (wait for the dial tone), and then dial 1 followed by the area code and number.

Time Zone

Paris is six hours ahead of Eastern Standard time and one hour ahead of U.K. time. So when it is noon in New York and 5 p.m. in London, it is 6 p.m. in Paris.

Tipping

Service is supposedly included at your hotel, but the custom is to tip the bellhop about 7F ($1) per bag, more at expensive hotels. If you have a lot of luggage, tip a bit more. Don't tip housekeepers unless you do something that requires extra work. Tip a few dollars if a reception staff member performs extra services.

Although your *addition* (restaurant bill) or *fiche* (café check) will bear the words *service compris* (service charge included), always leave a small tip. Generally, 5 percent is considered acceptable. Remember, service has supposedly already been paid for.

Tourist Information

The **French Government Tourist Office** (☎ 410-286-8310; Internet: www.francetourism. com) has offices at 444 Madison Ave., 16th Floor, New York, NY 10022-6903 (Fax: 212-838-7855); 676 N. Michigan Ave., Chicago, IL 60611-2819 (Fax: 312-337-6339); and 9454 Wilshire Blvd., Suite 715, Beverly Hills, CA 90212-2967 (Fax: 310-276-2835).

The main tourist information office (for information at 2.23F/30 cents per minute, dial ☎ 08-36-68-31-12; Fax: 01-49-52-53-00; Internet: www. paris-touristoffice.com) is at 127 Champs-Elysées, 8e, near the Arc de Triomph end. It's open daily 9 a.m. to 8 p.m. (low season Sundays, 11 a.m. to 6 p.m.).

There are also offices in all the train stations (except Gare St-Lazare) and at every terminal of both Charles de Gaulle and Orly airports. The tourist office hands out *Paris Selection,* a monthly events magazine, but *Pariscope* (www.pariscope.fr) available at any newsstand, is much better and more in-depth. To reserve tickets for shows and exhibitions, dial ☎ 01-49-52-53-53.

Water

Tap water in Paris is perfectly safe, but if you're prone to stomach problems, you may prefer to drink mineral water.

Part IX
The Part of Tens

WHILE TRYING TO FIND THE RENTAL RETURN AREA AT MIAMI INTERNATIONAL AIRPORT, FRANK AND MONA DISCOVER BERMUDA.

In this part . . .

Believe it or not, honeymooners may be more likely to ruin their trip than other travelers. We don't want that to happen, so we created a list of ten things to watch out for. You have enough to worry about with your wedding, so let us help make your honeymoon a breeze.

How about treating yourselves to the ultimate honeymoon — and we mean ultimate? Take a look at the top ten over-the-top resorts in the Caribbean and see if you want to indulge.

Chapter 35

Top Ten Mistakes Honeymooners Make

By Risa R. Weinreb

- -

In This Chapter

▶ Avoiding common honeymoon gaffes

▶ Preventing a crisis on your honeymoon

- -

*O*kay, we assume that you are marrying Mr./Ms. Right. After that, here's the countdown on the most common-yet-moronic ways couples mess up their honeymoon. Fortunately, all these goofs are preventable.

Leaving too Soon after the Wedding

Saturday night reception? Sunday morning 8 a.m. flight to Maui? Puh-leeeease! You wear yourself out before you even start your honeymoon with a schedule like that. Solution: Wait a day or two before departing on your honeymoon.

Booking the Bride's Airline Tickets under Her Married Name

Airline check-in personnel and immigration officials verify that the name of the person on the airline ticket matches the name on the passport or other identification. Solution: Book the tickets under the bride's maiden name.

Not Booking an Oceanview-or-Better Room

Sure you want to save money. But odds are that you'll be grievously disappointed if you end up facing the garbage dumpster instead sea-forever blue water. Even if you don't think that you're going to spend a lot of time in your room, you'll be sorry if it isn't special. Solution: Check around for the best deal that gives you at least a peek at paradise.

Not Booking a King-Size Bed

Double doubles just don't cut it romantically. Solution: Make sure that the king-size set-up is confirmed in writing.

Packing Contraceptives in Check-In Luggage

When airlines lose your bags, even for 24 hours, it's bad not having your favorite pair of shorts. But it's dismal to get short shrift in the bedroom department. Solution: Keep contraceptives in your carry-on bags, along with other honeymoon necessities, like a bathing suit.

Not Telling Everyone You're Honeymooners

Airline personnel, hotel front-desk clerks, and even supercilious maitre d's generally go out of their way to be helpful to newlyweds. (Besides, with those virginally shiny gold rings and eyes locked on each other, you're not fooling many people anyway.) Why not get the best? Solution: When you're making reservations, be sure to mention it's your honeymoon.

Counting on Renting a Car If You're under 25

The car's reserved, you have your confirmation number, and you're relying on having your own wheels to get around. But many car rental companies only rent to people over age 25. Solution: If you are under 25, double-check the agency's rental policy.

Not Budgeting Beforehand

Talking about money isn't romantic. Arguing about it after your new spouse blows $500 on a near-life-size carving of a dolphin is worse. Solution: Before you go away, set up a tentative budget and decide where you plan to splurge: shopping, dinners out, or gambling at the casino.

Trying to Do Too Much

No time for a room-service breakfast because you're booked into that 9 a.m. snorkel trip? Unable to linger in that marvelous corner cafe because you scheduled a massage? Women and Men Who Love To Do Too Much often try to cram in too many activities. Solution: Leave plenty of free time in your itinerary so that you can relax and enjoy what you see.

Not Making Sure that Your New Rings Fit

We have encountered at least six honeymooners who have spent the first day of their vacation mourning the loss of their new gold bands, which slipped off in the water. (Cold makes fingers shrink, remember.) Solution: If it doesn't fit, don't swim in it until you can get it properly sized.

Chapter 36

The Caribbean's Top Ten Over-the-Moon Honeymoons

By Echo & Kevin Garrett

• •

In This Chapter

▶ Indulging your sweetie's ultimate fantasy

▶ Finding honeymoon hideaways that cost more than the wedding

• •

*T*alk about the ultimate honeymoon! The following resorts are considered to be among the most fabulous — and most expensive — resorts in the world. Some are more affordable than others. Take a look and see if any capture your hearts.

Bitter End Yacht Club, Virgin Gorda

The Bitter End Yacht Club, on Virgin Gorda in the British Virgin Islands, is a casual, rustic resort, only reachable by sea. Bitter End — named for a sailing term which means the last stop before open seas of the Atlantic — is comprised of a collection of 95 villas and suites — some beachside, and some dotting the lush hillsides overlooking the North Sound (a protected, deep water harbor). For the ultimate in luxurious privacy, you can charter a Freedom 30 live-aboard yacht (100 watercrafts are available for guests). The most secluded and scenic beachfront digs have king-size beds, giant showers, and a wraparound veranda strung with a hammock for two. **Information: ☎ 800-872-2392** or 284-494-2746. Fax: 284-494-4756. E-mail: binfo@beyc.com. Internet: www.beyc.com. **Rates:** $500–$700 double or suite. Rates include all meals. Packages available.

Cap Juluca, Anguilla

This Moorish dream set on one of the Caribbean's finest crescent white sand beaches almost appears like a mirage at first: Arches, domes, and turrets adorn blindingly white villas edging the beach. Request a villa with a bathroom that includes a giant tub for two, a roomy shower, and glass walls with a view onto your own private sun terrace. Book the Juluca Ritual for Two and your villa is strewn with flowers while the two of you are pampered with a massage and a private bath is drawn. The new chef also works magic in the property's imaginative restaurants. **Information:** ☎ **888-858-5822** or 264-497-6666; Fax: 264-497-6617; Internet: www.capjuluca.com. **Rates:** $1,235-$5,140.

The Carenage, Canouan Island

Carenage Bay, on Canouan Island in St. Vincent & the Grenadines, offers a unique blend of relaxation and discovery on one of the few remaining untainted Caribbean islands. Carenage Bay, a $200 million luxury resort, offers 155 rooms and suites spread across 200 acres on the remote side of Canouan's Carenage Bay. The resort features many beautiful white sand beaches, a par-72 golf course designed by Roy Case, several private yachts, tennis, watersports, and scuba diving, a health and fitness center with spa facilities, one of the Caribbean's largest freshwater pools, and a deluxe European casino. **Information:** ☎ **888-ROSEWOOD;** Internet: www.rosewoodhotels.com. **Rates:** The seven-night Duet Package is available year-round and features champagne upon arrival, massage therapy for two, a boat excursion to the Tobago Cays, and a personal golf cart for the week. Package rates start at $3,200 per couple. Rates include breakfast, lunch, and dinner at any of the resort's four distinct restaurants.

The Cotton House, Mustique

Situated on a picturesque hillside on Mustique Island in St. Vincent & the Grenadines, and surrounded by the Caribbean and Atlantic, this restored eighteenth-century coral warehouse and sugar mill found new life as one of the Caribbean's most exclusive inns. We almost hesitate to use the word "inn," because it fails to convey the beauty of this 20-room unspoiled hideaway on this tiny island, just three miles long and half as wide. It's fitting that Cotton House started out as a wedding gift for a princess. It boasts niceties such as its own Equestrian Center and private sailing charters on request. **Information:** ☎ **877-240-9945** or 784-456-4777; Fax: 784-456-5887; E-mail: cottonhouse@caribsurf.com; Internet: www.cottonhouseresort.com. **Rates:** $900-$1,250.

Four Seasons Resort, Nevis

All the travel magazines consistently rate this jewel as one of the top resorts in the Caribbean, thanks to its service and its beauty. Accommodations are housed in two-story gingerbread-rimmed cottages along Pinney's Beach, one of our favorites. The beach concierge spritzes guests with Evian to cool them as they sun. **Information:** ☎ 800-332-3442; Internet: `www.fourseasons.com`. **Rates:** The "Romance in Paradise" package includes seven-nights accommodations, daily breakfast and dinner, and ground and water transfers for $7,100.

Golden Eye, Jamaica

Wanna stay at James Bond's birthplace? Ian Fleming built this simple house in 1946; his invention, 007, was conceived here in 1952, and Fleming later named it Golden Eye. Set on a bluff overlooking a small cove, Golden Eye is surprisingly simple at first glance. But then you start to notice all the playful touches. In homage to an international spy like 007, the main house is outfitted with over-size Indonesian bamboo couches, four-poster beds, batik fabrics, and African art. Bath "gardens" have been added near each of the three bedrooms, giving guests outdoor showering and bathing options (one has a clawfoot tub imported from London and now whimsically set in the middle of a rock garden). **Information:** ☎ **800-688-7678** or 876-974-3354; Fax: 876-975-3679. **Rates:** Winter, $650 bungalow for two. For $5,000 you can sleep in Ian Fleming's three-bedroom house. Discounts of up to 20 percent in off-season. Rates are all-inclusive.

Jumby Bay, Antigua

A lush, tropical, 300-acre private enclave, Jumby Bay is accessible only by boat and lies two miles north of Antigua. A tranquil haven for naturalists, the island is home to endangered species of turtles, rare birds, and sheep. Guests walk or bike paths lined with wild orchids leading to the 39 suites and 11 villas, which are outfitted in traditional West Indian designs. Oversize baths with showers adjoining private gardens inspire romance. Dinner is served in the 230-year-old English plantation manor. Honeymooners favor the picnics prepared on request and enjoyed in privacy on Pasture Beach, one of three powdery white beaches framed by the azure-blue Caribbean Sea and the Atlantic Ocean. **Information:** ☎ **800-237-3237** or 268-462-6000; Fax: 268-462-6020; E-mail: `jumbyb@candw.ag`; Internet: `www.jumbybayresort.com`. **Rates:** $950 for a Junior Suite, to $5,000 for a four-bedroom villa; rates are all inclusive.

Little Dix Bay, Virgin Gorda

Set on a fabulous crescent strand of white sand beach, nestled amid the lush hills of Virgin Gorda, is the elegant Little Dix Bay, a intimate resort designed by Laurance Rockefeller in 1964 to make the most of its natural surroundings while catering to the rich. We find the setting absolutely romantic and the service excellent without being obnoxious. The mood at this gracious and upscale 500-acre retreat is peaceful and unhurried. Little Dix is the sort of place where ladies always want to have their most chic beach cover-up close at hand. (Honeymooners flock here during the summer when rates drop dramatically.) The romance package includes all the basics plus a day sail, picnic, sunset cocktail cruise, and massage for two. Package starts at $6,300 in the winter. **Information:** ☎ **888-767-3966** or 284-495-555. Fax: 284-495-5661. Internet: www.rosewoodhotels. com or www.littledixbay.com. **Rates:** $450–$600 double.

Necker Island, British Virgin Islands

We promised you Fantasy Island, and here it is. Your host: British entrepreneur and adventurer Richard Branson, owner of Virgin Atlantic Airways, Virgin Megastores, and 100 other companies. The 74-acre Necker Island is ringed by a coral reef and within sight of Virgin Gorda. It's also the most expensive at a staggering $19,000 to $29,500 a day. That gets you (and, if you choose to invite them, up to 25 of your closest friends and relatives) the entire island and a staff of 30, including two gourmet chefs, to attend to your every detail of your wedding — it's an enormously popular spot for tying the knot — or your every honeymoon whim. **Information:** ☎ **800-557-4255** or 284-494-2757; Fax: 284-494-4396; Internet: www.neckerisland.com. **Rates:** $29,500 a day.

Four times a year, during "celebration weeks," the price drops to $12,000 for the week per couple.

Peter Island Resort, British Virgin Islands

If you tire of sailing the BVIs' pristine waters in your yacht, drop anchor at Peter Island. The Resort is an 1,800-acre, 52-room boutique escape that allows couples to snorkel in secluded coves or cast-off on the resort's sailing yacht. "Honeymoon," the most intimate of the five beaches necklacing the island, offers two lounge chairs beneath a thatch hut. At White Bay Beach, you can order up a custom-made gourmet picnic lunch complete with fine linens, china, and flatware. You won't feel entirely cut off from civilization, though, not with the resort's satellite television, the *New York Times* by fax at breakfast, telephones, and, of course, the Internet. **Information:** ☎ **800-346-4451,** 800-323-7500, or 284-495-2000. Internet: www.peterisland.com. **Rates:** $705–$970 two-bedroom villa. Rates include transfers to island and all meals.

Making Dollars and Sense of It

Expense	Amount
Airfare	
Car Rental	
Lodging	
Parking	
Breakfast	
Lunch	
Dinner	
Babysitting	
Attractions	
Transportation	
Souvenirs	
Tips	
Grand Total	

Notes

Fare Game: Choosing an Airline

Travel Agency:_____ Phone:_____

Agent's Name:_____ Quoted Fare:_____

Departure Schedule & Flight Information

Airline:_____ Airport:_____

Flight #:_____ Date:_____ Time:_____ a.m./p.m.

Arrives in:_____ Time:_____ a.m./p.m.

Connecting Flight (if any)

Amount of time between flights:_____ hours/mins

Airline:_____ Airport:_____

Flight #:_____ Date:_____ Time:_____ a.m./p.m.

Arrives in:_____ Time:_____ a.m./p.m.

Return Trip Schedule & Flight Information

Airline:_____ Airport:_____

Flight #:_____ Date:_____ Time:_____ a.m./p.m.

Arrives in:_____ Time:_____ a.m./p.m.

Connecting Flight (if any)

Amount of time between flights:_____ hours/mins

Airline:_____ Airport:_____

Flight #:_____ Date:_____ Time:_____ a.m./p.m.

Arrives in:_____ Time:_____ a.m./p.m.

Notes

Sweet Dreams: Choosing Your Hotel

Enter the hotels where you'd prefer to stay based on location and price. Then use the worksheet below to plan your itinerary.

Hotel	Location	Price per night

Menus & Venues

Enter the restaurants where you'd most like to dine. Then use the worksheet below to plan your itinerary.

Name	Address/Phone	Cuisine/Price

Places to Go, People to See, Things to Do

Enter the attractions you would most like to see. Then use the worksheet below to plan your itinerary.

Attractions	Amount of time you expect to spend there	Best day and time to go

Going "My" Way

Itinerary #1

☐ _____
☐ _____
☐ _____
☐ _____

Itinerary #2

☐ _____
☐ _____
☐ _____
☐ _____

Itinerary #3

☐ _____
☐ _____
☐ _____
☐ _____

Itinerary #4

☐ _____
☐ _____
☐ _____
☐ _____

Itinerary #5

☐ _____
☐ _____
☐ _____
☐ _____

Itinerary #6

☐ _____
☐ _____
☐ _____
☐ _____

Itinerary #7

☐ _____
☐ _____
☐ _____
☐ _____

Itinerary #8

☐ _____
☐ _____
☐ _____
☐ _____

Itinerary #9

☐ _____
☐ _____
☐ _____
☐ _____

Itinerary #10

☐ _____
☐ _____
☐ _____
☐ _____

Notes

Index

• *H* •

• *V* •

• *W* •

FOR DUMMIES
BOOK REGISTRATION

We want to hear from you!

Visit **dummies.com** to register this book and tell us how you liked it!

✔ Get entered in our monthly prize giveaway.

✔ Give us feedback about this book — tell us what you like best, what you like least, or maybe what you'd like to ask the author and us to change!

✔ Let us know any other *For Dummies* topics that interest you.

Your feedback helps us determine what books to publish, tells us what coverage to add as we revise our books, and lets us know whether we're meeting your needs as a *For Dummies* reader. You're our most valuable resource, and what you have to say is important to us!

Not on the Web yet? It's easy to get started with *Dummies 101: The Internet For Windows 98* or *The Internet For Dummies* at local retailers everywhere.

Or let us know what you think by sending us a letter at the following address:

For Dummies Book Registration
Dummies Press
10475 Crosspoint Blvd.
Indianapolis, IN 46256

FOR DUMMIES ™

BESTSELLING BOOK SERIES